Sweet Chestnut **19**

Birch **17**

Hornbeam **19**

Poplar **15**

Willow **16**

Elm **22**

Hazel p. **214**

Judas-tree **29**

Whitebeam **25**

Lime **35–36**

Katsura Tree **23**

Bay **24**

Dove-tree **37**

Cockspur
Thorn **25**

Snowy Mespil **26**

der **18**

Beech **19**

Raoul **19**

Paulownia **39**

Catalpa **39**

Zelkova p. **254**

Not to scale

A FIELD GUIDE TO THE
Trees of Britain
AND NORTHERN EUROPE

A FIELD GUIDE TO THE

Trees of Britain

AND NORTHERN EUROPE

Alan Mitchell

with 40 colour plates by
PREBEN DAHLSTROM AND EBBE SUNESEN

and 640 line drawings by
CHRISTINE DARTER

COLLINS
St James's Place, London

William Collins Sons & Co Ltd
London · Glasgow · Sydney · Auckland
Toronto · Johannesburg

First published 1974
Second edition 1978
© Alan Mitchell, 1974

ISBN 0 00 219213 6

Made and Printed in Great Britain by
William Collins Sons & Co Ltd Glasgow

CONTENTS

6   CONTENTS

COLOUR PLATES

PREFACE

A popular book on trees should enable a reader to identify any tree in his neighbourhood and in parks and gardens he may visit. It also needs to be fairly simple to use. It would be easy to meet both requirements if there were only a hundred or two trees normally seen outside botanic gardens, but this is not the case at all. There are only thirty-five species of tree (as defined in this book) native to the British Isles but five hundred more species from the entire temperate world and two hundred more varieties of various species can easily be encountered by anyone looking for trees in parks and gardens. If botanic gardens be included, and big garden-collections, some specialising in rare and tender species, the number of species rises to about 1,700. Bedgebury National Pinetum grows 220 species and 200 varieties of conifer alone, while 540 tree-species have been counted so far in Westonbirt, and Borde Hill has somewhat more.

So many species and varieties are so widely planted that to omit any but the most rare and restricted would render the book misleading to the casual reader, and of little use to the more serious seeker after trees, who is the very person the book should help and encourage. When a book on trees is taken on its first outdoor trial, it hardly needs to be said that the first tree seen, in the town park or churchyard, is not in the book. It should be in this one. The only chance that cannot be guarded against is that some reader may elect to start in Tresco Abbey, Caerhays Castle or Casa di Sole, gardens full of trees found nowhere else in northern Europe. The great collections like these, in which the British Isles are uniquely and fabulously rich, cannot be fully covered in a book like this. The generality of parks and major gardens must be covered, although they include hundreds of rare trees. If these trees were excluded, the reader would be misled because some are found in ordinary front gardens and city parks, while a few are in unexpected places in towns and villages. Therefore to be sure that even the common trees are correctly identified, the rarer ones resembling them must be included. It makes the book more complex, but it is necessary in order to make it useful and trustworthy. If, for example, the five rather rare Asiatic rowans were omitted for simplicity, the reader seeing one of them in gorgeous autumn colour in a town car-park would be forced to conclude that it was a slightly odd form of the common Mountain Ash, and he would lose the knowledge of a very valuable group of trees, or find the book of little use, letting him down when most needed.

A walk through some suburban roads, especially some fairly recent ones in residential areas is as good as a visit to an arboretum. This makes life more interesting for those who have an eye for and interest in trees. Many of the most striking trees seen, though, are relatively rare, or at any rate, are not in most of the popular tree-books. It is just this sort of tree-watching that needs encouragement and can lead to a full and life-long interest. The many stately homes open to the public are mostly set amongst fine collections of trees. Here again, many are too infrequent to have found their way into general tree-books, but these are the very places where an interest in trees might be started and a tree-book must try to include every one likely to be seen.

Hitherto there has been a large gap in books on trees. There are the complex botanical manuals, nearly comprehensive, but unable to exclude any woody plant so that half of them is taken up by shrubs, heaths, rhododendrons and climbers. At the other end of the range, nearly all popular books have been engrossed in details of folk-lore, witches, ancient remedies and uses, clogs and withies. They scarcely leave the hedgerows and are quite useless in a park or garden as they hardly admit exotics. Illustrated books on trees for the garden include many exotics, but none is described beyond a few words.

This book is designed to describe in systematic detail every tree species and cultivar (variety) found in parks, gardens large and small, towns and countryside, and to provide guides and keys with which to identify them. Not many of them are native to Europe and very few are native to the British Isles. Since, however, the climate of the British Isles allows many trees to flourish better than on the continent of Europe, and most of them were introduced first to Britain, so any tree growing in Europe north of the Mediterranean littoral is almost certain to be growing and have the biggest specimens in British gardens.

This book cannot encompass enough species to be wholly comprehensive for botanic gardens and specialist collections. To do so it would need to be three times as long, and the keys and guides for identifying species would have to be more than three times as complex. This would be impossible while keeping the book simple to use. Even so, many very rare species have been included where there are prominent specimens in such collections, so that even in Kew, Westonbirt, Wakehurst Place, Bodnant, Hergest Croft, Dawyck and Powerscourt, a high proportion of the specimens will be in the book. Anyone sufficiently interested and competent to try to identify those omitted, is already in the botanical manual class.

HOW TO USE THIS BOOK

The **trees in the book** include every species and large-growing cultivar to be seen in the countryside, parks and gardens of Europe north of the Mediterranean littoral. The only trees within this region not included are some of great rarity confined to the botanic gardens, the major specialist collections and sub-tropical gardens. It must be appreciated that barely a tenth of all the trees is native to the region, the majority coming from China, Japan and North America and grown widely in the temperate world. This book may be of some use in any of these areas.

A tree is defined for this work as a woody plant that commonly achieves a height of 6 m (20 ft) on a single stem. This definition excludes shrubs (except that the author has been persuaded to stretch it to include the Hazel as an abundant countryside species which might be thought to be a tree and thus may be sought in these pages).

The **endpapers** at the front and back of the book show a typical leaf or spray of foliage of each of the common genera of tree, represented by one of the species most frequently seen. This should be some guide to a beginner, referring him to the correct groups in most cases, but it has severe and unavoidable limitations. Some genera include leaves of very disparate shapes. In *Sorbus* one pinnate type and one simple ovate type can be included, and two very different shapes of poplar leaf can also be included. The oaks and maples, however, display so many kinds of leaf-shape that to include other, less typical forms would blur the simplicity which is the main aim.

The **coloured plates** include nearly all the common trees and also many less common, and a few rare, in which some feature of leaf, bark or flower is well shown in colour.

The **line drawings** cover almost every other tree except for the colour-variants, and include series of cones and numerous outlines drawn from individual trees displaying well-developed typical crowns. A 3 cm line indicates scale.

The **English name** given is the most usual or most appropriate one where there are already established names. In many cases, largely the rarer trees included here, there is no accepted English name. A botanist would prefer to keep it that way, but for wider use and for uniformity, it has been thought better to invent a name or bring out an obscure name. There is perhaps little point in giving "Hiba" for *Thujopsis dolabrata* as few people know it and no one uses it. It is really better to become familiar with the botanical name but such "English" names may be more useful to those who are unfamiliar with Latin or Greek. For trees with names like *Chamaecyparis pisifera* 'Filifera Aurea' there is no easy way out. To call it the "Golden Thread-foliaged Sawara Cypress" is nearly as long, less understood, and sounds just as precious.

The **botanical name** of each tree is given next. The authorities mainly followed are, for conifers and taxads, *A Handbook of Coniferae and Ginkgoaceae* by Dallimore and Jackson, 3rd Edition, revised by Harrison; and for the rest, *A Manual of Cultivated Trees and Shrubs* by A. Rehder, 1949 edition. A few have been changed to bring them in line with the *Kew Handlist*, the revision of *Trees and Shrubs Hardy in the British Isles* which is now being prepared and *Hillier's Manual of Trees and Shrubs*. In a few other cases, the author has used his own judgement. For the rules and methods of botanical nomenclature, see p. 16.

The **natural distribution** follows the name of the species and geographic varieties. For native species this is largely from *Flora of the British Isles*, 2nd edition, 1962, by Clapham, Tutin and Warburg, but in the elms the author has made his own surveys. For garden hybrids and cultivars, the place of origin is given, where known, and the date either of origin or of distribution; or where these are known to be many years apart, both are given.

The **date** following the natural range is the date of introduction into Great Britain. In most cases this is also the date of first cultivation anywhere as an exotic. Usually the first introduction was by seed and many plants were raised. In a few instances the introduction was of a single plant. A second date is then given for the next, more general introduction.

The **distribution in the British Isles** follows the date of introduction, and is from original observation, and in as much detail as seems valid. It should be helpful in showing, for example, that the possibility of finding quite a number of species is small if one is north of the English Midlands or far from the west coast. There are two main difficulties here. One is that many species have not been seen by the author in a large region north of the Trent, but seem to be flourishing in the Royal Botanic Garden in Edinburgh, a rather cold place, and in a few gardens in S.W. Scotland. There is always the chance that some collector's garden in Yorkshire or Cumberland may have a good specimen. The other is that there are many enthusiastic collectors with small gardens who grow species well beyond their general range. For example, one in Surrey has *Cornus capitata* growing quite well but to include Surrey in the general range would be misleading when the next nearest outdoor tree is probably on the Isle of Wight; another collector in Surrey grows trees found otherwise no nearer than Torquay.

The **frequency** of each species is also given with some attempt at precision, as this is also very helpful in gauging the general likelihood of having found a certain species. The terms used are much less generous than those used in other works. A tree should not be called "common in cultivation" if less than a hundred specimens of any measureable size are known. A good proportion of the 1,700 species grown must remain decidedly rare until they can be obtained at local nurseries, and many of these species, being found as fine trees in some large gardens open to the public, are included in this book.

Abundant has been used only for general countryside trees that occur as dominant tree-species over considerable areas, e.g. ash, and for a few species which are almost universal and usually in numbers in most gardens, e.g. Lawson Cypress.

Very common and *common* are used for trees which occur in numbers in any area with trees, in almost any garden, park or churchyard, without being the dominant species.

Frequent implies occurrence in almost any group of gardens or parks but usually in small numbers and not always present even in single large gardens.

Infrequent implies occurrence limited to well-stocked gardens or parks and single trees here and there perhaps in town gardens in most areas, but absent from the general run of parks and gardens.

Uncommon implies possibly absent from quite large areas but cannot be called "rare" in the country as a whole.

Rare implies almost confined to the best-stocked gardens; very few specimens in any one district (within the range given), probably absent from many large areas.

Very rare and *collections only* are used for trees of which less than 20 specimens have been measured by the author, and these are almost or quite confined to gardens in which trees are planted for their botanical interest rather than for landscaping, foliage or flowers. Many of the best known gardens are, in fact, of this kind, the famous landscaping at Stourhead and Sheffield Park, for example, is combined with considerable collections of rare species.

Very rare indeed is used where the author has measured less than ten specimens, sometimes less than five. These species are confined to botanic gardens and the most comprehensive collections like Borde Hill and Jermyn's House which are really very informal and very large botanic gardens. They are included only where a specimen is prominent in a much visited garden or the species is more frequent on the Continent. Some are confined by their tenderness to a few gardens in the extreme south or west.

The **height** and, where it may be useful or interesting, the **girth** follow the distribution in the British Isles. When only one height is given it is that of the tallest currently known specimen in the British Isles. This may seem to exaggerate the likely height in any one district, but has been adopted because a large number of species have not yet been in cultivation long enough to have attained their top height. The specimens whose heights are cited will soon be taller and others will be as tall as the figure quoted increasingly as the years go by. Where one tree has been found much taller than any other of its species, the general height of the majority of tall specimens is given, with the outstanding top height added in parentheses. Heights are in metres. The girth is the circumference in metres, measured at five feet (1.5m) above the highest point of the ground at the base.

The spread, beloved of gardening books, is NOT given. It is greatly dependent on surroundings and is nearly meaningless.

The **descriptions** are from fresh foliage on growing trees. Only in one or two instances of flower or fruit not being available has recourse been had to published works. There has been too much copying in tree-literature. Before the newly introduced species had made much growth here, it was necessary to copy from the authorities of its native country or from the collector's notes, but this is not now necessary for any species in this book except for the male flowers of *Metasequoia*. It has been the author's experience, for example, that in many cases trees grown in Britain produce leaves larger than those given in Rehder's Manual, and that old descriptions being usually from dried herbarium material omit some very useful features of colour.

The **sizes of leaf** given relate more to the largest leaves likely to be found than to the smallest. Most trees may bear dwarfed leaves, and leaves can be found in various stages of growth, so this end of the scale is little help in identifying a tree. By contrast, the largest leaves on each specimen are often a very good diagnostic feature. The entry "to 24 cm" implies that the largest leaves on specimens show no particular mean size below this, but leaves are unlikely to be found larger than 24 cm. The entry "20–26 cm" implies that on most trees the mean larger, healthy leaves are 20 cm, but leaves to 26 cm may well be found.

Under **Growth** some particularly striking examples of rapid growth are given for the most vigorous species and, where known from original observations, the period of height-growth. Also, where a reasonable estimate can be made, the likely life-span.

Under **Similar species** the reader is referred to the species most likely to be difficult to separate from the one under discussion (this can include only those similar species which are also in the book. There may be others which are too rare to be mentioned). Where the related species are not sufficiently similar to cause confusion or where there are none, some features of the species may be summarised under **Recognition**.

The **keys** (pp. 34–46) have been constructed from notes on fresh foliage and from specimen leaves preserved between sheets of transparent plastic. They are not strict botanical keys: that is, closely related species may key out widely separated if it is simpler that they should. To be botanically correct, the key should be largely based on features of flower and fruit. Since these are not often available, and can be together only after preservation, such keys are maddening for the amateur to use. In this book, the keys are based on features of the leaf, primarily, for use with collected samples of foliage, at home. Subsidiary features of the shoot are used, as this is usually with the leaf sample and, where particularly useful in the field, features of bark or crown may be added in parentheses. For elms and poplars, in which leaves are difficult to separate, keys for crown and bark types separate the main populations in the field in the simplest way.

INTRODUCTION TO TREES

A tree may be defined as a woody, perennial plant which can attain a stature of 6m or more on a single stem. The stem may divide low down, but it must do so above ground-level. This definition has been used as the criterion for inclusion in this book. Thus the Hawthorn qualifies because there are a few specimens over 10m tall with a single bole, although this plant is seen almost everywhere only as a low shrub with many stems. The Elderberry and the Dogwood, however, do not qualify for inclusion. The Hazel has been given the benefit of the doubt. It has been necessary to exclude all shrubs as this is a book on trees and needs all its space to include a sufficient number of them to be complete for use in ordinary gardens and parks. A few cultivars of conifers have been included which do not quite qualify according to the definition. This is because they are sure to be seen and many readers may look for them in this book. Few other popular books of trees include them and it is felt that this one should.

What is a tree?

The term "tree" is quite different in kind from the terms "fern", "moss" or "grass". Each of those is a group of plants closely related. For example, every grass is in the single Family Gramineae, and every plant in that family is a grass (or reed or bamboo) and readily seen to be such. But trees occur scattered throughout Families, Orders and even Classes. The flowering plants are divided into two great Classes, *Gymnospermae* and *Angiospermae*. These are further divided into Orders as shown:

CLASS	ORDER	PLANTS
	Cycadales	*Cycas*, like a tree-fern
	Gnetales	shrubby or trailing plants
Gymnospermae	Ginkgoales	one species – a TREE
	Taxales	small TREES
	Coniferales	nearly all TREES, a few shrubs
Angiospermae	Dicotyledons	herbs, shrubs and TREES
	Monocotyledons	herbs, bulbs, grasses and TREES

Within the vast assemblage of families in Dicotyledons, the occurrence of trees is random. Some samples are:

Primulaceae	Herbs only (Primrose, Cowslip). No trees or shrubs.
Cruciferae	Herbs and a few small shrubs. No trees.
Scrophulariaceae	Herbs (Foxglove, Figwort). One genus of tree, (*Paulownia*).
Rosaceae	Herbs (Salad Burnet), shrubs (*Potentilla*) and trees (rowans, cherries, etc.)
Fagaceae	Trees (oaks, beeches, chestnuts)

Nomenclature and taxonomy

Taxonomy is the subject of the correct botanical name for each tree, and its formulation is made according to the rules of Nomenclature. These subjects are allied to, but different from *classification*, which is the relationships among the species; the allocation of species to genera and genera to families. A taxon is a group – family, genus, species, variety, are all taxa (plural). It is also a general term for the members of these groups. Thus ten species and five varieties are together 15 taxa.

In everyday life we talk about an oak or a larch. These are general terms each covering several kinds of tree. To particularise which oak or larch, we say "Turkey oak" or "European larch". In botanical naming, the general ("generic") name comes first, to indicate first the group or "genus" (pl. "genera") followed by the particular ("specific") name, indicating the sort or "species" of tree within the genus. All the usual oaks are in the genus *Quercus* and all the larches are in the genus *Larix*. The Turkey Oak is *Quercus cerris* and the European Larch is *Larix decidua*.

The full name of the Turkey Oak is, however, "*Quercus cerris* L.", the "L." being part of the name. It stands for the name of the botanist who first validly published this combination of names, and distinguishes it from any other "*Quercus cerris*" that may have been allotted to another species of oak, but invalidly, by another botanist. "L." is unique in being a botanist's name reduced to a single initial. It stands for Carl von Linné, who wrote under the Latinised form of his name, "Linnaeus", and first established the consistent system of "binomial" (binominal) nomenclature, that is, the two names – the generic followed by the specific. The names of other botanists in this context are usually reduced to the first syllable, as in "Lamb." for Lambert, and "Mill." for Miller, or are given in full. Apart from Linnaeus one other name is often reduced to initals, this time two: "D.C." for de Candolle, an eminent Swiss botanist. A name is "valid" if it was the first unambiguous one for the species published in a work which is consistently binominal and conforms to a variety of the rules of nomenclature.

Early botanists had fewer species to name and put them in few and wide genera. For example, Linnaeus grouped most of the conifers he knew in one genus, *Pinus*. He called the Norway Spruce "*Pinus abies*" and the European Larch "*Pinus larix*". It later became apparent that the spruces and larches formed good genera on their own, and should be removed from the pines. The genus *Picea* was established for spruces and the genus *Larix* for Larches. A "priority rule" ensures that where possible, the original specific epithet is transferred to the new genus. The Norway Spruce thus becomes "*Picea abies* L." – but Linnaeus never wrote this combination of names. So the "L." is put in parentheses, and the author of the new combination is added, thus "*Picea abies* (L.) Karsten". To do the same thing with the name for the European Larch would result in "*Larix larix* (L.)". This repetition of the same word is known as "tautonymy" and is a sin in botany, although perfectly logical, and normal in zoology. To avoid this disaster, the name given by Linnaeus is dropped and the first valid name under the new genus is used or, if there is none, a new one is coined. This was "*Larix decidua*" published by Phillip Miller, so the full name is "*Larix decidua* Miller".

The result here is not particularly happy since the deciduous character in no way distinguishes this larch from any other, but it is more important to establish the rules for consistent naming than to worry as to whether the resulting names make good distinctions. A similar example is *Sequoia sempervirens*, where the specific epithet meaning "evergreen" seems redundant now, but was a very good feature when it was first described, for at that time, the only related tree known was the deciduous Swamp Cypress, *Taxodium distichum*. The redwood was thus first distinguished as *"Taxodium sempervirens"*, the only evergreen species in the genus.

Species with a wide or a fragmented natural range must gradually evolve into a number of new species. Minor genetical changes constantly arise in all species, and in these instances they will not be able to spread through the whole population of the species. Scots Pines in Spain differ in many minor features from those in Central Siberia or in Scotland with which there can be no exchange of pollen. Eventually they will differ so widely that they will be classed as separate species and, at a later period, they would not even interbreed if brought together. Various stages of this process are found in many species, and where there are good distinctions among them and no intermediate grading, the different forms need to be named. So a wild population distinct in form from that of the plant originally described is called a "variety" (var.), while the original plant is called the "Type" of the species. For example, the Pyrenean form of the Black Pine (*Pinus nigra*) is *Pinus nigra* var. *pyrenaica* and the Corsican form is *Pinus nigra* var. *maritima*. The varietal name first given to a geographical population remains unchanged, even when the specific name of the tree is subsequently revised. And it takes precedence over earlier classifications of the form as a full species.

Thus the Corsican Pine, first known as *Pinus laricio*, was later regarded by Aiton as a form of the Scots Pine and then called *Pinus sylvestris* var. *maritima* Aiton. Today regarded as a form of the Black Pine, its name becomes *Pinus nigra* var. *maritima* (Aiton).

In gardens and nurseries variants arise among seedlings or, rarely, as branch-sports, i.e. shoots on a normal plant which show some minor genetical change, usually variegation in colour. These are then propagated by grafting or cuttings. They thus differ from geographical varieties in not being found as a wild population, in arising as a single plant, and in being identical when multiplied, as this is done vegetatively, not by seed. However widely planted they are, these remain pieces of the same tree. They are like the Bramley Seedling apple; that is, they are one *clone*. For a long time, such forms have been treated as varieties and named accordingly. A few "cv." names cover more than one clone.

Now they are called cultivars (cultivated varieties), "cv." for short. Their nomenclature is ruled by "The International Code of Nomenclature of Cultivated Plants". This is simple. No authors' names are required. The cultivar name is printed in normal type, not italics, and either follows directly the specific epithet and is in single quotes, or has "cv." in front and no quotes. For example: either *Acer palmatum* 'Senkaki' or *Acer palmatum* cv. Senkaki. The old varietal names were in latinised form and may be used if given to the plant before Jan. 1st 1959, but names given since that date must be in the vernacular. An example of each is: *Fagus sylvatica* 'Pendula'; *Gleditsia triacanthos* 'Sunburst'.

Hybrid trees

A hybrid organism is one whose male parent is in a different taxonomic group from its female parent. There can be three different degrees of hybridity. Where a species has been divided into two or more subspecies or varieties, a cross between a pair of these will be an intra-specific hybrid. An example would be the seedling resulting from the pollen of a Polish Larch on the cone of a type larch from Switzerland. Such hybrids are of interest to tree-breeders but are not generally known nor markedly different in appearance from their parents, which will be similar to each other except in minor points.

The usual use of the term hybrid is for inter-specific hybrids, in which the parents are of different species. The Lucombe Oak is an example, where the female was a Turkey Oak which was pollinated by a Cork Oak. When giving the parentage of a hybrid it is customary to put the parents in alphabetical order, but it is better to put the female (seed) parent first. This is because it should normally be known from what species the seed was picked, but it may often be speculation as to which species was the male parent. The convention for writing the botanical name for a hybrid between two species is to put "×" in front of the new specific epithet given to the hybrid. For example, "*Larix × eurolepis* Henry".

The third kind of hybrid is the inter-generic hybrid in which the parents are in different genera. These are much rarer and depend on the two genera being very closely related. Since each seedling arises from the fusion of a single cell from each parent, these cells must be closely similar or they could not unite to make a viable organism. The only example in this book is the Leyland Cypress, a cross which has occurred both ways between *Cupressus macrocarpa* and *Chamaecyparis nootkatensis*. The correct way to write the botanical name of an inter-generic hybrid is to put a capital "×" in front of the generic name which has been given to this group of hybrids (this can be a group, because there may be several species in each genus and hybrids between other species in these two genera may arise). The example given, Leyland Cypress, is thus "×*Cupressocyparis leylandii*". Two other hybrids in this genus are known. Other inter-generic hybrids occur in Rosaceae, notably between the Medlar and the Hawthorn, but these are too rare to be treated in this book.

When hybrids occur between species, the *less* closely related the parents are the more vigorous is the hybrid between them, and in features like growth, size and fruit-production hybrids usually exceed either parent. This feature, known as "hybrid-vigour" or "heterosis" is the basis of much crop-breeding. It has several origins, but the simple one is that the cross between a species which bears masses of small fruit and one that bears few but large fruit may yield hybrids bearing masses of large fruit. Features like vigour and good-fruiting tend for good genetical reasons to be dominant and thus to be shown by the offspring. The great vigour of the Leyland Cypress may arise from one parent growing where it has hot, very dry summers and the other parent growing naturally where summers are cool and damp. The hybrid could have inherited the ability to grow fast in either kind of weather and thus outgrow both parents in the mixed summers of this country. Most tree-hybrids are fertile, unlike the few hybrid animals known. The resultant offspring cannot, however, be regarded as the same sort of hybrid as their parents, for those were true hybrids which have a father of a different species from their mother. The offspring have parents of the same (hybrid) species. They are distinguished by being called "second-generation" hybrids, F_2 for short, and the parents (true hybrids) are F_1 (first filial generation). Seed collected from F_2 trees will give rise to F_3 trees, and so on. Heterosis diminishes fast in these generations and is seldom much in evidence in F_3 trees.

Wood structure

In hardwoods (i.e. not conifers, Ginkgo nor palms) the wood contains large cells called *vessels*. In some trees, like the oaks and ashes, those vessels which are laid down during the early part of the season are large, but a fairly sudden change to small vessels occurs near the middle of the season. In cross-section, therefore, the wood shows rings of large cells separated by rings of small cells. Such woods are called *ring-porous*. In some other trees, such as beech and birch, the vessels are of similar, rather small or mixed sizes throughout the season. These are called *diffuse-porous* timbers. The difference between these two types is easily seen and is the first important feature used in determining the genus of the tree from which a sample of wood is derived.

Hardwood timber contains two other kinds of cell. The *fibres* are usually thick-walled, narrow, sharp-ended cells found fairly uniformly through the annual ring. The *parenchyma* are thin-walled brick-shaped cells which are mainly arranged in radiating *medullary rays*. It is these that give the "figure" or graining in timbers like the oak, where they are very large, and are most prominent on the face which is parallel to the rays, that is, the radial face. The oak wood showing this is referred to as "quarter-sawn" oak.

Coniferous, or "softwood" timbers have only two kinds of cell. The "vessels" and "fibres" of hardwood timbers are united in an intermediate form of cell, the *tracheid* which combines the functions of the two kinds, and the *parenchyma* which are much the same as in the hardwoods.

The *vessels* and *tracheids* are the conducting tissues forming long, wide tubes joined end to end. Vessels have large plates at the ends with perforations to permit the flow of sap, or sometimes they are joined with no end-plates at all. *Tracheids* are joined by a long overlap and their side-walls communicate by rows of holes. The fibres of hardwoods are entirely for strengthening, allowing the vessels to be thin walled for better conduction of sap. In softwoods there are no fibres and the tracheids have to be strong and thick walled as well as good conductors of sap, hence a long overlapping arrangement and small pits in their walls are necessary to permit the flow of sap through thick-walled, rigidly joined cells. The *parenchyma* is storage tissue, holding reserves of nutrients during the winter when the sap is scarcely flowing, ready for the time of greatest need, in spring when growth must start before the new leaves and roots are functioning.

These cells are all functional for a limited period only. After a variable period typically 20–30 years, they become *lignified*, their hollow interiors fill with lignin, a hard, durable substance, and they become "wood". The active cells are thus in the outside ring of timber, anything from 1 cm thick in very old trees, to perhaps 30 cm thick in very vigorous young trees. This ring, the *sapwood* is often pale and seldom at all durable. Inside it is the *heartwood* of dead cells of greater strength and durability, and often of much darker or redder colour than the sapwood. It is the heartwood that provides the structural strength in the bole and branches of a large tree.

How a tree grows

The essential difference between the growth of woody plants like trees, shrubs and some climbers, and other plants is that these perennial woody stems increase in diameter every year. In other plants the sites of actual growth, the dividing cells or *meristem* is confined to the buds and root-tips, as *apical meristem*. In trees, however, there is a complete covering of meristematic cells, called the *cambium*, enveloping shoots, branches, bole and roots (except in the Monocotyledons). This cambium can be seen as a usually wet thin bright green layer when bark is removed from a living shoot, between the bark and the wood.

Every season the cambial cells divide to produce many layers of new cells on each side, the many large layers on the inside becoming wood cells or *xylem*, and the small layers on the outside becoming *bast* or *phloem*. Outside the bast a

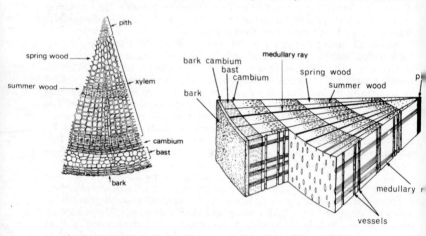

Left, cross-section of a conifer stem, showing two annual rings. *Right,* cross-section of a hard-wood stem, distinguished by the presence of vessels and medullary rays.

small bark-cambium grows a layer of bark cells each year on its outside. The xylem cells on the inner side, push the cambium and all the outer tissues farther out each year and so increase the diameter of the stem. The centre of the stem was derived from the apical meristem of the bud and is of a different character. It is called the *pith.* In other plants this original tissue is the final thickness of the shoot. The additional thickness added annually by the cambium of woody plants is called *secondary thickening.* In some Monocotyledons, including the palms, the secondary thickening is not in added rings (see below).

When the cambium of a tree starts dividing in spring, it makes large, thin-walled cells on its inner side. This is *spring wood*. As the season progresses the cells made are progressively smaller and often darker, until those made at the end of the season, in late October, are very small, thick-walled and dark. Thus the next spring wood of large pale cells grows immediately on the smallest and darkest cells. This creates a visible ring, the *annual ring*, plainly seen when the stem is cut across. Some trees like the birch and holly show no change in colour and a less marked sorting of large and small cells. The annual rings in such wood may scarcely be evident unless a dye or ink be applied, when the late or *summer wood* will take up more stain. By counting the rings back to the pith, taking care to omit "false rings" which are incomplete rings caused by severe set-backs to growth from pests or frost, the age of the branch or bole can be ascertained. Such rings are formed only in trees growing in climates which impose a stoppage of growth, whether by a winter or by a dry season. Trees from Equatorial rain forests will therefore not show them.

The Monocotyledons grow in a completely different manner. They have no complete covering of cambium, and thus normally no "secondary thickening" and in many the stem remains the same thickness as when it was first grown. In the palms bundles of meristematic (cambium-like) cells within the wood are left beneath the growing point and connect with it after it grows away, and these cause limited expansion. The growing-points are confined to the very few buds, usually a single, central, large bud. The growing-point is near the tip inside the stem and new leaves grow out of the tip. The growing-point moves up the centre, pushing out new leaves vertically, the previous leaves gradually becoming horizontal all round the stem.

The cycle of growth. In temperate climates with marked summers and winters, the first move in the spring is the growth of new feeding-roots. This occurs early in March, as the soil warms to around 5°C and is active before the aerial parts show any growth. Water and nutrients can be extracted from the soil only by the root-hairs and these last only a few weeks. Only those just behind the root-tip are active, and so continued growth of the tree depends on the constant growth of the fine, white new roots. Last year's root-hairs had died the previous autumn, so the first new growth depends on the mobilisation of the nutrients stored in the parenchyma cells. Once new root-hairs have grown, the water and nutrients can be drawn up the vessels or tracheids to the expanding shoots and leaves. In the leaves, the green pigment, chlorophyll absorbs energy from daylight and uses it to synthesise the carbohydrates, starch and cellulose by a complex series of processes, from water and from the carbon dioxide in the air. The energy which the plant needs directly for growth, raising its shoots and so on, it acquires (as do animals) from the oxidation of the carbohydrates.

There are thus the two opposing processes at work in a leaf. The building up of carbohydrates can occur only during daylight and this process liberates oxygen. The oxidation of these substances can occur at any time, and liberates carbon dioxide. In daylight, much more oxygen than carbon dioxide is given out, but in the dark only carbon dioxide is released.

The starches made in the leaves are required wherever growth is taking place in the plant. This includes the roots, and the stream of sap taking them to the roots is conducted down the bast, the tissues outside the cambium and just under the bark. This is why it is important not to damage trees beneath the bark. A cut all round the tree to the depth of the cambium (which is not far in) will cut off all the nutrients from the roots. They will soon use up all the stored nutrients and then they can grow no more. New root-growth is essential to the tree, so although a tree so "ring-barked" will leaf out normally or remain in apparent health for a while, it must soon die. A partial ringing or girdling, however, concentrates the nutrients in the crown of the tree and slows root-action and strong growth. It thus causes heavy fruiting and is often done for this purpose on fruit trees.

The leaves lose moisture to the air and this creates a gradient of dryness within the tree. Owing to the operation of the process of *osmosis*, a cell will abstract water from an adjacent cell until the two are equally moist. In this way, the sap is drawn up the tree. In normal life a pump cannot draw water up a column for more than 9 m or the column will break at this point and a vacuum will arise. If normal processes only were operating in a tree stem, no tree could be more than 9 m tall. The conducting tubes in a tree are however, so narrow that *capillary attraction* is important. This alone, whilst of some help, is insufficient to explain a column being drawn up 100 m of stem. Other effects enter here, one of which is that water in tubes of a certain very small bore has an adhesion which allows it to be drawn up more like a solid rod.

Osmosis is also the means by which the root-hairs extract water from the soil. The hairs contain sap with nutrients dissolved in it at greater concentration than the salts in normal soil-moisture. The hairs are semi-permeable membranes and the solutions each side will exchange water and solutes until the concentration is the same each side. The weak solution therefore enters the hairs and is drawn up into the plant. If, however, an excess of fertiliser, salt or some other soluble matter, is in the soil, the moisture moves the other way, out of the root hairs, and the plant may die of drought or "scorch" however wet the soil may be.

The leaves are complex organs involved in gaseous exchange. They need to take in oxygen and carbon dioxide and also to release the same gases as both processes, photosynthesis and oxidation, are carried out. When gas is released, some water must go too. In order to control the loss of water, the gases enter and leave through pores with surrounding cells which control the opening. The pores are *stomata* (singular *stoma*) and the special cells are *guard-cells*. Photosynthesis does not require full, strong sunlight to work at a maximum rate, but just bright daylight. When the sun is strong, the leaves lose water from their surfaces as well as from the stomata and lose it faster than the roots can, in dry soil, supply it. As stress sets in, the guard cells collapse across the stomata, partially blocking them and cutting down the flow of gases and loss of moisture. Photosynthesis is thus also diminished.

The manner of growth. It is often absurdly assumed that the branches rise with the growth of the tree and obvious signs of damage to a main stem 15 m up may be credited to some early misfortune near ground-level. That this is nonsense a moment's thought will show. If it were true, all old trees would have a long clean bole, whereas many are heavily branched to the base. A child's swing hung from a branch would slowly rise out of reach. With new branches visibly beginning each year at the top of the tree and getting larger, if the old ones were coming up from below, branches would have to be thrown out at some point. A very odd tree would result. All new growth is, in fact, an extension from a stationary bud.

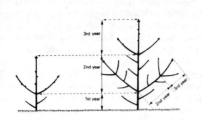 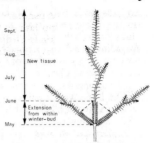

Methods of growth in conifers. *Left,* in spruces, pines etc. the whole year's growth takes place between May and July, by expansion of existing bud tissues. *Right,* in larches, cedars and hemlocks the bud tissue likewise expands in spring, but is then followed by further growth.

All normal trees, hardwood or softwood (but not the Monocotyledons like palms) end the year's growth with a central bud surrounded by side-buds. The side-buds extend branches and the central bud usually continues the axis of the branch or tree. In most conifers this is very regular for much of the tree's life, resulting in a conic and tall crown with the branches in whorls. Poplars, the Wild Cherry and a few other broad-leafed trees grow in this way for many years, but the majority soon lose the central axis and become diffusely branched, and seldom show any whorls.

In *Eucalyptus* no bud is made and growth in the warmer parts of the country is continuous except for brief pauses in the coldest spells. Cypresses and some conifers related to them just stop for the winter with no distinct bud. The Monkey-puzzle also has peculiar growth, often merely pausing for the winter in the middle of growing an unbranched shoot.

The terminal buds are of three kinds, depending on the manner of growth of the tree. They can be large and contain, already laid down, the entire, unexpanded shoot for the next year. They can be of medium size and contain the first portion of the next year's shoot, or they can be small, containing only the first leaves and perhaps a very small part of the shoot. The conifers show these features best. The pines, spruces and silver firs have large buds which rapidly extend the complete growth for the year. Even before the new growth is fully expanded, the terminal bud can be seen for the growth of the following year. For this bud to fill with the next year's tissues needs time during the growing season, so expansion of the current year's shoot is rapid and growth ceases by about early July and the rest of the season is devoted to filling the bud. This requires sunshine but little water, so this mode of growth suits trees which grow in places with hot, dry summers, although it is far from confined to them. Some pines grow two whorls or even three in a season, but with the exception of the anomalous growth of the Monterey Pine, these whorls do not represent separate periods of growth; they are all in the original bud and can be seen as swellings on it during the winter.

The larches, hemlocks and cedars have fairly small buds. These contain about one fifth of the next year's shoot in a vigorous tree, but if misfortune strikes or the tree is shaded or unhealthy this is all that will be grown. Normally this expands moderately rapidly and reaches full length by late June, after which the tip lays down new tissues and expands them continuously. In larches the two kinds of growth can be distinguished as the new leaves are larger and more spreading and the shoot makes slight curves. With only a small bud to be filled for next year, the growth of the shoot can occupy nearly all the growing season, and, in fact the larches grow on until October, as late as almost any tree.

The cypresses, sequoias, Metasequoia and some other trees have either no real bud or a very small one. Growth starts early and very slowly, as the new shoot has to be made, but it can go on all the season as no tissues have to be made for the winter bud.

Poplars and willows grow in the same way as this last group of conifers. In poplars the new shoot grows with increasing rapidity and with longer leaves as the season progresses, and stops suddenly only in late September. Oaks, maples and beeches grow in a modified form of the first category. The large buds suddenly extend the pre-formed shoot, the vigorous terminal shoots extending as much as 20–30 cm in a week. They then stop after a few weeks and either grow no more or make another, similar burst of growth in late July and then stop again for the rest of the year.

In Catalpa and Paulownia, the terminal bud either does not appear or is killed by the winter. A side bud takes over, starting late in the season from very small beginnings and growing slowly until the late summer. Then it grows rapidly until stopped in mid-growth by cold weather and the tip is inevitably too soft to survive the first frost.

In many trees a proportion of the lateral buds along the length of a shoot remains unopened in the following and succeeding years. They become covered by the bark, but move out with the cambium so that they are always near the surface. They are an insurance against the old age or premature death of the main shoot. When the main shoot is damaged or cut off, they erupt from beneath the bark and grow out. These are *epicormic* shoots. The burrs of Common Oak are a mass of these buds and when the bole is suddenly given more light, by the crop being thinned or a neighbouring tree dying, or, when the top dies, they grow out as sprouts. In fruit-trees especially, and *Acer negundo*, *Cotoneaster frigidus* and others, long sprouts arise from the upper sides of branches particularly if the tree starts to die from various causes other than old age. These are called "water-sprouts". Very few conifers have these epicormic buds so in general conifers cannot be coppiced nor can they regenerate a dying crown.

Estimating the age of a tree

The height and spread of a tree reach a maximum size then stop increasing and after a variable time start to decrease as senility sets in. Neither of these features can thus be measured to give an estimate of age except in young trees. But the circumference of the bole of any tree must increase in some measure during every year of its life. The age of the tree is thus some function of the circumference alone. The circumference (girth) is measured at 1.5 m (5 ft) from the highest point of the surrounding ground.

It would seem that much calculation and many graphs would be needed to cope with the changes in the increase in girth with advancing age, different species and differing individual vigour. It so happens, though, that trees of the most diverse species very largely conform to the simplest possible rule Only metrication robs us of the final touch – the mean growth in girth of most trees *with a full crown* is one inch (2.5 cm) a year. A tree 8 ft (2.44 m) in girth is usually about 100 years old. Grown in a wood, it will be 200 years old, and in an avenue, or slightly hemmed in, it will be 150 years old. This has been found to be true of hundreds of specimens of almost every species, coniferous or broad-leaved, of the large growing trees.

Such a rule needs some refining. The simplicity arises from the fact that early growth in almost any tree is rather faster than one inch of girth per year, then there is a period of about that rate, followed by a long period of a slower rate. So for much of its life, a tree's girth is near one inch for each year of its life. Evidently allowance should be made for young trees and for very old trees, and there are also species which are, when growing normally, much faster, and a few much slower than the general rule allows.

Young oaks on a good site often grow 1.5–2 in a year for their first 60–80 years. From then until they are about 20–22 feet (6–6.6 m) in girth they maintain the "standard" rate. Thereafter they slow further, the decrease depending on the loss of leafing crown. They seldom survive with a slower rate than one inch in 5–6 years. The major exceptions are:

Normal growth 2–3 in per year (rarely to 6 in in Wellingtonia):
Wellingtonia, Coast Redwood, Low's Fir, Grand Fir, Cedar of Lebanon, Monterey Cypress, Sitka Spruce, Douglas Fir, Western Red Cedar, Western hemlock, Cricket-bat Willow, Black Italian and other hybrid poplars, Wingnuts, *Nothofagus* spp., Red and Chestnut-leafed Oaks, Hungarian and Turkey Oaks, Tulip-tree, London Plane, and most *Eucalyptus* spp.

Normal growth soon falling much below 1 in per year:
Most small-growing trees, Scots Pine, Norway Spruce, Yew (see below), Horse Chestnut and Common Lime.

The Yew has a unique growth. Many yew-trees have achieved the standard inch for the first 100 years, but from few good data, it is apparent that they soon fall to about half this rate and gradually, over 4–500 years fall to 1 in in 5–15 years, whilst the crown is still in full vigour and increasing its spread annually. Without an earlier record of its girth, it is thus very difficult to estimate the age of a large yew and few can be properly measured. A rough guide is 8 ft – 100–150 years old; 16 ft – 300–400; 20 ft – 500–600; 30 ft – 850–1,000.

Height

An instrument designed to measure tree-height is called an Hypsometer. Modern hypsometers are simple, robust and rather expensive. They are basically a well-damped pendulum which shows directly on a different scale for each of several suitable ranges (distances from the tree) the length of tree below and above the level of the observer's eye.

Heights can be measured fairly accurately with simpler, or even makeshift equipment. The simplest of all, but quite accurate if used with care, is a length of grass, bracken or other stem, or string. A length is broken, cut or folded to the exact distance from the eyeball to the farthest stretch of the grasping finger and thumb (this length is constant for any one observer). The stick is then held at this distance, by its middle and quite vertical (string must be held by the top to hang, and is more difficult to use). The tree is then aligned, using one eye and moving back and forth until the tip and base are exactly in line with the upper and lower end of the stick or string. A mark is scored on the ground at this point. The height of the tree is now the precise distance of this mark from the centre of the tree at its base. This can be measured by a tape or by pacing. (One should establish how many paces one takes on different kinds of ground to measure, say, 30 m.)

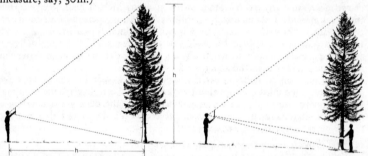

Simple ways of measuring the height of a tree. *Left,* with a stick equal in length to the full stretch of the grasping fingers from the eyeball.   *Right,* with a ruler notched at 1 inch. The corresponding mark on the tree is then one twelfth of its height.

A somewhat more sophisticated method requires a ruler and a second person. The ruler is notched at the one inch mark and is held vertically at a fixed distance from the eye (full stretch is the easiest constant distance), and the tree aligned so that it lies exactly between the 0 and 12 in. The second man stands by the tree and is guided ("up a little. No, down a bit.") until he has a narrow piece of white (paper, cloth, chocolate wrapper) exactly in the notch, centred on the one-inch line, to the satisfaction of the observer. He marks this point on the tree. The height of this point above the ground, *in inches*, is the height of the tree in *feet*. That is so because it is one twelfth of the total height. For trees over 80 ft tall, the correct point for the marker cannot be reached, so a notch on the half-inch mark is used, and the resulting height of the marker in inches is *half* the height of the tree in feet. For use with metric scales, a 30cm rule notched at 3 cm would cause the mark to be one tenth of the height of the tree.

At all times when measuring heights it must be realised that only in spire-topped trees (usually young conifers), is the apparent top shoot as seen from, say 30 metres, the true top. In most trees, especially broadly domed or widely branched trees, shoots on the nearest branches appear to be well above the true top-centre. It is easy to make a Cedar of Lebanon 40m tall by aiming at a tip which is really on a branch spreading far towards you, when the centre and highest point may be less than 30m above the ground.

In *estimating* heights without experience, it is almost invariable that trees of 7–15m true height are under-estimated and trees of 30m and over are grossly over-estimated. In general, a narrow, columnar or spire-like tree, like a Lombardy poplar, looks much taller than it really is, and broad and domed trees look less tall than they are. Really tall trees, of 50–60m seldom look anything like their true height, however, because the upper parts are much foreshortened to an observer beneath, and they may be among other very tall trees which give the eye a wrong scale by which to judge. Only when on its own, towering out of normal woodland-height trees does the giant show plainly its great height.

Flowers

The sexual organs of plants compose the flowers and can be arranged in various ways. A single flower can be entirely male, or entirely female, or both combined. In this last case, it is called a *perfect* flower. Flowers may arise singly or on special structures devoted to bearing a number of flowers. This structure is an *inflorescence* and can take many forms, for example the catkins of hazel and the panicle of horse-chestnut. The equivalent terms cannot be applied to the conifers as the analogous structures are uncertain; each conifer "flower" may represent a group of flowers or a single compound flower.

The arrangement of the flowers of each sex on the tree can also take many forms. In the simplest form, found in the more primitive conifers like yews and the Monkey-puzzle, but also in the much more highly evolved willows, hollies and the Osage Orange, each tree has flowers entirely of one sex. These trees are either wholly male or wholly female. These are called *dioecious* plants from the Greek, "di–" meaning "two" and "oecos" a household – two households are necessary to contain both sexes.

Left and *centre*, dioecious plants, i.e. of separate sexes. Seen in primitive conifers and some broadleaves, e.g. poplars, willows, hollies. *Right*, plants with 'perfect' flowers – each flower conveying elements of both sexes – comprise the great majority of broadleafed trees.

Another arrangement is with male and female flowers (unisexual) on the on the same tree. Such trees are *monoecious* (one household). This is the normal system among conifers. Some broadleaves have the flowers grouped in unisexual inflorescences, when the male inflorescence almost always differs greatly from the female in shape and position. Male walnut flowers, e.g. are on long catkins on one-year wood; the few female flowers are singly at the tip of new growth. In alders and birches, the male catkins are longer and more pendulous than the often upright females, in short inflorescences above the males. In pines the females are red ovoids at the tips of strong shoots; the males are yellow ovoids clustered near the base of weaker shoots. In a rare form of monoecity, found in Euodia, the male and female inflorescences are identical in shape and position, each being at random over the tree, either wholly of male flowers or wholly of female (*unisexual*).

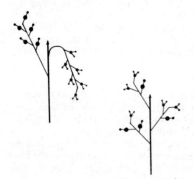

Monoecious plants. *Left,* with flowers of both sexes but on different inflorescences. Normal in conifers and found in many broadleaves e.g. oak, beech, hazel, plane. *Right,* a hermaphrodite plant, with flowers of both sexes borne on the same inflorescence. Not very common, found in e.g. Box, some maples, and some specimens of Sweet Chestnut.

In a few genera, male and female flowers are borne on the same inflorescence. These inflorescences are *hermaphrodite*. In the Box tree the female flowers are central and the males clustered around them. In some maples, the two sexes are randomly mixed. In some trees of Sweet Chestnut the female flowers are grouped towards the base of some small male catkins (but some trees are fully monoecious), and in the single poplar in the entire family which is not dioecious but hermaphrodite, the Chinese Necklace Poplar, the females are on the basal half of many male catkins.

Most of the "flowering" trees have *perfect* flowers, the female parts being the central style or styles, and the male part being the surrounding stamens tipped by pollen-bearing anthers. Among the trees not noted for their flowers, the elms also have perfect flowers. The term "*trioecious*" (three households) has been coined to try to convey the chaotic state of affairs in the flowers of the Common Ash and a few maples. Here the flowers can be male, female or perfect, and trees may be dioecious, monoecious or wholly or partially perfect, bearing flowers of any two kinds. Whole branches may be entirely female on an otherwise male tree, and the variations differ on a single tree from year to year.

The pollen from the male flowers or male parts of the flower is borne to the female flowers or parts either by the wind or by insects. All conifers are pollinated by the wind, as are most catkin-bearing trees like oaks, hornbeams, alders and birches. The willows are pollinated mostly by the wind, but, especially in the sallows, insects are also important. The Common Ash is wind-pollinated, but the Manna Ash, with petalled flowers is, like other trees with conspicuous flowers with petals, insect-pollinated.

The natural distribution of tree species

The immense variety of trees in cultivation includes species with every kind of natural distribution. Some of them occur in vast numbers across entire continents, whilst others are found only on one mountain or in one small valley in the entire world. Only one species occurs both in Eurasia and in America – the Common Juniper (though the Grey Alder of Europe has been regarded as conspecific with a very similar tree in North America). All other species are either strictly Old World or New World. Many *genera* are represented by species in both regions. There are pines, spruces, larches, birches, oaks and beeches in North America, and different ones across Europe and Asia to China and Japan. On the other hand, robinias are confined to North America, and the true cedars to the Mediterranean and India. Many genera have only one or two species and are confined to small areas particularly of Japan, Formosa or China. There is a striking parallel between the trees and shrubs in the South-east of the USA and those in S.E. China. Many genera have one or two species in both these widely spread regions and none at all in the rest of the world between them. The best known examples are the two Tulip-trees. Many other genera are common to these regions only but more widely spread in America, and in E. Asia, such as *Thuja, Tsuga, Magnolia* and *Catalpa*.

There are no species, and very few genera, of trees common to the temperate parts of both hemispheres. *Podocarpus* and *Sophora* are two of the exceptions, although only southern and northern species respectively appear in this book.

The conifers are, in the long view, retreating and becoming confined to mountains. The recent Ice Age caused a great deal of migration among trees and a number of conifers were left as mere relict populations. Two of these are European, the Serbian Spruce, found in only a single valley in Jugoslavia, and the Spanish Fir, found only around Ronda in the Sierra Nevada, S. Spain, where the three widely separated populations have been threatened by goats and fire.

In N. America the mountain chains run north and south. In Europe, the main ranges – Cantabrians, Pyrenees, Alps and Tatra – run east to west. This difference has had a profound effect on the species able to return north after the Ice Age. In Europe escape was difficult and possible through only a few gaps; many species must have perished *en bloc*. In N. America all could migrate southwards at their preferred elevation, ride out the storm in Mexico and then return in the same way. One group of species returned by the Coast Range, which by then was becoming eroded by the sea, and they finished up on the Monterey Peninsula, or in some cases, nearby areas of coast and off-shore islands. As the climate continued to become warmer and drier these trees would have migrated on north to Oregon and Washington, but the mountains went no farther, so they could not; nor could they move across the now hot, dry valley to the next range. So they are in or near Monterey as small relict populations, unable to grow to their full stature. This interesting group includes Gowen's Cypress, Bishop Pine, Monterey Cypress and Monterey Pine. These last two grow along short stretches of low cliff and over low hills, respectively, near Monterey where, at a considerable age, they rarely attain 20m in height. In Britain they can be 30m tall in 40 years, and in New Zealand the pine has grown 60m in a little over 40 years. (In San Francisco, 30 miles north of the natural stands, a Monterey Pine on an irrigated lawn has grown to 16m in five years.)

Among the 35 species of tree native to Britain, most have a wide distribution in Europe while some range to W. Asia, the Caucasus Mountains and N. Africa. That with the widest range is the Common Juniper which is found almost throughout the northern temperate world. The Scots Pine ranges from Spain across Europe and Russia to E. Siberia. Only some whitebeams, which may well be regarded as subspecies, and possibly the English Elm are *endemic* species, that is, found wild nowhere but in this country. In Eocene times, some 60 million years ago, this part of Europe was near the latitude of the present Mediterranean region. The Ginkgo, many magnolias and other trees grew around the shores of the sea which was then laying down the rocks of what are now the Hampshire and London Basins, and in other lowland parts. This rich flora became gradually more impoverished as the continent drifted into higher latitudes, and then about one million years ago, the Ice Age started. Succeeding waves cleared all Britain, with the exception of some probable refuges to the south-west which are no longer land, of all trees. The ice retreated for the last time only 11,000 years ago and migration back from Europe was rapid, but was stopped about 6,000 years ago when the land connection was breached. Only those trees which were already in N. France could have made the crossing in time. A few returned from the south western refuge; the Strawberry Tree and perhaps the Cornish Elm, but they remain in the south west. It needed the introductions made by man to make Britain the rich collection of trees it now is.

IDENTIFICATION

The process of learning to identify trees is a progressive one without an end. As beginners, we all puzzle over the differences between Lawson Cypress and Thuja even with foliage in the hand, and the existence of Nootka Cypress seems to complicate matters beyond solution. Some years later we will unhesitatingly identify all three, and more besides, at half a mile's distance from a passing train. Similarly, the snake-bark maples seem to be a confusing group, and some are seen mis-labelled in collections. After a season studying them, however, an indefinable "jizz", an unconscious combining of a number of minor features, allows almost infallible identification of the four most frequent species at 20 m range at least. This short-circuiting of the lengthy comparisons needed at first cannot be acquired from books alone – not even this one – although the guiding features upon which the "jizz" seems to be based have been stressed. It can be acquired only by frequent handling of the different foliages; observation of the whole tree, and thorough working out, preferably through a key, of what they must be. Once acquired, it is difficult to think back to the days when one had not this skill, and to write for those to whom a Norway Spruce seems very like a Douglas Fir.

How to learn. Everyone passes numerous trees almost every day without really seeing one of them. Town gardens and parks have a great variety of species and cultivars. If the trees passed daily are taken first and identified, they will then really be seen, and seen in every season until they are very familiar. These will then be a guide to a number of related trees or cultivars seen elsewhere. As the commoner species become known, the mass of unknown trees becomes much less forbidding, as well as smaller. Once the Common and Turkey Oaks are familiar in their considerable variation, an oak which is seen to be neither of these evidently differs in some ways which strike you, and these will be the pointers to identify it.

This book uses, as far as possible, features of the leaves for identification. Leaves can be collected and preserved easily. Large trees can spare a small shoot with a few leaves and these can be taken home and examined at leisure. In gardens, however, and with any small tree which may be rare, shoots should on no account be picked without permission. By autumn, however, a leaf or two of a deciduous tree can be gently removed just before it is about to be shed. In spring and summer, notes should be taken instead, and the more detailed these are and the longer the foliage is handled and described, the more that will be retained in the memory.

The notes should give: length and breadth of biggest leaf, and, if very different, of normal leaves; length of petiole; hairiness or otherwise of petiole and any unusual colour; shape of base and apex of leaf and general shape; lobing or toothing; shininess or otherwise above. The underside of a leaf usually tells much more than the upper. Note hairiness and whether confined to veins; any contrast with upper surface in colour or shine, and especially, any tufts of hair, any pegs or colour in the axils of the main veins, especially at the base. From these notes, any tree in one of the large genera should be identifiable from the key given. The notes should also contain details of bark, crown-shape, flowers or fruit, if seen.

Using keys. Do not be put off by the apparent complexity of the keys. They are easily used, great fun, and a splendid way to learn the features important in separating similar species. Using a key is like sitting a simple examination with all the answers before you. The keys are of two different kinds – broad guides and numbered dichotomous keys. First there are guides to conspicuous variants of colour, habit, etc. on pp. 34–5 and 38–42. They are mainly concerned with cultivars, which it is helpful to dispose of early on rather than include in the formal keys. These guides, with the guide to genera of broad-leafed trees on pp. 43–6, work by degrees of indentation: each pair or group of characters for selection is indented to an equal distance. Second, there are formal keys to the genera of conifers (pp. 35–7) and to species of the major genera in the main text. With these find the answer to Question 1. This will lead either to Question 2 or to another farther down the key, and soon these "either-or" options should lead inescapably to the species you have.

If it does not, but leads to a decision about a feature which the specimen lacks, or to a species whose flowers, fruit or other features under its full entry are obviously wrong, there are four possible causes: (1) The specimen is highly atypical in some feature which has been used in the key. This is always possible, but the keys have been made to encompass or avoid most likely variants. (2) The specimen is of a cultivar which is not in the key. The keys are long enough when made to cope with the species and a few of the most striking cultivar variants, but in conifers especially many have had to be omitted. Colour, weeping and fastigiate cultivars have the same foliage features in other respects as their parent types, and there should be no problem with them. Some leaf-variants, like cut-leaved forms are also omitted, but some help with these should be found in the guides on pp. 38–42. (3) The specimen is from a rarity beyond the scope of this book. (See Preface.) Nothing can be done about this, but it should occur only with specimens from the largest or most specialised collections. (4) You have made an error somewhere along the line. This may well not be your fault – you may have judged teeth as lobules, or the pubescence may be too fine or shed early on your specimen. Return to Question 1 and when a point arises where the choice of answer is not clear, take this time the alternative rejected last time. It is not, alas, possible to avoid a few ambiguities with such variable things as plants.

Confronted with a tree or shoot and leaves from a tree, quite unknown to them, different readers will start from different levels, depending both on the reader and on the species in question. Nearly everyone seeing an Indian Horse-chestnut would know that it was a Horse-chestnut, although many might need to turn to *Aesculus* to find out which one. On the other hand, nearly everyone is quite foxed by the Gutta-percha Tree, *Eucommia* which seems to be almost anything in general but nothing in particular. To many, a spruce is easily seen to be some kind of spruce, while to others it is just a conifer of some kind. But someone quite able to class one tree as a spruce may have no such knowledge to guide him with, say, a Wing-nut. Therefore almost everyone will need, at some time, to start from the beginning. Even the prime distinction between conifers and broadleafed trees cannot be assumed to be always easy to everyone. First, decide if the tree is a conifer (or Taxad) or broadleafed tree:

Conifer and Taxad

Veins parallel, not in a network; usually a resinous or aromatic scent can be obtained by crushing; usually annual growth is a whorl of branches at the base of a leading shoot; often leaves dark, hard, narrow and spine-tipped, rarely broad and flat; small and scale-like in many, needle-like in others. Male and female flowers always separate, never with petals; fruit a cone or berry-like or green and plum-like.

Broadleafed

Veins networked, parallel only in the immense leaves of *Cordyline* (a Mono-cotelydon); most have a vague green scent when crushed, a few have varied aromas but are not resinous; growth nearly always soon diffusely branched, not whorled; leaves usually flat and thin, some hard, dark and evergreen, but then flat, not needle-like nor linear.

Flowers with or without petals, perfect (i.e. bisexual) in many, separate male catkins in some, hermaphrodite catkins in a few.

Fruit very varied: capsule, pod, acorn, nut, berry, winged, etc.

If a Conifer or Taxad:

   1. If the foliage is golden, blue fastigiate or markedly pendulous, try the **guide to some variants of conifers** on p. 34–5, as these are not separated in the full Key, but can be quite easily identified if regarded as single groups, there not being very many of each.

   2. If the foliage is normal, use the end-papers as a first indication, then the **key to conifers**, p. 35. By following this, you should arrive at one or two possible genera. Turn to the general description of these genera and see if this narrows the field to one genus. If not, both will have to be searched for the species to fit your specimen, but the first few descriptions of species will prob-ably indicate whether the genus is the right one. With small genera, of few species, the descriptions will have to be compared, but the large genera, with many species all have keys. These should enable you to find which species you have merely by taking the relevant one of two statements and following through the numbers for a few such pairs until the answer appears.

If a broadleafed tree:

   1. If the leaf is very large (simple leaf with blade 25 cm or more long, or blade and petiole together more than 35 cm long; or compound leaf 50 cm or more long) try the **guide to broadleafed trees with outsize leaves**, p. 38.

   2. If the tree is very pendulous, fastigiate, golden-leaved, silver-leaved, variegated or cut-leaved, try the **guide to some variants of broadleafed trees**, p. 39.

   3. If the tree shows none of the features given in **1** and **2** (and even if it does, but not on the leaves you have) turn to the **guide to the genera of broad-leafed trees**, p. 43.

A GUIDE TO SOME VARIANTS OF CONIFERS

GOLDEN FOLIAGE
Scale-leaved

Slender, drooping thread-like shoots   *Chamaecyparis pisifera* 'Filifera Aurea', p. 67

Upturned bunches of plumes   *Chamaecyparis pisifera* 'Plumosa Aurea', p. 67

Blunt scales, broad conic crown   *Chamaecyparis obtusa* 'Crippsii', p. 66

Acute scales, narrow conic crown   *Chamaecyparis lawsoniana* 'Lutea', p. 62

Congested bunches on gaunt little tree   *Chamaecyparis obtusa* 'Tetragona Aurea', p. 66

Sprays banded gold, whitish and green, highly fragrant   *Thuja plicata* 'Zebrina', p. 81

Columnar; shoots at all angles, rounded (terete)   *Cupressus macrocarpa* 'Lutea', p. 70

Shoots of appressed scales mixed with shoots of spreading leaves

Columnar   *Juniperus chinensis* 'Aurea', p. 78

Leaves not scale-like

Flattened, margin gold   *Taxus baccata* cvs., p. 51

Needle-like

In pairs   *Pinus sylvestris* 'Aurea', p. 170

Single, gold only when new

Leaf more than 1 cm   *Picea abies* 'Aurea', p. 135

Leaf less than 1 cm   *Picea orientalis* 'Aurea', p. 136

BLUE or GREY FOLIAGE

Over 10 cm, slender, drooping needles   five-needled pines, pp. 155–65

4–8 cm, needles in fives, twisted   *Pinus parviflora*, p. 163

5 cm, leathery, standing above shoot   *Abies concolor* 'Violacea', p. 105

2–3 cm

Spreading round shoot, sharp, stiff   *Picea pungens* 'Glauca' group, p. 132

Parted beneath shoot, soft   *Picea engelmannii* 'Glauca', p. 133

1–2 cm linear

All round shoots; narrow, dense crown   *Tsuga mertensiana*, p. 147

In whorls on spurs; sharp; hard   *Cedrus atlantica* 'Glauca', p. 117

6–8 mm, free

Hard; clasping shoot; bushy; upright   *Juniperus squamata* 'Meyeri', p. 78

Soft, fluffy; spreading; broad conic tree   *Chamaecyparis pisifera* 'Squarrosa', p. 67

1–2 mm, free. Vertical sprays; narrowly columnar tree   *Chamaecyparis lawsoniana* 'Fletcheri', p. 61

Scale-like, closely appressed

Shoots at all angles

Open, gaunt crown; fleshy fruit   *Juniperus virginiana* 'Glauca', p. 78

Dense, conic crown; cones   *Cupressus lusitanica* 'Glauca', p. 71

Shoots in flat sprays
    Level; open, strong, conic tree   *Chamaecyparis*
                            lawsoniana 'Triomphe de Boskoop', p. 60

    Vertical; dense, small
        Grey-green, conic to ground   *Chamaecyparis lawsoniana* 'Fraseri', p. 60
        Grey-blue; bushy near base   *Chamaecyparis lawsoniana* 'Allumii', p. 60
        Narrow-columnar   *Chamaecyparis lawsoniana* 'Columnaris', p. 60

FASTIGIATE

Blue-green, needles in whorls   *Cedrus atlantica* 'Fastigiata', p. 117
Needles in pairs   *Pinus sylvestris* 'Fastigiata', p. 170
Scale-like leaves
    Foliage in plumes
        Dark green; tree very narrow, acute tip   *Cupressus sempervirens*, p. 72
          Bright green; tree moderately narrow,
                            Cupressus macrocarpa 'Fastigiata', p. 70
    Foliage in flattened plates
        Scales very long; foliage strongly scented   *Calocedrus decurrens*, p. 58
        Scales broad as long, minute, need crushing for scent
          Crown flame-shaped or broad columnar
                          Chamaecyparis lawsoniana 'Erecta', p. 61
          Crown very slender columnar   *Chamaecyparis lawsoniana* 'Kilmacurragh', p. 61

PENDULOUS

Branches pendulous   *Cedrus atlantica* 'Glauca Pendula', p. 117
Branches up-curved, shoots hanging
    Leaves needle-like
        Rounded cross-section, dark green all round   *Picea smithiana*, p. 126
        Flattened; silver bands beneath   *Picea brewerana*, p. 127
    Leaves scale-like
        Scale-leaves with long, free acute tips, bright green   *Juniperus recurva*
        var. *coxii*, p. 77; *Juniperus recurva* 'Castlewellan',   p. 77
        Scale-leaves appressed, deep green grey-green, or dark blue-green
          Branchlets remote, tree columnar, tip drooping
                          Chamaecyparis lawsoniana 'Intertexta', p. 62
          Branchlets dense, tree conic, tip nearly straight
                          Chamaecyparis nootkatensis 'Pendula', p. 63
        Foliage hanging on long threads, bunches of branchlets at long
        intervals
          Deep green or golden; scale-leaves long-acuminate
                          Chamaecyparis pisifera 'Filifera', p. 67
          Blue-green; scale-leaves acute   *Chamaecyparis lawsoniana* 'Filiformis', p. 61

KEY TO GINKGO, CONIFERS AND TAXADS

Fan-veined, broad-cuneate, broadly two-lobed, leathery, deciduous
    leaves, on spurs on old wood   *Ginkgo*, p. 50
Leaves linear, or, if broad, hard, spined and not on spurs   Conifer or Taxad: **1**

1. Deciduous, linear, soft, thin-textured, usually pale or bright green   **2**
    Evergreen, linear, scale-like, needle-like, chaff-like, hooked, spined or
    broad-triangular, usually hard   **5**
2. In rosettes on spurs from second year shoots   **3**
    Singly and flat each side of shoot   **4**

3. Spurs long and curved; leaf with pale margin   *Pseudolarix*, p. 123
    Spurs short and straight; leaf uniform above   *Larix*, p. 119
4. Alternate shoots and leaves; leaf slender   *Taxodium*, p. 94
    Opposite shoots and leaves; leaf·rather broad   *Metasequoia*, p. 95
5. Rosettes of 20–80 leaves on spurs on second year wood   *Cedrus*, p. 116
    Leaves neither in rosettes nor on spurs   **6**
6. Large, distant whorls of leaves 10–15 cm long   *Sciadopitys*, p. 91
    Not in whorls, or small leaves not more than five together   **7**
7. In bundles of 2, 3, 5 or, rarely, more; needle-like   *Pinus*, p. 150
    Not in bundles   **8**
8. Bud distinct; brown white or purple   **9**
    Bud indistinct, green; or absent   **13**
9. Second year shoot green or largely green   *Torreya*, p. 53
    Second year shoot not green   **10**
10. Leaf with sucker-like base; cone erect   *Abies*, p. 96
    Leaf not expanded at base; cone pendent   **11**
11. Bare shoots rough with peg-like pulvini   *Picea*, p. 124
    Bare shoots nearly smooth   **12**
12. Leaf soft, slender; bud acute, cone bracts lobed   *Pseudotsuga*, p. 148
    Leaf hard, bud very small, ovoid   *Tsuga*, p. 141
13. Leaf small, flat appressed scale   **14**
    Leaf a protruding scale or not scale-like   **21**
14. Leaf striped white above   *Austrocedrus*, p. 59
    Leaf not striped white above   **15**
15. Foliage in flattened, fern-like sprays   **16**
    Foliage in 3-dimension plumes   **19**
16. Lateral scales 5 times as long as broad   *Calocedrus*, p. 58
    Scales other than along shoots ± as broad as long   **17**
17. Scales 5 mm + broad; hard; glossy   *Thujopsis*, p. 82
    Scales smaller, narrower and, if shiny then soft   **18**
18. Cone globular, ripens woody   ×*Cupressocyparis Chamaecyparis*, p. 59
    Cone flask-shaped, leathery   *Thuja*, p. 79
19. Shoot stout, branching in 3s or 4s   *Athrotaxis*, p. 89
    Shoot slender; branching irregular   **20**
20. Free juvenile leaves at base or tip of shoot   *Juniperus*, p. 74
    Leaves uniformly appressed scales   ×*Cupressocyparis*, p. 68; *Cupressus*, p. 69
21. Leaves scale-like with tip or centre rising free   **22**
    Leaf not scale-like; linear or lanceolate   **27**
22. Leaves in whorls of three   **23**
    Leaves opposite or spiral on shoot   **24**
23. Leaf blunt, thick; striped white outside surface   *Fitzroya*, p. 74
    Leaf slender, acuminate; striped white inside   *Juniperus*, p. 74
24. Leaf big, 2–3 cm, hard, spined, broad-triangular   *Araucaria*, p. 57
    Leaf <2 cm not broad-triangular   **25**
25. Leaf 1–2 mm, free at tip only   *Athrotaxis*, p. 89
    Leaf with hard, rising incurved spine-tip   **26**
26. Spine <1 cm, dull green or grey   *Sequoiadendron*, p. 86
    Spine >1 cm, bright green   *Cryptomeria*, p. 87
27. Leaf thick, 10–12 mm, incurved   *Athrotaxis*, p. 89
    Leaf flat   **28**
28. Shoot with scale-leaves   *Sequoia*, p. 83
    Shoot without scale-leaves   **29**
29. Leaves mostly >10 cm; deep green, blunt   *Podocarpus*, p. 55
    Leaves <10 cm   **30**
30. Leaves mostly 5–7 cm, bright green; softly spined   *Cunninghamia*, p. 90
    Leaves rarely 5 cm   **31**

A GUIDE TO BROADLEAFED TREES WITH OUTSIZE LEAVES

Whether a leaf appears as very large or not depends to some extent upon its shape. A leaf of Common Ash seems quite ordinary when 35 cm long, but a nearly orbicular leaf, like that of American Lime, seems huge when 20 cm long. The leaf of Van Volxem's Maple seems outsize when the blade may be 15 cm long because it is on a petiole of over 20 cm long.

For inclusion in this section, the following criteria are used:

      Simple leaf = blade 25 cm long, or blade + petiole 35 cm long

      Compound leaf = 50 cm or more long

SIMPLE LEAF
Lobed
  Oak-like
    Lobes rounded; leaf to 40 cm   *Quercus dentata*, p. 246
    Lobes finely pointed; leaf to 27 cm   *Quercus borealis* (sprout), p. 232
  Sycamore-like
    Lobes shallow, coarsely toothed   *Acer velutinum* var. *van volxemii*, p. 335
    Lobes very deep, few large rounded teeth   *Acer macrophyllum*, p. 330
  Very broad; small acuminate lobes at corners   *Catalpa* × *erubescens*, p. 387
Unlobed
  To 50 cm+, thin; pale above, silvery beneath   *Magnolia*
                                          macrophylla, p. 262

  Less than 40 cm
    Oblique at base; ovate; abruptly acuminate
      Green beneath   *Tilia americana* (sprout), p. 360
      Grey beneath   *Tilia* × *moltkei*, p. 361
    Symmetrically cordate at base
      Petiole scarlet; leaf glabrous beneath   *Idesia polycarpa*, p. 364
      Petiole pink, yellow or green; leaf pubescent beneath
        Petiole soon glabrous (bark fissured)   *Catalpa speciosa*, p. 387
        Petiole densely pubescent (bark smooth)   *Paulownia*
                                        tomentosa, p. 383
        Petiole finely pubescent (bark scaly)   *Populus lasiocarpa*, p. 184

COMPOUND LEAF
Doubly compound; to 115 cm long   *Gymnocladus dioicus*, p. 303
Leaflets five or seven   *Carya* spp., p. 197
Leaflets 11 or more, toothed
  Rachis with sticky, dense woolly hairs   *Juglans* spp., p. 195
  Leaflets with 2–5 big teeth at base, each with a large gland
                                 Ailanthus sp., p. 310
  Leaflets serrated; oblique at base   *Pterocarya* spp., p. 191
Leaflets 11–13, entire, terminal leaflet large   *Rhus verniciflua*, p. 314
Leaflets, 20–30, entire, terminal often lacking   *Cedrela sinensis*, p. 312
Radiate-compound; Horse Chestnut-like; leaf-span to 60 cm, petiole to 42 cm
                                  Aesculus turbinata, p. 354

A GUIDE TO SOME VARIANTS OF BROADLEAFED TREES

VERY PENDULOUS
Simple leaves
  Long, slender   *Salix alba* 'Tristis', p. 189
  Green, broad
    Rough   *Ulmus glabra* 'Camperdown', p. 249
    Smooth
      Bud stalked   *Alnus incana* 'Pendula', p. 211
      Bud sessile, slender   *Fagus sylvatica* 'Pendula', p. 221
  Silvery   *Pyrus salicifolia*, p. 291
Compound leaves
  Bud black   *Fraxinus excelsior* 'Pendula', p. 380
  Bud hidden   *Sophora japonica* 'Pendula', p. 306

STRICTLY FASTIGIATE
Leaf white beneath   *Populus alba* 'Pyramidalis', p. 181
Leaf as broad as long   *Populus nigra* 'Italica', p. 183
Bark white and black   *Betula pendula* 'Fastigiata', p. 206
Leaf wavy-edged; few teeth   *Fagus sylvatica* 'Dawyck', p. 221
Leaf broadly lobed; flat ended *Liriodendron tulipifera* 'Fastigiatum', p. 265
Leaf serrate
  Petiole and under leaf woolly   *Malus tschonoskii*, p. 290
  Glabrous
    Veins parallel right to edge   *Carpinus betulus* 'Columnaris', p. 213
    Veins curve in   *Prunus* 'Amanogawa', p. 295
Leaf compound
  Doubly compound, to 40 cm *Koelreuteria paniculata* 'Fastigiata', p. 357
  Singly compound
    Only basal leaflets free   *Sorbus thuringiaca* 'Fastigiata', p. 281
    All leaflets free
      Leaflets entire   *Robinia pseudoacacia* 'Fastigiata', p. 308
      Leaflets serrate   *Sorbus aucuparia* 'Fastigiata', p. 278

GOLDEN-LEAFED (NOT VARIEGATED)
Simple leaf
  White underside   *Populus alba* 'Richardii', p. 181
  Ovate-acuminate
    8–10 × 8 cm   *Populus* 'Serotina Aurea', p. 186
    20 × 22 cm   *Catalpa bignonioides* 'Aurea', p. 387
  Elliptic
    15 × 9 cm   *Ulmus glabra* 'Lutescens', p. 249
    5 × 3–5 cm
      Harsh above   *Ulmus procera* 'Louis van Houtte', p. 250
      Smooth above   *Ulmus carpinifolia* 'Wredei', p. 252
  Lobed
    Oak-like   *Quercus robur* 'Concordia', p. 245
    Sycamore-like   *Acer pseudoplatanus* 'Worleei', p. 334
    Lobes entire, thread-pointed   *Acer cappadocicum* 'Aureum', p. 326

Golden-leafed (*contd.*)
Compound Leaf
  Leaflets few, 3–7, large   *Acer negundo* 'Auratum', p. 350
  Leaflets many, 13–36, small
    Entire   *Robinia pseudoacacia* 'Frisia', p. 309
    Toothed   *Gleditsia triacanthos* 'Sunburst, p. 302

STRONGLY VARIEGATED
Variegated white (silvery, not cream)
  Compound leaf   *Acer negundo* 'Variegatum', p. 350
  Simple leaf
    Holly leaf, several cvs   *Ilex aquifolium*, p. 315
                         Ilex × *altaclarensis*, p. 316
    Three-lobed   *Acer rufinerve* 'Albolimbatum', p. 344
    Oblong-lanceolate, large   *Castanea sativa* 'Albomarginata', p. 223
    Rounded, small, hairy above   *Ulmus procera* 'Variegata'ᶜ p. 250
    Beech leaf   *Fagus sylvatica* 'Albovariegata', p. 221
    Big ovate, deltoid poplar leaf   *Populus candicans* 'Aurora', p. 185
Variegated pale cream or pale yellow or gold
  Compound leaf   *Acer negundo* 'Aureomarginatum', p. 350
  Simple leaf
    Holly leaf, several cvs.   *Ilex aquifolium*, p. 315
                         Ilex × *altaclarensis*, p. 316
    Unlobed leaf
      Thin, small, entire, in layers   *Cornus controversa* 'Variegata', p. 373
      Poplar leaf (can be flushed pink)   *Populus candicans* 'Aurora', p. 185
      Beech leaf   *Fagus sylvatica* 'Luteovariegata' p. 221
    Lobed leaf
      No terminal lobe   *Liriodendron tulipifera* 'Aureomarginatum' p. 265
      Lobes with many coarse teeth, Sycamore leaf   *Acer*
                           pseudoplatanus 'Variegatum', p. 334
      Lobes with very few, large teeth, Plane leaf   *Platanus*
                          × *hispanica* 'Suttneri', p. 273
      Lobes with several large teeth drawn out to fine points
                     Acer platanoides 'Drummondii', p. 322

SILVERY LEAVES (all season, first two; new foliage only, the rest)
Long slender leaf
  Small, pendulous tree; hairy leaf   *Pyrus salicifolia*, p. 291
  Large, open tree; leaf nearly glabrous   *Salix alba* 'Sericea', p. 189
Leaf lobed or coarsely toothed   *Populus alba*, p. 181
                           Populus canescens, p. 181
Leaf oblong or ovate-lanceolate, 8 cm   *Pyrus elaeagrifolia*, p. 291
Leaf thick, nearly round, to 20 × 15 cm   *Sorbus cuspidata* 'Mitchellii', p. 283
                              S. 'Wilfrid Fox', p. 283
Leaf ovate, to 8 cm   *Sorbus aria* and cvs., p. 281
Leaf ovate-lanceolate, to 22 cm   *Sorbus cuspidata*, p. 282

VERY DEEPLY CUT LEAVES

Leaves with ribbon-like lobes cut almost to the midrib belong to such easily separated genera that a key is not necessary. However, it could save much searching through cultivars to refer to the list below.

Compound Leaf	*Juglans regia* 'Laciniata', p. 191
Simple Leaf	
Beech	*Fagus sylvatica* 'Heterophylla', p. 221
Birch	*Betula pendula* 'Dalecarlica', p. 206
Alder	*Alnus glutinosa* 'Imperialis', p. 210
Lime	*Tilia platyphyllos* 'Laciniata', p. 358
Maple	*Acer platanoides* 'Lorbergii', *A.p.* 'Dissectum', p. 323
Oak	*Quercus robur* 'Filicifolia', p. 245

A GUIDE TO TREES WITH PROMINENT FEATURES OF BARK

BROADLEAFED TREES

Mahogany-red; highly polished	*Prunus serrula*, p. 293
Bright orange-red; flaking and rolling	*Acer griseum*, p. 341
Deep orange-red; flaking finely	*Arbutus andrachnoides*, p. 375
Bright orange	
Uniform; scaly	*Betula albosinensis*, p. 203
With large white patches	*Myrtus apiculata*, p. 367
Pale or pinkish orange	*Sorbus aucuparia* 'Beissneri', p. 278
Pale brownish orange; glossy	*Prunus maackii*, p. 300
Dull orange-brown	
Spined foliage	*Maclura pomifera*, p. 260
Rough, cordate leaf	*Morus nigra*, p. 259
Bald, smooth	
Pink, red and yellow	*Arbutus andrachne*, p. 375
Red and pink	*Arbutus menziesii*, p. 376
Flesh-pink and grey	*Stewartia sinensis*, p. 363
Blue-grey, brown, yellow, etc.	*Eucalyptus* spp., p. 367–71
Dark pinkish-red; rolling up	*Betula albosinensis* var. *septentrionalis*, p. 203
Bright pinkish-red; bands of lenticels	*Betula utilis* var. *prattii*, p. 203
Pure white	
A little creamy; shiny	*Betula utilis*, p. 203; *B. jacquemontii*, p. 203
Dead white; chalky	*Betula platyphylla* var. *szechuanica*, p. 206
Dull white	
Banded or patterned grey	*Betula pubescens*, p. 207
Marked black in diamonds	*Betula pendula*, p. 205
Creamy white; small black diamonds	*Populus canescens*, p. 181; *P. alba*, p. 181
White	
Tinged pink	*Betula ermanii*, p. 202
Tinged orange	*Betula maximowiczii*, p. 202; *B. papyrifera*, p. 206
With dark purple; banded with lenticels	*Betula papyrifera*, p. 206
Brown	
Big flakes leaving yellow	*Platanus* × *hispanica*, p. 273; *Parrotia persica*, p. 271
Small scales leaving orange	*Stewartia pseudocamellia*, p. 363
Crumbling to leave orange	*Zelkova carpinifolia*, p. 254

Broadleafed trees (*contd.*)

Bright green, boldly striped white	Snake-barked maples, p. 341

Corky

Deeply

Yellowish-grey or cream	*Quercus suber*, p. 235
Grey-pink	*Quercus variabilis*, p. 233
Dull grey; compound leaf	*Phellodendron amurense*, p. 310
Shallowly; grey or cream-grey	*Quercus × hispanica* 'Lucombeana', p. 236
Cork on twigs only	*Ulmus × hollandica*, p. 252; *U. carpinifolia*, p. 250;
	Liquidambar styraciflua, p. 269; *Acer campestre*, p. 328

Very shaggy

Long plates; grey	*Carya ovata*, p. 198; *Carya laciniosa*, p. 199

Strips and rolls

Blackish red	*Betula nigra*, p. 205
Grey-blue, brown, yellow	*Eucalyptus* spp., pp. 367–71

CONIFERS

Bright orange; flaking and rolling	*Pinus patula*, p. 167
Bright orange-brown	*Sequoia*, p. 83; *Cryptomeria japonica* 'Elegans', p. 88

Dull orange-brown

Flaking and rolling	*Abies squamata*, p. 112
Stripping a little	*Metasequoia*, p. 95; *Taxodium distichum*, p. 94

Red-brown

Thick and fibrous	*Sequoiadendron giganteum*, p. 86
Prominently ridged	*Cunninghamia lanceolata*, p. 90

Pinkish-red

Small scales	*Pinus sylvestris*, p. 170; *P. resinosa*, p. 171; *P. densiflora*, p. 174
Big plates	*Pinus ponderosa*, p. 167
Pinkish-yellow; big plates	*Pinus ponderosa*, p. 167

Dark red

Shiny in places	*Thuja standishii*, p. 81
Fissured and scaly	*Pinus sylvestris*, p. 170
Dark purple, flaking to leave yellowish	*Cupressus glabra*, p. 72
Multi-coloured. Grey-brown flaking to leave white,	
yellow, red and purple	*Pinus bungeana*, p. 169

Very shaggy

Long strips	*Juniperus recurva* var. *coxii*, p. 76
Strips and rolls	*Abies squamata*, p. 112; *Picea asperata*, p. 131

Corky

Deeply

Dark brown	*Pseudotsuga menziesii*, p. 148; *Abies concolor* var.
	lowiana, p. 105
Pale grey or cream	*Abies lasiocarpa* var. *arizonica*, p. 114
Shallowly; pale grey	*Abies concolor* var. *lowiana*, p. ˜05

TREES WITH SPINES ON THE BOLE

Short, broad-based, single spines	*Kalopanax pictus*, p. 371
Long, bunched, bright green when new	*Gleditsia triacanthos*, p. 302
Slender, single, on short shoot	*Crataegus* spp., pp. 274–76

A GUIDE TO BROADLEAFED TREES

A full key which separated each genus of broadleafed tree would have to be based on flowers and fruit.

But since it is baffling and infuriating to have leaves of a tree but be prevented from finding out what it is because you have no flowers nor fruit (a frequent occurrence, especially when seeing young trees), it seems better to have some sort of guide working on leaves alone, even if it must often end by leaving rather a wide choice of genera as possible choices. The **guide to genera** below, therefore, is intended to be of use without flowers or fruit, but brings these in as secondary features in some places where no other distinction is made by foliage alone. Each line in a section implies a *negative* to the lines above it.

EVERGREEN

Blue-grey, doubly compound, linear leaflets	*Acacia (dealbata)*, p. 301
Blue-grey, leathery, aromatic	*Eucalyptus*, p. 367
Pale bright green, margin strongly waved	*Pittosporum*, p. 364
Yellowish dark green	
Strap-shaped, 1 m or more long	*Cordyline australis*, p. 389
Oblong-ovate, 8–16 cm long	*Magnolia*, p. 262
Elliptic or lanceolate, 1–3 cm	*Buxus*, p. 313
Blackish; may be grey at first	
Serrate	
Leathery, thin; petiole red	*Prunus*, p. 291
Hard	
1–3 cm	*Nothofagus*, p. 216
6–9 cm, glabrous shoot	*Arbutus*, p. 374
Partly compound; densely pubescent shoot and petiole	*Eucryphia*, p. 362
Softly spined teeth	*Quercus*, p. 224
Hard, sharp spines on wavy margin	
Broad, 3–8 cm across	*Ilex*, p. 315
Narrow, 1–2 cm across, black	*Phillyrea*, p. 383
Entire	
Petiole red	
Margin finely crinkled	*Laurus*, p. 268
Margin plane, underside glaucous	
8–12 cm	*Arbutus*, p. 374
5–20 cm, oblanceolate, broad midrib	*Drimys*, p. 266
Golden beneath	*Chrysolepis*, p. 224
Opposite	
Shapes variable	*Acer (sempervirens)*, p. 327
Uniformly elliptic, mucronate	*Myrtus (apiculata)*, p. 367
1 cm or less	*Nothofagus*, p. 216
Grey-brown, hairy beneath	*Quercus (ilex)*, p. 237
Thin, brilliantly glossy; dense	*Ligustrum (lucidum)*, p. 382
Stiff, broad; among spined leaves	*Ilex*, p. 315
Narrow	
Lanceolate, aromatic	*Umbellularia*, p. 268
Linear, to 20 cm, not aromatic	*Embothrium*, p. 267

DECIDUOUS
Simple

ENTIRE, or waved with a few small teeth   25 cm or more long
    Triangular *Paulownia*, p. 383
    Acuminate *Catalpa*, p. 386
    Oblong or obovate *Magnolia*, p. 262
  Less than 20 cm long
    Mixed with leaves with curved lobes *Sassafras*, p. 269
    White beneath *Cotoneaster*, p. 274; *Pyrus*, p. 291
    Orbicular
      Veins fanned; underside glaucous *Cercis*, p. 301
      Dark green, about 2 cm *Fagus* (*sylvatica* 'Rotundifolia'), p. 222
      Pale green, 10–15 cm *Styrax* (*obassia*), p. 378
    Margin waved
      Obovate-orbicular; underside brown pubescent *Parrotia*, p. 271
      Obovate-oblong; underside white pubescent *Mespilus*, p. 277
      Few teeth *Fagus*, p. 220
      Glaucous beneath, veins fanned *Cercis*, p. 301
      Fruit a tiny acorn *Quercus*, p. 224
      Flowers late summer, white, in spikes *Oxydendrum*, p. 374
      Flowers spring, among four white bracts *Cornus*, p. 372
      Flowers small, globose, green *Nyssa*, p. 365
      Very glossy deep green; flowers urn-shaped *Diospyros*, p. 376
      Shoot green, spiny *Maclura*, p. 260
SERRATE   Cordate, ovate-acuminate
    Leaf + petiole 30 cm or more *Idesia*, p. 364
    Teeth incurved; petiole slender *Populus*, p. 180
    Teeth coarse
      Base oblique *Tilia*, p. 357
      Leaf thin, veins prominent *Davidia*, p. 366
      Leaf thick, rough with hairs *Morus*, p. 259
      Opposite *Acer*, p. 318
      Torn veins exude latex *Eucommia*, p. 271
      Fruit abundant cylindric catkins *Betula*, p. 201
      Fruit woody, cone-like *Alnus*, p. 207
  Cuneate to rounded, ovate
    Petiole with large, stiff hairs *Corylus*, p. 214
    Petiole with long, soft hairs
      Three basal veins curving away from margin *Celtis*, p. 258
      Glossy leaf; long thorns *Crataegus*, p. 274
    Petiole with dense, fine wool *Malus*, p. 285; *Sorbus*, p. 277
    Few, large teeth *Nothofagus* (*fusca*), p. 220
    Fruit woody, cone-like *Alnus*, p. 207
    Teeth, small fine, sharp; fruit a berry *Amelanchier*, p. 284
    Teeth broad-based, crenate *Zelkova*, p. 254
  Orbicular; apex rounded
    Opposite *Cercidiphyllum*, p. 261
    Long spurs terminated by single leaves *Tetracentron*, p. 266
    To 20 × 15 cm; white beneath *Sorbus*, p. 277
    Teeth few, large, curved *Populus* (*alba* group), p. 181
    Densely hairy above *Ulmus* (*procera*), p. 249

Petiole slender; fruit a catkin   *Betula (pubescens)*, p. 207
Oblong-lanceolate
  Teeth large, at ends of parallel veins only
    Bright glossy green   *Castanea*, p. 222
    Dull green or glossy dark green   *Quercus*, p. 224
  Teeth also between ends of main veins
    Teeth minute   *Oxydendrum* p. 374
    Teeth broad-based, crenate   *Zelkova*, p. 254
    Glands at distal end of petiole   *Prunus*, p. 291
    Underside white as if painted   *Populus* (Balsam Poplars), p. 184
    Underside white with fine wool   *Sorbus*, p. 277
    Entire base; dull above, shiny beneath; flowers white *Stewartia*, p. 363
    Fruit
      Tufted with white cotton   *Salix*, p. 187
      A nut in a disc   *Ulmus*, p. 247
      A cylindric catkin   *Betula*, p. 201
      Winged or partly enclosed   *Carpinus*, p. 212
      Hop-like, white in summer   *Ostrya*, p. 214
      Globose in star-like calyx   *Styrax*, p. 377
      Four-winged flanges   *Halesia*, p. 378
      Tiny prickly involucre   *Nothofagus*, p. 216
LOBULATE, small lobes themselves toothed
  5–8 × 2 cm; shoot slender   *Nothofagus*, p. 216
  White-pubescent beneath   *Sorbus*, p. 277
  Oval or obovate   *Alnus*, p. 207
  Oblique, ovate-acuminate   *Tilia*, p. 357
LOBED
  Palmate – deeply divided into long, radiating lobes
    Opposite; thin, cut to base or very near *Aesculus*, p. 351; *Acer*, p. 318
    Alternate
      Thick; coarse teeth; petiole stout   *Ficus*, p. 260
      Finely serrated; petiole slender   *Kalopanax*, p. 371
    Palm leaves   *Trachycarpus*, p. 390
  Not palmate
    Opposite
      Veins beneath, glabrous   *Acer*, p. 318
      Veins beneath, downy
        Flower-buds show in winter; bark smooth   *Paulownia*, p. 383
        No flower-buds in winter; bark rough   *Catalpa*, p. 386
    Alternate
      Entire
        Long mid-lobe, two side lobes curved in   *Sassafras*, p. 269
        No mid-lobe, truncate top   *Liriodendron*, p. 265
      Finely serrated
        Shallow lobes; spines on shoot and bole   *Kalopanax*, p. 371
        Lobed half way, triangular lobes   *Liquidambar*, p. 269
        Doubly serrated; bud green ovoid *Sorbus (torminalis)*, p. 281
      Coarsely serrated
        Lobing variable   *Morus*, p. 259
        Small, dark; thorny   *Crataegus*, p. 274
      Few, relatively large teeth
        To 8 × 7 cm, dark green; shoot thorny   *Crataegus*, p. 274

Palm *Trachycarpus,* p. 390
  To 20 × 20cm; bud shiny red, hidden by petiole;
  fruit globose on catkin *Platanus,* p. 272
  Elliptic; fruit an acorn *Quercus,* p. 224
Compound, composed of at least some free leaflets
 PARTIALLY compound – basal leaflets free *Sorbus,* p. 277
 RADIALLY compound *Aesculus,* p. 351
 DOUBLY compound or part doubly
  Entire; whitish beneath; shoot bloomed violet *Gymnocladus,* p. 303
  Finely serrate or waved; shoot green *Gleditsia,* p. 302
  Lobulate, toothed; shoot pale copper *Koelreuteria,* p. 356
  Coarsely toothed, rachis red *Dipteronia,* p. 318
 SINGLY compound
  Even-compound – no terminal leaflet
   Leaf to 65cm; rachis orange, warty, stout *Cedrela,* p. 312
   Leaf to 25cm; rachis green, slender *Gleditsia,* p. 302
  Odd-compound – terminal leaf (usually) present
  Petiole surrounds lateral bud
   Leaflet obovate, to 10cm long, entire *Cladrastis,* p. 303
   Leaflet acuminate, finely serrated *Phellodendron,* p. 310
   Leaflet notched, oval, to 5cm, entire *Robinia,* p. 308
  Bud outside petiole
   Leaves opposite
    Entire
     Leaflets three *Acer,* p. 318
     Leaflets 5–7; rachis stout *Fraxinus,* p. 379
    Toothed
     Uniformly finely serrate *Euodia,* p. 309
     Coarsely toothed; leaflets 15, serrate *Dipteronia,* p. 318
    Leaflets 3–7, few large teeth or many, irregular *Acer,* p. 318
     Serrated distantly or remotely *Fraxinus,* p. 379
   Leaves alternate
    Few large basal teeth with glands *Ailanthus,* **p.** 310
    Entire
     Leaflets three *Laburnum* p. 307
     Leaflets 9–15, pubescent beneath *Sophora,* p. 306
     Leaflets stalked, 7–13 *Rhus (verniciflua),* p. 314
     Lateral leaflets sessile; 3–7(9) *Juglans (regia),* p. 195
    Serrated
     Leaflets 3–9
      Finely serrate *Carya,* p. 197
      Coarsely serrate; terminal leaflet ovate *Picrasma,* p. 311
     Leaflets 9–25
      Leaf 20cm or more; pith divided into chambers
       Bud without scales; fruit winged *Pterocarya,* p. 191
       Bud with scales; fruit globose *Juglans,* p. 195
      Leaf to 20cm; pith not chambered
       Leaflet sharply serrate but entire at base *Sorbus,* p. 277

Gymnospermae

A class of primitive plants in which the ovule is borne naked on a scale, and not enclosed in an ovary. There are five Orders in this class: Cycadales, Gnetales, Ginkgoales, Coniferales and Taxales. The last three are of tree form and are together loosely referred to as "Conifers".

Ginkgoales, an Order now represented by only one species, the Ginkgo, is very distinct in many features from all other living plants. The Order **Coniferales** is now held to include all the other families of conifers except the yews and Torreyas, which have been separated as the Order **Taxales** (along with three other genera not in outdoor cultivation here). It is thus more correct now to speak of "Conifers, Taxads and Ginkgo" when referring collectively to the Gymnosperms which are of tree form.

The reproductive organs of Gymnoperms may be regarded as homologous either to a single compound flower of higher plants or as groups of single flowers, and strictly each group should be called a "strobilus". Male flowers are, correctly, "microsporophylls" and female flowers are "megasporophylls" but neither of these terms, nor "strobilus", is used in this book, where "flower" is regarded as more euphonious, more readily understood, and equally applicable.

The flowers are always either male or female, never both or "perfect". In Ginkgos, Taxads and some of the more primitive Conifers, the sexes are on different trees (dioecious) and in the rest they are on the same tree and usually on the same shoot (monoecious) but on separate peduncles. Rarely, in *Larix* and *Cunninghamia*, for example, freak inflorescences occur with both sexes mixed.

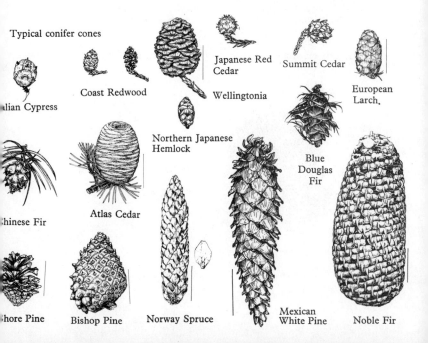

Typical conifer cones

Japanese Red Cedar

Summit Cedar

Coast Redwood

Wellingtonia

European Larch.

ulian Cypress

Northern Japanese Hemlock

Blue Douglas Fir

Atlas Cedar

Chinese Fir

hore Pine

Bishop Pine

Norway Spruce

Mexican White Pine

Noble Fir

Plate 1 **GINKGO, YEW, ARAUCARIA**

Primitive Conifers

Male and female flowers on separate trees.

1. Maidenhair Tree *Ginkgo biloba* 50

(a) Tree of about 18 m in summer.
(b) Whorl of leaves on a spur.

A frequent tree in cathedral close, large town garden and city park in the southern half of England and Wales.

2. Common Yew *Taxus baccata* 51

(a) Shoot from male tree, with both open and closed flowers.
(b) Shoot from female tree, with open flowers.
(c) Shoot with ripe fruit. The fleshy aril contains the highly poisonous seed.
(d) Young tree of about 3 m.

The longest living of our trees; widely spreading and often burred and sprouty with age. Almost all the biggest are in very old churchyards.

3. Chile Pine *Araucaria araucana* 57

Shoot. The stem is bright green for much of the season and may be largely hidden by the rigid spiny leaves (see drawing p. 57).

N.B. Heights given are of the specimens illustrated, not an indication of height when fully grown, for which see the main text.

Chile Pine, mature specimen

1a

1b

2a

2b

2c

2d

3

1

3a

3b

4

5

YEW FAMILY TREES AND ALLIES   Plate 2

Fruit like a small plum or a minute cone.

1. **California Nutmeg-tree**   *Torreya californica*   53

   The hard, spiny leaves rise from the shoot at varying angles. Bruising them releases a pungent scent of turpentine.

2. **Chinese Cow's-tail Pine**   *Cephalotaxus fortuni*   54

   The leathery, soft-pointed leaves lie flat on each side of the shoot. The upper shoot is from a male tree bearing flowers.

3. **Fastigiate Japanese Cow's-tail Pine**   *Cephalotaxus harringtonia* 'Fastigiata'   54

   (a) Plant 4 m high.
   (b) Shoot (which grows vertically) showing leaves of decreasing length towards the end of the year's growth.

4. **Plum-fruited Yew**   *Podocarpus andinus*   55

   The leaves are soft, and can often be bluish-green. A dense, often bushy tree with smooth black bark.

5. **Prince Albert's Yew**   *Saxegothaea conspicua*   56

   The leaves are hard and spine-tipped; the cones are ovoid, 1 cm

   A bush, or sometimes a narrow tree, with reddish-brown scaling bark like a yew.

lifornia Nutmeg-tree   Chinese Cow's-tail Pine   Willow Podocarp (p. 55)   Prince Albert's Yew

GINKGO FAMILY *Ginkgoaceae*

A family remote from all other trees and plants, although sharing some features with Cycads (which resemble tree-ferns); important in Jurassic times but long reduced to a single genus with a single species. Deciduous.

MAIDENHAIR TREE or GINKGO *Ginkgo biloba* L. **Pl. 1**
Chekiang Prov., China 1758. Frequent in S. England in big gardens and parks, and some small town gardens and city parks; rare north of the Midlands and in Ireland. Most frequent around London and in the Bristol-Bath-Yeovil area. Not seen north of Perth. 28 × 4m.
Bark. Young: brown-grey with corky pale brown fissures. Old: dull-grey, coarsely networked ridges and wide fissures, deepening with age. Sometimes deeply fluted, often with bosses.
Crown. Typically tall and slender, straight pole-like stems with few short branches. Some wider, columnar, with stronger, more numerous branches. A few are dense, much forked and shapeless, or many-stemmed, widening out at the top (e.g. original tree at Kew).
Foliage. Shoot pale green, glabrous; second year woody, pale fawn. Bud flat-conic, red-brown. Leaf emerges bright yellow-green in late April, becomes rich, dark green; leathery, fan-shaped, closely ribbed with fan-like veining. Spirally set on new shoots; in small whorls from big spurs on older wood. On new shoots, petiole 2 cm and leaf to 12 × 10 cm, cleft nearly to base, each half again shallowly cleft. On spur shoots, petiole to 4.5 cm and leaf to 6 × 8 cm, shallowly two-lobed and irregularly toothed. Bright yellow in October, fall in early November.
Flowers and fruit. Each tree is either male or female, but few flower to reveal their sex. The few known female trees are tall and narrow-crowned (Britain and most of USA; broad and bushy notably in Pennsylvania). Male catkins, thick and yellow, 6–8 cm, emerge with the leaves; erect, 3–6 together. Female flowers, like long-stalked tiny acorns; 1–2 on 4 cm pedicel which is pale yellow and widens to join the fruit at a yellow boss. Fruit globular to ovoid, 2.5–3 cm, smoothly uneven surface bright pale green, sub-shiny, ripening late in autumn to yellow then brown and rotting with a putrid smell.
Growth. Erratic; generally rather slow as in some years no new growth is made, but shoots of over 60 cm can be grown. Mid-May to end August. Almost free of pests and diseases (but not immune to Honey-fungus). Long-lived: Kew tree 210 years, flourishing.
Recognition. Foliage unique; but bare crown in winter, spiky and with spurs on branches, can resemble some pear-trees.

YEW FAMILY *Taxaceae*

Five genera, only two of which are in cultivation. They are distinguished from the true conifers by their single ovule, not on a scale, but surrounded when ripe by a fleshy aril, resembling a berry.

YEWS Taxus

A genus spread across the northern hemisphere and geographically distinguishable as six species, but several are very similar.

COMMON YEW *Taxus baccata* L. **Pl. 1**
Europe, Atlas Mts, and Asia Minor to Persia. Native to chalk downs in S. England, limestones in the north and in oakwoods on other soils. Very common in parks, gardens and shrubberies, widely planted for hedges in gardens and for topiary. Huge and ancient trees common in church-yards from Kent to Devon and in Monmouth, Hereford, Merioneth and Denbighshire. Some are about 1,000 years old and have girths of 9–10 m (see p. 25). They are all hollow, but this has no effect on their health. 10–25 m.
Bark. Reddish-brown and purplish, scaling away to leave dark red or brown patches.
Crown. Broad to very broadly conic when single-stemmed, irregularly spreading when multi-stemmed. Branches stout and level or a few upturned; shoots may be pendulous. Bole none, short, or long and slightly sinuous; often much burred or partly covered by dense growth of sprouts.

Common Yew

Foliage. Shoot green for three years, grooved below leaves. Bud minute, ovoid and green; most trees have some greatly enlarged into leafy top-shaped galls caused by Yew-gall midge (*Taxomyia taxi*). Leaves set spirally round erect shoots, in a rank each side of side-shoots, pointing forwards and arching downwards; linear, abruptly narrowed to a sharp point; 2–4 cm long to 3 mm wide, very dark green, shiny or dull, ridged above; underside yellow-green matt and dull.
Flowers and fruit. Each tree either male or female. Male flowers small, globular, along the undersides of shoots of the previous year. They become yellow and shed clouds of pollen in February. Female trees have minute, solitary green flowers, scarcely noticeable until the fleshy aril swells, and by mid-September turns bright red, with a deep cavity holding the seed; 1 × 0.6 cm.
Growth. Young trees will add 20–30 cm a year in height, and 2–3 cm a year in girth. Old trees have long ceased growth in height, and growth in girth declines to 0.5 cm a year; very old trees down to 0.1 cm or less each year.

'ADPRESSA' 1838 Chester. Frequent. Female, bush

'Adpressa'

to 10m; fine, densely borne shoots, some pendulous; leaves oblong-elliptic, acute, to 1 cm. A golden form is a pretty bush.

'DOVASTONIANA' 1777 Westfelton, Salop. Infrequent. Single-stemmed wide-spreading male; long level sinuous branches; new growth slightly arched; branchlets hang in curtains. Vigorous and very distinct. 7m.

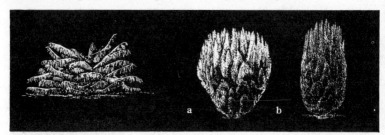

'Dovastoniana'   Irish Yew: typical trees of (a) E. and (b) W. Britain

'FASTIGIATA' Irish Yew (*T.b.* 'Stricta', 'Hibernica') 1780 Co. Fermanagh. Common; in every churchyard and most large gardens throughout these islands. Upright bush, female (male known), nearly black leaves spirally set round shoots; making many-topped broad columnar crown broadening to near the top. Grows best in western parts, making long-conic tops (Fig. b); flatter and broader in the east (Fig. a) 15 m. Only *Cephalotaxus harringtonia* 'Fastigiata' (p. 54) resembles it, but has much bigger leaves and is less branched. 'Fastigiata Aurea' is a golden form, and slower growing.

'FRUCTU-LUTEO' 1817 Ireland. Large bushy tree, like the type, but the fruits ripen bright yellow. Rare, but peculiarly attractive when in fruit. 12m.

There are several bushy forms of *T. baccata* with leaves variously margined and variegated in shades of yellow.

Similar species. *Torreya* spp. (p. 53) differ from yews in bark and longer, more spined leaves; *Cephalotaxus* spp. (p. 54) have bigger, broader leaves of pale green, and both genera have white bands on the undersides of the leaves. For differences from other yews, see *T. cuspidata* and *T. celebica* (below).

JAPANESE YEW   *Taxus cuspidata* Sieb. and Zucc.

Japan 1855. Very rare. A broad, bushy tree with hard, spine-tipped dark leaves, 2–3.5 cm long, *deep gold or brownish-yellow beneath, held stiffly up* from each side of the shoot. Female trees have numerous fruit, rather bunched, pale scarlet, 7–8mm long. 8m. This species has crossed with *T. baccata* and produced a range of hybrids, *Taxus × media* Rehd. (1900 Massachusetts), intermediate between the parents. Of these, 'Hicksii', a fastigiate form is the least rare. It has 2 cm leaves, shortly spined, pale green beneath, and bright scarlet, shiny fruit.

Japanese Yew

CHINESE YEW *Taxus celebica* (Warburg) Li
China 1908. Very rare. Broad, bushy, with *sparse foliage* and bare lengths of
shoot without leaves. *Leaves slender, pale yellowish-green,* flat each side of shoot,
some curving backwards, 1.5 cm long. Male flowers sparse, in axils, 2 mm ovoid,
green and brown. Fruit sparse, 2–3 together, 5 mm, ovoid, green with dark olive
cap. Still green in October – rarely ripens. 8 m.

NUTMEG-TREES Torreya

Six species, USA, China and Japan, with a plum-like, green fruit, and hard
spine-pointed leaves.

CALIFORNIA NUTMEG *Torreya californica* Torrey   **Pl. 2**
N. Coast Range and C. Sierra Nevada California 1851. Infrequent; in a few
large gardens, mainly in south and west. 20 × 3 m.
Bark. Pale red-brown or grey-brown; very shallow network of ridges.
Crown. Pointed conic, broad at base, open. Straight, *whorled,* horizontal
branches; rather pendulous shoots.
Foliage. Shoot green first year, with reddish patches by second year, red-
brown third year. Bud *conic,* finely pointed, brown above, glossy green beneath.
Leaves widely spaced, rigid, linear, long and narrow, slightly tapered, 4-5 ×
0.3–0.5 cm, dark glossy green with bright green broad margin above, two narrow
whitish bands beneath; usually irregularly pectinate and often *curved upwards.*
When crushed, the foliage emits an oily sage-like scent. Male flowers, one at
the origin of each leaf, ovoid 3 mm, pale green spotted yellow until shedding
pollen in May. Fruit obovoid, 4 cm, green, striped dull purple when ripe.

JAPANESE NUTMEG *Torreya nucifera* Sieb. and Zucc.
Japan 1764. Rare, 9 × 1 m. Gaunt slender small tree, branches irregular,
level; second-year wood bright orange-brown, third year mahogany; leaves
much *smaller* than *T. californica,* 3 × 0.25 cm, dark green with bright green
margins above, two silvery bands beneath; abruptly short-spined, very regularly pectinate and parallel, *down-curved.* When crushed, the foliage emits a
strong rather sage-like scent. Male flowers towards base of shoot, beneath each
leaf, ovoid, 2 mm, whitish-green. Fruit as *T. californica,* but smaller, 2 cm.
Similar species. *Cephalotaxus* spp. have non-spiny, leathery, more densely
set leaves with broad white bands beneath, and scaly bark. *T. californica* (above).

Chinese Yew

California Nutmeg

Japanese Nutmeg

COW'S TAIL PINE FAMILY *Cephalotaxaceae*

Seven species from S.E. Asia, formerly united with the yews; fruit olive-like, taking two years to ripen.

COW'S TAIL PINE *Cephalotaxus harringtonia* K. Koch var.
  drupacea (Sieb, and Zucc.) Koidzumi   **Pl. 2**
China, Japan 1829. Infrequent. Low bush, rarely a small, broad tree, densely crowned, often pendulous.

Foliage. Shoot green for three years, ribbed by leaf bases. Bud green, globular 1mm. One rank of leaves each side of the shoot rising above it and slightly curving inwards to form a *narrow V-shape*, like a dove's wings, often vertical, flatter in shaded parts; broadly linear, to 5 × 0.3 cm, abruptly pointed, leathery, *bright* matt *yellowish-green* above, two broad pale or silvery bands beneath.

Flowers and fruit. Male plants usually densely covered with pairs of globular, pale cream, then brown flowers on 2–4mm stalks beneath each pair of leaves. Pollen March to May. Female plants have two pairs of knobbly globose flowers on curved stalks at base of shoot. Fruit obovoid, 2.5 × 1.5 cm, smooth pale green striped dark green, ripening shiny brown.

  'FASTIGIATA' 1861 Japan. Infrequent; some large gardens. 6m. Broad cluster of erect stems with very dark green leaves spreading all round, strongly *decurved*;

Cow's Tail Pine

2–7 cm, marked into years of growth by sectors of long leaves decreasing to short leaves. Shoots unbranched in upper parts, lower parts often have untidy projecting side-shoots, sweeping downwards with leaves in flat ranks. Flowers not seen. **Pl. 2.**

Similar species. *Taxus baccata* 'Fastigiata' (p. 52) grows bigger, is smaller in all parts, and has vertical shoots densely clothed in short, spreading side-shoots.

CHINESE COW'S TAIL PINE *Cephalotaxus fortuni* Hook.   **Pl. 2**
C. China 1848. Uncommon S. and W. England, Wales. Rare elsewhere. 10m.

Bark. Red-brown, purplish in places, coarse square scales and long shreds lifting away.

Crown. Single, bare stem, often leaning; heavily foliaged upper half on level branches, or may be bush. Foliage very handsome where growing well.

Foliage. Shoot green for three years, much ribbed. Bud 4mm, dark green, globular, with long acute free tips to scales. Leaf *glossy* deep yellowish-green or dark green, long (5–9 × 0.5 cm), ridged, *parallel*, flat-ranked, slightly *down-turned* at tips, tapering gradually to a fine point; two broad grey or white bands beneath.

Flowers and fruit. Male flowers whitish, ovoid, 3mm on short stalk at base of each leaf. Fruit ovoid, 1.5–2 × 1 cm; at first bright glaucous blue, later glossy

Chinese Cow's Tail Pine

'Fastigiata'

pale whitish-green striped green, then darkens, ripening brown and red-brown, shiny; borne in bunches of three to five at the nodes.
Similar species. *C. harringtonia* var. *drupacea* (p. 54) has shorter, raised leaves, and is denser and more bushy.

YELLOW-WOOD FAMILY   *Podocarpaceae*

Seven genera, five of which are very rare in cultivation. Very variable. Male flowers in catkins.

YELLOW-WOODS   Podocarpus

A hundred species; tropical mountains south to Chile and New Zealand, north to Japan and Mexico. Most have the sexes on separate trees and hard, leathery leaves.

PLUM-FRUITED YEW   *Podocarpus andinus* Peoppig ex Endl.   **Pl. 2**
Syn. *Prumnopitys elegans* Phil.
S. Chile 1860. Frequent in large gardens in west of Britain, uncommon in east. Rare as hedge. Hardy. 15 m (20 m at Bicton).
Bark. Smooth, black, becoming coppery grey with age, wrinkled.
Crown. Often many-stemmed, each rising to a conic top; dense, but shoots project with bare lengths between tufts of short shoots.
Foliage. Shoot green for two years. Bud minute green ovoid, a few scale-tips projecting. Leaf: in young plants, deep green, rigid, spine-pointed, 2 cm, lanceolate, spreading; in adult, bright, slightly bluish-green, to 5 cm, linear, crowded and forward-pointing at shoot-ends, more two-ranked behind, often twisted showing two broad pale grey-blue bands beneath, *soft*.

Plum-fruited Yew

Flowers and fruit. Male flowers terminal and axillary, 3–4 cm, erect, blue-grey narrow heads of 7–8 ovoid yellow flowers, 1–2 mm. Female flowers terminal and axillary, erect and nodding, 2–6, curved, slender, conic, blue-green, on 3 cm peduncle. Fruit: 2–6 in bunch hanging on pale yellow-green peduncle, oblong-ovoid, 15–20 mm, apple-green, with raised white speckles.
Similar species. *Saxegothaea* (p. 56) differs in drooping branches, purplish flaking bark; leaves very dark green, curved, hard, spine-pointed, bright blue-white banded beneath.

WILLOW PODOCARP   *Podocarpus salignus* D. Don
Syn. *P. chilinus* Rich.
Chile 1853. Infrequent; in some of the larger gardens, mainly in S. and W. England and Ireland. 20 m.
Bark. Orange or red-brown, shaggy with coarse, vertical, papery, purplish strips peeling off.
Crown. Often many-stemmed, irregular in shape, rather open.
Foliage. Shoot green for two years, then dull grey-brown. Bud minute, a mere thickening of the shoot, ending in a few dark brown scales and filaments. Leaf deep rich shiny green, well-spaced in an irregular largely flat arrangement, alternate, curving forwards, slender, 5–12 cm long, soft, flexible. Underside pale matt yellow-green with yellow midrib.

Willow Podocarp

TOTARA   *Podocarpus totara* D. Don ex Lamb.
New Zealand. Rare; confined to some large gardens in
Sussex, S.W. England, Argyll and Ireland. A dense, often
bushy tree to 15m resembling faintly a small-leaved thin,
straggly, yellowish-grey Monkey-puzzle, with brown-grey,
coarsely peeling bark. Leaves linear-lanceolate, 2 × 0.4cm,
abruptly tapered to spine, grey-green above, *yellow-green*
beneath, all round shoot, stiff, leathery, rather distant.

Totara

CHILEAN TOTARA   *Podocarpus nubigenus* Lindl.
Chile, Argentina 1847. Similar to *P. totara*, but with
bright, fresh or yellowish-green foliage. Bark purple-brown,
stripping spirally. Leaf 3–4.5 × 0.5 cm broadest near middle,
stiff, narrowing to sharp point; dark bright green above,
two *broad whitish-green bands* beneath separated by broad
yellow midrib; spread straight forward beneath the shoot;
some above vertical and bent backwards. 19 × 3m (Heligan,
Cornwall).

Chilean Totara, with underside of leaf

PRINCE ALBERT'S YEW   Saxegothaea

A single species.

PRINCE ALBERT'S YEW   *Saxegothaea conspicua* Lindl.   **Pl. 2**
Chile, Argentina 1847. Rare; mostly in southern and western gardens, and in
Ireland. 17m.
Bark. Smooth, dark reddish- or purplish-brown, flaking
coarsely with age, the big, thin rounded flakes leaving areas
of pink. Deep flutes and cavities on the bole. Like *Taxus
baccata* (p. 51).
Crown. Can be slender and conic or broad and bushy;
branches drooping, finer shoots *pendulous*.
Foliage. Shoots crowded above branches and hanging from
the ends, green for 3–4 years marked by a broad white band
from the base of each leaf. Distant whorls of 3–4 branchlets
on main shoots. Leaf 1.5–2.5 cm × 2 mm, unfolds tinged
purple, soon dull, dark green, linear but *curved, hard,*
sharply pointed, rather closely set in two ranks, but lying
unevenly, two bright white bands beneath; apple-green
midrib and margins; gives grassy aroma when crushed.   Prince Albert's Yew
Flowers. Female flower becomes conelet at end of short shoot, an ovoid,
bright powdery blue-grey rosette of out-curved scales; 5 × 10mm; frequent
summer and winter. Male flowers 1 mm, dark purple, ovoid, 10–20 per shoot at
bases of distal leaves.
Similar species. *Podocarpus andinus* (p. 55) is sometimes confused.

CHILE PINE FAMILY *Araucariaceae*

Thirty-six species with large cones and hard scale-leaves, found in Malaysia, Oceania (many confined to New Caledonia), Australasia and S. America. Two genera: *Agathis* with 21 species (one rare in Irish gardens), and *Araucaria*.

ARAUCARIA

Fifteen species with whorled, horizontal branches and spirally set scale-leaves of varying size. Male and female flowers on separate trees in most species. One tender species, the Norfolk Island Pine, *A. heterophylla (excelsa)*, frequent as a pot plant and growing to 30m at Tresco, Isles of Scilly.

CHILE PINE or MONKEY-PUZZLE *Araucaria araucana*
(Molina) K. Koch   **Pl. 1**
Syn. *A. imbricata* Pavon

Chile, Argentina 1795. Common all over Britain and Ireland; best growth in the west from Devon to Argyll. 26 × 3.5 m.

Bark. Dark grey, wrinkled or slightly fissured around old branch-scars, and vertically into broken ridges, with visible annual layers; often exuding resin.

Crown. Domed, from tall and narrow to short and very broad. Vigorous young trees conic, whorled and open. Some crowns dense with epicormic shoots on stem.

Bole. Invariably straight and cylindric, often from a pedestal of roots; sometimes root-suckers sprout at base or many yards away.

Foliage. Shoot bright green, formed of plates, 1 × 1.5 cm, each bearing a leaf. Leaf very hard and leathery, dark shining green, yellow towards the margin, finely lined with stomata; broadly triangular, 3–4 cm long, 1 cm across the base, sharply pointed with a brown spine; forward, curving out to nearly vertical; all around the shoot.

Flowers and fruit. Male flowers terminal, several together, long-ovoid, 10 × 6 cm, long-tapered scale-tips deflexed; shed pollen in June but remain on tree, dark brown for months. Female flower solitary,

Chile Pine

on upper side of shoot, globular. Matures in two years to large, green, golden-spined globe, to 15 cm across, then breaks up while still on tree. Seed large and edible (preferably roasted), 4 × 2 cm, bright brown.

Growth. Unusual in that each whorl of branches may represent two or one and a half years of growth, or the normal one year. Slow to establish and seldom adds 30 cm a year. Mid-May to August.

Similar species. Slightly resembles *Cunninghamia* (p. 90) or *Podocarpus totara* (p. 56) but both differ from it too much to cause confusion.

CYPRESS FAMILY *Cupressaceae*

A very large family of 18 genera, many not in cultivation in the open. Juvenile foliage, grown for first 1–2 years: free linear spreading leaves. Adult: normally small, scale-leaves, sometimes mixed with juvenile. Cones small; in *Juniperus* fleshy like a berry.

NORTHERN INCENSE CEDARS Calocedrus

Formerly united with *Libocedrus*. Three species, in California, China and Formosa. Closely related to *Thuja*.

INCENSE CEDAR *Calocedrus decurrens* (Torrey) Florin
Syn. *Libocedrus decurrens* Torrey

Mid-Oregon to S. California 1853. Frequent generally, but in Scotland and Ireland more confined to largest gardens. 35 × 4 m.

Bark. Dark reddish-brown, fissured into coarse plates which curl outwards at top and bottom, even on young trees.

Crown. *Narrow-columnar* with a *rounded top*, often 'pencil-slim', especially in E. England, or broadly columnar, which is rare in England, normal in Ireland. Dense and bright green, usually down to the ground or to a short bare bole. Forked stems are frequent. Branches very small, even those from the base, short and upswept. Old, or exposed trees in dry areas, have patches of bare twigs in much of the upper crown, but retain a distinctive tuft of green foliage at the top. (In native region, all trees have broad, conic, open crowns with level branches, becoming gaunt and columnar with great age.)

Foliage. Shoot green at first then red-brown. Leaves long, narrow, over-lapping scales, broadening towards the triangular tips, the points curved inwards.

Incense Cedar

These are borne in fours – upper, lower and laterals; rich, bright green above, yellower beneath. Crushed foliage has a strong *scent of shoe-polish* or turpentine.

Flowers and cone. Both sexes on the same tree; male flowers 3-4 mm, drop-shaped and golden, profuse in some years, on the ends of minor branchlets. Cones small, 2 cm, pointed, only two fertile scales, pale yellow in late summer, in some years massed over parts of crown.

Growth. May-August. Young trees may add 60 cm a year. Very healthy.

Similar species. The crown of *Chamaecyparis lawsoniana* 'Erecta' (p. 61) has a more conic, pointed top and is more bushy, broader, with more curved sides, longer branches and darker foliage.

SOUTHERN INCENSE CEDARS   Austrocedrus

A single species from Chile.

CHILEAN INCENSE CEDAR   *Austrocedrus chilensis* (D. Don) Florin and Boutelje

Syn. *Libocedrus chilensis* (D. Don) End.

Chile, Argentina 1847. Rare; mostly in south and west, not reliably hardy in north-east. 15 m.

Bark. Nearly smooth, dark coppery-brown; small grey scales.

Crown. Neat; columnar base to slightly round-shouldered cone on a clean, straight bole with few branches which are level then upswept.

Foliage. Shoot bright green, soon pale yellow-pink, then dark fawn. Branchlet sprays horizontal or upcurved. Scale-leaves in fours, median pair almost obscured by large lateral pair which have projecting *blunt incurved points*. Deep bluish grey-green above, often with a *bright white band*; bright white, broad band beneath.

Chilean Incense Cedar

Flowers and cone. Male flowers 3 mm, cylindric, nodding at tips of smallest branchlets or erect, yellow and green, shedding in mid-April. Cone 8 mm; rare.

Recognition. The shape, bark and sage-green colour of the crown are distinct. *Chamaecyparis obtusa* resembles this most, and in shaded foliage its leaves project, but are smaller, bright green and unmarked above.

"FALSE" CYPRESSES   Chamaecyparis

Six species of cypress with foliage in flattened sprays, and with small cones. N. America, Japan and Formosa. Three species have a multitude of cultivars. The key cannot encompass these, but nearly every variant, however bizarre, has the aroma of its parent species when the foliage is crushed.

Key to Chamaecyparis species and Cupressocyparis leylandii

1. Sprays very short, dense, bunched, upright; very slender; when
      crushed give warm gingery scent   *thyoides*, p. 68
   Sprays long, open, flat, not bunched   **2**

2. Leaves blunt and obtuse, bright green, marked bright white
      beneath   *obtusa*, p. 63
   Leaves acutely pointed   **3**

3. Leaves against strong light show translucent spots; points
      incurved; aroma of sour parsley   *lawsoniana*, p. 60
   Leaves without translucent spots; points spreading   **4**

4. Foliage fine, slender shoots; light or bright green   **5**
   Foliage thick, heavy, dark or medium green   **6**

5. Foliage bright green, slightly upturned sprays, marked bright
      white beneath, aroma of acrid resin   *pisifera*, p. 66
   Foliage pale, bronzed green; sprays arch down at tips; pale
      green beneath, aroma of seaweed   *formosensis*, p. 68

6. Sprays pendulous, harsh, dull, dark green   *nootkatensis*, p. 62
Sprays less pendulous, smooth, brighter green or greyish;
leading shoot kinked   7

7. Sprays of plume-like shoots in two planes; leaves with grey
marks   × *C. leylandii* 'Haggerston Grey', p. 69
Sprays fern-like, flat, in one plane except towards tip; leaves
uniform deep green   × *C. leylandii* 'Leighton Green', p. 69

LAWSON CYPRESS *Chamaecyparis lawsoniana* (Murr.) Parlatore **Pl. 3**
Klamath and Siskiyou Mts. N.W. California and S.W. Oregon at 4–6,000 ft.
1854. Abundant as type and as numerous cultivars in town and suburban
gardens, parks, cemeteries and churchyards in all parts. Very hardy, occasionally browned by cold, dry winds in severe winters. 38 m (1970 but still growing
taller), 4 m girth. (37 × 3.4 m at Doune House, Perth.)

Bark. Smooth at first, dark brownish-green, slightly shiny;
becomes purplish grey-brown, vertically fissured into long
plates. Oldest trees have coarse, vertical plates lifting
away at the ends.

Crown. Tall, narrowly conic with *drooping leading shoot;*
dense and nearly to the ground in open-grown trees.
Forked stems frequent, often repeatedly forked. Foliage
pendulous, branches uniformly small; a few big basal limbs
on old trees, often layered in a ring.

Foliage. Shoot soon dull pinkish-brown, then purplish.
Leaf scale-like, rather dark green above, *translucent gland*
in centre of median leaves; pale green beneath, joints
between scales white; new long shoots thread-like and
drooping. Crushed foliage gives a resinous, parsley-like
scent.

Flowers and fruit. Most trees bear abundant flowers of   Lawson Cypress
each sex. Male flowers terminal on finest branchlets, 2 mm,
slate-black scales edged white, becoming crimson at end of March when 5 mm
long, shedding pollen in April then withering and falling off. Female flowers
terminal on small branchlets well behind tips of sprays, slate-blue, 5 mm,
open in April and a few throughout the summer; turn green and globose, often
bloomed blue-white, then open as woody cones, purple-brown, 7 mm, globular; scales wrinkled and with small central spine.

Growth. May–September. Young trees can make shoots of 80 cm, but over
long periods mean growth is not more than 30–45 cm a year.

'ALLUMII' 1890. Dull blue-grey foliage in vertical plates; yellow-green inner
surface, narrowly conic crown from bushy base 15 (22 m). Common; small formal
gardens (Fig. A, p. 61). 'Fraseri' (1891) is similar, but less blue and remains
narrow at the base. Frequent. 10 m.

'TRIOMPHE DE BOSKOOP' 1895 Holland. Outer foliage pale blue-grey;
crown broad-columnar, rather open, with good, single bole. 25 m. Frequent;
vigorous.

'COLUMNARIS' 1941 Holland. Pale grey-blue foliage in upright plates;
crown very slender, columnar, pointed. To 11 m so far. Now frequently planted
(Fig. B, p. 61).

'ERECTA' 1855 Knaphill, Surrey. Foliage bright deep green in vertical plates; crown flame-shaped, pointed, dense and usually many-stemmed, or much forked and short-boled. Common. 25 m (Fig. C, below).

'GREEN SPIRE' ('Jackman's Variety') Pre-1947 Woking, Surrey. Very tight, neatly fastigiate with stout, straight bole and pale green foliage in vertical plates.

'GREEN PILLAR' 1938 East Grinstead. As 'Green Spire' but paler, tinted slightly golden (Fig. D, below).

'KILMACURRAGH' Distributed 1951, Co. Wicklow. Very narrow, fastigiate with bright green foliage in vertical plates, like 'Erecta' but much narrower, more columnar.

'YOUNGII' pre-1874 Milford, Surrey. Rare; some big collections; more frequent in W. Surrey. A very shapely, narrowly-conic tree to 20m. Foliage dark green in hard fern-like sprays, ultimate branchlets upcurled and bearing profuse male flowers; sprays long, held level or somewhat drooped.

'POTTENII' 1900 Cranbrook, Kent. Crown dense, ovoid-columnar, bottle-shaped, acute. Pale green feathery foliage; small sprays arching out from vertical shoots; leaves semi-juvenile, with slender, forward-pointing tips, grey-green above, very pale beneath, dusted grey. 13 m. Common (Fig. E, below).

'FLETCHERI' 1913 Chertsey. Foliage blue-grey, feathery, juvenile; long-pointed leaves, 2mm, opposite pairs spreading; shoots upright in lower crown; crown dense and columnar, often broad and many-stemmed with many pointed tops. To 13 m. Common. (Fig. F, below).

'ELLWOODII' 1929 Bishops Waltham. A smaller, narrower, more grey-green, adult-foliaged form of 'Fletcheri', with dense, tight, vertical shoots from the base; regarded as dwarf, but to 11m so far. Common. A cream-variegated form is now in commerce (Fig. G, below).

'Intertexta'

'FILIFORMIS' 1878 Holland. Broadly columnar or conic crown, from which hang long slender thread-like branchlets bearing

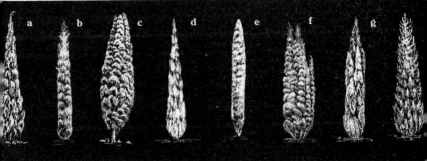

Distinctive shapes of Lawson Cypress cultivars: **a** 'Allumii', **b** 'Columnaris', **c** 'Erecta', **d** 'Green Pillar', **e** 'Pottenii', **f** 'Fletcheri', **g** 'Ellwoodii', **h** 'Wisselii'

occasional dense bunches of grey-green short branchlets. Infrequent. 10m (20m at Bicton, Devon).

'INTERTEXTA' 1869 Edinburgh. Foliage distant, sparse, rounded, hard, dark green, pendulous; crown narrow-columnar, but forks high and top splays out with age. 23m. Uncommon.

'WISSELII' 1888 Holland. Foliage dark blue-green and pale blue-grey in dense, short tufts, radiating, vertical at ends of branches like turrets; crown narrow-columnar; bole stout, may fork. Looks slow-growing, but soon very fast – to 25 × 3m in 50 years. In spring whole crown turns crimson with dense male flowers. Frequent (Fig. H, p. 61.)

'LUTEA' c. 1870 Tooting. Foliage bright gold shading to white inside; crown narrow-columnar, conic near top, dense, pendulous, appears dark inside. Cones bright grey-blue; bark orange-brown, finely scaly. Parent of many other golden cultivars, which are more broadly conic and not pendulous. Common, valuable in garden-design. 15m. (23m.)

'Wisselii'

'WINSTON CHURCHILL' 1945 East Grinstead. Brilliant gold, dense, conic form of 'Lutea', not pendulous; basal foliage in vertical plates.

'STEWARTII' 1920 Ferndown. Foliage gold shading to green, in long, ascending arched fern-like sprays; crown conic. Very distinct when young with projecting sprays of branchlets decurved below the shoot. 15m. Frequent.

Similar species. *Ch. nootkatensis* (below) differs in shape of crown, bigger cone and yellow male flowers. *Thuja plicata* (p. 81) can confuse beginners, but aroma, bigger, broader shining leaves, erect leading shoot and stringy bark all distinguish.

NOOTKA CYPRESS *Chamaecyparis nootkatensis* (D. Don) Spach

Alaska, to N. Oregon 1854. Much less common than Lawson Cypress, but frequent in parks, gardens and churchyards. Very hardy. 25 (30) × 3m.

Bark. Brown-orange, pink-brown or grey-brown shallowly fissured vertically or spirally into narrow stringy strips.

Crown. Remarkably *regular*, conic, rarely forked but often with heavy low limbs upturning; broad and obtuse-topped in Ireland. Upper branches regular in size, small, slightly ascending. May bush out and layer at base. Bare and open internally.

Foliage. Shoot soon rich purplish orange-brown. *Pendulous* sprays, *harsh* if rubbed the wrong way, dull dark green, paler and yellower beneath; fern-like, flat, thick, branchlet systems to 20 × 4cm, regularly alternate. When crushed gives heavy, oily, unpleasant aroma. Scales with fine, spreading points and pale margins, ridged towards the tip.

Flowers and fruit. Males abundant, massed at tips

Nootka Cypress

of hanging branchlets, yellow from autumn to late April when they pollinate and fall. Female flowers slate-blue on shorter branchlets behind males, a few open at all times; ripening into green, plum-bloomed cones taking two years to mature, globular, nearly 1 cm across, each scale with a large curved spine, finally dull brown.

'LUTEA' ('Aurea') 1891. Infrequent except in N. Ireland. In early summer, new shoots pale yellow, pendulous, soon dull yellowish-green and in winter differing from the type only in a faint yellowish tinge to the outer foliage. 20 m.

'PENDULA' 1884 Holland. A rather gaunt tree with upturning branches from which the foliage hangs in curtains. Quite distinct from even the most pendulous normal form of the type. The foliage is dark yellowish-green when young and it is then a strikingly ornamental tree, but becomes dull and less attractive with age. Cones 2 cm, conspicuous bright navy blue in summer.

Similar species. *Ch. lawsoniana* (p. 60) is distinct in crown, foliage and aroma. The foliage of the hybrid × *Cupressocyparis leylandii* can be very similar (see key, p. 59). The crown of all forms of Leyland Cypress is columnar (below).

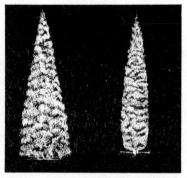

Nootka Cypress   Leyland Cypress (p. 69)   Hinoki Cypress

HINOKI CYPRESS *Chamaecyparis obtusa* (Sieb. and Zucc.) Endl. **Pl. 3**
Japan 1861. Frequent in large gardens in western parts, rare in the east or in small gardens or parks except as young plants of 'Crippsii'. Hardy. 23 × 3 m.

Bark. Rufous, fissured shallowly into coarse, grey-brown parallel strips, sometimes shaggy and grey; soft, stringy.

Crown. Medium broad-conic, interior open. Bole very straight and cylindrical; some fork at about 2 m. Branches few; level at first, then upturned. Shoots near top project and are very slender and arched.

Foliage. Branchlet systems obovate, lateral ones curved back. Shoot soon dull orange-brown. Leaf, very small, closely pressed, *blunt-tipped* scales clothing the shoots. Bright shiny green above, brightly patterned with white where scales overlap each other beneath. Crushed foliage has a sweet, resinous scent, sometimes like Eucalyptus.

Flowers and cone. Male flowers minute, dull yellow, pollinating in April, soon shed. Cones bright green in summer, become orange-brown, 1 cm across; a very small curved ridge on each of the eight scales.

64

Plate 3   **CYPRESSES**

Leaves scale-like, closely appressed to shoots.

1. Lawson Cypress *Chamaecyparis lawsoniana*   60
  (a) Young tree 5 m high showing drooping leading shoot.
  (b) Shoot with ripe cone.
  (c) Shoot with new cone, two male flowers about to shed pollen
    and two ready to drop off having shed their pollen.

2. Smooth Arizona Cypress *Cupressus glabra*   72
  (a) Tree 10 m high.
  (b) Foliage of the form with few white resin-dots (see p. 73).
    Various shades of grey-blue; when crushed it has a scent of
    grapefruit.
  (c) Shoot with ripe cone. These adhere to the shoot in bunches
    for many years.

3. Monterey Cypress *Cupressus macrocarpa*   70
  (a) Young tree 12 m high, broadly columnar, usually unforked
    and more spire-topped in England, broader in Ireland.
  (b) Old tree 27 m high. Some are broader and more open,
    while some are more dense.
  (c) Foliage and maturing cone. Crushed foliage has a lemon
    scent. Old cones adhere for years, dark brown.
  (d) Male flower about to shed pollen.

4. Sawara Cypress (Golden Thread-foliaged form) *Chamaecyparis pisifera* 'Filifera Aurea'   67

  Hanging spray. The acute-scaled foliage has an acrid resinous
  scent when crushed. Young trees are very bright gold and may
  be beehive-shaped or slender and gaunt.

5. Hinoki Cypress *Chamaecyparis obtusa*   63
  (a) Underside of shoot showing the pattern of bright white
    markings.
  (b) Strong shoot with young cone.

Sawara Cypress 'Filifera Aurea'

Hinoki Cypress

1a

b

1c

2a

3a

2b

3b

2c

4

5a

5b

3c

3d

THUJAS, JUNIPER

Plate 4

Leaves scale-like or mixed with small, sharp needles.

1. White Cedar   *Thuja occidentalis*   80

(a) Upper surface of shoot: matt, with raised "gland" on each scale.
(b) Under surface: very matt, pale green, unmarked.

Older trees seldom look healthy, having dull foliage hanging in a lifeless way; it is short-lived, but may be seen as a clipped hedge.

2. Western Red Cedar   *Thuja plicata*   81

(a) Cone ripe in autumn.
(b) Shoot showing glossy rich green upper side. The underside is marked by pale green bands. Handling the foliage, however lightly, produces a strong scent of pear-drops.
(c) Outline of young tree 10m high. The leading shoot is always erect.

This tree is usually luxuriantly healthy and appears likely to live to a great age in Europe. It is commonly planted as a screen or clipped hedge.

3. Korean Thuja   *Thuja koraiensis*   80

(a) Upper side of shoot bearing mature cones. The scales are always matt but can be pale 'green, dark green or blue-grey.
(b) Underside of shoot showing broad silvered markings. In most specimens this silvering largely obscures the margins also.

A small, slow-growing tree whose foliage when crushed gives a scent like that of a rich almond-cake.

4. Hiba   *Thujopsis dolabrata*   82

(a) Shoot showing upper side with glossy, hard broad scales.
(b) Shoot showing underside with well-defined pattern of thick white markings and glossy pale green margins.

5. Golden Chinese Juniper   *Juniperus chinensis* 'Aurea'   78

Spray showing typical mixture of juvenile and adult foliages. This male form can be a good deep yellow and is much planted in town gardens. The juvenile foliage is hard and prickly

Growth. Slow; few add as much as 30 cm a year, but girth can be added quite fast – to 3 cm a year for 60 years.

'CRIPPSII' 1901 Tunbridge Wells. Squat, conic, open when young, with very bright pale golden young foliage if grown in the open, greener in shade; slow, to 13 m so far. Frequent, even in very small gardens. 'Aurea' is an earlier form, dull yellow, but more vigorous; infrequent.

'TETRAGONA AUREA' 1876 Japan. Densely bunched, golden, partly quad-rangular foliage in vertical tufts; green interior or in shade; young trees gaunt, narrow, branch ends upswept; older many-topped, columnar and broad. 10 m. Infrequent. (The green form, introduced 1873, has been lost to cultivation.)

'FILICOIDES' 1861 Japan. Slender and gaunt; few level branches, upturned at ends, with long, flat, dense, fern-like sprays hanging from them. Rare. 15 m.

'LYCOPODIOIDES' 1861 Japan. Conic or narrow crown; open, gaunt; short branches upswept, with dense bunches of fasciated, thickened, erect sprays, dull dark green but showing much blue-white. Alleged dwarf; to 15 m but very slow. Infrequent; mainly S.W. England.

Similar species. No other cypress has blunt scale-leaves in flat sprays, but *Austrocedrus chilensis* (p. 59) is somewhat similar.

Cultivars of Hinoki Cypress: **a**, 'Tetragona Aurea'; **b**, 'Filicoides'; **c**, 'Lycopodioides'

SAWARA CYPRESS *Chamaecyparis pisifera* (Sieb. and Zucc.) Endl. Japan 1861. Uncommon as the type but cultivars very common, town gardens, parks, churchyards. Very hardy. 20 m (23 × 2.5 m at Killerton, Devon).

Bark. Rich chestnut-brown; close, parallel, narrow, deep fissures; ridges strip finely, may be grey.

Crown. Conic, often broad from forked stem, open; branches level but may bend down and layer at base.

Foliage. Shoot dull pinkish-brown. Leaf bright shiny green, small appressed scale abruptly acuminate with *fine, incurved point*, in dense, flattened sprays. Beneath, each scale

Sawara Cypress

is bright white at base. Crushed foliage has acrid, resinous aroma.

Flowers and cone. Male flowers minute, pale brown, terminal on fine branch-lets; shed pollen in April. Cones densely clustering a little behind males, pea-like, grey-green, ripening brown on upper side first; each of the ten scales with minute point in centre.

Growth. Slow: about 20 cm a year, May–September.

'AUREA' 1861 Japan. Rather rare. Like type, but new growth bright gold, changing to green during the summer.

'PLUMOSA' 1861 Japan. Broad, flat-topped column of flat-pinnate dense feathery, juvenile foliage. Each scale free, 2 mm, dark green, with long, spreading point. Pale yellowish new shoots against dark green make crown paler in summer. Bole usually forks at 2 m. Broad-conic when young. Common in parks and gardens, in towns especially, but less than the following form:

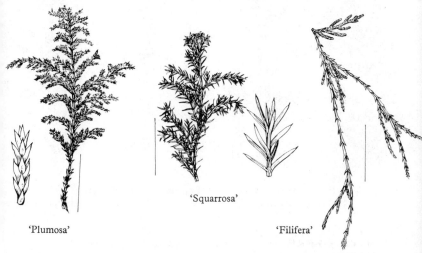

'Squarrosa'

'Plumosa'   'Filifera'

'PLUMOSA AUREA' a bright golden form when young, paler with age, some-times reverting to green. 24 m. Common in town parks, gardens and churchyards.

'SQUARROSA' 1843 Japan via Java. Conic with obtuse top, rarely on single straight stem to tip, more often forked at 2 m. Soft, blue, fluffy foliage of com-pletely free, forward-spreading, linear leaves, 5–6 mm long; light green above, very broad bands of pale blue-grey beneath; in dense bunches. Quite common. 20 m (25 m).

'BOULEVARD' ('Cyanoviridis') 1934 USA. A semi-dwarf form of 'Squarrosa', very blue if grown in partial shade; now much planted in rock gardens. Threat-ening to exceed 6 m.

'FILIFERA' 1861 Japan. Very broad, many-stemmed bush; shoots hang like threads, with small bunches of side-shoots at long intervals. Dark green, very open crown. 20 m. Infrequent.

'FILIFERA AUREA' 1889 Japan. Beehive-shaped bush or gaunt few-branched tree; as 'Filifera' but bright gold. 12 m. Infrequent. **Pl. 3.**

Similar species. The type is very like *Ch. formosensis* (below). The cultivars are very distinct.

FORMOSAN CYPRESS *Chamaecyparis formosensis* Matsumura

Formosa 1910. Rare; in gardens like Nymans, Stourhead and Westonbirt, and Irish gardens. 13m. Differs from *Ch. pisifera* in broad crown on *wide U-shaped* lower branching; yellow-green, *slightly bronzed* foliage, downcurved at shoot-tips; crushed foliage smells of *seaweed*; leaves *not* marked beneath in bright white. A tree of enormous size in Formosa, but very slow here and really thriving only in Ireland.

a   b

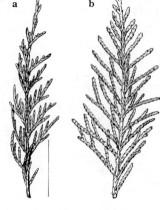

Formosan Cypress   White Cypress,   Leyland Cypress cultivars:
                        with ripe cone   **a,** 'Haggerston Grey'; **b,** 'Leighton Green'

WHITE CYPRESS *Chamaecyparis thyoides* (L.) Britten Sterns and Poggenberg

Maine-Florida-Mississippi near the coast 1736. Rare; mostly in collections and major gardens. Very hardy. 14m.
Bark. Dark brown or dull grey-brown, peeling in layers of long strips.
Crown. *Flame-shape*, narrowing to rounded tip.
Foliage. Two colour forms: green and blue-grey. Little bunches of *short*, flattened branchlets, each of fine (1mm across) ultimate divisions. Leaves minute scales, many with a resin-gland; dark grey-green or pale blue-grey, white at base, well marked white beneath. When crushed, gives warm gingery scent. Male flowers red, ovoid, 2mm.
Growth. Very slow; rather short-lived.

HYBRID CYPRESSES × Cupressocyparis

A hybrid genus covering crosses between species of *Chamaecyparis* and species of *Cupressus* (see Key, p. 59). At least three exist, but only one, the Leyland Cypress is commonly grown. Commonly, two distinct forms of this are seen both of which arose at Leighton Park, but a third, grey-leafed form, also from Leighton is likely to be much planted soon. A fourth, which arose after 1940 at Ferndown, Dorset ('Stapehill') is in commerce. This last has foliage similar to 'Leighton Green' but less dense and rougher to the touch.

LEYLAND CYPRESS ×*Cupressocyparis leylandii* (Jacks. & Dallim.) Dallim. Leighton Park, Welshpool 1888, 1911. Large trees in some major gardens; young trees and hedges now common everywhere. Extremely hardy. To 31 m in 50 years.

Bark. Dark red-brown with shallow, vertical fissures.

Crown. Narrowly columnar, tapering to slightly *leaning*, one-sided, sparsely clothed leading shoot. (In western Ireland broad-conic.) New shoot in June-July leans at tip. Below the top, dense with regular, numerous, steeply ascending branches, retained live to the base. (See Fig. p. 63).

Foliage. Two clones with different foliage, 'Haggerston Grey' and 'Leighton Green', are common:

'HAGGERSTON GREY' 1888. Female parent Nootka Cypress. Main shoots with minor shoots pointing forwards, each with narrow, pinnate *branchlet-systems in two or more planes* in plumes. Scale-leaves dark green above, often grey at base; yellow-green beneath. Flowers and cones very rarely borne. This is the more usual form.

'LEIGHTON GREEN' 1911. Female parent Monterey Cypress. Main shoots unbranched, bear directly *two flat ranks of pinnate flat, branchlet systems*, each system broader and larger than on 'Haggerston Grey'. Scale-leaves coarser and sharper, uniform dark green above, paler and yellowish beneath. Male flowers and cones frequent in some years. Cone 2–3 cm, globular, each scale with prominent process.

'NAYLOR'S BLUE' 1911, is rare but should soon be in commerce. Foliage somewhat intermediate between the two described, *dark grey, bluish when new*.

'CASTLEWELLAN' is a gold-tipped form with plumose spray.

'ROBINSON'S GOLD' is a flat sprayed form brilliant in early summer.

Growth. Very rapid on a variety of soils and sites. Shoots of 1 m are common and a steady 5 cm of girth is added annually. Growth in height is from May to end September; to 10 cm a week in July.

Similar species. 'Leighton Green' is like Nootka Cypress (p. 62) in foliage only, but is smoother, more yellowish beneath and brighter green above, and less pendulous. The columnar crowns are quite distinct.

TRUE CYPRESSES Cupressus

Twenty species, from USA, Mexico, and from the Mediterranean to China. Foliage systems angular, cones 1–4 cm.

Key to the less rare species of Cupressus

1. Leaves with acute, free, spreading tips — *lusitanica*, p. 71
   Leaves with blunt, appressed tips — 2

2. Cone 2.5–4 cm across — 3
   Cone 1–2 cm — 5

3. Leaves blue-grey, much white-spotted   *glabra*, p. 72
Leaves green, unspotted or sparsely spotted   **4**

4. Leaves bright green, branchlets slightly club-ended; lemon-
scented if crushed   *macrocarpa*, below
Leaves dull, dark green, branchlets tapered; nearly scentless
when crushed   *sempervirens*, p. 72

5. Long slender sprays of short shoots, right-angled to each other;
leaves dark grey-green   *goveniana*, p. 71
Broad sprays; shoots long, ± sparse, flattened basal sprays;
leaves bright yellow-green   *torulosa*, p. 73

MONTEREY CYPRESS   *Cupressus macrocarpa* Hartw.   **Pl. 3**
On low cliffs at Cypress Point and Point Lobos, near Monterey, California
1838. Common in most lowland areas in parks, gardens and churchyards;
abundant near coasts in W. Britain. Has been much used as a hedge but Leyland
Cypress now preferred. 37 × 7 m (35 × 7.3 m at Montacute House, Somerset).
Bark. Brown, shallowly networked with ridges; oldest trees grey with thick
ridges lifting away.
Crown. Young: columnar with conic top, either broad, or narrow, with spiky
level shoots on the leader which is straight and erect, unlike that of Leyland
Cypress. Old: hugely spreading, flat-topped with long, level heavy branches,
like Cedar of Lebanon, or ovoid, but in Ireland, a vast obtuse triangle. Young
trees in Ireland are broader, with long, narrow plume-like shoots projecting at
45° from horizontal as they are in Monterey. Dense, dark green or yellowish-
green, often heavily branched from low down, sometimes many-boled.
Foliage. Dense bunches of forward-pointing shoots clothed in scale-leaves,
soon dull brown-pink; on old trees leaves shorter and thicker, almost fleshy,
bright, dark or yellowish-green; *fragrant of lemon* when crushed. Each scale-
leaf has a dark-centred point closely appressed, with a pale margin.
Flowers and cone. Male flowers on small shoots on basal half of side-shoots
behind females; 3 mm green and yellow, ovoid, yellow late May, shed pollen in
mid-June; female flowers on central stronger shoots clustered on outer end of
previous year's growth, ovoid-cylindric, 6 mm bright green strongly deflexed
scales with dark purplish between, early to mid-June; ripening to big globose
lumpy cones, 3–4 cm long, shining purple-brown, 7–8 large scales, with curved
boss in centre, margins finely waved.
Growth. Very rapid in the west, to 30 m in 40 years then height growth almost
stops, but girth increases very rapidly, up to 6–7 cm a year being long maintained. Age-limit not yet reached here.

'LUTEA' 1892 Chester. Dull golden foliage, slower growing, probably more
hardy, good against sea-winds. 26 m. Frequent.
'DONARD GOLD' 1946 Co. Down. A brighter form of 'Lutea'. Infrequent.
'FASTIGIATA' probably 1838 California. Very narrow, columnar, at least
until quite old; branches small, fastigiate, eventually fanning out from the base
when very big. Rare. 32 m.
Similar species. *C. sempervirens* p. 72, *C. goveniana* p. 71, *C. lusitanica*
below.

MEXICAN CYPRESS or CEDAR OF GOA *Cupressus lusitanica* Mill.

Mexico, Guatemala. Before 1680. Uncommon and not reliably hardy except in S.W. England where large trees survived 1962–3. 30 m.

Bark. Brown, closely and shallowly fissured into vertical, peeling strips, often spiralled.

Crown. Conic; more open than in *C. macrocarpa*, especially near the top; branch-ends project. Usually a single, straight bole, circular in cross-section; branches curved sharply upwards.

Foliage. Scale-leaves with free, *spreading, acute* tips. Dark grey-green. 2–3 year wood on young trees is purplish-red bearing glaucous or dark foliage. Vigorous shoots sinuous, (straight in *C. macrocarpa*). Only faint resinous aroma when crushed.

Cone. Globular, small, 1.5 cm, few scales each with small, sharp, recurved boss; bloomed *blue-grey*. Later shiny deep purple-brown.

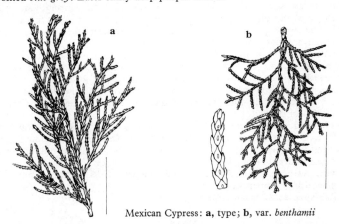

a
b

Mexican Cypress: **a**, type; **b**, var. *benthamii*

'GLAUCA'. Foliage as in the type but blue grey. Fine, rare tree. 20 m.

var. *benthamii* (Endl.) Carr. 1840 Mexico. Very rare, except in Devon and Cornwall, where some 27 m. Usually narrowly conic on splendid cylindrical stem but may be broad and branchy. Foliage bright *shining green* in short bunches of *fern-like, flattened* short sprays, scale-tips not spreading, minor branchlets *sinuous*.

Similar species. *C. macrocarpa* p. 70; *C. goveniana* (below).

GOWEN CYPRESS *Cupressus goveniana* Gord.

Two small groves near Monterey, California. 1848. Rare, some large gardens mainly in the south. 23 m (at Wakehurst Place, Sussex).

Bark. Pale brown and grey; shallow vertical ridges.

Crown. Columnar, from very narrow to broad; dense, upswept. (Broad, conic, open in California.)

Foliage. Young plants blackish grey-green, with some *white spots*; few or none on older trees where foliage bright green; tightly pressed scale-leaves. Smallest branchlets all *at right-angles* to each other in various planes in short minor sprays, making long slender major sprays or. dark red-brown shoots.

Flowers and cone. Male flowers ovoid-cylindric, 3 mm, yellow. Females globular, 5 mm, bright yellow. Cones clustered *at base* of shoot, dark shining grey-brown, 1.5–2 cm, each scale with horizontal ridge with central upcurved hook.

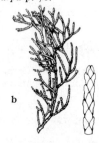

Similar species. *C. macrocarpa* (p. 70) and *C. lusitanica* (p. 71) differ in aroma, in angles of smallest branchlets, and always unspotted foliage.

ITALIAN CYPRESS   *Cupressus sempervirens* L.

Mediterranean, north to Switzerland, east to Persia 1500. Uncommon; most frequent in Somerset, uncommon to rare in other parts. Reputedly not hardy, but old trees in East Lothian unharmed in 1963. Occasional in small gardens and churchyards. 15 (23) m.

Bark. Brown-grey spirals of shallow, scaling ridges.

Crown. Columnar, often vary narrowly, and tapering finely to a slanting top. Some square-topped and broader, a few more spreading.

Foliage. Dark dull green, almost *scentless* when crushed; very closely pressed scale-leaves; branchlet ends tapering; densely bunched, thick and curved upwards in old trees.

Flowers and cone. Male flowers ovoid, greenish, 3 mm. Cones large, like Monterey Cypress, but more spread over crown, shining green at first, then persisting dark red-brown finally *dull grey* when old; lumpy ovoid, 4 × 3 cm, scale margins deeply sinuous.

Growth. Surprisingly fast when young; annual shoots to 80 cm, but soon very slow. May–September.

Similar species. *C. macrocarpa* p. 70.

a   b

c

Italian Cypress: **a,** foliage with cone; **b,** from old tree; **c,** cone

SMOOTH ARIZONA CYPRESS   *Cupressus glabra* Sudw.   **Pl. 3**
Syn. *C. arizonica* var. *bonita* Lemmon

Central Arizona 1907. Frequent, and increasingly planted, even in small gardens and as hedge. Sold as "*C. arizonica*" "*C.a. bonita*" or "*C.a. conica*". Hardy. 20 m.

Bark. *Purple*, soon *blistering* and flaking to leave red-brown or yellow circular patches. Older trees with some grey ridges flaking.
Crown. Rounded-conic (ovoid), even, and moderately dense; upswept branching.
Foliage. Shoot soon bright orange-brown. Sparse systems of branchlets, wiry and spreading nearly at right-angles, clothed in *grey-blue* and *grey-green*, closely pressed scale-leaves, some with a central white spot. Crushed foliage has aroma of grapefruit.
Flowers and cone. Male flowers often abundant making crowns partly yellow all winter. Cone large, 1.5–2.5 cm, clustered, persistent; scales glossy brownish-green and bloomed grey, margins pink, small curved central spine; cones ripen dark purple-brown and are retained on the tree for many years.
Growth. Rather slow; annual shoot to 50 cm, mid-May to end August in young trees.

'PYRAMIDALIS' 1928. Much brighter silvery blue-grey; thick dense upswept foliage, projecting tips vertical; a prominent white spot on nearly every leaf. Very attractive.
Similar species. Confused with *C. arizonica* (below) but bark quite different. Dense blue-grey, shapely crown, easily recognised.

ROUGH-BARKED ARIZONA CYPRESS *Cupressus arizonica* Greene

Arizona to Mexico 1882. Rare, but large trees in older collections are this species, not *C. glabra*. 22 m. Differs from *C. glabra* in greenish-brown, *finely fissured stringy bark*, with thin, short plates, often spiralled, and dull grey-green or bright green foliage often lacking white spots.

BHUTAN CYPRESS *Cupressus torulosa* Don

W. Himalaya and W. China 1824. Uncommon, mostly in south and west, in Ireland and Perthshire. Hardy. 28 m (26.5 × 4.4 m at Nettlecombe, Somerset).
Bark. Dark grey-brown; regular, narrow, shallow ridges, spiralled, curving away or flaking.
Crown. Rather broadly conic, rounded top; upswept branches; dense.
Foliage. Bright yellowish-green. Basal ultimate shoots *long, curved, slender*; outer shoots slender, bunched, pendulous. Leaves with incurved acute points in ± flattened sprays. Crushed foliage has *grassy scent*. Young plants blue-green.
Cone. Small, 1 cm, green then dark red-brown, each scale with minute decurved spine.

Bhutan Cypress: **a**, type; **b**, var. *corneyana*

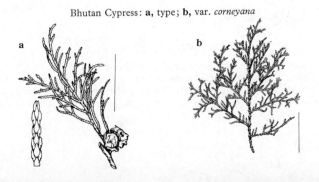

var. *corneyana* (Knight and Perry) Carriere. *c.* 1847. Rare; less frequent than the type. Yellowish or dull green, remotely branched thin shoots; sprays less flattened, irregular, twisted at tips.

Similar species. *C. lusitanica* (p. 71) has glaucous cones, more branched, less pendulous much shorter shoots, and leaves with free, long-acute tips.

FITZROYA

A single species distinguished by blunt outcurved leaves in whorls of three and cones with three whorls of three scales each, the lowest and often the middle, sterile.

PATAGONIAN CYPRESS or ALERCE *Fitzroya cupressoides*
(Molina) Johnst.
Syn. *F. patagonica* Hooker f.

Chile, Argentina 1849. Infrequent; largely confined to south and west, north to Argyll, and Ireland. Hardy once established. 18 × 1.9 m (Killerton, Devon).

Bark. Dark red-brown, deeply ridged, lifting away; clear boles greyer; shallow strips.

Crown. Vase-shaped; strong upswept branches arching out; young trees more conic; stem forks low. Branches curled; foliage pendulous.

Foliage. Pendulous sprays; leaves in whorls of three, spreading, thick, *blunt*; dark blue-green, prettily marked with two white bands on each side; 2–4 mm.

Flowers and cone. Female flowers abundant, 5 mm yellowish-brown rosettes of pointed scales, three spreading, three erect, in April, becoming glossy green, lumpy, globose, 6–12 mm, with conic, protruding scales, three large, three small, with whitish between; large ones with pale triangle with raised tip in centre of scale; ripening brown and opening very widely. Male flowers less frequent, 2 mm, drooping.

Growth. Very slow, but 2–5 year plants can make 30 cm shoots; June–October.

Patagonian Cypress, with cones and enlarged whorl

Similar species. Leaves are also whorled in threes in some Junipers, but sharp-pointed, and slender.

JUNIPERS Juniperus

Sixty species from most of the northern hemisphere from the tropics to the Arctic Circle. Fleshy cone-scales unite to form a "berry". Leaves of two kinds: acicular, free-standing, usually sharp, linear, awl-shaped, or triangular; scale-leaves overlapping, appressed, small. A few species bear both kinds of leaves;

all species have acicular leaves when young seedlings. A difficult group to identify, but the seven given are the only ones seen away from a few special collections. The key works only for these.

Key to the less rare of the Juniperus species

1. Acicular leaves only   **2**
   Overlapping scale-leaves, at least in part   **4**

2. Pendulous, soft shoots; leaves in whorls far apart; bright
      shining green above, blue-white beneath   *rigida*, p. 76
   Upright or nodding shoots; leaves crowded   **3**

3. Leaves big (2 × 0.3 cm), pale, fresh, rich green   *drupacea*, p. 76
   Leaves small (1.5 × 0.2 cm); grey-green   *communis*, p. 75

4. Nodding bunches of overlapping, long bright or grey-green
      scales with fine, white free tips   *recurva*, p. 76
   Slender, spreading sprays of minute, appressed dark green
      scales; tufts of acicular leaves on shoots behind, or mixed
      with scales.   **5**

5. Scale-leaves dark-centred, patterned by pale margins; when
      crushed give sour smell; juvenile leaves mostly at base of
      shoot; fruit 7 mm   *chinensis*, p. 77
   Scale-leaves appear nearly uniform, dark green; when crushed
      give smell of paint or soap; both kinds of leaves finer;
      juvenile leaves at ends of most adult shoots; fruit 3–5 mm *virginiana*, p. 78

COMMON JUNIPER *Juniperus communis* L.
Native; chalk-land in south, limestones in north,
shallow peats in pinewoods in N. Scotland; N.
Europe to S.W. Asia, N. America. Very rare in
gardens. Rarely over 6 m.
Crown. Usually a pointed shrub, bent or twisted,
dense becoming gaunt, or low, broad with many
pointed tops.
Foliage. Acicular leaves in whorls of three,
spreading, sharply pointed; inner side concave
with broad, white band, outer light grey-green; to
1 cm long. Shoot pale brown. Crushed or dried
foliage scented of apple.
Flowers and fruit. Male flowers on separate
trees from females, solitary, yellow; fruit green,
globular, ripening to blue-bloomed then, after 2–3
years, to black.
Growth. Very slow, only a few cm a year.

Common Juniper

'HIBERNICA' ('Stricta') 1838 Scandinavia. Irish Juniper.
Frequent in gardens. 8 m. Very narrow, pointed-columnar;
dense, close blue-grey foliage, *upright*, on upright branches,
tips slightly outturned.
   'SUECICA' 1768. Flame shaped, branches upright, shoot-

Irish Juniper

tips curve abruptly to *level* or slightly drooped, dense, short; leaves 1–1.4 cm. Uncommon; rock and formal gardens. Angle of shoot-tips distinguishes this from 'Hibernica'.

Similar species. *Fitzroya* (p. 74) differs in its thick, blunt leaves, banded white both sides.

SYRIAN JUNIPER *Juniperus drupacea* Labill.

Greece, Asia Minor and Syria 1854. Uncommon; in a few large gardens. 19 × 1.2 m (Brickendon, Herts.).

Bark. Orange-brown, shredding finely and vertically.

Crown. Narrowly conic or conic-columnar, sometimes with long clean bole; very dense. Old trees can be broad-columnar or ovoid; young may fork into two close, conic crowns.

Foliage. Much the biggest leaves of any juniper, lanceolate tapering to fine point, crowded, *shining fresh rich green*, two white bands on inner surface; *rigid and spiny*, 1.2– 2.5 × 0.3 cm.

Syrian Juniper

Flowers. Only male known; rich green in bud, ovoid in twos and threes at base of leaves; numerous.

TEMPLE JUNIPER *Juniperus rigida* Sieb. and Zucc.

Japan, Korea 1861. Uncommon, mostly in S. England. 7 (13) m.

Bark. Dull brown; long grey strips peeling away.

Crown. Pendulous and bushy, or gaunt, single-stemmed with few upswept branches and foliage hanging from their ends.

Foliage. *Hanging* slender shoots white, pink or pale green becoming pale orange-brown, with prickly-pointed but *soft* leaves in *sparse whorls* of three. Curious pinkish-yellow from a distance. The leaves have a narrow blue-white central sunken band on inner side. 1.5–2 cm long, convex and shining bright green outer side, with translucent yellowish spined apex.

Flowers and fruit. Male flowers clustered among leaves, globular, 2– 4 mm. Fruit on separate trees strung closely along shoots; globose, lumpy, 1 cm pale bluish-green, spotted white, ripening dark purple bloomed white; often very numerous.

Temple Juniper: **a,** female shoot and flower (×3); **b,** male shoot and flower (×3)

DROOPING JUNIPER *Juniperus recurva* Buchan.-Ham.

E. Himalaya, Burma, China 1830. Infrequent, mostly in W. and N. Britain; biggest in Ireland. 16 m (18 m Castlewellan, Co. Down).

Bark. Grey-brown, willow-like, ridges peeling away.

Crown. Broad-based, narrowing to pointed conic top. Young plants ovoid bushes. Short, nodding shoots from upturned branches. Open; bare in lower parts of old plants which may be partly reclining. Dead foliage retained inside crown for a few years, dull orange-brown.

Foliage. *Short, nodding shoots* of rather bunched branchlets; narrow, acute, *dry and rustling leaves* small, crowded forwards, quite hiding shoots, pale, rather grey-green, long white fine points; inner surface with two central *narrow white* bands, 5–8 mm.

Flowers and fruit. Male flowers on ends of inner shoots, 4mm green and yellow. Fruit *olive-brown*, glossy, 1 × 0.4 cm.

'CASTLEWELLAN' Co. Down. Rare. Many slender stems arching out and hanging down like fishing rods; foliage brighter green, fully pendulous.

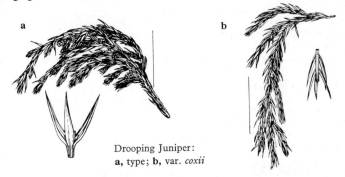

Drooping Juniper:
a, type; b, var. *coxii*

var. *coxii* (Jack.) Melville. Coffin Juniper. N. Burma 1920. 11m. Now about as frequent as the type. Bark more orange-brown, bole draped in *loose strips*. Richer green and *long pendulous* shoots of well-separated whorls of three leaves, the shoot visible between. Leaves 8–10mm, inner side with two *broad green-white* bands. Retained dead leaves brighter orange. Usually quite different from *J. recurva* in the hand, but intermediates are known.

CHINESE JUNIPER *Juniperus chinensis* L.

China, Japan 1804. Common; town parks and gardens, churchyards in all parts. 18m.

Bark. Dark cigar-brown, stringy; long, twisted, narrow strips peeling away.

Crown. Single-stemmed trees narrowly conic, often not quite straight; later an open narrow-domed top. Many-stemmed trees (from low forking or division) broad-conic. Light, open, untidy crown, yellow with male flowers in winter. *Bole deeply fluted* or several stems fused.

Foliage. Acicular tufts at *base* of branchlets, less often mixed with scale-leaves; sharp, rigid; glaucous-blue inner side; in whorls of three or in opposite pairs, nearly 1 cm. Scale-leaves very small, tightly appressed to shoot, dull, dark green; *pale margins* make pattern. Crushed gives faint or strong catty smell.

Flowers and fruit. Sexes usually on separate trees. Male small, terminal, yellow, abundant and prominent from autumn until shedding pollen in early

April. Fruit irregularly globular or top-shaped, *6–7 mm,* bright
glaucous-white; two years ripening.
Growth. Slow in height and girth. Average for height less than
15 cm a year although young plants may grow 50 cm a year.

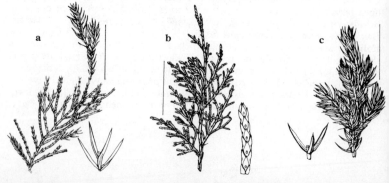

'AUREA' 1855 Milford, Surrey. Distributed 1872. A good
golden, narrowly columnar or many-columned, flat-topped
male form, frequent in town gardens and parks. 12 m. **Pl. 4.**
    'KETELEERII' Belgium pre-1910. Rare. A handsome,
regularly narrow-conic dense grey-green female form with   'Keteleerii'
scale-leaved foliage; juvenile foliage confined to a few interior shoots. The leaves
are shining and the frequent fruit are bloomed blue-green.
Similar species. *J. virginiana* (below).

PENCIL CEDAR   *Juniperus virginiana* L.
Quebec to Texas 1664. Frequent, but less so than *J. chinensis*. 15 m. Similar to
J. chinensis, but both kinds of foliage *finer,* slender, the adult shoots frequently
tipped by spreading juvenile leaves and when crushed aromatic of *paint or soap;*
scale-leaves with very narrow pale margins; fruit ripen in one year, *3–5 mm.*
Slow-growing, not very long-lived. Dark and untidy crown.

'CANAERTII' 1868 Belgium. A rare, striking tree: a dense, upright column
of bright green dense mainly adult foliage scattered with pale blue-grey fruit
soon brilliant blue-purple. 10 m.
    'GLAUCA' pre-1855. A narrow upswept, open-crowned tree with pale soft-
grey mostly terete adult foliage in upright sprays. Fruit pale blue-grey and
lilac. Infrequent. 12 m.

FLAKY JUNIPER   *Juniperus squamata* Buchan.-Ham.
Himalayas, China, Formosa 1836. Very rare, very slow and very dull shrub.

'MEYERI' 1914 China. Frequent, many being planted in small gardens, parks,
and shrubberies on trading estates. Young plants conic, dense, dark steely-blue
and grey-blue, until 1.5 m. Older plants to 8 m, spread in odd shapes with
conic spires widely spaced, open in lower half showing pink-brown papery bark.
Short crowded shoots surrounded by leaves in whorls of three, 1 cm long, sharply
pointed, bright blue-green outer surface; inner bright blue-white with faint green
margins and midrib. Dead leaves adhere pale pink-brown.

a, Pencil Cedar, type; **b,** 'Glauca'; **c,** Flaky Juniper 'Meyeri'

THUJA

Six species from N. America, China, Japan, Formosa. Five in cultivation. Called "*Arbor vitae*" in books but not in life. Similar to *Chamaecyparis* but with urn-shaped cones with thin scales, and larger, broader leaves. Seedlings have acicular leaves at first. Adult foliage appressed scale-leaves in flattened sprays.

Key to Thuja species

1. Foliage in vertical sprays, both sides same colour   *orientalis*, below
   Foliage spreading, flattened sprays, underside differing from
   upper   **2**

2. Underside uniform pale yellowish-green   *occidentalis*, p. 80
   Underside marked with pale green, white or wholly white   **3**

3. Underside bright white almost all over   *koraiensis*, p. 80
   Underside with narrow streaks of greenish-white   **4**

4. Foliage smooth, shiny; when handled emits powerful aroma
   of apples or pineapple   *plicata*, p. 81
   Foliage hard, dull, stiff, nodding; when crushed gives sweet
   aroma   *standishii*, p. 81

OLFACTORY TABLE FOR *Thuja* SPECIES

No scent	*orientalis*, below
Fruit-cake with almonds	*koraiensis*, p. 80
Sweet, as in cheap sweets, lemony	*standishii*, p. 81
Cooked apples, with cloves	*occidentalis*, p. 80
Pineapple; crushing not needed	*plicata*, p. 81

CHINESE THUJA

Thuja orientalis L.
China 1752. Infrequent. More often in city and town gardens and churchyards than in big gardens. Most frequent in Midlands, through Oxford and Wilts., in villages and towns. 15 m.

Bark. Dull red-brown, shredding into vertical strips from narrow ridges.

Crown. Narrow upright-branched, ovoid in young trees; shapeless gaunt and broad at the top with *bare upcurved branches* in old trees.

Chinese Thuja

Foliage. Thick, blunt scales dark *green both sides*, in *vertical plates*, free apices incurved.

Flowers and cone. Male flowers very small, dull yellow on tips of branchlets, nodding. Cone ovoid, upright; strong, hooked processes around the top in two rows; 1 cm, bright glaucous bloom in summer.

Growth. Very slow; hardy but seldom healthy or long-lived.

'ELEGANTISSIMA' 1860. Starts as dwarf, pointed, narrowly flame-shaped, upright; foliage brightly tipped gold in summer, yellowish-green in winter. Becomes broad, ovoid, to 7m. Young trees frequent in patios and around new buildings; old trees occasional in cottage-gardens.

'Elegantissima'

KOREAN THUJA *Thuja koraiensis* Nakai

Pl. 4

Korea 1918. Rare; collections and a few large gardens. Narrow, sparsely branched, conic, the branches up-curved towards the tips; sometimes low and bushy. Slow-growing: 10m to date. Foliage either fresh bright green or bluish grey-green, sometimes silvery grey; unique in completely *silvered underside*, or all silver except slender margins and midrib which are green. Shoot coppery-orange. Minor sprays broad, over-lapping. When crushed gives scent of rich almond-filled fruit cake. Male flowers black-tipped green, 1 mm globules on down-curved shoots. Cones, 2–3 pointing forwards from the tips of minor shoots, or erect; 10mm, Korean Thuja conic-ovoid; bright yellow-green, few scales, each tipped black.

WHITE CEDAR *Thuja occidentalis* L.

Pl. 4

E. Canada and USA 1536 or 1596. Frequent as numerous cultivars, mostly dwarf. Type infrequent, sometimes used for hedges. 20m.

Bark. Orange-brown, shredding in vertical ridges.

Crown. Thin, open, conic with narrowly rounded top and upswept branches; less often dense, rich green.

Foliage. Often hangs lifelessly, yellowish-green; on young trees held in distinctive *twisting* upright sprays. *Underside uniformly pale, yellowish*; aromatic of apples (see table p. 79).

Cone. Yellow, often so abundant that crown appears golden; upright, soon splitting open to base of scales, then hanging.

Growth. Very slow, about 20cm a year maximum. Trees of 10m plus usually lean, soon blown down; White Cedar short-lived but will grow well in very wet soils.

'FASTIGIATA' 1865. Narrowly conic, less columnar and tidy than 'Spiralis'; upright slender branches. 10m.

'SPIRALIS' 1923. Neat, very narrow pointed column of rich dark green foliage, bronzing slightly in winter and which is in short dense, flat sprays, slightly curved, spirally set on short, upcurved branches. 10m.

'LUTEA' Far superior to the type: strong-stemmed, dense-crowned, robust; new foliage bright gold. 17m. Rare.

'RHEINGOLD' Frequent in small gardens; rounded-conic, often many-stemmed; to 4m, pale gold all over, browning a little but still a good colour in winter, some orange in spring. When small this plant bears partially juvenile foliage.
Similar species. *Thuja plicata* (below) has a similar but stronger aroma, brighter, luxuriant foliage streaked white beneath, dense crown.

WESTERN RED CEDAR   *Thuja plicata* D. Don   Pl. 4
Syn. *Thuja lobbii* Hort. ex Gord.
Alaska to California, east to Idaho 1853. Very common as specimen, park, shelter or garden tree except in cities or big towns. Occasional as forest-crop, usually planted under old hardwoods or larch; much used for hedges. 41 × 5 m (40 × 5.5 m at Bicton, Devon).

Bark. Dark purplish red-brown; wide ridges broken into strips and lifting plates; rather soft, very thick. Bole much fluted with age.

Crown. Narrowly conic to erect tip, broadening with age, especially if very large branches near base; these sweep upwards or may layer and make huge rings of vertical, vigorous boles; second rings may layer outside the first. Old trees have open crowns at the top, and may die back if big layers compete.

Foliage. Appressed scale-leaves, oblong-obovate, blunt, aromatic even without handling; shining rich green above, paler and streaked whitish beneath; flattened. Minor sprays narrow, lanceolate. Shoot coppery-brown, then red-brown, later purplish-brown. Fruity aroma, of pineapple, often scents the air around the tree.

Western Red Cedar

Flowers and cone. Male flowers minute, terminal on smallest shoots, pale yellow, inconspicuous, not common; shed invisibly fine pollen in March. Cones on stronger shoots of same trees, abundant on many; leathery ovoids, 1 cm, erect, spreading or pendulous; at first green, pale yellow all summer, turn brown in late autumn; 1.5 × 0.5 cm acute; scale tips spreading as spines.

Growth. Rapid in damp cool areas, shoots to 90cm, trees to 25m in 30 years but slow above 30m. April–September.

'ZEBRINA' Around 1900. Frequent parks and gardens. 25 × 2.6m. Broad regular conic crown; variously broadly barred pale or bright yellow or largely yellow foliage. Best and brightest in Ireland. Sturdy tree of steady growth, more slender and open in some shade.

'SEMPERAURESCENS' 1923. A strangely rare, very shapely, narrow, conic form, yellowish mossy green becoming almost orange-yellow with new growth. Groups at Westonbirt but very few other trees known. 20m.

Similar species. Lawson Cypress has darker crown with drooping leader and different flowers and cones, duller less flattened foliage, narrower scale-leaves and parsley scent. For differences from other Thujas see Key (p. 79) and descriptions of other species.

JAPANESE THUJA   *Thuja standishii* (Gord.) Carr.
Syn. *Thuja japonica* Maxim.
Japan 1860. Infrequent; in many of largest gardens and collections in each

country; many of the best trees are in Ireland. 20m (21 × 2.6m at Coed Coch, Aber-
gele, N. Wales).

Bark. Rich *dark red*; big, coarse plates
lifting away and strips peeling from their
sides; often spiralled; shiny and smooth in
parts.

Crown. *Broadly conic* rather open inside,
strong, *low U-shaped* branching, the
branches curving sharply upwards 1–2m
from the bole.

Foliage. Shoot coppery-orange then red-
brown. Foliage *hard*, matt, either pale
yellowish-green or with new shoots grey;
terminal shoots upright with *nodding tips*,

Japanese Thuja

bright but narrow grey-white streaks beneath; sweetly aromatic of lemon,
eucalyptus or sweets when well crushed. Male flowers on nodding tips, 1mm
ovoid purple-black. Cone erect ovoid-cylindric 13 × 7mm, bright green ribbed
scales with outcurved margins, deep cigar-brown when ripe.

Similar species. *Thuja plicata* (p. 81) but features above all distinguish.

THUJOPSIS

One species, formerly united with *Thuja*.

HIBA   *Thujopsis dolabrata* (L.f.) Sieb. and Zucc.   **Pl. 4**

Japan 1853 (one plant; died) 1859, 1861. Common in larger gardens down the
west from Argyll to Cornwall and in Ireland, infrequent east of English midlands. 15m (22m Cornwall-Dorset, 20 × 2.4m Tregrehan, Cornwall).

Bark. Dark red-brown; finely shredding strips and strings which may be grey
or pale brown and look as if scratched away by a cat. In tree-form, areas of
smooth, rich, burnt sienna; strips of pale orange.

Crown. Two forms: **1.** Narrow single-stemmed tree; few short branches, level
or depressed at first, soon upturned; foliage rather thick, pendulous. Frequent in
Cornwall and Ireland. **2.** Broadly conic formed of central stem surrounded by
20–40 layered stems, interior ones equal to central, all straight, cylindrical,
inner ones clear of branches for some 4m; foliage spreading, sprays smaller.
Normal form.

Foliage. Bright rich or yellowish-green, *glossy, hard. Lateral scale-leaves projecting*, broad triangular to 7 × 4mm with incurved abruptly pointed tip;
beneath, a rich green margin, the rest *pure white like thick paint* in a curved
streak (supposedly hatchet-shaped: Latin *"dolabra"*, a hatchet.)

Flowers and cone. Male flower ovoid blackish green nodding at tip of
branchlet. Female flower blue-grey, ripening to woody ovoid cone 1–2cm soon
opening widely.

Growth. Very slow, may be only a few cm a year but best trees have averaged
nearly 30cm.

'VARIEGATA' An unstable form with some shoots pale cream. These occur
here and there on many of the biggest trees, which may thus have been planted
as this cultivar.

Similar species. Thujas (pp. 79–82) have smaller leaves, softer, without bold
white stripes beneath, and much narrower shoots.

SWAMP CYPRESS AND SEQUOIA FAMILY
Taxodiaceae

A primitive family of ten genera, mostly with only one surviving species each, 14 species in all. Leaves hard and scale-like, or linear, long or short; or soft and deciduous. Cone globular, woody or leathery, may be persistent.

SEQUOIA

A single species. Scale-leaves on leading and fertile shoots; linear, spreading, two-ranked leaves on laterals.

COAST REDWOOD   *Sequoia sempervirens* (D. Don) End.   **Pl. 5**
Narrow belt by coast from just in Oregon to south of Monterey, California. In north parts many exceed 100m in height; tallest tree in world is one of these 112.4m ("Howard Libbey"). Introduced via Russia 1843. Frequent; parks and large gardens; poor and thin in towns. 42×7m; 25–30m in exposed places; 40×6.7m at Taymouth Castle, Perths. Huge trees S.E. and N. Ireland.

Bark. From bright *rufous red* to dark reddish-brown, usually the latter on old trees which have deep fissures dividing thick intertwining rough-edged ridges. Very thick, soft, stringy. Finely stringy and brightest where constantly picked at by the public.

Crown. Broadly columnar; pointed, open and whorled when young, flat-topped with age or exposure. Thin with age so daylight shows through to base of long, level or slightly drooping branches.

Bole. Columnar with little taper, clean of branches only where in dense woods or pruned; occasionally encircled by huge boss for 2–3 m from ground. Often with sprouts around base.

Foliage. Shoots green, speckled white (under lens) surrounded by green *scale-leaves* 6–8mm long; side-shoots with two flat rows of linear, hard, sharply pointed leaves, 1.5–2 cm dark green above (often grey when new), white band each side of midrib beneath.

Flowers and cone. Male flowers drop-shaped, 2 mm terminal on smallest side-shoots, pale whitish-yellow all winter, pale yellow when shedding pollen in February but usually scorched brown by frost. Cones on same tree on stouter shoots, small, 2 cm, globular; wrinkled scales turning red-brown.

Ripe and dry cones

Growth. Very rapid in damp soils and shelter, to 1.3m annually. Mid-May to late September. Trees to 30m in 30 years in S.W. England. Foliage scorched brown by cold winds in some years, without harm. Can live to 2,600 years in California but mostly 700–1,000 years. "Howard Libbey" is just over 500 years. Still thriving here at 125 years. Withstands shade better than any other conifer, if sprouting from stump. Coppices vigorously: big stumps can produce a circle of new trees as at Montacute House, Somerset.

Plate 5   REDWOODS AND ALLIES

Rufous or brown fibrous bark, hard foliage; rather small cones.

1. Wellingtonia   *Sequoiadendron giganteum*   86

(a) Typical tree 45 m high. The spire point is often maintained
but many trees have the apex rounded after being struck by
lightning.
(b) Shoot and spray. The hard foliage emits a strong scent of
aniseed when crushed.

The tallest tree in nearly all lowland areas, in parks, larger
gardens and churchyards.

2. Japanese Red Cedar   *Cryptomeria japonica*   87

Spray with two portions of the male flower remaining at the tip
and a ripe cone. The leaves are much longer than in the Wellingtonia, and bright glossy green.

3. Coast Redwood   *Sequoia sempervirens*   83

(a) Typical tree 35 m high.
(b) Shoot and spray, upper side. The hard leaves have two
white bands on the underside.

Grows best in the west but often seen in town parks, slender-
crowned and thinly branched.

4. Chinese Fir   *Cunninghamia lanceolata*   90

Shoot, showing the long, pliant but spined leaves, which have
two broad silvery bands on the underside. The tree is in many
of the larger English gardens. It has a rich rufous-red bark and
is often rather gaunt.

Japanese Red Cedar   Chinese Fir

1a

1b

2

3a

3b

4

DAWN REDWOOD, SWAMP CYPRESS, JAPANESE UMBRELLA PINE

Plate 6

1. Dawn Redwood *Metasequoia glyptostroboides*   95

(a) Young trees 6–8 m high.
(b) Young cone. Trees ten years old have borne a few cones in hot summers, but do not generally flower in N. Europe.
(c) Spray showing short shoots borne in opposite pairs. These shoots are shed in late autumn.

This tree, first introduced in 1948, is now in many large gardens in the south, where it grows very fast for the first ten years, then more slowly unless in damp and sheltered sites.

2. Swamp Cypress *Taxodium distichum*   94

(a) Tree of 25 m, with "knees" in wet soil.
(b) Spray of foliage with alternate deciduous shoots.

A frequent tree in London suburbs and in S. England, this grows perfectly well in ordinary soils.

3. Japanese Umbrella Pine *Sciadopitys verticillata*   91

Shoot of this strange tree with scale-leaves showing as mere bumps on the shoot (left) and long leaves fused together in pairs, deeply grooved on the undersides (right).

Swamp Cypress   Japanese Umbrella Pine

'Adpressa'

'ADPRESSA' ('Albo-spica') 1867. Rare. New shoots narrow and creamy-white, older shoots pale blue-grey; leaves short, scale-like, 4–8 mm. Shortest at each end of shoot. Two bright blue-white bands beneath, central white band above, near tip. 23 m.

'GLAUCA' pre-1874. Foliage bluish-grey, rather shorter than type. To 23 m. Rare.

Similar species. As a tree, none is similar, but foliage of yew can be confused. *Sequoia* has shorter, duller, stiffer leaves, white-banded beneath where yew is yellow-green, and *Sequoia* has scale-leaves along the stems.

SEQUOIADENDRON

A single species formerly united with *Sequoia* but differing mainly in the foliage being entirely of scale-leaves, and thus the whole aspect of the foliage and tree is quite different.

WELLINGTONIA, GIANT SEQUOIA, BIG TREE, MAMMOTH TREE or SIERRA REDWOOD

Sequoiadendron giganteum (Lindl.) Buchholz   **Pl. 5**
Syn. *Sequoia gigantea* Lindl.

Sierra Nevada, California. Use of the name "California Redwood" is deprecated; it causes frequent confusion with *Sequoia sempervirens* which is also a Californian redwood. Confined to isolated groves on the western slopes, from 5,000 to 8,000 ft., which include famous trees like "General Sherman" (82.9 × 24.1 m), "Grizzly Giant" (61 × 22 m at 2.4 m) and "General Grant" (81.5 × 24.3 m). Has been found over 100 m tall and to 27 m in girth. Lives for up to 3,400 years. Introduced in 1853 from Calaveras Grove to Gourdiehill, Perth (August) and to Veitch's at Exeter (December). Very common; pointed crown a feature of all wide views except among mountains. Frequent, but not thriving, in towns. Many huge avenues to mansions; specimens on lawns, in churchyards and by roadsides. Rare in W. Ireland. 46 × 8 m at Castle Leod, Ross-shire 50 × 6.5 at Endsleigh, Devon.

Bark. Oldest trees *dark pinkish-brown*, almost blackish and burnt-looking in places; some others brighter, rufous or pale orange-brown. Very *thick, soft* and fibrous. Can be, and often is, punched with impunity. Deep wide fissures, separate complex, shredding ridges; also usually deeply fluted.

Crown. Tall, narrowly conic even in tallest trees except where rounded by lightning-damage, standing out above surrounding trees; dense but patches of light between big branches hung with dark foliage. Top branches ascending, then a sector of level branches; below this increasingly heavy long and drooping branches, all *curving up* and *upswept* at the ends.

Bole. In open, as nearly all are, very rapid taper for 1–2 m, then cylindric, finally evenly tapered to tip. Some trees, possibly from Mariposa Grove, and not the oldest, with redder bark have boles almost without basal taper and without flutes.

Foliage. Shoot stout, pale or grey-green finely speckled white. Branchlets, hard *cords* of small grey or dark green scales, blue-grey at base on young shoots, deep green and shiny on old, with sharp, slightly spreading tips, 4–7 mm;

the sprays upright on shoot-ends, pendulous and outturned elsewhere. Main shoots curve upwards in long
sweep. Strong aniseed smell when crushed.

Flowers and cone. Male flowers terminal on smallest
shoots, solitary, but densely borne, tiny droplets, nearly
white all winter, pale yellow when shedding pollen in
March–April, pale brown if frosted at that time.
Female flowers erect on 2 cm scaly stalk from main
shoot, bright green ovoid, 1 cm, each scale with slender
erect, 2 mm pink-yellow spine. Cones: one (two) on
long stalks drooping from main shoots, bunched, some trees
very numerous in patches, green then dark brown,
two years ripening (remain on tree 20 years in California

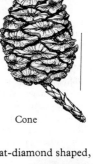

Cone

but only a few years here) ovoid, blunt 8 × 5 cm the scales flat-diamond shaped,
wrinkles running from a central fold.

Growth. Young trees only moderately rapid in height, shoots
of 60 cm, rarely 1 m, but steady growth continues; some trees
45 m tall and 100 years old adding 45 cm annually. Growth in
girth is extremely rapid: 5–8 cm annually is usual, 15 cm
known and many of the oldest trees maintain 5–8 cm. Never
blow down but occasionally die from a root-fungus. Frequently
struck by lightning.

'AUREUM' 1856 Cork. Slower; more dense, shoots upswept, outer sprays dull yellow. 20 m. Rare.
'PENDULUM' 1863, marketed 1873, Nantes, France. Either
very narrow, tall, to 28 m, or bent arched and upswept again in
curious shapes. Branches short arising and continuing

'Pendulum'

pointed almost vertically downwards; on arched trees some turn upwards. Rare.
Similar species. *Cryptomeria japonica* (below) differs in bright green foliage
and long curved points to leaves and bark coming away in long strips.

CRYPTOMERIA

A single species with long-pointed scale-leaves and cones with short spines on
the scales.

JAPANESE RED CEDAR   *Cryptomeria japonica* (L.f.) Don   **Pl. 5**
China, Japan. 1842 from China, 1861 from Japan. Frequent, locally common,
but seldom in small or town gardens. Best growth in western areas. 37 × 5 m
(36.5 × 4.3 m at Endsleigh, Devon).
Bark. Orange to red-brown then dark brown with age. Thick, soft, fibrous;
deep vertical parallel fissures. With age strips peel away or hang round the bases
of branches.
Bole. Sharp taper above roots then very cylindrical into crown. Old trees in
the west, especially, may have big woody hanging pap-shaped protuberances,
particularly around bases of branches.
Crown. Narrowly *conic with rounded apex*, dense only in patches, *bright green*.
Often with heavy low branches level or depressed for 2–3 m then upswept,
occasionally layering in a ring.

Foliage. Branchlet systems sparsely branched into long, often pendulous final branchlets, all clad in bright or yellowish-green, sub-shiny, hard, forward-curved leaves, rhombic in cross-section, to 1.5 cm long. Bases of leaves have tall keel running down the shoot. Chinese form, which all the oldest trees must be, has longer leaves, and more lax shoots than the Japanese, and a more open, pendulous crown.

Flowers and cone. Male flowers ovoid, 3 mm, clustered along terminal 1 cm of final branchlets, yellow-brown throughout winter, bright when shedding pollen in February; abundant and colour whole crown of some trees; borne from fifth year. Female flowers terminal on shorter stronger branchlets of same tree, frequent on trees five years old, abundant on older trees; green rosettes nodding like opening buds. Cone globular 2 cm on stalks now upturned, rough with five or six short curved spines on each scale. Ripen in one year, remain woody and dark brown for some months.

Cone

Growth. Rapid in cool damp areas, shoots more than 1 m, but less than half this in warm dry areas where height growth ceases at about 25 m. Mid-May to late September, but often ceases in early August.

'LOBBII' 1853 Japan via Java. Uncommon but locally frequent; in some gardens outnumbers the type (e.g. Westonbirt). Differs from type in open *unevenly bunched crown*, dense tufts of shorter foliage erect or partly so at branch-ends. The apex is a similar dense bunch. (36 m in height at Endsleigh, Devon; 5.3 m in girth at Boconnoc, Cornwall).

'ELEGANS' 1861 Japan. Frequent. Can be upright and conic with broadly rounded top, or broadly columnar, but often arched, bent, branchy, many columns, or sprawling. Bark *bright rufous* shredding in fine strips. Foliage permanently juvenile, bluish-green in summer, deep red or bronzy, purple-brown in winter; slender, soft leaves spreading, 2 cm, spirally set on bright green twisted shoots, and blue-green and shiny on both sides. 20 m. Slow-growing and inappropriately named.

'Lobbii'

'CRISTATA' 1901. Narrow tree, alleged dwarf, to 10 m high. Foliage partly in fasciated erect bunches. Rare.

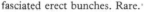

'Elegans'

'Cristata'

TASMANIAN CEDARS Athrotaxis

Three species from Tasmania, related to *Cryptomeria*.

Key to Athrotaxis species

1. Leaves completely pressed to shoot, thick, fleshy; branchlets
   sparse, in threes on main shoots   *cupressoides*, below
   Leaves with free, spreading tips, hard; branchlets irregularly
   set on main shoots   **2**

2. Leaves 1–2mm adpressed at base, free tip incurved   *laxifolia*, below
   Leaves 1cm spreading, showing white on inner side   *selaginoides*, p. 90

SMOOTH TASMANIAN CEDAR *Athrotaxis cupressoides* Don
W. Tasmania 1857. Rarest of the three; large gardens in S.W. England. 10m.
Bark. Pinkish-brown and grey-brown, slightly shredding.
Crown. Conic with broadly rounded top, very open.
Foliage. Rounded shoots clad in bright or pale green closely pressed scales;
sparsely branched; whorls of three branchlets only dividing again here and
there.
Cone. Pale green in summer, 1–1.5cm globose, tips of scales decurved; orange
in autumn.

Smooth Tasmanian Cedar

Summit Cedar

SUMMIT CEDAR *Athrotaxis laxifolia* Hook.
W. Tasmania 1857. Uncommon; least rare of the three, mostly in the south and
west. Rare in E. Scotland north to E. Ross-shire. 18m (19 × 2.3m at Scorrier
House, Cornwall).
Bark. Pale red-brown or coppery, deeply fissured and shaggy.
Crown. Broadly conic with rounded top, fairly open.

Foliage. *Young leaves and shoots pale yellow* turning deep green; hard, spreading then incurved tips, 1–2 mm, convex, ridged.

Cone. Conspicuous at ends of shoots, bright pale green turning successively whitish, yellow and bright orange, finally brown; ovoid 2 cm across; each scale broad ovate-acuminate, tip free, curved out as spine; bracts protrude between scales, yellowish; very freely borne.

KING WILLIAM PINE   *Athrotaxis selaginoides* Don

W. Tasmania 1857. Rare; in largest gardens of S. and S.W. England, in S.E. Ireland, where it reaches 17 m and N. Ireland.

Bark. Dull red-brown, peeling away in long vertical strips.

Crown. Conic, tufted especially at the top, branching rather upright.

Foliage. Shoot bright apple-green, very smooth; leaves less crowded than in above two species, free and spreading, rigid and sharp, forward slightly incurved points; rich shining green outside, two bright bluish-white broad bands on inner face, 1–1.2 cm.

Cone. In pairs on 2–3 cm peduncle, brilliant glossy green, ovoid 3 cm, each scale with pale decurved spine at tip. Ripens orange then brown.

Similar species. This is rather like some junipers, but shiny rich dark green outer surface to leaves which are thick and hard distinguish it from them all in the absence of cones.

King William Pine

CHINESE FIRS   Cunninghamia

Two very similar species from China and Formosa respectively; the latter very rare and scarcely distinct as yet in cultivation.

CHINESE FIR   *Cunninghamia lanceolata* (Lamb.) Hook. f.   **Pl. 5**
Syn. *C. sinensis* Rich.

S. and W. China 1804. Infrequent S. and W. England, rare elsewhere. 20 m (32 × 2.4 m at Bicton, Devon).

Bark. Chestnut-brown, regularly lined vertically with parallel narrow, shallow fissures; finely stringy.

Bole. Straight and without taper between branches.

Crown. Columnar or conic with domed top; gaunt as few branches, but hanging foliage of vigorous trees hides the wide gaps between branches. Rusty-brown inside crown from retained dead foliage; outside shining deep green. Low forking or several stems occasional.

Foliage. Shoot pale *shiny* green, clasped by leaf bases. Leaf broad-based tapering evenly to fine point, 3–7 × 0.4 cm spirally set but twisted to lie more or less in two somewhat rising ranks then curled downwards towards tip. Above: dark glossy green, edges and midrib raised, two narrow bright white lines often at base; beneath: two broad bands of silver or whitish-green. Flexible but not soft; some bend up to point backwards.

Flowers and cone. Male flowers small in a terminal bunch of 2–16, occasionally a few around base of female flower, early May. Female

Chinese Fir

flowers often numerous, terminal, yellow, orange and pale green acute scales; squat cylindric-ovoid, 12 × 8 mm. Cones terminal, glossy bright green until October, cylindric-ovoid; 2–3 × 2–3 cm; scales narrowing to rounded tip with small brown spine; margins white-fringed; stiff, hard, held vertically, tip convex; apex of cone a muddle of projecting folds.

Growth. Slow to establish and slow when old, even in Devon and Cornwall, but young trees can make shoots of 60 cm for some years and add 3 cm a year in girth. Hardier than reputed; has grown to 18 m in 35 years in a very frosty part of Kent and grows in S.E. Scotland.

'GLAUCA' Rare. Foliage has a silvery sheen from blue-grey bloom on deep green leaves.

Similar species. The very rare *C. konishii* Hayata (Formosa) has leaves only 2–4 cm and is less hardy. *Araucaria araucana* (p. 57) has slight resemblance from afar but bark and foliage completely different.

SCIADOPITYS

A single aberrant species in which the leaves are fused in pairs and spring from whorls with scale-like leaves at the base of and in between whorls.

JAPANESE UMBRELLA PINE *Sciadopitys verticillata* (Thun.) Sieb. and Zucc. **Pl. 6**

Japan 1853 (died); 1861. Infrequent; not in towns; uncommon in north and east. 15 m (23 m at Benenden, Kent).

Bark. Dark brown or grey, coarsely stripping away.

Crown. Tallest are narrowly conic with a slender spire-top, many are broadly conic or multi-stemmed tall bushes with many pointed tops; dense where thriving, otherwise open.

Foliage. Well-spaced *whorls* of deep shining green (yellowish where not thriving), parallel-sided, *deeply grooved* leaves to 12 × 0.4 cm; the whorls some 3.5 cm apart on buff-brown shoots with darker bud-like knobs which are the tips of long scales. The arrangement of leaves recalls umbrella ribs – hence the English name. Beneath: bright yellow-green, grooved; tip rounded, notched by the groove; each "leaf" consists of two fused together along this groove.

Flowers and cone. Male flowers small globules, yellow, in terminal bunches of a dozen. Females terminal, ovoid-cylindric, 15 mm, dark green dusted silver. Cones often densely borne by quite young trees, ovoid, 5–7 × 7 cm; scales fleshy and grooved, green then brown with rolled-down margin, fragile, loose.

Plate 7　　　　　　　　**SILVER FIRS**

Leathery, blunt leaves (except *A. bracteata*, p. 115).

The cones of Silver Firs, with the exception of the blue cones of both the Nikko Fir and the Delavay's Fir group, are confined to the shoots near the top of tall trees. They break up whilst still on the tree in autumn, so that they are not found on the ground and are seldom seen at close quarters.

1. Common Silver Fir　*Abies alba*　　　　　　　100

  (a) Young tree 8 m high showing regular whorls arising from the end of each year's growth.
  (b) Spray. Leaves shorter than *A. grandis*. Scattered hairs along the shoot.
  (c) Mature cone ready to disintegrate in November. Cones are borne only around the top of the tree. In summer they are green and brown. The scales may be more covered by the protruding and down-curved bracts than in this cone.

Now a rare tree in E. England, common in the west and in Scotland.

2. Noble Fir　*Abies procera*　　　　　　　114

Foliage of a form with fairly blue leaves but not as pale as 'Glauca'. The brown foliage-bud of a side-shoot for next year is visible.

A sturdy tree found in nearly every major garden and most common in Scotland.

3. Giant or Grand Fir　*Abies grandis*　　　　　　　104

Shoot showing the long and short leaves lying flat each side of the olive-green stem. Bruised leaves emit a strong scent of oranges.

4. White Fir　*Abies concolor* 'Violacea'　　　　　　　105

The long, thick leaves, the same colour each side, stand up from the shoot. This is the blue-foliaged form.

Noble Fir

Giant Fir

1a 1b 1c 2 3 4

1

2

3a

3b

3c

CEDARS   Plate 8

Leaves on older wood in whorls. Barrel-shaped cones taking 2–3 years to ripen after autumn flowering.

1. Deodar   *Cedrus deodara*   118

Long shoot with spirally set first-year leaves and short, spur-shoots developing. Young Deodars are often pale grey-blue, but older trees are dark green.

2. Blue Atlas Cedar   *Cedrus atlantica* 'Glauca'   117

Shoot and leaves. This bright blue-grey form is one of the commonest conifers in parks and large gardens.

3. Cedar of Lebanon   *Cedrus libani*   116

(a) Young tree 10 m high. The leading shoot nods at the tip, whereas that of the Deodar droops fully. Young trees like this are much less familiar than the huge, spreading trees into which they soon grow (see figure below).

(b) Ripe cone. The cones of these three cedars are very alike and spend two years a pale blue-green before they ripen. They stand erect from level branches. Male flowers look like un-ripe small cones 3–4 cm tall, bright grey green in summer, pinkish-brown towards autumn. They expand and shed pollen in October.

(c) Shoot and foliage. The colour can vary from deep green to grey-blue.

Many other conifers are called "cedar", e.g. Red Cedar (*Thuja plicata*), Port Orford Cedar (Lawson Cypress), Japanese Cedar (*Cryptomeria*) and Pencil Cedar (*Juniperus virginiana*), but the only true cedars are the four species of *Cedrus*.

Deodar   Blue Atlas Cedar   Cedar of Lebanon

Growth. Moderately slow; fastest young trees to 12 m in 40 years, older trees much slower.

Recognition. Whorls of big, grooved, long leaves unique.

DECIDUOUS CYPRESSES   Taxodium

Three closely allied deciduous species (one sub-evergreen) which shed branch-lets as well as leaves. Confined to E. and S. USA and Mexico.

SWAMP or BALD CYPRESS   *Taxodium distichum* (L.) Richards **Pl. 6**
Delaware to Texas and up the Mississippi to Missouri 1640. Frequent in S. England, prominent in London and some suburbs, infrequent north of Midlands and in Wales, uncommon in Ireland, rare in S. Scotland, a big tree near Perth, but absent in the north. Hardy but needs warm summers for proper growth. 35 × 5.4 m.

Bark. Pale reddish-brown, numerous small vertical or spiralled shallow fissures; stringy.

Crown. Conic, either broad or narrow, with *domed top*. Fresh green, pale in June, darker later; central stem persisting to the tip and fine dense branching show in winter. Boles of some trees much twisted.

Foliage. Among the last trees to leaf out; only a haze of green by June. Shoots reddish, very slender; new growth bluish-green; spirally set leaves on long shoots; side shoots shed in autumn, *alternate*, 10 cm long set with 80–100 thin soft slender leaves each 10 × 2 mm also *alternate* and in two flattened ranks; fresh, pale green becoming dark; two grey bands beneath. Fox-red or dark brown mid-October to mid-December.

Flowers and cone. Male flowers prominent on some trees throughout winter as catkins 5–6 cm long at the end of each shoot, in threes or fours; stout, central one longest, bearing flower buds 2 mm ovoid, yellow and green; catkins lengthen in March, become 8–10 cm long, slender, dull yellow in April. Cones can be, but often are not, on the same tree, globular with few scales, thickened edges and minute central spine; 3 × 2.5 cm bright green ripening purplish, on short stalk.

Growth. Rather slow, even young trees adding little more than 30 cm a year. Mid-June to early September. Thrives in normal soils if not too dry. Often grown by side of fresh water where some trees produce "knees" over a wide area like wooden ant-hills to about 40 cm high with domed tops, often depressed below thick rounded rim. They contain spongy tissue and help the aeration of roots permanently under water, and are properly known as "pneumatophores".

Similar species. *Metasequoia* (p. 95) has opposite shoots and leaves.

POND CYPRESS   *Taxodium ascendens* Brongn.
Virginia to Alabama 1789. Uncommon; confined to S. and W. England. Not hardy in the east. 23 m. *Gaunt*, open-crowned, few-branched. *Erect tufts and lines* of slender 10–15 cm shoots with small scale-like leaves, 6–8 mm, all round, strongly forward, minutely pointed. Bright green. These shoots rise vertically from each side of woody branches up to 3 cm diameter. A striking sight in June when fresh green erect shoots 4–5 cm, pale-tipped, stand up from every twig and small branch. Bark dark brown, coarsely ridged like a willow.

'Nutans'

'NUTANS' S.E. of USA. Probably 1789 with the type. Grown as 'Glypto-strobus' sometimes, or "*Taxodium distichum pendulum*". Most *T. ascendens* are of this form, which is not distinct in the wild. Differs only in that branch ends curve *sharply downwards*, the slender shoots rise above them, become horizontal, then hang down. 15 × 2.3 m, Knaphill, Surrey.

METASEQUOIA

A single surviving species somewhat resembling *Taxodium* and, like it, de-ciduous but with branches and leaves opposite.

DAWN REDWOOD or WATER FIR *Metasequoia glyptostroboides*
Hu et Cheng **Pl. 6**

E. Szechwan and N. E. Hupeh in S.W. China. Discovered 1941, described 1944, introduced 1948. Frequent in England where every large garden and park, and many small ones, soon acquired one; infrequent in N.E. England, Ireland, Wales and S. Scotland; few north of Perth. Hardy but needs warmth to grow properly. 21 m (1976); 18 × 1.9 m, Cambridge B.G.

Bark. Young branches and boles pale orange-brown with big flakes of dark brown coming away. Older stems and branches dark red-brown or orange-brown, stringy, in shallow ridges.

Crown. Fairly narrowly conic, open, branches ascending. Very sparse and with more level branches when grown under shade. The boles of most of the bigger trees taper rapidly for two metres and slowly and evenly above this, the basal 2 m deeply hollowed beneath branches. Slender trees often sinuous.

Foliage. Buds show green in early March; leaves fully out in early May. Shoots pinkish-green or pale purple, slightly winged. Leaves in two flattened ranks, thin, soft, flat, linear, 2–4 cm long 2 mm across. Fresh pale or greyish-green, often purple-tinted at first, later rich darker green above, *grey-green* beneath; oppositely set on 12 cm deciduous lateral shoots and on leading shoots. Turn pale pinkish-yellow in October then salmony to brick-red and, in good years, deep ruby-red in November. Buds *beneath* some branchlets not axillary (unique to this species and, occasionally *Sequoia sempervirens*) and often clustered.

Flowers and cone. Male flowers, not yet seen in the open in Britain (1972); small ovoids, 2–5 at base of each pair of leaves on the last 20 cm of main shoot and its side-shoots. These side-shoots are not shed until April, so together re-semble a flowering panicle. Cones occurred in the hot summers of 1955 and 1959 and a few have been noted since; green, globular, or cylindric 1.2–2.5 cm on a long 5 cm stalk; scales with grooved, swollen ends.

Growth. Initially very rapid, on good damp soil shoots of 1 m normal. Slows down by tenth year unless in light woodland or very sheltered, where this rate has been maintained so far. Early May to mid-September, up to 8 cm a week in July.

Similar species. *Taxodium distichum* (p. 94) has similar but alternate foliage; *Metasequoia* is larger leaved, softer green, more loosely crowned with an acute apex.

PINE FAMILY *Pinaceae*

A family of ten genera and about 200 species, with linear, flat, or needle-like leaves and woody cones with spirally arranged scales bearing two seeds each. This includes many of the familiar conifers like cedars, larches, pines and spruces. Arctic Circle to just south of Equator.

SILVER FIR   Abies

About 50 species of northern temperate regions as far south, in mountains only, as Mexico and Algeria. Regular symmetrical growth ensures a main axis of growth right to the tip. Differ from spruces and Douglas firs in erect cones breaking up while on the tree and foliage neither harsh nor soft but smooth, leathery and rarely acute. Leaves arise from sucker-like bases on shoot leaving circular scars when they fall.

Key to Abies species

Notes: A Side-shoots often show more pubescence than main shoots, and
this feature in the key applies to them.
B The colour of the shoot is brighter and more easily seen from beneath.

1. Shoots (side) uniformly and conspicuously pubescent   2
   Shoots glabrous or with pubescence scattered, or in grooves,
   or exceedingly fine   9

2. Leaves all round the shoot, crowded forwards, brilliant white
   beneath; pubescence orange-brown   *delavayi* var. *georgei*, p. 111
   Leaves pectinate, or distinctly parted beneath   3

3. Leaves pectinate, or widely parted above also   4
   Leaves not parted above shoot, lying forward on or standing
   above it   6

4. Pubescence white; leaves 1.5–2 cm, curved inwards, often
   upswept, yellow-green, strongly fragrant   *sibirica*, p. 103
   Pubescence brown; leaves 3 cm or more, not curved in, nor
   upswept nor fragrant   5

5. Pubescence pale coffee-brown, short, dense; leaves parallel,
   slender, not notched   *borisii-regis*, p. 101
   Pubescence dark brown, long, not dense; leaves variously
   forward, broad, notched   *delavayi* var. *fabri*, p. 111

6. Leaves with bright white bands beneath only, no stomata
   above   7
   Leaves with pale bands above and beneath   8

7. Leaves to 3 cm, 2nd year shoot grey-brown; foliage scented of
   tangerine; (bark smooth and blistered)   *amabilis*, p. 103
   Leaves to 2 cm, 2nd year shoot red-purple; foliage slightly
   ginger-scented; (bark dark grey, freckled pale)   *mariesii*, p. 104

8. Leaves densely covering shoot from above, flat, grooved *procera*, p. 114

Leaves spreading to show shoot from above; rounded, keeled *magnifica*, p. 115

9. Pubescence on shoots confined to grooves or lines **10**

Pubescence uniform and very fine or thinly scattered or absent **13**

10. Leaves 4 cm or more, broadly banded brilliant white beneath, lower ones arched; big bud 1 cm *spectabilis*, p. 109

Leaves 1–4 cm, thin white or broad green bands beneath; bud 5–8 mm **11**

11. Leaves perpendicular, broad, stiff, yellow-green *firma*, p. 107

Leaves all forward, more or less slender, grass- or very deep green **12**

12. Buds dark red, whorled; foliage a dense mass of forward grass-green leaves, sticky and fragrant when crushed; second year shoot dark grey *sachalinensis*, p. 103

Bud dark purple; leaves dark green, not notably fragrant; second year shoot pale pink-grey *delavayi* var. *faxoniana*, p. 111

13. Leaves not pectinate beneath shoot, a proportion spreading beneath **14**

Leaves pectinate beneath shoot, spreading each side or swept above **25**

14. Leaves radiating all round shoot, perpendicular to it, stiff **15**

Leaves beneath shoot lying forwards, flexible **18**

15. Leaves with stomata (grey or white) above and below **16**

Leaves with stomata beneath only **17**

16. Stomata grey above, bright white beneath; leaves 1–2 cm straight, broad, leathery *numidica*, p. 108

Stomata grey-green above and beneath; leaves 0.5–1 cm, some curved backwards, all thick, rigid *pinsapo*, p. 113

17. Leaves ± equally above and beneath shoots, well spaced, to 3 cm long *cephalonica*, p. 106

Leaves many more above than beneath shoot, crowded forwards *cephalonica* var. *appollinis*, p. 106

18. Leaves without stomata above **19**

Leaves with stomata above **21**

19. Leaves slender, densely parallel, grass-green; shoot pale brown, stomatal bands beneath narrow *sachalinensis*, p. 103

Leaves not slender, inner leaves erect or forwards, deep blue-green; shoot orange or brown, stomatal bands beneath broad **20**

20. Bud pale brown; side-shoots pubescent; (bark brown)
                                                   delavayi var. *fabri*, p. 111
     Bud dark red; shoots glabrous, roughened; (bark grey)
                                                   delavayi var. *forrestii*, p. 111

21. Stomata on upper surface dusted evenly all over; shoot orange-brown   **22**
     Stomata on upper surface in two bands or irregularly banded and obscure; shoot pink or brown   **23**

22. Shoot rough, glabrous   *delavayi* var. *forrestii*, p. 111
     Shoot smooth, glabrous (or densely pubescent) *delavayi* var. *georgei*, p. 111

23. Leaves shiny pale green both sides, stomata above (under lens) banded irregularly; shoot shiny pale pink
                                           pindrow var. *brevifolia*, p. 109
     Leaves grey- or dark-green, stomata clearly visible on upper side   **24**

24. Leaves beneath brilliantly white-banded, 1–2 cm long   *koreana*, p. 112
     Leaves with dull grey bands each side, 2–4 cm long   *lasiocarpa*, p. 114

25. Leaves pectinate above also, $\pm$ flat each side of shoot   **26**
     Leaves above shoot narrowly parted or all across shoot   **30**

26. Inner (upper) leaves strongly forwards; shoot purple and brown, ribbed   *fargesii*, p. 111
     Inner leaves parallel with outer; shoot fawn, olive or pink   **27**

27. Shoot shiny, glabrous, pink; bud large pale brown   *chensiensis*, p. 110
     Shoot olive, green or fawn-grey, pubescent; bud small, dark   **28**

28. Shoot dull grey or fawn, pubescence scattered, dark; leaves 2–3 cm   *alba*, p. 100
     Shoot olive or green, very finely pale pubescent; leaves 3–5 cm   **29**

29. Shoot olive, second year grey-brown; leaves 3–4 cm; (bark grey, cracked)   *grandis*, p. 104
     Shoot green, second year copper-brown; leaves 4–5 cm; (bark blackish, fissured)   *concolor* var. *lowiana*, p. 105

30. Leaves above shoot distinctly parted by narrow or wide 'V'   **31**
     Leaves above shoot not parted, lying along or standing above shoot   **41**

31. Bud slender, fusiform, pale brown, pointed, 1.5–2 cm; leaves long, 4–5 cm, stiff, sharply spined   *bracteata*, p. 115
     Bud ovoid or globose, blunt, red or purple, 1 cm long   **32**

32. Leaves with broad, bright white bands beneath   **33**
     Leaves with narrow white or greenish-grey bands beneath   **35**

33. Shoot white or buff, deeply grooved; leaves parallel, all slightly forward   *homolepis*, p. 110
     Shoot dark brown, orange or purple, ribbed or smooth   **34**

34. Shoots shiny purple, mahogany and brown; leaves slender
   glossy   *sutchuenensis*, p. 112
   Shoots orange-brown; leaves not slender, matt *delavayi* var. *forrestii*, p. 111

35. Shoot pale yellowish or pinkish   **36**
   Shoot green or purple   **40**

36. Shoot pale yellow-brown, or buff, finely pubescent   **37**
   Shoot pink or grey-pink, shiny, glabrous   **39**

37. Leaves broadening from narrow stalk, hard, rigid   *firma*, p. 107
   Leaves parallel-sided from base, leathery   **38**

38. Bud deep, bright purple; shoot grooved or ribbed; leaves not
   arched, parallel forward   *delavayi* var. *faxoniana*, p. 111
   Bud red-brown, shoot smooth; leaves arched, upper ones
   forward or rising   *cilicica*, p. 102

39. Shoot shiny pink, or reddish beneath, ribbed and cracking;
   leaves to 2 cm, inner ones vertical, some recurved   *recurvata*, p. 107
   Shoot ashen-pink, very stout, smooth; leaves 5–7 cm arched
   forwards and sideways   *pindrow*, p. 109

40. Shoot green; leaves 3–5 cm, two blue-grey bands on upper
   surface   *concolor* var. *lowiana* (southern form), p. 105
   Shoot purple, mahogany and brown; leaves to 2.5 cm, deep
   shiny green without stomata above   *sutchuenensis*, p. 112

41. Leaves along mid-line of shoot erect; side leaves upswept   **42**
   Leaves along mid-line lying flat along shoot; side leaves
   spread flat   **46**

42. Leaves to 2.5 cm only; shoot purple-brown; (bark orange-
   brown, flaking)   *squamata*, p. 112
   Leaves more than 3 cm, usually 4–5 cm   **43**

43. Leaves blue-grey above, thick, rounded; shoot yellow-green
                                                 concolor, p. 105
   Leaves green above, thin, flat; shoot pink or brownish   **44**

44. Leaves bright green with no stomata above; shoot shiny
   pink-buff   *holophylla*, p. 108
   Leaves green or dark with some stomata above   **45**

45. Shoot red-brown, shiny, glabrous; leaves 3–4.5 cm, stomata
   above at tip and in two bands on some leaves   *bornmuellerana*, p. 102
   Shoot yellow-brown; leaves 2–3 cm, pale tips and sometimes
   central band of stomata above   *cilicica*, p. 102

46. Leaves banded pale blue-grey above; shoot yellow-grey
                                   lasiocarpa var. *arizonica*, p. 114
   Leaves dark green or dark greyish-green above, without
   bands   **47**

47. Leaves sparse, 5–7 cm long, hard, arched, greenish bands
      beneath   *pindrow*, p. 109
    Leaves dense, to 3.5 cm, leathery, straight, white bands be-
    neath   **48**

48. Bud pale brown; not resinous; shoot olive-brown   *nordmanniana*, p. 101
    Bud purple or red, very resinous; shoot fawn or grey   **49**

49. Leaves brilliantly white beneath, deep green above, slightly
      shiny   *veitchii*, p. 102
    Leaves dull grey-white beneath, dull grey-green above   *nephrolepis*, p. 102

COMMON SILVER FIR *Abies alba* Mill.   **Pl. 7**

Syn. *A. pectinata* D.C.
Europe; France, Corsica, the Alps, Tatra, south to Balkan Mountains 1603.
No longer the commonest silver fir planted, Grand, Noble and Caucasian Firs
being much more frequent in large gardens, but old trees still very common in
parts of the west and north, particularly in Devon, Cornwall, Lake District,
Perthshire, Argyll and Co. Kerry; infrequent to rare in E. and S.E. England.
48 × 6 m (has been 55 m).

Bark. Dull dark grey, smooth with resin blisters on young trees, shallowly
square-plated at moderate age; deeply and narrowly cracked into small square
plates in old trees.

Crown. Regularly whorled, symmetrical, narrowly conic until some 35 m tall;
old trees in woods have long, clean, often slightly sinuous boles; in the open,
huge low branches extend level for many metres, then curve sharply upwards
to vertical. Rather open; old trees thin at top. Typically
seen as bent, often largely dead, herring-bone-branched,
forked top standing above beech or oak canopies.

Common
Silver Fir

Foliage. Shoot dull grey-buff with scattered dark small
hairs. Leading shoot of vigorous young plant, shiny,
pale grey, rather creased surface, no hairs; very short
leaves very widely separated; top whorl of side-shoots
curving upwards and similar. Bud ovoid, red-brown,
rather resinous. Leaves of varying length to 2 cm in
lowest row, parted and spreading each side of shoot in
several layers; dark green above, two narrow white
bands beneath.

Flowers and cone. Male flowers globular, densely set along underside of
shoots of older trees almost to ground level. Female short-ovoid, yellow-green.
Cones packed on top few branches of old trees, 15 cm tall, acute conic tip, erect,
pale green turning brown.

Growth. Slow for few years; annual shoot about 45 cm when 1.5 m high, may be
70–80 cm later; late May to July. Side-shoots flush early May, rarely frosted.

Growth. Very slow for several years then rapid for a long period, annual shoots
of 80 cm common; early May to July. Side-shoots flush in April and are often
frosted. Life span to 300 years in Scotland, seldom 200 in England.

Similar species. *A. nordmanniana* (below). *A. borisii-regis* (p. 101) much more
like *A. alba*, but has dense pale brown-pink pubescence on shoots and more
slender leaves.

CAUCASIAN FIR   *Abies nordmanniana* (Stev.) Spach
W. Caucasus; N.E. Turkey 1848. Frequent but mostly in large gardens especially in north and west. 40 × 4.5 m. (28 × 4.6 m, Powerscourt, Co. Wicklow.)
Bark. Dull grey, smooth; areas of fine fissuring into thick square plates on old trees.

Crown. Conic for many years then variably narrow-columnar with pointed top. At senility does not fan out or broaden but dies back from pointed or flat narrow top. In health rather dense. In young plants shoots at base of leader straight, ascend only slightly, not curved up as in *A. alba.*

Foliage. Shoot grey-green or olive-brown; scattered dark hairs, sometimes very few. Second year pink-brown. Foliage varies from impoverished to exceedingly luxuriant and dense; leaves from yellowish-green 2 cm to deep bright green 4 cm, always grooved, parallel-sided, abruptly ended and notched, two bright white bands beneath; margins often slightly rolled under; all leaves pointing forwards, those on top covering shoot; firm, leathery and shiny. Fruity aroma when crushed.

Caucasian Fir

Flowers and cone. Male flowers small, globular, clustered thickly along underside of previous year's shoots over most of crown. Females cylindric, 8 cm, bright pale green. Cones clustered erect on upper side of a few branches near top of old trees, cylindric 10–15 × 3.5 cm tapering to domed top, green until September when start to turn orange-brown; scales rather large; bracts exserted 6–7 mm and strongly deflexed.

Growth. Very slow for several years then rapid for a long period, annual shoots

KING BORIS'S FIR   *Abies borisii-regis* Mattf.
Balkan Mountains 1883. Rare; unrecognised in some large gardens. 30 × 3 m. A vigorous rough tree, many-topped when large, strongly branched, with rough dull dark grey bark. Foliage most like *A. alba*, but shoot *pale coffee-brown* from fine *dense hairs*; leaves 3–4 ranks each side of shoot, closely set, 3 cm, slightly forward-pointing, slender, straight, rich shiny green and grooved above, narrow bright white bands beneath. Cone 12 × 4 cm, ovoid-cylindric, bracts spread straight out, pale purplish-green; crowded near top of tree.

King Boris's Fir   Bornmüller's Fir   Cilician Fir

BORNMÜLLER'S FIR   *Abies bornmuellerana* Mattf.
Asia Minor. A rare species related to *A. nordmanniana* and *A. cilicica* (below).
Distinguished by smooth purplish-black bark, stout shiny *glabrous red-brown
shoots* and long dense leaves 3–4.5 cm standing *nearly erect* above, parted below,
the shoot, with *white stomata at tip* and often in lines on upper side. 25 × 2.5 m.

CILICIAN FIR   *Abies cilicica* (Ant. and Kotschy) Carr.
E. Asia Minor, Syria 1855. Rare. 25 m. Resembles *A. nordmanniana*, but variable; usually pale *golden brown* shoot, side-shoots at least short pubescent, more
slender leaves usually *more pointed*, much more sparse on shoot and rising curved
forward at 45° from it, *pale-tipped*, even a patch of stomata. Often easiest to tell
by dark *grey smooth bark* with big systems of *black rings* centred on prominent
scars from fallen branches.

VEITCH'S SILVER FIR   *Abies veitchii* Lindl.
C. Japan 1879. Infrequent but quite widely planted even in some small gardens.
25 m.

Bark. Grey or grey-brown, smooth but lined horizontally; patches nearly white on some old trees. Bole
always *deeply fluted* with large *hollows under branches* or
branch-scars.
Crown. Narrowly conic, finally columnar; branches of
lower crown often swept up so foliage on them shows
silvered undersides – like rime at a distance. Upper
crown open, branches level or slightly depressed; bigger
trees often flat-topped
Foliage. Shoot pale buff or grey, slightly ribbed, variably pubescent. Bud reddish-purple. *Leaves all pointing
forwards*, at sides 45°, fully forward on top, lowest rank
curving below level of shoot; dense, dark ± shiny
green and grooved above, two broad *bright silver bands
beneath*; broadening gradually to abrupt notched tip;
to 2.5 cm. Resinous aroma when crushed.

Veitch's Fir

Flowers and cone. Males 2–3 cm, cylindric, red, erect or along underside
of shoot; females erect, 2–3 cm, bright red, become 6–8 × 2.5 cm, blue-purple
cones, smoothly wrinkled, blunt, cylindrical with slender bract-tips exserted
2–3 mm, brown when ripe; borne on quite young trees, densely on old trees.
Growth. First five years growth most rapid of all *Abies*, third year shoot to
15 cm, fourth year to 60 cm. Last *Abies* to shoot – in mid-June, growing until
August. Short-lived; biggest and oldest trees dead at 80–85 years.
Similar species. *A. nordmanniana* (p. 101) has brown buds. *A. amabilis*
(p. 103) has white buds, different fragrance, flatter and wider sprays. *A. nephrolepis* (below).

EAST SIBERIAN FIR   *Abies nephrolepis* Maxim.
E. Siberia, N. China 1908. Rare; similar to *A. veitchii*,
differing in: *pink-grey* dull *warty* bark; denser neatly
conic crown, level branches; leaves closer, shorter
(1–2.5 cm), *dull* grey-green above, dull white beneath
in thin bands, narrower (1.5 mm); buds expanding in

East Siberian Fir

April. Crushed foliage is sticky and has paint-like scent. Shoots "square-ended" (not tapered by shorter terminal leaves). Bole only slightly fluted, if at all. 15 (24)m. Male flowers 8mm yellow-green; females 2.5cm, conic, bright green tipped pink.

SAKHALIN FIR   *Abies sachalinensis* Mast.

N. Japan, Sakhalin and Kurile Islands 1879. Rare. 23m.

Bark. Blackish or purple-brown smooth, horizontally lined with lenticels or *red-brown blisters.*

Crown. Narrowly conic; dense slightly upswept branches; epicormics frequent.

Foliage. Shoot grey-brown *shallowly ribbed*; fine pubescence of same colour in the grooves. Second year dark purplish-grey. Bud dark *purplish red-brown* clustered at tip of shoot; purplish-white resin. Leaves densely clothing shoots for five years or more, all forward-pointing, pectinate beneath, rising somewhat above, straight, parallel-sided to blunt double-tip, bright green becoming deep green, minute pale patch at tip above, two narrow white bands beneath; very slender, 3–3.5 × 0.1 cm. Leaf buds open very early. Crushed leaves are sticky and scented like cedarwood oil.

Cone. 6 × 4cm, pink-purple, numerous scales spreading level.   Sakhalin Fir

SIBERIAN FIR   *Abies sibirica* Ledeb.

N. Russia; Turkmen; Siberia 1820. Very rare, scarcely in cultivation in Britain; many so labelled are *A. sachalinensis* (above). Differs from *A. sachalinensis* in pale *yellow-brown buds in cluster* joined by *pearly resin*; shoot pale fawn or *honey-colour, smooth; short, dense, white* pubescence; leaves more densely covering shoot, often much curved inwards, some laterals curved outwards, 1.5–2cm; paler yellowish-green, stomatal lines on outer half above. From beneath the foliage is a distinctive whitish yellow-green. Scent similar but stronger. (Described from Finnish foliage.) (Scone Palace 14m.)

BEAUTIFUL or RED FIR   *Abies amabilis* Dougl. ex Forb.

British Columbia to Oregon 1830. Infrequent; in large gardens and collections mainly in north and west. 32 × 4m.

Bark. Purplish-grey, smooth horizontal blisters of resin until old when dull grey, corky, still blistered in parts.

Crown. Narrowly conic, sometimes broad; shapely, dense; lower branches sweeping down and curving up.

Foliage. Shoot pale greenish-brown or grey with variably dense whitish pubescence often absent on young trees; second year grey-brown. Bud globular soon white with resin. Leaves to 3 × 0.2cm on vigorous trees, side ones spreading lax and curved, middle ones straight *radiating forwards fanned out close* to shoot; new leaves often glaucous grey, second year rich dark glossy green and grooved above, two broad silver bands beneath. Parallel-sided to abrupt tip, usually notched. *Aroma of tangerines* when crushed.

Beautiful Fir

Flowers and cone. Male flowers abundant, fairly large globules on underside of shoot; female seldom seen, near top of tree, red; cone long-ovoid, very smooth, purplish ripening brown, 10–15 cm.

Growth. Extremely variable, partly from origin of seed. After very slow start for several years some trees in west and north-west grow leading shoots of nearly 1 m with *appressed side-shoots* near the middle and rapidly produce very stout boles and tall, luxuriant trees; in the south-east many remain slow and of poor growth. Leading shoot grows from early May to early July.

Similar species. *A. mariesii* (below) often confused; *A. nordmanniana* (p. 101) and *A. veitchii* (p. 102) differ in buds and narrower sprays, harder leaves, less pressed down on shoot; bark, and scent of foliage.

MARIES'S FIR   *Abies mariesii* Mast.

C. Japan 1879. Rare; some trees grown as this sp. are *A. amabilis*. 22 m (Dawyck).

Bark. Silvery, smooth, *freckled* with dark grey lenticels and marked by black circles round *big branch-scars*.

Crown. Narrowly conic, rather open, small branches sweeping gently down and then outwards.

Foliage. Shoot underside *brown-pink or pale orange*, with *dense, fine* orange or buff pubescence; second year red-brown or dark orange. Bud globular, very resinous, soon white. Leaves to 2 cm, deep glossy green or, at first, glaucous-grey, grooved above, two broad silver bands beneath; 0.2 cm broad, abruptly ended and notched, forward over shoot but not pressed down close to it nor radiating widely; aroma when crushed warm and gingery. *Expanding bud crimson.*

Maries's Fir

Flowers and cone. Male flowers expand to 4–6 cm long, pale yellow catkin with dark grey scales by mid-May. Cone 10 × 5 cm, long-ovoid, smooth, dark blue-purple.

Similar species. *A. amabilis* (p. 103) has longer, relatively narrower, more fanned out leaves and differs in other features emphasised.

GIANT or GRAND FIR   *Abies grandis* Lindl.   Pl. 7

N. Vancouver I. and interior southern B.C. south to Navarro River, California. Native trees once known to 100 m. 1832. Frequent, locally common; on increasing scale as plantation tree; present in many big gardens but not near cities. 50 × 6 m. (56 × 5.4 m, Strone, Argyll; 51 × 5 m, Bodnant.)

Bark. Young trees brownish-grey with resin-blisters; dull grey or purple-grey when old, cracked into small square plates in places.

Crown. Regularly narrow-conic with very whorled level branches until some 30 m then broad-columnar. Open grown trees may have a few very heavy branches low, turning sharply upwards; closer grown long slender branches hang far down. With age, top fans out – not flat. Tall trees whose tops have broken out may break into six or so trunks at 30 m above ground rising vertically close together and growing fast.

Foliage. Bud small, 2 mm usually hidden among leaves, cylindric-ovoid, rich deep purple, later white with resin. Shoot *olive-green*, very finely pubescent at first, second year dull greyish red-brown. Leaves very *flat-pectinate*, 2–5 cm, shorter

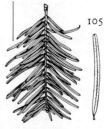

ones above but lie nearly flat in roughly three sizes together; upper surface grooved, shiny, bright mid- or
slightly yellow-green or dark; margins sometimes rolled
under; two bright narrow silver bands beneath; highly
aromatic with *fruity orange-flavour*.

Flowers and cone. Males small for *Abies* on inner
lengths of the underside of side-shoots in upper crown
of old trees, purplish, resinous, ovoid, 2mm, seen only
when squirrels or high winds break and drop shoots.

Giant Fir

Cone small, cylindric 7–9 × 4 cm, tapered, smoothly wrinkled, seen when light
green, near apex of some old trees, ripen red-brown.

Growth. One of the very fastest conifers for height and timber volume; slow
for first five years, soon shoots of 1 m common and 1.5 m occur; mid-May to
early July. To 40 m in 50 years.

Similar species. *A. concolor* var. *lowiana* (below) is an intergrade between
A. grandis and *A. concolor*. In the Cascade Mountains of C. Oregon and the
Siskiyou Mountains, *A.c.* var. *lowiana* and *A. grandis* occur together. Trees in
Britain with foliage like *A. grandis*, often larger, but with blackish, rough bark,
and copper-brown second-year shoots, are *A. concolor* var. *lowiana* and probably
from those regions.

COLORADO WHITE FIR   *Abies concolor* (Gord.) Hildebrand
S. California, Utah and Colorado to Mexico 1873. Less
frequent than the variety and one cultivar; thrives only
in a few areas in north and west notably Northumberland and Argyll, rare elsewhere. 46 × 4 m (Cragside).

Bark. Dark grey, *smooth*; many resin-blisters.

Crown. Conic, rather open, older trees obtusely pointed
at the top.

Foliage. Shoot *stout yellow-green*, second year grey-
brown; bud very resinous, globular; leaves dull *uniform
blue-grey* both sides, except for green midrib beneath,
thick, leathery, to 5.5 × 0.2 cm, all upswept, standing
well-spaced and nearly *vertical*. Crushed foliage or
broken shoots give a strong lemon-balm aroma.

Cone. Smooth, apple-green in summer, 12–15 × 4 cm,
domed, cylindric; near apex of tree only.

Colorado White Fir

'VIOLACEA' 1875. Infrequent; parks and gardens; to 18 m, narrow-conic
crown, leaves as *A. concolor* held vertically but a little smaller and a bright blue-
grey. **Pl. 7.**

var. *lowiana* (Gord.) Lemm. Low's Fir. Mid-Oregon south to Siskiyou Mts.
and Sierra Nevada, California 1851. Uncommon, but not confined to largest
gardens. 45 × 5 m (46.5 × 4.8 m at Durris, Kincardine). Intergrade from
A. grandis in N. to *A. concolor* in S. Very distinct in cultivation and most specimens can be sorted into one of two distinct forms: the first with foliage
nearly as *A. grandis*, the second approaching *A. concolor*. These are called
"northern" and "southern" here, but in Oregon they are in fact less evident than
they should be and a few "southern" types occur. In general two features alter

in foliage: leaves lie flat in north, curve increasingly
upwards to south; leaves have no stomata on top
and are green in north; increasing stomata and grey-
blue colour with distance south.

A: *Northern*. Bark black, rough, fissured. Crown
narrow, tall, columnar, forked about half height in
old trees (at about 20m). Foliage: leaves green above,
5–6cm, held nearly flat; shoot pale brown, rather
slender, copper-brown in second year.

Low's Fir

B: *Southern*. Bark dark brown, corky; deep buff-orange fissures from early age
like Douglas Fir, or grey, corky, with few fissures. Crown conic, usually narrow,
oldest trees with many leading shoots from near top making a dome. Foliage:
leaves grey-green to bluish, parted each side of shoot but inner rows curving
up at 45°; 4.5–5.0 cm; shoot bright green; second year dull orange-brown. (In
California the bark is blackish, with big curved grey ridges, the same as in
Oregon.) Cone flat-domed, barrel-shaped, 12 × 7 cm; smooth, green turning
bronzed then brown.

Growth. Rapid after third year; northern form nearly as *A. grandis*, southern
form slower in height but more rapid in girth.

GRECIAN FIR　　*Abies cephalonica* Loud.

Mountains of Greece 1824. Infrequent, but in East Anglia
often the only big *Abies*; in some big gardens everywhere.
36 × 5 m. (39 × 3.3 m, Bodnant.)

Bark. Smooth, dark brown tinged orange, becoming grey
with black fissures forming squarish plates lifting away.

Crown. Broadly conic or ovoid at first. Old trees open
grown have numerous heavy, low and spreading branches,
wide and flat-topped, some branches often broken; in
woods long stout bole may be sinuous and may fork high
but some straight single stems. Rather rough tree.

Grecian Fir

Foliage. Shoot pale, shiny brown; second year orange or
bright brown. Bud large in young vigorous trees, small in
old; red-brown, thinly resinous. Leaves to 3 cm, *radiate all round shoot*, somewhat more on top; arise from large sucker-like bases and narrow stalks and
broaden to 0.2 cm; *stiff*, leathery, usually *spined* at tip, dark shiny green above
and grooved, two bright but narrow white bands beneath.

Flowers and cone. Male flowers densely clustered beneath shoots over much of crown, globular; cone 15 ×
5 cm, brownish, resinous, cylindric with conic apex,
ripens brownish green; bracts deflexed; numerous on
wide, level upper branches.

Growth. Among the first *Abies* in leaf and frequently
frosted badly so early growth often slow but, once
growing well, it is very sturdy and makes rapid increase
in girth until old; slower in height with shoot seldom
more than about 45 cm.

var. *apollinis* (Link) Beiss. Rare, but some big trees.
Leaves much more densely borne and nearly all above

var. *apollinis*

shoot and lying forwards at varying angles to almost flat; often round-tipped.
31 × 4m.

Similar species. Other *Abies* with radiating leaves include *A. pinsapo* (p. 113):
shorter, rigid leaves, with stomatal lines on both sides; *A. numidica* (p. 108) and
A. × vilmorinii (p. 113): shorter leaves without bright white bands beneath.

MOMI FIR   *Abies firma* Sieb. and Zucc.

S. Japan 1861. Uncommon; large gardens, collections, rare elsewhere. 25 (33) ×
3m.

Bark. Grey-pink, smooth, horizontal resin-blisters, becoming flaky; old trees
pale grey, thick, corky and roughened; orange-pink areas.

Crown. Conic, rather broad; level branches, rounded top. Young trees with
branches rising straight and stiffly at 45°.

Foliage. Shoot pale grey-brown or honey-coloured,
grooves often cracked and finely pubescent, shining pinkish-
brown or orange in second year. Bud stout, ovoid, blunt,
shiny, red and green. Leaves vary in shape and size but
markedly *thick, leathery* and stiff and so *narrowed at base*
yet broad above that against the light a broad band of daylight runs along each side of the shoot. Yellowish-green,
pale or dark above; usually *pale green beneath* but sometimes grey or whitish bands. 2–3 cm. Vigorous young shoots
very stout with leaves to 4 cm × 0.3 cm tapering to two
short spines; several dense rows parted each side of shoot

Momi Fir

by a "V". Spined leaves can be on one part of a branch and shorter round-
ended leaves which are the usual adult foliage on another.

Flowers and cone. Female flower near top of tree, cylindric-ovoid, 2.5 × 1.5
cm, long scales bright green, faintly margined yellow-pink. Cone 8 × 3.5 cm,
cylindric-conic, deep yellow-green; scales with wide, low-curved margins,
finely toothed; bracts exserted 3–4 mm, bright yellow-green.

Growth. Shoots can be very stout and vigorous after 4–5 years; fast from about
15 to 40 years, slow when old.

Similar species. *A. recurvata* (below) has similar stout leaves green beneath,
but shorter, more erect; *A. homolepis* (p. 110) has leaves brightly silvered beneath.

MIN FIR   *Abies recurvata* Mast.

W. Szechwan, China 1910. Infrequent; collections and a few gardens. 20 m.

Bark. Pink-brown or orange-brown, *fine flakes* with grey centres; small papery
vertical rolls.

Crown. Narrowly conic or columnar, open; *small level branches*. Bole frequently
bears epicormic shoots.

Foliage. Bud ovoid, knobbly. Shoot
shining pinkish-grey or orange, glabrous,
pink-buff in second year, cracking open.
Leaves like smaller *A. firma* being similarly
pale *green beneath* but some standing above
shoot and some of these *curve backwards*
especially on second-year shoots; sharply
pointed on young trees, rounded on older;
thick, hard, dark yellow-green, 2–2.2 cm.

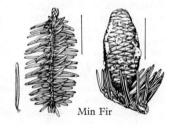

Min Fir

Cone. Ovoid tapered narrowly to base, domed top, 6 × 3 cm, dark purple-blue; bract-tips exserted 2 mm, but closely appressed.

Similar species. Some sprays and crown very like *A. firma* (p. 107) but shiny glabrous first-year shoot, shorter leaf and browner, more flaky bark and narrower crown distinguish.

ALGERIAN FIR   *Abies numidica* De Lannoy ex Carr.

Mt. Babor, Algeria 1862. Infrequent; in many large gardens, rare elsewhere. Best *Abies* in towns and dry areas. 27 m.

Bark. Salmon-pink-grey, smooth, curly cracks at base; later orange-pink or purplish-grey patterned by close shallow fissures making small rounded plates.

Crown. Rather broad-conic, sturdy; older trees broad-columnar with pointed or flat top and *dense layers* of branches slightly *curved downwards*. At distance, dense grey-black foliage with pinkish-orange stem showing between.

Foliage. Shoot shiny green-brown; pale orange-brown in second year. Bud small, conic, pale red-brown, chocolate or coppery, knobbly; long-pointed basal scales. Leaves very *densely set* and small, 1–2 cm, all over upper side of shoot, slightly parted beneath except on strong shoots and second-year shoots; mid leaves shortest and vertical, almost *as broad as long, thick*; all leathery, stiff, bluntly *rounded*, dark bluish-green with pale grey bands above, or grey or white triangular patch near tip; two white bands beneath.

Algerian Fir

Cone. 13 × 5 cm, slightly ovoid cylinder abruptly narrowed to a conic beak; smooth, whitish-green tinged lilac.

Growth. Very rapid in girth from 15 to 50 years; moderate in height.

Similar species. *A. pinsapo* (p. 113) leaves are thicker and lack white bands beneath. No other has such short, dense leaves with upper surface marked strongly with grey and white (but see *A. squamata* p. 112).

MANCHURIAN FIR   *Abies holophylla* Maxim.

Manchuria; Korea 1908. Rare; collections; a few big gardens in the west. 17 m.

Bark. Grey-pink to purple, pink or orange-buff; smooth, finely flaky.

Crown. Conic, fairly open, lower branches sweeping down.

Foliage. Shoot stout, slightly ridged, shiny *smooth corky-pink*. Bud globular, 7 × 5 mm, resinous bright red-brown or pale brown. Leaves to 3.7 × 0.1 cm, very slender, parallel-sided to short point or blunt; all swept slightly forward then straight up *vertically* above shoot; rarely spread somewhat each side; bright glossy green above, two grey-green, rarely white, narrow bands beneath.

Manchurian Fir

Cone. 12 × 3.5 cm, cylindric, smooth, pale green.

Similar species. *A. pindrow* var. *brevifolia* (p. 109) differs in having consistently round-ended leaves spreading all round the shoot and purplish broader cone.

PINDROW FIR   *Abies pindrow* (Royle) Spach
Afghanistan to Nepal 1837. Rare in England and
Ireland, infrequent in Scotland. Older trees fail and
die back in south-east; thrive only in north-west and
extreme north. 25 × 2.5 m (35.5 × 4.1 m at Castle
Leod, Ross-shire).
Bark. Dull grey, crinkled but scarcely fissured, with
black between flat ridges.
Crown. Narrow-conic to columnar, some old trees
fork several times.
Foliage. Shoot *very stout*, pale ashy pink, smooth,
glabrous. Bud large, 5–7 mm, globular, resinous,
dark red and white, apex pale green. Leaves partly
spread over upper side of shoot, forward and up-
ward-pointing, mainly in strongly *arched ranks*

Pindrow Fir

at each side; 5–7 cm, often ending in two short pale spines; dark shining green
above, two greenish-grey bands beneath.
Cone. 12 × 6 cm, ovoid-cylindric, smooth; scales slate-blue, margins steeply
rounded, edged grey.

   var. *brevifolia* Dallim. and Jacks. Has shorter (2–4 cm) blunt light green leaves
all round the shoot, shiny both sides, whitish-green bands beneath. Cone as
type but dark purple edged brown. Rare. 13 m.

HIMALAYAN FIR   *Abies spectabilis* (D. Don) Spach
Afghanistan to Bhutan at higher elevation than *A.
pindrow* and spreading farther east but intergrading
with it. 1822. Infrequent; mainly confined to western
and northern gardens. 30 m. (28 × 4 m, Gosford
Castle, N. Ireland.)
Bark. Dull pinkish-grey, rough and craggy with
irregular brown fissures, flaking and shredding; more
orange-pink in smaller trees.
Crown. Irregular, broadly columnar, soon flat-
topped, *few heavy level branches*, many new top-
shoots and level epicormic sprouts on bole.
Foliage. Shoot very stout, deeply ribbed, red-
brown or grey-brown, brown hairs in furrows. Bud
blunt, knobbly, ovoid 1 cm, yellow-brown, white
with resin. Leaves widely parted above shoot,
arching downwards, parallel, very densely set, long,

Himalayan Fir

to 6 cm, dark green and grooved above, ending in
blunt yellow tip, two broad brilliant white bands beneath.
Cone. 12–18 × 7 cm, smooth, pale grey-blue, domed,
cylindric, may stay on tree, dull dark purple, until spring.

   var. *brevifolia* (Henry) Rehd. Western form, differing in
narrow shapely crown, smooth bark, less stout shoot, leaves
crowded, parted by only a narrow "V" above, almost all
round shoot beneath, only 3–4 cm long, deep blue-green,
narrow pale stripe on upper surface, two greenish-white
stripes beneath. Rare; a few western and Scottish gardens.
20 × 3 m (34 × 2.9 m at Taymouth Castle, Perths.).

var. *brevifolia*

Similar species. *A. pindrow* (p. 109) is very closely related but in cultivation it is quite different. Huge sprays brilliantly silver beneath resemble some in *A. delavayi* (p. 110) group, but leaves much longer than all except *A. fargesii* (p. 111) which are not brightly silvered beneath.

NIKKO FIR   *Abies homolepis* Sieb. and Zucc.
C. Japan 1861. Infrequent; in some big gardens and a few small. Better near towns than other *Abies* except *A. numidica*. 32 × 3 m.

Bark. Distinctive pink shade in pale grey and shredding finely; older trees purplish grey-brown cracked into fine flakes.

Crown. Sturdy rather broadly conic with spiky appearance until big when less regular, broadly columnar,
level-branched, domed. Epicormic shoots commonly on
the bole.

Foliage. Shoot shining *white* to pale buff, glabrous
deeply *grooved* into plates, second year pink-brown. Bud
blunt, white with resin. Leaves usually well parted above
shoot and spreading *perpendicular* to it, somewhat stiff,
shining green above or at first glaucous-grey, grooved,
narrowed at base, bluntly tipped and notched; two
bright white bands beneath.

Nikko Fir

Flowers. Males open to striking, bright yellow-green,
red-tinged, cylindric ovoids; 2.5 cm. Females cylindric, 2 cm, bright deep red, soon lengthening to 3.5 cm and turning plum-purple.

Cone. Barrel-shaped, 8 × 4 cm, purple-blue, smooth, with red tips to scales, ripening brown, borne freely even on low branches; often encrusted with white resin.

Similar species. *A. chensiensis* (below) is similar in some forms but the shiny pink shoot is smooth. *A. spectabilis* (p. 109) differs in hairs in grooves of darker shoots, much longer arched leaves, also in bark and crown.

CHENSIEN FIR   *Abies chensiensis* Van Tiegh
S.W. China 1907. Several forms of this rare tree are in cultivation. It is charac-
terised by glabrous pink or yellow-brown shiny shoots, hard leaves in two spreading ranks rather flat each side of the shoot, yellowish-green above with greenish-white bands beneath and tipped by two sharp spines. The length varies from 2.5 to 5 cm, the bands beneath may be bright white and the spine may be single. The bud is large, knobbly, pale and resinous. Forms occur which have long leaves rising from the shoot and recurved – grading into *A. recurvata*.

DELAVAY'S SILVER FIR   *Abies delavayi* Franch.
S.W. China. Frequent in collections and larger gardens particularly in north and west and Ireland but only as one of the varieties. Trees labelled "*A. delavayi*" are usually var. *fabri*, or var. *forrestii*. The type is known at Edinburgh R.B.G., Benmore and in a few forest-plots. It has pale brown scaly bark, slightly ascending branches crowded with short upright shoots on their upper side, prominent red-brown globular buds, bright orange shoot very finely pubescent and *bright green* foliage, each leaf *curled down along its margins* hiding much of the broad bright white bands beneath but showing the bright green midrib.

var. *forrestii* (Rogers) Jacks. Forrest's Fir. Yunnan, Szechuan 1910. The most frequent form, growing strongly in Scotland and Ireland; often short-lived in S. England. 20 × 2 m.

Bark. Grey, smooth, some flaking patches, few broad black wandering vertical fissures.

Crown. Conic, regularly whorled, open; stout ascending branches.

Foliage. Shoot bright orange-brown, occasionally red-brown, glabrous but finely roughened; second-year deep purplish red-brown striped white. Bud small, 3 mm, glob-ular, dark shiny red, partly white with resin. Leaves *crowded forwards all round the shoot* or slightly parted above, those beneath lying well forwards; slightly shiny deep blue-green above, often bloomed blue-grey at first, shallowly grooved,

Forrest's Fir

abruptly notched at tip, 2–4 cm; two brilliantly white broad bands beneath.

Cone. Frequent on quite young trees, barrel-shaped, flat-topped, 9 × 4.5 cm, blue-purple; bracts exserted as fine spikes to 5 mm long, the broad, toothed base of some just showing. Flower 4 cm, deep purple-blue.

var. *georgei* (Orr) Melville. Yunnan 1923. Uncommon; collections only. 16 × 1.5 m. Differs from var. *forrestii* in dense orange-brown pubescence on shoot, leaves shorter to 1.5 cm and more bloomed grey; bud soon pure white with resin and cone *cylindric* 9–12 × 5 cm, bracts exserted 8–9 mm, pointing upright except those near the base; wavy brown-edged bases well exposed. Probably a high elevation form of var. *forrestii*.

var. *fabri* (Craib) Hunt. W. Szechuan 1903. Often grown as "*A. delavayi*"; somewhat less frequent than var. *forrestii*. 16 × 1.5 m. Differs from var. *forrestii* in *brown scaly bark* with wide shallow fissures and scaly ridges; dark brown pubescence on brown or orange shoots, especially side-shoots; leaves darker, not bloomed, pectinate below shoot and well parted above; cone long-ovoid, 5–8 × 2–3 cm, bracts exserted only as 2–3 mm spines, mostly twisted. Variable in colour of shoot, and length and arrangement of leaves.

var. *faxoniana* (Rehd. and Wils.) Jacks. N.W. Szechuan 1911. Very rare; a few collections. 17 × 1.3 m. Bark with shiny patches pinkish or purple; shoot slender golden-brown; bud dark red or rich purple; leaves nearly pectinate or rising above shoot, pale-tipped, usually banded beneath greenish-white, sometimes bright white. Some have pubescent grooves in the shoot. Some are very near var. *fabri*.

FARGES'S FIR   *Abies fargesii* Franch.

W. China. Hupeh and Szechuan 1901. Rare; a few collections only.

Bark. Pink-grey, very smooth.

Crown. Conic, open; whorled branches, upper ones level, lower drooping then curving upwards gracefully.

Foliage. Shoot stout, *rich purple*, mahogany, orange-brown and pale brown on the same tree, with minute white curly pubescence in slight grooves. Second year shiny pale orange-brown striped white. Bud ovoid, knobbly, yellow-brown, 5–6 mm. Leaves large thick *leathery* more or less pectinate above and below, laterals slightly forward, inner leaves strongly

Farges's Fir

forwards, some rising; 4–4.5 cm, *glossy*, deep yellowish-green above tapering to a two-pointed tip, two narrow *grey-green* bands beneath, prominent midrib between them. Margins slightly revolute.

Similar species. This beautiful tree is a giant-foliaged form of *A. sutchuenensis* and is distinct from the others of the *A. delavayi* group in its deep yellowish-green, not blue-green, large leaves and purple shoots.

SUTCHUEN FIR   *Abies sutchuenensis* (Franch.) Rehd. and Wils.

W. Kansu, China 1911. Rare; many collections and a few gardens, mainly in the west; in Scotland and Ireland.

Bark. Pinkish-grey, finely fissured and flaky.

Crown. Narrowly conic, open; occasionally fails to grow a leading-shoot and makes a wide, flat bush.

Foliage. Bud ovoid, knobbly, purple-red-brown, 6 mm. Shoot slender, deep, rich, shiny *purple-red* also mahogany to orange-brown on same tree. Leaves pectinate below, slightly parted above, upper leaves forward and rising, some with underside pointing outwards, some bending below shoot, many with tips bent down; *glossy very dark green* grooved above, two broad bands bright or greenish-white beneath; 1–2.5 cm; narrow but thick, bluntly rounded, often notched at tip.

Cone. 7 × 3.5 cm, cylindric, bluntly domed, dark blue-purple, bracts exserted as small spines.

Sutchuen Fir

Similar species. This is a small-foliaged form of *A. fargesii* (p. 111) separated adequately by the length of leaf.

FLAKY FIR   *Abies squamata* Mast.

W. Szechuan, China 1910. Rare, but in some collections and very distinct because of the bark. 15 m.

Bark. Rich *orange* and pinkish-brown; big *papery flakes* rolling up and hanging on bole.

Crown. Conic, rather open in lower half.

Foliage. Shoot glabrous or nearly so, purple-orange-brown. Bud ovoid to 6 mm; purple, white with resin. Leaf short, to 2.5 cm, parallel-sided, abruptly short-pointed, very *grey above* with stomata at tips and in grey band down centre on dark grey-green; two broad grey-white bands beneath; rather *stiff*, pectinate below, standing densely perpendicular and *nearly vertical* above.

Cone. Tall-ovoid, deep purple-blue, 5.5 × 3 cm, bracts long exserted 6–8 mm and decurved.

Flaky Fir

KOREAN FIR   *Abies koreana* Wils.

Korea 1913. Bushy form from Quelpaert I. grown as flowering shrub. Mainland form scarcer, to 10 m so far. Infrequent.

Bark. Shiny dark olive-brown to black, freckled conspicuously with lenticels.

Crown. Very broad, low-conic (bushy form), narrow conic as tree, branches level.

Foliage. Shoot pale brown or pink-grey, slightly pubescent. Bud small ovoid, pale brown soon pure white with resin. Leaves *short*, 1(2.5) × 0.2 cm, *blunt* and notched, rarely sharp; nearly all round shoot, vertical and some recurved above, some bent forwards beneath; dark green above often with white near the tip, two broad very bright white bands beneath which may obscure midrib.

Korean Fir

Flowers and cone. Male buds small and globular, *crowded among leaves* of side-shoots all over crown, ovoid, 4–5 mm; open to conspicuous clusters, bright yellow, 1 cm. Females on upper side of shoot, 2–5 cm tall, slender, yellowish-green, whitish-pink or pale purple; slender bracts decurved. Cone 5–7 × 2–3 cm, long barrel-shaped, usually pointed at top, deep blue, bracts exserted, brown, strongly decurved. Ripen pale brown. Much covered by white resin. Borne freely all over crown when tree little more than 1 m tall.

SPANISH or HEDGEHOG FIR   *Abies pinsapo* Boiss.

Ronda, S. Spain 1839. Infrequent; gardens, parks and churchyards especially in E. England where few *Abies*. 33 m.

Bark. Dark grey roughly freckled at first then fissured irregularly into lifting plates. Oldest trees black, finely roughened.

Crown. Conic at first rather open with tapered top. Old trees: dense mass of fine shoots, mostly dead or dying, twiggy, rough; opened-out tops.

Foliage. Bud ovoid, knobbly, 3–5 mm, purple-brown with pale brown tips. Shoot green-brown becoming orange-brown. Leaves crowded equally *all round shoot* standing *perpendicular* to it, older leaves curled backwards; short, 1–1.8 cm × 2–3 mm, *thick stiff* leathery; sucker-like bases, broadly rounded tips, variably grey-green to *grey-blue both sides*, two broad bands grey-green each surface, or upper surface dusted white and bands beneath blue-white ('Glauca').

Flowers and cone. Males big, globular, red before and, at edges, during shedding of pollen in late May; cones clustered around top of tree, cylindrical, tapered, about 10 cm, pale green during summer, often very numerous.

Similar species. *A. cephalonica* (p. 106) and its hybrid with *A. pinsapo*, *A.* × *vilmorinii*, Masters (Paris 1867) also have leaves all round the shoot. Neither has quite as many below, both have longer leaves, 2.5 cm or more, not densely packed, dark shiny green above and sharply pointed. *A.* × *vilmorinii* differs from *A. cephalonica* in the dull pale green bands beneath the leaf and widely spaced thick leaves, and is very rare. Cone 11 × 3 cm, purplish

Spanish Fir

A. x *vilmorinii*

H

ALPINE FIR   *Abies lasiocarpa* (Hook.) Nutt.

W.N. America. Very rare, stunted and sickly in cultivation; superb slender spires high in Cascade Mountains.

var. *arizonica* (Merriam) Lemm. Cork Fir. Arizona, Colorado, New Mexico 1903. Infrequent, small highly ornamental tree. 20 m.

Bark. Young trees greenish-grey with wide, pink, corky fissures. Older trees thick, corky rough, yellowish-grey.

Crown. Narrowly conic, usually elegant and regular to tip, but if broken can form many-headed candelabra-crown.

Foliage. Shoot ashy grey, slightly hairy. Leaves slender, rising forwards from shoot at sides, lying close to it and forwards down the centre; appear bright deep blue from grey-green upper side with central bright white band; two white bands below; 2–3 cm, bluntly rounded. Crushed foliage scented of balsam.

Cork Fir

Cone. Sometimes numerous near top, crowded, 15 × 7 cm, barrel-shaped, brown; pubescent scales; disintegrating early.

Similar species. Resembles rich blue form of *A. concolor violacea* (if there were one) with small leaves, or may be mistaken at distance for a deeper blue form of *Picea pungens* 'Glauca' (p. 132).

NOBLE FIR   *Abies procera* Rehd.   **Pl. 7**

Syn. *A. nobilis* Lindl.

Washington and Oregon 1830. Common; small-scale use in forestry in western mountains, widely planted in gardens especially in north and west, but scarcely grows in towns. 47 × 5.2 m (47 × 4.7 m at Taymouth Castle, Perths.).

Bark. Pale silvery grey or dull purple. Smooth at first with resin-blisters then shallowly cracked; oldest whether silver or purple have a few large fissures, the parts between shallowly cracked.

Crown. Narrowly conic at first, always liable to lose top in exposure; older trees broad-columnar, flat-topped, branches level; dead tops distinct with two to three heavy, twisted branches near apex.

Foliage. Shoot pale reddish-brown, very finely pubescent, largely *hidden by crowded leaf-bases*. Leaves *strongly parted below* shoot sweeping up at sides, those on top spreading forwards and then upwards nearly to vertical, to 1–3.5 cm slender (1–2 mm) leathery, *grooved and flattened*, bluntly tipped, dark grey-green; grey stomata above in two thinly scattered lines, broad near tip, two grey-white bands beneath; *bluish-white general colour*, 'Glauca', not really separable, in best form is bright bluish-white each side of new leaves.

Flowers and cone. Males globular, crowded along underside of shoots over most of crown of older trees, about 6 mm across, *bright crimson before shedding pollen*; females cylindric, 4–5 cm, yellow-green; slender scales tipped orange. Cones slightly tapered to a low domed top; 20–25 × 8 cm, pale purplish-brown but appear pale green as bracts of this colour, broad at base, protrude and bend down sharply, covering most of the cone; the cones hang sideways from weaker shoots bent by their weight, erect on strong shoots in the upper half of the crown; may be borne on trees only 5 m tall.

Noble Fir Cone

Growth. Slow for a few years then fast, shoots to 80cm in north and west; lower in south and east. Mid-May to late June.

Similar species. *A. magnifica* (below).

RED FIR *Abies magnifica* Murr.

Oregon and California 1851. Uncommon; occasional in big gardens mainly in north; notable in Perthshire, where to 37 × 4.5m. Differs from *A. procera* as follows:

Bark. Dull grey or purplish-grey, thick, corky, finely rough-ened, some curved fissures; thick ridges around *prominent*, numerous whorled *black branch-scars*. (Old trees are deep red in California, hence name. A few here also show some dark red.)

Crown. Very symmetrically conic then columnar; branches even-sized in young trees, level, ascending in older trees in upper crown, often curved up in lower but may be depressed at origin; *strongly whorled*, short. Bole *stout*, often barrel-shaped at base then tapering sharply through crown.

Foliage. Dark rusty brown shoot visible from above; leaves spreading widely sideways from under shoot, those on top curving up then to the side and some curling back above shoot; to 4cm noticeably longer than *A. procera*, slender and lax, ridged, thickish, *almost rounded* (can be rolled).

Red Fir

Cone. 20 × 10cm, big domed barrel, smooth, pale golden green, on a few large trees in good summers. In var. *shastensis* (Oregon; California) bracts exserted.

Red Fir   Santa Lucia Fir

SANTA LUCIA FIR *Abies bracteata* (D. Don) Nutt.

Syn. *A. venusta* (Dougl.) K. Koch

Santa Lucia Mountains, Monterey, California 1853. Infrequent; in large gardens mainly in S.W. England, rare in Scotland, north to Deeside. 25m (39 × 3.3m, Bodnant, Clwyd).

Bark. Purplish-black, much wrinkled and lined around branch-scars. Young trees smooth dark grey heavily lined around scars.

Crown. Narrowly conic; when 20m and above, upper crown a narrow spire of whorled short branches with hanging foliage; lower crown broad with long branches sweeping gently down with drooping fans of long branchlets.

Foliage. Shoot smooth, sub-shiny, olive becoming dark red-brown. *Bud 2cm long, narrow, acutely pointed* like a beech bud, and pale brown. Leaves parted, lower ones spreading each side of shoot and somewhat forwards, upper rising from shoot, strongly forwards, a few above middle of shoot; widely spaced; to 5 cm, *hard, sharply spined*, dark green above, two bright white bands beneath Whole spray on large scale.

Cone. Seen rarely on biggest trees only, 10 cm, extraordinary for long 5 cm bristly, protruding bracts; bright green in July.

Similar species. *A. pindrow* (p. 109) has foliage nearly this size and arrangement but paler green abruptly double-pointed, lacking bright white below, less hard; pale shoot and globular bud distinguish. Other big-foliaged *Abies*, like *spectabilis, chensiensis, fargesii* also at once separable by bud.

CEDARS   Cedrus

The true cedars are a closely related group of four species from the Mediterranean and the Himalaya. They are the only evergreen conifers in which the leaves on second year and older shoots are borne in dense whorls on short spur-shoots. Cones erect like *Abies*, disintegrating on tree, but spend at least two years ripening. Flowering September–November. The old tag: ascending – Atlas level – Lebanon, down – Deodar works quite well when applied only to the young *tips* of the branches.

CEDAR OF LEBANON   *Cedrus libani* A. Richard   Pl. 8

Mt. Lebanon, Syria; S.E. Turkey 1638. Very common in parks, large gardens churchyards, even in towns and cities. 40 × 8 m (40 m in height at Petworth House, Sussex; 8.2 m in girth at Blenheim, Oxon.).

Bark. Dark grey, smooth at first, becoming shallowly networked with small fissures, into short scaly ridges; in old trees these are dull brown and separated by wider, deeper fissures.

Crown. Gaunt and conic at first, rapidly spreading in the open until short bole bears many huge branches low down, rising from bole, arching over and descending nearly or quite to ground; upper bole usually breaks into several vertical limbs, upper branches *level*, all branches *layering out to extensive flat plates o* dense, short, curved, vertical shoots. Many such trees flatten into wide 'table tops' at only 15–20 m especially in towns; others have open tops of slender arched branches. Old trees suffer much breakage from wet snow. In woods, may have long, straight bole, high, level branches.

Foliage. New growth nodding on old trees, level on young, with leaves singly and sparsely all round pale brownish shoot which has fine pale coffee-brown pubescence; leaves slender, curved out, lax, 2 cm; older wood has spur-shoots bearing whorls 10–20 leaves to 3 cm, sharp fairly stiff, dark green, blue-green grey or blue-grey. Bud ovoid, brown, the tips of outer scales very dark.

Flowers and cone. Male flowers pale grey-green, 5 cm, tall-conic, erect; female flower terminal on spur, 1 cm, ovoid-cylindric, bright pale green, often tinged rosy-purple, in October. Cone first year grey-green purplish by mid-summer 8 cm, barrel-shaped; lumpy, low-pointed top, ripens grey and pink-brown scale margins purplish, some white resin; 9 × 6 to 15 × 7 cm.

Growth. Slow for several years, and never rapid in height, (to 35 cm a year) but becomes very rapid in girth; most of the vast and apparently ancient specimens were planted since 1800.

'AUREA' Rare; narrow, densely layered crown with bent top, becoming very broad; leaves bright gold, varying a little with season. 15 m.

ATLAS or ALGERIAN CEDAR   *Cedrus atlantica* (Endl.) Carr.

Atlas Mountains in Algeria and Morocco 1841. Common, but mainly as 'Glauca' which is one of the most planted of all decorative conifers. The type is frequent in large gardens, parks and churchyards. Thrives better in hotter and drier areas than will most conifers. 33 × 6 m (× 6.3 m, Corsham Court). Some trees are so similar in foliage to *C. libani* that the crown needs to be seen, and even then a few cannot be identified for certain.

Bark. Dull dark grey, smooth at first then dark cracks make large plates; old trees dull brownish grey with crowded narrow fissures leaving short, narrow, scaly plates.

Crown. Broad-conic when young with branches ascending strongly right to their tips; later very broad but less spreading than *C. libani* and nearly always *obtusely pointed*; big branches ascend and level out but seldom droop, nor do they bear such large plate-like areas of shoots; bole often clean for a few metres.

Foliage. New shoots ascending slightly. Bud ovoid, light red-brown with blackish tips to scales, 2–3 mm. Leaves on long shoots 2–2.5 cm; on spurs 1–2 cm about 45 on each spur; rounded in section, spined, shiny deep green.

Flowers and cone. Male flower ripens pink-yellow in mid-September to 4 cm long curved; female flower 1 cm, cylindric, domed, scales dark green, with pale margins, appears bright, fresh green from distance; late September.

Atlas Cedar

Cone to 8 cm, often hollowed at apex; first year 5 × 3 cm, pale green scales tipped lilac; later dull purplish, ripens pale brown-purple.

Growth. Soon rapid from good small plants, shoots to 60 cm, increase in girth rapid, to 2.5 m in less than 50 years.

'GLAUCA' 1845. Occurs in parts of natural range, with intermediates. Very common, part of nearly every civic and private planting in gardens of any moderate size. 32 × 4 m. Leaves bright blue-grey or whitish, crown more shapely, bark pale grey finely fissured. **Pl. 8.**

'FASTIGIATA' 1890, Nantes. Rare, striking tree, narrowly columnar and fastigiately branched, widening somewhat with age. Bark dark grey cracked into square plates. 20 m.

'GLAUCA PENDULA' 1900. Curious and magnificent when well-grown (which it rarely is) arching down from 10 m in one-sided fan of few stiff branches right to ground. Leaves grey-blue. Difficult to start, best trees grafted high on rootstock of the type, or carefully trained from lower grafting.

'Fastigiata'   'Glauca Pendula'

DEODAR   *Cedrus deodara* (Roxb.) G. Don ex Loud.   **Pl. 8**
W. Himalayas and Afghanistan 1831. Very common in large and small gardens, churchyards and town parks. 36 × 5 m. (37 × 4.5 m Whitfield House.)
Bark. Dark grey-green and smooth at first then dark brown or black closely fissured into small vertical plates of pale, ashy grey.
Crown. Conic to a narrow *spire-top* with *drooping leading shoot*. Young trees pale grey or silvery leafed becoming dark green with age. Oldest trees broader
and may have big low branches or long clean boles but, whether broad or narrow, they keep a pointed top. Some fork high and have two equal spire-tops. Upper branches level or slightly depressed, lower sweep gently down.

Foliage. New shoots conspicuously *arched*, pale pink-brown, densely pubescent, their spiral-set leaves soft, curved out, 3–5 cm dark green; faint grey lines each side. Bud pointed, 1 mm orange, free scale-tips pale brown. Whorled leaves 3–3.5 cm. In a form sometimes called 'Robusta' (properly a grey, more pendulous form) the spurs are far apart and leaves thick dark yellowish-green, 5–6 cm, staying in half-opened bunches. Many of the biggest trees have this foliage.

Deodar

Flowers and cone. Male flower erect, conic-ovoid grey-green turning pink, 4 cm in early October; dark purple, 6–7 cm and curved before shedding pollen at end of October. Female flower ovoid-cylindric, 5–6 mm, bright pale green, some pink-tipped. Cones less often seen and often on branches or trees with no males; barrel-shaped to 14 cm.
Growth. Soon rapid in height with shoots to 1 m; growth in girth quite rapid to about 2.5 m then usually very slow. Some original trees thriving at 135 years but dying or dead trees commonly seen of 100 years or less.

CYPRUS CEDAR   *Cedrus brevifolia* (Hook. f.) Henry
     Syn. *C. libani* var. *brevifolia* Henry
Paphos Forest, Cyprus 1879. Rare; often grown as dwarf conifer but known so far to 21 × 1.3 m (Borde Hill, Sussex).
Bark. Dull dark purplish-grey, a few deep blackish flat-bottomed cracks, which become more numerous.
Crown. Moderately narrow-conic, straight single bole and stem. Branches level, drooping at the ends holding flat plates of dense deep green foliage.
Foliage. Shoot pale green-brown, downy, second year pink-brown. Bud ovoid, brown, resinous, 2–3 mm. Bases of leaves pale orange. New shoot with basal leaves to 1.5 cm, spur-leaves *0.7–1.2 cm*, rich green or blue-green, both with fine white lines above, sometimes yellowish. New shoots mark-edly arched.

Cyprus Cedar

Cone. 12 × 5 cm, ovoid, long-tapered from base, abruptly narrowed at tip like a lemon to a small beak, smooth pale green, then yellow-brown, margins purple.

Similar species. Sickly *C. libani* have short leaves and may be confused but the leaves are never as short, and their crowns are broad, and shed many of their needles.

LARCHES Larix

Ten closely related species, three spread widely across the northern circumpolar plains, seven montane relict species in small, scattered areas in mountains to the south. Deciduous; long shoots with spirally set leaves, short shoots on older wood, spur-like, bearing leaves in whorls. Softly woody cones falling complete from tree after one or many years but ripening in one year. Light-demanding pioneer species of very rapid early growth. One hybrid used in forestry, several others known.

EUROPEAN LARCH. *Larix decidua* Mill. **Pl. 9**
  Syn. *L. europaea* D.C.
Alps from Savoy to Tyrol and east to near Vienna; varieties in Sudeten and Tatra Mountains and on Polish Plain. About 1620. Locally abundant; forests, coverts, shelter-belts, roadsides, gardens and parks but not in large towns. 45 × 5.5 m.
Bark. Greenish grey-brown and smooth at first, soon fissured vertically; in plantations may be uniform grey for 70 years plus; old single trees pink-brown with deep, broad, scaly ridges.
Crown. Narrow-conic, main branches whorled but minor branches between; regular until height-growth ceases then broadens and top may flatten and stout level branches grow irregularly high in crown while lower branches, now very big, droop. Very old trees in open massively branched low, the biggest branches often turning abruptly upwards some 2 m out from bole. Foliage pendulous.
Foliage. Shoot *pale yellow* or pale pinkish, glabrous, grooved from leaf-bases. Leaf 2–3 cm but on leader of vigorous young tree can be 6 cm. Spur-leaves emerge bright green in March, darken somewhat by summer and are golden by the end of October. Narrow, parallel-sided to blunt tip; rich green above, variably grey-green beneath. Many young trees have silvery or glaucous foliage on long shoots.
Flowers and cone. Males on underside of weak shoots or all round hanging shoots, open late March as *whitish discs*, often pale purple round edge, raised slightly in centre, become yellow as pollen shed a week or so after; females towards ends of strong shoots from an age of 5–10 years, 1–6 per shoot, many more on old wood; rosy-red, pale green or white; erect, to 1 cm, on 0.5 cm scaly stalk, first open two weeks before male; turn red-purple then green, ripen into brown cone, tall-ovoid, bluntly rounded, or pointed ovoid-conic 2–4 × 2–3 cm; scales rounded, tips turn slightly inwards, rarely slightly outwards. Many trees retain dead cones for ten years or more.

European Larch cone

Growth. Very fast: seedlings can grow 30–40 cm first year, transplants (two years old) to 1.3 m. Those planted out check one year – shoot only 30–80 cm – then next year can grow 1.5 m. To 18 m in 18 years. Leading shoots may be unbranched, have several short branchlets half way up around slight kinks in the shoot or have strong shoots in lower half decreasing to small ones near top. Growth starts in May at 2 cm a week increasing to 8–10 cm weekly in June, checks slightly as sinuous sections grown, then speeds up through August and September growing the top straight section at 8–12 cm a week and stops in early October. Less vigorous trees stop in early August.

var. *polonica* (Racib.) Ostenf. and Larsen. **Polish Larch.** Hills on Polish plain 1920. A few plantations and collections. Bark dark grey soon *deeply and roughly fissured brown,* bole usually *sinuous,* shoots hang from branches, *very slender white;* cone very small 1.5–2 cm ovoid or flat-topped, soon green, scales incurved. The larch in the Sudeten and Tatra Mountains is intermediate between this and the type and is of vigorous straight growth. It is now preferred to other forms in forests.

SIBERIAN LARCH   *Larix russica* (Endl.) Sabine
Syn. *L. sibirica* Ledeb.

N. Russia and east in Siberia to River Yenisei 1806. Very rare; very few collections. Large trees once thought to be this species are *L. decidua.* Usually fails here as leafs out in January and is frosted. 3 m. Shoot slender, very pale buff, usually *pubescent.* Leaves slender, to 4 cm grey blue above with two widely separated pale grey bands beneath. Cone 3 cm, scales *pubescent.*

JAPANESE LARCH   *Larix kaempferi* (Lamb.) Carr.
Syn. *L. leptolepis* (Sieb. and Zu.cc) Endl.

C. Honshu, Japan 1861. Common. Plantations cover huge areas in western hills; some shelter-belts, coverts, etc. in all parts but less frequent in gardens than *L. decidua,* although withstands town air better. Used in reclamation of mine-tips, etc. 37 × 3 m (37 × 2.7 m at Blair Atholl, Perths.).

Bark. Reddish-brown, scaly; sometimes vertical flakes lifting away.

Crown. Broadly conic, seldom as narrow as *L. decidua,* often with very long, low branches sweeping out and slightly up; upper branches also bend up somewhat towards tips; branchlets do not hang. Stands look orange-brown in winter from distance.

Foliage. Shoot usually *dark orange-red* but may be dark brown or dark purple and bloomed grey. Leaves much broader and greyer green than *L. decidua* especially on vigorous young trees, 3.5–4 × 0.1 cm, two *broad grey bands* beneath; more densely leafy, shoots more densely set.

Flowers and cone. Males lie densely along underside of all but main shoots, globular, smaller than *L. decidua,* open yellow, *droplet-shaped* and shed pollen in Feb.–March. Females 1–8 along outer parts of strong shoots and singly terminating some feeble

Japanese Larch

shoots, Feb.–March, usually pink and cream, some pink and green or yellow, more dumpy than *L. decidua,* ripen to brown, flattened-bun-shaped cones with edges of scales *strongly turned out and down* like a woody rose, 3 × 3 cm. Usually profuse and starting at 4–10 years old.

Growth. As *L. decidua* (p. 119), but on poor soils much superior and usually more rapid in growth in girth. Leading shoot always bears side-shoots.

HYBRID LARCH or DUNKELD (HYBRID) LARCH

Larix × eurolepis Henry   **Pl. 9**

First arose about 1897 at Dunkeld, Perthshire, noticed 1904. Hybrid *L. kaempferi × decidua*, intermediate between these species in all characters except growth which on all but the best sites is superior to either parent. 32 m × 2.5 m.

Bark. Reddish-brown like *L. kaempferi*.

Crown. Intermediate, usually good shape, medium-conic.

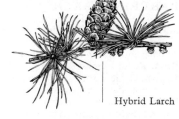

Foliage. Intermediate: shoot pale orange or varying from pinkish to pale brown or red-brown. Leaves on vigorous leading shoots to 8 cm, broader and greyer than *L. decidua*; on older wood bright green above and 3.5–5 × 0.2 cm; pale grey-green bands beneath.

Hybrid Larch

Flowers and cone. Males intermediate; females bigger than in *L. decidua*, bright red, pink, yellow-green, bright pale green, white or red and white. Cone *taller* than in *L. decidua*, 3.5–4 cm, 2–2.5 cm across, scales *abruptly bent out* but not curled down at tip, pale brown. Fruits even earlier in life and more prolifically than either parent. Young trees may grow female flowers and cones on very short sprouts from the bole.

Growth. First year to 55 cm, second year to 1.7 m; fifth year to 6 m total height recorded in my garden; May to October. Leading shoot usually with side-shoots if vigorous.

Similar species. The distinctions between the hybrid and *L. kaempferi* can grade to nil because much seed has been taken from plantations where these are mixed. More seed comes from plantations of trees themselves hybrids, and this second generation shows all variations between the original parents. True hybrids differ from *L. kaempferi* in paler shoot, longer leaf less whitish beneath and long-conic cones with scale-tips spreading or upwards, not curled down.

TAMARACK   *Larix laricina* (Du Roi) K. Koch   **Pl. 9**

Alaska to Newfoundland, south to Minnesota 1739. Rare; few even in collections but occasional in large gardens. 21 × 1.5 m

Bark. Dull pink or pinkish-brown, *finely flaking*; no fissures.

Crown. Slender, conic, good length of straight bole but axis lost in *twisting often hooped branches* well below top of big trees; short slender twisting branches bear bunches of *curled, fine* shoots. Young trees have strongly ascending, slender branches.

Foliage. Shoot slender, pinkish, bloomed; leaves very slender, 2.5 cm long, those on long shoots with two broad grey bands above and beneath, those on spurs with bands beneath only; dark green above.

Tamarack

Flowers and cone. Males very small, numerous but not dense; females small, 0.6–0.8 cm, deep red, numerous over outer crown, ripen to small blunt, cylindric cones, 1.5 × 1 cm; few rounded scales, curved in at tips.

Similar species. *L. gmelinii* (below) has small cones but broader with more scales, stouter red shoots and different crown. *L. decidua* var. *polonica* has small cones and slender shoot but shoot white and bark deeply fissured and grey. Trees too young to cone are unmistakable with narrow crown of few, very slender, rather wavy shoots, upright near top.

DAHURIAN LARCH   *Larix gmelinii* (Rupr.) Kuzeneva
Syn. *L. dahurica* Trautv.

Siberia, east of River Yenisei along which it hybridises with *L. sibirica* which ranges west of this river. 1827. Rare; in collections. Usually rather stunted as it comes into leaf in late January and is damaged by frosts. 19 m.

Bark. Reddish-brown, roughly scaling.

Crown. Conic, rather open, slender at top, when thriving, but mostly low, bent and dense; flat plate-like masses of foliage bending down.

Foliage. Shoot dark red or pink-brown, slightly ribbed, variably hairy, always hairy in two varieties from far south-east of range; leaves very slender, to 4 × 0.05 cm, blunt, emerge and remain *bright shiny grass-green* above, keeled and with two whitish, narrow bands beneath.

Flowers and cone. Males small; females bright yellow-green in spring; conelets rich rosy purple in summer, often densely borne; cone 2–2.5 × 1.8 cm, squat, many scales, with broad, rounded apex,

Dahurian Larch

slightly curved out at margin, ripening rather shiny pale brown on stalks 5–7 mm.

SIKKIM LARCH   *Larix griffithiana* Carr.

Sikkim, Nepal, Bhutan, Tibet 1848. Rare; confined to a few gardens in S. and W. England and in Ireland. 21 m.

Bark. Red-brown, scaly.

Crown. Broadly conic with heavy branches in the few old trees; younger trees mostly gaunt, few branches, bole slender, straight; branches with few shoots which are *long, pendulous, stout,* and *rich orange-red.*

Foliage. Long leaves, shiny deep green, 3–4 cm; two narrow greenish white bands beneath; 30–40 on a spur.

Cone. Numerous, erect, on hanging shoots, dark purple-brown, very tall, *cylindric,* slightly tapered, 6–11 × 2 cm; bracts protruding as 1 cm long fine points, upper ones arched, lower depressed against cone. Conelets 4–5 cm, purple with deflexed bracts.

Similar species. Sometimes confused with the

Sikkim Larch

Chinese *L. potaninii* Batalin (China 1904) in which the cones are 5 × 2.5 cm, long-ovoid, dull purple or blackish, bracts pale purple and brown, long-exserted, vertical; shoots tan brown not pendulous; slender leaves golden-green.

WESTERN LARCH   *Larix occidentalis*
Nutt.

British Columbia, Oregon, Washington, Idaho, Montana, where it has reached a larger size than any other larch, over 60 m. 1881. Rare; collections and some large gardens. 24 m. Has been tried in plantations.

Bark. Purplish-grey, deeply and widely fissured into flaky-edged ridges.

Crown. Narrowly conic, broadening with age, rather open.

Foliage. Shoot stout pale *orange-brown*; leaves 3–5 cm on prominent spurs; keeled beneath, bright grass-green above and below.

Cone. Tall-ovoid, 3–5 cm, rich purple in summer with yellow and orange bracts, ripen purple-brown; bracts protrude as long, spreading or down-curved points.

Western Larch

GOLDEN LARCH   Pseudolarix

A single deciduous species related to Larix with cones that disintegrate when ripe, and male flowers bunched on spurs.

GOLDEN LARCH   *Pseudolarix amabilis* (Nels.) Rehd.   **Pl. 9**
S.E. China 1853. Rare; large gardens mainly in S. and S.W. England. 12(22) m (18 × 2.4 m at Scorrier House, Cornwall).

Bark. Pale grey or brownish-grey, thick, cracked into square, lifting plates.

Crown. Broadly conic or even squat; long level branches; narrower in shade.

Foliage. Bud: terminal brown, ovoid, surrounded by fine whiskery scales; side-buds globose, pink-brown. Like a large coarse larch; *long, curved spurs thickest at their tips*, bear 15–30 bright pale green leaves, *pale-margined* above, two broad pale bands beneath; 3–7 cm long 0.3 cm wide; single leaves on pink-buff shoots (later purple), curved forwards and twisted above shoot. Turn gold in October then bright orange then foxy brown.

Golden Larch

Flowers and cone. Males replace leaves on some spurs, about 20, on slender 5 mm stalks, cylindric to 5 mm; females on different branches, become bright pale green, leathery cones 5–6 × 4.5 cm with large triangular acute, thick scales, straight and slightly spreading leaving a hollow apex; resemble a small globe-artichoke.

Growth. Slow; apical shoot frequently killed by frost when young. June to September.

SPRUCES Picea

Some 50 species over most of N. hemisphere except Africa. Bare shoots rough with peg-like bases of shed leaves; cones pendulous when ripening; bark thin, scaly, not deeply fissured. Foliage harsh to touch and may be spiny.

Key to Picea species

Note: Side-shoots used for arrangement of leaves as several species have leaves all round main snoots but not normally on side shoots.

1. Leaves spreading all round shoot, some pointing downwards   **2**
   Leaves parted beneath shoot, spreading flat or upcurved, each side   **9**

2. Leaves all round shoot equally in all directions   **3**
   Leaves mostly above shoots, a few spreading beneath   **7**

3. Leaves round in cross-section, green all round   **4**
   Leaves flattened, white bands beneath   **5**

4. Shoots stout, spreading; bud whitish-brown, dull   *schrenkiana*, p. 127
   Shoots less stout, long and pendulous; bud red-brown shiny   *smithiana*, p. 127

5. Leaves 1–1.5 cm, densely crowded, blue-grey in mass; shoot spreading, short   *mariana*, p. 131
   Leaves 2–3.5 cm, not crowded, deep green or bright green in mass; shoots pendulous   **6**

6. Leaves 3–3.5 cm, sparse, curved outwards, slender blackish-green; shoots hanging   *brewerana*, p. 127
   Leaves 2–3 cm, straight, bright green above, silvery blue beneath; shoots mostly pendulous   *spinulosa*, p. 130

7. Bud shiny chestnut-red; leaves very stout, spined, rigid, curved, yellow-green   *polita*, p. 131
   Bud pale brown, papery, dull, often like rosette; leaves not spined, less rigid but sharp and stiff, blue-green or blue-grey   **8**

8. Shoot pale pink to red-brown; leaves to 1.5 cm, upper ones forward; bud without long basal scales   *asperata*, p. 131
   Shoot yellow or purplish; leaves to 2.5 cm, usually blue-grey, upper ones erect; bud with long basal scales   *pungens* and cvs., p. 132-3

9. Leaves square or round in cross-section   **10**
   Leaves much flattened   **18**

10. Leaves uniformly coloured on all surfaces   **11**
    Leaves dark green above, blue-white bands beneath   **17**

11. Leaves less than 1 cm, rounded at tip   *orientalis*, p. 136
    Leaves more than 1 cm, usually acutely pointed tip   **12**

12. Shoot shining white, glabrous; leaves at side curve upwards, grey   *glauca*, p. 133
    Shoot dull, not white, often pubescent   **13**

13. Leaves pale blue-grey, often round-tipped; shoot golden-
brown *engelmannii* 'Glauca', p. 133
Leaves dark or bright green **14**

14. Shoot dull grey-pink or brown; finely pubescent; leaves forward, one leaf spreading widely from each bud *obovata*, p. 135
Shoot orange or red-brown **15**

15. Shoot orange; leaves dark blue-green, stiff, well-spaced
rising above shoot at ± 45°; bud large *koyamai*, p. 134
Shoot red-brown; leaves bright or deep green; bud small **16**

16. Bud with slender, long, dark scales at base; leaves short,
1.3 cm, wiry, bright green, usually curved upwards and
inward; shoot markedly pubescent *rubens*, p. 134
Bud without long basal scales; leaves 1.5–2.0 cm, upper ones
forward close to shoot; shoot glabrous or finely pubescent *abies*, p. 135

17. Shoot white or buff, stout; (crown wide, long upcurved
branches) *bicolor*, p. 136
Shoot bright or pale orange, not stout; (crown narrow-conic,
dense) *glehnii*, p. 137

18. Shoot pubescent, pinkish-brown **19**
Shoot glabrous, white or pale buff **20**

19. Leaves with blunt, broad, tips; those above shoot often
partially erect, dark bluish-green; (crown narrow, columnar
or conic; bark orange, scaly) *omorika*, p. 140
Leaves abruptly acute, those above shoot pressed close to it;
grey, pale bluish or dark grey-green; (crown broad-conic;
bark grey, few fissures) *likiangensis*, p. 138

20. Leaves leathery, blunt or short-pointed, rising from shoot *jezoensis*, p. 137
Leaves hard, spiny-tipped, those above shoot pressed close
to it **21**

21. Leaves 2–2.5 cm, parted flat beneath shoot, long-spiny points,
narrow white bands beneath; (crown dense) *sitchensis*, p. 139
Leaves 1–1.6 cm, parted in "V" beneath, side ones depressed
each side, short-pointed, two broad bands beneath often
coalesce; (open crown) *brachytyla*, p. 138

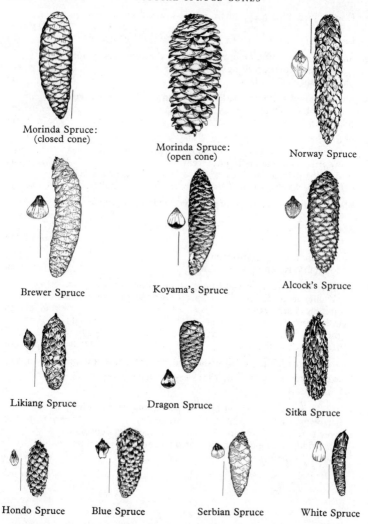

Morinda Spruce: (closed cone)

Morinda Spruce: (open cone)

Norway Spruce

Brewer Spruce

Koyama's Spruce

Alcock's Spruce

Likiang Spruce

Dragon Spruce

Sitka Spruce

Hondo Spruce

Blue Spruce

Serbian Spruce

White Spruce

All spruce cones are pendulous. They are soft and leathery, and ripen brown, white (Sitka) or purple. They fall complete, the larger ones often when still closed, and high winds may cause some to be shed when still green. Within each species they are fairly uniform in size and shape. They all ripen within one year and none is retained on the tree for a second year. Most open when dry, though e.g. Sitka, Blue Colorado and Hondo barely do so.

MORINDA or WEST HIMALAYAN SPRUCE

Picea smithiana (Wallich) Boissier   **Pl. 10**
Syn. *P. morinda* Link

Afghanistan to Nepal 1818. Infrequent but in many large gardens. 38 × 3.5 m.

Bark. Dull purplish, shallowly broken into large round scales, sometimes grey.

Crown. Slender *spire of level branches* upcurved at ends, and long *hanging branchlets*; dense in parts, thinning with age, often forked into two spires when central axis usually reaches each tip. Sometimes broad and domed.

Foliage. Shoot pale cream, shining, much grooved or ribbed. Bud ovoid, 8 mm, shiny *purple-brown* with some white resin. Leaves on *hanging shoots*; long, slender, well-spaced, forward-curved, rounded in section, uniformly shining dark green, *spread nearly equally around shoot*, abruptly sharp-pointed, 3–4 × 0.1 cm.

Flowers and cone. Male flowers large, 4 cm, ovoid at ends of hanging shoots; pollen shed in June. Cone cylindric, tapered each end, 12–15 cm, bright pale green, smooth, shiny in summer, ripen to shining brown; numerous scales closely set, convex, smoothly curved tips.

Morinda Spruce,
cones closed and open

Similar species. *P. schrenkiana* (below) is very similar. *P. brewerana* (p. 127) is unlikely to reach half the size, has flat leaves, is very much more dense and dark in crown and has a pubescent shoot, but is often confused with this.

Morinda Spruce   Schrenk's Spruce   Brewer Spruce

SCHRENK'S SPRUCE   *Picea schrenkiana* Fischer and Meyer

C. Asia to China 1877. Rare; collections. 20 m. Similar to *P. smithiana* in foliage but *not pendulous*. *Bud creamy pale brown*, pulvini finely pubescent. Leaves *stouter*, harder, straighter, less numerous beneath shoot than above, paler green, 3–3.5 × 0.15 cm, *obtuse* or abruptly short-pointed. Cone 8 × 3 cm ovoid-cylindric, curved, grey-brown and purple-black, resinous.

BREWER SPRUCE   *Picea brewerana* Wats.   **Pl. 11**

Oregon–California boundary, on ridges at 6,000 ft, in the Klamath and Siskiyou Mountains. 1897. Frequent; older trees confined to large gardens and collections but much recent planting in parks and smaller gardens. 12 m. (19 × 1.5 m.)

Plate 9   **LARCHES**

Deciduous trees; leaves on older wood in whorls. Cones with leathery or softly woody scales.

1. European Larch   *Larix decidua*   119

    (a) Young tree, ten years old, 8 m high, in winter.
    (b) Shoot with spirally set leaves on new growth and whorled leaves on spurs of last year's growth.
    (c) Shoot with fully ripe cone. Some trees retain old cones for years.

2. Hybrid Larch   *Larix × eurolepis*   121

Shoot with three male flowers after shedding pollen and one cone from the previous season. The shoots are varying shades from pink to orange-brown. The cone is taller than that of the Japanese Larch with scales less decurved.

3. Tamarack   *Larix laricina*   121

    (a) Shoot in spring with one male flower about to open and two female flowers opening. They become vertical and deep red.
    (b) Old cones open, with the seed shed.
    (c) Spray showing slender shoots which are often pinkish, usually bloomed lilac.
    (d) Tree of about 15 m in winter, showing the slender habit and shoots.

4. Golden Larch   *Pseudolarix amabilis*   123

    (a) Second-year shoot with young spurs.
    (b) Old spurs showing their annual rings.

A tree of broad growth and level branches, seldom seen of much stature except from Cornwall to Surrey. The cones reak up when still on the tree. The foliage turns bright gold in October and becomes foxy red by November.

Golden Larch

a

1b

1c

2

3a

3b

3c

3d

4a

4b

1

2a

2b

3

4a

4b

5a

5

SPRUCES   **Plate 10**

Hard, sharp leaves; cones hanging, confined to near the top of trees except when trees mature. Bark scaly, never fissured.

1. Sitka Spruce *Picea sitchensis*   139

Spray showing the hard spiny leaves. The shoot is usually white. The flat leaves have two broad blue-white bands on their undersides. The main tree of forestry in W. Britain and capable of very strong growth on upland peat sites. Has attained much greater stature than any other spruce.

2. Black Spruce *Picea mariana*   131

(a) Spray showing the very short, fine, blue-grey leaves. The shoot is brown and pubescent.
(b) Ripe cones, which may be in dense clusters near the tops of quite small trees.

A small, dense, bluish tree.

3. Tiger-tail Spruce *Picea polita*   131

Spray with its stout, rigid, fiercely spined leaves. The shoot is stout and white.

4. Likiang Spruce *Picea likiangensis*   138

(a) Female flower opening.
(b) Three male flowers before shedding pollen.

The tree is spectacular when in full flower in early May. The leaves are flattened, and blue-grey above on long-pubescent cream or pink shoots.

5. Morinda Spruce *Picea smithiana*   126

(a) Spray showing the long, slender leaves which are quad-rangular in section and the same green on each face.
(b) Tree 27 m high. The hanging shoots are the longest of all spruces except Brewer (see Pl. 11).

Likiang Spruce

Bark. Small trees dull pinkish-grey, freckled paler, branch-scars prominent with cracks each side. Older trees dark purplish with hard, circular flakes.

Crown. Spiky top with *side-shoots curved up* competing with leader untidily; mid-crown branches level, upswept at ends, hung with *curtains of branchlets to 2m long*, branches dense but radiate with space between curtains as no spreading lateral shoots; lower branches sweep somewhat downwards.

Brewer Spruce

Foliage. Shoot slender, pink-brown, finely pubescent. Bud blunt, pale ovoid; red-brown pubescent; terminal buds with incurved, whisker-like scales at tip. Leaves slender, *flattened*, 2–3.5 cm long, pointing forwards, many curving gracefully outwards, well-spaced; at first rich green and shiny above, later deeper green, almost black from mid-distance, two narrow white bands beneath; abruptly fine-pointed.

Flowers and cone. Male flowers large, globular, 3 cm, several towards the ends of hanging shoots, often numerous on old trees; female flowers clustered on branches near top of bigger trees, bright red 4 cm, erect; cone 10–12 × 2.5 cm, cylindric, irregular, *long-tapered to base*, abruptly to apex, purple ripening to light red-brown; scales round-topped, incurved, flexible; patches of white resin.

Growth. Slow, seldom exceeds 25 cm a year. Seedling trees have ascending slender branches, without pendulous shoots until about 1.5 m high; preferable to be patient than to plant grafts which are densely pendulous too low down and poorly shaped and usually one-sided.

Cone

Recognition. Unique crown of hanging, blackish foliage, (but see *P. smithiana*, p. 127).

SIKKIM or EAST HIMALAYAN SPRUCE
Picea spinulosa (Griffith) Henry
Sikkim and Bhutan, Himalaya, about 1878. Rare; collections and a few large gardens. 25 m.

Bark. Pale or pinkish-grey, cracked into circular plates. Oldest trees purplish-grey, shallowly fissured like an oak.

Crown. Very *open*; sparse long shoots arching out from ascending branches near top, lower branches bear short pendulous branchlets. Broad conic top, broad columnar below.

Foliage. Shoot white becoming pale pink-brown in second year. Bud blunt ovoid, light brown, shiny with resin. Leaves 2–3 cm, rather crowded, all *pointing forwards* and straight, *close to shoot and all round it*, slender, sharply pointed, light or rich green above, two *broad silvery bands below*, often united.

Flowers and cone. Female flower dark red, 2 cm; soon 4 cm, purple. Cone seldom seen, 8 × 3 cm, cylindric-ovoid, slightly curved; yellow-green, ripens shining brown.

Growth. Older trees rather slow but some younger trees have made shoots nearly 1 m long.

Similar species. Open crown, pendulous shoots and leaves

Sikkim Spruce

all round shoot pointing forwards distinguish from *P. sitchensis* (p. 139) and *P. likiangensis* (p. 138). *P. brachytyla* (p. 138) has broader leaves parted beneath shoot.

BLACK SPRUCE *Picea mariana* (Mill.) Britten, Sterns and
Poggenberg **Pl. 10**

Syn. *P. nigra* (Ait.) Link

All Canada except tundra; northern USA 1700. Uncommon outside the major gardens for conifers but occasional in small, roadside gardens. 15(21) × 2 m.

Bark. Pinkish-grey, flaking roughly, becoming dark purple with fine grey flakes.

Crown. Conic, sometimes narrowly conic or with narrow top, sometimes broad, always *densely branched*, *blue-grey from distance*, low branches occasionally layered.

Foliage. Shoot pinkish-brown, pubescent; leaves slender, crowded densely all round shoot, small, 1–1.5 cm, soft, those on top pressed forwards, dark green above, two bluish-white bands beneath. Crushed gives menthol aroma (cough-sweets) or balsam.

Flowers and cone. Male flowers small, conic, numerous and crimson. Females crowded in upper crown, small, erect,

Black Spruce

deep red. Cones crowded, hanging in bunches, ovoid 3–4 cm purplish, ripening shiny red-brown. Borne already by trees less than 3 m tall.

Growth. Very slow, usually 15–25 cm a year, June and July.

Similar species. *P. rubens* (p. 134) is closely related also with small leaves but rich green all round, wiry and upcurved, none below shoot. Intermediates occur.

TIGER TAIL SPRUCE *Picea polita* (Sieb. and Zucc.) Carr. **Pl. 10**

Japan 1861. Infrequent; large gardens and collections, one or two churchyards. 18 × 3 m (25.3 × 2.3 m at Stourhead, Wilts.).

Bark. Grey-brown-pink, dark orange, or purplish, rough with large scales of irregular shapes.

Crown. Rather narrowly conic; regular level branching but untidy within, much dead branching retained. Yellowish at distance. Frequent epicormic sprouts.

Foliage. Shoot *stout, shiny cream-white*, becoming buff; bud shining chestnut-red, rounded or short-pointed leaves *all round* the shoot; the stoutest of any spruce, curved forwards, rigid, 1.5–2 cm, very *sharply pointed* and painful to grasp even lightly, yellowish green, some dark.

Tiger Tail Spruce

Cone. 6 × 4 cm, ovoid, pale grey-green with golden margins to scales, ripen to 10 × 5 cm, deep brown.

DRAGON SPRUCE *Picea asperata* Mast.

W. China 1910. Variable tree from wide area of mountains, several forms introduced under various names. Infrequent; collections, a few large gardens, rare elsewhere. 20 × 1.5 m.

Bark. Dark brown, dark grey or purplish-brown, rough; *large papery scales* peeling away and hanging.

Crown. Broadly conic, long *stout branches curving upwards*, each with its plume of short but dense branchlets separated from adjacent branches. Swellings where branches leave bole.

Foliage. Shoot stout, grooved into distinct plates, pale, white at first, soon pinkish-brown, or dusky brown. Bud stout, conic, 1 cm, pale brown, scales free at tips, often spread in rosette. Leaves crowded, *radiating all round stem* but usually more above, slightly forward at sides, much more so on top, some beneath bend backwards; 1.5–2 cm, *bluish-green* with two fine grey lines on each side, *rigid*, abruptly tipped by yellow spine.

Flowers and cone. Male flowers on older trees only, bunched at ends of earlier years' growth, crimson-purple until shed pollen mid-April, ovoid, 3 cm. Females near top, 5–6 cm, deep red, then purple; cones, at first shining green, some scales edged dark purple, later pale brown 8–14 × 2.5 cm, tapering long cylindric, often numerous.

Similar species. Probably likely to be passed as *P. abies*, but rougher, more sturdy as young tree, more open-crowned with age and rigid leaves all round stout shoot, and papery bark.

Dragon Spruce

COLORADO SPRUCE   *Picea pungens* Engelm.

E. Rocky Mts. USA 1862. Type tree very rare; blue or grey cultivars very common everywhere in gardens and parks of all sizes and in towns. 24 m.

'GLAUCA'   **Blue Spruce** (1877).   **Pl. 11**

Bark. Purplish-grey or brown, coarsely flaky, some flakes ash-grey.

Crown. Narrowly conic, sometimes bent; branches level, rather dense, down-swept in biggest trees.

Foliage. Shoot shiny cream-white or pale yellow-brown, (deep purple-brown in some other cultivars). Bud ovoid-conic, 6 mm with long slender scales around

base and papery pale brown scales often curving out in rosette. *Leaves all round shoot* but majority above and *up-swept*, perpendicular curving forwards; lower ones spread; 1.5–2 cm, *stiff*; (dark green in type with pale lines on all four faces), bright blue-grey in common cultivars.

Cone. Long ovoid-conic, often curved 10–12 × 4 cm, purplish-brown ripening grey-brown, scales thin, papery; pale wavy margin finely-toothed.

Blue Spruce cone

Varieties are named selected seedlings from the bluest forms occurring within the natural population in Colorado. 'Koster' ('Kosteriana', ten selections in 1908) is the commonest brightly coloured form with broad white-bloomed bands on each side of the leaf. 'Moerheimii' (1912) is whitest; dense and conic.

Similar species. See *P. engelmannii* 'Glauca' (below). *P. asperata* (p. 131) shares recurved bud-scales and stiff bluish leaves all round shoot but differs in crown, bark and shorter leaves.

ENGELMANN SPRUCE *Picea engelmannii* (Parry) Engelm.
N.W. America 1864. Very rare. Type differs from the cultivar given below, in having green leaves with 2–3 white bands above and two broader white bands beneath. 27 m.

'GLAUCA' With the type in the S. Probably 1809. Infrequent, occasional in gardens, and resembles a rather superior Blue Colorado Spruce. Crown slightly narrower and much cleaner, bark *orange* with fine, papery flakes; leaves *parted widely* beneath the shoot, lie close along the upper side, *soft and flexible*, blue-grey with two white bands above and beneath. Shoot pale pinkish-brown and pubescent near pulvini, minor shoots pendulous. Crushed foliage gives a menthol scent. 15 m (31.5 m Fairburn, Ross-shire).

Engelmann Spruce

Cone, 5 × 2 cm, cylindric, slightly curved, each scale brown with a purple base.

WHITE SPRUCE *Picea glauca* (Moench) Voss
Syn. *Picea alba* Link
Canada, Alaska and northern USA. By 1700. Uncommon; collections. 15 m (28 m in Rhinefield Drive, New Forest).

Bark. Young: pink-grey stippled vertically in white; shallow curving cracks. Old: purplish grey with large circular plates.

Crown. Narrowly conic, open, at first slender and slightly gaunt, more dense and slightly round-topped when old.

Foliage. Shoot clean white and shiny or bloomed pale pink; faintly grooved. Bud pale orange-brown, ovoid, smooth. Leaves numerous but standing well clear of each other, all point slightly forwards, nearly all *stand above shoot*, rounded in section, *grey or pale blue-green* with white lines all round but a little whiter below; stiff but slender. Aroma when crushed said to be "mousey" or foetid, but varies with strength and can be fruity like blackcurrant syrup or sharp like grapefruit. Very even in size, 1.2–1.3 cm.

White Spruce

Cone. Narrowly cylindric, tapering to blunt tip, 5–6 × 1.5 cm soft copper-brown to bright pale orange; scales smoothly rounded, convex.

Similar species. *P. mariana* (p. 131) has pubescent shoot and finer leaves all round the shoot.

KOYAMA'S SPRUCE *Picea koyamai* Shiras.

C. Japan; Korea 1914. Rare; collections only. 18 m.

Bark. Dark purplish-brown flecked with ashy flakes and strips.

Crown. Sturdy and conic, branches ascending, rather dense.

Foliage. Shoot bright orange or brown, buff beneath, hairy in grooves, at least on side-shoots. Bud large, 1–1.5 cm, conic, sharp, pale or purplish-brown, papery scale-tips free around apex. Leaves quadrangular in section, dark blue-green with fine white lines on all sides, strongly parted beneath shoot where perpendicular or slightly backwards, standing clear above shoot and *forwards at 45°*, rather stiff, abruptly bevelled to a point, 1–2 cm; aroma when crushed is strong, rather sweet and like chrysanthemum leaves, or rosemary. Regularly spaced, not crowded.

Koyama's Spruce

Flowers and cone. Male flowers upcurved, 2 cm, yellow, shed pollen in June. Cone cylindrical, bluntly pointed apex, in summer shiny rich green, scales edged purple one side of cone, silver the other – looks lilac-coloured – ripens 5–10 × 3 cm pink-brown, striated scales, margin smooth, purple edged silver.

Growth. Difficult to establish and slow for years but then rapidly builds up large girth and shapely crown with long leading shoot.

Similar species. Most like bluish leafed *P. abies* (p. 135).

RED SPRUCE *Picea rubens* Sarg.

Syn. *P. rubra* (Du Roi) Link

Nova Scotia to North-eastern USA pre-1775. Uncommon; seldom outside collections. 27 × 2.5 m.

Bark. Rich purplish-brown, sometimes dark grey, finely flaking; old trees with small concave plates.

Crown. Narrowly conic and long-pointed; lower branches bend down then sweep upwards; dense.

Foliage. Shoot pale orange or red-brown, densely pubescent or with hairs scattered in grooves. Bud ovoid, red-brown, surrounded by long-pointed, slender brown scales from base. Leaves slender to 1 mm across, well-spaced, curving forwards and upwards, wiry and short, 0.8–1.5 cm, nearly round in section, abruptly short-pointed, *grassy green* in first year, becoming deep green; glossy. Aroma when crushed like candle-wax or apples.

Red Spruce

Flowers and cone. Male flowers crimson, curving upwards when open, 1 cm long. Cone long-ovoid, often in bunches, 3–5 cm, pale orange-brown when ripe; scales convex, slightly toothed, crinkled.

Similar species. Other short-needled spruces with brown, hairy shoots are *P. orientalis* (p. 136) the leaves of which are shorter, blunt, straight, pressed close, and *P. mariana* (p. 131) which has leaves all round shoot, bluish-green and straight, but intermediates occur between this and *P. rubens*.

NORWAY SPRUCE *Picea abies* (L.) Karst. **Pl. 11**
Syn. *P. excelsa* Link

Europe from Alps to Scandinavia and Balkans to Russia, merging eastwards into Siberian Spruce, *P. obovata*. Probably before 1500. Locally abundant, generally common; forest plantations, Christmas-tree crops, game-coverts, shelter-belts, upland farms, gardens. Frequent, if seldom happy or well-placed, in suburban gardens ex Christmas-tree. 43 × 4 m.

Bark. Until about 80 years old coppery-brown, shredding finely into small, papery scales; old trees dark purplish, cracked into hard, smooth, rounded, small plates.

Crown. Regularly conic, branches whorled, ascending in upper parts, others level; descending from lower crown of old trees. Thins much with age. Oldest trees may have big low branches bent abruptly to vertical; forked stems rare. In one form, shoots hang in lines from level branches ascending at tips; seen in a small proportion of the trees everywhere; this is called the 'Comb' form of spruce.

Foliage. Shoot at branch-ends stiff, fairly stout; on branchlets: small hanging, slender; dull orange-brown, grooved, usually glabrous; some (illustrated) pubescent from eastern parts of range. Bud dark brown, ovoid-conic, 5 mm. Leaves spreading each side of and *above* shoot, well parted beneath, upper ones pointing forwards; four-sided, each side the same dark green with a few fine white speckled lines; *hard, stiff*, pointed, 1–2 cm.

bud

Norway Spruce

Flowers and cone. Male flowers at ends of weak hanging shoots on old trees only; 1 cm, globular, crimson then yellow in late May. Female flowers crowded on upper few whorls, except in old trees where spread over crown, dark red, erect, turn down early, ripening, green cone hangs down, turning brown by autumn; 12–15 cm long; cylindrical, broadly rounded apex; width, when open, 5 cm. Scales with smoothly rounded broad or variably acute, crinkled tips.

Growth. Rapid in height when young, 1 m shoot quite common, but slow above 20 m. May–July. Life-span here little over 200 years.

'AUREA' New shoots pale gold in May and June; mostly green from July but some have leaves striped yellow all the year. Rare. 28m (Westonbirt).

'VIRGATA' Snake-branch Spruce 1854. Monstrous rare form in a few large gardens. Needles 2–2.5 cm all round thick pale orange shoots, *no branchlets*, just long branches dividing into a few, arching, branchless shoots. Vigorous, to 20m.

Similar species. *P. asperata* (p. 131) has sharper, stiffer, bluer needles, some pointing downwards; *P. koyamai* (p. 134) needles bluer and stiffer, buds much larger, *P. orientalis* (p. 136) and *P. rubens* (p. 134) have hairy shoots and shorter leaves.

SIBERIAN SPRUCE *Picea obovata* Ledeb.
European Russian to E. Siberia 1908. Rare; sometimes a bushy, low tree, can be

shapely with level branches curving up towards the tips.
Eastern counterpart of *P. abies*. Greyish or buff shoot; bud
6–7 mm orange-brown; lateral leaves may droop below shoot
each side, one leaf by each bud on the shoot standing straight
out; leaves dull, or shiny green all round, slender, 1–1.2 cm,
bevelled abruptly to sharp point. Crushed foliage has a sweet
resinous scent. Female flower ovoid-cylindric deep red, 5 cm.
Cone 5–8 × 4 cm, ovoid-cylindric, curved; scale-tips strongly
decurred, rich dark brown.

Siberian Spruce

ORIENTAL SPRUCE   *Picea orientalis* (L.) Link   **Pl. 11**
Caucasus and N.E. Asia Minor 1839. Frequent all over Britain and Ireland.
33 × 3.5 m. (35 m at Bowood, Wilts.)
Bark. Young trees grey-fawn, roughly speckled. Old trees pinkish-brown,
narrow, circular cracking, forming regular small raised plates.
Crown. Narrowly conic, densely branched in old trees. Young vigorous trees
have upper crown very open; long slender shoots, often *much curved* and *twisted*.
On older trees spiky, new, *slender shoots project* straight from crown.
Foliage. Shoot whitish becoming pale brown, pubescent, often densely. Bud
small, ovoid-conic, red-brown, basal scales with red tips just free. *Leaves the
smallest of any spruce*, 0.6–0.8 cm, upper ones closely pressed; shiny dark green,
round-ended, nearly square in cross-section. Main shoots have leaves all round;
side-shoots have parting beneath.
Flowers and cone. Male flowers ovoid-conic, pointed, deep red then yellow
when shedding pollen, beneath the ends of small branchlets. Female flowers
near top except in oldest trees when sparsely all over crown, red. Cone 7 × 2.5
cm, curved and pointed, purplish grey-green as ripening, then ashen-brown,
resinous.
Growth. Slow when very young or rather old, but very rapid between ten and
50 years, in height and girth.
   'AUREA' 1873. New shoots bright yellow, most turn green by midsummer.
Very striking mid-May to end of June. Rare. 10 m.

Similar species. Sickly *P. abies* (p. 135) are short-leaved but never so short
nor round-ended. *P. rubens* (p. 134) has narrower, curved needles, long-pointed
scales at base of bud and red-brown shoots.

ALCOCK'S SPRUCE   *Picea bicolor* (Maxim.) Mayr
Japan 1861. Rare; collections and biggest gardens. 18 (25) m.
Bark. Dull orange-grey or pinkish-grey, very flaky, later with square plates,
grey-purple.
Crown. Broadly conic or squat; long, gently *upcurving branches* from low on
bole each with narrow dense system of branchlets.
Foliage. Shoot stout, white becoming pale orange, usually glabrous. Leaves
four-sided, lower sides with broad white bands, upper dark bluish-green with
two narrow lines of white. Parted below shoot and curved forwards, those
above shoot forward or nearly erect; 1–2 cm, crowded, rather stiff.
Flowers and cone. Male flowers erect, curved, 2.5 cm dull purple-red, opening to 4 cm and shedding pollen in late May. Female flowers terminal, erect,
ovoid-cylindric 4 cm, deep red. Cone ovoid-cylindric, 8–12 × 5 cm, purplish,
ripening pink-brown, the numerous scale-margins purple and often sharply
curved out and down.

Similar species. Very like *P. jezoensis* (p. 137), but leaves not flat. Also resembles *P. glehnii* (below), the only other spruce with square-sectioned leaves much whiter beneath than above.

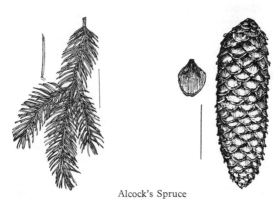

Alcock's Spruce

SAKHALIN SPRUCE *Picea glehnii* (Schmidt) Mast.

N. Japan and Sakhalin 1877. Rare; collections. 21 m. Similar to *P. bicolor* in foliage, but shoot *bright orange*, usually densely pubescent. Crown neat, dense narrow-conic; leaves short, 1–1.5 cm., rhombic cross-section.

Bark. Often rich chestnut-brown; can be dark purple-grey, and very flaky.

Flowers and cone. Female flowers rich red 5 cm. Cone 5 × 1.5 cm, fusiform, pink-purple, resinous.

Sakhalin Spruce

HONDO SPRUCE *Picea jezoensis* (Sieb. and Zucc.) Carr

Korea, Manchuria and Japan (1861), 1879. Only var. *hondoensis* Rehder, Hondo Spruce, from Honshu, thrives, and is described here. Frequent in larger gardens, and collections, rare elsewhere. 30 × 3 m.

Bark. Young trees dark brown finely speckled white; older trees pale dull grey or purplish, smooth, cracked deeply into irregular rectangular plates which may still have white speckling.

Crown. Narrowly conic, dense and untidy along branches but open between; branches level then descending in lower crown.

Foliage. Shoot stout, smooth, *white, shining, grooved*. Bud very smooth, shiny orange-brown, globose. Leaf-buds crimson when unfolding, fat; leaves flat, rich shiny green above, two broad very white bands beneath, both sides keeled; strongly parted below shoot and swept up each side; upper leaves forward, pressed close in new growth, more erect on older shoots; stiff and with short, sharp points. 1.5 cm.

Flowers and cone. Male flowers often pro-

Hondo Spruce

fuse, crimson, droplet-shaped, lengthening and showing yellow as pollen shed mid-May. Female flowers spread well over crown, bright red. Cone cylindric, slightly curved, tapered, 5–8 cm, papery, crinkled scales, jagged margin with 2–3 teeth, incurved, reddish-brown.

Similar species. *P. bicolor* (p. 136). *P. sitchensis* (p. 139) has bluer, stiffer, more slender spreading and sharper leaves; less dense. *P. brachytyla* (below) has leaves more silvered beneath, abruptly pointed, pressed down on shoot, and more open crown.

SARGENT SPRUCE   *Picea brachytyla* (Franch.) Pritz.

W. and C. China 1901. Infrequent; collections and a few large gardens. 26 × 2.5 m so far.

Bark. Young trees: smooth pink-grey freckled with rows of white resin-spots. Older trees: pale grey, purplish or brown in places, shallowly cracked into round plates 5–8 cm across.

Crown. Conic, open and sparse in upper parts, denser lower where smallest shoots are pendulous from rising ends of long, straight branches.

Foliage. Shoot white to pale buff, rather slender, shiny and smooth except for fine grooves; old bud scales orange-brown adhere at base. Bud ovoid, shiny with resin, light chestnut. Leaves flat, light green above, *solid silver-white* beneath, midrib often quite obliterated; keeled both sides, short, blunt to abruptly sharp point, upper leaves *pressed down* on to and *below shoot*; strongly forward-pointing. 1–1.6 cm.

Cone. Spindle-shaped, long-tapered to top, 10–12 × 3 cm, slightly curved, purple and brown; scales with broadly rounded margins, the tips reflexed.

Sargent Spruce

Growth. This tree of lovely foliage is remarkably rapid in growth. One of the two tallest trees, both 26 m, is only 36 years old.

Similar species. *P. jezoensis* (p. 137). *P. spinulosa* (p. 130) has softer leaves all round pendulous shoots.

LIKIANG SPRUCE   *Picea likiangensis* (Franch.) Pritz.   Pl. 10

S.W. China 1910. Infrequent; collections and some large gardens, often many in each. 20 × 2 m. (23 × 2.0 m, Powerscourt, Co. Wicklow.)

Bark. Pale grey, scaly, a few vertical black fissures.

Crown. Broadly conic, rather open; long branches ascending, bare on interior lengths.

Foliage. Shoot pale pinkish-brown or grey, grooved, usually very pubescent. Bud conic-ovoid, shiny red-brown or purplish, resinous. Opening leaf-buds like hanging droplets. Leaves somewhat flattened, *bluish-green* above finely lined white (but see varieties below), two broad white or grey bands beneath 1.5–1.7 cm, lateral leaves curving outwards, upper ones forward along shoot and rising from it, densely set, bevelled at the tip, lower leaves bend forwards from *backward-pointing pulvini*.

Likiang Spruce

Flowers and cone. Both profuse, a remarkable sight in early May when covered with big, crimson, globular male flowers opening cylindric, yellow, on small shoots, and erect, scarlet, ovoid-cylindric, 2 cm female flowers terminal on all stronger shoots. Cone 5 × 1.5 to 13 × 4 cm, slightly tapered, cylindric, scales deep blue-purple edged plum purple in June, ripen pale brown; wavy incurved margins, reddish at the base, flexible.

Varieties. A very variable tree introduced in various forms as different species, now reduced to two varieties which are given below and very different from the type. The first is nearly as frequent as the type. Another form, now merged with the type, is a sturdy beautiful grey-blue tree grown as "*Picea yunnanensis*".

var. *purpurea*

var. *purpurea* (Masters) Dallimore and Jackson. 1910. Described as having more hairy shoots and purpler cones, but these are respectively variable and not always available. At once recognised by its *dense conic top of multiple competing leaders* and dark grassy green colour. The bark is *orange-brown and flaky* and the shorter (1.5 cm) deep green leaves are *pressed down* around the shoot as in *P. brachytyla*, those at the side curving outwards, greyish white beneath, not bright. Cone smaller, 5 × 2.5 cm, fusiform, rich plum-purple in summer. To 22 m.

var. *balfouriana* (Rehder and Wilson) Hillier. Similar but lacks the vertical shoots around the leader and has darker green leaves banded dull grey-green beneath, on densely long-pubescent pink-cream shoots. Leaves 1.2–1.5 cm. Bark brown and scaly. Rare. To 20 m.

SITKA SPRUCE   *Picea sitchensis* (Bong.) Carr.
Kodiak Island in Alaska to Caspar in Mendocino County, California, in a narrow strip along the coast, best developed on the Olympic Peninsula, Washington, where many are 80 m tall. 1831. Locally abundant; the main forest tree of western Britain, planted by the hundred million since 1920; old and large trees in all policies and larger gardens in Scotland and western parts, less common in E. England and absent from town parks or gardens. 53 × 7.5 m (53 × 5 m at Murthly Castle, Perths.; 47 × 6.2 m, Drumtochty Glen, Kincardineshire).

Bark. Young trees dark grey, speckled, flaking, very soon purplish with coarse, lifting scales.; old trees purplish-grey, cracked into small, lifting plates.

Crown. Narrow-conic with long spire even on some very tall trees; upper branches ascending, draped with dense, rather hanging branchlets, lower branches on isolated trees heavy, rising and arching widely over and down with numerous branchlets radiating stiffly at all angles. Boles often have numerous small epicormic sprouts.

Sitka Spruce

Foliage. Shoot white, becoming pale buff, grooved and rather knobbly. Bud blunt ovoid, pale brown, purplish with resin. Leaves flat but strongly keeled, at first radiating all round shoot but later all but a few on lower side are parted and very *straight out flat from shoot, upper ones pressed down* close to shoot along

middle; bright green above; fresh light green
at first then deeper, somewhat shiny with two
narrow white bands except on those towards
base of shoot; two bright blue-white bands beneath; rather slender, 2–3 cm, *sharply pointed*,
hard, stiff. From short distance foliage appears
dark *blue-grey*.

Flowers and cone. Male flowers sporadic, blunt
ovoids, 25 × 15 mm, pale yellow or purple; female
flowers crowded around top of some trees, pale red
or green 2–5 cm; cone short-cylindric, blunt 5–
8 cm, pale green, ripening *nearly white*, scales, *thin*,
papery, with *crinkled* coarsely toothed margins.

Sitka Spruce

Growth. Extremely rapid from third year from seed; annual shoots in fifth year
1–1.5 m. Early May–early August then, if soil moist, "second-growth" until late-
September. This "second-growth" has a whorl of short branchlets at its base,
shoot bright apple-green turning red-brown, deeply grooved, and leaves to 5 mm
broad at base and +3 cm long. In a warm, damp Somerset valley a 47-year-old
tree is 42 m tall, 3 m in girth.

Similar species. Large trees are much bigger in height and girth than any
other spruce. Foliage is most like *P. likiangensis* (above) or *P. jezoensis* (p. 137),
but leaves longer, harder, and spined; shoot never hairy. Plated purplish bark
is distinct, though similar to *P. glauca* (p. 133).

SERBIAN SPRUCE *Picea omorika* (Pančić) Purkyně   **Pl. 11**
Drina Valley, Jugoslavia 1889. Frequent; in some small gardens even near
towns, many larger gardens and parks and a few small forest plantations. Can
thrive on limestone or on deep acid peats and in frost-hollows. The best spruce
in polluted air. 28 × 2 m (25 m at Sheffield Park, Sussex).

Crown. Distinctively spire-like, slender columnar or narrowly conic. Great
variation in density: pencil-slim trees very dense, conic trees often quite open
with upper branches level, lower branches elegantly sweeping down then
curving out and upwards.

Bark. Orange-brown; fine papery scales shredding off; big trees hard square
flakes or plates. Bole often swollen at branch-junctions, hollowed beneath.

Foliage. Shoot pale buff, finely grooved, pubescent; later dull pinkish-brown.
Terminal bud hidden by tuft of leaves; lateral bud pale brown with red-brown
tips free. Leaves 1.2–1.8 cm long, to 2 mm broad,
flat, keeled, broad and blunt or abruptly acute at tip,
upper leaves radiating forwards pressed close to shoot,
lower spreading sideways often curved and somewhat
below shoot; fresh grass-green at first above then
deep or dark bluish-green; two broad white bands
below. The narrowest and most pendulous trees
have bluer, softer leaves all standing up from
shoot, to 2.5 cm long.

Flowers and cone. Male flowers large globules
on hanging side-shoots, crimson in early May just
before shedding pollen; female flowers bright red
on branches nearest top, bend down as dark purple-
blue rather lumpy spindle-shaped pointed cones on

Serbian Spruce

thick curved stalks, ripening dark brown, 6 × 3 cm; scales closely pressed, shallowly rounded with fine, uneven toothing and some patches of resin.
Growth. Rapid; shoots in fifth year from seed to 1.2 m. Short season – mid-May to early July – may grow 15 cm in one week in mid-June; may add short second-growth early August.
Similar species. *P. mariana* (p. 131) and *P. rubens* (p. 134) have crowns approaching this shape but have very different foliage. Among other flat-leaved spruces, the broad blunt leaf-tips are unique. Hybrids with *P. sitchensis* with crowns intermediate in breadth are increasingly seen.

HEMLOCKS   Tsuga

The only connection between these coniferous trees and the Umbelliferous herbs called Hemlocks is the aroma of the crushed foliage. The first one known in Europe (*Ts. canadensis*), was thought to have a similar aroma. It seems to be more like menthol and rather fruity, but crushed *Ts. heterophylla* has an aroma very like another Umbellifer, Ground-elder. Nine species, of which one is aberrant and a rather mysterious hybrid. Related to the spruces, but with softer, delicate foliage ánd, except for the eccentric species, very small, rounded cones. N. America, Himalayas and E. Asia.

Key to Tsuga species

1. Leaves parted each side above shoot   **2**
Leaves not parted above shoot   **7**

2. Shoot with prominent, long pubescence   **3**
Shoot glabrous or very finely short-pubescent   **4**

3. Leaf banded white beneath; leader long, drooping   *heterophylla*, p. 142
Leaf greyish-green both sides, very slender; leader short, nodding at tip   × *jeffreyi*, p. 147

4. Leaf broad, blunt, notched, densely set   **5**
Leaf slender, tapered, round-tipped, scarcely notched, sparsely set   **6**

5. Shoot orange, finely white pubescent (under lens); leaves regularly spaced, brilliant white bands beneath   *diversifolia*, p. 146
Shoot pale brown, glabrous, shining; leaves irregularly placed, often dull white bands beneath   *sieboldii*, p. 146

6. Shoot shining brown; leaves slender, sparse, dark green above, bright white bands beneath   *caroliniana*, p. 143
Shoot pale buff; leaves relatively broad, yellowish-green above, dull greenish-white bands beneath   *chinensis*, p. 143

7. Leaves radially set, thick, bluish or dark grey   *mertensiana*, p. 147
Leaves parted beneath shoot, lying forwards above   **8**

8. Leaf 1–3 cm, rigid, crowded over top of shoot   *dumosa*, p. 146
Leaf 0.5–1 cm, not rigid, single line only over top of shoot, reversed showing underside   *canadensis*, p. 143

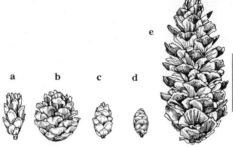

Cones of Hemlocks: **a** Western Hemlock, **b** Chinese Hemlock, **c** Eastern Hemlock, **d** Northern Japanese Hemlock, **e** Mountain Hemlock

WESTERN HEMLOCK   *Tsuga heterophylla* (Raf.) Sarg.   **Pl. 12**
Syn. *Ts. albertiana* (Murray) Senecl.

S.W. Alaska to Siskiyou Mountains and Coast Range in Mendocino County, N. California. To over 70 m in Rainier N.P., Washington. 1851. Common in large gardens, policies and plantations, especially in Scotland. Often planted under hardwood crops. Infrequent in E. England; or near big towns. 45 m at Benmore, Argyll; 38 × 5.3 m at Scone Palace, Perths.; × 5.7 m Drum Ho., Co. Tyrone.

Bark. At first dark grey-green, smooth. Small trees purple-brown, circular flakes lifting away; old trees dark brown, flaking and shredding, **or dark grey** finely fissured; usually fluted boles.

Crown. Regularly conic, narrow until growth in height wanes then broader. *Spire-top* retained to great age, with distant, slender, ascending slightly arched, spirally set shoots near the top and *leading shoot* which *arches* widely over into a 'dropper', hanging often 50–60 cm. Main crown dense, dark green mass of delicate leaves and slender shoots, rather pendulous from straight branches ascending at 45°, gently curved over at tips, low branches on big trees drooping. Single stem straight to the tip; forked or mis-shapen trees very rare.

Foliage. Shoot brown above, cream beneath, ribbed, with dense, long curly, pale brown hairs. Bud small globular, brown; white in spring when expanding. Leaves parted each side of shoot, of mixed sizes, upper rows 0.5–0.7 cm lowest rows 1.5–1.8 cm, 0.2 cm broad, oblong, slightly tapering to rounded tip. Bright fresh green and very matt at first becoming dark green and shiny; two broad bright white bands beneath.

Western Hemlock

Flowers and cone. Male flowers dense amongst leaves on side-shoots right to the ground on old trees, scattered on most trees, none on younger trees; very small globular, bright red turning pale crimson, then whitish-yellow as pollen shed in late April when it adheres to leaves like white dust. Female flowers terminal on 2–3 cm shoots, nodding, ovoid, 6 mm, rich plum-purple. Cones all over old trees on ends of small shoots, pendulous, blunt ovoids, 2–3 cm, few scales; green, often purplish or plum-purple, ripening pale brown.

Growth. Very rapid on light sands or on heavy loams; annual shoots commonly 1 m can be 1.5 m; mid-May to end August. Growing shoot always points downwards; much of 'dropper' straightens during June but leaves the terminal 20 cm or so hanging for rest of growing season. Clips into beautiful, dense hedge.

Similar species. *T. chinensis* (p. 143), *T. canadensis*, (p. 143).

CHINESE HEMLOCK   *Tsuga chinensis* (Franch.) Pritz.
C. and W. China 1900. Rare; conifer collections only; 12m.
Rather dense, broad-based tree or bush with foliage like
Ts. heterophylla but shoots nodding and with *narrow pale
green bands* beneath leaves which are more sparse, make a
spiky shoot and are a paler *yellowish-green* above. Bark at
first has curving patterns of dark green-grey scales, then
dark brown and grey, very flaky; later coarse, oak-like
fissuring occurs. Male flowers singly on one-year shoot;
1–5 bunched on two-year shoot, dull purple, 8mm. Female
terminal on very short shoot, nodding, rosy-purple, 6mm.

Chinese Hemlock

Cone 3 × 1.3 cm long-ovoid, green bronzing red-brown. Scales large, rounded,
appressed. (15 × 1.5 m Bodnant.)

EASTERN or CANADIAN HEMLOCK   *Tsuga canadensis* (L.) Carr.
Pl. 12

E. Canada and USA from Lake States to Alabama 1736. Frequent; large
gardens, smaller gardens and parks in some areas, more in eastern areas than
Ts. heterophylla and nearer towns. Useless in forestry; inferior hedge to *Ts.
heterophylla*. 32 × 4m.
Bark. Young trees orange-brown with flaking ridges; old trees dark dull
purplish-grey much fissured into coarse network of broad, shallow ridges;
corky; fissures pale brown and smoothish.
Crown. Irregular, broad, obtusely pointed, usually heavily
branched from low on bole and loses main axis but, if
single, the bole is sinuous.
Foliage. Shoot cream-brown with dense, curly pale rufous
hairs. Bud 1–2mm, ovoid, green with brown tip bearing
grey pubescence. Leaves mainly in 2–3 rows each side of
shoot but *one row* neatly arranged *along centre line of shoot*
and twisted so white-banded *underside* is *uppermost*;
broadest at base and *tapering gradually* to rounded tip;
fresh green above at first, then dark; two broad bright
white bands beneath; 1–1.2 × 0.1 cm. Young shoots often
arched.

Eastern Hemlock

Flowers and cone. Male flowers very small, 3mm, globular, yellow-green,
crowded along shoots 2–3 years old; shed pollen mid-May. Females 6mm
terminal, pale green. Cone like *T. heterophylla* but smaller; to 1.5 × 1 cm ovoid-
conic, scale margins slightly thickened; ripens coffee-brown.

CAROLINA HEMLOCK   *Tsuga caroliniana* Engelm.
S. Alleghany Mountains, USA 1886. Rare; collections
only; 10m. Small dense tree or tall bush with shining
red-brown or pale pinkish-brown shoots, pubescent in
grooves; distinguished by *spiky narrow foliage*. Leaves
sparse, distantly set and at irregular angles each side of
shoot, *very slender* and brightly white-banded beneath
blackish-green above. Male flowers 4mm red-purple;
females pale purple 3mm. Cone long-ovoid 2.5 × 1.5 cm,
orange-brown with thin, tall, round-topped scales.

Carolina Hemlock

Plate 11   **SPRUCES** (Contd.)

1. Serbian Spruce   *Picea omorika*   140

    (a) Tree 15 m high. All are distinctively narrow, some conic, as
      in the illustration, and some columnar.
    (b) Spray with flat, blunt-ended leaves.
    (c) Spray showing broad white bands beneath leaves.

2. Norway Spruce   *Picea abies*   135

    (a) Young tree of 12 m in late spring with side shoots emerging
      from last year's leading shoot. At other times of year the
      leading shoots appear bare of side shoots.
    (b) Spray with mature cone.

3. Blue Colorado Spruce   *Picea pungens* 'Glauca'   132

Shoot with rigid, spined leaves arising all round.

A very popular tree for small gardens.

4. Oriental Spruce   *Picea orientalis*   136

Spray showing the very short, bevelled-ended, glossy green
leaves. The shoot is orange-brown and pubescent.

5. Brewer Spruce   *Picea brewerana*   127

Spray of the slender, flattened leaves. The shoots hang in long
curtains from up-curved branches making a dense, dark tree.
It grows slowly and none has yet achieved one half of the
stature quite usual in older Morinda Spruce, the other very
pendulous spruce.

Serbian Spruce   Norway Spruce   Blue Colorado Spruce   Oriental Spruce

1a

1b

1c

2a

2b

2c

3

4a

4b

4c

DOUGLAS FIRS, HEMLOCKS   Plate 12

Relatively small or very small, hanging cones, usually borne over the whole crown of older trees.

Douglas Fir   *Pseudotsuga menziesii*   148

(a) Tree of 20 m open-grown. In regions more favourable to this tree it has a more regular, narrow habit.
(b) Spray with mature cone. The soft foliage has a strong fruity scent and is banded with white beneath.
(c) Female flowers opening.
(d) Male flowers about to shed pollen. Some at this stage are crimson around the edges and white in the centre.

Western Hemlock   *Tsuga heterophylla*   142

(a) Young tree 12 m high. The leading shoot remains drooping so long as the tree is still increasing in height, even in trees over 40 m tall. Always a shapely tree.
(b) The undersides of the leaves have broad blue-white bands.
(c) Spray and immature cone. Female flowers are bright crimson. The leaves are parallel-sided.

Mountain Hemlock   *Tsuga mertensiana*   147

Spray with mature cone. The leaves, variably blue-grey, arise from all round the shoots, making short shoots look like the spurs of a cedar. The cones cluster around the top of the tree and are much bigger than those of any other hemlock.

Eastern Hemlock   *Tsuga canadensis*   143

(a) Underside of leaves, similar in colour to those of Western Hemlock.
(b) Spray showing leaves tapering from the broadest part near the base. A line of leaves normally shows well lying along above the shoot, with their white undersides uppermost.
(c) Cone nearly ripe.

Douglas Fir

Western Hemlock

Mountain Hemlock

SOUTHERN JAPANESE HEMLOCK   *Tsuga sieboldii* Carr.
S. Japan 1861. Infrequent; collections and some large gardens. 15 m.
Bark. Dark pink-grey, smooth at first with horizontal folds, later cracking into
squares and becoming flaky.
Crown. Usually multiple-stemmed from base, broadly
conic, pointed, rather dense outside.
Foliage. Shoot pale *shining buff* varying to white or pale
brown, glabrous; bases of leaf stalks red-brown. Bud
narrow-based ovoid, dark orange, scales convex. Leaves
densely set in *irregular* flat rows, *broad and stubby*,
variable in length 0.7–2.0 × 0.2 cm; blunt, notched tips,
shining dark green above, two broad not very bright
white bands beneath.
Flowers. Male flowers terminal on weak shoots, minute
2 mm, globular, cherry-red. Female nodding ovoid,
purple, 5 mm.

Southern Japanese
Hemlock

Cone. Pendulous, ovoid-conic, blunt, 2.3 × 1.3 cm, scales flat-topped; very
dark brown.
Similar species. *T. diversifolia* (below).

NORTHERN JAPANESE HEMLOCK   *Tsuga diversifolia* (Max.)
   Mast.
N. and C. Japan 1861. Much less seen than
Ts. sieboldii; rare outside collections. 15 m.
Differs from *Ts. sieboldii* in bark orange-
brown shallowly fissured pink and flaking
vertically; bud rich purple-red; shoot *bright
orange* or red-brown, with fine pale pubescence
visible under lens; crown low-domed, more
dense; leaves less crowded at least on underside of shoot, more *regular*, *parallel* on second
year shoot, darker, harder, 1 × 0.2 cm, and
brilliantly white-banded beneath. Very dis-
tinct from beneath, with regular broad silvery leaves on orange shoot.

Northern Japanese Hemlock

Flower and cone. Female flower terminal on long or short shoot, dull purple,
ovoid, 5 mm; soon pale green with centre and margin of each scale purple.
Cone cylindric-ovoid, 1.8–2.8 cm dark brown; scales slightly convex and
ridged; pendulous.
Similar species. *T. sieboldii* (above).

HIMALAYAN HEMLOCK   *Tsuga dumosa* (D. Don) Eichler
   Syn. *Ts. brunoniana* (Wall.) Carr.
E. Himalayas 1838. Rare; mostly in Ireland and in S.W.
England, a few in Surrey, Sussex and Kent. 20 m.
Bark. Old trees like an old larch – pinkish, heavily ridged
with broad, shallow, flaky fissures.
Crown. Small trees ovoid, pendulous bushes; older trees
multiple stems from low or one or two sinuous boles;
broad, irregular, open.
Foliage. Shoot pale pink-brown, with fine, scattered

Himalayan Hemlock

pubescence; pendulous. Leaves forward-pointing over upper side of shoot, rigid, distant, large, to 3 cm, tapering from base or middle to rounded end; grooved above; two broad silvery bands beneath. Conelet acute ovoid, blue; 2 cm.

Similar species. The very rare *Tsuga yunnanensis* (Franchet) Masters (China 1908), has softer leaves narrower, pectinate and depressed below shoot, variable in length and in brilliance of the underside.

MOUNTAIN HEMLOCK *Tsuga mertensiana* (Bong.) Carr. **Pl. 12**
Syn. *Ts. hookeriana* Carr.

Alaska to Sierra Nevada, California 1854. Infrequent; in roadside gardens in parts of Scotland, Surrey and such coniferous areas; in large gardens, especially C. Scotland. 20 m. (31 m at Blair Castle, Perths.).

Bark. Dark brownish-orange, finely fissured vertically into rectangular flakes.

Crown. Bushy at first then long spire arises, very narrow and straight with leading shoot nodding at its tip. Branches slightly drooping, each with a narrow *dense system of pendulous* branchlets separated from adjacent branches; more compact where thriving in cool, damp places. Pale grey exterior, blackish interior.

Foliage. Shoot pale, shining brown; short-pubescent. Leaves set *radially* making *short shoots look like the spurs of a cedar*, pointing forwards along shoot, *thick*, narrow, 1.5–2 cm long, smooth rounded tips, uniform dark *grey-green to grey-blue all round.*

Mountain Hemlock

Bright blue-grey trees are grown as 'Glauca' but in native stands trees vary from deep green to pale grey, so the distinction is doubtful.

Cone. Like a spruce-cone, clustered on top shoots, pendulous, cylindric, tapered, to 7 × 3.5 cm (open) with many thin scales; green, ripening deep red-brown.

Growth. Depends on the origin of the seed, far northern seed gives very slow, semi-dwarf trees. Normal trees very slow for ten years or more then quite rapid – hence bushy bases to spired crown. Largest trees in Scotland are growing quite fast.

Similar species. This is an eccentric species in cone and in leaf-arrangement, and none is similar except its hybrid, *T. ×jeffreyi* (below)..

JEFFREY'S HYBRID HEMLOCK *Tsuga × jeffreyi* (Henry) Henry

Hybrid *Ts. mertensiana × heterophylla* not known wild until very recently (Washington 1968 and British Columbia 1970), but raised several times in Britain from Hemlock (and even Rhododendron) seed collected in British Columbia. 1851 Edinburgh. Rare as tree but several recently planted. 14 m. Ovoid bush when young with upswept upper shoots and curious olive-grey coloured foliage. Older trees very like *Ts. mertensiana.* Differs from *Ts. mertensiana* in leaves being *sparse*, spreading each side of shoot and some pointing backwards, *flat* and slender, 1–1.5 cm long, light yellowish-

Jeffrey's Hybrid Hemlock

green both sides; bark deep blackish-brown, finely fissured orange, very scaly. One tree has branches rooting and layered stems arising from them.

DOUGLAS FIRS Pseudotsuga

Five species: two from western N. America, two from China, one from Japan.
Cones with exserted bracts which have three long points; buds slender spindle-
shaped, foliage very soft in all but one species. *Ps. menziesii* and its var. *glauca*
are the only forms likely to be seen, but two others are in cultivation.

Key to Pseudotsuga species

1. Leaves hard, spiny, 4–5 (8) cm   *macrocarpa,* p. 149
   Leaves soft, rounded or notched, 2–3 cm   **2**

2. Leaves notched; shoot glabrous   *japonica,* p. 149
   Leaves rounded; shoot pubescent   **3**

3. Leaves green, pectinate; bud scales entire   *menziesii,* below
   Leaves blue-grey, rising across top of shoot; bud-scales
   fringed   *menziesii* var. *glauca,* p. 149

DOUGLAS FIR   *Pseudotsuga menziesii* (Mirb.) Franco   **Pl. 12**
Syns *P. taxifolia* (Lamb). Brit.; *P. douglasii* Carr.

N. British Columbia to N. California and Rocky Mountains to Mexico 1827.
Locally abundant; common everywhere except near cities and the centres of
large towns; small and large gardens, shelter-belts, game coverts and plantations. 55 × 7m, tallest tree in Britain in 1970 (two Grand Firs equal or taller by
1973); many stands from New Forest and Somerset to Argyll and Inverness have
dominant trees of mean height 40–50m (55m in height at Powis Castle, Monts.,
53m in height at Hermitage, Dunkeld; 6m in girth at Dunkeld Cathedral,
Perths.).

Bark. Young: dark grey-green, resin-blistered. Pole-sized; purple-brown,
finely cracked vertically. Old: from nearly black or dark purple all over to pale
grey-brown with thick, corky, very deep, wide pale brown fissures. Best-shaped
trees have long tawny-brown fissures from early age; rough-branched forms
usually have very corky, dark bark.

Crown. Until top-height reached, slender, regularly conic; branches whorled,
light, ascending; leading shoot slender, curved near tip where young trees have
small whorl of shoots showing 'second-growth'. Old trees flat-topped with heavy,
level branches in upper crown; often huge low branches bending sharply upwards; foliage in dense, heavy, pendulous masses. Some trees thinly crowned;
a number forked; big crowns much broken by gales and snow.

Foliage. Shoot pale green, finely pubescent, sometimes red in young plants.
Bud pale brown, to 7mm, smaller and often bright deep red on minor shoots,
slender *spindle-shaped* like a beech. Leaves readily emit strong, sweet, *fruity-
resinous aroma*; any green colour from yellowish to dark blue-green dusted
glaucous grey above; two variably bright white bands beneath; soft, 2–2.5cm,
rising above and spread each side of shoot with some pointing forwards below.

Flowers and cone. Male flowers close on underside towards tip of last year's
shoot, not dense; open whitish blunt and conic, often plum-purple at edges,
pale yellow and more pointed as pollen shed, early to mid-May. Females also
towards tip but at sides of shoots, 1–3 rarely 5–6 per shoot, open to erect conelets crimson, purple, green or whitish. Cone 5–8 × 2.5cm, hangs green, ripens
dull brown, *three-pronged bracts* project like tongues and point straight towards
tip, middle lobe 1.5cm, whole bract 0.5cm broad at base.

Growth. Very rapid indeed: annual shoots of 1 m common, sometimes 1.5 m in young trees, to 30 m in 30 years, 50 m in 70 years. Early May–late July.

var. *glauca* (Mayr) Franco. Blue Douglas Fir. E. Rocky Mountains, Montana to Mexico 1876. Uncommon but locally frequent in gardens in coniferous areas like S.W. Surrey. 25 m. Slender tree with small branches, distinguished by black, scaly or *pewter-grey* and *black-fissured* bark; fringed bud-scales, *blue-grey, thick leaves* of first year *standing above the shoot*; crushed foliage has little scent; cone fusiform, light copper-brown, 5 × 2.5 cm, bracts long-exserted spreading or *bent right back* towards stalk, to 1.4 × 0.6 cm.

Blue Douglas Fir

'STAIRII' Golden Douglas Fir. *c.* 1870 Wigtownshire. Rare. Slender tree to 20 m, occasionally bushy; with dull golden rather pendulous foliage.

LARGE-CONED DOUGLAS FIR *Pseudotsuga macrocarpa* Mayr

San Gabriel and San Bernardino Mountains, S.W. California 1910. Rare; a few gardens and collections only. 18 m.

Bark. Dull grey; wide, shallow, parallel brown fissures.
Crown. Rather broadly conic; very whorled, slightly descending branches, rather open. (In California, long, thinly foliaged descending branches like *Sequoia sempervirens*.)
Foliage. Shoot pale red-brown, fawn or olive, becoming grey; slightly pubescent. Buds red, apex pale, to 8 mm. Leaves ± parted each side of shoot, curving forwards, *hard, stiff*, slender, abruptly sharp-pointed, yellowish or dark, shiny green above, two bright white bands beneath; only slightly aromatic when crushed, 4–5 (8) × 0.2 cm.

Large-coned
Douglas Fir

Cone. 8–18 cm, bracts only slightly protruding, straight (not known here).

JAPANESE DOUGLAS FIR *Pseudotsuga japonica* (Shiras.) Beiss.

S.E. Japan 1910. Very rare. 12 m. A small tree, seldom thriving.

Bark. Dark grey-pink, irregularly cracked.
Crown. Slender, gaunt; level branches.
Foliage. Short shoots tend to stand above branches in *flat layers* and have blunt, notched, yellowish, often curved leaves broadly banded bright white beneath, *spread all round* the pale whitish-green and brown, glabrous shoot; 2.5 cm, no fragrance. The shoot retains at its base some chaffy dark brown and white bud-scales from the ovoid red-brown buds.

Japanese Douglas Fir

Cone. Often numerous 5 × 3 cm, narrow-tipped, dark grey-brown; very few scales, each basal one large with big, smooth very convex curve; bracts exserted, shorter ones straight, longer ones decurved.

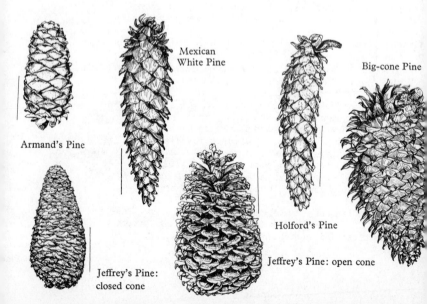

150

PINES Pinus

Eighty species in northern hemisphere and across Equator to Java; biggest number in Mexico. Seedlings bear spirally set silvery blue, serrated linear leaves (primordial leaves), the axil of each then bears a short shoot, undeveloped, ending in a bundle of needles (adult leaves). Needles in bundles of two, three or five normally but strong shoots of a two-needle pine may bear a few bundles of three, four and five needles and a few species are inconstant but basically three or five-needled. In two-needled pines each needle is semi-circular and usually rather stiff, in three and five-needled pines each needle is triangular and with five needles derived from the division of a single shoot, they are very slender, often lax and blue; these trees are thus distinguishable from a distance. Male flowers (more accurately "strobili") clustered around base of new shoot, sometimes along four-fifths of shoot. Female flowers ("strobili") at tip of new shoot or, in a few species, in a whorl some way below the tip.

Pine cones develop from the enlarging flower only during their second summer so are nearly two years old when ripe, except in *P. pinea* in which a third season is needed. The general shapes accord roughly with whether the species bears its needles in bunches of two, three or five. The cones of two-needled pines tend to be small (except *P. pinea*), globose or conic; they open widely and are retained in many species for many years on the tree. Three-needled pines tend to have massive cones, globose or conic, often retained many years on the tree. Five-needled pines have predominantly cylindric cones with thin, pliable scales, but a few (*P. cembra, flexilis, armandii*) have short-cylindric cones with thick scales; none is retained long on the tree once ripe; many are very resinous.

Typical pine cones

Mexican
White Pine

Big-cone Pine

Armand's Pine

Holford's Pine

Jeffrey's Pine:
closed cone

Jeffrey's Pine: open cone

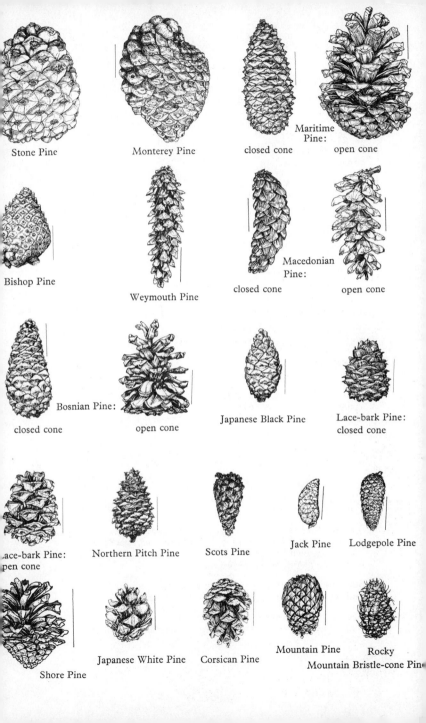

Stone Pine

Monterey Pine

Maritime Pine:

closed cone

open cone

Bishop Pine

Weymouth Pine

Macedonian Pine:

closed cone

open cone

Bosnian Pine:

closed cone

open cone

Japanese Black Pine

Lace-bark Pine:
closed cone

Lace-bark Pine:
open cone

Northern Pitch Pine

Scots Pine

Jack Pine

Lodgepole Pine

Shore Pine

Japanese White Pine

Corsican Pine

Mountain Pine

Rocky Mountain Bristle-cone Pine

Key to Pinus species

(Based primarily on foliage, for use with picked shoots, but secondarily on cones and tree features for use in field.)

1. Leaves in pairs   **2**
Leaves in bundles of three or five   **22**

2. Leaves 3–10 cm long   **3**
Leaves 10–20 cm long   **15**

3. Bud-scales free at the tips   **4**
Bud-scales appressed at tips or coated in resin   **9**

4. Bud-scales curved outwards or rolled down   **5**
Bud-scale tips straight, vertical   **6**

5. Shoot whitish-green; leaves crowded, deep green   *densiflora*, p. 174
Shoot grey-green and orange-brown; leaves sparse, light green   *halepensis*, p. 172

6. Shoot orange-brown; leaves 6 cm, stiff, dark grey-green; cone scales long-decurved   *uncinata*, p. 174
Shoot pale, yellowish or greenish   **7**

7. Bud silky white; shoot golden-brown   *thunbergii*, p. 173
Bud red-brown; shoot whitish, pink, green-fawn   **8**

8. Leaves 9–10 cm, slender, deep green   *densiflora*, p. 174
Leaves 3–7 cm, thick, broad, bluish   *sylvestris*, p. 170

9. Bud with long, sharp point from broad base; scales papery-edged, foliage whorled   **10**
Bud cylindric, or ovoid, short-pointed; bud-scales not papery-edged   **11**

10. Shoot pale brown, ± bloomed grey, second year grey-brown; young cones bright deep blue; crown neat; bark smooth, grey   *leucodermis*, p. 173
Shoot dark green-brown, second year dark orange-brown; young cone pale brown; crown rough, bark deeply fissured and scaly   *nigra* var. *nigra*, p. 171

11. Bud slender, straight, pale brown; shoot slender, smooth; cone pointing forward, smooth; branches depressed; bark orange-brown fissures   *banksiana*, p. 178
Bud ovoid or bright red-brown or twisted   **12**

12. Bud straight; leaves blue or deep grey-green, cone not prickly   **13**
Bud twisted; leaves bright or dark green, cone prickly   **14**

13. Bud cylindric; leaves bluish, foliage not whorled   *sylvestris*, p. 170
Bud ovoid; leaves deep grey-green, foliage in short whorls   *uncinata*, p. 174

14. Leaves 6–9 cm, flattened, spreading; crown open *contorta* var. *latifolia*, p. 175
Leaves 4–5 cm, slender, crowding close to shoot; crown dense
contorta var. *contorta*, p. 174

15. Upper bud-scales free at tips, usually strongly decurved   **16**
Upper bud-scales scarcely free, not decurved; usually tightly
pressed or enclosed in resin   **18**

16. Leaves slender, flexible, 12–15 cm, fairly dense *halepensis* var. *brutia*, p. 173
Leaves stout, stiff shorter or longer, sparse   **17**

17. Leaves 10–12 cm, dark green; cone squat, smooth, 10 × 10
cm   *pinea*, p. 170
Leaves 15–20 cm, pale grey-green; cone oblique-conic, 10
× 5 cm   *pinaster*, p. 169

18. Bud long-cylindric, tapered, purple-white with resin on dark
red-brown; leaves stout; cones adhering all over tree,
stoutly prickled   *muricata*, p. 178
Bud short-cylindric or conic, sharply pointed, cones soon
shed, smooth   **19**

19. Shoot shining yellow-brown; leaves 12–18 cm, twisted
nigra var. *maritima*, p. 172
Shoot orange or orange-brown; leaves straight   **20**

20. Shoot bright orange; leaves snapping cleanly when bent
sharply; foliage markedly whorled; bark of branches red-
brown   *resinosa*, p. 171
Shoot yellow-green or pale orange; leaves not snapping when
bent sharply; foliage not markedly whorled, bark dark
purple-grey   **21**

21. Leaves slender, 15–18 cm, grey-green   *nigra* var. *cebennensis*, p. 172
Leaves stout, 10–15 cm, dark green   *nigra* var. *caramanica*, p. 172

22. Leaves in bundles of three (predominantly)   **23**
Leaves in bundles of five (occasionally more, or some in threes)   **29**

23. Leaves less than 15 cm   **24**
Leaves more than 15 cm   **26**

24. Leaves very slender, lax, bright, deep green; cone 12 × 9 cm,
ovoid   *radiata*, p. 165
Leaves not slender, stiff; cones 4 cm long   **25**

25. Leaves serrate to touch, dark grey-green, slightly twisted;
shoot orange-brown or whitish-green (epicormics); bark
roughly fissured, orange-brown   *rigida*, p. 166
Leaves very smooth to touch, dark yellow-green, straight;
foliage sparse, shoot olive-green. Bark smooth, colourful
bungeana, p. 169

26. Leaves bright greyish-green, very slender and pendulous; bark bright orange   *patula*, p. 167
Leaves blue-grey or dark green, stout, spreading; bark not orange   **27**

27. Bud bright orange, to 6 cm long, some scale-tips free; leaves 25–30 cm, blue-grey, widely spreading, often crinkled   *coulteri*, p. 168
Bud dark red-brown, to 4 cm long; leaves 15–23 cm, rather forward, straight   **28**

28. Shoot shining red-brown or green-brown, without bloom; leaves dark green, cone ovoid, to 9 × 5 cm; bark red-brown to cinnamon, scaly   *ponderosa*, p. 167
Shoot pale blue-grey ± bloomed violet; leaves pale grey; cone broad-based ovoid 18 × 7 cm, opening to 15 cm across; bark nearly black   *jeffreyi*, p. 167

29. Leaves similar colouring on inner and outer surface   **30**
Leaves blue-white inner surface, green or blackish outer surface   **32**

30. Leaves about 8 cm, dark green, bundles scarcely open first year; shoot pale apple-green; short shoot dark grey, thick, spur-like   *flexilis*, p. 156
Leaves more than 10 cm, grey-green or blue to grey, spreading   **31**

31. Shoot very stout, dark orange-brown or bright orange; leaves 25–28 cm, pale blue-grey; (crown broadly domed)   *montezumae*, p. 163
Shoot not stout, pale grey-blue, bloomed; leaves 10–20 cm, dull grey or green-grey; (crown gaunt, tall)

montezumae var. *hartwegii* p. 164

32. Leaves densely curved forward over shoot, hard, short, 2–4 cm, persisting five years or more, bright green outside first year; shoot densely pubescent, reddish (Foxtail pines)   **33**
Leaves not crowded forwards along shoot nor persisting more than four years; soft   **34**

33. Foliage spotted white; leaves abruptly short-pointed (cone with long spreading spines)   *aristata*, p. 164
Foliage not spotted white; leaves tapering to slender spine, second year leaves curving less closely than in *P. aristata*; (cone without spines)   *balfouriana*, p. 165

34. Shoot densely and obviously pubescent   **35**
Shoot glabrous or slightly and finely pubescent   **38**

35. Shoot red-brown from long pubescence of that colour   **36**
Shoot buff or olive, very short pubescence, pale   **37**

36. Leaves 7–9 cm; main shoots abruptly upturned; cut leaf shows two resin-drops; (crown dense and columnar)   *cembra*, p. 155
Leaves 10–12 cm, main shoots in long curve; cut leaf shows three resin-drops; (crown open, conic)   *koraiensis* p. 156

37. Shoot buff or copper brown; foliage separated in whorls, palish green outside surface; bud with free and decurved scales *monticola,* p. 159

Shoot dark olive-green; foliage not whorled, leaves forward along new shoots, dark green outer surface; bud with straight acute scales *lambertiana,* p. 162

38. Leaves 4–10 cm **39**
Leaves 12–20 cm **41**

39. Leaves 4–8 cm, twisted, blue-green outer surface; bud with scales free at tip, foliage layered above branches; (cone erect, ovoid, scales incurved) *parviflora,* p. 163

Leaves 8–10 cm, slender, straight, forward along strong shoots, dark green outer surface; (cone pendulous, curved, narrow-cylindric) **40**

40. Shoot bright green, glabrous; (cone scales incurved at tip; tree densely columnar) *peuce,* p. 158

Shoot brownish pale green, pubescent on pulvini; (cone scales strongly curved out at tip, tree open, wide crown) *strobus,* p. 157

41. Shoot pale green, bloomed violet, stout; leaves 18–20 cm *wallichiana,* p. 156

Shoot deep, bright or brownish-green, slender; leaves 12–18 cm **42**

42. Shoot deep green, exuding resin, glabrous; foliage confined to tip of shoot; new leaves hanging in nearly closed bundles, not slender; (crown open; branches level; cone ovoid 14 ×5 cm) *armandii,* p. 159

Shoot pinkish-green or bright green, pubescent (under lens); leaves very slender; cones long-cylindric, tapered, 18–30 cm, orange **43**

43. Shoot apple-green; cone variable in breadth and taper; leaves 14–18 cm, deep glossy green outer surface; (bark fissured orange-brown) × *holfordiana,* p. 162

Shoot pinkish-fawn-green; cone variable in length always long-tapered; leaves 12–15 cm, pale or mid glossy-green outer surface; (bark deep purple, deeply cracked into squares) *ayacahuite,* p. 162

AROLLA PINE; SWISS STONE PINE *Pinus cembra* L.

Alps, Carpathians 1746. Frequent; large gardens, sometimes small gardens and town parks. 17 × 2 m (27.5 × 3.3 m at Taymouth Castle, Perths.).

Bark. Dark grey or orange-brown, shallow broad fissures red-brown; dark lifting scales.

Crown. *Columnar; short level branches* turning up at ends retained down to ground level.

Arolla Pine

Foliage. Shoot green-brown covered in *short, dense, brown* pubescence. Bud ovoid-conic sharply pointed, pale brown, long acute scales pressed close to point. Needles shining dark green outer surface, inner blue-white from fine white lines; bundles of five not opened fully, densely set, forward-pointing; mass of papery scales at bases; 7–9 cm.

Arolla Pine

Flowers and cone. Male flowers bunched at base of short shoots, in ring 3–5 cm deep; ovoid, purple-tinged, open yellow, 3 cm. Female ovoid, dark red. Conelet rich plum-purple, 1 cm. Cone 8 × 6 cm, tall blunt ovoid, scales swollen, hard, large, tips projecting; deep blue through the summer, ripening glossy red-brown; on old trees only. Seed held until after cone shed; often eaten out of cones on ground by mice and squirrels.

Growth. Slow but steady, seldom more than 30 cm a year; best in north and north-western regions.

KOREAN PINE   *Pinus koraiensis* Sieb. and Zucc.
E. Asia 1861. Rare. Foliage similar to *P. cembra* but needles longer, 10–12 cm, *spreading and lax*, brighter green outer and blue-white inner surface when healthy but some are sickly with short yellowish needles. Expanding shoots rich, dark red, early May. Bark *pink-brown* or purplish, and grey, flaking into small, lifting scales. Crown wider *conic and open*. Male flowers crimson. Attractive when young. 19 m. Cone conic, 15 × 8 cm, deep blue-green.

LIMBER PINE   *Pinus flexilis* James
E. and S. Central Rocky Mountains to 10,000 ft. and above in Sierra Nevada and White Mountains 1851. Rare; some collections mostly in S. England. 17 × 2 m.
Bark. Smooth, horizontally wrinkled, dull pink-grey; later brown shallowly cracked.
Crown. Sturdy, lower branches level, clothed in short, dark grey, knobbly, flexible shoots; upper branches ascending, *projecting* widely with foliage *closely appressed*.
Foliage. Shoot pale apple-green; fine brown pubescence. Bud pointed, cylindric-conic, to 1.3 cm; free scales red-brown, closely pressed scales pale. Leaves in fives, closely held in widely spaced bundles; pulvini dark grey, wrinkled; leaf 8 cm *dark green all round*; quite smooth, entire margin. Sheath pale red-brown soon shed.

Limber Pine

Flowers and cone. Male flowers in shallow ring at base of shoot; ovoid, 5 mm, yellowish-green. Cone conic, long-tapered from broad base, 12 × 5 cm; scales thick, those at the base reflexed; dark orange-brown, very rounded, slightly toothed margins; much resin.

Similar species. Tree like a sturdy broad *P. strobus* (p. 157) but leaves similar colour on all surfaces and entire; in widely spaced bundles; green shoot and different cone distinguish.

BHUTAN PINE   *Pinus wallichiana* Jacks.   **Pl. 13**
   Syns. *P. excelsa* Wall.; *P. griffithii* McClelland
Afghanistan to Nepal 1823. Common; in large gardens, often in town parks and gardens. 35 × 3 m.

Bark. Very shallow fissures of orange- or pink-brown between small grey ridges; rather oak-like.

Crown. Conic, open and whorled when young and growing fast, later rough, wide, heavily branched, with wide-spreading drooping branches; oldest trees much broken by snow, often dead at the top.

Foliage. Shoot stout, pale grey-green, thickly *bloomed violet-grey* at first; somewhat ribbed, glabrous. Bud orange and grey, cylindric, often pointed; scales free at tips. Length varies greatly with vigour of shoot. Leaves in fives, *bluish-grey* (green outer, blue-white inner surfaces) lax, very slender, forward and pendulous, some bundles with each needle crimped at same point; 18–20 cm long.

Flowers and cone. Male flowers from tenth year or earlier and on all older trees, crowded on basal part of new shoots, scattered farther up long shoots; ovoid-cylindric, 1–2 cm, pale yellow when shedding pollen in early June. Female flowers 1–2, on 3–4 cm stalks like clubs at ends of shoots, on trees from eighth year; erect, 2.5 cm, pinkish in first year; second year become cones, hanging and banana-like, dark blue-grey and green, encrusted in resin, clear or white; mature to woody, dark brown, white-resined, curved, cylinders 20–30 cm long, opening to 10 cm across. Basal scales near stalk small and usually bent back.

Growth. Fast when young – 28 m in 40 years known; later growth in girth very slow when height growth ends. Mid-April to mid-July. Ultimate age here likely to be about 150 years, oldest trees now senile.

Similar species. *P. strobus* (below) often confused but differs widely; *P. ayacahuite* (p. 162) and *P. × holfordiana* (p. 162).

WEYMOUTH PINE   *Pinus strobus* L.

Eastern N. America, Newfoundland to Georgia where once known to 80 m tall. 1705. Frequent; mostly as rather broken, blackish old trees; few young ones since planting discouraged by Blister-rust disease which is killing many of the older trees. Occasional in parks and churchyards near towns. Named after Lord Weymouth who planted many at Longleat in early eighteenth century.

Bark. Blackish, purplish or grey-pink; narrow, short fissures.

Crown. Young tree narrowly conic, open, with slight bend in leading shoot; older tree irregular but with several narrow, conic apices until very old when flat-topped. Branches often upswept, upper ones always with spiky, narrow shoots spreading widely, dense in places but thins with age when lower crown dies.

Foliage. *Shoot slender*, bright green when new, then pale green-brown, not bloomed; minute hairs on pulvini and on the slight ridges below. Bud ovoid-conic, pointed, orange-brown, the tip dark brown with long pointed scales appressed.

Weymouth Pine

Leaves in fives 8–12 cm (short) staying *close together in bundles* and forward close to shoot, none on inner length of shoot; dark green, blackish from distance but fine white lines on inner surfaces, very slender.

Flowers and cone. Male flowers small 6 mm ovoids, whitish, tipped bright cerise, on basal 3 cm of new shoot. Females terminal 1–4, slender, cylindric-conic, incurved 1.5 cm, pale pink; first year cone straight, 9 × 2 cm, bright green, each scale tipped lilac. *Cone small*, 10–15 cm (very rarely 25 cm) pointed, slightly curved, narrow, 4–5 cm broad when convex scales open and *curve outwards*; some resin.

Growth. Young trees can grow fast but not for long. Leaders to 1 m long are slender and *slightly sinuous* with needles *tufted near the top*, sparse in the middle, absent from the lower part. Age limit 200 years at most.

Similar species. *P. lambertiana* (p. 162) is most similar but shoot fully pubescent. *P. wallichiana* (p. 156) confused with it but much longer leaves and cone and stout bloomed shoot.

MACEDONIAN PINE   *Pinus peuce* Griseb.

S.W. Balkans 1864. Infrequent; large gardens, a few high altitude plantations recently planted. 20 m (31 × 3.8 m at Stourhead, Wilts.).

Bark. Young trees: grey-green, finely cracked with red-brown. Old trees: smooth areas dark purple, cracked areas blackish, or dull grey all over finely fissured into short narrow plates.

Crown. Neat, *broadly columnar*, conic tip, dense to ground at all ages when open-grown, upswept upper branches, often heavy basal branches but keeps a good shape.

Foliage. Shoot greyish from bud, soon bright *apple-green, smooth*. After nearly one year, brownish. Bud cylindric, abruptly pointed, grey-white with hairy fringes on scales which are free at the tip. Leaves in fives, bundles *densely set*, slender, 8–12 cm not spreading widely, dark blue-green, white lines on all surfaces, fine on outer, broad on inner. Lower third of shoot bare of leaves.

Macedonian Pine

Flowers and cone. Male flowers clustering close to the base of small shoots, conic, pointed, shed pollen mid-June when upcurved, 12 mm and purplish-yellow. Female flowers terminal, slender ovoid, open pale green and pink, soon rosy and deep plum-purple, 18 mm. Cone 10–15 × 3.5 cm (closed), curved at base and slightly at tip, cylindrical, resinous, bright deep green, ripening in September to dark red-brown, scales grey-tipped, convex, tips incurved.

Growth. Steady but not fast, shoots to 50 cm when young and nearly as much thereafter so far. Early May–early July. A robust and healthy tree resistant to Blister-rust and exposure.

Macedonian Pine cones, closed and open

Similar species. *P. armandii* (below) also has green shoots but sparse, pale, stouter leaves. *P. strobus* (p. 157) has similar cones.

ARMAND'S PINE   *Pinus armandii* Franch.

W. China 1897. Rare; many collections except in Scotland. 18 m.

Bark. Smooth at first with shallow curving cracks, grey-purple; later dark purple, deeply cracked into rough, large square plates.

Crown. Broadly conic and open; long, *level, sinuous* branches bare of foliage except near tips; markedly whorled, often asymmetric.

Foliage. Shoot deep or yellowish-green, shiny with minute blobs of resin which later become small white lumps, glabrous. Bud small, 0.5 cm, ovoid, pale red-brown, resinous. Leaves in fives rather *sparse* at *ends of shoot* only, *drooping* in closed bundles, bright shiny green, sometimes dull greyish outer surface, pale whitish-green inner surface, 12—14 cm, many bunches sharply curved near their base. Bare base of shoot bears 2 mm brown scales.

Armand's Pine

Flowers and cone. Male flowers ovoid, 8 mm, whitish-green with cerise tip in long whorl to 10 cm long, shed pollen mid-June. Females 1–3 at tip of shoot, 2 cm, erect, on 3 cm stalk, bright red. One year cone erect ovoid 6 × 4 cm blue-green. Two year cone on 3 cm stalk, conic-ovoid or *barrel-shaped*, domed, 8–14 × 5 cm; erect; scales *thickened*, incurved; deep shining green ripening orange-brown becoming dark purple-brown. "Twinned", double cones frequent on some trees.

Similar species. *P. ayacahuite* (p. 162), *P. wallichiana* (p. 156) and, in glabrous green shoot, *P. peuce* (p. 158).

WESTERN WHITE PINE   *Pinus monticola* Dougl. ex D. Don

British Columbia to Montana and California 1831. Old trees now rare due to deaths from Blister-rust; smaller trees infrequent. 30 m. (37 m Patterdale Hall.)

Bark. Smooth dark grey, blistered becoming purplish, narrowly fissured, smooth and blistered between fissures.

Crown. Broadly columnar with tapering, conic upper parts. Appears from moderate distance to have black foliage on clean, shiny dark grey branches. Young trees fairly dense, old trees thinly crowned.

Foliage. Shoot brownish-green, *coppery*, very *finely and densely* pubescent. Bud ovoid-conic, sharply pointed with long free tips to scales, dark orange-brown. Leaves in fives densely set, 10 cm, *straight and stiff*, dark blue-green outer surface, inner white with fine lines. Length of bare shoot between annual tufts of foliage.

Cone. Usually numerous in *hanging bunches*, to 22 × 4 cm long-conic tapering to slender point, pur-

Western White Pine

Plate 13   **PINES**

Needles in bunches; cones two years ripening, often very woody and spined, especially the ovoid cones; long cones at first leathery.

1. Maritime Pine *Pinus pinaster*   169

   (a) Shoot (bent for convenience: it is straight in life) expanding in June, with female flowers open at the tip and one-year cones at the base, starting to enlarge.
   (b) Mature cone, unopened and shining rich brown.

2. Monterey Pine *Pinus radiata*   165

   A very familiar tree in S.W. England and in Ireland.
   (a) Leaves, three in a bundle, slender, bright green.
   (b) Close-up of bark of old tree. Crevices can be 15 cm deep.
   (c) Cone, closed but many years old. Whorls of cones often stay tightly fixed on tree for twenty years or more.

3. Corsican Pine *Pinus nigra* var. *maritima*   172

   (a) Leaves, two in a bundle, greenish-grey. On young trees they are very twisted.
   (b) Tree 43 m high showing typical crown.
   (c) Spray with vertical bud lengthening and one-year conelet at base.
   (d) Dried and open old cone.

   This tree is the main forest-tree of the sandy areas and shallow peats in Eastern and Midland England.

4. Bhutan Pine *Pinus wallichiana*   156

   (a) Mature, open cone as found beneath the tree. It looks too good to leave there but the white resin transfers to fingers and clothes readily, and off them again far less readily.
   (b) Spray showing slender leaves in bundles of five, more usually deep blue-grey, and pendulous.

   A tree seen surprisingly often in gardens on the outskirts of towns. It becomes broad and irregular in crown.

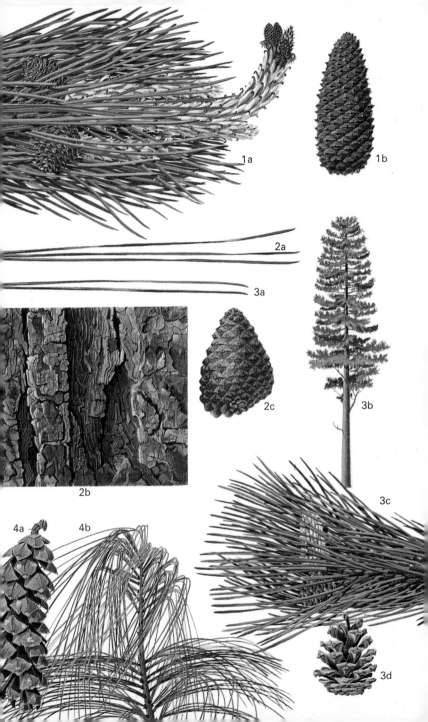

1a

1b

2a

3a

2b

2c

3b

3c

4a 4b

3d

PINES (Contd.)

Plate **14**

1. Western Yellow Pine   *Pinus ponderosa*   167

(a) Leaves, three in a bundle, long and fairly stout.
(b) Spray showing winter-buds. Shoot brown and green, shining.
(c) Cone with spreading or decurved spines.

Jeffrey's Pine, somewhat less frequent, has a bloomed grey-blue shoot; greyer leaves and a cone much broader and bigger, particularly when dry and open.

2. Scots Pine   *Pinus sylvestris*   170

The common pine, semi-wild in S. England, truly wild in N. and C. Scotland.
(a) Leaves, two in a bundle, short, thick and blue-grey.
(b) Spray with maturing cone, deep glossy green.
(c) Opening cone.

3. Japanese Black Pine   *Pinus thunbergii*   173

Golden brown shoot; conspicuous silky white bud in winter.

4. Bosnian Pine   *Pinus leucodermis*   173

Cone in late summer, maturing from deep cobalt blue to purple.

The tree is a dark-leafed, two-needle pine of a most shapely ovoid habit and clean grey bark. A few trees are narrowly conic.

Japanese Black Pine

plish-brown, on short, stout stalk; scales numerous, lower ones much ben
towards stalk.
Similar species. *P. lambertiana* (below) less whorled more lax foliage, *P*
ayacahuite (p. 162) has longer leaves and less densely pubescent shoots.

SUGAR PINE   *Pinus lambertiana* Dougl.
Mid-Oregon to S. California where known to 75×12m 1827. Rare. Old tree
all killed by Blister-rust but healthy young trees in some gardens and collec
tions. Similar to *P. strobus* in short needles (10cm) in fives closely pressed for
ward along shoot, but shoot dark olive-green with pale *red-brown pubescence ai*
over. Broken twigs give strong citrous scent. Leaves crowded almost to base o
shoot, spread widely near shoot-tips, deep green outside, brilliant blue-whit
inside, slightly twisted. Cones probably no longer seen here; largest of the pines
cylindric to 45×10cm.

MEXICAN WHITE PINE   *Pinus ayacahuite* Ehrenb.
Mexico to Guatemala 1840. Infrequent; collections. 25m.
Bark. Dark purplish-brown, densely and coarsely flaking or in rough squar
plates; wide, shallow fissures pinkish-buff inside on some trees.
Crown. Young trees open with slightly sinuous leading shoot, broadly conic
old trees dense towards conic pointed top, lower branches *long, sinuous, level.*

Foliage. Shoot pale green, pinkish and
brownish-green, very fine pale pubescence.
Bud ovoid-conic 6–7mm, smooth pale red-
brown, a few scales free at the tip. Leaves in
fives *spreading*, slender, 13–15cm, sometimes
kinked, dark blue-green on young trees (some
older trees dull grey-yellow-green); bright
blue-white inner surfaces.

Flowers and cone. Male flowers small,
8mm, widely spaced (1.5cm apart) along
15cm of long shoots; pale green with bright
pink tip or pale yellow. Female flowers 2–3   Mexican White Pine
terminal, erect on 2cm stalks, bright red; conelets bright green; scales tippe
blue-green and orange. Cone pendulous on a stout 2cm stalk; long, conic
tapering to long point, variable in length (20–40cm) and in width, when ope
(6–15cm) and in degree of curvature of scales: some have only basal scale
well reflexed, others have most reflexed and basal extremely so. Pale orange
brown scales with dark purple-brown apices.
Similar species. *P.* × *holfordiana* (below); *P. armandii* (p. 159).

HOLFORD'S PINE   *Pinus* × *holfordiana* A. B. Jacks.
Hybrid raised at Westonbirt in 1904, identified from the
cones in 1933. Seed from *P. ayacahuite* pollinated by *P.*
wallichiana beside it. Four original groups and others at
Westonbirt, single trees in many other collections and
gardens. 28×3m. Very vigorous.
Bark. Similar to *P. wallichiana*, *orange-brown*, finely
fissured
Crown. Young trees vigorous and sinuous, wide, level
sinuous branches; old trees conic, level-branched; bole
often swept at base, crown open.

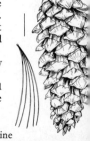

Holford's Pine

Foliage. Shoot more slender than *P. wallichiana*, pale green with fine buff pubescence. Bud long, 5–7mm on side-shoots, broad cylindrical base, conic top, pale green-brown. Leaves in fives, slender, straight, 14–18cm, blue-green (deep glossy green outer surface, white inner).

Cone. Broader than *P. wallichiana*, 20–30 × 8cm and more tapered but mostly much less so than in *P. ayacahuite* and scales point forwards except tiny ones by the 4cm stalk. Orange turning dark orange-brown. Very resinous.

Similar species. Like a long-leafed *P. ayacahuite* (p. 162) but broader and with orange bark. Differs from *P. wallichiana* (p. 156) in pubescent, not bloomed, slender shoot. Cone varies from near Mexican white Pine (as on p. 150) to much broader.

JAPANESE WHITE PINE *Pinus parviflora* Sieb. and Zucc.

Japan 1861. Frequent in large gardens, occasional in small gardens, commonly in 'Japanese-style' gardens. Usual form probably a Japanese semi-dwarf selection; to 10m, a few of the normal wild form to 25m (Stourhead, Wilts.).

Bark. Purplish-grey with areas of curling, blackish scales.

Crown. Usual form low; wide, *level or drooping branches* carrying foliage on the upper side *in layers* of short, spreading branchlets. Tree form broad columnar, level light branches. Vigorous young trees broad, shapeless; upcurved branches.

Foliage. Shoot greenish-white, very finely pubescent. Bud ovoid, pale orange-brown, scale-tips free. Leaves in fives, 5–8cm, *short, twisted, blue-green* outer surface, blue-white inner.

Japanese White Pine

Flowers and cone. Male flowers fairly well-spaced on basal 10–12cm of every new shoot, ovoid, 3mm, green and white in bud, 5mm yellow and brown when shedding in mid-June. Female flowers abundant from an early age, 1–4, terminal, erect, ovoid or conic, rosy-pink turning rich purple, rarely bright pale green, 12mm. One-year cones spreading from every node, bright green convex scales blue-green at the tip; ovoid-cylindric. Ripe cone soon opening to barrel-shape, 5 × 3.5cm, pale orange-brown then dark purplish. On strong growth, cones radiate from nodes; on old trees with flat branching they stand above the layer of foliage.

Recognition. In tall or short form, the leaves are more twisted than in any other pine, and bluer in the low-crowned form; the layered foliage, crown and cones are equally distinct.

MONTEZUMA PINE *Pinus montezumae* Lamb.

Mexico 1839. Uncommon; some large gardens in S. England from Sussex to Hereford, in S.W. Scotland and in Ireland. 20m.

Bark. Grey-pink, shallowly fissured by wide vertical cracks into short knobbly ridges.

Crown. Unique broad dome of huge blue-grey upswept tufts.

Foliage. Shoot very *stout*, ribbed, shining *orange-brown*, up-curved. Needles on outer third, inner length bears big brown forward-curved scales,

Montezuma Pine

elaborately toothed. Bud cylindric, pointed, deep red-brown or purplish, crusted white with resin; 2 cm or more. Leaves mainly in fives but bundles of 3–8 found, slender straight 25–30 (45) cm long, *blue-grey* spreading stiffly.

Flowers. Male flowers in long clusters at base of expanding shoot; cylindric-ovoid, 1.5 cm, deep purple before ripe.

Cone. Unexpectedly small (6–10 cm) barrel-shaped, brown or dark purple; tiny prickle on each scale.

var. *hartwegii* (Lindl.) Engelm. Hartweg's Pine. Mexico 1839. Infrequent; collections and a few gardens in S. and W. England and Ireland. 25 m. Much less spectacular, narrower tree than the type, rather gaunt, needles shorter, 13–18 cm three or five together, grey or yellowish-green; shoot not stout, pale green, *bloomed violet*, later green-brown. Bud 2.5 cm red-brown, much fringed tips or scales free. Bark pink-grey with wide brown fissures, very scaly, like young *Pinus sylvestris*. Cone 10.5 × 5 cm long-ovoid-conic, grey-pink then pale *orange-brown*.

Similar species. The only other hardy pines with very long blue-grey needles are three-needle pines with very different crowns and cones (see *P. jeffreyi* p. 167 and *P. coulteri* p. 168).

ROCKY MOUNTAIN BRISTLE-CONE PINE *Pinus aristata* Engelm.

Colorado, Arizona, Mexico 1863. (It has recently been suggested that the oldest trees in the world are not this species but an allied one, *Pinus longaeva* Bailey, with a cone like *P. aristata* but shorter-spined and foliage very like *P. balfouriana*. It is found in California, Utah and Nevada. The oldest living tree found was nearly 5,000 years old. This species was not in cultivation in Europe, until seedlings were raised in 1972.)

P. aristata is rare, mainly in collections. Small, slow-growing, 9 m so far. A "Fox-tail" pine (as is *P. balfouriana*), holding foliage 10–15 years, close on long branchlets.

Crown. Narrow with slightly projecting, upswept branch-ends.

Foliage. Bud 4 mm, pointed; large, basal, dark red-brown scales free. Leaves in fives, short, abruptly short-spined, 2–4 cm; thick, stiff, dark outer surface with occasional large *white spot* of resin; blue-white on inner surface, crowded around and *curved forward* on to the orange, densely pubescent shoots. Crushed leaves have a scent of turpentine.

Cone. Frequent on young trees; first year ovoid, spiny, dull purple, 2 × 1.5 cm, second year 5–6 cm with spreading brown 6 mm spine on each scale.

Rocky Mountain Bristle-cone Pine

Similar species. *P. balfouriana* (below) is the other "Fox-tail" pine.

FOX-TAIL PINE *Pinus balfouriana* Jeffrey ex A. Murr.
N. Coast Range and C. Sierra Nevada, California 1852. Rare; confined to a few collections, notably the Royal Botanic Gardens, Edinburgh. 10m. Like *P. aristata* (p. 164) but needles slightly longer, 3.5–4 cm and *finely spined, unspotted* and, on two-year-old shoots, curving in farther out from shoot; crushed leaves have a sweet resinous scent quite unlike the turpentine scent of *P. aristata*. Bud without free basal scales; cone without spines.

MONTEREY PINE *Pinus radiata* D. Don   **Pl. 13**
    Syn. *P. insignis* Dougl.
Small areas around Monterey and Cambria, California 1833. Abundant in S.W. England especially near coast and in Ireland, frequent in west north to Ross-shire, infrequent in E. England, rare in E.

Scotland. 30 × 7m (44 × 3.4m at Cuffnells, Lynd-hurst, Hants.).
Bark. Dull grey, rugged, deeply fissured into thick, ± vertical, short parallel ridges; oldest trees often blackish-purple; fissures to 15 cm deep.
Crown. Conic, long-pointed when young; dense high dome when old, clothed to ground in the open and heavily branched; where more crowded, the dome is high on a long bole which is untidy with snags and dead branches. Wide-spreading branches droop low; heavy ones may rest on ground. Crown *bright green* from close to, blackish from distance. May shed big branches laden with whorls of old cones in snow or gales.

Monterey Pine

Foliage. Shoot pale greyish or whitish-green, becoming pale brown, glabrous. Bud cylindric, abruptly pointed, red-brown, purple-grey with resin. Leaves in threes densely set, very *slender*, straight, *bright green*; old needles orange-brown before falling, 10 (15) cm.
Flowers and cone. Male flowers crowded at base of new shoots, visible by March, bright yellow when pollinating March-April (February in S.W.). Cone, squat, ovoid, very asymmetrical at base, 12 × 9 cm clustered in threes to fives around shoot, glossy brown; scales big, woody, rounded ends protruding far on those at base on outer side. *Retained on branches or trunks*, even when these 25 cm diameter and 40 years old.

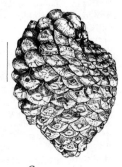

Growth. Shows extraordinary vigour and peculiar timing – has grown annual shoot of 2.5 m in Britain and in New Zealand has grown 60 m in 40 years. May start in early January in far S.W. and grow on until October. Elsewhere may grow only from May to July or add another shoot from August to October. Some grow two whorls of branches in a season.

Cone

Similar species. *P. muricata* (p. 178) shares many features, but needles are in pairs and cone-scales have prickles. *P. rigida* (p. 166) also similar, and three-needled.

KNOBCONE PINE   *Pinus attenuata* Lemmon

Hills of California and S. Oregon at 5–6,000 ft. 1847. Very rare; a few collections from S. England to N. Wales. 20 × 2 m (25 × 3.1 m Bodnant, N. Wales).

Bark. Grey-pink, rather smooth, flaking finely; old trees dark brown, ridged and fissured.

Crown. In America: bright green, narrow, with central stem encrusted in pale brown deflexed cones. In Britain: *open*, gaunt; *wide-spreading ascending strong branches*, sinuous and with *long-conic cones appressed in whorls*; dark green leaves.

Foliage. Shoot green-brown. Bud stout, cylindric, pointed, 4–5 cm dark brown encrusted with white resin. Leaf in bundles of three, slender, 14–16 cm grey-green, on outer half of shoot.

Flowers and cone. Male flowers profuse, closely packed on long lower sector of shoot, globular, 5–6 mm, yellow when shedding pollen in early May. Females in whorls of 3–5 half way up strong shoots on stout red-brown stalks 1 cm long; 1.5 cm, ovoid, pink-brown with upraised prickles. Cones in whorls pressed down against shoot, pale green ripening dark brown, 13 × 6 cm, long-conic, oblique based; outward-pointing scales with stout spreading spines, others minutely spined; held tightly on the tree for up to 20 years.

Knobcone Pine

Growth. A tree of rapid early growth but slow later and short-lived.

Similar species. Resembles *P. radiata* (p. 165) in persistent cones and leaves in threes, but crown and shape of cone quite distinct.

NORTHERN PITCH PINE   *Pinus rigida* Mill.

E. N. America 1743. Rare; mostly collections in S. England. 20 m.

Bark. Brown, deeply fissured into thick ridges.

Crown. Irregular, rather broad and domed; bole bears only major branches and *sprouts*; open, but patches of dense, *slender sprouts* also on large branches make it less sparse.

Foliage. Shoot pale orange-brown, often crinkled on surface. (Epicormic sprouts white). Bud very slender cylindric-conic, dark red-brown, some free scale-tips and white resin. Leaves in threes, thick, stiff, somewhat twisted, dull grey-green, 8–9 cm (on sprouts to 12 cm).

Flowers and cone. Male flower 8 mm ovoid, purple-red, opening to 2.5 cm in early June. Female flowers, three below tip of new shoot, bright crimson with decurved 6 mm scales. Cone small, 3–4(7) cm, symmetrical, cylindric,

Northern Pitch Pine

pointed or barrel-shaped; scales thin, flat, shining yellowish-brown with curved prickle, borne rather bunched and held on tree for many years, dull red-brown.

MEXICAN PINE *Pinus patula* Schlecht. and Chamisso
Mexico pre-1837. Rare; Ireland and from Cornwall to Sussex in a few large
gardens. 10m. (17.5 × 2.3m at Tregothnan).

Bark. *Orange,* smooth; big brownish
papery rolls remain attached. Biggest
trees purplish-grey and ridged on
lower bole.
Crown. Broadly conic, pointed,
often forked; branches level, curving
up at ends.
Foliage. Shoot pale fawn-green,
bloomed pink-white. Bud slender
cylindric, curved; scales pale brown,
free at tip. Leaves in threes, very
slender, 18–20 cm, pale or bright green *hanging.*

Mexican Pine

Cone. Clustered and persistent, 10 cm oblique, curved conic.

WESTERN YELLOW PINE *Pinus ponderosa* Dougl. **Pl. 14**
Rocky Mountains, S. British Columbia to Mexico. To 70m in Siskiyou Mts,
Oregon 1828. Frequent in large, occasional in smaller gardens over Britain,
especially in Scotland; very rare in Ireland. 32 × 3m
(39 × 4m at Powis Castle, Monts.).

Bark. Old trees: big, flat plates pale brownish-yellow, pink
and dark red, scaly at edges, separated by wide shallow
fissures. (In USA mostly pink-brown; no yellow seen. In
C. Oregon one forest where bark bright chestnut-brown.)
Young trees: dark grey-pink; red-brown vertical fissures.
Crown. Nearly *conic,* upper branches ascending; heavily
branched but pointed top until old; long, bare, stout shoots
hang down, curling upwards to end in tuft of long needles;
open in lower parts, dense towards top.
Foliage. Shoot stout, orange-brown or reddish and green,
shiny above, yellowish beneath. Bud cylindric, pointed pale
red-brown, white resin often at base; tips of scales free of
resin. Leaves in threes; crowded, dark green-grey or
blackish-grey, stiff, 17–22 cm.

Western Yellow Pine

Flowers and cone. Male flowers deep rich purple, ovoid, 2 cm, lengthen and
curve to 4 cm, cylindric, when shedding pollen in June. Female flowers 1–5
terminal, ovoid, dull red, soon deep purple conelets 2 cm, ovoid; deflexed
scales. Cone variable 7–10 × 4–5 cm, rarely longer; ovoid, acute; scales with
minute spine, curved down from transverse ridge; dark brown. Leaves base on
tree when shed.
Similar species. *P. jeffreyi* (below). The two species are still often confused.

JEFFREY'S PINE *Pinus jeffreyi* Murr.
S. Oregon to S. California at above 5,000 ft. 1852. Less frequent than *P.
ponderosa* but equally widespread; infrequent in Ireland. 30 × 3m (38 × 3.8m
at Scone Palace, Perths.).
Bark. Nearly *black, smooth* overall but areas of numerous, narrow, deep fissures.
(In California, when 50 × 5m, orange-brown, ridged; or pink-brown, shallowly
plated.)

Crown. Conic and shapely; branches of regular, moderate size, slightly ascending. Oldest trees may have wide tops of up-curved, spreading branches.

Foliage. Shoot stout, pale brown bloomed *blue-grey*. Bud dark red-brown, cylindric, pointed; scales at sides with free, short tips. Leaves in threes, 16–23 cm, stout, stiff *bluish-green* or *grey*, spreading.

Cone. First year to 0.5 kg in weight, dark purplish-brown, cylindric-ovoid, 12 × 6 cm. Becomes typically very broad, flat-based to 18 × 7 cm (when open, × 15 cm), pale brown, beehive-shaped with small, sharp recurved prickles, but some less broad-based. A variable amount of the base

Jeffrey's Pine

is left on the tree when the cone falls, leaving a hollow in the base.

Similar species. *P. ponderosa* (p. 167). *P. coulteri* (below) much more confusing but has thickly ridged bark, wide-spreading branches, quite different cone and very large, orange buds.

BIG-CONE PINE *Pinus coulteri* D. Don

S.W. California 1832. Rare; in collections and a few gardens mainly in S. and W. of England and in Wales. 28 × 4 m (died). Now 20 × 2.5 m.

Bark. Black or purplish-grey-brown; thick ridges or big plates divided by wide, deep fissures. Young trees pale grey, cracking.

Crown. Broad; long slightly-drooping branches on old trees; young trees gaunt with few branches, upturned at ends.

Foliage. Shoot very stout, ridged and glaucous, pale bluish-white, becoming red-brown; long bare inner part with brown, narrow scales. Bud pale *orange*, *fat*, to 6 cm, sharp-pointed; some outer scales usually free. Leaves in threes, very *stout, stiff*, usually crinkled in second year, grey, 25–30 cm.

Flowers and cone. Male flowers rather scattered or densely borne on basal lengths of new shoot for 6–12 cm, stout ovoid, 2 cm, pink-purple becoming yellow when pollinating in early June. Cones near top of tree, massive ovoid 20–35 × 15–20 cm weighing to 2 kg, oblique at base; scales pale brown, thick ends drawn out into broad, flattened, rigid and very sharp hooks 2 cm long, spreading and upcurved, except for those at base which point downwards.

Similar species. *P. jeffreyi* (above). The rare **Digger Pine**, *P. sabiniana* Douglas (California 1832) has similar-shaped cones, less massive, less hooked with thinner, *down-curved*, less rigid scales. It is a very open-crowned, thin-branched, slender-shooted tree, three-needled with similar but more slender and duller grey leaves, 20–25 cm long held very level on slender blue-white shoots. It grows in a few southern collections. 20 m.

Big-cone Pine

LACE-BARK PINE   *Pinus bungeana* Zucc.
N.W. China 1846. Rare; confined to S. and E. England. 13 m.
Bark. Unique, smooth grey-green and olive-brown. Flakes come away and leave white patches which turn successively yellow, pale green, olive, rufous, purple and purple-brown.
Crown. Usually low, often bushy, rarely narrowly conic (notably at Wisley).
Foliage. Shoot pale olive-green becoming dark grey-green. *Bud stands 5 mm clear of leaves,* pointed ovoid, dark red-brown, with scales decurved all over. Leaves in *threes, sparse,* dark yellow-green held rather close in bundle, 6–8 cm, clean and smooth-looking. Side shoots widely spreading.
Flowers. Male flowers 6 mm, ovoid, dull yellow.
Cone. Short-stalked ovoid 4 × 3.5 cm, dark brown, few scales, thick, wrinkled, with spreading 3 mm spines.

Lace-bark Pine, with cones, closed and open

MARITIME PINE   *Pinus pinaster* Ait.   **Pl. 13**
   Syn. *P. maritima* Poir
Coast of C. and W. Mediterranean pre-1596. Frequent in South. Small forest plantations restricted to New Forest and Wareham areas and behind some southern sand-dunes. Small semi-wild populations in W. Surrey and N. Hants. Infrequent in other parts of England and Wales. Rare in Scotland and Ireland. 34 × 3 m.
Bark. Young trees pale grey, deeply fissured pale or red-brown; old trees deep purple, blackish or reddish, divided by deep, narrow fissures into small square shiny plates.
Crown. Young trees: bole curved at base, broad whorls of branches widely spaced, open. Old trees: long, bare sinuous boles, level branches, wide, flat tops; cones adhering to branches.
Foliage. Vigorous new shoots stained dark red on pale green, normal shoots stout, pink-brown above, pale olive beneath, glabrous. Bud bright red-brown with pale margined scales fringed with silvery hairs, those near the tip with apices bent out and rolled down; 1–2 cm. Leaves in pairs, *stout* semi-circular and *long,* 15–20 cm, *pale grey-green.*
Flowers and cone. Male flowers scattered along basal third of new shoots, shed pollen in June; female flowers 3–5 around terminal bud, dark pink, ovoid, 1 cm.

Cones persistent along branches, often in clusters, sessile, oblique-based, conic, pointed, curved, bright *shining brown*, 10 × 5 cm, each scale with a broad ridge and upcurved prickle. Sometimes used as ornaments.

Maritime Pine cones, closed and open

SCOTS PINE *Pinus sylvestris* L.   Pl. 14
Scotland; Spain to mid-Siberia, north to Lapland. Abundant, semi-wild on heaths in S., C. and N.E. England, truly wild in C. and W. Highlands; widely used in forestry but less planted now; frequent in landscaping of old parks. 35 × 5 m.

Bark. Young trees pale grey with scaly ridges or finely scaly orange-red. Older trees variable from "crocodile-skin" small, shallowly divided plates, pink tinged yellow or grey, to deeply fissured black and dark red and scaly. In upper crown, orange-brown, finely scaly; pink in old trees.

Crown. Conic and whorled until height growth ceases then becomes flat-topped on long, bare, straight bole. Many variants in native areas like Black Wood of Rannoch.

Foliage. Shoot pale greenish-brown, glabrous; strong shoots finely ribbed. Bud cylindric, pointed, brown or dark red, some with white resin, a few scales just free at their tips. Leaves in pairs, short on old trees, 5–7 cm, twice as long on vigorous young plants (may be in threes or fours), *blue-grey-green* (deep green closely and finely lined bluish-grey), often twisted, *thick and broad*.

Flowers and cone. Male flowers clustered at base of weaker new shoots, bright yellow, occasionally crimson before they shed pollen in late May; female flowers 1–5 at tips of new, strong shoots, pale pink then dark rosy-purple by June, globular with scales protruding; become conic, bright green and down-turned next year. Following year, dull grey-brown, woody cones, pointed ovoid, 5–8 cm.

Growth. Mid-May – early July. Young trees often grow 1 m a year. Life-span about 250 years, possibly 400 in Scotland rarely.

'AUREA' Nursery origin. Leaves bright gold from December to May; new growth grey, whole tree a sickly grey-green tinged yellow in summer. Slow, rather rare; splendid in winter-flowering heather-garden. 12 m.

'FASTIGIATA' Nursery origin 1856. Very rare but splendid narrow spire with slender nearly vertical branches. 8 m. (Wisley, Surrey, 7 m.)

Similar species. *P. densiflora* (p. 174) has similar bark but differs in leaves and cones. *P. resinosa* (p. 171) also similar bark high in crown.

STONE PINE *Pinus pinea* L.
Mediterranean. Probably pre-1500. Uncommon; mainly in S. England but a few in S. Scotland and Ireland. 22 × 3 m. Seedlings retain blue-grey juvenile single, serrate-leafed foliage for 4–5 years, and occasional juvenile shoots for ten years or much longer where damaged by browsing cattle.

Bark. Red-brown or orange, deeply fissured grey, forming large vertical plates. Young trees deeply fissured with orange.

Crown. *Broad dark dome* from short bole, often dividing low, into several limbs; branches *radiating*.

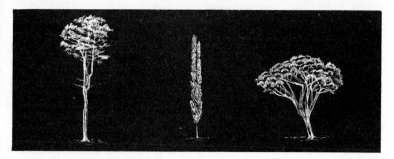

Left, Scots Pine; *centre*, 'Fastigiata'; *right*, Stone Pine

Foliage. Shoot curved, pale green-buff; orange pulvini. Bud 1 cm ovoid bright chestnut, scales deeply fringed whitish, tips curved out. Leaves in pairs, fairly stout, often twisted, 12–15 cm dark greyish-green, rather sparse.

Flowers. Male flowers ovoid, 13 mm, orange-brown when shedding pollen in late June.

Cone. Big, 10 × 10 cm, globose, flat-based, pale, slightly shiny brown, smooth scales with rounded ends and roughened grey or red-brown centres from which radiate five fine folds.

RED PINE   *Pinus resinosa* Ait.

Eastern N. America; Nova Scotia to Pennsylvania 1756. Rare; in a few collections. A handsome tree resembling *P. ponderosa* with the bark of *P. sylvestris*. Dense crown of level then upswept branches with *stout orange shoots* bearing dense *whorled* masses of long needles in pairs. Needle dark green, 10–15 cm, very slender, *snaps cleanly* when bent sharply. Strongly scented of lemon-balm. Bud conic, long-pointed, chestnut, 2 cm. Cone 4–5 × 2.5 cm ovoid-long conic, shining pale orange-brown, often borne in threes. 20 m (Borde Hill).

Red Pine

AUSTRIAN PINE   *Pinus nigra* Arnold var. *nigra*
Syn. *P.n. austriaca* (Hoess) Badoux

Austria, C. Italy and Balkans 1835. Common; often in shelter-belts by coast or on calcareous soils, also in gardens on outskirts of towns, churchyards and railway embankments. 33 × 4 m.

Bark. Blackish-brown, pale purple-grey or dark grey, coarsely ridged, very scaly.

Crown. Usually irregularly ovoid, from short bole, open and untidy below. Less often narrow, from a straight single bole and level dense branches. Usually appears to be grimy with soot. Foliage *black, short, whorled*.

Foliage. Shoot stout, *ridged, yellow-brown* or green-brown, *shining*. Bud pale brown, squat, abruptly long-pointed; on side-shoots buds deep in white, papery, loose scales. Leaves in pairs, dense, stiff, nearly black, 10–15 cm, straight first year, older leaves curved forwards in short whorls.

Flowers and cone. Male flowers in shallow ring at base of short, upturned shoots of new growth, opening conic, upcurved to 3 cm long, yellow, early June. Cone ovoid, pointed, 5–8 cm long, yellowish-brown becoming dull grey-brown.

CORSICAN PINE *Pinus nigra* var. *maritima* (Ait.) Melville **Pl. 13**
Syns. *P.n. laricio* (Poir.), *P.n. calabrica* (Loud.), *P.n. corsicana* (Loud.)
Corsica, S. Italy, Sicily 1759. Very common or common almost everywhere:
parks, gardens, churchyards, copses, for shelter and in large areas of forest; on
sandy heaths, heavy clays, over chalk or on shallow peats. 35 × 4 m (44 × 3.3 m
at Stanage Park, Radnor; 4.7 m in girth nr. Llanfacreth, Merioneth).
Bark. In plantations pink-grey finely flaking, shallowly fissured; old single
trees pale or dark grey, heavily ridged, flaking coarsely; less often pink-grey
plates, some large and concave.
Crown. Narrow, regular cone or column with evenly spaced, *small level*
branches, rather open throughout; old trees broadly flat-topped, more heavily
branched, occasionally with heavy low branches drooping; usually with single
main axis to top.
Foliage. Shoot stout, slightly ridged, pale yellow-brown.
Bud brown 1.5–2 cm, rather squat, abruptly pointed longer
than var. *nigra* and lacks papery scales, often white with
resin. Leaves in pairs *slender, lax*, 12–18 cm, *grey-green* well
spaced on shoot, much twisted on young trees.
Flowers and cone. Male flowers barrel-shaped 1.3 cm
tightly clustered, pale yellow-green heavily speckled dark
purple. Female flowers bright rosy pink, ovoid, 5 mm mid-
June. Cone as var. *nigra* (p. 171).

Corsican Pine

CRIMEAN PINE *Pinus nigra* Arnold var. *caramanica* (Loud.) Rehd.
Crimea; Asia Minor 1790. Uncommon. A very vigorous form, somewhat
intermediate between vars. *nigra* and *maritima*. Old trees are distinct by the
trunk dividing from about 6 m into five to ten vertical stems looking like organ-
pipes. Shoot yellow-green, shiny. Leaf hard, ± stout, straight, dark, 10–15 cm.
Cone narrow-conic, knobbly; scales with protruding centres. 42 × 5 m.

var. *cebennensis* (Gren. and Godr.) Rehder, **Pyrenean Pine** (*Pinus n. pyrenaica* Gren. and Godr.) S. France and Pyrenean Mts 1834. Rare; S. England.
Broad crown of *descending* branches, *orange shoots* and slender grey-green
leaves 12–15 cm long; buds often obscured by white resin; smooth ovoid-conic
cone. 23 × 2.5 m. Dense pale foliage in layers in solid dome highly distinctive.

ALEPPO PINE *Pinus halepensis* Mill.
Mediterranean 1683. Very rare; a few collections in
S. England, notably big trees at Kew, to 16 × 2.5 m.
Seedlings retain juvenile foliage for several years.
Bark. Deep purple-brown with wide orange fissures,
older trees with short, narrow plates flaking to terra-
cotta.
Crown. Narrow as a young tree, domed on stout
bole when old; twisting branches and a mass of fine
twigs with old cones retained.
Foliage. Shoot slender, pale greenish-brown or
orange. Bud red-brown, cylindric, small; 1 cm;
scales free and down-turned, fringed grey. Leaves in
pairs on outer half of shoot only, *sparse*, 6–9 cm,
shining *bright green*.

Aleppo Pine

Flowers. Female flowers 1–3 a little below tip of shoot, pink, ovoid, 1 cm.
Cone. Borne in decurved whorls of three, ovoid, pointed, 5–7 × 3cm, bright reddish-purple-brown.

var. *brutia* (Ten.) Elwes and Henry. Cyprus, S. Italy 1836. Very rare indeed. To 12 × 2.5m at Kew. Differs from type in leaf and cone. Leaf 15–16cm, darker; cone *pointing forwards* on stalk 1 cm *thick*; ovoid, pointed curved top, 9 × 4.5 cm.

BOSNIAN PINE   *Pinus leucodermis* Ant.   **Pl. 14**

Balkans 1890. Uncommon; some large gardens in all parts, thriving on chalk and limestones as well as on acid soils. 20 × 2m.
Bark. Clean, *smooth greenish-grey* at first with fine vertical cracks; pale grey with whitish areas, other parts shallowly cracked into small squares when larger.
Crown. Neat, dense, regular, ovoid or conic; branches curving upwards.
Foliage. Shoot bloomed glaucous blue-grey at first, later pale brown. Bud large squat, abruptly long-pointed; loose papery basal scales, dark red centres, whitish broad margins. Leaves in pairs, very dense whorls separated by nearly equal lengths of shoot bare except for big brown scales (or male flowers in season); needles blackish-green, stiff, 6–9cm, pointing forwards.
Flowers and cone. Male flowers crowded on basal 5 cm of new shoot; ovoid-cylindric, 2 cm, purplish or yellow-orange before opening in mid-June. Female flowers 3–5 at end of shoot become deep blue-purple conelets 1.8 cm with small spreading spines. Enlarge and turn bright blue during second year, conic-ovoid, pointed, 7cm; dull orange-brown as ripen then purple-brown; small reflexed spine on lower scales.
Similar species. *P. thunbergii* (below) differs widely in bark and crown; *P. nigra* var. *nigra* (p. 171) differs similarly and neither has bloomed shoots nor blue conelets, but both are similar in foliage.

JAPANESE BLACK PINE   *Pinus thunbergii* Parl.   **Pl. 14**

Japan 1861. Rare; a number of large gardens and collections especially in S. England. 23 × 2.5m.
Bark. Dark grey or dark purplish-pink, deep interlacing fissures.
Crown. Young trees stiffly upright, conic, later columnar, becoming irregular, *leaning at the top* with age. Old trees dense yet gaunt as *long branches wander far out*, tufted at short intervals along their length but with few or no laterals. Bole often leans; forking in mid-crown is usual.
Foliage. Shoot stout *golden-brown*; bare lengths with scales. Bud *silky white* with long-fringed scales, most striking when expanding; cylindric, sharply

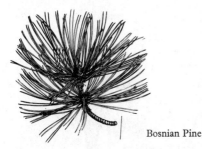

Bosnian Pine

pointed. Leaves in pairs remaining close in dense forward-pointing whorls separated by lengths with scales; *rigid, thick,* sharply spined, 7–10cm, grey-green close to, blackish from short distance. Basal sheath ends in two long filaments.

Flowers and cone. Male flowers numerous in small whorls, yellow with pollen in mid-June. Females absurdly numerous, often clustered in place of needles, 70 or more on about 20cm of shoot, dark pink-red becoming rich plum-purple conelets; cone normally 4–6 × 3.5cm, minutely prickled, flat-based, conic, dark grey. Much smaller when densely clustered.

Japanese Black Pine

Similar species. *P. leucodermis* (p. 173,) *P. nigra* var. *nigra* (p. 171).

JAPANESE RED PINE   *Pinus densiflora* Sieb. and Zucc.

Japan 1854. Rare; collections only. Resembles Scots Pine in bark but has bright grey-green shoots; leaves *slender*, forward-pointing bright, deep *shining green*, 9–10cm long in pairs; long whorls, 9–10cm of pale brown male flowers, and small, pointed cones (5 × 3cm) in clusters of 3–5 retained on the tree for years. A sturdy, rather low tree, soon flat-topped or domed. 15m. (21m Borde Hill.)

MOUNTAIN PINE   *Pinus uncinata* Mill. ex Mirb.

Syn. *P. mugo* Turra var. *rostrata* Hoopes

Pyrenees and Alps. *P. mugo* is a spreading bush. *P. uncinata* is the tree-form, 20m. Rare; occasionally in forests at high altitude and in some collections.

Bark. Grey-pink cracked into small squares, becoming *blackish* with curling scales.

Crown. Conic, broad or narrow; lower branches level then curved up. Dark, sturdy tree.

Foliage. Shoot orange-brown; purple-brown in second year. Bud ovoid 1cm, red-brown. Leaves in pairs, very dense and *whorled*; basal sheath broad, re-curved and persistent; needles 6cm, *rigid*, grooved inside, dark grey-green; new whorls markedly paler.

Flowers and cone. Male flowers very numerous, clustered at base of every small shoot, pollinating in mid-June. Female flower terminal, ovoid; purple. Cone 5cm, pale brown ovoid-conic *basal scales curiously drawn downwards,* some curved outwards.

Similar species. *P. contorta* var. *latifolia* (p. 175).

BEACH or SHORE PINE   *Pinus contorta* Dougl. var. *contorta*

Alaska to N. California within about 200km of coastline. 1855. Uncommon in collections, but recently planted over thousands of hectares of high peatlands in

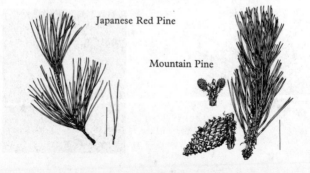

Japanese Red Pine

Mountain Pine

Wales, Scotland and Ireland and on some southern hill-peats. 25 × 3 m (32 × 2.9 m at Bodnant, Denbighs. 27 × 3.7 m at Ashford Castle, Co. Mayo).

Bark. Rich brown fissures break the dark bark into prominent squares, oldest trees deeply fissured vertically.

Crown. Young trees: broad bushy base and long spire of very vigorous shoot from centre; often swept at base of bole. Old trees: dense bushy domed or spired crown, usually tall and rather narrow; rarely a broad, domed bush (two notable examples at Wisley).

Foliage. Shoot greenish-brown, wrinkled; second year orange-brown striped white. Bud dark brown long cylindrical, often twisted (hence "contorta") especially when expanding; very resinous. Leaves in pairs very densely set, *closely clothing* long vigorous shoots of young trees, more spreading on older shorter shoots;

Shore Pine

deep green on trees of southern origin when young, bright yellowish-green on older trees; 4–5 cm.

Flowers and cone. Male flowers sometimes in third year from seed, in dense whorl, shed pollen in April. Female dull dark red, 2–4 at tip of, or half way along, shoot. Cone conic-ovoid, 5 cm, minutely prickled, light pink-brown in whorls of two to four *pointing back down stem*, variably persistent, opening to blunt ovoid.

Shore Pine cone

Growth. Buds lengthen very early (in March), growth ceases by early July. Annual shoots of nearly 2 m seen on southern Shore Pines on many moorlands. The more northerly the origin the more double-whorled shoots occur, the annual leading shoot bearing a whorl of branchlets rather above the middle.

var. *latifolia* Wats. **Lodgepole Pine.** Northern, inland B.C. to Washington and E. Rocky Mountains to Col. 1854. Rare in gardens, but plantations on some high, inland moors, especially in N.E. 20 m.

Bark. Finely scaling dark red-brown.

Crown. Much less dense than var. *contorta*, open and conic, often up-swept, bole straight but often forked.

Foliage. Leaves in pairs, *spreading*, not

Lodgepole Pine

densely set, *broad*, twisted, dark green, 6–10 cm.

var. *murrayana* (Balf.) Critchfield. Oregon Cascades and California south to Mexico 1853. A slow-growing, shapely, conic tree with open crown and shortish dark needles, 4–4.5 cm, falling after one or two years. This has been grown more by accident than design in some plantations, seed having been sent from the wrong area. (One, 408 years old at Bluff Lake, San Bernardino, is 6 m in girth.)

Similar species. P. *banksiana* (p. 178) resembles Shore Pine but cone points upwards along shoot, foliage sparse and bark differs. P. *uncinata* (p. 174) resembles Lodgepole Pine but foliage denser, darker and stiffer, bark darker and cones have unique basal scales.

Plate 15   **POPLARS**

Resinous buds; flowers on catkins, sexes on separate trees (in all but one species).

1. White Poplar   *Populus alba*   181

    (a) Outline of an unusually sturdy specimen. Most trees lean slightly and have rather flattened systems of shoots (see figure p. 181).

    (b) Leaf showing some white down adhering to upper surface.

    (c) Underside of leaf.

2. Lombardy Poplar   *Populus nigra* 'Italica'   183

    (a) Tree of moderate age, about 20 m high.

    (b) Leaf.

3. Black Italian Poplar   *Populus × euramericana* 'Serotina'   186

    (a) Outline of mature tree about 25 m high. Many trees develop stout upswept branches (see figure below).

    (b) Normal leaf from crown (on suckers, or stool-shoots, leaves of this and many poplars are often much bigger and of rather different shapes).

4. Railway Poplar   *Populus × euramericana* 'Regenerata'   186

Tree of 20 m. Arching branches with fine, often hanging shoots.

5. Grey Poplar   *Populus canescens*   181

Leaf from crown of large tree. Young, vigorous trees bear some leaves the same shape as in White Poplar similarly felted on under surface but less bright, greyer white and soon without white down on upper surface.

6. Aspen   *Populus tremula*   182

Leaf. The lack of hairs beneath distinguish this from leaves of similar shape of Grey Poplar. Leaves flutter easily giving a shimmering effect.

7. Berlin Poplar   *Populus × berolinensis*   185

Leaf has distinctive cuneate base. The underside is slightly whitish green.

Black Italian Poplar

1 2a 2 3 4

WILLOWS, WINGNUT   Plate 16
Trees of exceedingly rapid growth.

1. White Willow   *Salix alba*   189
Tree 20m tall in winter.

2. Weeping Willow   *Salix alba* 'Tristis'   189
(a) Tree of about 15m.
(b) Hanging shoot and leaves.

3. Crack Willow   *Salix fragilis*   188
By midsummer many leaves are 15cm long and a rich, glossy green. Often more frequent by lowland rivers than is the White Willow.

4. Caucasian Wing-nut   *Pterocarya fraxinifolia*   191
Densely pubescent bud without bud-scales. Some leaves have an even number of leaflets, but the majority have an odd number. This tree suckers profusely and widely and thrives best by water. In summer it is hung with long catkins of winged fruit.

Chinese Wing-nut (p.194)   Hybrid Wing-nut (p.194)

Caucasian Wing-nut (p.191)

JACK PINE *Pinus banksiana* Lamb.
E. Canada, near Arctic Circle to Lake States pre-1783. Rare; in a few large gardens. 21 m.
Bark. Orange-grey, striped vertically by shallow grey fissures.
Crown. Thin, irregular; narrow and leaning with slender point when young but soon flattens. Shoots slender; crown twiggy with long, slender drooping branches, lined with whorls of cones.
Foliage. Annual shoot usually three whorls on all main shoots; slender. Bud slender, cylindric, light brown,

Jack Pine

shiny with resin. Leaves in pairs, sparse, short (3–4 cm), *broad, twisted*, yellowish.
Flowers and cone. Male flowers numerous on minor shoots, yellow, shed pollen in May. Female globular, pale rose red. Cones frequent and persistent, 3–6 cm, lumpy ovoid, pointed, in pairs or threes *facing forwards* along shoot. Old cones on trees quite smooth grey-brown, or covered in algae and moss.

BISHOP PINE *Pinus muricata* D. Don
Scattered, small colonies on coast of California and adjacent islands 1846. Infrequent; in some large gardens north to Perthshire and in W. Ireland, and now planted on west coast for shelter. Northern narrow, blue form rare. 29 × 3 m (27 × 4 m at Ebernoe, Petworth, Sussex).
Bark. Dark grey; thick parallel ridges and deep fissures running up bole far into crown. Young trees early fissured orange-brown between grey bark.
Crown. Trees from the two most northerly sources (Big Lagoon and Noyo River, Mendocino): tall, narrowly conic and pointed; trees from more southerly sources; broadly domed, long branches level or slightly arched downwards with whorls of cones persisting back to bole; up to 70 whorls on oldest trees. Leaves in short, *whorled* bunches; rather open foliage.
Foliage. Shoot green to orange-brown; bare length between whorls has broad, curved bracts. Bud cylindric, tapered, very resinous, purplish-brown or red-brown with some white resin. Leaves in pairs 7–15 cm, in whorls, stiff, curved; grey-green often yellowish towards base on broad (southern) trees, dark blue-grey on tall, narrow (northern) trees.
Flowers and cone. Male flowers, small, narrow ovoids, 7 mm packed in long narrow whorl along up to 25 cm of new shoot, each on a red-brown, lanceolate, slender bract; dull yellow. Female flowers 2–5 in a whorl well below the tip, ovoid, 1.5 cm bright pink-red centre; long upcurved scales shading to pale yellow. Mid-June. Cone heavy ovoid, oblique, 8 × 7 cm, very firmly held in whorls on branches or trunk; scales with *sharp prickle*, some at base of outer side convex, protruding 6–7 mm; deep red-brown.
Growth. Best forms are remarkably vigorous on poorest soils; shoots of over 2 m, and trees of 13 m in 11 years, at Bedgebury, Kent.
Similar species. *P. radiata* (p. 165) is similar from distance and in bark, crown (often) and in adhering cones, but *P. radiata* is a three-needle pine and its cones have unarmed scales, its brighter green needles not in tufts, are slender and pendulous, and the crown is more dense.

Bishop Pine

Angiospermae

Ovules borne in a closed ovary which at maturity becomes a fruit. The dominant plant group of this Age, includes all the non-coniferous higher plants. Stature varies from minute creeping plants a few mm tall to *Eucalyptus regnans* 100m tall. Flowers range from minute bunches of stamens without petals as in the oaks to showy and substantial structures with large petals as in Magnolia. The tree-species included in this book are scattered among 49 families. Some of these families consist almost entirely of trees (e.g. *Fagaceae, Juglandaceae, Ulmaceae*); some have a vast array of species of which a small proportion only is trees (e.g. *Rosaceae, Leguminosae*) and a few have but an exceptional tree species among numbers of herbs and shrubs (e.g. *Bignoniaceae, Scrophulariaceae, Liliaceae*).

Dicotyledoneae

Stems formed of bark, wood and pith, increasing in size annually by the addition of a ring to the wood (secondary thickening) (see p. 21); leaf veins in a network; first leaves from the seed a pair of cotyledons. In some trees these remain in the seed (e.g. *Quercus, Aesculus*) or are conjoined as in *Fagus*.

WILLOW FAMILY *Salicaceae*

Large family of over 300 species, all but one either a willow or a poplar. Male and female flowers on separate trees (dioecious) except in *Populus lasiocarpa*, both in catkins opening before the leaves in most species: seeds surrounded at base by long, silky hairs.

POPLARS Populus

Mainly very fast-growing trees reaching large sizes, with resinous buds and alternate, petioled leaves. About 30 species from the N. temperate regions, and numerous hybrids.

Key to the commoner species and Hybrid Poplars by shape of crown

1. Fastigiate (i.e. branching erect)   **2**
  Not fastigiate   **3**

2. Narrowly columnar; bark dull grey, shallowly ridged; (leaves
  bright green)   *nigra* 'Italica', p. 183
  Broadly columnar, widening towards the top; bark black,
  grey, cream and white, pitted black; (leaves silvery beneath)
              alba 'Pyramidalis', p. 181

3. Conic, or broadly columnar narrowed to apex   **4**
  Domed or widely spreading   **5**

4. Shoots dense, slender, partly pendulous   'Eugenei', p. 186
  Shoots sparse, widely whorled, moderately stout, not pendulous; (leaves emerge orange-red)   'Robusta', p. 187

5. Bark on branches partly cream or white   **6**
  Bark uniformly grey or brown   **7**

6. Lightly branched, leaning, rather flat-topped *alba*, p. 181
  Massively branched, tall, high-domed *canescens*, p. 181

7. Upper branches short, level; crown narrows towards top
               tremula, p. 182
  Upper branches ascend to make huge, broad dome or flat top **8**

8. Main branches arch outwards   **9**
  Main branches curve inwards or nearly vertical   **10**

9. Bark brown, branches massive, shoots in dense clusters on
  deeply arched, wide-spreading branches *nigra* var. *betulifolia*, p. 182
  Bark grey; branches not massive; relatively narrow, open-
  topped, vase-shape; many snags and dead shoots; long,
  slender shoots partly pendulous. Female only
              'Regenerata', p. 186

10. Branches similar sizes, upswept or radiating   **11**
  Branches few massive, many small, strongly incurved **12**

11. Small, gaunt, very rough-barked   *lasiocarpa,* p. 184
Very vigorous, large, densely crowned, upswept, smooth or
  smoothly shallow-ridged bark   *trichocarpa,* p. 184

12. Very open; swept to one side, shoots stout and distant;
  male; (leaves emerge late and orange)   'Serotina', p. 186
Fairly dense, regular, globular; shoots close; female; (leaves
  emerge early, green)   'Marilandica', p.187

WHITE POPLAR   *Populus alba* L.   Pl. 15
C. and S. Europe, C. to W. Asia. Introduced at an early unknown date. Frequent, locally common in garden-boundaries, roadsides and parks, often on sandy coasts where abundant sucker-growth makes useful shelter. 18 m.

White Poplar

Bark. Dark grey-green, furrowed, becoming black and deeply pitted or coarsely cracked at base and to 5–6 m up, above which are patches of creamy white or grey, smooth but pitted with small black diamonds.
Crown. Broadest near top which is *usually leaning* to one side, branches twisting, level, drooping slightly, shoots slender, twisted, foliage strikingly white.
Foliage. Shoot green densely covered in white wool, second year pale brown. Bud ovoid, orange-brown with white pubescence. Leaf unfolds white from dense hairs, later upper surface shiny, dark grey-green; five-lobed on strong growth, to 9 × 8 cm, main lobe has 1–2 lobules each side; some leaves with short, sharp, distant teeth. Small leaves nearly round 5 × 5 cm irregularly sinuate, to three-lobed; all truncate to rounded at base. Shoot, petiole and underside coated with thick white hairs. Petiole flattened, 3–4 cm.
Flowers and fruit. Catkins out before the leaves in late March, 4–8 cm long, males crimson and grey, females pale green, forming fluffy seeds.

'PYRAMIDALIS' 1872 Turkmen. Uncommon, locally frequent in parks or as street tree in towns. Fastigiate like a rather broad Lombardy Poplar with a much more open crown broadest near the top; the white, black-pitted areas of bark prominent. Short-lived; biggest trees usually dying. Syn. 'Bolleana'. 25 m.

'RICHARDII' 1918 Holland. Infrequent; parks and gardens. Leaves bright yellow above, greyish-yellow beneath when fully out; often rather patchy colouring but can be striking.

Similar species. Much confused with *P. canescens* (below) which is a stronger growing tree attaining much greater size, but *P. alba* leaf is pure white beneath and crown is paler grey in summer.

GREY POPLAR   *Populus canescens* (Ait.) Sm.   Pl. 15
Probably not native; Europe and W. Asia. Intermediate or hybrid between *P. alba* and *P. tremula.* Locally common, mainly in river valleys, north to Easter Ross, and especially in Dorset, Wiltshire and C. Ireland. 38 × 5.1 m. (Birr Cas.)
Bark. Dark grey with diamond-shaped pits when young; big boles dark brown or nearly black, regularly networked by thick ridges, upper bole largely silvery white or pale cream with horizontal lines of black diamond-shaped pits.

Crown. Narrowly conic at first until over 20m high; old trees high multiple domes, broadest well below the top; rather few massive, ascending branches, somewhat pendulous and dense exterior shoots; large bole carried well into crown; upper parts sinuous; soft pale grey in leaf until midsummer then deep green and pale grey.

Foliage. Shoot greyish green-brown at first thickly covered in white, scurfy pubescence, readily rubbed off. Bud ovoid-conic, red-brown with white hairs at base, yellow or pink-brown towards the glabrous tip, rather appressed. Leaf unfolds silvery with dense hairs, later deep glossy grey-green above, remaining covered below in dense, greyish-white pubescence. Vary from orbicular, 7×7 cm with big, irregular, curved teeth each side, to shallowly five-lobed, truncate, 8×8 cm, acute main lobes with crinkled and lobulate margin; minor lobes with a few small, pointed teeth. Petiole flattened, pubescent, 5 cm.

Flowers and fruit. Male trees bear catkins enlarging from short, thick, silky and grey to reddish-purple 3–4 cm long in March, yellow with pollen in early April for a few days, then shed. Female trees very rare; catkins enlarge green in mid-April, develop white wool on the seeds and fall by the end of April.

Similar species. *P. alba* (p. 181) bright white under leaves.

ASPEN   *Populus tremula* L.   **Pl. 15**

Native, locally abundant in N. and W. Scotland, frequent over much of the country on damp sites on hillsides, in rocky valley-bottoms, hedges and copse-edges; less frequent in S.E. England. 20 m.

Bark. Greenish-grey, very smooth, wrinkled and lenticelled horizontally; sometimes lenticels are deep pits enlarged by Green Woodpeckers; older trees pale grey or brownish, shallowly ridged at base but noticeably smooth through crown.

Crown. At first conic, open, lightly branched, later broader and less regular but still open and lightly branched, bole leaning, branches twisting, lower branches level. Often grows as a thicket of suckers from an earlier tree. In leaf pale grey-green, often yellowish, leaves flutter to show light greenish-grey undersides.

Foliage. Shoot shiny deep brown. Bud: leaf-bud yellow and deep brown, laterals appressed, narrowly conic; terminal ovoid-conic, 7–10 mm; catkin-buds prominent towards the tip of most shoots, ovoid, pointed, shiny chestnut-brown, 1–1.2 cm. Leaf ovate-orbicular, truncate or broad-cuneate, very short-acuminate, 4–6 × 5–7 cm, with blunt, curved, irregular teeth and slightly crinkled margin; unfold coppery-brown; still tinged in late May, then dull rich or greyish-green above, pale grey-green beneath; petiole very flattened, whitish, 4–6 cm. Autumn colour a good clear yellow late in October.

Flowers and fruit. Male trees bear profuse, thick grey-brown catkins, yellowish in mid-March when shedding pollen, then dull brown and soon shed. Female trees about as common as males, with green catkins, 4 × 0.5 cm with red-brown bracts and grey hairs, becoming woolly and white in mid-May and shedding the woolly seeds soon after.

BLACK POPLAR   *Populus nigra* L.

Native as the var. *betulifolia* (Pursh) Torr. Europe; this variety confined to N.

and W. Europe. Uncommon as very
large tree by country roadsides and in
fields, occasional in parks and gardens, but
much used as the "Manchester Poplar" in
industrial Lancashire and Cheshire around
playing-fields, railways and factories and
by roads. 30 × 5 m.

Bark. *Grey-brown*, very deeply fissured
into *short*, broad ridges.

Crown. Young trees densely-twigged
ovoid; old trees with huge spreading domes
of a few massive low branches ascending
then *arching* out and over, bearing *up-swept dense bunches* of straight shoots from
the upper side; *bole burry* and short.

Black Poplar

Foliage. Shoot slender, whitish and pale yellow, brown towards the tip; second
year pale fawn-grey, shiny and smooth. Bud: terminal, narrowly ovoid-conic,
pointed, 7 mm, shiny chestnut-brown; lateral closely appressed, straw-yellow
and pale brown. Flower buds less appressed, large, glossy bright green. Leaf
unfolds pale brownish-green or khaki, soon bright glossy green, deltoid to
ovate-deltoid, abruptly short-acuminate, long-acuminate or acute, 5–8 × 6–8 cm,
with forward, curved, hooked teeth, and thickened, translucent margins. Underside pale green, reticulate. Petiole flattened, 3–4 cm. Autumn colour soft yellow.

Flowers and fruit. Male catkins grey becoming crimson and 5 cm long just
before shedding pollen in late March. Female catkins greenish-white 6–7 cm
long, shedding white woolly seeds in June.

Similar species. *P. × euramericana* (p. 186), which, with other hybrids, has
replaced this species as a countryside tree, is a very different tree.

'ITALICA' **Lombardy Poplar** **Pl. 15**

N. Italy 1758. Common everywhere except in hilly country, best developed in
lowland river-valleys especially the middle Thames and middle Severn basins.
Too often planted in lines for which it is most unsuitably fragile. 30 × 4 m
(36.5 m at Marble Hill, Twickenham). Many look taller but are deceptive.

Bark. Dark grey, smooth and sub-shiny at first, soon dull and shallowly ridged.

Crown. Varies with the clone, of which there are several, but the true (male)
form is *fastigiate* and *narrowly columnar* to a tapered apex until old when
several stems form a narrow, flat top and soon die back or are damaged by
lightning. Bole burry and sprouty, deeply fluted and buttressed.

Foliage. Shoot shiny pale yellowish-brown, with scattered small groups of
long, dark lenticels. Bud very slender, conic on outer parts of shoot, appressed,
pale *chestnut-brown*, 8 mm; on inner parts, ovoid-conic,
appressed, shiny dark red, 6 mm. Leaf deltoid to ovate short-
acuminate, 6 × 4.5 cm, with regular, small, curved teeth;
bright green, glabrous. Petiole 2.5 cm, flattened, yellowish-
green.

Flowers and fruit. The true form is male only, the catkins
expanding in early April, *deep red*; red and yellow when
shedding pollen in mid-April.

'Gigantea' ('Foemina') Frequent. Few heavy ascending

'Italica Gigantea'

branches, rather open crown broadening to near the top like a glass or inverted triangle. Female, flowering late April; long, 12 cm, curved pale bright green catkins ascending and arched.

'PLANTIERENSIS' 1855 Metz. Similar to 'Italica' but with hairy petioles and shoots at first; nearly glabrous by midsummer. From many seen in Herefordshire, this form seems to have more healthy, shiny, brighter foliage and columnar, square-topped crown, less tapered. Probably common.

CHINESE NECKLACE POPLAR   *Populus lasiocarpa* Oliv.

C. and W. China 1900. Rare; some gardens in all parts but most in S.W. England. 15 m. (21 × 2.1 m Bath B.G.)
Bark. Brownish-grey fissured shallowly and vertically, rough and peeling off branches; biggest boles grey with oak-like fissures strongly spiralled at base.
Crown. Gaunt; long level branches swept upwards at the ends; few laterals; upper branches radiating.
Foliage. Shoot stout, green, densely hairy at first. Bud large, long-pointed, conic, bright shining green. Leaf *very big*, 20–35 × 20 cm on pink, flattened 20 cm petiole; cordate, ovate-acuminate, finely serrulate or forward crenate, finely pubescent beneath; the veins red towards base.
Flowers. Thick yellow catkins on male trees, 20–25 cm long, open before leaves in early May. Fruit either on separate 20–25 cm catkins with 20–25 well-spaced rounded green fruits covered in long pale fawn wool, or 5–6 fruit on basal 6–8 cm of male catkin.

Chinese Necklace Poplar

WESTERN BALSAM POPLAR   *Populus trichocarpa* Hook.

Alaska to California 1892. Common; shelter-belts, roadsides, gardens small and large, occasional plantations, north to Easter Ross. 35 × 3 m.
Bark. Dark green-grey and smooth until quite large, then dark grey, shallowly fissured.
Crown. Young trees narrowly conic, pointed with leading shoot 2 m or more long; in late summer, leaves increase in size to apex. Branches whorled, ascending, very numerous, mixed untidily with epicormic sprouts and old snags. Old trees with broad brush-like tops as branches nearly upright and lower ones sweep up level with central stem.
Foliage. Shoot slightly angled, yellowish, becoming rounded, shiny and reddish. Terminal bud long slender and pointed, shiny red-brown slightly hairy; slightly curved, 3 cm; lateral bud closely appressed, brown, 1 cm. Leaves well out and bright yellowish-green early in April; big, long-pointed nearly oblong or broad-ovate; thick and heavy to the touch, 10–30 cm long; finely crenate teeth; dark green above, white as if painted beneath, often rather yellowish, also rusty near veins. Autumn colour a good Western Balsam Poplar
yellow turning pale brown contrasting with still white underside. Petiole 2 cm, broadening at base, stout, pale green variably stained crimson.

Flowers. Male trees bear thick, 8 × 1.5 cm, dull crimson catkins before the leaves in early April, often shed before releasing pollen. Female flowers green, more sparse on catkin; fruit shed in May, covered in white wool.

Growth. The most vigorous tree grown in Britain (exceeded by *Eucalyptus globulus* in Ireland), has grown to 30 m in 15 years; shoots of 2 m are common until the tree is over 20 m tall. Growth starts slowly in May when the expanding buds emit a powerful fragrance of balsam detectable at more than 100 m and present, but less strongly, during hot weather until midsummer. Shoots grow at increasing speed to a maximum in mid-August and stop by early September. Stool-shoots may grow on later and can be over 4 m long.

Similar species. *P. tacamahaca* and several hybrid balsams all similar and known by the white undersides to the long, thick leaves. *Populus tacamahaca* Miller, **Eastern Balsam Poplar** (Eastern N. America 1689) is found in a few gardens especially in the Midlands, to 37 m. It is distinguished from *P. trichocarpa* by *numerous slender suckers* around the base for many yards; bark with pink fissures, cleaner bole; more upswept branching; longer petiole, 5–7 cm and shoot not winged or angled. The leaf is the same oily yellowish-white beneath and equally variable on the same shoot; mean about 9 × 6 cm. The veins curve in elegantly until parallel with the nearly entire margin. Hybrids between *P. trichocarpa* and *P. tacamahaca* are now much used for planting in odd corners of rich, moist soil. The one most planted, **'TT 32'** is narrow, erect and extremely vigorous. A recent production being widely planted for ornament is *Populus* × *candicans* **'Aurora'**. Easily recognised as the only variegated poplar, its dark green leaves are blotched pale green and cream with some pink. The amount of cream in the leaf varies with the time of the season when it emerged and the vigour of growth. It can be a striking object in midsummer with big bunches of white leaves like water-lilies at the tip of each branch. Shoot red-brown and terete, petiole white or red, 4–7 cm, leaf truncate, deltoid, 10 × 8 cm. Approx. 15 m Aylesbury (by canal bridge).

BERLIN POPLAR *Populus* × *berolinensis* Pl. 15

A hybrid between *Populus laurifolia* and, probably, the Lombardy Poplar. Berlin, about 1800. Rare, largely confined to collections but occasional survivors of more general planting. More successful and frequent on the Continent. 25 × 3 m.

Bark. Dull grey irregular, narrow ridges, with corky pale buff fissures.

Crown. Upswept and dense; crowded, densely leafed branches and vertical epicormic shoots; broadest near the flat top in old trees, not far below pointed top in young trees.

Foliage. Shoot bright green at first (red in places on epicormic sprouts), ripens greenish-fawn, slightly winged, faintly pubescent at first, soon glabrous. Leaf *long-cuneate*, obovate or lanceolate, some rounded at base; acuminate; regular, shallow, forward-hooked teeth; to 8 × 6 cm bright green above, midrib nearly white; *slightly whitish* beneath; petiole to 5 cm slender.

Flowers. Male trees thought to grow better than females, so survivors probably mostly male with crimson catkins in late April.

Similar species. Resembles a small-leaved, dense and sprouty *P. trichocarpa* (p. 184) but narrow, small leaves much less white beneath.

HYBRID BLACK POPLARS *Populus* × *euramericana* (Dode) Guinier
Syn. *P.* × *canadensis* Moench
This name covers all the numerous hybrid poplars which have arisen from
crossings between the European *P. nigra* and the American *P. deltoides* since
about 1700, but the cultivar name alone is better.

'SEROTINA' **Black Italian Poplar**   **Pl. 15**
France 1750. Very common, in cities, towns, parks, gardens and river valleys,
by railways and as screen round water-towers and factories. 45 × 6.3 m.
Bark. Pale *grey*, fissured deeply, vertically and peculiarly regularly, fissures
running straight for 10 or 20 m and parallel, separated by acute ridges. A
disc cut from the bole looks like a cog-wheel.
Crown. Clean bole for 3–4 or sometimes 15 m without any burrs or branches,
then a few large branches level at first then curving upwards finally nearly
vertical, some curved inwards making huge, *open-cup* crown, usually swept
rather to one side of the tree. Shoots stout, distant, upward, not pendulous.
Foliage. Shoot stout, bright green; second year light brown. Bud 2 cm, sharp
pointed, shiny green. Leaves emerge in *late May, reddish-brown,* turning light
fresh grey-green then darkening somewhat but pale undersides gives general
crown a light colour. Spread thinly and evenly over whole crown. Leaves
8 × 8 cm, with petiole flattened, 2–6 cm often reddish; truncate, 4–5 small teeth
along basal margin, deltoid, acuminate; margins thickened and translucent
under lens, scalloped by curved teeth. Vigorous young trees may bear leaves
14 × 11 cm.
Flowers. A *male* clone, only. Catkins lengthen in April, turn bright red in mid-
April, shed pollen and fall before the end.
Growth. Very rapidly makes huge tree until branches begin to be shed by
150 years at most. Can grow 2 m a year, over 30 m in 30 years and rapidly makes
a large bole.
Similar hybrids. 'Robusta' (p. 187) when young; 'Marilandica' (p. 187) a
female clone, and 'Regenerata' (below) also female.

'SEROTINA AUREA' **Golden Poplar**. 1871 Belgium. Fairly frequent in towns
and parks. 30 × 3 m. Leaves a good golden colour by mid-June. More branchy,
not cup-shaped, more dense, irregular conic or domed crown on smaller
branches.
'REGENERATA'   **Pl. 15**
France 1814. Should be named "Railway Poplar" as common by main lines
into cities, in coal-yards and sidings, also on embankments elsewhere, London
parks, village greens, cress-beds and shelter-belts. Often pollarded. 30 × 3.2 m.
Superficially resembles 'Serotina', but differs in every detail:
Bark. Pale grey, sometimes ridged as in 'Serotina', fissures usually shorter, and
shallow.
Crown. Bole untidy, cluttered with shoots and snags; rather *slender* branches,
ascending then arching over and fanning outwards, slender shoots spreading
and hanging from them.
Foliage. Shoot pale yellow-brown, shiny. Bud 5–6 mm, narrowly conic, at first
glossy green then glossy dark brown. Leaves emerge pale brown in late April,
remain tipped brown until mid-May, then bright pale green, and are unevenly
spread over crown. Petiole 3–5 cm. Leaf 8 × 8 cm, short acuminate or obtuse;
teeth curved hooks.

Flowers. A *female* clone only. Slender, bright pale green catkins like caterpillars hang in dense rows in late April as leaves unfold. They drop, covered in white wool, in late July.

'ROBUSTA' 1895 France (*P. deltoides*×*P. nigra* 'Plantierenses'). Frequent, roadsides, small plantations and a few collections in valleys in S. England. 30m. (40×4m, Bowood, Wilts.). Differs from 'Serotina' in more regular, and leafy ovoid-conic crown maturing with more but smaller branches evenly spaced; broad-conic, not cup-shaped. Also in leaf three weeks earlier much brighter orange to red-brown, a fine sight in mid-April. Leaves larger, 9 × 9 cm or more, deep glossy green, deltoid-acuminate with incurved teeth from base, main veins white, irregular; undersurface matt. Petiole 6–9 cm patterned pinkish-yellow. Stool shoots grow 3–4 m in a year and bear leaves to 19 × 13 cm. Flowers: male clone only. Deep, bright red catkins in early April, 8–10 cm, so many and prominent as to identify the tree.

'Robusta'

'EUGENEI' **Eugene's Poplar.** (*P.* 'Regenerata' × *P. nigra* 'Italica') 1832 Metz. Introduced to Kew 1888, two of which are now 36 × 3.3 m. Lombardy Poplar was one parent and this shows in the columnar and densely branched ascending crown of younger trees. Old trees have a few big branches level, then upswept. Shoots slender, straight and pendulous. Sometimes in plantations. Can be 30 × 2 m in 30 years. Leaves flush pale brown soon green, 9 × 8 cm, very truncate, round-based deltoid, acuminate with very shallow incurved teeth. Petiole slender, 5 cm. On plants cut down annually, leaves can be 12 × 12 cm.

Eugene's Poplar

'MARILANDICA' *c.* 1800. Introduced to Kew 1843 where now 35 × 5.2 m. Infrequent but occasional in city parks and by roads.

Bark. Old tree *dark grey-brown*, reddish in places, deeply fissured.
Crown. Remarkably *globular, densely* branched, when young; open when old.
Shoots. Green and winged. Leaves flush green; very triangular.
Flowers. *Female* clone only. Green catkins mid-April; fluffy white fruits in June.

WILLOWS   Salix

Some 300 species from all parts of the North Temperate Zone, the Arctic Zone and some from the tropics and South Temperate Zone. 19 native to Britain, from large trees 30 m tall to a tiny shrub of 3 cm. A difficult group, as all 19 are thought to have hybridised with at least two of the others and some with many more. *Only those species growing to tree-size are included here.* In all willows the male and female flowers are on separate trees except on occasional trees of Weeping Willow.

BAY WILLOW   *Salix pentandra* L.

Native in N. Wales and north of the Midlands; uncommon, by rivers and rare in gardens. 10m (21m, died 1971). Pyrenees to Asia Minor, north to N. Norway.

Bark. Brown-grey, finely fissured by narrow orange buff cracks.

Crown. Broad, low dome, dense and dark in leaf.

Foliage. Shoot glossy, olive-green. Bud ovoid-conic, 5mm, pale brown. Leaf 10 × 4.5cm oblong-lanceolate, acuminate, finely and evenly serrulate, *deep glossy green* above, glaucous beneath; midrib pale yellow above. Little obovate leaves, 1.5cm are mixed with normal leaves. Petiole 8mm.

Bay Willow

Flowers. Male catkins cylindric, 2–6cm on leafy, pubescent stalks; open bright yellow among leaves; females a little smaller curving to erect. Stamens five or more.

Similar species. Only *S. fragilis* (below) also has big, shiny leaves but these are much longer and much paler.

CRACK WILLOW   *Salix fragilis* L.   **Pl. 16**

Native north to Perthshire, planted farther north and in Ireland. Abundant beside lowland rivers in S. England, often pollarded. Europe and W. Siberia to Persia. 18 × 3.5m.

Bark. Dull, dark grey; scaly when young, later a network of thick ridges.

Crown. Broadly conic, long slender upswept branches with widely spaced *rather pendulous* leaves. Old trees with heavy, twisted, low branches; broadly domed. Pale orange shoots in March, before leaves appear.

Foliage. Shoot yellow then green-brown spreading very straight from larger shoot at 60° and snapping off cleanly at the base very readily. Bud yellow, pale green or brown, closely appressed, long-pointed conic. Leaf slightly silky at first, soon smooth, narrowly lanceolate to finely tapered often twisted point, 12 × 2cm (19 × 5cm); glabrous grey-green or glaucous beneath, *rich glossy green* above; petiole 1–2cm.

Flowers. Male catkins yellow, 2–5cm; female green 10cm by May; each fruit 7mm very slender, soon fluffy white.

Similar species. Shape and position – pollarded or not, in numbers along rivers – shared only by *S. alba* (p. 189) but *S. fragilis* has much more regularly placed, longer leaves which are soon bright green, and a more open crown.

CONTORTED WILLOW   *Salix matsudana* Koidzumi 'Tortuosa'

China 1925. A cultivar of a very rare species; now quite commonly planted and common in small gardens. To 17m in ten years at Oxford Botanic Garden.

Bark. Pale grey-brown, rather shiny, becoming pale grey and fissured.

Crown. Unmistakable; short bole, 2–3 very sinuous upright stems soon diffusing into slender upright shoots *curling in large arcs*; the exterior of fine shoots *contorted* in a sharp curve each 3cm of their length, some pendulous.

Foliage. New shoots very pale yellow-green, bearing crisped and curled boat-shaped leaves 8 × 1cm on

Contorted Willow

petioles of 0.5 cm. The leaves appear during early March and are matt, bright
pale green with a few persistent long silky hairs; glaucous beneath; long-
acuminate, with very small, distant, forward, thickened, hook-tipped teeth.

WHITE WILLOW   *Salix alba* L.   Pl. 16
Native all over Britain except in N.W. Scotland. Europe, N. Africa to C. Asia.
Common along lowland riversides and valleys; usually less numerous than
S. fragilis. 25 m.
Bark. Dark grey, thick ridges in a close network.
Crown. Tall, rather shapeless and billowing, main branches ascending, smaller
ones spreading with slender shoots rather pendulous; blue-grey in leaf. Younger
trees conic, acute.
Foliage. Shoot *slender*, light grey-pink to olive-brown, densely pubescent; at
narrow angle from main shoot and not brittle at base. Bud very small, 2 mm,
dark pink with grey pubescence and narrow curved beak. Leaves held densely
at all angles, dark blue-grey; silky white pubescence above, short matted white
beneath, 7–8 × 1 cm on petiole 0.5 cm; lanceolate, long-acuminate; shallow,
sharp, forward serrate.
Flowers. Catkins on leafy stalks; males yellow; females slender, green soon
fluffy white with seed; both 4–6 cm.

'TRISTIS' **Weeping Willow**   Pl. 16
Syns. *S. vitellina* var. *pendula* (Rehd.), 'Chrysocoma'
(France, c. 1800?). Common by large rivers and in gardens and parks equally
on dry or damp soils, and in suburban gardens. Best developed along the River
Thames above Kew, in Cambridge and Cheltenham. 22 × 4 m.
Bark. Pale grey-brown, regularly networked by rather shallow ridges.
Crown. Irregularly broad-domed; large branches sinuous in big curves, long
slender shoots hanging straight down.
Foliage. As in the type but shoot pale yellow in summer, becoming brighter
and richer yellow during spring; leaves unfold very early bright pale green,
larger, 10 × 1.5 cm, shiny above and finely pubescent, bluish-white beneath,
very finely pubescent.
Flowers. Male catkins slender, curved upwards 7–8 cm yellow when leaves
well out in mid-April. Normally only a male clone; occasional female flowers on
male catkins.
Recognition. This is the common Weeping Willow, often called "*S. baby-
lonica*" which is a Chinese, brown-twigged, rare tree of poor growth here.

'CHERMESINA' **Coral-bark Willow** ('Britzensis') 1840 Germany. Frequent
in gardens and plantings near lowland rivers and lakes. 25 m. Sometimes cut
regularly to make a small plant with long, colourful shoots in winter. Young
trees narrowly conic with rather incurved, upswept branches. New shoots
dark red, becoming *bright orange-red* in winter and spring; leaves pale slightly
yellowish-grey distinguish in summer. (30 × 3 m Glasnevin B.G., Dublin.)

'SERICEA' **Silver Willow** ('Argentea'). Fairly common, widely distributed
in parks and gardens. Smaller and much slower than the type; striking in the
landscape and easily recognised by *bright silver-white* leaves throughout the
season. Leaf slender, lanceolate, 10 × 1.5 cm, covered in silky white long hairs.

'COERULEA' **Cricket-bat Willow** c. 1780 Suffolk. Commonly grown for
cricket-bats in Suffolk and Essex especially, around margins of low-lying fields,

besides dykes and streams; sometimes in plantations; uncommon elsewhere, in parks, gardens and by roads. Differs from the type in: crown conic upright and narrow; branches at 45° or less from trunk; shoots very slender, *purple*; leaves deep *blue-greyish-green*. 25 × 4 m. One of the fastest growing of all trees in Britain, to 20 × 2 m in 15 years, 24 m in 19 years.

GOAT WILLOW, SALLOW, PUSSY WILLOW   *Salix caprea* L.

Native, found everywhere in damp woodlands, scrub and hedges. Europe to N.E. Asia. 16 × 1 (4) m.

Bark. Pale grey, smooth; shallow and wide fissures of pale brown.
Crown. Bushy and often low on a sinuous bole; trees open-crowned with ascending branches.
Foliage. Shoot at first grey with long hairs, soon smooth, shiny, deep red-brown. Bud ovoid, slightly pointed, 3–4 mm, bright red. Leaf variable in size, shape and toothing. Oval, lanceolate or obovate, rounded at base, obliquely short-pointed, 6–10 × 3–6 cm, shallowly crenate or entire; on a *dark red*, very *pubescent* petiole 1 cm long; grey-green above often

Goat Willow

wrinkled and downy; glaucous beneath with soft dense hairs.
Flowers. Male buds expand to show silver hairs for weeks before the dense stamens emerge with golden tips; inflorescence ovoid, 3 cm, usually abundant in full flower throughout March but occasional trees from late December. Female trees with similar buds, but flowers 5–6 cm, some 200 whitish-green styles arch over; soon bright pale green, each fruit 7 mm flask shaped; in mid-May turn erect, covered in brown wool, white within a few days; fluffy seed shed by end of May.
Similar species. The native sallows are a complex group, and several species, subspecies and hybrids occur, most of which pass as Pussy Willow when in flower. All except the next species are strictly shrubs and so are outside the scope of this book. *S. caprea* is distinct from other tree willows in its rather thick, often short and knobbly shoots and upright shrubby growth.

GREY WILLOW   *Salix cinerea* L.

Same distribution here and abroad as *S. caprea*. Differs from *S. caprea* mainly in slender shoot remaining densely covered in short *brown pubescence*; bud dark red-brown covered in long hairs; large *stipules* at the base of the leaf and usually narrower leaf. Pubescence beneath is often rust-coloured along the veins. If the bark is stripped from a two-year shoot, it reveals fine ridges absent in *S. caprea*. Very seldom of tree-form.

Grey Willow

VIOLET WILLOW   *Salix daphnoides* Vill.

S. Europe, C. Asia, the Himalayas 1829. Infrequent; almost confined to well-planted small gardens. 9 m. (19 m Glasnevin B.G., Dublin.)
Crown. Upright then spreading, open. Branches slender.
Bark. For several years, bright blue-white bloom covers the dark purple bark which later shows. Young plants, or those cut back frequently, have long shoots blue-white to the base.

oliage. Shoot dark, shining purple after shedding some hairs; cond year bloomed. Bud narrowly conic, blackish purple, lateral ids closely appressed. Leaf lanceolate, acuminate, 6–8 × 2 cm; ry shallow, fine serrulation; dark rather shiny green with broad, hite midrib above, glaucous grey-green beneath; petiole crimson ove, colour spreading on to midrib, pale yellow beneath, 3–5 m. Stipules bright green, 2–3 mm, ovate, serrate. Leaf remains een into November.

lowers and fruit. Male catkins like Sallow (p. 190), bright llow, 5 × 2 cm in March; females more slender, grey-green. Seed aring white fluff.

rowth. Very vigorous for a few years, the Violet Willow soon ows from 1–2 m a year, as the arched branches decline in vigour,) 20–50 cm a year. The rare ideal – the fast growing-tree which rely grows too big.

ecognition. The blue-white bloom, thinning here and there er the purple bark to give a violet tinge, most striking in winter, always visible to identify this attractive tree.

Violet Willow

WALNUT, HICKORY AND WING-NUT FAMILY *Juglandaceae*

rees with rather substantial, sometimes huge, pinnate leaves and with male owers in short or very long catkins; female flowers on the same tree solitary or on short or very long catkins.

WING-NUTS Pterocarya

ight species: six from China, one from Japan and one from the Caucasus ountains. Very vigorous trees usually suckering widely around the base and ith naked buds and chambered pith.

AUCASIAN WING-NUT *Pterocarya fraxinifolia* (Lamb.) Spach **Pl. 16** Syn. *Pt. caucasica* Mey.

aucasus Mountains to N. Persia 1782. Infrequent; some large gardens and arks north to Edinburgh, beside open water or in damp soil. 25 m. (35 × 5.5 m : Melbury, Dorset.)

rown. Either short, rugged bole, strong branches curved up in a cup shape, r many-stemmed, wide open clumps of long, sinuous boles. Small branches vel, long ones slightly drooped.

ark. Dull grey, a coarse network of broad shallow ridges.

oliage. Shoot green-brown slightly bloomed purple, smooth. Bud without ales, slender, 2 cm, two leaves pressed together, rich brown with very short ubescence. Leaves alternate, compound, to 60 cm with (7) 21 (27) opposite aflets on a smooth, *round*, yellow-green rachis swollen at the base to a bulb cm across. Leaflets crowded, overlapping, floppy, oblong, curved to a narrow oint, middle ones largest to 18 × 5 cm, all pointing somewhat forwards, unqual at base, sessile, forward-serrate, bright shiny green above, paler beneath ith pale brown or white, long, stellate hairs each side of midrib. Autumn olour bright yellow in October.

Plate 17   **WALNUTS, BIRCHES**

Male and female flowers separate but on the same tree.

1. Common Walnut   *Juglans regia*   195

(a) Bud, leaf and fruit.
(b) Male catkins.
(c) Female flowers at tip of new growth.

2. Black Walnut   *Juglans nigra*   195

Leaf. The numerous, toothed leaflets together with the dark, rugged bark make this a very different tree from the Common Walnut even at a distance.

3. White-barked Himalayan Birch   *Betula jacquemontii*   203

(a) Leaf which has 7–8 pairs of main veins.
(b) Bark, shining white and without the black diamond marks of Silver Birch.

This species merges into *Betula utilis* which has 11–12 pairs of main veins.

4. Northern Chinese Red-barked Birch   *Betula albosinensis* var. *septentrionalis*   203

(a) Leaf, which can be 15 cm long.
(b) Bark.

5. Silver Birch   *Betule pendula*   205

The common Silver Birch of dry, sandy heaths, and on mountainsides; replaced by the Downy Birch on wet soils and boggy areas.

(a) Shoot. Leaves much less rounded and more irregularly toothed than the leaves of Downy Birch.
(b) Shoot in April with male catkin about to shed pollen.
(c) Immature male catkins in midsummer.
(d) Tree 15 m tall showing pendulous crown of mature tree.

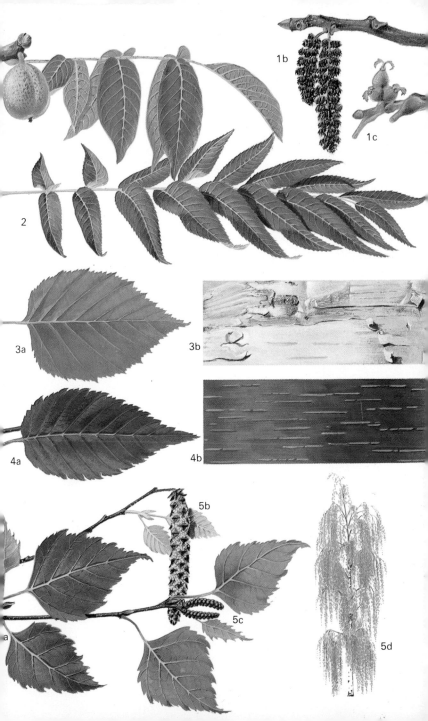

1a

1b

1c

1d

2

3a

3b

4a

4b

ALDERS

Plate 18

Mostly trees of rapid growth; bud on a stalk (except Green Alder), flowers of each sex separated but on the same tree, fruit woody, cone-like.

1. Common Alder   *Alnus glutinosa*   210

    (a) Old, open fruit.
    (b) Shoot with leaves, immature fruit, next year's male catkins
        and the smaller female catkins, in late summer.
    (c) Male catkins shedding pollen.
    (d) Tree about 20 m tall.

2. Green Alder   *Alnus viridis*   207

    Shoot with immature male catkins and showing the unstalked winter-bud. This plant, rare in Britain, can be a shrub or a small tree.

3. Italian Alder   *Alnus cordata*   211

    (a) Immature fruit, summer.
    (b) Shoot and foliage with next year's female flowers and the
        larger male flowers.

    A handsome shapely tree of rapid growth, occasional in city parks and by roadsides.

4. Grey Alder   *Alnus incana*   211

    A useful tree for rapid growth on dry and difficult soils; planted in land-reclamation schemes, on coal-tips, etc.
    Shoot in summer with:
    (a) Next spring's male catkins, and
    (b) Next spring's female catkins.

Flowers and fruit. Male flowers thick, yellow catkins unfold with the leaves, rarely in mid-March, usually late April; 5–12 cm, greenish, shed in mid-May; females 10–15 cm, slender, strung with 3 mm flowers, with bright pink stigmas; lengthen to 25–50 cm and bear fruit thinly scattered along basal half, densely but unevenly on outer half, each fruit surrounded by whitish-green, circular wing 2 cm across.

Recognition. Wing-nuts are known by: wide crowns of level branches with alternate, large, rather hanging, bright green compound leaves; fruit-catkins in summer, and their suckering habit. This species is separable from the two below mainly by the smoothly rounded rachis and tendency to grow as a clump of boles.

CHINESE WING-NUT   *Pterocarya stenoptera* DC.

China 1860. Rare; largely confined to collections in S. England and Ireland. 18 × 2.2 m (24 × 3 m at 0.6 m, Kew).

Bark. Pink-grey; very shallow, broad, interwoven ridges.

Foliage. Differs from *Pt. fraxinifolia* in shoots with long, pale brown hairs shed during summer, shorter leaves to 30 cm with 15–19 (11–21) leaflets, and rachis *broadly winged*, flanges between leaflets broadening at base of each pair to 7 mm across and there serrate. Rachis also with stiff white pubescence at the base, often to the end of the season.

Fruit. Wing oblong-elliptic, half the width of the elliptic wing of *P. × rehderana*; green at base, rest white and pink.

HYBRID WING-NUT   *Pterocarya × rehderana* Schneid.

A hybrid between the two previous species. 1879, introduced 1908. Rare; collections mainly in S. England and in Ireland. Differs from other wing-nuts in the rachis having *narrow flanges* pressed together along the top or reduced to a groove, and abundant female catkins to 45 cm long with about 60 fruit densely set below bare basal 5 cm. A tree of immense vigour to 17 × 2.1 m in 22 years at Kew; largest bole × 3.3 m; 26 × 2.8 m in 43 years at Birr Cas., Co. Offaly.

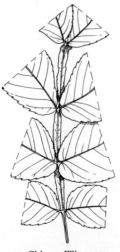

Chinese Wing-nut

Hybrid Wing-nut

WALNUTS Juglans

Fifteen species from N. and S. America and Asia. Pith is chambered as in *Pterocarya* but not in *Carya*. That is, the centre of the shoot is closely divided by transverse parallel plates.

COMMON WALNUT *Juglans regia* L. Pl. 17

S.E. Europe to China. Introduced in early times. Common, especially S. and S.W. England, less frequent north to beyond Inverness. 23 × 3 m.

Bark. Very pale grey, smooth between wide, deep fissures; branches shiny grey in young trees, later paler and fissured like the bole.

Crown. Widely spreading with big, very sinuous low branches; lace-like in winter from many twisting branches and rather bunched, short small shoots.

Foliage. Shoot stout, shiny, dark yellow-green, soon dark brown, smooth. Bud very squat, broad, dark purple-brown. Leaves alternate, pinnate, 20–45 cm, usually seven (three to nine) leaflets, terminal one largest on 4 cm petiole, elliptic or obovate, to 20 × 10 cm; side ones decrease in size towards base of leaf, subsessile, oblique at base, oblong-ovate, outermost pair to 18 × 8 cm, basal pair down to 3 × 1.5 but usually 8 × 4 cm. Dull, dark yellow-green with yellowish veins swinging away from margins; thick, *leathery*. Margins *entire*, except for some smallest leaflets shallowly and irregularly toothed. Crushed leaves have a scent like shoe-polish. Leaves *unfold orange-brown* in mid-May (rarely late April) and remain this colour until mid-June.

Flowers and fruit. Thick, short male catkins 5–10 cm, axillary, on last year's shoot, dark yellow mid-May to early June. Female flowers terminal, on new shoots, 2–5, with green pubescent, flask-shaped ovaries and yellow styles: 1 cm. Nut ripening in long, hot summers; fruit globose, smooth, dark green, 4–5 cm.

'LACINIATA' Rare, small tree; leaves 25 × 20 cm with nine leaflets cut to midrib into narrow irregularly toothed lobes. The rachis and veins are dark purplish.

'Laciniata'

Recognition. All other walnuts and hickories have serrated leaves. The chambered pith separates walnuts from all other trees except wing-nuts. It is shown in an obliquely broken or cut twig.

BLACK WALNUT *Juglans nigra* L. Pl. 17

Eastern USA, S.E. Canada to Texas pre-1656. Infrequent; parks and gardens in S. and E. England, best trees confined to area from Thames Valley and Wilts. to E. Anglia. Rare in Scotland and Ireland but one fine tree in Ross-shire. 30 × 6 m (Mote Park, Kent).

Bark. Dark brown or black, rarely grey, closely patterned by diamond network of narrow, thick ridges with deep hollows between.

Crown. Tall dome, occasionally wide, usually on a fine straight bole, often long, with a large symmetrical head of radiating, slightly twisting large branches. In summer densely hung with long shiny leaves.

Foliage. Shoot pale brown, or orange and densely finely pubescent; bud pointed, complex folds, pale brown; grey pubescence. Leaf alternate, pinnate, to 45 cm or more with 11–23 leaflets, usually 15, often 14 (terminal leaflet missing), widely spaced, 4 cm apart, opposite or nearly so, a few alternate, sub-sessile, longest in the middle of the leaf where to 9 × 3 cm, unevenly rounded ovate-lanceolate, acuminate, shallowly forward-*serrate*; *flushes yellow-green*, later rich, dark shiny green above, paler beneath and finely pubescent, especially on midrib.

Flowers and fruit. Male catkins 3–5 from distal buds, on last year's shoot, cylindric, thick, spreading, bright lime-green turning yellow, 5–10 cm, pubescent; females terminal in fives, 6–8 mm, grey-green; fruit solitary or in pairs, green, smooth, globose, 3–5 cm, highly fragrant if bruised.

Growth. Very fast-growing on rich damp soils in hot areas but difficult to start; slow outside the region mentioned. 45 cm first year from seed.

Similar species. *J. cinerea* (below) also has toothed, numerous leaflets.

BUTTER-NUT *Juglans cinerea* L.
E. N. America, New Brunswick to Georgia 1633.
Very rare; S. England, S. Scotland and Ireland.
24 × 2 m, Cliveden, Bucks.

Bark. Similar to *J. regia* but purplish-grey and less coarsely fissured pink.

Foliage. Buds *white or pink*, pointed. Leaf to 60 cm, leaflets 9–15–17, thin, bright green above, glaucous and finely pubescent beneath. Rachis *finely pubescent*. Crushed foliage has strong scent of sweet hay or paint.

Fruit. To 12 or more on pubescent, spreading catkin to 15 cm long.

Similar species. Leaf bigger than either *J. nigra* (p. 195) or *J. regia* (p. 195), thin, bright green; bark quite unlike *J. nigra*, crown slender, un-evenly conic in all but oldest trees, rachis less thickly pubescent and sticky than *J. mand-schurica* (p. 197) or *J. ailantifolia* (below).

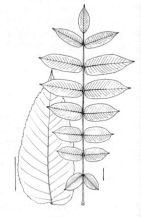

Butter-nut

JAPANESE WALNUT *Juglans ailantifolia* Carr.
　Syn. *J. sieboldiana* Maxim.
Japan 1860. Rare; in several collections and some big gardens in Great Britain and Ireland; some notably good at Edinburgh R.B.G. 18 × 2 m.

Bark. Striped pale and dark grey with shallow fissures.

Foliage. Shoot and rachis densely covered in *sticky dark reddish, short pubes-cence* also on veins beneath leaflets. Leaf huge, 80–100 cm with 11–17 leaflets, glabrous, shiny bright green above, rather *abruptly* tapered to short point, finely toothed.

Flowers and fruit. Male catkins 15–30 cm; female flowers June, striking, bright deep red, flat stigmas on 10 cm, erect, pubescent spike; fruit globose, 5 cm densely covered in sticky down.

MANCHURIAN WALNUT *Juglans mandshurica* Maxim.

Manchuria and N. China 1859. Very rare, almost confined to southern botanic gardens in England but more widely planted in N. Europe. Bark pale grey-pink with wide buff fissures. Shoot and leaf-stalk with sticky pubescence. Leaf to 70 cm, leaflets 15, terminal on 3 cm petiolule, laterals subsessile, oblique, oblanceolate; white fluff in axils beneath, *acuminate*, matt yellow-green above, veins reddish beneath; scarcely toothed.

Manchurian Walnut

HICKORIES Carya

Twenty species in eastern N. America, one in China, one in Tonkin. Only nine American species grown here. Pith in shoots solid; leaf compound, 3–17 leaflets opposite, serrate. Male flowers on three-pronged catkin; females clustered at tip of new shoot. A group of fine trees, seldom planted and often seen wrongly named when they are, as most descriptions rely much on fruit for identification and are vague about those and about the leaves. A few hybrids are known, and some species are rather variable.

Key to Carya Species

1. Bud bright, deep yellow; slender, pointed; terminal leaflet
sessile; leaf to 25 cm; leaflets usually nine   *cordiformis*, p. 197
Bud pale green and/or brown; ovoid; terminal leaflet stalked or
subsessile; leaflets three to seven, rarely nine   **2**

2. Larger leaves 20–30 cm; rachis glabrous, leaflets five or three,
rarely seven; terminal leaflet subsessile   *glabra*, p. 198
Larger leaves 45–70 cm; rachis pubescent, at least at first;
terminal leaflet with petiole 1–4 cm   **3**

3. Leaflets five, rarely seven; terminal petiole stout; shoot deep
purple-brown, becoming glabrous; leaves often thick and
oily, yellowish-green, ciliate; (bark soon very shaggy)   *ovata*, p. 198
Leaflets seven, rarely five or nine; terminal petiole slender;
shoot green-brown or yellow-pink, densely pubescent;
leaves thin, hard, parchment-like, deep green   **4**

4. Pubescence on shoot hard; leaf coarsely serrate, shoot yellow
and dark pink; (bark smooth, or finely folded)   *tomentosa*, p. 199
Pubescence on shoot soft; leaf crenate; shoot green-brown;
(bark with raised curling plates, later shaggy)   *laciniosa*, p. 199

BITTERNUT *Carya cordiformis* (Wangh.) K. Koch
Syn. *C. amara* Nutt.

E. America, Quebec to Louisiana 1689. Uncommon but the most frequently seen of the *Caryas*; in a number of the larger gardens and collections in S. and

S.W. England, S. Scotland and E. Ireland. 26 × 3 m.

Bark. Pale grey, smooth at first, later shallowly wrinkled, pink and orange in the grooves; older trees with
grey or grey-brown network of small ridges with grey
scales lifting away and orange, curly fissures of varying
depth.

Crown. Elegantly conic, pointed until old; many light
long ascending straight branches. Occasional epicormic
sprouts.

Foliage. Shoot slender, bright green, speckled with
white lenticels. Bud slender with *curved tip*, deep *bright
yellow*. Leaves compound, *nine* (seven, rarely eight)
leaflets on finely pubescent rachis, terminal leaflet *long-
cuneate* but *sessile*; lateral leaflets subsessile, oblique at
base, middle longest, to 15 cm, leaf to 25 cm. Leaflets
dark yellowish-green, sharply forward-serrate, finely
pubescent beneath on veins. Bright golden in mid-
October.

Bitternut

Flowers and fruit. Not conspicuous; male catkins in threes, 5–7 cm. Fruit
in pairs or threes, pear-shaped or rounded, 2–4 cm, yellowish, four-winged
above middle with short, dense pubescence at first.

PIGNUT   *Carya glabra* (Mill.) Sweet
   Syn. *C. porcina* (Michx.f.) Nutt.

Ontario to Alabama *c.* 1750. Very rare; a few collections and large gardens in
S. and W. England and E. Ireland. 22 × 1.5 m.

Bark. Grey-purple, smooth, becoming a beautiful smooth purple finely
wrinkled into rusty and black folds.

Crown. Fairly broad, pointed; in summer covered in small, dark leaves like a
pear-tree at a distance.

Foliage. Shoot brown-green, second year shiny red-brown, slender. Bud very
small, 6–8 mm, ovoid, yellow-green becoming orange-brown. Leaves compound,
small (for the genus), to 18 (30) cm, rachis green or dark pink, glabrous, leaflets
five, three on small leaves, rarely seven; slender, terminal subsessile, laterals
sessile, sharply forward-serrate, dark green, rather oily, firm, glabrous beneath
except for small tufts in vein-axils. Terminal leaflet largest, to 18 × 10 cm.
Brilliant yellow in autumn, turning orange.

Flowers and fruit. Very like those of *C. cordiformis* above.

Similar species. *C. ovalis* (Wangh.) Sargent, New York to Florida, is very
rare and closely related but has stout shoots dark red and usually seven leaflets
per leaf.

SHAGBARK HICKORY   *Carya ovata* (Mill.) K. Koch
   Syn. *C. alba* Nutt.

Quebec to Texas 1629. Uncommon; second to *C. cordiformis* in frequency but
mainly in S. and W. England. 24 × 1.8 m (17 × 4.4 m Antony House, Cornwall).

Bark. Pale grey, shaggy from early age, thin rough plates 10–20 cm at first,
50–60 cm later, curved far from bole at each end.

Crown. Broad and rather gaunt; few branches *arching widely* out.

Foliage. Shoot *stout*, green, finely pubescent at first; later deep purple-brown with pale, oval lenticels, soon glabrous. Frequent large ring of brown hairs at basal node. Bud large, 1–1.5 cm, ovoid, pale green inner scales, brown outer. Leaves compound, large, 45–65 cm on *thick* rachis which is soon glabrous except for dense *pubescence* on *large, bulbous base*; leaflets five (three, seven) thick and oily, yellowish-green, rarely thin and dark; terminal leaflet on *stout* petiole of 2.5–4 cm. Three terminal leaflets largest, obovate, to 35 × 20 cm. Entire at base for 2–3 cm, then crenate, thick small teeth with small tufts of white hairs between, cuneate base also ciliate; soon glabrous beneath. Fine golden autumn colours.

Shagbark Hickory

Flowers and fruit. Males terminal spray 3–4 catkins each 10–15 cm, dividing into three 3 cm from base; minute green flowers, mid-June. Fruit similar to *C. cordiformis*, 2–3 together on stout stalk, 4 × 3.5 cm, four grooves; obovoid, yellow-green; short dense pubescence, later smooth green, speckled white.
Similar species. The other hickories with large leaves, *C. laciniosa* (p. 199) and *C. tomentosa* (below) usually have seven leaflets.

MOCKERNUT   *Carya tomentosa* (Lamb.) Nutt.
Syn. *C. alba* K. Koch
Ontario to Texas 1766. Rare; collections in S. England and in Ireland. 22 × 1.6 m.
Bark. Quite smooth and grey in young trees, faintly striated orange and greenish, later shallow brown fissures develop and divide the now purplish bark into short, smooth ridges; some trees patterned silvery-grey on black.
Crown. Young trees slender and conic, older trees broader, less regular.
Foliage. Shoot dull brown with *stiff*, short, *dense* pubescence, rarely shed. Bud big, 2 × 1.5 cm, ovoid, whitish-green inner scales, outer dark red-brown with dense hairs. Leaf compound, very large, to 50 cm, seven (rarely five or nine) leaflets on stout, yellow-pink rachis with hard, dense pubescence and swollen base; terminal three leaflets largest, central one on *slender* 2–4 cm petiole; speckled white beneath when newly unfolded, usually *fragrant* (grass or paint scents noted), coarsely and shallowly crenate except for basal 2 cm, with occasional tufts of hairs between teeth; dark shiny green above, dense pubescence on veins beneath; hard and parchment-like. Brilliant gold in late October.
Flowers and fruit. Male catkins dense, three-pronged, 15 cm, dull yellow in June. Females two, terminal in a green 4–5 lobed involucre, 6 mm; centre red-brown. Fruit sessile, two, globose, 3–4 cm, four deep grooves; green faintly speckled white.
Similar species. The big seven-parted leaf is only like *C. laciniosa* (below).

BIG SHELL-BARK HICKORY   *Carya laciniosa* (Michx.f.) Loud.
Syn. *C. sulcata* Nutt.
New York to Oklahoma 1804. Rare; in many collections in S. England; less rare than *C. tomentosa*. 18 × 1.6 m.

Bark. Grey with shallow orange fissures and, from the first, curiously overlaid by loosely adhering, dull grey, long, irregularly *curving scales*; becoming shaggy with long strips, narrower than in *C. ovata* but similarly bent away at each end.

Crown. Rather open and narrow, irregular; broadly conic when young.

Foliage. Shoot greenish-brown or orange, finely soft-pubescent. Bud bigger even than in *C. tomentosa*, to 2.5 cm, ovoid, whitish-green inner scales (two), outer brown and hairy. When opened, big obovate, silky red-brown bud scales adhere, deflexed 6 × 3 cm, until early June. Leaf compound, the largest of the Caryas, 50–75 cm, seven (rarely five or nine) leaflets on finely soft-pubescent rachis, with bulbous base; terminal largest, to 37 × 15 cm, on *slender short* petiolule 1 cm or subsessile; crenate, yellowish-green with yellow veins, dull, thick and hard, pale beneath and reticulate, slightly pubescent veins; lanceolate; terminal obovate-lanceolate; all acuminate. Not fragrant. Yellow in autumn.

Big Shell-bark Hickory

Flowers and fruit. Similar to *C. cordiformis* (p. 197) but rarely seen.

Similar species. Bark of young trees distinct although can be similar in *C. ovata*; foliage very similar to *C. tomentosa* (p. 199).

PECAN   *Carya illinoensis* (Wangenh.) K. Koch
    Syn. *C. pecan* (Marsh) Engl. and Graebn.
South-western USA. Planted in Virginia, has grown 40 m in 110 years. Extremely rare. Wisley; Cambridge B.G. 13 long-lanceolate leaflets. Bark pale grey coarsely flaked.

BIRCH, ALDER, HORNBEAM AND HAZEL
FAMILY *Betulaceae*

A hundred species in all north temperate regions and S. in Andes to N. Argentina. Leaves alternate, male flowers in catkins and females on the same tree in spikes, clusters or catkins.

BIRCH Betula

About 40 species in N. America, Europe and Asia south to the Himalaya. Trees with rapid early growth in full light and on poor soils; among the first species to colonise bare ground but short-lived and soon replaced by others which can grow in some shade. Most species fruit heavily, early in life and regularly. Strong timber, much used in plywoods.

Key to Betula species

1. Leaf lanceolate, long-acuminate, to 17cm, bark red
albosinensis var. *septentrionalis*, p. 203
    Leaf not as above   **2**

2. Leaf to 10cm broad, orbicular to ovate   **3**
    Leaf not as above   **4**

3. Petiole and underside of leaf glabrous   *maximowicziana*, p. 202
    Petiole and underside of leaf pubescent   *medwediewii*, p. 204

4. Shoot pubescent   **5**
    Shoot glabrous; often warted   **9**

5. Leaf bright green, ovate; petiole reddish, grooved   **6**
    Leaf dull or dark green; petiole neither red nor grooved   **7**

6. Veins 7–8 pairs; bark bright white   *jacquemontii*, p. 203
    Veins 9–14 pairs; bark white or brown   *utilis*, p. 203

7. Leaf deeply serrate or lobulate, whitish beneath   *nigra*, p. 205
    Leaf evenly and shallowly serrate, green beneath   **8**

8. Leaf oblong-ovate, to 12cm, 9–12 pairs veins   *lutea*, p. 204
    Leaf orbicular to ovate, 6cm, 5–7 pairs veins   *pubescens*, p. 207

9. Veins prominent and parallel, 7–11 pairs   *ermanii*, p. 202
    Veins neither prominent nor very parallel   **10**

10. Petiole pubescent   **11**
    Petiole glabrous   **13**

11. Leaf thick, dull, diamond-shaped, 6–8 pairs veins   *papyrifera*, p. 206
    Leaf thin, oblong-ovate, 10–14 pairs veins   **12**

12. Leaf evenly doubly toothed; bark red-brown   *lenta*, p. 204
    Leaf unevenly doubly toothed; bark yellow-brown   *lutea*, p. 204

13. Leaf 4 × 3cm, six pairs veins; bark marked black   *pendula*, p 205
    Leaf to 11 × 8cm, 7–9 pairs veins; bark chalky white
platyphylla var. *szechuanica*, p. 206

MAXIMOWICZ'S BIRCH   *Betula maximowicziana* Reg.
Japan *c.* 1890. Rare; many collections and some large gardens. 20 × 2 m.
Bark. White, smooth, striped horizontally grey-brown becoming orange and
pale pink in parts, the rest white. Young trees dark red-brown.
Crown. Unusually *strong-branched* and broad for a birch, long branches rising
at 45°, well-spaced, make a domed top.

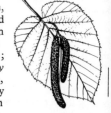

Foliage. Shoot *orange-brown* when young, glabrous,
lenticelled; older trees shining green, turning brown. Bud
ovoid-conic, sharply pointed, glossy green. Leaf: on
young trees unfolds pale orange from dense, fine hairs
when slightly older, glabrous but coppery-purple-brown;
on old trees quite smooth and shiny, rich green, *very
large*, to 14 × 11 cm deeply cordate at base, broad-ovate,
acuminate. 10-12 pairs veins each ending in a finely
pointed tooth projecting well beyond the teeth between
them; dull beneath, often finely pubescent on veins.
Petiole 3–4 cm green, may be dark red by October

Maximowicz's Birch

Flowers and fruit. Male catkins 3–5 together, yellow and dark brown, 4–5 cm
long in winter, 10–12 cm when open. Fruit cylindric 2–7 cm *in twos and threes*.
Recognition. The big, broad leaves like a lime-tree are unlike those of any
other birch.

ERMAN'S BIRCH   *Betula ermanii* Chamisso
N.E. Asia, Japan 1890. Rare; in collections and some large
gardens. 20 × 2 m (20 × 2.5 m at Westonbirt, Glos.).
Bark. White at first, in young trees strikingly so, later peeling under branches into shreds and with horizontal pink
stripes, older trees *pink* or dull pink, very shredded, leaving grey beneath; shreds hang in bunches under branches.
Crown. At first narrowly ovoid-conic, later broadly conic,
upper branches white as far as small shoots.

Foliage. Shoot dull brown with conspicuous pale, raised
lenticels. Bud 5–10 mm conic, pointed, appressed, glossy
green and brown. Leaf 6–9 × 5–6 cm on broad, *grooved* pale
yellow petiole, 2 cm long and pubescent at first; 7–11 pairs of
impressed parallel veins; truncate or broad-cuneate, triangular-ovate, acuminate, sharply and deeply serrate,
dark shiny green above, fine pale brown pubescence beneath; small, darker tufts in vein-axils.

Erman's Birch

Fruit. Abundant, slightly club-shaped cylindric, 4 × 1.2 cm, scales vertical,
appressed; mostly erect in summer, persisting on the tree through the winter.
Similar species. *B. utilis* (below). Handsome dense, shiny foliage with parallel
conspicuous veins, and often cuneate leaf distinguish *B. ermanii*. In winter the
numerous fruit and pink bark hanging in fine strips under branches are charac-
teristic of larger trees.

HIMALAYAN BIRCH *Betula utilis* D. Don

The Himalaya. 1849. Rare; some collections and, like the next species, now sought after for smaller gardens. 17 × 1.5 m.

Bark. Curiously variable; normally mainly *white* with greyish patches but some from China smooth shiny deep browns and greys in a large scaly pattern and in var. *prattii* Burkill (W. China 1908) *bright red-pink* banded by large white lenticels.

Crown. Ovoid with strong ascending branches; later broad-conic or domed.

Foliage. Shoot with long sticky hairs. Bud spreading, 8 mm, brown base, green tip. Leaves hard and often shiny dark green, 5–8(14) × 3–8 cm ovate-acuminate, rounded at base, 10–14 pairs of impressed veins; often slightly lobulate; fine, sharp slightly hooked double toothing, pubescent or woolly on veins and in axils beneath. Petiole stout, grooved, pubescent, dark red or yellow.

Himalayan Birch

Similar species. Intergrades with *B. jacquemontii* (below).

WHITE-BARKED HIMALAYAN BIRCH *Betula jacquemontii* Spach

Pl. 17

W. Himalayas 1880. Rare; older trees in a few large gardens; now more widely planted. 14 × 1.3 m.

Bark. In good forms, the brightest white of any tree, shiny and smooth except for periodic shedding and renewal, tinged cream in places. Many are, however, hybrids with *B. pendula* raised from seed of trees growing here, and these show grey and black patches in the bark. The true form differs from *B. utilis* in ovate-acute leaf with only 7–9 *veins*, scarcely pubescent beneath and coarsely doubly toothed. Some trees, with very white bark, have 10–12 pairs of veins on the leaf and may be more properly referred to *B. utilis* (above).

White-barked
Himalayan Birch

CHINESE RED-BARKED BIRCH *Betula albosinensis* Burk. **Pl. 17**

C. and W. China 1901. Rare; collections and some large gardens. 20 × 1.5 m.

Bark. Bright orange finely flaking or coarsely rolling up and redder, rarely purplish-grey, orange and brown mixed.

Crown. Upright branching and a mass of rather fine twigs.

Foliage. Leaf 4–7 cm, ovate, rounded at base, acuminate, doubly serrate, often slightly lobulate, 10–14 pairs of veins, dark yellow-green above, paler and sparsely silky on veins beneath.

var. *septentrionalis* Schneider. W. China 1908. The most frequently seen form and, contrary to general belief, has usually a much duller bark, dark pink to dark red, peeling in long papery, adhering rolls. Foliage much more sparse, shoots dark grey with white lenticels, leaves often huge, to 17 × 10 cm lanceolate, long-acuminate, very sharply, doubly serrate, dark green above, veins beneath silky-haired and with tufts in axils. Flowers: male catkins 6 × 0.5 cm. Fruit cylindric, domed, 4 × 1 cm; acuminate bracts pointing forwards.

Chinese Red-barked Birch

Similar species. The bark is similar only to *B. utilis* var. *prattii* (an even more rare tree) but lacks prominent band of lenticels, rolls away more and is (in the variety) duller and redder. Var. *septentrionalis* has the longest leaves of any birch, but grades into the type and that grades into *B. utilis*.

TRANSCAUCASIAN BIRCH *Betula medwediewii* Reg.

N. Persia 1897. An interesting, bushy little tree, to 6 m, planted in a few gardens, largely for its bright golden autumn colour. From a stem with silvery grey-brown, flaking hazel-like bark and seldom 30 cm long, branches *radiate* then sweep upwards bearing large, dark, *alder-like* leaves, to 14 × 11 cm deeply ribbed by 10–13 pairs of veins; ovate to nearly round, with big, persistent stipules at the base. Petiole 3 cm, deeply grooved, long-pubescent. Shoots sprout from along the branches making the broad, cup-shaped crown somewhat dense. Male catkins from 2–4 terminal axils, 8 × 1 cm, pale yellow tinged red.

Transcaucasian Birch

CHERRY BIRCH *Betula lenta* L.

Eastern USA, Maine to Alabama 1759. Rare; largely confined to collections in each country. 15 × 1.5 m.

Bark. Dull purplish-grey or dark brownish-grey curling into narrow rolls or coarse scales; occasional reddish patches like the bark of a cherry.

Crown. Globose; shoots slender, rather sparse, radiating.

Foliage. Shoot olive-purple-brown; long pubescence largely shed in summer except at tips. Leaves widely spaced, 8–13 cm, cordate base, ovate-acuminate, *regularly* doubly serrate, the teeth *at vein-ends projecting, aristate*; 9–12 pairs of sunken veins; bright green, paler beneath; young leaves densely white-pubescent beneath, later on veins only. Brilliant but brief gold and orange shades in late October. Bruised shoots emit strong scent of oil of wintergreen.

Cherry Birch

Fruit. Nearly sessile, erect ovoid-oblong, 2–3.5 cm, spreading scales glabrous.

Similar species. *B. lutea* (below) is very similar in foliage and has the same scent from crushed shoots. It differs largely in the bark, less regular double toothing, more and persistent pubescence on leaves, and ciliate scales of the fruit.

YELLOW BIRCH *Betula lutea* Michx.

Syn. *B. alleghaniensis* Brit.

E. N. America; Newfoundland to Tennessee 1767. Rare; collections and large gardens in each country, slightly more frequent than the preceding species. 16 × 1.6 m. (20 × 1.9 m Tilgate Park, Sussex.)

Bark. *Brown and yellowish-grey* "walnut" colour, some silvery sheen, partly ashen-grey, pink or pale orange, peeling in crisp rolls or more shaggy with papery rolls.

Crown. Ovoid with widely radiating then level branches; shoots at acute angles; very distant, sparse leafing.

Foliage. Shoot dull grey-brown, long-pubescent at first, later glabrous; leaves almost as *B. lenta*, 8–11 × 4–6 cm; deep green, coarsely and *irregularly* double-serrate, plane, 12–15 pairs of veins, petiole 1–2 cm, pale green, long-pubescent, grooved.

Yellow Birch

Long-pubescent on veins beneath and tufts in axils, often until leaf-fall. Autumn colours bright yellow; two weeks earlier than *B. lenta*. Crushed or skinned shoots give oil-of-wintergreen scent.

Fruit. Numerous, erect, short-cylindric, 3 × 1.5 cm with spreading scales, like a spruce-cone, bright green, ciliate (under a lens).

Similar species. *B. lenta* (p. 204).

RIVER or BLACK BIRCH   *Betula nigra* L.

Eastern USA, Minnesota to Florida 1736. Rare; a few large southern gardens have several, e.g. Windsor Great Park, and Wisley; even street trees near Woking, Surrey, but in very few collections. 17 × 1.5 m. Hollycombe, Sussex.

Bark. At first pink-buff to orange with long papery grey or dark brown bunches of adhering strips; older trees *dark reddish* or blackish-brown flaking in *large rolls* and tatters which hang from branches, even from small branches high in the crown.

Crown. At first rather bushy, narrow, upswept; as a tree, a clean, sinuous bole, few large ascending branches, fine, dense shoots somewhat pendulous; broadest near the top, arching out.

Foliage. Shoot red-brown, long-pubescent; leaves 3–12 × 2–8 cm, broad-cuneate, ovate-rhombic (diamond-shaped), *deeply and elegantly doubly* toothed, large teeth almost lobules, 6–10 pairs of veins; deep glossy green above, white beneath at first

Black Birch

with dense white pubescence, later pale green, the hairs still on veins.

Fruit. Erect on stout pubescent peduncle, cylindric, tapered to the base, 3 cm; scales green with curled margins tipped brown-purple.

SILVER BIRCH   *Betula pendula* Roth   **Pl. 17**
Syn. *B. verrucosa* Ehrh.

Native in all parts on light soils and shallow peats. Europe and Asia Minor. Abundant on heaths and gravels, hills and moorlands, wood-edges and scrub, in gardens on light soils; valuable as street tree and as cover for establishing beech-woods or specimen trees. 30 × 3 m.

Bark. At first shiny red-brown like cherry-tree, later pinkish-white with horizontal, broad, pale grey bands and some dark grey scaling patches, finally white with *big black diamonds*; often deeply fissured at base into small black knobbly plates.

Crown. Young trees narrow, conic, pointed and upswept. Older trees slowly lose pointed top to become high-domed, with *long pendulous* branchlets. Bole usually deeply fluted.

Foliage. Shoot dark purplish-brown, roughened by *raised white warts*. Bud: young trees blunt ovoid, 3 mm, dull purple-brown; mature trees conic ovoid, 4 mm, shiny green. Leaf 3–7 cm, truncate, slightly rounded-triangular, acuminate; six pairs of veins to protruding, acuminate teeth separated by 2–3 small triangular teeth. Petiole slender, 1.5 cm, glabrous.

Flowers and fruit. Male catkins 2–4 together on ends of small shoots, visible all winter when pale purple-brown, 2 × 0.3 cm, curved; lengthen to 3 cm and pale yellow as pollen shed in April. Female flowers six or so on branched stalk standing erect from shoot at base of some male catkins, open pale green, 1–1.5 cm, turn down and thicken to fruit, 2–3 × 0.4 cm, gherkin-shaped, turning brown in late autumn and breaking up, helped by birds (redpolls, siskins, gold-finches, tits) during winter.

Growth. Seedlings may be nearly 1 m tall, and shoots of 1 m common in early years. To 15 m in 20 years or less but later growth very slow. In the south matures at 50–60 years and dies back and breaks up rapidly, but in C. Scotland can be healthy at 180 years.

'DALECARLICA' Discovered in Dalecarlia, S. Sweden in 1767. Many large gardens; recently in favour for street planting. Smoothly rounded bole, soon white, later patterned in grey; narrow pendulous crown from upright branching. Leaves 6 × 5 cm cut deeply into narrow, angular lobes and lobules each with big acute teeth. Petiole slender 3–4 cm. 30 × 1.7 m at Tay-mouth Castle, Perths.

'Dalecarlica'

'FASTIGIATA' Narrowly conic-columnar with sinuous nearly vertical branches, becoming narrow at base but broader columnar above, truncheon-shaped. Leaves very dark. Rare, but in a few city parks and large gardens. 22 m.

'TRISTIS' Very rare splendid tree with widely spread twisted branches from which shoots hang in curtains of twisty small twigs.

'YOUNGII' c. 1900, Milford. An untidy dense mass of shoots falling off a grafted mop-head on a stem, seen in many gardens, but can be small tree to 9 × 1 m with 2–3 layers of dense shoots, long-pendulous on the outside and domed, pendulous apex. Leaf smaller than in the type.

SZECHUAN BIRCH   *Betula platyphylla* var. *szechuanica* (Schneid.) Rehd.

'Fastigiata'

W. China 1908. A variety of the Manchurian Birch grown in some gardens for its *chalky white* bark, strikingly unmarked well into the crown and coming off on the hand as a *fine powder*. Shoot pale brown, *very rough*; leaves to 12 × 9 cm leathery, with 6–8 main pairs of veins; coarsely and doubly crenate, orbicular-ovate, acuminate, glabrous beneath, dotted with shiny spots. 15 m. Female flower 4 cm, slender

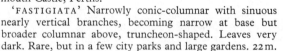

CANOE BIRCH or PAPER-BARK BIRCH
Betula papyrifera Marsh.

Szechuan Birch

N. N. America; Labrador to British Columbia (Alaska as var. *kenaica*); south to Pennsylvania 1750. Uncommon; large gardens and a few parks in each country but few if any north of Edinburgh. 20 × 2 m.

Bark. Varies greatly with origin of seed. Typically smooth and white with *cream, pink* and *pale orange* shading, less often deep pink, and purple strongly marked by horizontal bands of lenticels.

Crown. Strong branches ascending, shoots rather stout, leaves *distant.*

Foliage. Shoot dark brown much roughened by pale warts.

Canoe Birch

Bud 6–8 mm, slender-conic, appressed, green and brown. Leaves variable in size, 4–10 cm long, rather thick, very *matt* dark green, on *stout*, hairy petiole 1.5–3 cm long; putty-knife shaped, truncate or rounded at base, ovate-acuminate with few veins for the size (6–10 pairs); doubly toothed; pale beneath with tufts in basal axils, and scattered black dots.
Flowers and fruit. Male catkins large, to 10 cm when ripe; fruit 4 × 0.8 cm.

DOWNY or WHITE BIRCH *Betula pubescens* Ehrh.
Native and common on badly drained heaths and damper soils generally where it replaces *B. pendula* locally; abundant in the Scottish Highlands. Rarely if ever deliberately planted in gardens, present in a few. Europe and N. Asia. 25 × 3 m.
Bark. At first red-brown as in *B. pendula*, becoming smooth *greyish*-white, variably banded horizontally grey or brown, sometimes with fine grey lacework patterns, often remaining brownish and cherry-like until big; *never with black diamonds*.

Crown. Irregular, soon losing pointed top, rather spreading and *twisting branches*, shoots spreading, crowded, not pendulous.

Foliage. Shoot greyish red-purple, covered in *short, soft*, shiny white hairs. Leaf differs from *B. pendula* in being more *rounded*, often nearly circular, 5–6 × 5 cm, broadest near middle, not near base, *uniform* crenate toothing; glistening white hairs on veins beneath; petiole densely pubescent. Shoots of old trees may be glabrous.

Downy Birch

Similar species. *B. pendula* (p. 205).

ALDERS Alnus
Thirty species across northern hemisphere, south to Peru and W. China. Male catkins long with flowers in threes; females on short catkins often erect, ripening to woody, ovoid cone-like structures. Buds of all species given here except *A. viridis* are stalked, and with 2–3 unequal scales. Most thrive best in damp, cool sites, but *A. incana* thrives in poor drier soils and is much used in reclamation of waste heaps.

GREEN ALDER *Alnus viridis* DC. Pl. 18
Mountains of Europe 1820. Rare; confined to a few collections. 5 m. An erect-branched shrubby plant, rarely a small tree. Bud 1.2–1.5 cm not stalked, purplish-red, shiny, long-pointed. Leaf 6 × 4.5 cm on grooved petiole 1.5 cm; truncate, rounded-ovate, obtuse, with very fine, sharp, spreading teeth, 8–9 pairs of veins; pubescent on petiole and midrib beneath, dull matt green above, paler beneath with small tufts in vein-axils.
Flowers and fruit. Male catkins thick and long, 5–12 cm, yellow in late April. Females stand in bunches of 5–8, erect, pinkish-green, 1 × 0.4 cm, ripening to hanging bunches of large ovoids, 2 × 1.5 cm, green in summer then pale red-brown with 15–20 layers of very small scales, remaining (nearly black) until spring.

Plate 19   BEECHES, HORNBEAM, SWEET CHESTNUT

1. Common Beech   *Fagus sylvatica*   220
    (a) Mature tree 25 m tall.
    (b) Shoot, leaves and winter-buds.
    (c) Ripe fruit opening to show seeds.

2. Hornbeam   *Carpinus betulus*   212

    Shoot in summer, with leaves and immature fruit. Male flowers are on catkins, emerging from their buds in March.

    A tree of heavy clay soils especially.

3. Rauli   *Nothofagus procera*   217
    Shoot with leaves and ripe fruit.

    A tree of exceptional vigour now planted in many gardens.

4. Sweet Chestnut   *Castanea sativa*   223
    A species introduced very long ago, now naturalised on light soils.
    (a) Immature fruits at base of withered small, late male catkin. The normal, long male catkins bear no fruit and have been shed.
    (b) Shoot with leaves.
    (c) Strong young shoot, grooved and purple-brown.

Hornbeam

Rauli

Roble Beech (p. 216)

OAKS **Plate 20**

Trees of very variable foliage but all having acorns for seeds.

1. English Oak *Quercus robur* 244

Native and widespread but replaced on light soils and in the western hills by another native – the Sessile Oak.
(a) Leaf, showing auricles at the base and very short petiole.
(b) Acorn, showing long stem.
(c) Old tree in exposed position.

2. Red Oak *Quercus borealis* 232

(a) Acorn, ripening in the second year.
(b) Leaf, which is matt both sides.
(c) Close-up of bark, which can remain smooth and silvery for many years.

3. Cork Oak *Quercus suber* 235

An evergreen tree with a wide, low crown and distinct bark.
(a) Close-up of bark.
(b) Leaf.

4. Scarlet Oak *Quercus coccinea* 230

Leaf (enlarged compared with that of the Red Oak). Glossy on both sides.

5. Holm Oak *Quercus ilex* 237

Leaf from a low shoot or young tree. Normal crown leaves of mature trees are entire. The underside is covered in a white felt.

A very densely crowned, dark evergreen tree.

6. Sessile Oak *Quercus petraea* 243

A handsome native tree much less seen in S.E. England than the English Oak.
(a) Leaf, showing only a trace of an auricle and a longer petiole than in the English Oak. Some leaves are fully cuneate at base, and all are more regularly toothed, of better substance and less galled than those of English Oak.
(b) Acorn, which is sessile, growing directly on the shoot-tip.

7. Turkey Oak *Quercus cerris* 235

(a) Acorn-cup and acorn in summer.
(b) Leaf in late summer when the short, grey hairs have worn off, and the surface is somewhat glossy. Many leaves are narrower and more angularly toothed than this is (see figure p. 235).

COMMON ALDER *Alnus glutinosa* (L.) Gaertn. **Pl. 18**

Native, lining open water in all parts, up to 1,600 ft, by rocky streams or fens and carrs. Rare as specimen tree. Europe to Siberia and N. Africa. 22 × 2 m (26 × 3.7 m at Sandling Park, Kent).

Bark. Purplish-brown at first, soon dark grey-brown cracked into square plates; old trees grey and like Common Oak, finely fissured into small, vertical plates.

Crown. Broadly conic, pointed, branches ascending at first, later more level; rather open.

Foliage. Shoot green becoming rich purple above by October, with raised orange lenticels, slightly zigzag. Bud on 3 mm stalk, smooth, green at first turning purple from tip downwards, 7 mm, narrow. Leaves open pale orange-brown on young plants; broad-cuneate, obovate, broadly rounded and slightly indented end, 10 × 7 cm, margin slightly waved, irregularly and very shallowly toothed, sub-shiny, very dark green, seven pairs of white veins, pale beneath with tufts of long, untidy hairs in vein-axils. Petiole 2–3.5 cm, with fine rough speckles increasing in size towards base of leaf. Sprout-leaves often lobulate. Leaves retained late on tree and fall dark green in November.

Flowers and fruit. Male catkins 3–5 together, dull purple in winter, 2–3 cm, opening over a long period in any one area from March to late April, dark yellow, 5 cm. Females in short erect clusters, 3 mm, dark purple, open dark red, 5–6 mm, ripen to green ovoids 8–15 mm, dark brown and woody when ripe.

Growth. Very rapid when young; shoots 1 m frequent.

Recognition. The obovate leaves distinguish from other species.

'LACINIATA' Uncommon. Like the type but with leaves cut to about half way into 6–7 triangular, acuminate slightly toothed lobes. 20 m.

'IMPERIALIS' 1853. A small slender tree leaning at the top and with weak branches bearing leaves cut deeply, sometimes to the midrib, into slender acuminate lobes, rich green, thin, on slender petioles

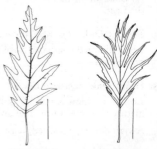

'Laciniata'   'Imperialis'

2–4 cm long; stipules prominent, ovate, bright pale green, contrast with leaves. Quite different in aspect and leaf from 'Laciniata'. Infrequent, by lakes or in damp parts of parks and gardens. 15 × 1.1 m (Thorp Perrow, Yorks.).

OREGON or RED ALDER *Alnus rubra* Bong.

Syn. *A. oregona* Nutt.

N.W. America; Alaska to California and Idaho. Pre-1880. Curiously rare; occasional in large gardens and parks. 20 × 2 m.

Bark. Smooth, pinkish leaden-grey with, on young trees, vertical lines of pale lenticels. (Strikingly silvery in western USA.)

Crown. Conic and spire-topped at first, becoming broad with level branches. Widely domed even when only 9 m tall.

Foliage. Shoot slightly angled, at first greenish with long loose hairs, soon dark red and glabrous. Bud dark red sometimes pale green; petiole 2.5–3.5 cm yellow or

red; leaf to 10–12 × 7 cm with 10–15 parallel, reddish
veins to lobules which each have 2–4 sharply mucronate
little teeth on basal edge, usually entire distal edge;
oval or ovate-lanceolate, obtuse or short-pointed,
rounded at base, dark green above, *greyish* beneath,
rusty pubescence or orange colour remaining on veins;
extreme margins minutely but strongly *decurved.*

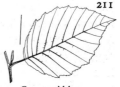

Oregon Alder

Flowers and fruit. Male catkins 3–5 together to 15 cm; fruit 3–6 together,
barrel-shaped, 1.2–2 cm.

Growth. Exceedingly rapid for a few years; unreliable thereafter except on
good sites. To 15 m in 15 years.

Similar species. Lobulate leaves like *A. incana* (below) but shoot differs in
being soon glabrous and red, leaves usually less broad and more lobed, with
minutely decurved margin.

GREY ALDER   *Alnus incana* (L.) Moench   **Pl. 18**

Europe, Caucasus Mts. 1780. Rare as garden tree, more often on reclaimed tips;
a few small plantations mostly in Scotland. 25 × 2 m.

Bark. Smooth *deep grey*, green-tinged with flaky small vertical lenticels; older
trees dull dark grey with a few deep wandering fissures, paler grey well into
crown.

Crown. More or less conic; broad with age.

Foliage. Shoot red-brown above, olive beneath, orange lenticels, covered in
grey, short pubescence; pale *shiny grey* when older. Bud purple-red, curved,
8 mm on stalk 2 mm. Leaves distant, 4–5 cm apart, *ovate*, sometimes nearly
round, to 10 × 10 cm on petiole 2.5–3 (8) cm; 9–12 pairs of veins (or veins each
side as they may be alternate), small lobules about the middle, sharply toothed,
base of leaf entire; dull green above, greyish beneath, pubescent all over or
later on veins alone. Deep green until falling in late November.

Flowers and fruit. Male catkins 3–4 together open in February to 5–10 cm.
Female flowers 3–8 on pale brown finely pubescent stalks, ripen to ovoids, 1 ×
0.8 cm.

'AUREA' Small tree, distinctly rare, with smaller leaves golden all summer
and shoots yellow, turning orange in winter.

'LACINIATA' ('Incisa' 'Pinnatifida') Rare. Leaves small, deeply cut into 6–8
pairs of slender, toothed lobes. Pubescent shoot distinguishes this from other
cut-leaf alders.

'PENDULA' Rare. Mound-like tree of long-pendulous branches. 6 m.

'RAMULIS COCCINEIS' Uncommon but more planted now than other
cultivars; orange-red shoots and bright red leaf-buds and catkin-bud-scales in
winter. Leaves gold in summer – a form of 'Aurea'.

Similar species. *A. rubra* (p. 210) also has lobulate leaves but much more
markedly so, with decurved margin.

ITALIAN ALDER   *Alnus cordata* Desf.   **Pl. 18**

S. Italy and Corsica 1820. Uncommon; in some parks and large gardens, also
beside main roads in a few places (Esher; Basingstoke by-pass). 27 × 3 m.

Bark. Pale brown-grey becoming dull grey, smooth but blistered and with a
few vertical, shallow, wide fissures.

Crown. Majestically conic to maximum heights; *dense* for an alder. Resemblance to a luxuriant pear-tree much reinforced by the shining, dark pear-like leaves.

Foliage. Shoot dark brown above, paler beneath, slightly zigzag; bud ovoid 5mm on 5mm stalk, pale green densely speckled red-brown in places; leaf 5–8 × 5–7cm, ovate, short-acuminate, cordate, entire base, the rest shallowly serrate with forward, slightly mucronate teeth, dark *glossy* green above, paler beneath with *large tufts* of pale *orange hairs* in vein-axils and long hairs flat each side of base of midrib. Petiole 3 cm. New leaves in summer tinged orange. The foliage remains green late into autumn, falling green and grey in November.

Flowers and fruit. Male catkins in threes (fives), in winter 2.5 cm, cylindric tapered at tip, pale purplish, shed pollen variously from February to April when golden and 7–10cm long. Females erect above males. 1–2 on stout 2–5 cm stalk, ripen to ovoid fruit 2.5 × 1.8 cm.

Recognition. A very distinctive tree in crown, bark and foliage, large flowers and fruit. Very handsome and of rapid growth. To 16m in 19 years.

HORNBEAMS   Carpinus

Twenty-six species from all north temperate regions. Male catkins enclosed in a bud during winter. Fruit are nutlets in bunches, each with a large bract.

HORNBEAM   *Carpinus betulus* L.   Pl. 19

Native to S.E. England with isolated areas in Somerset and Monmouth. Europe from Pyrenees to S. Sweden, east to Asia Minor. Common in S.E. England mainly as hedgerow tree, pure woods in parts of Epping, Hatfield and Hainault Forests (Essex) and in Herts. and a component of many woods. Planted north to Sutherland. Frequent, parks, roadsides, gardens and as a hedge, retaining dead leaves all winter if kept within the bounds of a cone 8–9 ft high. Some woods pollarded as in Epping Forest. 30 × 4m, old pollards to 8m in girth.

Bark. Pale silvery-grey finely striped pale brown and paler grey. Smooth patches with fine network patterns of grey, separated by deep, black, irregular fissures. Old trees with raised network of flat ridges. Boles deeply fluted and usually eccentric, oval.

Crown. Irregular ovoid or broadly conic, old trees reversed-conic spreading to a high dome; bole *sinuous* and deeply fluted and holed; branches ascending and sinuous, shoots very fine and straight.

Foliage. Shoot dark brownish-grey with sparse long hairs, slender, slightly zigzag, seen close to. Bud very slender, sharp-pointed, appressed closely, 6–7mm. Leaves alternate, oblong-ovate, short-acuminate, cordate, slightly oblique, about 15 *pairs of parallel veins*; finely and sharply *double toothed*, sometimes almost lobulate, 8–10 × 5–6.5 cm on 1cm reddish petiole; sub-shiny both sides, very dark green above, yellower beneath with small white tufts in vein-axils. Good yellow then old-gold in autumn.

Flowers and fruit. Male catkins expand in March to 2.5–5 cm, bright yellow-green near-to, brownish in the mass, from reddish outer scales. Females, terminal nodding, 3 cm, slender, bright green with pink stigmas. Fruit cluster 6cm long with about eight pairs of nutlets, 6–8mm, each pair near the base of a green bract, 3.5 cm long, with a small lobe spreading each side near the base.

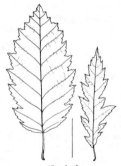

'Fastigiata'   'Incisa'

'FASTIGIATA' ('Pyramidalis') 1885 Europe. Widely planted as street-tree and in gardens and town-parks where ideal for somewhat formal but always attractive shape. Smooth grey bole usually clean for 2 m bearing a densely straight-twigged ovoid, pointed crown, like an ace-of-spades. Leaves brighter and more shiny green than in the type, held very densely and rather level. Colours bright gold, then orange-brown in autumn. Fruit and male flowers less evident. 16 m.

'COLUMNARIS' Rare. Strictly fastigiate and columnar.

'INCISA' (Includes 'Quercifolia') Broad and bushy; small leaves with triangular lobes. Some forms narrowly lanceolate, deeply lobed. Big old trees in a few gardens and parks (Jephson Gardens, Leamington) on some of which part of the crown has reverted to normal foliage. 10 (20) m.

EASTERN HORNBEAM *Carpinus orientalis*
Mill.

S.E. Europe, Asia Minor 1739. Rare; some collections in S. England. 11 m. A small tree with small leaves, 2–5 cm ovate, folded somewhat along the 11–15 pairs of veins; doubly toothed. The bark is purplish-grey, prettily streaked in buff, smooth. The bracts of the fruit are like small leaves and are sharply serrate, deep green.

Eastern Hornbeam with fruit

JAPANESE HORNBEAM *Carpinus japonica* Bl.

Japan 1879. A rare but very handsomely foliaged tree in a few collections and large gardens. 10 m.

Bark. Smooth, grey-purple or dark green with pink, wavy stripes.

Foliage. Shoot red, lenticelled, pubescent; leaf 5–10 cm ovate-lanceolate, acuminate, sharply forward-serrate, 20–22 *pairs parallel* veins, every third tooth aristate, projecting and rising; glossy deep green; stipules green, persistent.

Fruit Big ovoid bunch 5 × 3 cm of incurved

Japanese Hornbeam with fruit

bracts each 2 cm with 4–5 coarse teeth, bright pale green becoming pink-green flushed crimson by August.

HOP-HORNBEAMS   Ostrya

Seven species in north temperate regions. Similar to hornbeams, but male catkins naked during winter and fruit enclosed by bladder-like involucre.

EUROPEAN HOP-HORNBEAM   *Ostrya carpinifolia* Scop.

S. Europe, Asia Minor pre-1724. Rare; collections and big gardens. 19 × 1.5 m.
Bark. Smooth grey-brown at first, soon peeling and deep-brown fissured, later either oak-like, purplish-grey, or fissured into squarish, loose flakes which, on falling, leave orange-brown patches.

Crown. Broadly conic, young trees slender-topped, old very broad. Sometimes many, spreading boles (as at Killerton Chapel, Devon).
Foliage. Shoot brown or red-brown very pubescent; minute raised orange lenticels. Bud ovoid, pointed, shiny green. Leaf 5–12 × 3–6 cm ovate-acuminate or acute, rounded at base, very sharply and doubly serrate, 12–15 pairs of veins; thick, hard, dark glossy green above, paler beneath with small tufts in vein-axils; petiole 3–4 mm, soft-pubescent.

European Hop-hornbeam with fruit

Fruit. Hanging in *hop-like bunches* 3–5 cm long, *white* in summer or greenish, with long hairs, about 15 ovoid bladders each 1.5–2 cm long enclosing a nutlet.
Similar species. *O. virginiana* (Mill.) K. Koch. Eastern N. America 1692. In some large collections differs only in "glandular" (blob-tipped) hairs on shoots and petioles, and in having fewer veins.

HAZELS   Corylus

Fifteen species across north temperate regions, only four truly qualify as trees. Female flowers hidden in bud except for protruded red styles; fruit a large nut surrounded by a leafy involucre.

TURKISH HAZEL   *Corylus colurna* L.

S.E. Europe, Asia Minor, W. Asia 1582. Infrequent; collections, some large gardens and a few parks and smaller gardens north to Edinburgh. 22 × 2.2 m (22 × 2.8 m at Syon Park, Middx. 25 m Brocklesby Park).
Bark. Pinkish-brown with rather oak-like fissuring, later dark brown scaling coarsely.
Crown. Conic with rather stout, very level twisting branches.
Foliage. Shoot densely covered in glandular hairs, as is petiole. Leaf large, heavy, hanging, to 12.5 × 12.5 cm on reddish petiole 2.5 cm; broad-ovate or obovate, cordate, abruptly acuminate, slightly puck-

Turkish Hazel

ered, doubly toothed, tending to lobulate, shining dark green.

Flowers and fruit. Male catkins 5–7 cm; fruit clusters of 5–6; involucre of 20 linear acute lobes, 3 × 2 cm recurved, densely set   with stout soft prickles, bright glossy green.

Recognition. The only hazel of tree-stature normally seen with a good stout bole. The rough bark, conic crown and level branching help to identify in winter.

COMMON HAZEL   *Corylus avellana* L.

Native to all parts except the Shetlands; found in places up to 2,000 ft. All Europe to 68°N and Asia Minor. Abundant on chalk, limestone, neutral and mildly acid soils, as coppice, hedgerows and under-shrub in woods; nut walks in gardens. 12 m.

Bark. Shiny grey-brown, soon raised in small, curling strips.

Crown. A tall, broad bush, sometimes from a short bole.

Foliage. Shoot pale brown covered in long, stiff hairs with swollen tips ("glandular"). Bud ovoid, smooth. Petiole stout, densely glandular-pubescent. 1.5 cm. Leaf to 10 × 10 cm orbicular or obovate, cordate base, sharp, triangular, unequal teeth; harshly hairy, deep green above, softly white-haired on veins beneath.

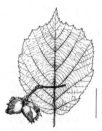

Flowers and fruit. Male catkins brownish-yellow in autumn, opening pale yellow, to 5 cm long from late December to late April in different years and places; main period mid-February. Female flowers brown ovoids 3–5 mm with bright deep red styles exserted 2 mm a few days after pollen of same tree is shed. Nuts 1–4 together, compressed ovoid, 1.5–2 cm long, whitish-green ripening pale pink-brown, in green involucre of two bracts overlapped, 1 cm long with teeth 3–5 mm deep and sparse long white hairs.

Common Hazel

'CONTORTA' **Corkscrew Hazel** *c.* 1870 Gloucestershire. Erect bush of much contorted stems, shoots and twigs. Infrequent.

BEECH, OAK AND CHESTNUT FAMILY
Fagaceae

A huge family of some 1,000 species found almost all over the world outside
the Tropics. Nearly all are trees, a few are shrubs; many are evergreen. Leaves
alternate, stalked; male flowers in slender catkins, spikes, or pendent, globose
female flowers solitary, in threes or on short spikes or at the base of the male
catkin; fruit a nut partly or wholly enclosed in an involucre or cupule.

SOUTHERN BEECHES Nothofagus

About 20 species in S. S. America, Australia, New Zealand and New Guinea.
The majority are evergreen mostly with very small leaves, but the three most
grown here are deciduous.

Key to Nothofagus species

1. Leaf entire   **2**
Leaf serrated or with few large teeth   **3**

2. Leaf plane   *solandri*, p. 219
Leaf margins decurved, tip raised   *solandri* var. *cliffortioides*, p. 220

3. Teeth few, large, incurved; thin texture   *fusca*, p. 220
Serrated   **4**

4. Leaf thin, bright green or darkish, deciduous   **5**
Leaf thick, hard, blackish or pale grey; evergreen   **7**

5. 15–18 pairs parallel veins; shoot stout, green   *procera*, p. 217
4–7 pairs of veins; shoot slender, brown or red-brown   **6**

6. Seven pairs of veins; leaf to 8 cm   *obliqua*, p. 216
Four veins each side; leaf to 4 cm   *antarctica*, p. 218

7. Leaf 1 cm, orbicular or triangular   **8**
Leaf to 3 cm, elliptic to ovate-lanceolate   **9**

8. Toothing blunt, double; pits in lower vein-axils beneath, (bark
shiny, cherry-like)   *menziesii*, p. 219
Serrate; fairly uniform; no pits in axils (bark orange-brown
and grey, scaly)   *cunninghamii*, p. 219

9. Leaf oval, evenly serrate, stipules orange   *betuloides*, p. 219
Leaf ovate to lanceolate; irregularly serrate   *dombeyi*, p. 218

ROBLE BEECH *Nothofagus obliqua* (Mirb.) Bl.
Argentina, Chile 1902. Infrequent; some large gardens everywhere, north-east
at least to Aberdeen; a few small plantations. 30 × 3 m (23 × 3.3 m Sunningdale,
Nsy, Surrey).
Bark. Smooth and pale grey becoming widely fissured by shallow black cracks
later brownish-purple cracked by wide buff fissures into square, curling plates.

Crown. Slender and conic, later opening out at the top with *arching* branches and strikingly *regular herring-bone* shoots which *fan downwards and outwards* in slender sprays. Large branches remain silvery-grey high in the crown.

Foliage. Shoot *slender*, dark red above, light yellow-brown beneath, slightly pubescent. Bud prominent, ovoid, 5 mm light brown. Leaf 5–8 cm, ovate-oblong, sharply and irregularly toothed, variably lobulate especially on late-season leaves which may have 4–5 well-marked lobules each with 2–3 coarse teeth each side; 7–11 *pairs of impressed veins*; slightly oblique base, deep green, paler beneath, glabrous. Petiole 5 mm, pink or dark red above. Late shoots hold crinkled stipules. Autumn colours yellow and crimson.

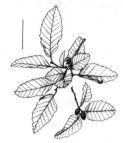

Flowers and fruit. Male flowers solitary, inconspicuous, tufts of stamens; fruit one at the base of each leaf pale bright green, ovoid 8 × 5 mm, roughened by outcurved 1 mm scales between four smooth ribs.

Roble Beech

Growth. An extremely vigorous tree frequently growing 1.5 m in a year, and has grown 26 m in 22 years at Windsor. Growth starts slowly in April and is rapid from mid-May to early September. Seedlings spring up in abundance near groups of fruiting trees.

Similar species. *N. procera* (below); *N. antarctica* (p. 218).

RAULI *Nothofagus procera* (Poepp. and Endl.) Oerst. **Pl. 19**

Argentina, Chile 1913. Infrequent; some large gardens everywhere north to Aberdeen, particularly in western areas; a few small plantations. 26 × 3 m (26 × 2.7 m at East Bergholt Place, Suffolk; 25 × 2.5 m at Muncaster Castle, Cumbs.).

Bark. Dark grey-green much marked by lenticels at first, then silvery-grey finely striped horizontally in grey, brown and pink, later duller greenish-grey with many evenly spaced, dark, broad fissures running far up bole and larger branches. Frequent small bosses on bole.

Crown. Young trees: *whorled*, stout ascending shoots in a narrow cone; old trees: broadly conic, upper branches ascending, lower level; foliage dense and somewhat pendulous.

Foliage. Shoot green, then dark brown much *roughened* by small warts. Bud narrowly conic, angled, 1 cm, bright chestnut-brown. Leaf 4–8 cm, (17 × 6) on yellow-green petiole, 5–10 mm; ovate-lanceolate or oblong-ovate, acute or rounded, 15–20 *prominent, impressed pairs of veins*; finely serrulate and slightly wavy margin on bigger leaves, often slightly lobulate on smaller; fresh yellow-green to somewhat dark; silky hairs on veins beneath. *New leaves copper-brown.* Autumn colours pale gold with some crimson.

Rauli

Flowers and fruit. Male flower on green 1.5 cm pedicel, flattened globose 1 cm: pale pink-yellow bracts and long brown-green anthers. Fruit at base of each leaf, *1 cm, deep green, covered* in filigree of deeply laciniate appendages.

Growth. Extremely vigorous in both height and girth, rapidly building a stouter more persistent bole than does *N. obliqua*. Shoots to 1.6 m in a year frequent, to 14 m in nine years from seed and a girth of 2 m in 30 years. Buds start to unfold in March, often held back from full expansion by cold weather until late April. Height growth occurs between late April and early September and may attain 15 cm in a week.

Similar species. *N. obliqua* (p. 216); *Carpinus betulus* (p. 212) has long hairs on the shoot, deep green more sharply serrate leaves and differs also in buds, bark and crown.

ANTARCTIC BEECH   *Nothofagus antarctica* (Forst.) Oerst.

Argentina, S. Chile 1830. Uncommon; large gardens in all parts. 15 × 1.3 m.
Bark. Dark grey-brown early and deeply fissured pink or orange, irregularly divided into rough plates with papery surfaces. Rarely like *N. menziesii*.
Crown. Sparse and irregular, often broad, larger branches twisted, shoots slender, *herring-bone pattern*; bole sinuous, tree *often leans*.
Foliage. Shoot red-brown above, olive-grey beneath, short-pubescent. Bud ovoid, red-brown, shiny, some violet bloom, 5–6mm. Leaf 3 × 2cm, unfolding bright, shiny green, on petiole 1–2mm; oblong-ovate, obliquely rounded or subcordate base, unevenly toothed, *crinkled* and slightly cupped, 4–5 pairs of veins; deep glossy green, paler beneath.

Antarctic Beech

Fruit. Closely alternate, at base of each leaf on side-shoots, sessile, erect, ovoid, angular, four-winged, shining green edged deep red, 6–7mm.
Growth. Rapid when young, shoots to 1 m. Soon becomes slow.
Similar species. Lenga, *N. pumilio* (Poepp. & Endl.) Krasser, introduced 1960 may now be seen. It differs in very regular double toothing and *7 pairs* of veins.

DOMBEY'S SOUTHERN BEECH   *Nothofagus dombeyi* Bl.

Argentina, Chile 1916. Rare; some collections and large gardens in all parts, large trees only in Cornwall, Cumberland, Ireland and far west generally. 27 × 3 m.
Bark. At first smooth dark blackish-grey, horizontally *wrinkled*. Later widely and shallowly fissured and, on biggest trees, coming away in dark brown strips leaving rich orange or with big irregular grey-purple plates lifting away.
Crown. Evergreen. Upright rather open *ovoid* with long vertical upper branches bent slightly outwards towards their tips. Older trees broad-conic, often multiple stems from low on bole. Blackish from mass of tiny evergreen dark leaves.
Foliage. Shoot very slender, red-brown above, apple-green beneath. Bud minute, 1mm, brown ovoid. Leaf varying from oval to lanceolate, broadest below middle 2.5–4 cm, jagged toothing very *unequal*, very short petiole visible only from beneath shoot; hard, shiny, black-green above, *smooth, matt pale green* below with only midrib visible, often densely set and overlapping, *black specks all over* seen under lens or when dried. New leaves bright green, closely set on arched shoot. Male flowers 2–3 on branched red pedicel, pale cream tube; pink anthers.

Dombey's Southern Beech

Growth. Tender at first, soon a hardy and most attractive tree of quite rapid growth: very rapid in Ireland.
Similar species. *N. betuloides* (p. 219), has regularly toothed leaves.

SILVER BEECH *Nothofagus menziesii* Oerst.
New Zealand *c.* 1850? Infrequent in Cornwall and Ireland, in most large gardens; rare east to Surrey and Sussex and north-west to at least Wigtownshire. 19 × 2 m (Nymans).
Bark. Striking smooth, *shiny purple-brown* or, less often, silvery-grey, closely ringed by *long, thick bands* of lenticels.
Crown. Usually a broad, upright bushy tree on many stems from low on the bole. Young trees slender, and *pale grey leafed.*

Foliage. Shoot slender, pubescent, dark brown; older shoots often orange. Bud conic, dark red, 2–3 mm. Leaves evergreen, *orbicular,* 1 × 1 cm, with deep, *blunt* double-toothing; pale grey, almost silver on young plants, dark glossy green on older trees; underside pale green, sub-shiny; minute, deep hairy *pits each side* in axils of *two basal pairs* of veins.
Similar species. *N. solandri* (below) and var. *cliffortioides* (below) have entire leaves, and black bark. *Nothofagus cunninghamii* Oerst (Tasmania) is much closer, and differs in more triangular or deltoid leaf, doubly toothed and without the pits beneath. The bark is brown or grey-green freckled orange,

Left, Silver Beech; *right, N. 'Cunninghamii'*

and scaly. This species is more rare, but is found in the same regions, north to Argyll. (19 × 1.3 m Mt. Usher, Co. Wicklow.)

OVAL-LEAFED SOUTHERN BEECH *Nothofagus betuloides* (Mirb.) Oerst.
Chile 1830. Less frequent than *N. dombeyi*; a few gardens in S. England, Wales, Cumberland and Ireland. 25 × 2.5 m.
Differs from *N. dombeyi* in a tighter, denser crown, orange-brown shoots, slightly clammy foliage, oval leaves broadest at middle with *regular,* crenate teeth, speckled whitish, not usually black; veins often pink. Stipules retained in summer, bright red-brown. Male flowers bright deep red, hang like *fuchsia,* slender tube 1 cm, ten stamens exserted 3 mm.
Similar species. *N. dombeyi* (p. 219).

Oval-leafed Southern Beech

MOUNTAIN BEECH *Nothofagus solandri* var. *cliffortioides* (Hook. f.) Poole
New Zealand 1880? Rare, mostly in far south, west and Ireland, but also Edinburgh. 20 × 1.5 m (22 × 2 m at Nymans, Sussex).

This tree is a variety of the only other entire-leafed evergreen Nothofagus, *N. solandri* (Hook) Oerst, Black beech, which differs only in the leaf being *flat* and slightly larger. Introduced after 1914 it is rare, from Sussex to Wigtownshire and in Ireland. 17 × 1.5 m.

Mountain Beech with typical leaf from the side

Black Beech

var. *cliffortioides* has blackish, smooth, very ribbed bark and peculiar crown of widely spaced flat *layers* of crisp, *wiry* shoots crowded with evergreen, tiny leaves above the sparse, level branches. The long leading shoot leans and the few upper branches rise and *wander far out* as slender spikes. Leaf 1 cm, entire, matt grey-green, buckled so the margins curve down and the *blunt tip rears up*. Male flowers cluster among the leaves in May, like translucent red berries 2 mm long.

RED BEECH *Nothofagus fusca* Oerst.

New Zealand. About 1910. Rare; some collections from Cornwall to Sussex, Hereford, E. Ireland and Edinburgh. 20 × 1.5 m (26 × 2.6 m at Nymans, Sussex).

Bark. Dark grey, deeply and finely scaling.

Crown. Slender when young, branches few and level. Large trees high-domed, rather open.

Foliage. Leaves evergreen, many remaining on tree yellow and dark red; ovate, 3–5 × 2 cm with 3–6 big incurved forward-pointing teeth; thin, papery; smooth matt upper surface, slightly shiny beneath, dull, often yellowish-green or deep green both sides; veins beneath dark red.

Red Beech

Growth. Has grown 11 m in 29 years in Edinburgh so is evidently more hardy than is usually credited. In the south, shoots can be 0.6 m.

BEECHES Fagus

Ten species from all north temperate regions, except N.W. America and C. Asia. Male flowers in bunches on slender stalks; nuts in four-parted, woody involucre.

COMMON BEECH *Fagus sylvatica* L.   Pl. 19

Native to S.E. and Midland England. Europe except N. Scandinavia and replaced by *F. orientalis* south and east of N. Bulgaria. Dominant and climax tree on chalk and some well-drained sands. Much planted in policies, woods, gardens and parks in all parts. Frequent in shelter-belts, especially in S. Scotland, also as garden-hedges. Old pollarded trees in many areas. Survives moderately polluted air but not water-logged soils. 40 × 6 m (36 × 6.2 m at Longleat, Wilts.).

Bark. Smooth, silvery-grey, often slightly roughened and less often with rippled patches or a fine network of ridges.

Crown. Young trees: slender, conic, rather gaunt. Old trees: hugely domed, usually much branched; occasional survivors of the fellings of two wars with 15–20 m straight, cylindrical bole. Variants common on chalklands include one with stiff, brush-like ascending shoots and one with long, arched branches like fishing-rods. A few of the oldest trees have branches rooting as layers.

Foliage. Shoot dull purple-brown, lenticelled and slightly zigzag. Bud *slender, long-pointed*, 2 cm, many scales, each red-brown at base, the rest light brown. Leaf to 10 × 7 cm oval or obovate, slightly oblique at cuneate base, with wavy margin and short teeth at the end of each of the 6–7 *veins* each side; acute at tip. Fresh green and silky-white hairy at first, then dark, shiny green above, pale and shiny beneath with long hairs on larger veins and in axils. Petiole 1–1.5 cm, hairy. Autumn colour starts with pale yellows in early October, leaves fall rich orange-brown to rufous in early November.

Flowers and fruit. Flowers emerge with the leaves in early May. Male flowers pale yellowish globose bunch of stamens on 2 cm stalk, shed in vast numbers to carpet the ground in mid-May. Female on a short, stiff, hairy stalk; green globose head of fine white filaments. Nuts triangular in section, often concave sides, shiny deep brown, two in four-lobed involucre pale brown outside, with prickles, whitish inside, 2.5 m long, opening widely. Heavy "mast" years usually follow hot summers of the previous year.

Growth. Height growth and lengthening of side-shoots occur in two periods; long, greyish-green, hanging shoots expanding very rapidly during two weeks in May, and again in late July. Shoots of up to 1 m on young trees. First leaves unfolded are on shaded, slender shoots deep in beechwoods; these are green in late April, 2–3 weeks before the upper crowns show any green.

'PURPUREA' **Copper Beech** pre-1700 Europe. This includes all "copper" ("cuprea") and red-leafed forms. They flush brownish-pink but soon assume the heavy, dark, blackish-purple colour which disfigures so much of our landscape. Grossly overplanted in villages, rectory gardens, churchyards, parks and all commemorative plantings. Only 'River's Purple' a superior dark red form can, occasionally, be excused. 32 × 5 m.

'ZLATIA' 1892 Serbia. A much too rare form in which the leaves emerge a fresh light golden colour but turn green by August. 19 × 1.9 m. Westonbirt.

'TRICOLOR' 1879 France. Rare form with pinkish margins to white-spotted green leaves.

'ALBOVARIEGATA' pre-1770. Rare, strikingly white variegated.

'LUTEOVARIEGATA' pre-1770. Unaccountably extremely rare. 23 m Westonbirt, Willesley Drive; none other noted. Leaf variegated and margined pale yellow.

'Dawyck'

'DAWYCK' ('Fastigiata') **Dawyck Beech** c. 1860 Dawyck, Peebles. Increasingly planted by roads and in formal parts or approaches to parks and gardens. Fastigiate; rather curving, upright small branches; like Lombardy Poplar but curving branches protrude here and there and foliage much superior. 27 m.

'PENDULA' 1820 Europe. Frequent in parks and gardens. Varies from tall and narrow to widely spreading with layered branches rising as an outer ring of trees; long-pendulous shoots, new shoots at first rise vertically to 5–6 m from top of crown and gradually droop down into main crown. 28 × 4 m.

'HETEROPHYLLA' ('Laciniata') 1820 Europe. **Cut-leaf** or **Fern-leaf Beech.** Frequent in parks and gardens, often in towns (notably in Bath). A mixture of forms with leaves variously cut and lobed, the last leaves at the ends of shoots often willow-like, long and strap-shaped. Normal

'Pendula'

leaves may be cut into triangular or long, narrow lobes, or have a long sinus almost to the midrib in the middle ('Aspleniifolia').

Where branches cut or damaged, ordinary entire leaves will appear, with leaves of intermediate shapes, because the plant is a *"chimaera"* with inner tissues of ordinary beech overlaid by tissues of the Cut-leaf form. 25 × 3.5 m.

'CRISTATA' 1836. Rare. Gaunt tree with long, wandering slender branches and clustered leaves which are sessile, some nearly round and deeply triangular-toothed, in bunches which remain partly closed. 23 × 2 m.

'ROTUNDIFOLIA' 1870 Surrey. Rare. Attractive broadly-crowned tree with neat, small leaves, nearly round and entire, 1–3 cm. 19 × 2 m. 'Cockleshell' (1960, Winchester) is a form with only the smaller leaves.

'Heterophylla'   'Cristata'   'Rotundifolia'

ORIENTAL BEECH *Fagus orientalis* Lipsky

Asia Minor to Bulgaria in west, and Persia in east 1910. 18 × 1.8 m. Rare; a few collections in each country. Dark grey bark and *fluted* bole, upswept ovoid crown, many narrow forks in branching. Differs from preceding in distant branching and leaves, buds spreading, orange 1 cm, leaves long-cuneate, *obovate*, 7–10 pairs of *veins*, often cupped, *entire*, 8 × 3 cm (occasionally 14 × 7 cm). Handsome and very vigorous tree.

Oriental Beech

CHINESE BEECH *Fagus englerana* Seemen

C. China 1911. A rare and lovely small tree in a few gardens and collections. 15 × 1 m. Regularly and slender-branched, often forked low; bud exceedingly *slender*, 24 × 2 mm; leaf 10–13 × 6 cm, fresh, *light green*, curiously *deckled* wavy margin, slightly silvery beneath. In autumn orange-brown outer crown, golden interior.

Chinese Beech

CHESTNUTS Castanea

Ten species in southern parts of north temperate region. Male flowers on long, bunched catkins, female flowers at the base of the same catkin or on separate short catkin; seeds in threes in a globose, very prickly involucre.

SWEET or SPANISH CHESTNUT   *Castanea sativa* Mill.   **Pl. 19**

S. Europe, W. Asia, N. Africa. Probably introduced by the Romans. Abundant on light soils in S. England, formerly in large areas of coppice; in small woods, copses. Frequent everywhere in parklands and surrounds of estates, often in parks. Huge old trees on old estates, in avenues or lines, as far north as Ross-shire. 35 × 10 m (13.3 m, solid burrs, at Canford School, Dorset).

Bark. At first purplish-grey, smooth, later silvery-grey, smooth with a few vertical, dark cracks. Fairly old trees with grey or brown bark deeply fissured into small, vertical plates. Old trees dark brown with increasingly angled *spirals* of heavy ridges or a network of ridges.

Crown. Young trees conic, open, whorled, stout shoots. Middle-sized trees broadly columnar with narrow-domed tops. Older trees tall-domed or widely spreading with many low domes, huge low branches, twisting upper branches.

Sweet Chestnut

Foliage. Shoot stout, purple-brown, strong ones ribbed, at first with a grey bloom and long pubescence, lacking a terminal bud. Bud ovoid, red-brown, few-scaled. Leaf 15–20 × 9–10 cm (to 32 cm long on coppice-shoots) oblong-lanceolate, slightly cordate base, hard, glossy dark green, with about 20 *prominent, parallel* main *veins each side*, irregularly opposite and alternate, each ending in a large, abruptly spined tooth; paler and soon glabrous beneath. Petiole 2.5 cm yellowish or red. Autumn colour pale yellow in October turning rich browns in good years.

Flowers and fruit. Axillary bunches of cord-like catkins at end of June open whitish-yellow, 25–32 cm long, crowded with small male flowers each a mass of stamens, turn brown and fall in mid-July. Female flowers sometimes on small, separate spreading catkin, 5–6 cm long, 5–6 flowers; usually 1–2 at base of short, 10–12 cm catkin of unopened, yellowish rudimentary female or rarely male flowers, near tip of shoot. Female flower a 1 cm rosette of bright green, minutely hairy spines with a bunch of spreading, slender white styles. Fruit in bunches of 2–3, in light yellow-green 3 × 4 cm husk covered in sharp spines 1.5 cm long, radiating in clusters; interior white with silky, appressed hairs. Usually two nuts: one globose, the other smaller, concave; dark, shiny red-brown, narrowing to a tip bearing dead styles.

Growth. A vigorous tree in height and girth, continuing rapid increases in girth until 8–9 m round. Long-lived; two known to be 420 years old still thriving; probably the oldest exceeds 600 years.

'ALBOMARGINATA' 1864. Rare. Leaf broadly margined white; some inner leaves completely white.

'Laciniata'

'LACINIATA' 1838. Rare. Usually grown as 'Asplenifolia', a different form. Leaf with 20–30 long, narrow *lobes* drawn out into long filaments. Liable to revert. 15 × 1.7 m (Westonbirt).

CHINQUAPIN   Chrysolepis (Castanopsis)

Similar to *Castanea* but evergreen and fruit take two years to ripen. Connecting link with *Quercus*. One in N.W. America, thirty in E. Asia.

GOLDEN CHESTNUT   *Chrysolepis chrysophylla* (Hook.) Hjelm.

Syn. *Castanopsis c.* (Hook.) DC. Chinquapin (California).

Western USA, Oregon and California 1844. Rare; a few collections in each country. A large bush or moderately small tree to 16 × 1.5 m.

Bark. Grey; few sharp-edged vertical fissures.

Foliage. Shoot bright golden-green at first then brown above, green beneath, finely pubescent. Leaves *evergreen*, 6 × 2 cm, thick, leathery, ovate or lanceolate, abruptly narrowed to rounded point, entire. Dark shiny yellow-green above, coated with minute *golden scales beneath*; petiole 5 mm pubescent.

Golden Chestnut

Flowers and fruit. Flowers late July; big, terminal panicles of pale yellow-green catkins 2–8 cm long. Male flowers slender cream stamens, 8–10 mm across; females on short basal catkins, stigmas purple-red 1 mm.

Fruit in tight terminal bunches of about ten, altogether 3–4 cm across in summer; bright green spiny involucres as in Castanea, each 3–5 cm across when ripe.

OAKS   Quercus

Over 800 oaks have been described including numerous natural hybrids, from all N. temperate regions and at high altitudes in the tropics. Nearly all are trees and about half are evergreen. The one major feature common to all is the bearing of acorns.

Key to Quercus species

1. Leaf margin entire; straight or sinuous 2
   Leaves lobed or toothed 7

2. Evergreen 3
   Deciduous 4

3. Leaves thick, leathery, large, 11–14 cm, yellow-green beneath
                                                      acuta, p. 227
   Leaves thin, hard, small, 5–10 cm, fawn-grey pubescence
      beneath   *ilex*, p. 237

4. Leaves lanceolate, curved; margin thickened, sinuous; leaf 20–22
      × 3–5 cm   *petraea* 'Mespilifolia', p. 244
   Leaves oblong-lanceolate or obovate 5

5. Leaves obovate; mixed with three-lobed leaves *nigra*, p. 229
   Oblong-lanceolate; uniform 6

6. Petiole 0.5 cm, leaf thin, straight, 10 × 2 cm, soon glabrous
   beneath   *phellos,* p. 228
   Petiole 1.5–3 cm, leaf thick, curved, to 18 × 7 cm, hairy
   beneath   *imbricaria,* p. 229

7. Leaves remotely and finely serrate, otherwise entire   **8**
   Leaves serrated, lobed or lobulate   **9**

8. Leaves ovate, dark, thick, leathery, crowded   *acuta,* p. 227
   Leaves lanceolate, thin, pale, distant   *myrsinifolia,* p. 227

9. Leaves lobed*, deeply or obscurely and shallowly   **10**
   Leaves serrated or spined   **33**

10. Lobing obscure, irregular   **11**
   Lobing distinct and more or less regular   **14**

11. Leaves oblong-lanceolate; sporadic lobes in basal half; 15–20
   cm   × *leana,* p. 229
   Leaves obovate, long-cuneate; obscure lobes terminal   **12**

12. Leaves narrow, to 5 cm across, thin, dull   *nigra,* p. 229
   Leaves broad, 10–12 cm across, thick   **13**

13. Leaves glossy above, green beneath, to 12 cm long   *marilandica,* p. 229
   Leaves dull above, white or whitish beneath, 15–20 cm long
                                                   bicolor, p. 246

14. Lobes three, terminal   **15**
   Lobes more than three, lateral   **16**

15. Leaves thin, dull, to 5 cm across   *nigra,* p. 229
   Leaves thick, glossy, to 12 cm across   *marilandica,* p. 229

16. Lobes and teeth with filaments   **17**
   Lobes and teeth, rounded or acute, not filamented; or lobes
   entire, mucronate or not   **20**

17. Shoot pubescent; petiole and main vein stout; leaves hard
                                                   velutina, p. 230
   Shoot glabrous; leaves not hard; petiole not stout   **18**

18. Big tufts in vein-axils beneath   *palustris,* p. 231
   Very small tufts, usually none, in vein-axils beneath   **19**

19. Leaves glossy above and beneath; mid-lobe prominent,
   spreading widely between broad, rounded sinuses   *coccinea,* p. 230
   Leaves matt above and beneath; mid-lobe not prominent,
   pointing forwards between angular sinuses   *borealis,* p. 232

20. Leaves long-cuneate   **21**
   Leaves broad-cuneate, subcordate or auricled   **25**

*Distinction between many small lobes and serration is arbitrary; here more
than ten small lobes is called serrated.

T.B.E.   P

21. Leaves pubescent both sides, lanceolate; lobes distant
pyrenaica 'Pendula', p. 242
Leaves glabrous above and soon beneath, ovate or obovate; lobes close **22**

22. Leaves up to 13 cm long; semi-evergreen; lobes narrow, forward × *turneri*, p. 238
Leaves more than 15 cm, usually at least 20 cm long, fully deciduous; lobes broad, spreading **23**

23. Lobes obovate; sinuses deep, narrow *alba*, p. 245
Lobes triangular or rounded; sinuses shallow, broad **24**

24. Petiole 0.2–1.0 cm; leaves 15–20 cm, whitish beneath; basal half entire, evenly cuneate *bicolor*, p. 246
Petiole 3–5 cm; leaves 20–26 cm, green beneath, lobed irregularly almost to base *macrocarpa*, p. 246

25. Petiole pubescent **26**
Petiole glabrous **31**

26. Leaves up to 15 × 8 cm, petiole slender **27**
Leaves more than 16 × 10 cm, petiole stout and short **29**

27. Side-buds as well as terminal buds with whisker-like stipules; lobes triangular, not mucronate *cerris*, p. 235
Side-buds without persistent stipules **28**

28. Leaves hard, nearly evergreen, shiny above; lobes triangular and mucronate × *hispanica* 'Lucombeana', p. 236
Leaves soft, hairy above and matt, deciduous; lobes broadly rounded *pubescens* p. 243

29. Leaves 25–40 × 18–20 cm; lobes 5–8 per side, forward; resembles giant leaf of common oak *dentata*, p. 246
Leaves 16–25 × 10–15 cm; lobes 8–20 per side, some spreading; quite unlike leaf of common oak **30**

30. Lobes cut more than half way to midrib, larger ones lobulate and broad near tip, irregular, often cupped *frainetto*, p. 242
Lobes shallow, ovate, rounded; small lobule on largest lobe or lacking; rather regular, usually hooded *macranthera*, p. 239

31. Lobes shallow, evenly decreasing in size toward acute tip of leaf; 12–15 parallel veins; leaf 16–20 cm, often hooded; petiole often red *canariensis*, p. 238
Lobes irregular, some deep; 5–10 veins, not parallel; leaf obtuse or rounded, 8–15 cm **32**

32. Leaves auricled at base, crinkled, usually partly eaten, discoloured or covered in galls; acorns on long stalks; petiole 0.3–2 cm *robur*, p. 244
Leaves cuneate at base, plane, dark green, healthy and hard; petiole 1.5–3 cm; acorns sessile *petraea*, p. 243

33. Evergreen; leaves hard, blackish, spined   **34**
       Deciduous; leaves not hard, nor dark, nor spined   **36**

34. Leaves glabrous beneath except for vein-axils; orbicular,
       often hooded   *agrifolia*, p. 233
       Leaves densely felted beneath, elliptic or lanceolate   **35**

35. Adult leaves mainly entire; spined leaves entire near base,
       fawn pubescent beneath; (bark black, square-cracked)   *ilex*, p. 237
       All leaves with 5–6 spines each side from near the base; white
       or bluish-white beneath; (bark yellowish-grey, with deep
       corky ridges)   *suber*, p. 235

36. Teeth not aristate   **37**
       Teeth aristate   **38**

37. Teeth shallow, hooked; leaf elliptic   *pontica*, p. 238
       Teeth deep, triangular; leaf oblong-lanceolate   *castaneifolia*, p. 234

38. Leaves silvery pubescent beneath; teeth abrupt, distant; bark
       pink, corky   *variabilis*, p. 233
       Leaves green beneath, nearly glabrous; teeth close; bark grey   **39**

39. Bud green, narrowly conic; leaf to 20 × 6 cm   *acutissima*, p. 233
       Bud orange-brown, ovoid; leaf to 12 × 3 cm   *libani*, p. 234

JAPANESE EVERGREEN OAK   *Quercus acuta* Thunb.
Pl. 21

Japan 1878. Rare; mainly in S. England in a few large gardens,
also Edinburgh R.B.G. An *evergreen* bush, rarely a sturdy tree.
14 × 1.5 m (13 × 1.7 m at Caerhays Castle, Cornwall). Foliage
very *like a Rhododendron*.
Bark. Smooth, dark grey, wrinkled, sparsely dotted with pale
stomata.
Foliage. Shoots densely covered in pale orange wool which soon
rubs off. Bud pale yellow, conic. Leaves 10–14 × 2–6 cm densely
clustered at ends of shoots, oval with shoulders *narrowing to*
wool beneath, *entire* but wavy margin, sometimes obscure remote
teeth. Petiole 3–4 cm with orange wool shed late in season.
Fruit. Acorns 4–7 on a spike 6–8 cm long; 2 cm, pale orange-
brown, 4–5 more undeveloped.

Japanese
Evergreen Oak

BAMBOO-LEAFED OAK   *Quercus myrsinifolia* Bl. .
Pl. 21

China and Japan 1854. Rare; big gardens and collections in S.
England. 10 × 0.7 m.
Bark. Pink-grey, smooth or shallowly cracked with orange-
brown short, narrow fissures.
Crown. Usually several stems from near base, occasionally an
elegant, slender tree with slender, ascending branches.
Foliage. Shoot slender, dark olive, speckled white. Leaves *evergreen*, 10 × 2.5 cm, drooping delicately, *distant*, 3–4 cm apart,
narrowly lanceolate, cuneate base, acuminate, few small sharp

Bamboo-leafed Oak

teeth widely separated near tip, the rest entire; hard, *fresh yellowish green* above, *glaucous* beneath. Petiole 1.5 cm.
Fruit. Minute acorns crowded on a spike 3–4 cm long.

WILLOW OAK   *Quercus phellos* L.   **Pl. 21**
Eastern USA 1723. Infrequent; large gardens in S. England and Ireland. 25 × 3 m (25 × 3.7 m at Cobham Hall, Kent).
Bark. At first quite smooth and grey, later finely fissured with orange; old trees purple-grey roughened by horizontal wrinkles.
Crown. Domed; rather few ascending branches and dense mass of twigs.
Foliage. Shoot slender, red-brown; leaves deciduous, *entire*, oblong to lanceolate, cuneate base, acute tip, 5–10 cm usually 7–8.5 × 2 cm, dull yellow-green above, pubescent at first beneath, slightly shiny, flat, may be curved. Petiole 2–4 mm. Leaves expand yellow with red-tinted centres, in June.
Flowers and fruit. Female flowers axillary on middle of new shoot, minute 2 mm brown, ovoid-conic, stigmas deep red, soon black. First year acorns 2 mm globular, green and brown on shiny 2 mm peduncle. Ripe acorn 1 cm in shallow cup.

Willow Oak shoot with 1-year acorns

Similar species. *Q. imbricaria* (p. 229).

LUDWIG'S OAK   *Quercus × ludoviciana* Sarg.
Hybrid *Q. phellos × Q. falcata*. South-east USA 1880. Rare, handsome tree to 21 m at Caerhays Castle, Cornwall and 16 m at Kew. Bark smooth, dark grey finely striated pink; crown conic, rather upright. Buds small, bright red-brown. Leaf unfolds copper-brown, soon bright gold, then dark green; 10–22 cm, slender cuneate, two *large, forward, acute* lobes, project from outer half; irregular, acute, spine-ended or broad, rounded, obscure lobes or teeth variably present. Dense patches of long pubescence each side of midrib beneath. Petiole 1 cm. Glossy dark green until late November, then rich orange-red. Female flowers: three on decurved axillary peduncle; conic, 2 mm

Ludwig's Oak

BARTRAM'S OAK   *Quercus × heterophylla*
    Michx. f.
Natural hybrid *Q. phellos × Q. borealis*. Eastern USA pre-1750. Very rare; a few collections in S. England and in Ireland. 16 × 2 m.
Bark. Smooth, dark grey with swarms of fine pink fissures.
Crown. Rather open; spreading branches, upright near apex.
Foliage. Shoot glabrous; leaf lanceolate, oblong-elliptic or obovate, 5–8 cm, 1–4 small spined teeth or very shallow lobes each side; often hooded; dark shiny green above with pale impressed veins, shiny beneath with pale buff tufts in axils; turning pink, brown and red in autumn.

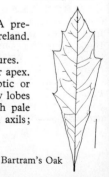

Bartram's Oak

SHINGLE OAK *Quercus imbricaria* Michx.

South-eastern USA 1786. Infrequent; a few large gardens and collections in all parts. 26 × 2 m.

Bark. At first grey, smooth but wrinkled and warty, later purplish-grey with very shallow, wide fissures.

Crown. Rather broad, domed, lower branches level, upper ascending. Epicormic sprouts on bole often numerous.

Foliage. Shoot orange-green to pink-brown. Bud to 1 mm, conic, dark brown. Leaf 13–18 × 5–6 cm, deciduous, *entire*, *crinkled*, margin waved; oblong-lanceolate acute often with 1–2 mm spine at tip, glossy dark green above with wide pale midrib, paler and soft-pubescent beneath. Petiole *1–3 cm*, often red above. Leaves open yellow; brilliant gold until mid-June.

Fruit. Acorn 1–2 cm, nearly globular in shallow cup with flat scales.

Similar species. *Q. phellos* (p. 228).

Shingle Oak

LEA'S HYBRID OAK *Quercus × leana* Nutt.

Hybrid, *Q. imbricaria* × *Q. velutina*. Occurring with the parents in N. America pre-1850. Rare; a few collections in S. England. 19 × 2.8 m. Bark dark grey, shallowly cracked into rough knobbly small plates. Leaf lanceolate 15–20 × 5–7 cm, *sinuous* margin irregularly or obscurely lobed or with 1–4 big spine-ended lobes; rounded base, slightly oblique; finely pointed tip; hard, glossy, dark green above, matt beneath with rusty long hairs each side of midrib.

Lea's Hybrid Oak

WATER OAK *Quercus nigra* L.

South-eastern USA 1723. Very rare; a few collections and large gardens in S. England. 18 × 2.5 m (16 × 2.7 m at Pylewell Park, Hants.). A sturdy, broadly domed tree with very *variable* leaves but always broadest near the outer end; deciduous but green on the tree until November. Some are spoon-shaped and almost entire with long-cuneate base and broadly rounded end, others have 1–2 minutely spined short lobes each side towards the tip; terminal leaves 8 cm, narrow and usually lobed, basal leaves to 12 × 5 cm, less lobed, often hooded, glossy deep rich green.

Similar species. *Q. marilandica* (below).

Water Oak

BLACK-JACK OAK *Quercus marilandica* Muenchh.

Eastern USA pre-1739. Very rare; a few gardens in S. England. 17 × 1 m. Similar to *Q. nigra*, but leaves much broader and crown heavily branched, rather upright. Leaves *hard and thick* to 12 × 11 cm on stout 2–3 cm petiole; variously lobed from one hugely broad, rounded shallow lobe each side to a terminal lobe each side making a nearly flat end to the leaf and sometimes with spines at the tip to 5 mm long;

Black-jack Oak

occasional single spine-teeth on obscure lobes; bright *glossy* green above, brown pubescence beneath shed during season. Midrib white, very broad until half way along leaf then breaks into three narrow veins. Shoot olive-green short curly buff pubescent. Acorn 1–2 on stout 5mm stalk, globular 8mm, pale pink brown.

BLACK or QUERCITRON OAK   *Quercus velutina* Lam.
Eastern and central USA 1800. Infrequent; collections and large gardens in England and Ireland, rare in Wales and Scotland. 20×2m (23.5×2.4m at Batsford Park, Glos.).

Bark. Dark grey, smooth at first, soon densely fissured into small squares, the vertical fissures more prominent and *orange* inside.

Crown. Conic when young, later domed with long, slightly ascending, often sinuous branches.

Foliage. Shoot densely short-pubescent, later nearly glabrous. Petiole stout, rarely slender, broad-based, yellow, 4cm. Leaves oblanceolate, 12–25cm; 3–4 deep, broad lobes each side, *often mis-shapen* with the last two lobes unequal and splitting the leaf, i.e. terminal lobe lacking and midrib dividing, at other times quite regular; lobes with a few spine-teeth; often hooded; *hard leathery* somewhat shiny both sides; brown pubescence beneath shed except *tufts* in axils and often scurf elsewhere; dark green turning deep brown in autumn. Main veins very prominent on underside.

Black Oak

Fruit. Acorn ovoid 1–2cm, half enclosed in loosely scaled cup.

Similar species. *Q. borealis* (p. 232) differs in bark, slender petiole, matt underside to regularly and more shallowly lobed, softer leaf.

SCARLET OAK   *Quercus coccinea* Muenchh.   **Pl. 20**
Eastern and central USA 1691. Frequent; in gardens, some roadside plantings but mainly in S. England; less frequent than *Q. borealis*. 26×3m.

Bark. At first silvery-grey, smooth with many warts and lines of large lenticels, later dark grey, finely fissured, still warty.

Crown. Young trees rather densely conic, old trees gaunt in lower half with few ascending then *widely spreading, wandering* branches; upper half strongly ascending branches and many fine shoots in a tall dome. Bole *sinuous* and slender.

Foliage. Shoot orange-brown or red-brown above, olive beneath. Bud ovoid, pointed; scales dark red or red-brown with fawn or grey pubescent margins near the tip. Leaf oblong or elliptic, variable but typically 12 × 10cm, truncate or broad cuneate base from *slender* 2.5–4cm petiole, three lobes each side, basal lobe perpendicular or reflexed, mid-lobes *widely* spread-

Scarlet Oak

ing, 3–4 cm deep, third lobe forward, the pair often unequal, each lobe with a few spined teeth each side; base of leaf *rising each side* of white midrib, veins to lobes often not opposite; dark shiny green above, paler and also *shiny beneath* with scarcely visible or absent tufts of hairs in axils. Autumn colour starts by *one or two branches* of leaves turning bright deep red while the rest of the crown is still green; later the whole crown is deep crimson and reds. When all the upper leaves have fallen, those on some lower shoots remain attached and brown until January.

Flowers and fruit. Male catkins 6–8 cm, bunched at tip of last year's shoot. Female flowers in leaf-axils of new shoot; 3–4 together; 2 mm, globose, pale brown, two minute black stigmas. Peduncle stout, 4 mm, bright green. Acorn ovoid 1–2 cm, in shallow, large-scaled cup.

Scarlet Oak

'SPLENDENS' A larger-leaved form with big glossy leaves to 18 × 13 cm on 4–6 cm petioles, in some gardens. This is a selected form, probably more reliable for bright reds in autumn. Apparently normal trees, however, may be labelled 'Splendens'.

Similar species. Oaks in this group (*Q. coccinea, borealis, palustris* and *velutina* pp. 230–232) are difficult as their leaves vary in size and shape. Those of *Q. coccinea* are usually more deeply lobed with more regular semi-circular sinuses than *borealis* and *velutina*, are glossy both sides and lack the prominent axillary tufts of *palustris*.

PIN OAK   *Quercus palustris* Muenchh.

North-eastern and north-central USA pre-1770. Uncommon; almost confined to S. England in large gardens and some parks. 26 × 3.7 m.

Bark. At first silvery-grey and smooth, soon darker and purplish-grey with pale vertical streaks; old trees very dark grey with pinkish-grey smooth, flat, wide ridges separated by pale, shallow fissures.

Crown. Young trees slender, straight-boled, many level branches and dense fine shoots; older trees narrowly domed on clean bole, a dense head of slender shoots, many pendulous.

Foliage. Shoot shiny olive-brown with white lenticels. Bud ovoid, dull grey-brown. Leaf elliptic-oblong, 8–15 cm on petiole 3–5 cm, broad or narrow-cuneate, 3–4 lobes each side, basal pair triangular, often without teeth, spreading, second pair biggest, 1–3 spined teeth each side, point slightly forwards, oblong-triangular; third pair very forward 0–2 teeth each side; bright green above, shiny pale green beneath and *conspicuous brown tufts* of hairs in vein-axils. In late autumn the leaves at the *tips of shoots* turn scarlet before the rest then all the leaves turn crimson then dark red.

Flowers and fruit. Female flowers axillary at base

Pin Oak

of new shoot, four on bright green, 2 mm pedicel, ovoid; stigmas dark red. First year acorn 3 mm on stout, appressed peduncle, dark brown. Ripe acorn on short, thick stalk, very small, 1–1.5 cm across, nearly hemispheric, shallowly enclosed in thin, finely hairy cup.

Similar species. *Q. coccinea* (p. 230).

RED OAK   *Quercus borealis* Michx. f.   **Pl. 20**
   Syn. *Q. rubra* du Roi

E. Canada and north-eastern USA, south and west to Texas 1724. Common; parks, amenity belts, gardens, roadsides; often seeding itself; less frequent in Scotland. 35 × 6 m (30 × 6.3 m at Cassiobury Park, Herts.).

Bark. Smooth, silvery-grey, sometimes with a few large warts; old trees variable: some silvery-grey with a few fissures, some brown-grey, some shallowly fissured into small rough plates.

Crown. Young tree conic, often very gaunt and distantly whorled; soon broad; old trees hugely domed from a short, straight, massive bole and usually dividing at around 2 m up, the branches

Red Oak

straight and radiating. Large sprouts at the base of some trees.

Foliage. Shoot dark brown, stout, glabrous, ribbed. Bud ovoid, pointed, dark brown. Leaf very variable in size and lobing but usually oblong-elliptic and acute in outline, 12–22 cm long (30 × 20 cm on strong sprouts and 24 × 12 cm on young trees), broad cuneate, to the 2(5) cm yellowish petiole which has a swollen reddish base (dark pink petiole and main veins in some big leaves). 4–5 lobes each side, 4–5 cm deep, shallower in some big leaves, each with 1–3 large teeth with 3 mm whisker at the tip; dark *matt green above*, pale *matt* and greyish beneath sometimes with minute tufts in vein-axils. When first unfolded, the leaves are a clear

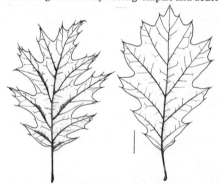

Red Oak – types of leaf

bright yellow for three weeks. Autumn colour starts *uniformly* over crown, young trees usually a good deep red, some older trees yellow and brown on each leaf, some cigar-brown all over, some deep red. A few young trees retain dead leaves all over the crown, but most trees of all ages shed every leaf before December.

Flowers and fruit. Male catkins slender, 5–8 cm; female flowers in axils of leaves on new shoots, two on 5 mm peduncle; dark red, 2 mm ovoid. First year acorns scattered along two-year shoot on short stalks, flat-globose, pale brown 3 mm. Ripe acorn 2 × 2 cm, flat-based ovoid, base recessed in centre; dark red-brown. Cup on stout stalk 1 cm long; 1.5–1.8 cm across, very shallow, incurved at rim, many layers of prettily patterned scales, smooth, pale pink-brown with purple margins. Trees from southern part of range (var. *maxima* (Marsh) Ashe) may be distinguished by more pendulous leaves, more deeply cut into six angular lobes each side and larger acorn.

Growth. A very fast-growing tree which can make shoots of 2.5 m in a year and rapidly builds a stout bole. Shoot-growth is made in two periods, mid-May to early June and again, in young trees, for two weeks in early August when 20 cm may be grown in a week. A few old trees are now collapsing and the life span is about 180 years.

'AUREA' Rare, striking tree; leaves boldly variegated rich yellow fading to paler yellow.

Similar species. *Q. palustris* (p. 231) big tufts in axils; *Q. velutina* (p. 230) pubescent shoot, and *Q. coccinea* (p. 230), leaf glossy both sides.

CALIFORNIAN LIVE OAK   *Quercus agrifolia* Née

California 1843. Rare; confined to oak collections in each country. 16 × 1.6 m. An evergreen tree rather like *Q. ilex* (p. 237) but the black bark is smooth striped brown, later fissured into large squares, and the leaves are nearly orbicular, obovate or elliptic, usually very hooded, 3–4 × 2 cm, hard with a variable number of very small spines along the margin; deep shiny green above, *slightly paler beneath* with *tufts in vein-axils*. Petiole 2–3 mm. Acorn conic-ovoid, half in cup, bright, shining green, 15–18 mm; cup with large brown scales edged purple.

Californian
Live Oak

JAPANESE CHESTNUT OAK   *Quercus acutissima* Carruth.

Korea, Japan, China, the Himalaya 1862. Rare; collections and a few large gardens in S. England and Ireland. 15 × 1 m. An attractive, open-crowned tree with dark grey bark roughly ridged and fissured. Leaves large, *glossy, oblong*, acute, *spine-edged*, 18–21 × 4–6 cm, 12–16 pairs of veins and long spiny teeth; petiole 1–2.5 cm; bud long-pointed and pale green like the shoot.

Similar species. *Q. libani* (p. 234), *Q. castaneifolia* (p. 234), *Q. variabilis* (below).

Japanese Chestnut Oak

CHINESE CORK OAK   *Quercus variabilis* Bl.

N. China, Korea, Japan 1861. Very rare; collections in S. England and in Ireland. 16 × 2 m. 18 × 1.6 m (Hollycombe, Sussex).

Bark. *Very thickly corky*, pink-grey or brown with deep short fissures or cavities and broad wavy ridges.

Crown. Rather open, strong level branches.

Foliage. Bud slender, acute. Very handsome leaves, obovate, acute, 20 × 10 cm with 15–18 pairs of parallel veins ending in an *abrupt whisker-like tooth* 6–7 mm long; rich glossy green above, midrib white; fine *silvery pubescence* beneath. Petiole 2.5–3 cm, curved, pale green.

Chinese Cork Oak

Similar species. Distinguished adequately from *Q. prinus* (p. 239) and *Q. castaneifolia* (p. 234) by corky bark, abrupt teeth and silvered underside of leaf. *Q. pontica* (p. 238) has similar veining and shape of leaf, although usually broader, but differs in its hooked teeth as well as in bark and underside of leaf.

CHESTNUT-LEAFED OAK *Quercus castaneifolia* C. A. Mey. **Pl. 21**

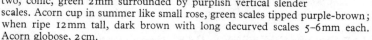

Caucasus, Persia and (variety) Algeria. 1846 to Kew where now 32×6m; elsewhere 20×3m. Rare; collections and some gardens north to Yorkshire and in Ireland.

Bark. At first black and smooth, later dark grey short lumpy ridges separated by deep orange fissures.

Crown. Conic and broad when young, hugely domed with age, stout straight upcurved shoots; branches swelling at the bole.

Foliage. Shoot stout, dark brown, speckled with white lenticels, hairy at first. Terminal bud large, pale brown, surrounded by whiskers to 1 cm long; laterals smaller, dark brown with shorter whiskers to 5mm. Leaf oblong-lanceolate, variable in size from 12–15 cm to 20×5 cm (as original at Kew), broadly cuneate, 9–14 pairs of parallel veins. Teeth obtuse triangles, faintly mucronate. Dark or blackish-green with yellow midrib above, glaucous and finely pubescent beneath with small buff tufts in vein axils and buff pubescence on veins. Petiole 2–4 cm, light green, finely pubescent.

Chestnut-leafed Oak

Flowers and fruit. Female flowers in terminal axils of new shoot, two, conic, green 2mm surrounded by purplish vertical slender scales. Acorn cup in summer like small rose, green scales tipped purple-brown; when ripe 12mm tall, dark brown with long decurved scales 5–6mm each. Acorn globose, 2 cm.

Growth. Remarkable, sustained and vigorous. Old tree at Kew has increased in girth by 300cm (10 ft.) in the last 60 years; 65 cm (26 inches) in the last 13 years. A young tree near the Main Gates increased in girth 63 cm (25 inches) in seven years, and is 15 m × 1.7 m when 22 years planted.

Similar species. Blunt teeth separate from finely acuminate teeth of *Q. acutissima* (p. 233) and *Q. libani* (below). Pubescent petiole and underside of leaf, whiskered side-buds and broad-cuneate leaf distinguish from narrow-acuminate, long, glabrous-petioled *Q. prinus* (p. 239).

LEBANON OAK *Quercus libani* Oliv.

Syria, Asia Minor 1855. Rare; collections. 20 × 2m. Bark dark grey to blackish, may be slightly corky with orange fissures. An attractive, open-crowned, straight-boled tree like *Q. acutissima*, differing in orange-brown bud; terminal bud surrounded by whiskers; olive-brown shoot roughened with lenticels, leaf lanceolate 10–12 × 3.5 cm; 10–12 pairs of veins and triangular, whisker-tipped teeth; dark glossy green, often hooded, pale beneath and pubescent at least on the veins. Petiole slender, 6–10mm. Leaf may be unequal at base. Acorn on short, extremely broad stalk 4mm long and 4mm across; cup covers fruit, top-shaped, flat-topped, 2 × 1.5 cm, pale green with brown scale-tips; sometimes to 5 ×2 cm. First year globular, 3mm, grey, tipped purple

Lebanon Oak

Similar species. *Q. acutissima* (p. 233), *Q. castaneifolia* (p. 234).

TURKEY OAK   *Quercus cerris* L.   **Pl. 20**
S. Europe; S.W. Asia 1735. Abundant in many parts of S. England as a country-side tree spreading like a native in hedgerows and woods, common everywhere as park tree in towns or deer-parks and roadside tree, big specimens as far north as E. Ross-shire. 38 × 8 m (39 × 7.1 m at Knightshayes, Devon).
Bark. Dull grey and roughly fissured from an early age; old trees finely and deeply fissured into dark, rough convex small plates.
Crown. Young trees open, slender, conic; older trees broadly domed, usually tall with long, ascending branches swollen at the base, and markedly straight shoots.
Foliage. Shoot light coppery grey or dull green-grey with short, dense pubescence. Bud ovoid, pale brown with long pubescence, all buds surrounded by *long, persistent, twisted* whiskers. Leaf very variable,

normally 9–12 × 3–5 cm with 7–9 lobes each side but leaves on sprouts and cut hedges may be 20 × 5 cm very fancily lobed and cut to the midrib for a length in the middle. Normal leaves cut one third to two thirds to midrib into triangular lobes, rarely mucronate; lanceolate or obovate-oblong overall, dark green and *rough above* becoming shiny; grey-brown woolly beneath at first, later woolly on veins only; petiole 2 cm, pubescent.
Flowers and fruit. Male flowers on 5–6 cm catkins in dense bunches, crimson before opening, brownish-yellow in early June often hanging on dead for months. Female flowers axillary to new leaves, 1–3, obovoid 5 mm, dark red stigmas; surrounded by pale yellow-pink slender scales. Acorn sessile, narrow, ovoid   Turkey Oak
2.5 × 1.4 cm in "mossy" cup 1 cm deep, 1.8 cm across
with long pale green scales drawn out to points, curled upwards in upper half, downwards in lower half, to 4 mm long. Occasional acorns big, 3 × 2 cm in cup 2 × 2 cm.
Growth. Very rapid and long maintained; many trees around Exeter of original date or soon after still flourishing 200 years old. Shoot made in two periods, June–July and late August, to 15 cm a week.
Similar species. Differs from *Q. robur* (p. 244) in rougher, darker bark, more upright crown, straighter branches and shoots, hairy shoots, lateral buds whiskered, rough leaves with angular lobes and acorn narrow in "mossy" cup with protruding scales, no burrs on bole. The hybrid *Q. × hispanica* 'Lucombeana' (p. 236) can be confused with *Q. cerris*.

CORK OAK   *Quercus suber* L.   **Pl. 20**
S. Europe; N. Africa 1699 or before. Infrequent but not rare; in large gardens and some parks particularly in S.W. England, also E. Anglia, rarer towards north as far as Morayshire; rare in Ireland particularly in east, less rare in south-west. 20 × 4 m (19 × 4.5 m at Antony House, Cornwall).
Bark. Young boles and small branches coarsely *winged* with dull grey thick flanges of finely ridged cork; old trees pale dull grey or *cream-brown*, short, interwoven corky ridges standing out 10 cm or so from dark narrow-based wide fissures, all the cork finely ridged (annual rings of growth). In Spain and Portugal the bark is stripped from the trees to become the cork of every-day use leaving the trunks a rich red colour.   Cork Oak

Crown. Low-domed, spreading, with low, heavy twisting branches.
Foliage. Shoot grey-green with dense grey-brown pubescence. Bud small, dark purple, 2 mm, ovoid. Leaf *evergreen*, oval, 4–7 × 2–3 cm acute, hard, margin crinkled or waved, often curved down, tip somewhat raised and arched, 5–6 shallow, spine-tipped lobes each side, dark ± shiny blackish-green above, grey or glaucous beneath with dense white pubescence. Petiole 1 cm, densely pubescent.
Fruit. Acorn ovoid-oblong, 1.5–3 cm long in fairly deep cup with elongated upper scales, ripens in one year.
Similar species. *Q.* × *hispanica* 'Lucombeana', (below) *Q. ilex* (p. 237).

SPANISH OAK *Quercus* × *hispanica* Lam.

A hybrid between *Q. cerris* and *Q. suber* occurring naturally in S. Europe. Only the following forms are grown:

'LUCOMBEANA' Lucombe Oak   Pl. 21

Exeter 1762. Common in parks and gardens in Devon and Cornwall, frequent in the rest of S. England, rare towards north and in Scotland and Ireland. 30 × 6 m. Many seedlings were raised and grafts were made from the first two trees. In 1789 six seedlings were selected for further propagation. Many early trees are grafts but more are seedlings and show a great variety of forms. Two main groups, probably corresponding nearly to the first cross and to the 1789 series respectively, cover most of the trees seen.
Type A. This type is common around Exeter, rare elsewhere.
Bark. Pale creamy grey finely divided into very small corky ridges or dark grey more deeply fissured into short non-corky ridges.
Crown. Very distinctive, open, few main branches arising from very *swollen bases*, level for several metres then ascending, holding an *outer fringe* of dark yellowish-green leaves in winter but losing most of them if February or March very cold and windy; upper crown tall-domed.
Foliage. Shoot pale grey-brown, densely pubescent. Terminal bud red-brown surrounded by whiskers, lateral without. Leaf nearly evergreen, oblong-elliptic 10–12 × 3–4 cm on petiole of 1 cm; 3–7 irregular, rounded, mucronate lobes each side, often with a wide, deep sinus near the middle of the leaf; deep *shiny* green above, grey-green with close pubescence beneath.
Flowers and fruit. Male flowers dense sprays of slender 4 cm catkins crimson before flowers open. Female flowers in leaf axils towards tip of new shoot; 2 mm, pubescent, surrounded by slender reddish scales. One-year acorns deep brown, minute, 1–2 on 1 cm peduncle. Acorn 2–2.5 × 1.4 cm, rich green until November of second season, one third in cup 1.5 × 2 cm, bright pale green, dense scales protruding 2–3 mm and radiating (not parted as in the narrower cup of *Q. cerris*).
Type B. This type less frequent round Exeter but more frequent elsewhere. Differs in:
Bark. Dark grey with deep, wide black fissures leaving rather smooth non-corky plates; rarely yellowish-grey, finely fissured   Lucombe Oak
and corky as in Type A.
Crown. Low, dense, *dark domes like Q. ilex* with heavy, twisting, low branches; leaves *largely retained* in dense masses until new leaves emerge in June; only hardest winters cause them all to fall by April.

Foliage. Leaf 4–6 × 2 cm; 4–5 triangular, mucronate lobes each side; unfolding silvery-grey in June.

'DIVERSIFOLIA' is a rare form seen in some collections with a pale, smooth but corky-fissured bark, *nearly fastigiate* branching and slender leaves *deeply cut* by a long sinus in the middle. 27 × 3 m.

'FULHAMENSIS' **Fulham Oak.** Probably of independent origin at Fulham soon after the Lucombe Oak. In a few collections. Bark pale pinkish-grey, deeply corky-fissured. *Slender* tree with a dense crown of branches *arching* out and bearing *pendulous*, slender shoots. Leaves flat, *oval*, 10 × 4 cm, evergreen but partly shed by spring, uniformly six-toothed each side, blackish-green above, paler and somewhat pubescent beneath.

Similar species. In winter the crown and foliage of Type A are unique, and Type B differs from *Q. ilex* (below) in the bark and lobed leaves. The foliage of Type A differs from that of *Q. cerris* (p. 235) (with which it is often confused because some have a very similar bark) in the persistent and dense pubescence on the shoot and under the leaf and by the lack of whiskers around lateral buds, the shiny upper surface of the harder broader leaf and in holding dark yellowish-green leaves on outer crown all the winter.

HOLM OAK *Quercus ilex* L. Pl. 20

N. Africa, S. Europe *c.* 1500. Common in parks and gardens everywhere except N. Scotland, abundant in many coastal areas particularly in S. and S.W. England, parts of E. Anglia and E. Scotland. 28 × 4.3 m at Killerton Chapel, Devon.

Bark. Brownish-black or black, shallowly cracked into small, square, thin, dry, and often curling plates.

Crown. Broad, domed, often on many stems or branched very low; upper branches slender ascending steeply, straight; densely leafy at all times, black in winter, yellowish and silvery in early summer, soon grey and black.

Foliage. Shoot slender, dull grey-brown with a close fawn wool. Bud minute, 1–2 mm, fawn; terminal bud with curled whiskers. Leaf *evergreen*, unfolding in June silvery-white then pale yellow, covered all over with dense hairs; upper side soon rough but shiny blackish-green, underside remains matt *dull fawn* and densely pubescent. Very variable in shape and toothing both on a single tree and among minor varieties and cultivars. In general lanceolate to oval, 5–10 × 3–8 cm; on sprouts and young trees variably shallowly spiny toothed, others usually entire, waved or sinuate; petiole 1–2 cm, woolly.

Holm Oak

Flowers and fruit. Male flowers in dense sprays of catkins 4–7 cm long, pale green and pink in bud; open a broad mass of stamens conspicuously *pale gold* against silvery-grey opening leaves and black old leaves in mid-June. Female flowers 2–3 on stout woolly, 1 cm, peduncles from outer axils, green-grey pubescent; 2 mm, tipped pink; late June. Acorn light green, 1.5–2.0 cm, one third to one half enclosed in cup of many rows of small, fawn, felted scales, the cup 1.2 cm across, 1.8 cm deep.

'FORDII' ('Angustifolia', 'Lanceolata') Leaf 5 ×
1 cm, entire and curled. Frequent.

'LAURIFOLIA' Leaf 10–14 × 3–5 cm long-lanceolate, very shiny, margins decurved. In some gardens.

'ROTUNDIFOLIA' Leaf nearly round, 8–10 cm;
acorn 3–4 cm, edible. Rare. There are many other
named and un-named with varying shapes of leaves.

'Fordii'

Similar species. *Phillyreas* (p. 383) with dense, thick,
much smaller opposite leaves; *Arbutus unedo* (p. 375) with finely serrated
leaves. *Q. × hispanica* 'Lucombeana' (p. 236) and *Q. suber* (p. 235) with a
different bark and foliage and the very rare *Q. agrifolia* (p. 233).

TURNER'S OAK   *Quercus × turneri* Willd.

Hybrid *Q. ilex × robur* pre-1783 London. Infrequent;
large gardens and collections mainly in S. England but
also in Scotland and Ireland. 17 × 3 m.

Bark. Smooth, purplish-grey, shallowly and coarsely
cracked.

Crown. Low dome, with heavy, low, twisting branches,
somewhat open interior, *some leaves retained green until
spring.*

Foliage. Shoot green, finely and densely pubescent.
Leaf obovate, cuneate to rounded base, or long-cuneate
6–12 cm, 2–3 shallow, forward teeth towards the tip,
or 6–8 all round, each broadly triangular, acute often

Turner's Oak

mucronate; shiny dark green above, pubescent on veins beneath. Petiole
4–8 mm.

Fruit. Acorns 4–8 on zig-zag tomentose 7 cm spike.

Recognition. A very handsome, low, domed, partly evergreen tree, identified
by the usually long-cuneate base and forward-pointing teeth.

PONTINE OAK   *Quercus pontica* K. L. Koch

Caucasus Mts. 1885. A most handsome and distinct, rare,
usually bushy tree found in a few gardens and collections
in each country. 8 × 0.8 m Kew.

Foliage. Shoots glabrous *very stout,* ribbed, greenish-
brown. Bud large, tall, conic, green scales edged brown.
Leaf large, flat, elliptic 10–18 × 8–11 cm, 13–17 *pairs of
prominent parallel* veins, and small acute, *curved spined
teeth;* bright, fresh green with yellow veins above; glaucous
beneath, hairy on the veins. Autumn colour yellow-brown.

Flowers and fruit. Male flowers 1–3 slender, pink-buff
catkins 5–10 (20 cm) long, flowers tinged dull purple.
Female flowers 4–5 crowded on 3 cm peduncles from
terminal axils of new shoot, globular, 5–6 mm pubescent;

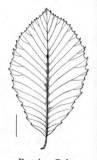

Pontine Oak

pale grey-green; stigmas large, purple-red; mid-June. Acorn ripens to 3–4 cm
long, ovoid, tapered each end, deep mahogany-red, in shallow, thin grey cup.

MIRBECK'S OAK   *Quercus canariensis* Willd.

Syn. *Q. mirbeckii* Durieu

Spain; N. Africa 1844. Infrequent; some gardens and collections in S. England

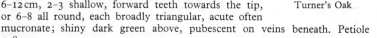

and Ireland, rare elsewhere. 20 × 4m (27.5 × 2.5m at Osborne House, I.o.W.).
Bark. Distinctively *dark grey* or blackish, deeply fissured into square rough, convex plates, slightly shaggy.
Crown. Young trees shapely, narrowly conic or ovoid with straight bole; old trees domed with ascending branches; in winter retains *some green leaves* mixed with brown ones.

Foliage. Shoot smooth green-grey tinged pink, glabrous after soft dense wool has rubbed off. Bud narrowly conic, 7mm, pale brown, of many scales fringed with white hairs. Leaf oblong-ovate to obovate, subcordate at base, 6–13 pairs of shallow, obtuse teeth largest where leaf broadest and *decreasing in size regularly towards the acute tip*, 10–15 × 6–8cm on petiole 1.5–2cm; on vigorous trees to 19 × 11cm, petiole 3cm and warty, softly woolly at first; on some trees all leaves strongly hooded, on others very plane. Petiole and basal veins on terminal leaves dark pink; upper side mid to dark green, usually shiny, underside paler, matt, pubescent at first. In autumn about half the leaves stay green.

Mirbeck's Oak

Flowers and fruit. Male flowers bunched at nodes, yellow, slender catkins, 4cm at end of May. Acorn-cup hemispheric, on 5–10mm stalk.
Similar species. Often resembles a luxuriant *Q. petraea* (p. 243) with shallow and small lobes, but bark and toothing (lobing) and acute leaf different. More like *Q. macranthera* (below) and *Q. muehlenbergii* (below). Hybrids with *Q. robur* occur when acorns from trees here are sown and these may be labelled "*Q. canariensis*" but the bark is pale grey and shallowly fissured and the leaves less handsome and substantial, and more auricled at base.

CAUCASIAN OAK   *Quercus macranthera* Fisch. and Mey.

Caucasus to Persia 1873. Uncommon; collections and a few large gardens in each country. 24 × 2.3m (Westonbirt.)
Bark. Purplish-grey, flaking coarsely.
Crown. Tall-domed, upper branches ascending.

Foliage. Shoot stout; dense pubescence orange-brown and persistent. Bud large ovoid, 8–10mm, *dark shiny red*, brown tip pubescent. Leaf obovate-lanceolate, to broad-ovate, acute, hard, parchment-like, usually hooded, fully deciduous on old trees, 15–23 × 10–14cm on pubescent petiole 1–2cm; cuneate, slightly auricled, 8–12 pairs of veins to forward-pointing, shallow ovate slightly out-curved lobes, decreasing in size regularly from broadest part of leaf to the tip; dark greyish-green above, grey-pubescent beneath or curly brown pubescence each side of midrib. Male flowers; pubescent catkins 5–8cm.

Caucasian Oak

Similar species. A handsome tree similar only to *Q. canariensis* (above) and sufficiently distinguished by the pubescent shoot, and dark red buds.

CHINKAPIN or YELLOW OAK   *Quercus muehlenbergii* Engelm.

Central and southern USA 1737. Very rare (fine tree in Kensington Gardens, London, 20 × 2.6m). Leaf *lanceolate, long-cuneate, long-acuminate* 18 × 8cm. 10–14 parallel veins to triangular lobes decreasing regularly in size from base of

Plate 21   **OAKS** (Contd.)

1. Japanese Evergreen Oak   *Quercus acuta*   227

An uncommon tree in southern gardens with foliage rather resembling that of a Rhododendron, and small acorns clustered on spikes. Dense orange wool on shoot and underside of leaf, easily rubbed off.

2. Bamboo-leafed Oak   *Quercus myrsinifolia*   227

An elegant rare tree in some southern gardens. The leaves are slightly silvered beneath, and the very small acorns are borne clustered on small spikes.

3. Chestnut-leafed Oak   *Quercus castaneifolia*   234

Leaf. A tree of great vigour and handsome foliage. Trees vary greatly in the size of their leaves.

4. Lucombe Oak   *Quercus × hispanica* 'Lucombeana'   236

   (a) Leaf from tree typical of the Exeter area; large and glossy and mostly shed in winter, a fringe of green leaves being left on the outside of the crown.
   (b) Leaf from tree of the kind more usual outside Devon remaining densely leafed in winter.

5. Willow Oak   *Quercus phellos*   228

An unusual deciduous oak from America. The Shingle Oak (p. 229) has similar foliage but larger glossier leaves on a longer petiole.

6. Hungarian Oak   *Quercus frainetto*   242

Leaf (reduced). A very vigorous tree growing a hugely domed crown on straight, radiating branches.

Lucombe Oak (see p. 236)

Type (a)   Type (b)   Hungarian Oak

1a

1

2

3b

4a

4b

4c

4d

ELMS Plate 22

Deciduous trees with leaves varying in size depending on their position on the shoot; deep red perfect flowers and membraneous fruit.

1. Wych Elm   *Ulmus glabra* 248

  (a) Leaf. Roughly hairy and very short-stalked. In Britain, the leaf is usually more ovate (see drawings below).
  (b) Ripe seed, shed in June after being prominent on the tree in bright green bunches before the leaves emerge.

2. Huntingdon Elm   *Ulmus × hollandica* 'Vegeta' 253

  Leaf has glossy upper surface and very oblique base. The smoothness and the 2 cm petiole distinguish this from Wych Elm.

3. English Elm   *Ulmus procera* 249

  The common countryside elm east of Plymouth and south of York, except in East Anglia.
  (a) Leaves nearly round, on some short shoots, and harshly hairy above.
  (b) Fruit, which is scarce, does not often develop seeds and is very rarely fertile.

4. Smooth-leafed Elm   *Ulmus carpinifolia* 250

  (a) Outline of a broad-crowned tree. Some are even broader and more pendulous; some are relatively narrow.
  (b) Fruit.
  (c) Shoot and leaves. The leaves are shiny and leathery above and variable in details of shape and toothing.
  (d) Flowers open in March, before the leaves.

  Common in East Anglia in a variety of minor forms.

Wych Elm leaves showing variation; right hand form most usual in Britain

leaf to tip; fresh *pale* green above, slightly glaucous beneath.
Petiole *slender*, yellow, 4 cm. Acorn, squat ovoid, 15 × 15 mm,
one third in grey-green cup of very small scales; sessile on shoot.
Usually grown as *Q. prinus* which has a bigger, broader leaf and
very short petiole.

Chestnut Oak

HUNGARIAN OAK   *Quercus frainetto* Ten.
     Syn. *Q. conferta* Kit.
S. Italy and Balkans to Hungary 1838. Infrequent; many large gardens in
England, north to Deeside on the east; Ireland. 30 × 3.5 m (27 × 3.9 m at
Holkar, Lancs. Fine trees at Osterley Park, Middx.).
Bark. Pale grey, sometimes a little brownish, closely fissured
by a network of deep cracks into very small, short ridges,
smooth overall.
Crown. A magnificent dome of straight branches radiating
from a point about 4–6 m up a straight, cylindric, stout bole.
Some specimens, and all the original ones, are grafted on to
Q. robur at ground-level, which may sprout from the base.
Foliage. Shoot pale brown or grey-green softly pubescent;
ridged on young trees. Bud ovoid-conic, 1 cm, many-scaled,
pale grey-brown, crimson on young trees as they unfold the
grey-green silky leaves and shoot. Leaf *oblong-obovate* 15–25
× 8–14 cm narrowing to auricled base and 2–12 mm petiole;
deeply cut from base to tip into 7–10 lobes each side, usually   Hungarian Oak
asymmetrically, the larger lobes beyond the middle of the leaf
themselves lobulate, broad, close, often overlapping and floppy; rich green
above, greyish and pubescent beneath.
Flowers. Females flowers in sessile cluster around terminal bud or on 3 cm
peduncle from terminal axils; 2 mm ovoid, pale brown; stigmas deep purple.
Growth. Many books repeat the startling error that this is slow, when it is
almost everywhere one of the fastest growing trees. The big trees in the Pagoda
Vista at Kew consistently add 5 cm annually to their girth as do most others.
Shoot-growth starts in early or mid-May with a rapid burst for four weeks, up
to 15 cm being added in the second week. Young trees have another equally
rapid spell of growth in mid-July.
Recognition. No other oak leaf is so deeply cut into so many lobes.

PYRENEAN OAK   *Quercus pyrenaica* Willd.
     Syn. *Q. toza* DC.
N. Africa, S. Europe 1822. A very rare tree related to *Q. cerris*, without whiskered lateral buds and with long leaves to 20 cm, irregularly cut to within 1 cm
of the midrib and hairy above. Mostly seen as 'Pendula'.

     'PENDULA' Infrequent; collections and occasional parks and gardens.
20 × 2.5 m (19 × 4.3 m Clonmannon, Co. Wicklow).
Bark. *Pale grey*, deeply fissured into small, *craggy square plates*.
Crown. Rather open, ascending twisting then *arched* branches and long, straight
pendulous shoots. Sometimes obviously grafted on a bole of *Q. cerris*.

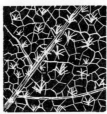

Foliage. Shoot bright green with grey pubescence, terminal bud with whiskers, very pale brown, ovoid-conic. Leaf grey-green, softly pubescent all over, 13–15 × 9 cm, six lobes a side, mid lobes ovate 2 cm broad, reaching half way to midrib; narrowly cuneate, sometimes slight auricles at base; often hooded. Petiole 8–10 mm densely pubescent.
Flowers. Male flowers spectacular *golden curtains* of catkins very late in season, at the end of June. (This is also the last oak into leaf.)

DOWNY OAK *Quercus pubescens* Willd.

Syn. *Q. lanuginosa* Thuill.

S. Europe, W. Asia, Caucasus. Introduced long ago, at unknown date. Although it grows quite rapidly into a sturdy tree, it is rare and found only in collections in each country. 20 × 2.8 m.
Bark. Dark grey, deeply and finely cracked into small, rough plates.
Crown. Like *Q. robur* but branches swollen at union with bole.
Foliage. Shoot brown, with dense, long grey pubescence. Bud pale orange-brown, grey at tip. Leaf obovate-lanceolate, 8–13 × 6 cm on very pubescent petiole 7–20 mm; broad-cuneate, 4–8 broadly rounded, forward lobes each side, becoming glabrous above and grey-green; *pubescent* beneath, by autumn hairy each side of midrib only.

Downy Oak

Flower. Females 1–3 on pale green 2 mm peduncles from terminal axils, pale brown, ovoid 3 mm, stigmas deep red.
Similar species. In effect, a dark-barked form of *Q. petraea* with pubescent shoot and petiole.

SESSILE or DURMAST OAK *Quercus petraea* (Mattuschka)

Lieblein **Pl. 20**

Native; dominant oak in N. and W. and often sparingly mixed with *Q. robur* on light soils and in hillside woods in the south. Europe and W. Asia. 30 × 8.5 m (41 m at Whitfield, Hereford, tallest of any oak in Britain; 34 × 6.6 m at Nettlecombe, Somerset; 28 × 9.3 m at Shobdon, Herefords.).
Bark. Grey, finely fissured and ridged, predominantly vertically.
Crown. Domed from a straight bole, branches *radiating*, straighter than in *Q. robur* and has a more open crown when in leaf as leaves *evenly spread*, not bunched. Crowns remain green and healthy where surrounding *Q. robur* eaten bare by larvae of Oak-leaf roller moth (*Tortrix viridana*).
Foliage. Shoot dark grey, partly purplish and bloomed grey. Bud large ovoid, *many-scaled*, each pale orange-brown tipped dark brown, finely white, long-pubescent. Leaf *cuneate* or sub-cordate base to a 1–2 cm long, yellow petiole narrow-elliptic acute, 8–12 cm × 4–5 cm (rarely 18 × 12 cm), 5–9 pairs of rounded lobes, dark green rather thick, leathery or hard, *very flat*, *healthy*.

'Mespilifolia' Sessile Oak

Flowers and fruit. Male catkins 5–8 cm. Female flowers terminal and in terminal axils on new shoot; 2–6, whitish, globular, 1 mm; stigmas red-purple, late May. Acorn rather shorter than in *Q. robur*, in groups 2–6 sessile, or sub-sessile on 5–10 mm peduncle.

'MESPILIFOLIA' Rare. 16 × 3 m. Leaf 20–22 × 3–5 cm, oblong-lanceolate, curved with entire, thickened, sinuous margin, occasionally with irregular shallow lobes or irregular teeth. Petiole often dark red.

Similar species. *Q. robur* (below). Intermediate forms are frequent with foliage of *Q. petraea* but acorns on peduncles of varying lengths. These are variants of *Q. petraea*. *Q. pubescens* (p. 243) differs mainly in its hairy petiole and shoot.

ENGLISH OAK *Quercus robur* L.   **Pl. 20**
   Syn. *Q. pedunculata* Ehrh.
Native in lowlands everywhere and dominant tree on basic loams and clays, reaching 450 m alt. on Dartmoor and in Co. Kerry. Europe, from N.E. Russia to S.W. Asia and to Spain. Abundant in parks, deer-parks, gardens and woods. Big old veterans most frequent in English Midlands; some of the best younger trees in Herefordshire and Shropshire. Old trees are frequently pollards with boles 2–3 m long; these live longer and become more stout in the bole than unpollarded trees, and have been 14 m round. Unpollarded trees to 37 × 10 m (11.4 m in girth, Fredville, Kent; 17 × 10.2 m "Major Oak", Sherwood Forest).

Bark. Pale grey, closely fissured into short, narrow, vertical plates.

Crown. Widely and irregularly domed; few massive, twisting low branches; often many sprouty burrs on bole; interior foliage and shoots more *bunched* and locally dense than in *Q. petraea*.

Foliage. Shoot green-brown slightly bloomed blue-grey, pale buff lenticels. Bud ovoid-conic, pointed, light brown. Leaf obovate-oblong, 10–12 cm × 7–8 cm, *auricled at base*; petiole short, 4–10 mm; 4–5 rounded lobes each side, cut half way to midrib by narrow, round-ended sinuses, the lobes wavy-edged with occasional teeth, dull dark green above, pale beneath. Underside by autumn often covered in small discs of Spangle-gall.

English Oak

Flowers and fruit. Male flowers on very slender catkins in thin bunches 2–4 cm long, brownish-yellow until shedding invisible pollen in early May when yellow-green. Female flowers terminal on new shoot, 1–2 peduncles 2–5 cm long, bearing globular pale brown flowers, 2 mm with dark red stigmas. Acorn 2–3 on *4–8 cm stalk*; 1.5–4 cm, long-ovoid, whitish-green, becoming dark brown, often wrinkled, in shallow cup.

Growth. Popularly supposed to be slow, really quite fast. When 50 years old a tree on a reasonable oak soil should be 20 × 2 m. For first 100 years annual increase in girth is 4 cm, for the next 150 years it is 2.5 cm, and thereafter decreases. Oldest pollards 12–13 m in girth may be 800 years old; unpollarded trees of 10 m girth are usually less than 400. Seedlings grow from a terminal side-bud, not the central bud, hence rather zigzag shoots. 60 cm may be grown in a year for a few years. The shoot is expanded rapidly in a few weeks from

late May and leaves are then varying shades of yellow and coppery-brown. Second-growth, often shown by red young leaves on trees, is made in July. Leaves unfold mid-April to mid-May with great variation in any population, and trees are known which are in full leaf in March every year. Autumn colour equally variable: main colour rich browns, orange-brown in some years, occurs in late October and during November but some trees still green until December. Young trees hold dead leaves in winter, often all over crown, or within "juvenile cone" the apex of which is about 3 m from ground.

'Fastigiata'

'FASTIGIATA' **Cypress Oak.** Occurs in natural stands in C. Europe. Variably fastigiate, from broadly flame-shaped to as narrow as a good Lombardy Poplar. Infrequent; fortunately now more used in formal plantings. 25 × 3 m.

'CONCORDIA' **Concord**or **Golden Oak.** 1843 Belgium. Leaves open bright yellow, greenish-yellow by late summer. Very rare. 13 × 1.5 m (Wilton House).

'FILICIFOLIA' pre-1860. Rare; a low, domed bush in a few gardens; very rarely a tree to 13 m (Kew). Shoot bright green, short, rather crowded with ovoid-conic, 5–8 mm pale brown smooth buds. Leaf 10–15 × 6 cm cut almost to midrib into 6–7 lobes each side, each lobe little more than a vein with a narrow, irregular, wavy or lobulate border, to 60 × 5 mm; underside closely pubescent.

This very slow-growing oddity with twisting branches and filigree leaves has a "Japanese Garden" look about it. It frequently bears so many Marble-galls that when they are rosy pink in early summer it passes for a flowering shrub. The abundance of galls and the uncommon stalked acorns imply that it is a form of *Q. robur* while the buds and pubescent underside of leaf indicate *Q. petraea*. A rather ill-defined hybrid between these oaks has been called *Quercus × rosacea* Bechst. so 'Filicifolia' is, by some, called *Q. × rosacea* 'Filicifolia'. *Q. robur* 'Hetero-

'Filicifolia'

phylla' (17 m, Kew), even more rare, has leaves to 20 cm, sessile, usually hooded and less deeply cut into curved lobes.

Similar species. *Q. petraea* (p. 243) but dull, insect-eaten, gall-infested, thin less regular leaves with auricles and the stalked acorns distinguish *Q. robur*.

AMERICAN WHITE OAK   *Quercus alba* L.
East and central USA 1724. Rare; a few collections and large gardens. 16 m.
Bark. Dark grey *shaggy*, lifting plates between deep parallel fissures.
Crown. Similar to *Q. robur*; neat broad-conic as young tree.
Foliage. Shoot shiny reddish above, green beneath. Leaf opening pale brown flushed violet, obovate, flat, soon dark

American White Oak

grey-green with 4–6 big elliptic round-ended lobes and often elegantly curved sinuses; 17–21 × 10–12 cm long; *narrow-cuneate* to 1–2 cm reddish petiole; whitish beneath. Some trees have smaller leaves, often very hooded, forward lobes at end. Glossy rich green above, bright glaucous beneath, petiole and midrib dark red. Autumn colour *rich purple*.

SWAMP WHITE OAK   *Quercus bicolor* Willd.
C. N. America from Quebec to Georgia 1800. Rare; some fine trees in collections. 25 × 3 m (21.3 × 2.8 m Syon Park, Middx.).
Bark. Pale grey with coarse network of blackish-grey thick ridges.
Foliage. Leaf broadly obovate or ovate tapering back to 1–10 mm petiole by a long cuneate base, 15–18 × 7–12 cm shallowly lobed beyond the middle or sinuately toothed, *whitish* and at first velvety beneath. New leaf bright yellowish glossy green. Good orange-browns in autumn.
Similar species. *Q. macrocarpa* (below), *Q. marilandica* (p. 229).

BURR OAK   *Quercus macrocarpa* Michx.
E. N. America, Nova Scotia to Texas 1811. Rare, collections only. 20 × 2 m. Similar to *Q. bicolor* but with *longer petiole* (3–5 cm) *and leaf* (20–26 cm) which is also relatively narrower, 10–12 cm across, narrow cuneate, lobing starts much *nearer the base* and is deeper, 6–8 irregular, rounded lobes, sometimes very asymmetrical. Acorn cup 2 cm deep, 2 cm across, purplish with pattern of raised scales.

DAIMYO OAK   *Quercus dentata* Thunb.
Japan, Korea and China 1830. Infrequent; several large gardens as well as collections. 15 × 1.5 m (14 × 1.5 m at Osterley Park, Middx.).
Bark. Blackish-grey, thick, corky, coarsely cracked.
Crown. Singularly gaunt; level branches usually low from a sinuous short bole; sometimes bunches of fine sprouts from short, thick branches.
Foliage. Shoot very stout, densely grey-pubescent. Leaf a giant form of *Q. robur*, slightly auricled, short stout hairy petiole, 1–1.5 cm long, blade 25–40 × 15–20 cm with forward-pointing lobes, relatively shallow on biggest leaves, very large on smaller, straight-sided round-ended. Most leaves retained on crown, brown and dead for part of winter.
Flowers. Females axillary near tip of new shoot, sessile, broad-cylindric 6–8 mm surrounded by pale brown, pubescent linear scales.
Similar species. *Q. robur* clipped in hedge may have leaf nearly as big, but petiole and shoot glabrous.

Daimyo Oak

Swamp White Oak

Burr Oak

ELM, ZELKOVA AND HACKBERRY FAMILY
Ulmaceae

A hundred and fifty species in both hemispheres. Leaves alternate, usually oblique at base; flowers perfect or monoecious, fruit winged or nutlet or drupe.

ELMS Ulmus

Eighteen species in north temperate regions east of Rocky Mts. and north of and in the Himalaya. Flowers perfect, out before leaves or late in autumn, fruit surrounded by membranous wing. A genus in which modern definition of species and hybrids is so different from that of early works that the long descriptions in those works are now quite baffling. It is, in detail, complex, but is readily simplified so that the usual variants of the eight species, varieties and hybrids commonly seen can easily be identified, often best at a distance by the crown, using the leaves for confirmation. The crowns may be distorted in areas close to the sea, but retain most of their characteristics. Leaves vary much on different parts of a tree and should be taken from short shoots rather than long new growth.

Key to the crowns of some mature elms

1. Conic; central axis persists to tip   **2**
   Fan-topped or domed; central axis fails below tip   **3**

2. Dense ascending small branches to symmetrical tip
   carpinifolia var. *sarniensis*, p. 251
   Few ascending branches, arching out a little and thinning out
   markedly below the slightly leaning, one-sided tip
   carpinifolia var. *plottii*, p. 252

3. Fan-top of arching branches with dense foliage close along
   upper sides; lower branches straight, ascending at 45° or less
   carpinifolia var. *cornubiensis*, p. 251
   Domed   **4**

4. Thin, open dome of stout shoots on few, large, strongly
   ascending sinuous branches leaving sinuous bole in narrow
   'V's (bark brown, small scales)   × *hollandica* 'Hollandica', p. 251
   Deep dome or multiple domes, dense or fairly so   **5**

5. Branches from bole massive and twisting, or small sprouts, not
   intermediate sizes; shoots slender, dense, short   *procera*, p. 249
   Branches from bole all sizes mixed   **6**

6. Branches radiating, with a long very straight sector; usually
   symmetrical deep dome   × *hollandica* 'Vegeta', p. 253
   Branches not radiating, seldom straight for long   **7**

7. Shoots very fine, often on long pendulous branchlets and
   crisped, short; crown tall, narrow   *carpinifolia*, p. 250
   Shoots stout; crown broad, irregular domes   *glabra*, p. 248

EUROPEAN WHITE ELM   *Ulmus laevis* Pall.

Syn. *U. pedunculata* Foug.; *U. effusa* Willd.; *U. racemosa* Borkh.

C. Europe to W. Asia. Very rare; one or two collections. 21 × 2.6m. A tree with an untidy crown as broad as it is high; arched branches with *fine sprouts and burrs* at short intervals, dull grey or pale brown bark with wide, shallow network of broad, smooth ridges, many sprouting burrs and deep flutes and buttresses to branches. Shoot dark red-brown, pubescent. Bud acute, small, dark orange-brown. Leaf broadly obovate from an extremely oblique base, one side curving to petiole some three veins above the other, 11 × 6cm but much smaller leaves

European White Elm

also always present; 10–14 veins one side, 13–17 the other, coarsely doubly toothed with strongly incurved teeth; finely pubescent above, grey pubescent beneath.

AMERICAN WHITE ELM   *Ulmus americana* L.

E. and C. N. America 1752. Rare; collections and a few gardens. 25 × 2.5m. Bark pinkish-brown or dark, coarsely ridged. Crown: widely arching branches; shoots slender, whippy, rather pendulous; frequent *burrs with pendulous shoots*. Leaf obovate-lanceolate, acuminate, very oblique at base, like *U. laevis*, very doubly toothed, *bright shining green but rough* above; white axil-tufts beneath; 10–15cm; petiole 3mm, densely pubescent at first.

American White Elm

WYCH ELM   *Ulmus glabra* Huds.   **Pl. 22**

Syn. *U. montana* With.

Native; scattered but frequent in S. England, abundant in W. and in N. Wales and from Yorkshire northwards especially by water. N. and C. Europe and W. Asia. Infrequent in parks and gardens, more often in town parks and churchyards especially as cultivars. 38 × 7m (29 × 5.6m at Glendoick, Perths.).

Bark. For many years smooth (hence 'glabra') and silvery-grey. Becomes dull grey finely cracked in black and gradually browner and ridged until deeply networked with broad ridges, dark grey-brown.

Crown. A broad, irregular, multiple dome; branches arching out, sinuous and nearly level, ending in *stout shoots* with laterals short and at right-angles; low branches massive, twisting, may rest on ground then turn abruptly upwards, burrs and sprouts frequent but suckers very rare. In woodland, a long, sinuous bole. Young trees sparsely branched but very leafy.

Foliage. Shoot stout, dark red-brown with dense, hard pubescence. Bud obtuse, ovoid, dull red-brown with reddish hairs. Leaf obovate, *shouldered* (less so in most British trees, see p. 241) abruptly long-acuminate, 10–18cm × 6–9cm on *short*, thick petiole 2–5mm long and hairy; very unequal at base; about 17 pairs of veins to larger teeth with smaller between, very *harsh above* and dark green, paler beneath with short, stiff white hairs on veins, less on blade; midrib stout.

Flowers and fruit. Flowers densely clustered close to shoots, dark purplish-red in early March or before; fruit large bright pale green broad obovate membrane slightly notched 2.5 cm across with nutlet in centre, prominent before leaves open in April and early May, in bunches 8 × 5 cm; turning brown before being shed in July.

'LUTESCENS' Infrequent in parks and gardens, locally common as street tree especially in fairly recent plantings of ring roads and housing estates. Leaves bright pale yellow. Much bigger leaf, smoother branches and wider crown than *U. procera* 'Louis van Houtte', under which name it is often planted. A very fine tree of rich colour. 15 m (25 m).

'Camperdown'

'CAMPERDOWN' **Camperdown Elm** 1850 Angus. The common weeping elm. Frequent town parks, gardens and churchyards. A broad head of spreading, tortuous branches grafted on a straight bole of *U. glabra* and weeping to the ground in a bower all round it. Leaves bigger, to 20 × 12 cm, nearly glabrous beneath and on pale green, slightly bloomed, sinuous shoots. Not to be confused, as it often is, with 'Pendula'. 12 × 2.8 m.

'PENDULA' 1816. Largely confined to town parks, churchyards and cemeteries. Frequent around N. London. Tall with good bole from which faintly depressed branches spread then fan out in drooping arrays of *herring-bone-like* shoots. Not fully pendulous as is 'Camperdown' nor are branches tortuous; leaves normal size. 20 × 3 m.

'Pendula'

'EXONIENSIS' **Exeter Elm** pre-1826 Exeter. Occasional in London and other city and town parks and a few gardens especially around Exeter and Tavistock. An upright brush of a tree very densely twigged; leaves in *upright bunches* not fully opening, smaller than in the type, rounded, coarsely serrate. 17 × 2.5 m.

Similar species. The big leaf is like only that of *U. × hollandica* 'Vegeta' (p. 253) but that is smooth and often shiny above with pale petiole 1–2 cm long and tufts in axils beneath, and scarcely "shouldered". *U. americana* (p. 248) differs in more slender leaf, glossy above.

ENGLISH ELM *Ulmus procera* Salis. **Pl. 22**
Syn. *U. campestris* Mill.
Confined to England and perhaps S.E. France, probably introduced in very early times to Bristol Channel region. Abundant in well-drained valleys and plains in Midlands and south-west to Plymouth, Okehampton and Bideford, replaced west of that line by *U. carpinifolia* var. *cornubiensis* (p. 251) and in East Anglia and E. Kent largely by *U. carpinifolia* (p. 250). Rare north of Vale of York. Rare and always planted in Ireland. 36 × 7 m (36 × 5.6 m at Holkham Hall, Norfolk).
Bark. Dark brown (black in city parks) deeply cracked into small square plates.
Crown. Conic with ascending branches when young. Typical mature trees

with massive, straight bole persisting half way or more
through the crown and bearing only a few, massive
twisting, ascending limbs and small sprouts spreading
from burrs; *no intermediate sizes.* Limbs rapidly diffuse
into dense domes of short, slender, curled shoots. In leaf,
denser and blacker green than other elms, outline
billowing like a thundercloud. Profuse suckering.

English Elm

Foliage. Shoot slender, reddish-brown, densely hairy.
Bud pointed ovoid, small, 2–3 mm, dark brown, slightly
pubescent. Leaf ovate to orbicular, varying in shape and size with position on
shoot: on side-shoots nearly *round*, 4 × 3.5 cm; on terminal shoots ovate, 10 ×
7 cm, both sorts oblique at base, short-pointed, very doubly-toothed, often
curled or puckered, dark green, harshly roughened above, white fluff each side
of midrib beneath; 10–12 pairs of veins. Petiole 5 mm, finely pubescent. Leaves
unfold early, in hedges by early April, on trees by early May, stay on late,
green until November, soft yellow to bright gold until early December.

Flowers. Profuse and regular, dark red, tufts of stamens, clustered on small
shoots, open late February to early March. **Fruit** irregularly borne and usually
sterile, in rounded membrane, seed close to notch at top.

Growth. Young trees (which are always root suckers from old trees) grow fast
with shoots of 60–90 cm but can be difficult to get started. Large boles probably
all hollow but live on until some 6–7 m round and 250–300 years old. A fungal
disease (Dutch Elm Disease) carried by the Elm bark Beetle is regularly seen in
areas with many elms and has been causing widespread damage in many
areas. The first sign is yellowing in June or July and early shrivelling of the
foliage of isolated branches. The next year these branches show as dead spikes

'LOUIS VAN HOUTTE' ('Vanhouttei') 1880 Holland. Golden-leafed rather
upright form seen occasionally in streets, parks and gardens. Differs from the
commoner *U. glabra* 'Lutescens' in smaller crimped leaves
densely and regularly set alternately; narrower crown, and
bark early furrowed and dark brown. Closely resembles *U.
carpinifolia* 'Wredei' (p. 252).

'VARIEGATA' ('Argenteo-variegata') pre-1770. Strikingly
variegated with white in spots, blotches and margins. A big tree
to 30 m uncommon in parks and large gardens, occasional at
roadsides when a length of hedge from its suckers will be similarly
variegated.

'VIMINALIS' 1817. A narrow, upright tree to 25 m with very
slender shoots and rather willow-like bark. Leaf 5 × 3 cm with very   'Viminalis'
double, deep, *curved* toothing to 1 cm deep. An unusual tree in a few gardens, as
is 'Marginata', a white-variegated form. Origin obscure; may be a form of
U. carpinifolia.

SMOOTH-LEAFED ELM   *Ulmus carpinifolia* Gleditsch   **Pl. 22**
Syn. *U. nitens* Moench

Possibly native in E. Kent and E. Anglia, but probably very early introduced.
The common elm of the Continent and much confused in early literature with
U. procera partly owing to both being called "*Ulmus campestris*". Europe,
N. Africa, S.W. Asia. Common countryside tree in Essex, Suffolk, Hertford -

shire and Kent east of Canterbury. Less common towards the Midlands, rare in Sussex, Surrey and farther west or north of the Midlands. 30 × 6m (26 × 6.1m at Dane End, Herts.).

Bark. Grey-brown with deep, *long, vertical fissures* and long, thick ridges. Branches pale grey with fine, black vertical cracks.

Crown. Typically tall, narrow domes from many nearly vertical limbs with branches of *all sizes* ascending from bole, *arching* over to end in long, pendulous branchlets with narrow systems of fine curled shoots. In Hertfordshire and adjacent areas, a form with a broader dome and less pendulous branchlets from fewer big branches is frequent.

Foliage. Shoot slender, soon glabrous, pale brown. Bud ovoid, shiny dark red, pale brown at tip, pubescent, 5mm. Leaf variable, typically elliptic, 6–8cm, very oblique at base, neatly crenate or doubly toothed, acuminate, *bright shiny green* above; white tufts in axils beneath. A form common in Hertfordshire has large, longer, darker leaves to 12 × 5cm. Petiole 5mm pubescent. Late in leaf, late May; still a pale, translucent crown when *U. procera* dark and opaque.

Flowers and fruit. Flower red with white stigmas in March. Fruit in elliptic membrane, cuneate at base, seed near closed notch.

var. *cornubiensis* (Weston) Rehd. Syn. *U. stricta* Lindl. **Cornish Elm.** Doubtful native to S.W. Ireland, especially in Blackwater and Bandon valleys, east to Clonmel, and to Cornwall and W. Devon, replacing *U. procera* west of the road Plymouth–Yelverton and Okehampton–Bideford, overlapping with *U. procera* from Plymouth to near Kingsbridge, outliers near Exeter.

Rare as planted tree elsewhere (see var. *sarniensis* (below)), but a few in Torquay; near Lyme Regis, Salisbury Cathedral Close, Regent's Park area, London; Savernake and Devizes, Wilts. and Walsingham, Norfolk. Also in Limerick, Gort and Ennis. 35 × 5m (37 × 3.5m by Salisbury Cathedral, Wilts.).

Bark. As type but darker brown, parallel ridges prominent.

Crown. Young trees conic, rather open, branches ascending at 45°. Old trees inland, vase-shaped, few large steeply ascending branches; top an *open fan* of arching branches, foliage dense closely above branches, none between, giving a *striped effect* of daylight and leaves. Near the sea, domed and swept in inland direction. *Rich bright green.*

Cornish Elm

Foliage. Shoot pale yellow-brown or chocolate above, green beneath. Bud minute ovoid, 2mm, dark red-brown. Leaf boat-shaped, i.e. cupped and narrow-elliptic, 5 × 3cm, 10–12 pairs of impressed veins; grey-white tufts in axils beneath, new leaves in summer bright yellow-green, older leaves shiny rich bright green; small regular teeth with secondary tooth on lower margin of each.

var. *sarniensis* (Loud.) Rehd. Syn. *Ulmus wheatleyi* Simon-Louis. **Guernsey, Jersey** or **Wheatley Elm.** 1836 Jersey. Common along by-passes, ring-roads and streets, in parks and avenues especially in the Midlands, general north to Edinburgh, occasional north to Elgin; rare in Ireland. Commonly called "Cornish Elm" but similar only when young. 30×3m (37×3.8m Wilton (Wilts.) by A30; 25 × 5.8m Avington House, nr. Winchester, Hants.).

Wheatley Elm

Bark. Often shorter ridges than in the type, almost square plates as in *U. procera*, but still strongly vertically fissured; big boles fluted.

Crown. *Conic*, even and regular except only the oldest few trees where top is narrowly domed; until then a single central stem persists right to the apex. Branches of all sizes from bole, densely ascending parallel at 45° or more steeply, the angle decreasing towards top where nearly vertical, longest sweep up at tips in *projecting conic sprays*. Young trees differ from var. *cornubiensis* of same age only in density and regularity of branching.

Foliage. Leaf as in var. *cornubiensis* but rounder, some obovate, 7 × 4.5 cm, *darker* green, veins wider apart, scarcely tufted in axils beneath. A golden-leafed form is occasionally seen as a young tree.

var. *plotii* (Druce) Tutin. Syn. *U. minor* Mill. **Lock Elm.** Locally frequent in N. Midlands, rare in collections. Resembles a more broadly conic form of var. *sarniensis* with *scanty* crown, the top 5–6 m very thin and more on one side of the tree than the other, and the leading shoot and branches nod slightly. The leaf is variable; like var. *cornubiensis* but less shiny and smooth above, also darker, 8 × 4 cm *obovate*, acuminate, deeply and doubly toothed; white tufts in axils beneath.

'WREDEI' Rare, golden-leafed form of the type *U. carpinifolia* with small, shiny leaves.

Recognition. *U. carpinifolia* and all forms are distinct in small leaves shiny above. The varieties are best distinguished by their crowns.

DUTCH ELM GROUP   *Ulmus × hollandica* Mill.

A group of hybrids between *U. glabra* and *U. carpinifolia* of which two are important here, but many others have been raised on the Continent.

'HOLLANDICA' Syn. *U. major* Sm. **Dutch Elm.** Probably introduced in about 1680. Common from Cornwall to N. Hampshire, absent (or almost so) from S. Hants., Surrey and Kent, one or two in W. Sussex, common Wiltshire north to E. Midlands, rare elsewhere, including Ireland, but biggest known are in Co. Tipperary (Marlfield). 35 × 5 m (34 × 4.9 m at Saltram House, Plymouth).

Bark. Distinctively cracked into shallow *small flakes*, usually cigar-brown, sometimes grey-brown. Oldest trees shallowly square-plated, slightly fluted; boles very smoothly rounded until 3 m round.

Crown. Open, thin, *shallow dome* on *sinuous* big branches arising in *steep, narrow "V"s* from sinuous bole. Stout shoots spreading out and slightly downwards. No burrs, but sucker shoots along branches often dense on upper side and vigorous root-suckers, both kinds often winged by corky ridges.

Foliage. Shoot stout, brown, with long hairs soon mostly shed. Bud ovoid, shiny red-brown. Leaf oval to ovate-acuminate, hard, very oblique at base, variable in size on same tree, commonly 12–15 × 8 cm, often buckled or puckered, impressed veins; more or less doubly crenate, the teeth often raised; dark and nearly smooth above, stiff, rough pubescence on veins and in axils beneath and on stout, pinkish 1 cm petiole.

Dutch Elm

Flowers and fruit. Flowers dark red, large, in late March;

fruit touching edge of 2 cm membrane, prominent pale golden-green before leaves in mid-May. Soon brown.

Growth. Very vigorous, sucker-shoots and young trees growing nearly 2 m in a season. Growth in girth continues vigorously making a bole 3–4 m round after 100–120 years. Oldest trees collapsing when 200 years.

'VEGETA' Syn. *U. vegeta* Lindl. **Huntingdon** or **Chichester Elm**. Raised 1760 from seed from Hinchingbrooke Park, Huntingdon. Frequent in streets, avenues and parks, rare in gardens or outside England. 36 × 4 m (35 × 4.9 m at Rendcombe, Glos.). Few survived by 1977.

Bark. Dark brown, sometimes grey, even network of broad, flat ridges leaving deep pockets; long ridges along larger branches.

Crown. Regular, tall dome from radiating branches on a straight, clean bole, the strong, ascending lower branches with a *long straight sector*, upper ones arching out, pendulous in old trees. Sucker-shoots frequent along branches in young trees.

Foliage. Shoot dull brown, slightly hairy. Bud prominently ovoid, shiny red-brown, sparsely hairy. Leaf elliptic, long-acuminate, 10–13 × 8 cm, coarsely and very doubly toothed, very oblique at base, one side rounded, usually curving in *to a vein first*; *long petiole*,

Huntingdon Elm

1–2 cm, pinkish yellow-green, finely pubescent; leaf leathery, smooth, shiny rich green above, tufted in axils beneath where midrib and veins white. **Pl. 22.**

Flowers and fruit. Flowers large, prominent, bright red in early April. Fruit prominent pale green in late April just before leaves emerge; usually sterile; bunches 6 × 6 cm, each seed obovate, notched, pale green, crimson in centre over seed; 2 cm.

'COMMELIN' Holland 1940 (1954). Narrow-crowned, smaller-leafed, Huntingdon-type hybrid raised and selected for superior resistance to Dutch Elm Disease. Recently much planted, but not resistant to the strain of disease rampant in 1971.

Similar species. Differs strongly from 'Hollandica' in bark and crown; *U. glabra* (p. 248) is more similar but has harsh leaves on very short petioles.

SIBERIAN ELM   *Ulmus pumila* L.

Siberia, Turkmen, Manchuria, Korea 1860. Rare; a few collections mainly in S. England. Elegant, nearly evergreen, small-leafed tree with a domed crown and grey, much-cracked bark. Shoot grey soon glabrous; leaf 5–8 × 5 cm, elliptic, acute, nearly equal at base, irregularly serrate, 10–12 pairs impressed veins; firm, bright green becoming dark greyish-green, soon glabrous beneath. Petiole 5–6 mm. Flowers in spring; fruit very small, 1 cm, present until June. Quite rapid in growth: 19.8 × 2.1 m in 45 years at Colesbourne, Glos.

var. *arborea* Litvin. (var. *pinnato-ramosa* Henry) 1894, Turkmen. Very rare; collections in England, Scotland and Ireland. 17 × 1.4 m.

Bark. Brown or grey, cracked orange, later hugely networked with broad ridges; often bearing numerous sprouts.

Crown. Flat-domed; twisting branches and exceedingly fine shoots, some very regularly arranged in herring-bone pattern.

Siberian Elm   var. *arborea*   Chinese Elm

Foliage. Shoot pale green. Leaf unfolding very early in March, *lanceolate*, acuminate, 5–7 cm, *lobulate* with 3–4 teeth on each lobule, or doubly crenate; shiny dark green, bright at first. Petiole 1 cm tinged dark red.

Similar species. The type is very like *U. parvifolia* (below) and confused with it. Larger leaf with more equal base, and spring flowering distinguish *U. pumila*. Var. *arborea* is very distinct in its slender leaf.

CHINESE ELM   *Ulmus parvifolia* Jacq.

China, Korea, Japan 1794. Rare and attractive nearly evergreen tree like *U. pumila*. Bark may be red-brown or dark grey, soon very cracked and flaking. Crown a dense dome, outside shoots somewhat pendulous with age. Leaf very small, 3–4 × 2 cm, fresh then dark green until late November, somewhat oblique at base, narrowly elliptic or obovate-lanceolate, 6–8 obscure pairs of veins; neatly forward-crenate, shiny above, sub-shiny beneath with white hairs each side of midrib, densely set on finely pubescent shoot. Petiole 1–2 mm, pubescent. Flowers in autumn. 16 × 1.5 m.

Similar species. *U. pumila* (above).

ZELKOVA

Five species, Caucasus, Crete and E. Asia, with attractively toothed alternate leaves similar in several ways to elms; fruits small nutlets.

CAUCASIAN ELM   *Zelkova carpinifolia* (Pall.) K. L. Koch

Syn. *Z. crenata* Spach

Caucasus Mts. 1760. Infrequent in large gardens and parks (city parks in Oxford and London). North to S. Scotland, rare in E. Ireland. 30 × 5 m (29 × 6.1 m at Pitt Farm, Chudleigh, Devon, 33 m at Capel Pk. Enfield; Syon Ho.).

Bark. Greenish-grey or pale buff, smooth, scaling to leave *crumbling orange*, circular patches.

Crown. Unique giant-ovoid of *scores of stems* from 1–3 m from the ground on a stout, very fluted bole, rarely (in woodlands) with a long, sinuous, smoothly rounded bole. Rarely grafted on elm. Shoots slender level curved upwards, sparse; hedges of suckers occasional (notably near Chudleigh, Devon). Some trees have a more normal crown with several big, upcurved branches.

Caucasian Elm

Foliage. Shoot slender, greyish brown-green, pubescent. Bud small, blunt ovoid, dark red-brown with white pubescence. Leaf elliptic, acute, 5–9 (15 on

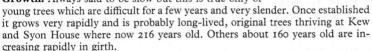

sprouts) × 3–5 (8)cm, 6–12 pairs of veins and large, very crenate teeth, ciliate; sub-sessile or 1–2mm petiole, dark dull or shiny green above, often rough with hairs, stiff white *hairs each side of veins* beneath; in autumn pale brown turning orange-brown.

Fruit. Uncommon in this country; solitary at base of each leaf, bright green (summer) globose, 5mm four-ridged or winged, rather lumpy.

Caucasian Elm

Growth. Always said to be slow but this is true only of young trees which are difficult for a few years and very slender. Once established it grows very rapidly and is probably long-lived, original trees thriving at Kew and Syon House where now 216 years old. Others about 160 years old are increasing rapidly in girth.

Similar species. The crown is unique but the foliage resembles that of *Z. serrata* (below).

KEAKI   *Zelkova serrata* (Thunb.) Mak.
    Syn. *Z. acuminata* Planch.
Japan 1862. Infrequent; in large gardens in each country and in some city parks, notably in London, 20 × 3m (19 × 2.5m nr Horsted Keynes, Sussex).
Bark. Until quite large, smooth pale grey, horizontally and finely striped pink, brown and orange and lenticelled. Bigger boles flaking, some with loose strips 15–25cm long leaving pale brown.
Crown. Broadly domed with branches spreading at a wide angle from a smoothly rounded bole; shoots very slender, straight; leaves pendulous.

Foliage. Shoot stiffly white-pubescent, later glabrous, red-brown, zigzag. Bud minute, 1mm blunt ovoid, dark red. Leaf 5–12 × 2–4cm on glabrous pale yellow petiole, 1.5cm; lanceolate, acuminate, about ten triangular, mucronate teeth each side, veins beneath finely white-pubescent 8–12 pairs; hanging on young trees in regular alternate rows, pale rather yellowish-green, often cupped. Autumn colour, yellow, pink and orange; very ornamental.

Keaki

Fruit. 5mm capsule at base of each leaf, green, smooth, laterally flattened; styles white; two points.
Similar species. *Z. carpinifolia* (p. 254), *Z. sinica* (below).

CHINESE ZELKOVA   *Zelkova sinica* Schneid.
China 1908. Rare; collections only. A most attractive tree, so far to 15 × 1.5m. Bark orange-pink roughened by short vertical lines of lenticels. Differs from *Z. serrata* in densely pubescent dark grey-brown more zigzag shoot, harder, darker leaf *cuneate and entire* for basal 2cm, 6×2.5cm, 6–8 pairs of veins; five shallow, forward sharp crenate teeth each side; pubescent beneath; petiole 3mm, *pubescent*, may be crimson beneath like the veins. Bud slender, pointed ovoid, 1mm green to red-brown; pairs of slender brown 2mm stipules adhering when leaves out. Yellow-

Chinese Zelkova

Plate 23 MULBERRIES, KATSURA TREE

1. Common Mulberry *Morus nigra*   259

Shoot with leaves, a ripening fruit and a ripe fruit. Leaves harshly hairy above.

2. White Mulberry *Morus alba*   259

Shoot with ripening fruit. It will become pink, then reddish when ripe. The leaves are smooth and shiny above.

3. Katsura Tree *Cercidiphyllum japonicum*   261

(a) Shoot showing leaves in opposite pairs (The Judas-tree (Pl. 29) bears alternate leaves).
(b) Ripe fruit pods from female tree. These are blue-grey until ripe.
(c) Male flowers.

An elegant tree, frequent, particularly in western gardens and noted for variety of autumn colours shown.

Common Mulberry, old specimen

Katsura Tree

1

2

3a

3b 3c

1a

1b

1c

1d

2

3

4a

4b

4c

5

TULIP TREE, SWEET GUM, BAY, PLANES Plate 24

1. Tulip-tree   *Liriodendron tulipifera*   265

(a) Flower-bud in early June.
(b) Leaf.
(c) Ripe fruit. These adhere to the tree through the winter.
(d) Open flower. The shades and amounts of orange, cream and
    green are somewhat variable.

2. Sweet Gum   *Liquidambar styraciflua*   269

Leaf from mature tree. On young plants the three main lobes
are more deeply cut. The leaves are all alternate (cf. maples
where all leaves are opposite). Much planted for autumn colour.

3. Sweet Bay   *Laurus nobilis*   268

Shoot and leaves showing crinkled margins.

4. London Plane   *Platanus × hispanica*   273

(a) Young tree 20 m tall.
(b) Leaf. Leaves vary greatly in depth and breadth of lobing.
    Many have less acute, broader lobes than this.
(c) Fruiting catkin. Some bear three or four fruit.

5. Oriental Plane   *Platanus orientalis*   272

Shoot with leaf, showing terminal bud hidden in petiole of a
leaf, as in all planes. The lobes are normally more deeply cut
and acute than in London Plane.

Tulip-tree, a large and old specimen

pink in autumn, then brown. Fruit at base of each leaf, 2 mm, deep green strongly veined pale green, irregularly conic-ovoid.

CUT-LEAF ZELKOVA *Zelkova verschaffeltii* Nichols.

Small broad tree of unknown origin, possibly Caucasian, first planted at Kew in 1886. Rare. Elm-like, small dark, thin, rough leaves 5–8 cm, cuneate, lanceolate, 5–8 pairs of very sharply acute, triangular, outcurving teeth; pale beneath, pubescent on veins. Fruit 1–2 in each axil, globose deeply grooved into two halves 4–5 mm,

Cut-leaf Zelkova

bright green. Bark like *Z. carpinifolia* (p. 254) (may be a form of it). Resembles *Ulmus procera* 'Viminalis' (p. 250) but leaf larger, tree broad and bark different.

HACKBERRIES; NETTLE-TREES Celtis

About 70 species in tropics and northern hemisphere; leaves three-nerved at base, usually hard, sharply serrate in middle but often entire basal half and long point; fruit small ovoid drupe.

SOUTHERN NETTLE-TREE
Celtis australis L.

Mediterranean and S.W. Asia 1796. Confined to collections. 10 m. Bark smooth, sparsely wrinkled, grey and pale brown, leaf 10–15 cm drawn out to *long twisted* point, sharply serrate, usually wavy, harsh above, white pubescence beneath, long on veins and on pale green 10–15 mm petiole.

Southern Nettle-tree

NETTLE-TREE *Celtis occidentalis* L.

E. N. America, Manitoba to Alabama 1636. Rare; collections in England and Scotland. 15 × 1.4 m.

Bark. Pinkish-grey, rough with big, hard flakes, *knobs* and short, *winged ridges*.

Crown. Domed; rather long arching shoots.

Foliage. Shoot brown with long, silky white hairs. Bud brown, closely appressed to shoot. Leaf ovate-lanceolate, 6–10 × 3–5 cm, oblique and rounded entire base, acuminate, hard, rough, occasionally all of one side entire, the rest with sharp, whiskered teeth or apex entire, dark shiny green above, dull yellowish-green beneath, silky on veins and on 1–2 cm petiole.

Fruit. Small and berry-like, hard, dark shining green then orange to dark purple, 7–10 mm long, ovoid on 1 cm slender stalk.

Nettle-tree

var. *crassifolia* (Lam.) Gray. 1812 Eastern USA. A form with larger leaves, 11–15 × 8 cm, serrate above the middle, thick, dull dark green; shoot more hairy. Leaves regularly and closely alternate each side of long, *arched* shoots. Rare. 15 × 2 m.

MULBERRY, FIG AND OSAGE ORANGE
FAMILY *Moraceae*

A thousand species, mainly in the tropics.

MULBERRIES Morus

Twelve species from temperate and subtropical regions of the northern hemisphere. Flowers on catkins, monoecious or dioecious. Fruit a syncarp composed of fleshy sepals, in appearance like a blackberry.

COMMON or BLACK MULBERRY *Morus nigra* L.   **Pl. 23**
W. Asia; about 1500. Frequent in parks and gardens, chiefly in S. England. 12 × 2 m.

Bark. Dark orange with wide stringy-sided fissures and many bosses and sprouty burrs.

Crown. Low broad dome, twisty branches from short bole, old trees leaning or procumbent, some of oldest have main stem buried in mound of soil leaving a low spreading mass of branches.

Foliage. Shoot stout, pale green becoming brown and purple-grey, fairly pubescent; large scattered lenticels. Bud stout ovoid-conic, shiny dark purplish red-brown. Leaf 8–12 × 6–8 cm (18 × 15 cm), broad-ovate, deeply cordate, curled, acute; irregularly and deeply double-crenate, sometimes three-lobed; *rough and hairy*; deep, slightly shiny green above, paler and pubescent beneath; petiole stout, hairy, 1.5–2.5 cm.

Black Mulberry

Flowers and fruit. Male flowers short, stout very pale catkins. Occasionally some branches entirely male. Fruit ovoid or globose cluster of drupes 1 cm, green in summer, by late July orange-scarlet and, just before falling, deep blackish-red and sweet to eat.

Similar species. *M. alba* (below) is rather different in general appearance but foliage is similar.

WHITE MULBERRY *Morus alba* L.   **Pl. 23**
China; long cultivated farther west; 1596 or before. Rare; a few collections and gardens in England and S. Scotland. 16 × 2 m. This is the species preferred by silkworms.

Bark. Dull green-grey or pinkish-brown, shallowly networked by flat, often wavy ridges; old trees dark orange-brown.

Crown. Tall, rather narrow, brittle; branches usually broken; less commonly low, domed.

Foliage. Shoot slender, straight, finely pubescent at first. Bud minute dark brown narrow-conic or ovoid; leaf variable, often some lobed, others not, lobes large and curved, at base or at tip of leaf, other leaves cordate or

White Mulberry

rounded at base, ovate-acuminate 10 × 8 cm (20 × 12 cm); big triangular teeth; abrupt entire tip; smooth glossy green or light green above; thin, flat; veins below pubescent; petiole 2.5 cm, grooved, slightly pubescent.

Flowers and fruit. Female flowers erect pale green cylindric heads, 9 × 6 mm, stigmas minute, black; pedicel 12 mm, axillary. Fruit as *M. nigra* but white, becoming yellowish, pink or purplish.

'PENDULA' A rare, domed, weeping small tree surrounded by hanging branches with big leaves, 20 × 12 cm, often lobed. A fine plant.

Similar species. Crown and bark unlike *M. nigra* (p. 259) until old; a paler, narrow tree easiest known by fruit and smooth upper surface of leaf.

MACLURA

A single species bearing thorns and a fruit which is a large globose syncarp; dioecious.

OSAGE ORANGE *Maclura pomifera* (Raf.) Schneid.

Central USA 1818. Rare; collections in England occasionally. 16 × 2 m (Kew Gardens).

Bark. Rich reddish orange-brown, deeply fissured into coarse ridges.

Crown. Irregular dome.

Foliage. Shoot green, zigzag, bearing 1 cm spines singly at the base of each small shoot and leaf. Leaf ovate, short-acuminate, or lanceolate, long-acuminate, mixed sizes in whorls, 3–10 cm, entire, slightly waved margin, dark glossy green above, paler beneath with white veins at first hairy; petiole 5 cm, pubescent.

Osage Orange

Flowers and fruit. Flowers: 4–5 globose heads 1 cm across on 1 cm green peduncles spreading from base of new shoot. About 30 green buds opening 2 mm across, yellow. Fruit common on the Continent, very rare here because it needs male and female trees adjacent; globose, finely wrinkled, bright pale green, with scattered dark remains of styles, 8 × 9 cm, hard, and weighing 0.25 kg when fresh; hard stringy white inedible pulp.

Recognition. Spiny, zigzag, green shoots and orange bark.

FIG TREES *Ficus*

About 600 species in the tropics and subtropics of both hemispheres. The large majority are evergreen. The flowers are internal in a hollow receptacle which becomes the fleshy fruit.

FIG *Ficus carica* L.

W. Asia. Long cultivated. Common in England; town gardens and parks, usually against a wall but sometimes standing free in the south, infrequent to rare farther north.

Bark. Pale grey, smooth, finely patterned in dark grey.

Crown. A spreading bush or small, leaning tree of somewhat upswept, stout, knobbly shoots.

Foliage. Shoot stout, ribbed and segmented, dark green; big leaf-scars. Terminal bud conic acute, pale green, lateral bud squat, purple or red-brown. Leaf big, broad, to 30 × 25 cm, hard, 3–5 lobed, a few unlobed; cordate base; lobes obovate obtuse, middle one largest, coarsely and bluntly toothed; sub-shiny dark green, rough with hairs above and beneath where veins prominent and white; thick, leathery; petiole 5–10 cm.

Fruit. Near tips of shoots; first winter small, dark green, pear-shaped, 1–2 cm long, ripening second year to familiar fruit. Styles within the cavity of the fruit.

Fig

KATSURA FAMILY *Cercidiphyllaceae*

One species from Japan and China. Male and female flowers on separate trees. Related most closely to Magnolias and Tulip-tree.

KATSURA TREE *Cercidiphyllum japonicum* Sieb. and Zucc. **Pl. 23**
Japan; China 1865. Infrequent but in most landscaped gardens and new plantings. 15 (25 m.)

Bark. Dull grey or fawn, shallowly and irregularly fissured, becoming shaggy in vertical strips.

Crown. Ovoid-conic, often many-stemmed but can be single and straight to narrow tip; lightly and regularly branched, shoots very slender upcurved or straight; arched and pendulous in upper crown of tall trees, evenly and distinctively strung with *prominent pairs of opposite buds*. Branches lined with leaves in interior of crown.

Foliage. Shoot red-brown above, green beneath, slender. Bud shiny dark brown, 1 mm. Leaf opposite 8 × 7 cm, slightly cordate, ovate, obtuse, or nearly round, with shallow rounded teeth, smaller leaves nearly entire; 5–7 veins *fanwise*, blue-grey or sea-green above, glaucous beneath, glabrous. Petiole red 2–4 cm. Leaf emerges bright pink. Autumn colour variable from year to year and tree to tree. Young trees usually scarlet and crimson in mid-October, older usually then pale yellow with some leaves pale pink. By late October, variously gold, pink, scarlet, crimson and plum-purple. May fail to colour in dry years.

Flowers and fruit. Male trees with small tufts of red stamens tipped grey and yellow, 4–5 mm, at each pair of buds in April before leaves unfold. Female trees with small bunches of dark red, twisted, erect, 5–6 mm styles, also at nodes. In summer they are blue-grey tinged crimson, with long drawn-out ends; 2–5 cm. Fruit clusters of 4–6 claw-like erect, shiny green pods, yellower at base, curved at tip, 1.5–5 cm long, densely borne along shoots.

Growth. Rapid, despite delicate appearance and damage to leaves of young trees by late frosts.

Similar species. *Cercis siliquastrum* (p. 301) has yellower-green alternate leaves, usually bigger, on longer petiole.

MAGNOLIA AND TULIP TREE FAMILY
Magnoliaceae

Eighty species, America and Asia.

MAGNOLIA

Thirty-five species in N. and C. America, the Himalaya and E. Asia. Evergreen or deciduous; bud with a single scale; large solitary terminal flowers with 6–15 petals or 'tepals' (sepals/petals); fruit a cone-like structure.

CUCUMBER TREE   *Magnolia acuminata* L.   **Pl. 39**
East and mid-western USA 1736. Uncommon; many large gardens and some parks north to S. Scotland and in Ireland. 26 × 2 m (25 m Tilgate Park, Sussex. 26 and 19 × 2.7 m Mote Pk. Kent).
Bark. Mixed rich orange-browns, purplish and deep brown narrowly fissured into short vertical ridges.
Crown. Conic, open and rather sparse as a young tree, rather upswept; old trees either conic and tall or broadly domed; stout spiky shoots curved upwards at the ends.
Foliage. Shoot stout, glabrous, green, later shiny red-brown. Bud pubescent with grey-green silky hairs; terminal, 1–1.5 cm, curved, cylindric; laterals 5 mm, appressed, flattened ovoid. Leaf elliptic to oblong-ovate, short-acuminate, 10–23 × 6–15 cm, margin often crinkled, entire; pale yellowish-green above, rarely dark and glossy; paler beneath and glaucous, finely pubescent as is the 2.5–3.5 cm petiole. Leaf-buds open conic, brilliant blue-grey in June.

Cucumber Tree

Flowers and fruit. Insignificant flower dull greenish-yellow, amongst leaves in June, campanulate, 6–8 cm high. Petal 6 × 3 cm, cupped, obovate, pale orange with green base. Fruit brilliant shocking pink in early autumn, then bright deep red, erect "cucumbers" 5–8 cm.
Growth. Young trees fairly fast, old trees slow. Long-lived.

LARGE-LEAFED CUCUMBER TREE   *Magnolia macrophylla* Michx.
South-eastern USA 1800. Several of the larger southern gardens grow this tree which bears the largest simple leaves which can be grown here. Gaunt small tree with few stout shoots *bloomed blue-grey*, turning pale orange-brown; leaf obovate narrowing towards base to *big auricles*, pale or deep green above with bright white midrib, bright glaucous beneath, finely pubescent, thin, 20–60 × 15–35 cm, petiole closely pubescent, 5–12 cm. Few leaves, whorled at ends of shoots. Flowers rare; pale brown with purple centre, 30 cm across.
Similar species. One other Magnolia with auricled leaves, *Magnolia fraseri* Walter, is rarely seen. South-eastern USA 1786. To 20 × 1.3 m (Leonardslee). Leaves smaller 20–40 × 10–20 cm, *glabrous* beneath. Flowers cream-brown, 20 cm.

Large-leafed
Cucumber Tree

JAPANESE BIG-LEAF MAGNOLIA

M. hypoleuca Sieb. and Zucc. Syn. *Magnolia obovata* Thunb.
Japan 1865. Infrequent in larger gardens in S. England
and Ireland. Gaunt, smooth grey-barked tree to 18 × 1 m
with whorls of slender upcurved branches and terminal
whorls of big, 30×15 cm pale green, oboval leaves;
pale glaucous and slightly pubescent beneath. Flowers
20 cm across, highly fragrant, cup-shaped, 6–9 petals
very thick, cupped, obovate, 10×4 cm, pale pinkish-
brown; crimson stamens and pistil; among leaves in June. Fruit striking,
cone-like, lumpy purplish-red, 10–12 × 5 cm, seed bright pink-red, 1 cm.
Similar species. *M. macrophylla* (p. 262) has bigger leaves, more glaucous
beneath and with large auricles.

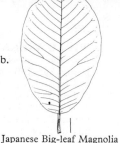

Japanese Big-leaf Magnolia

EVERGREEN MAGNOLIA or BULL BAY   *Magnolia grandiflora* L.

South-eastern USA 1734. Common against walls in England and Ireland, infrequent as free-standing tree in S. England and Ireland. 10 × 1.5 m.
Bark. Blackish-grey, smooth.
Crown. Broad-conic.
Foliage. Shoot fawn with dense, long, rust-coloured pubescence. Bud
oblique-conic, 1.5 cm green-brown, tip rusty-pubescent. Leaf evergreen,
8–16 × 5–9 cm, hard, thick, leathery, elliptic to obovate-oblong, entire
but often waved margin, glossy rich green above, matt and reticulate
beneath with thick rust-coloured pubescence. Petiole stout, 2–2.5 cm
densely pubescent.
Flowers and fruit. Flowers rather sparsely borne over long season,
from July to November, fragrant, white, opening pointed, conic then
narrow cup-shape and spreading the six thick petals wide to 20–25 cm
across. Fruit ovoid-cylindric, 5 × 3 cm on stout, curved orange-brown
stalk of which 1 cm is black finely pitted, and 5 mm brown-scarred
from stamens and petals; scales purplish-green, grooved, densely
pubescent.

'EXMOUTH' (var. *lanceolata*; var. *exoniensis*). Frequently planted as
flowering earlier in life; narrower leaf soon shedding the rusty hairs beneath to become green and glabrous.

'GOLIATH' Leaves broader than the type, green beneath, and
flowering younger.
Evergreen Magnol

Similar species. The only evergreen Magnolia with glossy green leaf. See
also *M. delavayi* (below).

CHINESE EVERGREEN MAGNOLIA   *Magnolia delavayi* Franch.

S.W. China 1900. Infrequent in gardens in S. England and in
Ireland, often free-standing but also against walls. 13 × 1.5 m.
Evergreen. Differs from *M. grandiflora* in thick, corky, pale
yellowish-white bark and big matt, *silvery grey-green leaf*, 25 × 18 cm
on stout petiole 7 cm long with a fine yellow groove along the top
and dense grey wool shed in stripes. Leaf oblong-elliptic, entire,
waved margin, whitish-green beneath with soft white pubescence.
Young leaves tinged coppery-brown. Flowers cream, 20–25 cm.

Chinese Evergreen Magnolia

WILLOW-LEAFED MAGNOLIA

Magnolia salicifolia (Sieb. and Zucc.) Maxim.
Japan 1892. Infrequent; large gardens in S. England
and Ireland. 13 × 1 m. A lightly branched, elegantly
domed tree, a spectacular mass of pure white flowers
in late April. Flowers open to 12 cm across before
the leaves. Shoot slender pale green, glabrous. Leaves
mixed sizes 4 × 1.5 to 12 × 3.5 cm *thin, cuneate,*
lanceolate, pale brownish shades on light green
above, greyish beneath, with prominent midrib.
Crushed leaves strongly aromatic, aniseed or sweet
heliotrope scent. Petiole very *slender* dark red above.

Willow-leafed Magnolia

Fruit at first blackish-green, 2 cm, ripening to become curved cylindric lumpy,
8 cm, bright yellow-green. Distinctive foliage in shape, colour and scent. Bark
smooth, pink-grey striated buff.

NORTHERN JAPANESE MAGNOLIA *Magnolia kobus* DC.

Honshu, Japan 1865. Shrubby. The variety is of good tree-
form and is hardier.

var. *borealis* Sarg. 1892 N. Japan. Infrequent; S. England,
Ireland. 12 × 1.8 m. Broadly conic, straight, sturdy tree with
level branches, dense short-jointed shoots at wide angles.
Leaves obovate 12–17 × 7–9 cm cuneate at base, *abruptly
pointed,* dark green and wrinkled above, *shiny dark green
beneath* and slightly pubescent. Petiole 1–1.5 cm. Flowers in
April, creamy-white, 12 cm across. Flower-buds grey with
dense pubescence, leaf-buds slender, 1 cm curved, green.

Northern Japanese
Magnolia

Similar species. *M. salicifolia* (above) has similar but more
prolific flowers but very different leaf and general aspect.

CAMPBELL'S MAGNOLIA *Magnolia campbellii* Hook. f. and Thoms.

Sikkim, Himalaya 1868. Infrequent; in many large gardens from Sussex to
Cornwall; by the west coast north to Argyll and in Ireland. 20 × 2.5 m (18
× 2.3 m at Wakehurst Place, Sussex).

Bark. Elephant-grey, smooth overall but finely roughened.

Crown. Broadly domed from a stout slightly sinuous bole; long upcurved
branches.

Foliage. Shoot stout, pale sea-green. Bud narrowly pointed, curved, conic,
4 cm, pubescent at first, bright yellow-green, later lilac. Leaf 17–20 × 10–11 cm
oblong-ovate, acute, rounded or subcordate base, entire, rather grey shiny green
above, white-pubescent beneath with 16 pairs of dark veins. New leaves emerge
rolled up, erect, dark purple-red. Petiole stout, 2.5 cm.

Flowers. High on trees 20 or more years old, damaged by March frosts, open
March (late Jan. 1975) before leaves; huge deep rosy-pink cups to 30 cm across
then petals drooping; 100 plus flattened stamens white with red centres.

'ALBA' is rare and has white flowers. To 19 m in 40 years.

'CHARLES RAFFILL' is a recent cross (1946) between this species and a
similar but rarer pale flowered form, the subspecies *mollycomata*. It flowers
when younger, bright purplish pink. Leaf abruptly acuminate, to 20 × 12 cm,
oblique base. 15 × 1.2 m.

VEITCH'S HYBRID MAGNOLIA *Magnolia × veitchii* Bean
M. campbellii × M. denudata

Exeter 1907. Similar frequence and distribution to *M. campbellii* and differing in taller, narrower crown, to 26 m so far (26 × 1.8 m at Caerhays Castle, Cornwall); flowers smaller, variably pink to nearly white, to 15 cm, earlier in life; and longer, narrower obovate leaf to 30 cm, pubescent on veins beneath, dull grey-green above; leaf-bud flattened-conic, 1–2.5 cm, pale green-grey, short silky pubescence. Flower-buds 5 × 2 cm, with long cream hairs.

TULIP-TREES Liriodendron

Two species, one each in China and N. America. Buds covered by two stipules, as is each new leaf, stipules remaining large on shoot; leaves with long petioles and broad, peculiarly truncate ends.

TULIP-TREE *Liriodendron tulipifera* L. Pl. 24

S.E. Canada to mid-western USA; about 1650. Frequent in gardens and parks north to N. Midlands, infrequent N. to C. Scotland and in Ireland. 36 × 6 m (34 × 5.7 m, Stourhead, Wilts.; 32 × 6.6 m at Woolbeding, Sussex).

Bark. Grey, evenly ridged in shallow network. Oldest trees pale orange-brown.

Crown. Young trees: conic to columnar, narrow-domed, straight-stemmed, regularly branched; old trees: often with buttressed heavy, low branches curving to vertical and carrying a tall, many-domed crown; open in winter, densely leafed in summer.

Foliage. Shoot smooth, at first bloomed lilac, then shiny greenish-brown to coppery red-brown, with prominent, raised leaf-scars. Bud laterally flattened obovoid, curved at tip, 1 cm, shiny red-brown. Leaf on older trees and normal shoots, four-lobed, basal lobes perpendicular, ovate-triangular, acute; terminal lobes spreading each side of indented truncate end of leaf, middle of leaf nearly parallel-sided, "corners" (lobes) acute, slightly "eared"; 10–15 × 15–20 cm, broad-cuneate to 5–10 cm petiole. Young trees, with larger leaves more indented; sprout-leaves to 16 × 23 cm on petiole 11 cm; 4–6 lobed, extra lobes small and basal, mid-leaf narrowed to a waist. Rich shiny green above, somewhat glaucous beneath with white veins sometimes papillate on midrib. Autumn colours bright gold, turning rich brown in good years, lasting until early November.

Flowers and fruit. Flower terminal, among leaves in mid-June, prolific only in hot summers, from ovoid, blue-green bud, 4 cm long. At first cup-shaped; petals blue-green at base, then a broad pale orange band shading to pale green; inside, a central cream cone with conic green top, surrounded by a ring of 5 cm, linear, fleshy erect stamens, cream coloured. Later the petals open widely and droop, and the stamens spread. Fruit dark brown, papery, erect, pointed, narrow, ovoid, persisting through winter, 4–5 cm.

Growth. Once above 1 m high, quite hardy and very fast-growing, particularly in south-west where can be 20 × 2.5 m in 40 years. Oldest trees, 280 years old, now decaying.

'AUREOMARGINATUM' Rare; smaller, slower form with pale yellow margins to smaller leaf; quite effective.

'FASTIGIATUM' Narrowly fastigiate at first, opening a little with age. Rare but being planted when obtainable. To 20 m.

CHINESE TULIP-TREE *Liriodendron chinense* (Hemsl.) Sarg.

C. China 1901. Rare; confined as large tree to collections in S. England and Ireland. 27 × 2 m. Bark as *L. tulipifera* but smoother and paler; in Ireland characteristically with large black circular patches of algae; shoot more strongly glaucous-bloomed; leaf from crown or from sprouts deeply waisted like sprout-leaf of *L. tulipifera*; to 22 × 25 cm, normally to 15 × 20 cm; petiole to 12 cm dull *pink* or dark *red*; leaves *unfold brown*, lobes sometimes rounded, and flat terminal edge may not be notched; glaucous beneath but varying from pale to metallic silvery; glossy dark green above. Flower, terminal on bright green shoot, open in mid-July, 6 cm across. When fully opened;

Chinese Tulip-tree

three large deflexed, yellow-green, obovate sepals, five petals, 4 × 1.5 cm, obovate, rounded, pale orange; about 50 stamens, pale orange, spreading flat with upcurved anthers. Style green, cylindric with conic top, 2.5 cm. A handsome tree of rapid growth, the leaves turning bright yellow in autumn.

TETRACENTRON FAMILY *Tetracentronaceae*

A single species, closely related to the Magnolias.

"SPUR LEAF" *Tetracentron sinense* Oliv.

C. and W. China 1901. Rare; some large gardens mostly in S.W. England but fine trees at Cambridge and Edinburgh Botanic Gardens. 15 × 1 m. A curious, lightly branched, shapely tree with a *single leaf terminating each long spur* alternately set along shiny red-brown shoots. Leaf cordate, 11 × 9 cm, ovate-acuminate, finely and *jaggedly* serrate along thick margin, 5–7 sunken fan-like veins; thick, deep green. Petiole 3 cm yellow or red, expanded at base over tip of spur. From spring to late winter a very slender green catkin 9–15 cm long hangs from each spur; flower-buds 1 mm tinged dark red in mid-May.

Spur Leaf

Similar species. General aspect, without catkins, is of sparsely foliaged *Cercidiphyllum* (p. 261) but leaves alternate, and single leaves on spurs at once distinguish from all other trees.

WINTER'S BARK FAMILY *Winteraceae*

A small family of aromatic evergreens related to the Magnolias.

WINTER'S BARK *Drimys winteri* Forst.

S. America from Tierra del Fuego north to beyond the Equator 1827. Confined to the far south and far west in Britain; rare except in Cornwall; reaching

Hants., Glos., and Wigtown. Frequent in Irish gardens. 15 × 2.5 m.

Bark. Smooth, pinkish-brown, aromatic.

Crown. Conic when young, and whorled especially in "latifolia" or "glauca" (see below); upright, open and bushy.

Foliage. Shoot smooth, crimson or green. Leaf oblanceolate or oblong-ovate, tapering to a narrow, rounded tip, cuneate, entire, glossy light green; midrib broad and pale green; underside light glaucous green with midrib very prominent. Crushed leaves have a sweet peppery scent, not very strong. Plants from an import in the 1920s have silvery-blue undersides, are hardier and more shapely. These have been called "latifolia" and "glauca".

Winter's Bark

Flowers. In big 10–12 cm open, terminal, loosely globular inflorescences, open in June, 4 cm across; seven decurved slender white petals; centre yellow, six ovaries in two-bracted involucre.

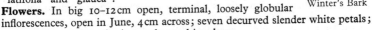

EMBOTHRIUM FAMILY *Proteaceae*

A family of many trees and shrubs in the southern hemisphere, of which only one genus of tree is grown here, other than in restricted areas of Cornwall and Ireland.

CHILEAN FIREBUSH *Embothrium coccineum* J. R. & G. Forst.

Chile, Argentina 1846. Frequent in western and southern gardens in England and in W. Scotland and in Ireland. Infrequent in east. 12 m.

Bark. Dark purplish-brown, slightly flaking; may be grey with algae;

Crown. Slender; one or more sinuous stems leaning somewhat outwards; small side shoots rather pendulous; usually evergreen.

Foliage. Shoot pale green, smooth. Terminal bud 15 mm, long-pointed, dark red. Axillary bud ovoid, scales spreading, dark purple. Leaf very variable on the same tree and among variant forms; elliptic and pale green to oblong-lanceolate and deep bluish-green; 5–15 (22) cm, long-cuneate or rounded, entire; underside pale blue-green. Petiole to 1 cm, bright green.

Flowers and fruit. Flowers late May and June (rarely October); spectacular bunches of scarlet tubes 5–10 cm, swollen at apex which opens to four segments; terminal and axillary. Fruit an oblong, grooved, buff-pink capsule, 3 × 1 cm, on dark red peduncle and bearing a dark red 3 cm persistent style at tip.

'NORQUINCO VALLEY' (1926) Hardiest; planted in colder areas. Some leaves narrowly lanceolate; flowers more densely wreathed along shoots. Becomes tall, gaunt and open with several vertical stems.

'Norquinquo Valley'

LAUREL FAMILY   *Lauraceae*

About 1,000 species, mainly tropical and evergreen.

LAURELS   Laurus

Two species from the Mediterranean region, evergreen and aromatic. One (*L. azorica* Franco) Canary Islands, very rare in S. England.

SWEET BAY or POETS' LAUREL   *Laurus nobilis* L.   **Pl. 24**
Mediterranean 1562. Common as tub-plant and shrub in S. England and Ireland, infrequently a tree to 15 m.
Bark. Dark blackish-grey, smooth, slightly wrinkled or cracked.
Crown. Broadly conic often to a narrowly conic apex; branches ascending.
Foliage. Shoot dark *purple-red* above especially near tip, green beneath. Bud narrow ovoid-conic, 3 mm, shiny deep red. Leaf evergreen, leathery, very dark green, lanceolate, (few obovate) cuneate, acute, hard, margin *finely crinkled* and toothed, 5–10 × 2.5–3 cm; basal veins *dark red*, others pale; yellow-green beneath; petiole dark purple-red, 6 mm. Rich fruity aroma when crushed.
Flowers. Opening to 1 cm across, pale yellow, in late April, 2–6 beneath each leaf, on 3–4 mm stalk, red and pale green in bud. Fruit 4 mm shining deep green, obovoid in summer; enlarging to 8–10 mm, turning black.
Similar species. *Prunus lusitanica* (p. 300) from which it differs in the leaf being very finely toothed, narrower and harder, on shorter petiole, also in flowers. Much more like *Umbellularia* (below).

UMBELLULARIA

A single species; evergreen and aromatic.

CALIFORNIAN LAUREL, OREGON MYRTLE or HEAD-ACHE-TREE   *Umbellularia californica* (Hook. and Arn.) Nutt.
Coast Range California and Oregon 1829. Rare; some gardens in S. England, mostly in south-west. 16 × 2.3 m (Kew).
Bark. Very dark grey, smooth, later cracked into shallow rectangles.
Crown. High dome on numerous straight ascending branches. Bole and main branches with many sprouts. Evergreen, dark yellowish grey-green.
Foliage. Shoot and petiole bright green; leaf 6–9 × 3 cm, oblong-lanceolate, cuneate, entire, *plane,* sub-shiny, smooth pale green above and below, midrib whitish, petiole slender, 5–6 mm. Flowers dull whitish-yellow in 2–4 terminal umbels of about ten each. Fruit obovoid 2.5 cm, purplish. Crushed foliage has a

Californian Laurel

rich, sweet fruity aroma, more pungent than *Laurus nobilis* and apt to cause a sharp headache some while after inhaling.

Similar species. *Laurus nobilis* (p. 268) from which it is separable by duller, greyish, usually relatively narrower, more sparse leaves in more open, upright crown.

SASSAFRAS

Three species, one each in N. America, China and Formosa.

SASSAFRAS *Sassafras albidum* (Nutt.) Nees
  Syn. *S. officinale* Nees
Eastern USA 1630. Rare; a few gardens in S. England. 18 × 1.9m.

Bark. Grey with short, spaced, black vertical fissures with abrupt horizontal widenings; sometimes purplish.

Crown. Upswept, dense, leafy dome, twisting branches. Suckers may grow far from bole.

Foliage. Shoot slender, bright green and lenticelled for several years. Leaves curiously varied shapes, all (usually) *long-cuneate* on slender 3.5 cm petiole and of thin texture, three-nerved well in from base, midrib white, often much widened in basal half. Some ovate, 10–12 × 5 cm, some with two, some with three large, *ovate lobes* the central lobe curving to a narrowed base; to 17 × 8 cm; all pale or deep sub-shiny green above on yellow-pink petiole; bright glaucous beneath. On old trees, lobed leaves are few, normal leaf elliptic 10 × 7 cm, glossy deep green on red petiole. Autumn colours yellow-pink and finally orange. Crushed leaf gives strong sweet aroma of *oranges and vanilla*.

Sassafras

Flowers. Male and female usually on separate trees. Pedicels at base of new shoot, 5 cm, red, erect or decurved each with few flowers, 8 mm, six narrow yellow sepals, no petals. Males with nine stamens and purplish anthers; females with six imperfect stamens. Early June.

Recognition. In leaf none has similar array of shapes; in winter and with oldest trees, the bark, slender green shoots; in summer glaucous underside and scent of crushed leaf.

WITCH-HAZEL FAMILY *Hamamelidaceae*

A large family mostly from warm temperate regions of both hemispheres, represented here by trees and shrubs notable for winter flowering or autumn colours or both. (*Disanthus*, *Fothergilla*, *Corylopsis* and *Hamamelis*).

SWEET GUMS Liquidambar

Three species, N. America, S.W. Asia, China and Formosa. Flowers in globose heads forming spiny, globose fruit.

SWEET GUM *Liquidambar styraciflua* L.   **Pl. 24**
Eastern and Southern USA 1681. Frequent in gardens and parks in S. and

Midland England and in S. Ireland, rare north to Edinburgh. 28 × 3 m (25 × 1.7 m at Mote Park, Maidstone, Kent).

Bark. Young trees pale grey or, if raised from root-suckers, dark brown with corky wings; becoming fissured into squares, later dark grey, rough with a network of thick ridges.

Crown. Young trees conic or ovoid, lower branches level upturned at ends, older trees domed, sometimes on long bole, usually broad with short bole. In winter rather spiky.

Foliage. Shoot pale yellow-brown or rich deep green, at first with short brown wool. Bud ovoid-conic, 5 mm, rich shiny green. Leaf rather maple-like but borne *alternately*, well-spaced, on long, grooved, slightly flattened petiole of 10–15 cm; on young trees, three-lobed, mid-lobe obovate or oblong, 10 cm long, on older trees, 5–7 lobed, truncate, to 15 × 15 cm, lobes ovate with incurved teeth; deep rich green and shiny above, sub-shiny below, small white tufts in vein-axils, thin brown wool on veins. Leaves unfold first half of May. Autumn colours notoriously variable in time and amount. Some bright scarlet in late September then deep red, some deep red late October, some green until November, then lemon and purple. Crushed leaves give sweet lemon soapy scent.

Flowers and fruit. Not often seen; on separate, erect, thick, green peduncles; males small, 5–8 mm globose on 5–10 cm spike, females larger, 1 cm dense cluster of yellow-green stigmas. Fruit hangs on tree through winter, 2–3.5 cm across on 5 cm stalk; globe of paired, rough, bulbous-based beaked vessels each 6–8 mm long, curved, dark purplish-brown.

Similar species. Often mistaken for a maple but leaves alternate. See below for differences from other *Liquidambars*.

CHINESE SWEET GUM *Liquidambar formosana* Hance

China and Formosa 1884. Very rare; only a few collections. Differs from var. *monticola* (below) in usually smaller, 9 × 10 (10 × 14) cm, yellow-green leaf, pubescent especially beneath, with rectangular-acuminate lobulate lobes, basal ones spreading widely, spikily and unevenly toothed.

var. *monticola* Rehd. and Wils. China 1907. Rare; large gardens and collections in S. England and in Ireland. Recognised by very hard, *dark*, three-lobed leaf,

Chinese Sweet Gum   var. *monticola*

10 × 14 cm; triangular lobes with hard, *jagged* teeth; *deep red* petiole 4–7 cm and *dark purple veins*. Leaves emerge red-brown and glossy, soon less shiny, very dark green, same beneath as above. Autumn colours distinctive orange, dark red and purple. A fine tree with narrow crown and rapid growth, to 12 × 1 m in 20 years. This variety is now regarded as not fully separable from the type.
Bark. Cream to grey. Crushed foliage scented as apples.

ORIENTAL SWEET GUM *Liquidambar orientalis* Mill.

Asia Minor 1750. Rare; a few collections in England and S. Scotland. Usually densely bushy, rarely to 8 × 1.5 m. Bark orange-brown coarsely cracked into

thick dark brown flakes; branches level; shoots fine
and level, shiny red-brown above, green beneath.
Bud glossy red-brown, pointed. Leaf small, 6 ×
6 cm on very slender petiole 3.5 cm long; 3–5 lobed
to two thirds of width, a blunt tooth at the shoulder
of each lobe and 1–2 obscure teeth beyond, or
serrate, *dull, matt* green above, sub-shiny beneath,
quite glabrous, truncate, lobes acute, ovate-oblong.

PARROTIA

A single species in which flowers open before the leaves.   Oriental Sweet Gum

PERSIAN IRONWOOD   *Parrotia persica* C. A. Mey.
N. Persia to Caucasus Mts. 1841. Frequent; most large gardens and many
small; most numerous and largest towards south and west. 8 × 1 m (15 m at
Abbotsbury, Dorset).
Bark. Pinkish-brown or grey-brown with some purplish and grey-green,
flaking in large squares to leave pink-buff and yellow. Resembles bark of
London Plane.
Crown. Broad with level lower branches and wide-spreading sparse upper
branches arching shallowly, usually from a
short bole but some have a sinuous clean bole
2–5 m tall.
Foliage. Shoot green-brown with fine, short
and stiff pubescence. Bud purplish-black,
finely pubescent. Flower-buds in summer
deep brown, decurved, ribbed, long-ovoid,
8 mm. Leaf obovate to orbicular, obtuse,
margin waved; emerges bright glossy green
in April as flowers fade; later dark, glossy
green, thick; 6–9 impressed veins each side;
underside covered at first in fine brownish
pubescence, some stained scarlet on veins.
Petiole 4–5 mm, pubescent. Autumn colour

Persian Ironwood

starts on a few upper branches early, mid-September, yellow, orange and
crimson; later whole crown deep red; a few trees remain bright yellow.
Flowers and fruit. Buds stalked, ovoid. Open mid-January to mid-March,
bunches of deep red stamens, 1.5 cm across. Fruit erect, 1–2 cm on stout
peduncle, pale green bracts around 3–5 deep brown nuts.

GUTTA-PERCHA FAMILY   *Eucommiaceae*

One species only.

GUTTA-PERCHA TREE   *Eucommia ulmoides* Oliv.
C. China 1896. Rare; a few gardens and collections in all parts
N. to Edinburgh. 14 × 1.5 m (13 × 1.4 m at Kew).
Bark. Pale grey, networked by deep, dark grey fissures.
Crown. Domed, rather broad and heavy with hanging glossy
deep green leaves.

Gutta-percha Tree

Foliage. Shoot olive-green, bloomed grey in patches. Bud ovoid, orange-brown. Leaf elliptic to oblong-ovate, cuneate, sometimes subcordate, long-acuminate, to 18 × 10 cm on finely pubescent, 2–3 cm, petiole, forward-crenate or doubly toothed, deep glossy green, veins impressed from above, raised and pubescent beneath.

Flowers. In April before leaves, sessile clusters, 1 cm, around bases of side-shoots; green and fawn. Fruit radiating 4 cm ovate-lanceolate, pale green.

Recognition. Sometimes known by being so puzzling without apparent clues, only dark, glossy, long-acuminate leaves. Instant check is to tear a leaf across and draw the pieces slowly apart, when *sap from the veins hardens into strings connecting the parts*. This also occurs in *Cornus* species – and *C. controversa* is somewhat similar to Eucommia in bark and foliage (p. 372).

PLANE TREE FAMILY   *Platanaceae*

PLANE TREES   Platanus

Six species, from N. America, Mexico, and S. Europe to India. Large or very large and long-lived deciduous trees with buds hidden in the bases of the petioles and bark peeling in thin plates. Male and female catkins separate but on the same trees. Fruit globular cluster of angular nutlets surrounded by long hairs.

ORIENTAL PLANE   *Platanus orientalis* L.   **Pl. 24**

Asia Minor, S.E. Europe, India; about 1550. Infrequent in parks and gardens in S. England, rare north of Midlands and in Ireland. 30 × 6 m (27 × 8.4 m at Rycote, Oxon.).

Bark. Pale pinkish-brown, fairly smooth, shedding large rounded plates to leave yellow patches.

Crown. Broadly and irregularly domed often extended far by large limbs resting on ground or layered; bole often with big burrs.

Foliage. Shoot yellow-brown, short-pubescent, later purple-brown with some violet bloom. Second year grey-pink and dark red-brown. Bud green-brown, furry base, dark red-brown pubescent with abrupt blunt beak, 7 mm. Leaf unfolds pale orange-brown from dense pubescence soon shed, to 18 × 18 cm, five main lobes cut to *within 5 cm of base* by *acute* sinuses; lobes acute, lanceolate, shouldered often with a tooth there, sometimes one more tooth towards tip, broad-cuneate, (long, slender-cuneate in the rare form 'Cuneata'), yellowish-green. Petiole 5 cm with red bulbous base, the rest yellowish, finely pubescent. Autumn colour a distinctive *pale bronzy-purple* and light brown.

'Cuneata'

Flowers and fruit. Sexes on separate catkins. Male 5–6 cm, outer half contorted, bearing 3–5 globular pale yellow-pink flower-heads, with yellow anthers. Female catkin 6–8 cm, bent half way, 2–5 flattened globose heads, 3–8 mm across, of dark crimson styles and stigmas in mid-May. Fruit on 15 cm catkin, 2–5, first one 8 cm down; 3 cm diameter, yellow-green to brown knobs with fine, hooked spiny balls.

Similar species. *P.* × *hispanica* (below).

LONDON PLANE   *Platanus × hispanica* Muenchh.   **Pl. 24**

Syn. *P. × acerifolia* (Ait.) Willd.; *P. × hybrida* Brot.

Hybrid between the Oriental Plane and the American Plane, *P. orientalis × P. occidentalis*. The latter scarcely grows in Britain and the hybrid probably arose in Spain or S. France in about 1650. First planted in England in about 1680 at Ely and Barnes, Surrey (both trees still magnificent and healthy). Abundant in town and city streets, squares and parks and frequent in large gardens in England S. of the Pennines, less common north to mid-Scotland, rare north to Ross-shire, infrequent in Ireland. 45 m at Bryanston, Dorset; 35 × 8.4 m at Bishop's Palace, Ely, Cambs.

Bark. Until large, dark grey or brown, large flakes falling to leave whitish-yellow patches; large boles reddish-brown or grey-brown with fine vertical fissures and folds.

Crown. Tall-domed on long bole; old trees immensely domed, tall and spreading, large branches twisting; bole sometimes heavily burred.

Foliage. Shoot at first pale green covered in loose white fluff, later orange-brown or purple-brown, bloomed lilac at base. Bud red-brown, ovoid, slightly curved tip, 6–8 mm on large, protruding base. Leaf unfolds pale brownish grey-green in mid-May from fine hairs soon shed. Shape varies greatly with clone, several of which are in use in London. Ely tree has typical, large leaves, to 20 × 23 cm, short-cuneate base sweeping round entire or with one tooth each side to basal lobes; five big lobes cut only to within 14 cm of base; central lobe (6 cm deep) with five curved teeth each side or five one side and three the other, each tooth large, mucronate, 2–20 mm deep; entire for last 3–4 cm to acute tip; rich, shiny bright green with dense close wool on veins above, paler beneath, the veins more woolly; petiole 5 cm, dull red-brown with dense, close brown wool. Variation in depth of lobing is considerable, one form has a leaf 14 × 12 cm with broad, triangular lobes cut one third to the leaf-base and with three curved teeth each side. Another, 11 × 11 cm, is abruptly cuneate and cut to half way. Young trees retain broad, ovate, toothed stipules.

Flowers and fruit. Catkin with 2–6 flower-heads, male and female on separate catkins, 6–8 cm long. Males yellowish, soon shed. Females crimson in mid-May, globose. Fruit brown, seeds scatter in spring, cylindrical, ringed by hairs at one end.

Growth. Remarkably vigorous even under very trying conditions, provided it has warm summers, hence biggest mostly south and east of Cotswolds. In park in C. London, one 23 × 3 m in 57 years. Such growth in (until recently) sooty air is due to short season in leaf and glossy leaf easily washed by rain. Other trees very late in leaf and liking the warmth of London are *Catalpa*, *Robinia*, *Liquidambar* and *Taxodium*. More important in streets is the ability of the roots to function in compacted and covered soil. Never known to blow down, rarely affected seriously by pest or disease, although some shoots killed annually after leafing out, by Anthracnose (*Gnominia veneta*). Trees nearly 300 years old are in full vigour, so this species promises to provide S. England with its biggest trees on a grand scale in the future.

'SUTTNERI' Very rare, strikingly white-variegated form, some leaves inside crown completely white. 22 × 2.5 m (Puttenham, Surrey).

Similar species. *P. orientalis* (p. 272).

ROSE FAMILY *Rosaceae*

A huge family of some 2,000 species of herbs, shrubs and trees. Distinguished by flowers with 4–5 sepals and 4–5 petals on the top of a receptacle holding the ovaries.

COTONEASTERS Cotoneaster

About 70 species from temperate Old World except Japan; all but one or two purely shrubs.

HIMALAYAN TREE-COTONEASTER *Cotoneaster frigidus* Wall. ex Lindl.

Himalaya 1824. Frequent in large gardens; to tree-size especially in west, north to Argyll. 17 × 1.5 m.

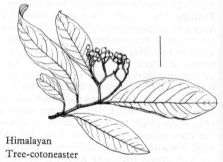

Usually short-boled, often leaning with long vertical sprouts from the bole, or many-stemmed; the ascending branches arch out to a broad-topped crown. Bark pale grey. Leaf semi-evergreen, elliptic or oblong-ovate, cuneate, obtuse, 6–12 × 4–6 cm, dark green above, whitish beneath with dense white hairs shed during season, entire. Many of the younger trees in cultivation are hybrids with *C. salicifolius*

Himalayan Tree-cotoneaster

and have narrower, more acute, crinkled leaves, whiter beneath. Flowers white in dense, hairy-stemmed flat heads 5 cm across; late June. Fruit ovoid 5 mm, bright red, prominent in late autumn.

Recognition. Pale bark and sprouty, often leaning bole, semi-evergreen leaves, and fruit.

THORNS Crataegus

Complex group proliferating in N. America (where there are between 300 and 1,000 species according to choice), and 90 in Europe and Asia. Nearly all unashamed shrubs, but our native thorns aspire to tree form in places and some small true tree-species are planted quite widely.

HAWTHORN or QUICKTHORN *Crataegus monogyna* Jacq.

Native, abundant nearly everywhere to 500 m, commonest hedge and scrub plant. Europe to Afghanistan. Occasionally a tree in parks or on village greens to 14 × 1.5 (3) m.

Bark. Dark orange-brown or pink-brown, narrowly cracked into rectangles; bigger boles fluted or flattened between rounded ribs.

Crown. Fanning out from fairly low, or narrow but rather shapeless. Taller (tree-form) rather upright.

Foliage. Shoot dark purplish red with straight sharp thorns 2.5 cm long. Leaf

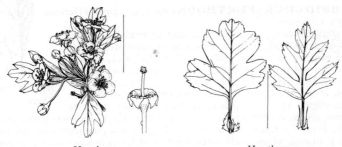

Hawthorn   Hawthorn

8 × 7 cm on petiole 3.5 cm, 1–4 lobes each side cut one half to two thirds to base, coarsely double-toothed, or 1–3 lobes (or large teeth) a side, which may be entire; truncate, abruptly cuneate, dark shiny green above, veins and petiole beneath dark pink with white pubescence at base of veins and in axils.

Flowers and fruit. Flowers densely borne, 16 or more in a bunch, buds white, globular, open white and fragrant mid-May, only one style, rarely two, surrounded by anthers bright pink then purple; petals cupped, overlapping. Fruit 8–10 mm, ovoid, dark red.

MIDLAND HAWTHORN *Crataegus oxyacanthoides* Thuillier
Syn. *C. oxyacantha* L.

Differs from *C. monogyna* as follows: much less common, mainly confined to heavy soils and in shade in S. England; leaf divided less than half way to base, styles mostly two, no axillary tufts beneath leaf. Hybrids between the two species are frequent.

'PAUL'S NEW DOUBLE SCARLET' 1858 Cheshunt. Common in town parks and squares. Flowers double, bright red.

Midland Hawthorn

COCKSPUR THORN *Crataegus crus-galli* L. Pl. 25
N. America, Quebec to Kansas 1691. Frequent, mainly in streets and small gardens, but much confused with *C. × lavallei* and *C. prunifolia.* See Table of Differences (p. 276). 6 × 1 m.

Bark. Grey, fairly smooth, becoming dark brown, slightly cracked.

Crown. Flat-topped, wide-spreading usually on clean bole of 2 m.

Foliage. Shoot dark purple-brown, glabrous; thorns frequent, shiny purple, slender, 4–8 cm. Bud dark brown. Leaf obovate, cuneate, rounded at apex, serrate above entire base, hard, dark green, *glabrous both sides,* 5–8 × 2–3 cm. Autumn colour rich orange.

Flowers and fruit. Erect inflorescence of *glabrous* stems, flower 1.5 cm across, white, end of May. Fruit 1 cm red, late October persisting through winter.

Similar species. The hybrids *C. × lavallei* (p. 276) and *C. × prunifolia* (p. 276). *C. crus-galli* is the only one of this group that is entirely glabrous; the orange autumn colour is also distinct.

HYBRID COCKSPUR THORN *Crataegus × lavallei* Hérincq

Syn. *C. × carrierei* Vauvel

A hybrid between *C. crus-galli* and another similar American
species; known before 1880. Frequent as street tree and in
some gardens, 14 × 1.5 m. Differs in: bark dark grey, coarsely
scaly; few but stout thorns 5 cm long; *dull green* shoot has *long
hairs*; leaf 8 × 4 cm, oblong-obovate, cuneate, acute, dark shiny
green above, pubescent beneath with pink midrib; inflorescence elliptic 10 × 5 cm, pale green, loosely woolly, about 20

Hybrid Cockspur
Thorn

flowers, 2.5 cm, orbicular petals (five); prominent *red disc*; anthers pink turning
black. Fruit 1.3–1.5 cm, orange-red speckled brown, pubescent near tip, persisting through winter. Late autumn colour of leaves *bronzy red* or remaining
dark green until falling in December. Very floriferous; handsome in flower, the
dark glossy leaves setting off the abundant white flower-heads.

BROAD-LEAFED COCKSPUR THORN *Cra-taegus × prunifolia* (Poir.) Pers.

A possible hybrid of unknown origin, cultivated by 1797.
Much planted recently in streets and on housing-estates.
Broad bush or low spreading tree. *Shiny dark chocolate-
purple* shoot and thorns (1.5–2 cm), leaf 8 × 6 cm, broad
ovate, obtuse, dark *glossy* green; fine pubescence on midrib
beneath; bud bright deep red; flowers in erect inflorescence,
red-tipped in bud; sepals long-acuminate and serrate,
petals broad, orbicular; anthers blackish; flower 1.5 cm.

Broad-leafed
Cockspur Thorn

Fruit dark red, shed in late autumn. Autumn colour orange to red and bright
crimson. Differs from *C. × lavallei* in relatively broader leaf, less pubescent beneath and in glabrous shiny shoot. Quite different in general aspect.

TABLE OF DIFFERENCES

	crus-galli	*× lavallei*	*× prunifolia*
SHOOT	glabrous, glossy	pubescent, dull	glabrous, glossy
THORNS	numerous	few	numerous
LEAF COLOUR	Dull yellowish-dark green	glossy blackish-green	glossy, dark green
(under)	glabrous	pubescent	base of midrib and veins pubescent
TOOTHING	entire basal third	entire to nearly half way	entire only to 1 cm from base
SHAPE	oblong-obovate, rounded tip	oblong-obovate, acute tip	broad-ovate, obtuse tip
AUTUMN COLOUR	early; orange	late; red or none	early-mid; orange, crimson, purple
INFLORESCENCE	glabrous	pubescent	pubescent
FRUIT FALL	Spring	Spring	Autumn

MEDLAR Mespilus

A single species allied to *Crataegus*.

MEDLAR *Mespilus germanica* L.
S. Europe, long cultivated. Rare. Very few large gardens; a few cottage-gardens; said to be naturalised in woods in S.E. England. 9 × 1.5 m.
Bark. Grey-brown fissured deeply into oblong, vertical, lifting plates.
Crown. Low, spreading, rather tangled.
Foliage. Shoot densely white-pubescent. Leaf oblong-ovate, 15 × 5 cm, entire, undulate, crinkled with sunken veins, dark yellow-green above, pale with dense pubescence beneath. Petiole 5 mm, densely pubescent; midrib pinkish near base.
Flowers and fruit. Flower 6 cm across; five acuminate, slightly rolled, linear sepals 4 cm long between five broad-

Medlar

ovate white petals; stamens white; anthers dark brown. Fruit globose, 5–6 cm, brown, the long calyx persistent and surrounding an open pit. Edible when over-ripe.

WHITEBEAMS AND ROWANS ("MOUNTAIN ASH")
Sorbus

More than 80 species from north temperate regions south to Mexico and the Himalaya. The whitebeams have simple leaves, sometimes lobed, and the rowans have pinnate leaves but there are several hybrids between members of the two groups which have partly pinnate or lobulate leaves.

ROWAN or MOUNTAIN ASH *Sorbus aucuparia* L. **Pl. 25**
Native in all parts, reaching nearly 1,000 m altitude in Scotland (higher than any other tree) and a notable feature of the landscape in W. Ross and Sutherland. Common in streets, gardens and parks everywhere. Europe, N. Africa, Asia Minor. 20 × 2.5 m.
Bark. Silvery-grey then light grey-brown, smooth until shallowly networked by a pattern of thin scaly ridges.
Crown. Irregularly ovoid; branches strongly ascending, few; open.
Foliage. Shoot dull purplish-grey, pubescent at first, soon glabrous. Bud long-ovoid; 1.7 cm; curved tip, outer scales dark purple with long dense appressed grey hairs; inner scales densely hairy. Leaf pinnate, to 22 × 12 cm, (9)–15–(19), leaflets each to 6 × 2 cm, sessile, oblique at rounded base, oblong, evenly forward crenate-serrate to within 1 cm of base, finely and densely pubescent beneath at first, later nearly glabrous; rachis terete below leaflets, grooved among them. Leaves unfold early in April, rarely colour before falling, except in N. Scotland where fine red and crimson until November.
Flowers and fruit. Dense inflorescence of woolly stems, erect or nodding, 10–15 cm across; flowers faintly creamy-white, 1 cm across, open in May. Fruit nearly 1 cm, yellow in late July, suddenly orange then scarlet within a few days in early August, soon attacked by Mistle-thrushes, Blackbirds and Starlings.

'FASTIGIATA' 1838. Narrowly fastigiate form used in street-planting; large dark leaves densely borne; large fruit.

'XANTHOCARPA' 1893 Scotland. Rare form with fruit ripening orange-yellow. Flowers later, prolific in domed heads. **Pl. 25.**

'BEISSNERI' 1899 Bohemia. Rare, by streets and in parks, much sought now. An upright tree most striking in winter with *copper-pink* to orange bark and in autumn with leaves *luminous gold*. Bark slightly waxed; shines when wet; dull grey bloom on orange-pink when dry. Leaves yellowish; leaflets deeply toothed or lobulate. **Pl. 25.**

CHINESE SCARLET ROWAN   *Sorbus* 'Embley'
Syn. *S. discolor* Hort.

China. *c.* 1908. Frequent in parks, around public buildings; infrequent in gardens. 17m, Sheffield Park. Shoot pale brown. Bud 1.5cm long-pointed, ruby-red. Leaves 17 × 10cm, 11–15 slender oblong-lanceolate leaflets deeply double-toothed, glabrous beneath. In autumn, margins broadly bright purple then whole leaf scarlet then deeper smoky red. Fruit 1cm orange-red. The true *S. discolor* has white fruit and may not be in cultivation. 'Embley' is of obscure origin; a Chinese form of *S. commixta* (below).

JAPANESE ROWAN   *Sorbus commixta* Hedl.
Korea, Japan and Sakhalin 1906. Infrequent; recent gardens and town plantings. 16m.

Bark. Smooth, silvery grey; pale brown lenticels.

Crown. Upright when young, older trees opening out towards the top.

Foliage. Shoot pale grey tinged pink; buff lenticels. Bud narrowly conic, *acute, deep shining red*, resinous, 2cm. Leaf compound, 20–30cm, 13–15 lanceolate, *acuminate* sub-sessile leaflets oblique at base, to 8.5 × 2.5cm, basal 2cm entire, very sharply serrate beyond; terminal leaflet often very oblique based, on 1cm petiolule; rather deep and glossy green above with much impressed veins, glaucous whitish green beneath. Autumn colours begin in early October when parts of outer leaves usually turn yellow then scarlet and the rachis ruby red. The whole crown becomes scarlet and purple by the third week.

Flowers and fruit. Flowers white, in open heads 8cm across. Fruit globose, 8mm, bright orange-red.

Similar species. In autumn, *S.* 'Embley' (above) assumes similar colours but starts with broad edgings deep purple. The shiny red slender bud is a good feature in summer or

Japanese Rowan

winter. This species is often grown under the name "*Sorbus matsumurana*" which is very rare and has the basal half of the leaflets entire.

KASHMIR ROWAN   *Sorbus cashmiriana* Hedl.
Kashmir. A rare rowan, seen in a few gardens, prominent in autumn because of the big white berries. Main branches upright with spreading or arched minor branches. Shoot grey, tinged purple-brown; bud long-conic with curved, pubescent tip, dark purple-red. Leaf 15–20 cm with 17–19 leaflets, each deeply serrate, 4–5 cm long, falling pale yellow early in October. Flowers pale pink. Fruit nodding on pale red pedicels, about 30 in a head, globular or ovoid, 12–13 mm, pure white with brown apex and five radiating dark lines; prominent in mid-October after the fall of the leaves.

HUPEH ROWAN   *Sorbus hupehensis* Schneid.   **Pl. 25**
W. China 1910. Frequent in many parks and gardens. A rowan known by its *silvery grey-green* leaves glaucous beneath, to 25 cm long, rather pendulous, 11–13 leaflets forward and very sharply serrate on the *outer half only*; grooved *pink rachis* red at base; pointed dark purple-red bud. Inflorescence hemispherical, open, 8–15 cm; flowers 8 mm, five oval, narrow-stalked petals; yellow centre; anthers pale purple. Berries pale green until autumn then *white or pink*, 6 mm on open red panicle 10–15 cm across. 14 × 1.5 m. Sturdy, upright tree when young.

SORBUS 'JOSEPH ROCK'
China. Now much planted. Fruit small, yellow. Leaf 15 × 6 cm; about 17 small oblong leaflets on rachis bright crimson at base; yellowish in summer, fiery crimson and purples in late autumn, setting off the yellow fruit well.

SARGENT'S ROWAN   *Sorbus sargentiana* Koehne
W. China 1908. A thick-shooted, open, broad bushy tree often grafted on a clean stem of *S. aucuparia*, now planted in many gardens and parks. Recognised

Sorbus 'Embley'   'Joseph Rock'   Sargent's Rowan by big, glossy, bright *deep red bud exuding clear resin*, stout dark brown shoot with oval white lenticels, *big* pinnate leaf to 35 cm with 9–11 leaflets, matt soft rich green; impressed veins, terminal pair of leaflets point forward overlapping small central leaflet; basal pair 5 cm long, outer to 13 × 4 cm; soft pubescent beneath. Inflorescence with long white hairs, flat-domed 15–20 cm across. Fruit numerous but very small 6 mm bright red. Autumn colour a splendid blaze of scarlet and gold. Leaves unfold dusky pink with grey pubescence.

VILMORIN'S ROWAN *Sorbus vilmorinii* Schneid.

W. China (1889) 1905. Infrequent; modern gardens and a few parks in England, rare elsewhere. 8 × 1 m.
Bark. Dark brown or grey, scaling.
Crown. Low, spreading; branches level or arched; sinuous.
Foliage. Bud ovoid-conic, acute, pubescent, dark brown. Shoot pale grey-brown; short-pubescent. Leaf emerging pale brown, compound on deeply grooved and *winged* rachis, 12 cm dark green above, 19–25 leaflets each 2 cm, oblong-elliptic with rounded, mucronate tip; outer half serrulate; subsessile; grey-green and reticulate beneath. Petiole scarlet at base. Autumn colour late, deep red.
Flowers and fruit. Flowers on slender-stalked heads to 10 cm across, each 6–7 mm, clear white. Fruit ovoid, 1 cm, dark red, turning dark pink, then paling to white flushed pink.
Recognition. The least rare of several species, distinctive in their small, narrow, dark leaves of many tiny leaflets and pale berries.

TRUE SERVICE TREE *Sorbus domestica* L.

S. Europe, N. Africa, W. Asia. Once held to be native due to a single, very old tree in Wyre Forest. Descendants of this tree known in a few gardens. Rare; a few parks and large gardens. 22 × 3 m (20 × 2.7 m in Kensington Gardens, London).
Bark. A rich mixture of oranges and dark browns finely fissured into small rectangles; sometimes pale brown ridges, narrow, dark fissures.
Crown. Domed with level spreading branches.
Foliage. Shoot with loose, silky hairs at first, olive-green to dark brown above; green beneath. Bud glossy, exuding resin, *bright green*, *ovoid*, 1 cm. Leaf pinnate, 15–22 cm, 13–21 leaflets, oblong, 3–6 cm long, 1 cm wide, entire near base, sharply and doubly serrate; soft-pubescent beneath, rather dark, yellowish-green above; rather pendulous.

True Service Tree

Flowers and fruit Flowers in May in slightly domed inflorescence 10 × 14 cm and long-pubescent, each flower 1.5 cm across, slightly greyish-cream. Fruit *large*, 2–3 cm long, apple or pear-chaped (var. *maliformis* and var. *pyriformis*) *green* tinged brownish-red.
Similar species. *S. aucuparia* (p. 277), distinguished by bark and bud.

BASTARD SERVICE TREE   *Sorbus × thuringiaca* (Ilse) Fritsch
Syns. *S. × hybrida* Hort., *S. pinnatifida*.
E. Europe. A hybrid between *S. aucuparia* and *S. aria* and
probably the commonest of several similar hybrids of *S.
aucuparia* and the whitebeam group. Infrequent; mostly in
streets and towns, also in some gardens. 14 × 1.5 m.

Bark. Dull grey, shallowly cracked.
Crown. Upright ovoid, larger trees mostly leaning, dense.
Foliage. Shoot soft pink-grey, purplish towards tip. Bud
8 mm, few-scaled, dark red-brown. Leaf oblong or ovate,
11 × 7 cm on 2 cm stout, red petiole, 1–4 pairs leaflets at base,
serrate towards the tips, the rest of the leaf lobed decreasingly
to its apex, dark grey-green above, dense white wool beneath. Bastard Service Tree
Flowers and fruit. Flowers white, 1 cm across in pubescent
inflorescence 6–10 cm across; fruit bright red, 1.2 cm across, 10–15 per head.

'FASTIGIATA' Narrower, more fastigiate form usually with clean bole
favoured around car-parks or where space is restricted.

WILD SERVICE TREE   *Sorbus torminalis* (L.) Crantz
Native north to Lincolnshire and Westmorland, the best growth is found below
the North Downs east to the Eden Valley, Kent. Europe north to Denmark;
Algeria, Caucasus and Syria. Infrequent in gardens. 22 × 2.8 m.
Bark. Dark brown and pale grey shallowly fissured into scaly plates.
Crown. Young trees conic, older trees tall-domed and spreading.
Foliage. Shoot shiny dark purplish-brown above, olive-brown beneath. Bud
globular, glossy green, 4–5 mm. Leaf ovate, 10 × 8 cm, lobed rather *like a maple*
but alternately borne, 3–5 pairs triangular-ovate lobes, variable basal pair
2.5 cm deep, spreading; next pair
largest, to 5 cm, forward; all finely,
usually doubly serrate; hard, shiny,
rather deep green both sides. Petiole
yellow-green, 2–5 cm. In autumn,
deep red, purple.

Flowers and fruit. Flowers white,
1.2 cm across, anthers yellow; in
loose, green, densely pubescent   Wild Service Tree
heads 10–12 cm across, May–June. Fruit obovoid, 1 cm slightly ribbed, *brown*,
speckled rusty.
Recognition. Regularly taken for a maple; no other *Sorbus* has a similar leaf.

WHITEBEAM   *Sorbus aria* (L.) Crantz   **Pl. 25**
Native from Kent and Herts. to Dorset and Wye Valley and in Co. Galway, on
chalk and limestone or on sandy soils near these. C. and S. Europe. Common;
much planted, very often as one of the cultivars, in streets; frequent in gardens.
20 × 1.9 m.
Bark. Grey and smooth, later with shallow, scaly ridges.
Crown. Irregularly domed, branches radiating and upswept.
Foliage. Shoot dark brown above, pale green below, with long hairs soon shed.
Bud dark brown at base, hairy white tip, rest greenish, ovoid 2 cm. Leaf elliptic,
variable in shape and size, usually 8 × 5 cm, irregularly shallow-toothed or

shallowly lobulate, clothed in long silvery hairs when young, becoming dull yellow-green above, remaining densely *white-pubescent* beneath. Petiole 1–2 cm. Autumn colour brief but fine yellows and pale browns in the wild; poor in gardens.

Flowers and fruit. Flowers 1.5 cm across in heads 5–8 cm across, white; fruit ovoid, green, some bright red by mid-September. Seldom numerous or conspicuous for long; soon eaten by birds.

'DECAISNEANA' ('Majestica') 1858. Frequent in streets, less usual in gardens where old trees develop broad columnar crowns with large upswept branches; to 20 × 2 m. Leaves larger and thicker, to 15 × 9 cm, obovate-lanceolate, or oblong-elliptic, *narrowly cuneate*; finely toothed, sometimes faintly doubly; deep green and glossy in summer. Narrower and much more sharply toothed than *S. cuspidata* (below). Fruit globose, 1.5 cm, scarlet finely speckled white, 5–10 in a head, on pale yellow pedicels.

'LUTESCENS' 1892. Frequent in street plantings of recent years. Neat, rather dense, ovoid, upswept crown; deep purple shoots contrasting in May with bright silvery unfolding leaves. Leaves smaller than in *S. aria*, become slightly yellowish-grey-green; autumn colour fleeting pale yellow.

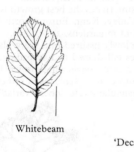

Whitebeam

'Decaisneana'

HIMALAYAN WHITEBEAM   *Sorbus cuspidata* (Spach) Hedl.
Syn. *S. vestita* Wall.
The Himalaya 1820. Rare but splendid fast-growing tree. 16 × 2.3 m at Borde Hill, Sussex.

Crown. Narrow, conic with few, stout, upturned branches becoming broadly conic.

Foliage. Shoot dark purple above, olive beneath, tomentose. Bud 6 mm, ovoid, green. Huge thick leaves to 22 × 14 cm, variable in shape, usually oblong-elliptic, broad-cuneate, acuminate, shallowly crenately toothed and variably lobulate;

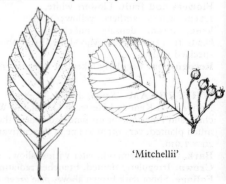

Himalayan Whitebeam

'Mitchellii'

deep ± shiny green above, densely white pubescent beneath, whole crown appear ing light grey-green.

Flowers. In heads 8 cm across on thick woolly peduncles; flower 2 cm, white, calyx and anthers dull purple; strongly scented of hawthorn.

Similar species. The variant grown as *Sorbus* 'Mitchellii' is a striking tree, now planted in many gardens, but rare as an older tree (Westonbirt pl. 1938, now 19 × 1.3 m). It differs only in the massively orbicular leaves to 20 × 18 cm, or broad-ovate 20 × 15 cm, entire base, beyond gradually toothed bluntly and unevenly. Petiole 1.5 cm. Found in the native Himalayan population. *S. aria* 'Decaisneana' has smaller, thinner, narrower lanceolate leaves, deeply toothed above the middle, more glossy, with impressed veins. The shoot is only 3 mm across, compared with 5 mm in *S. cuspidata*.

SORBUS 'WILFRID FOX'   (*S. cuspidata × aria*)

c. 1920 Surrey. Uncommon; recent plantings in some parks and gardens.

Bark. Purplish grey, scaling finely in patterns.

Crown. Narrowly erect when young; stout branches with small shoots.

Foliage. Shoot smooth, brown; small pale lenticels. Bud ovoid, 1 cm, green and red-brown. Leaf from lanceolate 14 × 6 cm to elliptic 16 × 10 cm; narrowly cuneate or nearly round-based; fine sharp teeth, uneven to shallowly lobulate; deep rather glossy green with 12–15 pairs of impressed veins; underside white tomentose. Petiole 2–3 cm grooved, pale green.

Flowers and fruit. Flowers similar to *S. cuspidata*. Fruit large, globose, 20 × 20 mm, yellowish-green ripening pale orange to brown.

Similar species. *S. aria* 'Decaisneana' and *S. cuspidata*.   'Wilfrid 'Wilfrid Fox' differs from the former in stout dark   Fox' brown shoots; much bigger green or brown fruit; petiole stouter, leaf thicker, usually broader; veins curving upwards towards margin. (In 'Decaisneana' the veins tend to arch over and curve slightly downwards to the margin.) *S. cuspidata* typically has much longer, narrower leaf, variably lobulate. In 'Mitchellii' the leaf is broader, more orbicular and much larger.

FOLGNER'S CHINESE WHITEBEAM   *Sorbus folgneri* Rehd.

C. China 1901. Rare: largely confined to major collections. 15 m (Leonardslee).

Bark. Purplish with dark fissures peeling at margins. Old trees ashen grey, smooth.

Crown. Elegant, slender branches, ascending then arched.

Foliage. Shoot dark red with long, forward tomentum soon shed. Bud narrowly conic, to 5 mm, dark red-brown. Leaf *obovate-lanceolate*, *cuneate*, to 10 × 4.5 cm; *rugose*; 8–9 pairs parallel veins; irregular, forward toothing; very dark green above, variably *silvered beneath* with dense pubescence. Petiole 1.7 cm, white tomentose. In autumn the upper surface turns orange, scarlet and crimson, the underside remains silver, making a spectacular display in early November.

Folgner's Chinese Whitebeam

Flowers and fruit. Inflorescence 10cm across; flowers small, white. Fruit yellow-green then red, flask-shaped with calyx adhering, 6–10mm.

Recognition. Distinctive narrow leaf silvered beneath and dark, rugose above. Some are mottled dull yellow.

SERVICE-TREE OF FONTAINEBLEAU *Sorbus × latifolia* (Lam.) Pers.

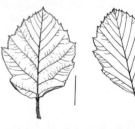

Service-tree of   Sorbus bristoliensis
Fontainebleau

A hybrid between *S. aria* and *S. torminalis* found in Fontainebleau before 1750, but differing only in details of lobing and the large size of the leaf from local native forms described as species: *S. bristoliensis* Wilmott, (Avon Gorge), *S. subcuneata* Wilmott (N. side of Exmoor), *S. devoniensis* Warburg (Devon and S.E. Ireland) and *S. × vagensis* Wilmott (Wye Valley). *S. × latifolia* is rare in parks and gardens and has *broad* leaves, to 20 × 12 cm with small, broadly triangular lobes from *near the middle*, hard, dark shiny green above, white-felted beneath, petiole 3.5 cm. 10 × 2.7m at Kilkerran, Ayrshire.

SWEDISH WHITEBEAM *Sorbus intermedia* (Ehrh.) Pers.   Pl. 25
Sweden, Baltic States and N.E. Germany. Introduced long ago. Frequent in town streets and parks, less common in gardens. 15 × 2m.

Bark. Dull purplish-grey, smooth except for wide, shallow, scaly fissures.

Crown. Dense, broad dome on short bole.

Foliage. Shoot soft pink-grey, purplish near tip, with long hairs soon shed. Bud green to dark red-brown, grey-pubescent, 8mm. Leaf elliptic, broad-cuneate, 8–12 × 5–7cm, lobes starting below the middle, 3–7 each side decreasing to teeth towards apex of leaf, largest cut a third or less to the midrib; lobes irregularly serrate with 3–5 teeth; dark green above, dense short white wool beneath. Petiole 2–5cm.

Flowers and fruit. Flowers densely borne almost like a large hawthorn, in heads 8–10cm across, each flower 1.2–2cm, dull white, circular petals, anthers pale pink. Fruit oblong-ovoid, 15 × 10mm, glossy green turning bright scarlet, on nearly glabrous olive-brown peduncles; about 20 in a bunch.

Similar species. Leaf narrower, smaller and with lobing starting nearer base than in *S. × latifolia*, and without free leaflets as in *S. × thuringiaca* (p. 281).

SNOWY MESPILS Amelanchier
About 25 species in the northern temperate regions south to Mexico. White flowers in terminal racemes.

SNOWY MESPIL *Amelanchier laevis* Wieg.   Pl. 26
E. N. America 1870. The only common species to make a small tree. True origin and name the source of much speculation. Often known as *A. canadensis* which it certainly is not, and recently named *A. lamarckii* Schroder. Naturalised on several heaths in Surrey, frequent in gardens in S. England. Bark smooth,

dark grey. Bushy and many-stemmed, sometimes gnarled old tree on bent single bole and with low, domed very dense crown of fine shoots. Leaves unfold in mid-April *coppery-pink* below slender *erect* inflorescences. Flowers spectacular but brief, star-like white, in conic head. Leaf ovate, 5 cm sharply and shallowly serrate, dull, rather yellowish dark green, colouring scarlet then deep red in autumn. Fruit globose, 6 mm, green turning dark red in July then blackish-purple, soon eaten by birds.

APPLES   Malus

About 25 species in north temperate regions from which a vast number of hybrids and cultivars have been raised both for fruit and for ornament. Formerly united with pears, whitebeams and rowans under *Pyrus*. Only a few of the commonest or most ornamental can be given here. See **Pl. 28** for typical *Malus*.

CRAB APPLE   *Malus sylvestris* Mill.   **Pl. 26**
Native, frequent to rare in hedgerows and copses everywhere. Europe and S.W. Asia. 10 × 3 m. Roadside trees, common in areas like the New Forest may often be seedlings of orchard apples, especially if the flowers are very pink.
Bark. Dark brown, deeply and finely cracked into small square plates.
Crown. Low-domed, usually one-sided; dense twisting branches.
Foliage. Shoot dark purple above, pale brown beneath, ribbed, with some greyish down later shed, *often thorny*. Bud 4–5 mm dark purple fringed with grey hairs. Leaf elliptic, abruptly acuminate, cuneate or rounded, slightly oblique, crenate-serrate; deep green above, whitish-green and pubescent beneath. 5–6 × 3–4 cm. Petiole 2.5 cm, grooved, densely pubescent, dark crimson towards base.
Flowers and fruit. Flowers with leaves in late May, white, faintly pink; fruit nearly globular, 2.5 × 2.8 cm depressed each end, glossy pale green speckled with large white spots, flushed or speckled red in autumn.

CHINESE CRAB   *Malus spectabilis* (Ait.) Borkh.
Not known wild. China pre-1780. Infrequent in large gardens. A large tree for an apple, to 12 × 2 m, with twisting, drooping branches, spectacular when in flower. Flower-bud *bright rosy-pink, globular*, becoming pale pink, then opening to 5.5 cm across, *slightly double* (6–8 petals) on pubescent 4 cm pedicel; stamens 1.5 cm spreading widely. Fruit 2 cm globose without cavity at base, yellowish; leaf 5–8 × 3 cm elliptic, base unequal, forward crenate, glossy above; petiole 1.5 cm, long-pubescent. Bark spiralled fine ridges, purple-brown, with thick grey scales.

Chinese Crab

Recognition. Big pink and pale pink semi-double flowers.

SIBERIAN CRAB   *Malus baccata* (L.) Borkh.
E. Siberia, Manchuria, N. China 1784. Infrequent in gardens, where it is a mass of small white flowers in May. Crown low-domed rather pendulous; bud very sharply conic; leaf 3–8 × 2–3.5 cm cuneate, *lanceolate*, acute, sharply serrate, on

Siberian Crab   var. *mandschurica*

slender petiole 2–5 cm, flowers 3.5 cm across, narrow elliptic petals, *widely parted*; on slender pedicels 2–6 cm; in fives; fruit abundant, glossy pale green, 8 mm in summer ripening to 2 cm, globular, bright red persisting on tree until spring.

Recognition. Small slender leaf on slender petiole; small fruit of good colour; narrow petalled wide white flowers crowded on shoots.

var. *mandshurica* (Maxim.) Schneid.
Japan, China to Amur River. Infrequent in gardens. A vigorous tree reaching larger size than the type, to 15 × 2 m. Broad crown, densely twigged; leaf broad-elliptic, petiole pubescent; pedicel pubescent; otherwise similar to type.

HUPEH CRAB *Malus hupehensis* (Pamp.) Rehd.
    Syn. *M. theifera* (Bailey) Rehd.
China 1900. Infrequent, but in some larger gardens and a few small. 9 × 1.9 m at Mount Usher, C. Wicklow.
Bark. Dull orange-brown coarsely fissured into vertical plates.
Crown. Broad; long, level, lower branches, ascending upper.
Foliage. Leaf 5–10 × 3–6 cm, ovate, short-acuminate, finely crenate on outer half, bright green; petiole 4–6 cm, slender, green, finely pubescent.
Flowers and fruit. Flowers standing out in open bunches on 4 cm pubescent pedicels, pink and glob-ular in bud, opening pure white, cup-shaped and 3–4 cm across at first, 5–6 cm across when flat; petals incurved, broad oval, overlapping; anthers

Hupeh Crab

yellow. Fruit ovoid-conic, 1.3 × 1.3 cm, on crimson pedicel; ripening from yellow and orange to red-purple.
Growth. Very vigorous; to 11 × 2 m in 40 years.
Similar species. *M. baccata* (p. 285) also covered in white flowers in early or mid-May, but *M. hupehensis* differs in stature, spreading flowers, pink buds, cupped flowers and overlapping petals.

PURPLE CRAB *Malus × purpurea* (Barbier) Rehd.
A garden hybrid commonly planted in streets, small gardens and around buildings. Crown exceedingly untidy, spreading with sparse, long, curved branches bearing in summer muddy red-purple-green, shiny leaves, ovate-lanceolate to elliptic, 3–5 cm long with dark red-purple midrib beneath. Briefly in early May, as the leaves unfold reddish, numerous dark red flower-buds open to reddish-purple flowers 4 cm across with obovate petals. In late summer there are abundant small red or purple apples.

Probably now being replaced by the cultivars below, but their distinctive features are rather vague in some cases, and trees which are very similar are sold under these names.

'ALDENHAMENSIS' 1912 Hertfordshire. Usually semi-double flowers, deep red, two weeks after *M. × purpurea*. Fruit flattened globose.

'LEMOINEI' 1922 Nancy. Larger, more erect; leaf to 10 cm, very variable in shape, sometimes with triangular lobes, unfolding crimson-purple; flowers larger, 5 cm, deep red-purple; petals obovate, flattened at apex. Fruit 12–18 mm, dark red.

'ELEYI' Pre-1920 Suffolk. Leaf ovate, 5–7 cm, short-acuminate, or obovate-lanceolate. Flower bright red-purple, 3–4 cm, petal oval; fruit conic-ovoid, 2.5 cm deep red. Flower more red than in the above forms.

'PROFUSION' Pre-1938 Holland. Hybrid from 'Lemoinei'. Leaf 8 × 3 cm, ovate, short-acuminate, crenate, opening red then purple-brown. Flower-buds globose, deep bright red, open cup-shaped at first then fully, when more purplish, 3.5–4 cm on brownish-purple pedicel 3–4 cm, densely held on long sectors of shoots. Bred for superior foliage, noticeable in summer.

'Profusion'   Hall's Crab

HALL'S CRAB *Malus halliana* Koehne
China, unknown wild. 1863 from Japan. Infrequent, small tree with open crown with rosy-pink flowers and neat dark leaves. Leaf lanceolate, 5 × 1.5 cm slightly glossed purple on dark green with exceedingly *fine, dark red margin*, on bright crimson 1 cm petiole. Rich pink buds open to show bright but paler pink inner side of petals, 3 cm; pedicel 3 cm, bright purple-red like the calyx; fruit 5–6 mm, globose, purple. Very attractive in flower.

MAGDEBURG APPLE *Malus × magdeburgensis* Schoch
Hybrid *M. spectabilis × M. pumila*. Infrequent; locally frequent. Cup-shaped crown, becoming slightly pendulous; in flower like a very densely flowered orchard apple, with bright pink buds and pale pink, globular, large semi-double flowers, opening at first in isolated clusters among pale green leaves, then in dense bunches closely clothing the branches in mid-May.

Plate 25   THORN, ROWANS, WHITEBEAMS

Trees of the Rose Family.

1. Cockspur Thorn *Crataegus crus-galli*   275

Leaf and fruit. The pedicels of the fruit are glabrous.

2. Hupeh Rowan *Sorbus hupehensis*   279

Single leaf and fruit. The leaf-stalk may be crimson, and the fruit will ripen with a pink or purplish tinge.

3. Rowan *Sorbus aucuparia*   277

Single leaf and ripe fruit. The fruit turns red rapidly in early August and in towns is at once raided by birds.

4. Yellow-fruited Rowan *Sorbus aucuparia* 'Xanthocarpa'   278

Fully ripe fruit of this rare cultivar of Rowan.

5. Beissner's Rowan *Sorbus aucuparia* 'Beissneri'   278

Close-up of bark when dry; when wet it is shining orange. A rare cultivar, but now much in demand for the bark colour, the neat upright shape and the autumn gold of its leaves.

6. Swedish Whitebeam *Sorbus intermedia*   284

Leaves, one showing white-felted underside, and ripe fruit. A tree much planted in streets and by roads.

7. Whitebeam *Sorbus aria*   281

Leaves; the larger showing the underside, and ripe fruit. The fruit are usually eaten or fall before achieving this bright red. A tree native to chalk downlands, and much planted in towns.

Cockspur Thorn

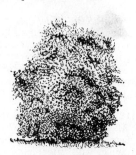

Swedish Whitebeam

1a

1b

3a

3b

4a

4b

SNOWY MESPIL, APPLES, PEAR   Plate 26

Trees of the Rose Family.

1. Snowy Mespil   *Amelanchier laevis*   284

   (a) Leaves in summer and autumn.
   (b) Flowers. When first open the inflorescence stands erect
     and the leaves are copper coloured.

2. Crab Apple   *Malus sylvestris*   285

   Flowers and leaves. Trees in the wild with pink in the flower
   are seedlings of domestic apples.

3. Pillar Apple   *Malus tschonoskii*   290

   (a) Leaves and shoot.
   (b) Tree 7 m tall in autumn. The leaves turn orange and
     scarlet on this narrow-crowned apple.

4. Willow-leafed Pear   *Pyrus salicifolia*   291

   (a) Foliage with ripening fruit. The leaves emerge pale silvery
     grey with dense hairs.
   (b) Outline of tall specimen, about 6 m.

Snowy Mespil

JAPANESE CRAB   *Malus floribunda* Sieb.
Japan 1862. Common in streets and gardens. A low-domed, broad-crowned
dense tree extremely profuse of single flowers among open leaves, red in bud,
opening pink and fading to white. Fruit sometimes prolific, 6–8 mm, yellow or
red on very slender 4 cm pedicel. Very early into leaf; flowers early May. Shoot
green, densely pubescent; leaf lanceolate or ovate-lanceolate shallowly toothed
basal two thirds, sharply on outer third; occasional lobules; cuneate, deep
green. Underside paler with fine pubescence. Petiole 3 cm, pinkish groove;
finely pubescent pale green, crimson base.

PILLAR APPLE   *Malus tschonoskii* (Maxim.) Schneid.   **Pl. 26**
Japan 1897. Rare as large tree (15 × 1.4 m at Leonardslee, Sussex), more
frequent as young tree and now much planted in streets. *Narrowly erect* crown,
long upright branches with few, spiky lateral shoots; leaf 10–12 × 6–8 cm, subcordate, ovate-oblong, acute; sharp, shallow teeth; thick, *leathery* glossy deep
green above, *white pubescence* beneath. Autumn colours *brilliant gold and scarlet*.
Flowers erect 4–5 together, pink in bud opening white with yellow boss of
stamens, fragrant, 2.5 cm. Fruit 1.5 × 2 cm flattened globular, shiny yellow and
deep red.

MALUS 'JOHN DOWNIE'
1875 Lichfield. Frequent in small gardens. 10 m.
Crown upright, later arched.Profuse pale pink
buds; white flowers, 3 cm; petals oblong-ovate
narrowing to slender stalk; pedicel 2.5 cm red
above; calyx deflexed, slender. Fruit in long
stalked bunches, conic-ovoid, 3.5 × 3 cm, glossy
scarlet and orange. Leaf glossy rich green,
6 × 2.5 cm, lanceolate, serrulate, subshiny and
glabrous beneath, on pubescent pale
green 2 cm petiole. A fine sight in fruit.

'John Downie'

MALUS 'GOLDEN HORNET'
Pre-1949 Surrey. A selection from a variety of a Japanese species. Now much
planted. Crown low with arched, pendulous shoots. White flowers, 3 cm;
leaves oblanceolate or elliptic, 6 × 3 cm, petiole 4 cm. Fruit in bunches of six
or more, wreathed along branches and weighing them down, pale bright yellow,
globular or obovoid, wrinkled, calyx-end protruded; 2.5 cm.

PEARS   Pyrus

About 20 species in the temperate regions of the Old World. Flowers in umbel-
like corymbs; flesh of fruit with grit-cells. See **Pl. 28** for typical *Pyrus*.

COMMON PEAR   *Pyrus communis* L.
Doubtful native; single trees occasional in hedgerows, and edges of woods;
parks and gardens. Europe and W. Asia. 15 × 2 m.
Bark. Deep brown or blackish, finely but deeply cracked into very small
squares.

Crown. Tall-conic, leaning or rounded at the top; ascending branches; narrow and spiky when young.

Foliage. Shoot brown often slightly pubescent sometimes with thorns. Leaf orbicular-ovate to elliptic, 5–8 cm, finely crenate on slender 2–5 cm petiole, glossy dark or yellowish-green.

Flowers and fruit. Flowers white, 2–4 cm across in heads 5–8 cm across, in April before the leaves emerge fully; fruit 2–4 cm pear-shaped or globose, brown. In many gardens, the largest and most floriferous pear is the old 'Pitmaston Duchess', which bears big yellow and russet fruit. In Gloucestershire and neighbouring counties many big old pears are survivors of perry-orchards grown for the making of cider, and can be any of a large number of small-fruited cultivars raised for that purpose. They often carry much mistletoe in this region.

WILLOW-LEAFED PEAR *Pyrus salicifolia* Pall.   Pl. 26

S.E. Europe, W. Asia 1780. Frequent in gardens and parks; usually known as *Pyrus salicifolia* 'Pendula'. A small, domed, slender-branched, *pendulous, pale grey-leafed* tree. Leaf 3–9 × 1–2 cm, long-acuminate, long-cuneate, covered at first in silvery hairs, later shiny green, entire, on petiole 3–15 mm. Flowers pure white, 2 cm, densely bunched buds tipped bright red, stalks white-woolly; fruit pear-shaped, 2–3 cm. A decorative little tree similar only to two other species, both much more scarce. *P. elaeagrifolia* Pallas (S.E. Europe 1800) has broader entire leaves (8 × 3 cm) on longer petioles (2–4 cm); fruit two, terminal, erect, 1 × 1 cm, green-tinged purple, and is thorny. *P. nivalis* Jacquin (S. Europe 1800) is taller, more upright, scarcely pendulous, not thorny and also has broader leaves 9 × 2–4 cm, pure white when new, dark green later, *forward serrate*; bud squat, deep purple-brown,   Willow-leafed Pear

flowers white, among white young leaves, fruit nearly globular 2 cm (in July) on 5 mm stout woolly stalk.

PLUMS, ALMONDS, APRICOTS, PEACHES, CHERRIES etc.
Prunus

About 200 species from temperate regions. Leaves alternate, flowers with five petals, five sepals and solitary style. See **Pl. 28** for typical *Prunus*.

MYROBALAN PLUM *Prunus cerasifera* Ehrh.

Balkans to C. Asia. Long cultivated. Locally frequent in S. England as a tall hedge or roadside thicket, less frequent in gardens. A spreading open-crowned small tree, covered in small pure white flowers among opening fresh green leaves in early March. Normally the first Prunus in flower, this is regularly mistaken for the Blackthorn, *Prunus spinosa* which is a dense, upright bush flowering more than a month later.

Foliage. Shoot green, minutely pubescent. Leaf oval or elliptic, obtuse, finely crenate, deep glossy green with impressed veins; 5 × 3 cm; underside paler, matt. Petiole 1 cm purplish-green with wide concave groove.

Fruit. 1–5 in bunch, globular, 2 cm, glossy pale green during summer, finally red; slightly grooved; on short, 5–10 mm pedicel.

'ATROPURPUREA' (*P. pissardii*) 1880 Persia. The form which, with 'Nigra', is almost always planted now. Common in town and suburban gardens and parks especially. The first common *Prunus* in flower, from late January to late March, depending on year, and in flower for several weeks. Flowers crowded along shoots and on spurs, pink in bud, opening palest pink then white, much smaller than in Almond, 2 cm. Best by busy roads where bullfinches rarely eat them. Leaves unfold towards the end of flowering, red at first, darkening all too soon to an unsightly dark purplish-red, ovate or obovate 5–8 cm, acute, obtusely toothed.

'NIGRA' Common. As preceding, except flowers rosy pink; a few days later in flower; summer foliage noticeably richer deep red-purple (Pl. 27).

DOUBLE CHERRY-PLUM   *Prunus × blireana* André
Very similar to 'Atropurpurea' (above). Arose in 1895, a hybrid between that and *Prunus mume*. Becoming frequent in street-plantings. Differing in rose-pink, double flowers button-like before fully open, and broader, ovate-acuminate leaves, 7 × 4 cm, which unfold red and become duller, greenish red-purple; midrib beneath bright crimson; shoot smooth deep red-purple.

ALMOND   *Prunus dulcis* D. A. Webb
Syn. *Prunus communis* Arcang, *not* Hudson, *nor* (L.); *P. amygdalus* Batsch.
W. Asia and N. Africa, cultivated since ancient times and wild range not properly known. Particularly common in the newer suburban gardens but short-lived so fewer in older gardens. Many of the larger-flowered forms commonly seen are *Prunus* 'Pollardii' – a hybrid between almond and peach, but scarcely distinguishable, except that the flowers are a little larger.
Bark. Nearly *black* deeply cracked into small squares.
Crown. Flattened globose; ascending branches, rather open.
Foliage. Leaf ovate-lanceolate, 7–12 cm, finely serrulate, dark or yellowish-green, often folded near base with midrib in a "V", also contorted and pink in early summer with Peach-leaf Curl, a fungal disease.
Flowers and fruit. Flowers open well ahead of leaves in early years, just ahead with much overlap in late years, some out before March in early areas like London, Southampton, Torquay and Gloucester, general by end of March, large, 3–5 cm across, singly or in pairs on short stalks, wreathed along young shoots, very pink. Fruit yellowish-green often tinged red, long-ovoid, about 4 cm, flattened, covered in dense hairs, numerous on some trees and may fall after leaves, when dark brown.
Recognition. The largest-flowered early *Prunus* and usually distinctive pink, but pale and white, also double cultivars occasionally seen. Large dull, rather hanging leaves, dark bark and big fruit identify in summer.

Double Cherry-plum

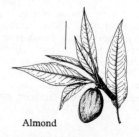

Almond

'Autumnalis'

'Umineko'

ROSE-BUD CHERRY *Prunus subhirtella* Miq.

Japan 1895. A small, dense erect tree with ovate leaves deeply and irregularly sharp-toothed and soft pink, paling clustered small flowers in April, with petals notched or toothed at their tips. Much less planted than 'Autumnalis'.

'AUTUMNALIS' Winter-flowering Cherry. Japan pre-1909. Common in gardens especially in towns. For some years with an open, ascending, spreading crown, later densely twigged. Shoot crimson, pubescent. Leaf 6 × 2.5 cm oblong-lanceolate, acuminate, sharply and very unevenly toothed. Petiole crimson 1.2 cm. The very pale pink bell-shaped flowers with fringed petal-ends start to open in October among the still green leaves. In bunches of 2–5 and on 8 mm stalks they continue to open in moderate numbers through the winter until early spring when the remaining buds, clustered near shoot ends, open together in mid-April, among young leaves.

'PENDULA' 1862 Japan. Low, spreading, very pendulous hummock, spectacular in white flowers in May. Frequent.

'ROSEA' is a semi-double pink-flowered form of 'Autumnalis'.

PRUNUS 'UMINEKO' *(P. incisa × speciosa)*

Rare. Very erect, densely set with 4 cm single white cup-shaped flowers with golden stamens and purple calyx among fresh green leaves in April. Shoot olive-green, smooth. Petiole grooved, pubescent, 1.5 cm. Leaf obovate, abruptly long-acuminate, 9 × 6 cm, sharp uneven toothing, a white spot at the base of each primary tooth; dark matt green; glabrous, sub-shiny beneath.

PRUNUS × HILLIERI 'SPIRE' *(P. incisa × sargentii)*

1956. Frequent; erect, narrow; dense, pale pink, single flowers 3 cm, when leaves reddish-purple. Leaf later yellowish-brown tinged, then dark green, 8 × 5.5 cm broad-obovate, abruptly acuminate, unevenly mucronate-crenate, ten pairs impressed veins; shiny glabrous beneath. Petiole 1.5 cm, dark crimson. Colouring well in autumn. Dark, leafy crown in summer is like *P. sargentii*, but nearly erect. The type is a broad bush with similar flowers and foliage.

TIBETAN CHERRY *Prunus serrula* Franch.   Pl. 27

Syn. *P. s.* var. *tibetica* Koehne

W. China 1908. Infrequent; gardens or even parks where good plantsmen in charge.

Bark. Where admired and stroked, bright, *glossy mahogany* with pale brown horizontal bands of lenticels; where out of reach or ignored deep blackish-purple, hard, curling scales, amid massed sprouts.

Crown. Broad-domed and dense with large branches arching out and strong shoots growing at a wide angle from them.

Foliage. Shoot purplish above, light brown beneath, short-pubescent. Bud ovoid, pointed, chestnut-brown, appressed to shoot, 6–7 mm. Leaf mixed sizes on same tree, from 4 to 12 × 3 cm, lanceolate, long-acuminate, rounded at base on 6–7 mm petiole, finely and sharply serrulate, dull dark green above; below midrib very prominent and white, all veins white-silky pubescent.

Flowers and fruit. Prolific, 2 cm, 2–3 together hanging on 4 cm green stalks, petals rounded, white but rather lost among fully expanded leaves in first half of May. Fruit oblong ovoid, 5 mm, on 4 cm, slender pedicel; bright green in summer. Grown entirely for the remarkable bark.

YOSHINO CHERRY *Prunus × yedoensis* Matsum.

Probably hybrid between *P. subhirtella* and *P. speciosa*; Japan 1902. Frequent; in large gardens (where flowers eaten in bud by bullfinches), increasingly planted by busy roads and by-passes, around factories and on trading-estates where bullfinches seldom go. Low, broad crown of stout branches gently arching downwards far from the bole. All shoots densely wreathed in short-stalked flowers in bunches of 5–6, pale pink in bud, opening nearly white and flat, 3–3.5 cm across, petals deeply notched; sepals dark pink, serrate; well before the leaves, in early April. Leaves slightly folded at base; to 15 × 7 cm elliptic-obovate, acuminate, very unevenly crenate with teeth drawn out to fine points, pubescent on veins beneath. Petiole 4 cm pale pink. Dull and coarse when not in flower. Fruit 1 cm obovoid on 2 cm pubescent pedicel. By June bright glossy red and yellow.

Yoshino Cherry

PRUNUS 'PANDORA' (Back-cross *P. × yedoensis × P. subhirtella*)

An extremely floriferous tree with masses of early, pale pink, nearly white flowers 1.5 cm across with leaves unfolding bronze at flowering time. Vigorous, upright tree (but can be rounded bush), very dark green in leaf.

SARGENT'S CHERRY *Prunus sargentii* Rehd.

Japan and Sakhalin 1890. Common in street and park plantings. Grafted plants to 10 × 3 m in 40 years.

Bark. Purplish-brown, smooth between close horizontal, raised, pale brown lines of lenticels.

Crown. Rarely grown as seedling when tall and spreading, many-stemmed from ground; usually grafted at 1.6–2 m on stem of *P. avium*, swollen at the union; many branches ascending at a wide angle, bearing fine short shoots. Often seen with green-leafed, white-flowered shoots of rootstock invading crown.

Foliage. Shoot dark red with pale brown lenticels. Bud dark red, conic, pointed. Leaf reddish-purple when unfolding before flowers fade then yellowish, finally dark green, elliptic-obovate, abruptly long-acuminate; to

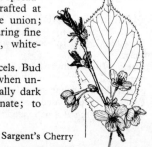

Sargent's Cherry

15 × 8 cm on stout, grooved deep red petiole 4 cm long; sharply toothed, with acuminate teeth. Autumn colour *early* and bright, often *scarlet* in early September well before other autumn colour, deep crimson and falling by the end of the month but some turn later and deeper red.

Flowers. Early, about mid-April, delicately and densely borne in 4–5 close pairs, rosy-pink, 3–4 cm across, usually untouched by bullfinches.

Similar species. Flowers less massed but densely through the crown, and much more pink than *P. cerasifera* (p. 291), forms of which may still just be in flower; much smaller and more bunched than in *P. dulcis* (Almond, p. 292).

Several hybrids have been raised from this species and share the autumn colours and similar flowers. One is given below.

PRUNUS 'ACCOLADE' (*P. sargentii* × *subhirtella*)

1952. Infrequent but widespread; broad, open, low-crowned tree known by mid-early, light pink, semi-double, bell-shaped flowers with fringed petals hanging below the shoots, 4 cm

'Accolade'

across, red in bud. Delicate and attractive. Leaf glossy bright green, 12 × 6 cm, ovate-lanceolate, closely and sharply serrate. Petiole 2 cm, purple-red, pubescent.

JAPANESE CHERRY *Prunus serrulata* Lindl.

The true species is not known for certain but probably a Chinese single-flowered tree early introduced to Japan. The original description was from one of the innumerable cultivars raised in Japan which was introduced in 1822. The following are a selection of some of the Japanese cultivars most planted and among the best. Some have been ascribed to various "species" in the past, e.g. "*P. lannesiana*", "*P. longipes*", but they are now treated as cultivars without a specific epithet but closely related to *P. serrulata*. They share big, sharply toothed leaves and pale gold and pink autumn colours. Classed collectively as 'Sato Sakura'.

'AMANOGAWA' After 1900. Common. Narrowly *fastigiate* to 6 m then opening rather when older and taller. Late mid-season, semi-double, pale pink large flowers on long stalks as the pale green leaves unfold slightly bronzed.

'Amanogawa'

'KANZAN' *c.*1913. The most abundant of these and rather over-planted; a poorly shaped dull plant all summer. Often wrongly called 'Hisakura'. Strongly ascending branches from graft-union, unfailingly weighted down with billowing masses of late mid-season large, bunched, semi-double pink flowers, mixed before they fade with bronze-purple leaves. Attractive in bud, with pink buds beneath bright red opening leaves. Leaf fairly dark green in summer; whitish beneath; obovate, acuminate, 18 × 9 cm; spreading aristate teeth, petiole red 3 cm; soft, luminous gold and pink, sometimes red, in autumn. Old trees with sparse, widely arching branches. **Pl. 27.**

'Shimidsu'

'SHIMIDSU' ('Longipes'). After 1900. Common. Among the last to flower, supremely attractive as big bunches of long-stemmed pink buds among violet-tinged pale green leaves begin to open to large, double, pure white flowers, 5–6 cm across; petals sharply toothed at fringe; on pedicels 3–8 cm with spiky, green bracts. Wide, slightly pendulous crown. Leaf to 15 × 7 cm oblong-obovate. acuminate; sharp aristate teeth; bright green. **Pl. 27.**

'FUGENZO' ('James Veitch') 1892 Tokyo. Uncommon; parks and old gardens Low, very broad crown of stout, widely spreading level branches. Flowers well after 'Kanzan', double, deeper rose-pink, young leaves bronze-red.

'SHIROFUGEN' ('Albo-rosea') c. 1900. Common. Last to flower except for 'Shimidsu' and differing from that in arching and pendulous branches; unfolding leaves deep purple-red, flowers similar but pinker at first then white, dull pink before falling. A superb sight in flower. Leaf 16 × 8 cm on dark red petiole; short-aristate teeth. **Pl. 27.**

'SHIROTAE' ('Mount Fuji') c. 1905. Frequent. Low-crowned; branches level then drooping; fairly early into flower with intensely white, semi-double, (some singles) very large flowers hanging in long-stemmed clusters below bright green unfolding leaves. Fades and browns before the very similar 'Shimidsu' opens its pink buds. Leaf 12 cm, long-acuminate; long aristate teeth. Pedicels to 20 cm on late flowers.

'CHEAL'S WEEPING' ('Kikushidare Sakura'), pre-1920. Common and unmistakable low tree with rather few branches arching to the ground, usually asymmetrically. Mid-season (late-April)

'Cheal's Weeping'

in flower with leaves opening pale green, branches are strung with big, fully double very pink flowers.

'HOKUSAI' 1866. Common. Stoutly branched small tree becoming globular or broad; a pale fore-runner of 'Kanzan', in flower two weeks before it. Flowers densely held in tight bunches, pale pink with a mushroom tint, semi-double opening flat and showing the boss of dark red stamens; 4–5 cm across, among pale brown opening leaves. Autumn colours bright orange and red.

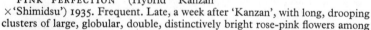

'Hokusai'

'PINK PERFECTION' (Hybrid 'Kanzan' × 'Shimidsu') 1935. Frequent. Late, a week after 'Kanzan', with long, drooping clusters of large, globular, double, distinctively bright rose-pink flowers among green or faintly bronzed young leaves. Deeper pink in bud, and flowers in various shades of pure pink unlike the uniform purplish pink of 'Kanzan'; fades pale pink. Long flowering period.

'TAI-HAKU' 1899. Frequent. The long-lost Great White Cherry of old Japan, discovered by Capt. Collingwood Ingram in Sussex. The *largest-flowered* cherry; mid-season; flowers

'Tai Haku'

strong along young shoots; in big globular bunches towards the tips of old shoots, large palest pink buds, opening pure white 6–8 cm across, broad petals *often overlapping*, entire or variably notched; *single*, with red centre; young leaves deep red; full leaf very big, 20 × 8 cm broad ovate, with long, aristate teeth; dark glossy green on 4 cm dark red petiole. Autumn colour scarlet.

'UKON' Strong-growing, rather upright at first then spreading, mid-season, large semi-double flowers on long stalks, opening pale slightly *greenish-yellow* fading to white, with red centres; young leaves yellow-brown. Unusual colour and now much planted. **Pl. 27.**

Approximate order of flowering of common forms of Prunus

Actual dates vary with season and locality but the sequence varies little although more amongst the early trees.

FIRST	*P. cerasifera*	Small white fls; green lvs.
	P.c. 'Atropurpurea'	Small pink then white fls, dark red-purple lvs.
EARLY	*P.c.* 'Nigra'	Small bright pink fls, dark red-purple lvs.
	P. dulcis	Large pink fls; later green lf.
	P. 'Accolade'	Light pink, bell-shaped; lf green.
	P. yedoensis	Medium white fls wreathed on shoots before green lf.
EARLY MID	*P. sargentii*	Small, massed pink fls; lf red-purple.
	P. 'Shirotae'	Large, white, hanging below green lf.
	P. 'Hokusai'	Large, bunched pale pink tinged brown fls; pale brown lf.
	P. 'Tai-haku'	Huge white single fls in clusters; deep red lf.
	P. 'Cheal's Weeping'	Very weeping; double pink; green lf.
LATE MID	*P.* 'Amanogawa'	Very upright, pink opening whiter.
	P. avium	Masses of single white fls; green lf.
	P. 'Ukon'	Large yellow-tinged fls later white with red centre; pale brown lf.
	P. 'Kanzan'	Massed bunches uniform purplish-pink nearly double fls; dark red lf.
LATE	*P. avium* 'Plena'	Small, globular very double white fls in dense lines; green lf.
	P. 'Pink Perfection'	Bright pink buds; big, globular pink fls paling; brownish, soon green lf.
	P. 'Shirofugen'	Pink buds; hanging, white, large dble fls; purple-red lf.
	P. 'Shimidsu'	Pink buds; hanging white, large dble fls; green lf.
	P. cerasus 'Rhexii'	Small white button-like fls; green lf.
	P. 'Fugenzo'	Deep rose pink; lvs still red at flowering.

WILD CHERRY or GEAN　*Prunus avium* L.

Native in all parts, common in many areas especially on clay over or near chalk, and common as garden and park tree. Europe, N. Africa, W. Asia. 30 × 4 m (17 × 4.5 m at Studley Royal, Yorks.).

Bark. Young trees dark grey-pink somewhat shiny, older trees purple-red, pale lenticels in prominent bands; oldest trees dark purple with wide, shallow blackish, scaly fissures, the ridges between partly grey-scaled; often much fluted.

Crown. Young trees to 20m or more, remarkably regular, conic with open whorled branching; old trees broad, dense, slightly downward-bent domes often on long boles in woodland. Frequently one or more branches is curved down by the weight of a large "witches' broom" of dense slender upswept shoots which leaf early and are cut back by frosts. This is caused by a fungus *Exoascus*.

Foliage. Shoot pale, bloomy red-brown above, fawn-grey beneath. Bud pointed ovoid, shiny red-brown. Leaf oblong-ovate or obovate, 10 × 4.5–7 cm, short-acuminate, sharply forward-serrate; petiole 2–3.5 cm, grooved, red above, yellow beneath, with 2–5 irregularly placed, stalked 'glands' near the leaf-base, leaf hanging and soft, pale beneath with small tufts in vein-axils. Autumn colours pale yellow and red.

Flowers and fruit. White flowers wreathed along shoots of young trees in short-stalked clusters, more bunched and longer stalked in old trees, very profuse, 2.5–3.5 cm across, opening just before leaves in mid-April. Fruit 3–5 in a bunch, ovoid, 2.5 cm on 3–5 cm red-brown pedicel; glossy yellowish turning bright red by July and eaten by birds before turning blackish-red.

'Plena'

'PLENA' By far the biggest in stature of the double white cherries, making a *large tree*, regularly crowded with globose fully double very white long-lasting flowers long stalked in spreading bunches, beginning as the green leaves unfold in early May, with the last of the Japanese cherries.

SOUR CHERRY　*Prunus cerasus* L.

S.E. Europe, S.W. Asia. Long cultivated. A parent of the Morello Cherry. The form grown as an ornamental tree is:

'RHEXII' Pre-1600. Frequent; gardens, especially small front gardens. (Romsey by-pass, with *P. avium* 'Plena'.) Small tree with flattened, rounded crown, rather untidy branching; noticed only when in flower in mid-May, the last cherry to flower. Flowers in bunches, each on 5 cm pedicel, white, very double, globular, 3 cm, finally opening to show green centre; hanging below green leaves which seem dark green

'Rhexii'

at a distance. Leaf bright green obovate, 6 × 4 cm, abruptly acuminate, broad-cuneate, very uneven, round toothing; petiole 2 cm, dark red. Unspectacular in comparison with, say 'Shimidsu' and dark, but pleasant.

BLACK CHERRY *Prunus serotina* Ehrh.

N.E. America, Ontario to Texas 1629. Uncommon, largely confined to some big gardens but in places used for amenity or game-covert and seeding itself. 22 × 2.5 m.

Bark. Dark purplish-grey, peeling early in raised, curved strips, becoming widely fissured brownish-pink.

Crown. Irregularly spreading out at a height from ascending branches, somewhat pendulous outside. Young trees may be broad and bushy.

Foliage. Shoot slender, dark purple-brown above, green beneath. Bud sharply conic, 5 mm green and brown. Leaf obovate or ovate, abruptly acute, to 12 × 3.5 cm, waved margin with thickened, forward, *incurved* teeth; dark *glossy* green above, paler and sub-shiny beneath, midrib prominent with bright orange or white *hairs perpendicular in patches* along each side of the basal half. Petiole almost nil to 1.5 cm, with glands at base of leaf enlarged into several green wings or minute lobes.

Flowers. 1 cm, white, on 10–15 cm cylindrical erect inflorescence.

Black Cherry

Fruit. Globular, 1 cm on pedicel 1 cm, glossy bright red, some turning dark purple.

Growth. Very vigorous, shoots on young trees nearly 2 m. Very late into leaf.

    var. *salicifolia* (Kunth) Koehne. Mexico to Peru 1820. A rare similar tree in some collections with narrower grey-green hanging leaves which lack hairs on the midrib beneath.

BIRD CHERRY *Prunus padus* L.

Native north of Midlands and in Ireland, common by streams in limestone areas as in N.W. Yorkshire. Planted frequently in gardens and sometimes in streets. Europe, Asia Minor. 15 m.

Bark. Smooth, dark grey-brown.

Crown. Young trees slender-branched, conic, upper branches ascending, lower level; older trees rounded, branches drooping.

Foliage. Shoot shiny dark brown. Bud tightly appressed, sharp, conic-ovoid, not unlike that of beech, dark brown at base, pale at tip. Leaf obovate or elliptic, to 10 × 7 cm, finely serrulate, firm and leathery with sunken veins, petiole stout, 2 cm grooved, dark red; two prominent red-brown lumpy glands by leaf; autumn colours pale yellows with some red, early.

Flowers. White, densely crowded on long spikes with leaves near base, spreading or forward-drooping 8–15 cm long, fragrant, in late May. Fruit globular, black, 8 mm.

Bird Cherry

Recognition. In flower the light green leaves distinguish from other spike-flowered cherries; out of flower rather delicate, fresh green slender-branched crown with cherry leaves.

    'PLENA' Rare. Conspicuous spikes of double, long-lasting flowers.

    'WATERERI' Frequent. Flower spikes much longer, to 20 cm, spread perpendicular; leaves with big tufts in axils beneath, sparse and remote on untidy, spreading pendulous shoots. Spectacular in flower.

MANCHURIAN CHERRY *Prunus maackii* Rupr.   **Pl. 27**
Manchuria, Korea 1910. Infrequent; large gardens and collections. 12 × 2.6m.
Bark. Young trees *smooth shiny honey-brown or gold*. Old trees pale and darker
orange coarsely and widely fissured grey.
Crown. Irregularly low-domed. Young trees narrow, upright.
Foliage. Shoot light red-brown. Bud dark red-brown, pointed. Leaf ovate to
lanceolate 8 × 5cm *almost entire* but minute peg-like teeth; dark green above;
veins below short-pubescent; petiole 1.5cm *densely pubescent*.
Flowers. Small, 1cm fragrant, white, on 4cm nearly globular erect spikes in
early May. Single long style.
Growth. Very vigorous; a bole 2.6m round was only 48 years old.
Recognition. Unique bark, for which planted, and toothing of leaf.

PORTUGAL LAUREL *Prunus lusitanica* L.
Spain, Portugal 1648. Very common as shrub and hedge or small tree, occasional
as larger specimen tree to 12 × 2.5m especially in Cornwall and Ireland.
Bark. Black and smooth, or slightly scaly.

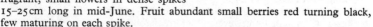

Crown. A domed, rather dense evergreen tree with level branches.
Foliage. Shoot dark red-purple above,
pale green beneath. Bud narrowly
conic, acute, bright deep red. Leaf
evergreen ovate-oblong, rounded base,
acute, coarsely forward serrate, thick,
leathery, deep glossy green above, very
matt yellow-green beneath, 8–12 ×
3.5–5cm; petiole 2cm, grooved, *dark
red.*

Portugal Laurel

Flowers and fruit. Cream-white, very
fragrant, small flowers in dense spikes
15–25cm long in mid-June. Fruit abundant small berries red turning black,
few maturing on each spike.
Similar species. *P. serotina* (p. 299) or var. *salicifolia* (which are deciduous).
Laurus nobilis (p. 268) but leaf of *Prunus* more leathery, more toothed without
crinkled edge and non-fragrant.

CHERRY LAUREL *Prunus laurocerasus* L.
S.E. Europe, Asia Minor 1576. Locally abundant
as shrub or hedge and widely spreading under-
shrub in woods; more rarely of near-tree form in
the far west, to 14m. Brown-grey, lenticelled
bark; shoot pale green; leaf large, 20 × 6cm,
obovate-lanceolate, glossy, bright yellowish-green,
obscurely toothed, on stout 2cm yellow-green
petiole. Fragrant whitish flowers in erect *short*
spikes begin to emerge in mild weather from
January, but do not open until early April or
later; fruit a large purple-black berry, 2cm.

Cherry Laurel

PEA FAMILY *Leguminosae*

About 7,000 species in 430 genera, mainly herbs and shrubs, from all non-arctic areas but most in warm or tropical regions. Flowers usually of five petals, three forming a "keel" and two forming "wings"; fruit a pod (legume); roots bearing nodules wherein are nitrogen-fixing bacteria, enabling many species to grow in very poor soils.

ACACIA

A large genus, with 400 species; world-wide, but largely tropical.

SILVER WATTLE or MIMOSA *Acacia dealbata* Link.

Silver Wattle

S.E. Australia and Tasmania 1820. Frequent S. Devon, Cornwall and Ireland; rare S.E. England where cut to the ground in hard winters but, against a wall, survives to attain 6m in about five years. To 15m in Ireland. Easily blown down.

Bark. Bright blue-green when very young; soon pale chocolate brown and very smooth even if corrugated. Older trees grey or nearly black; much fluted; some cavities.

Crown. Broadly conic; longer branches depressed.

Foliage. Shoot greenish-white with fine dense woolly pubescence, faintly ribbed, slightly zigzag. Leaf doubly compound, alternate, to 12 × 4cm. 10–12 pairs of leaflets (pinnae), no terminal leaflet; each leaflet held forwards, parallel with others, 3cm, divided into about 30 pairs of minor leaflets (pinnules) which are linear-oblong, acute 3–4mm long, raised above the common stem, often scarcely parted, finely pubescent, blue-green or yellowish-green each side.

Flowers. Large terminal inflorescence and small axillary ones, larger ones branched, bearing 20–30 globular bright yellow flowers about 3mm across. These are open in Devon in January and February. Imported by florists.

JUDAS-TREES, REDBUDS Cercis

Seven species in N. America, S. Europe and E. Asia.

JUDAS-TREE *Cercis siliquastrum* L.   Pl. 29

S. Europe; W. Asia pre-1600. Frequent in parks and gardens in S. England and East Anglia, rare beyond this to N. Wales. 12 × 1.7m.

Bark. Purplish and folded or ridged when small, later dull grey-pink with numerous fine brown fissures.

Crown. Low and irregular, usually one-sided dome, older trees largely decumbent, branches curving up from the ground.

Foliage. Shoot dark red-brown, overlaid in places by grey; lenticelled. Bud narrowly conic, appressed, small, 3–5mm dark red. Leaf alternate, nearly *orbicular*, 8–10 × 10–12cm slightly sinuate, *entire*, obscurely mucronate, pointed, veins fanwise; yellowish or dark green above, pale and glaucous beneath; petiole 5cm yellowish-green, dark red-brown at base. Leafs out pale brown.

Flowers and fruit. Flowers small, 2 cm pea-flower type, bright rosy-pink in mid-May in bunches of 3–6 from small shoots, big shoots and branches and even *directly on the bole* before or sometimes with the leaves. Fruit a pod 10 × 2 cm, very flat, bright pale purple in midsummer turning dull brown and remaining well into the winter; calyx at base bears about 15 whiskers 1 cm long.

'ALBA' White-flowered as long in cultivation as the type, but rare.
Similar species. Leaf is similar to *Cercidiphyllum* but larger, entire and petiole not scarlet. The alternate leaves of *Cercis* distinguish from *Cercidiphyllum* (p. 261).

HONEY-LOCUSTS   Gleditsia

Twelve species in N. America, tropical Africa and S. America, C., S.W. and E. Asia. Usually armed with branched spines on the bole. Alternate, pinnate and partly doubly pinnate leaf with base of petiole covering bud. Flowers with equal petals, not typical pea-flower.

HONEY-LOCUST   *Gleditsia triacanthos* L.
Mid-western USA *c.* 1700. Infrequent; almost restricted to East Anglia and S. England where occasional in city parks and gardens and large gardens generally. Very rare in Ireland (Birr Castle). 20 × 2.3 m (23 × 1.9 m at Pampisford, Cambs.).
Bark. Dark purplish-grey, wandering wide shallow scaly ridges and big bunches of ferocious *branched spines*, green when young, to 30 cm long (but see cultivar below).
Crown. Upright, widely spreading near the top where broadest; smaller branches twisting; shoots slender, sparse.
Foliage. Shoot slender, green, slightly zigzag, three spines usually by each bud. Leaf pinnate, usually without terminal leaflet, some doubly pinnate; when singly pinnate 10–15 cm long with 14–36 oblong-lanceolate leaflets 2–4 cm long, crenate-serrate towards the tip only; when doubly pinnate 20 cm with 8–14 *pinnae* each with 22 smaller (2 cm) leaflets; *glossy bright yellowish-green* or dark; briefly bright gold at end of October.
Flowers and fruit. Male flowers scattered along pubescent stalk 12 cm long, each 5–6 mm very pale yellow-green, five petals; campanulate, with anthers protruding. Female flowers on separate sparse

Honey-locust

racemes; pod 25 × 2.5 cm (30–45 cm long in warmer countries) thick-edged, twisted, thin and concave-sided, pale yellow-green in midsummer ripening brown, seen after hot seasons only.

'INERMIS' Bole and shoots *without spines*, fissures deeper and often with flanged, raised edges. Understandably the usual form in city parks and streets.
'SUNBURST' New form with leaves a rich gold, turning yellowish-green.

GYMNOCLADUS

Two species, N. American and China. Very large bi-pinnate leaf on stout, bloomed shoot. Five equal petals.

KENTUCKY COFFEE-TREE   *Gymnocladus dioicus* (L.) K. Koch
Syn. *G. canadensis* Lam.

Eastern USA pre-1748. Rare; a few large gardens in S. England and Ireland. 18 × 1.5 m (Nymans, Sussex).

Bark. Grey-brown, scaling in curved vertical lines and flaking shallow ridges; some big flanges.

Crown. Domed, open, with stout, knobbly, twisting shoots.

Foliage. Shoot very stout, glaucous-green, *bloomed violet, pink and purple,* knobbly from big, raised, concave grey leaf-scars. Bud very small, flat-domed, yellow-brown, bright orange as it swells. Leaf huge, double-pinnate, often 75 cm long, sometimes 115 × 60 cm; 0–3 basal pairs of simple leaflets, 6–7 alternate or opposite big pinnae with 6–14 small leaflets each; leaflets 5–8 cm long, ciliate, entire, rarely toothed, ovate, acute *pale fresh green* above, whitish beneath; whole leaf ends in feeble pinna of five short leaflets. Pink when unfolding, yellow in autumn, rachis remains on tree when leaflets shed.

Kentucky Coffee-tree

Flowers and fruit. Rare in these countries. Male trees with panicles 3 cm long, female trees with panicles 22 cm long, in USA; flowers long-stalked; 5 petals, white, striped green; calyx brown, pod oblong, 8–30 cm dark brown bloomed blue-purple.

Recognition. In winter, gaunt, scaly-barked tree with stout, glaucous shoots; in leaf unmistakable.

YELLOW-WOODS   Cladrastis

Four species in N. America, S. America, Australasia and E. Asia. Bud naked, hidden by base of petiole; leaf large, pinnate; flower white on large panicle.

YELLOW-WOOD   *Cladrastis lutea* (Michx.) K. Koch
Syn. *C. tinctoria* Raf.

Eastern USA, C. Alleghany Mts. 1812. Rare; a few collections and large gardens in S. England, E. Anglia and N. to Edinburgh. 10 × 1 m. Round-headed tree, lying down with age, with dark grey and smooth bark. Leaves large, pendulous, *bright green*, distantly pinnate, 20–38 cm long, 5–7(8) *widely spaced* leaflets which are obovate, abruptly acuminate, some with two lobules; veins impressed; glaucous beneath; petioles and rachis slender, green bulbous base of petiole covers several buds. Autumn colour bright yellow. Inflorescence 20–40 cm, 0–2 side branches,

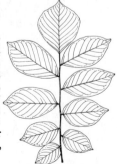

Yellow-wood

Plate 27   **PLUMS, CHERRIES**

Trees of the Rose Family.

1. Myrobalan Plum   *Prunus cerasifera* 'Nigra'   292
Dark-flowered form.

2. Prunus 'Kanzan'   295

Widely planted especially in streets; mid-late season, weighed
down with blossom.

3. Prunus 'Ukon'   297

Mid-season, opening with distinct yellow shade which is lost
after a week. Strong growing, widely branched.

4. Prunus 'Shirofugen'   296

Among the last into flower; drooping branches hung with
pink buds on long stalks, opening white beneath purplish leaves,
and fading pink weeks later.

5. Prunus 'Shimidsu'   296

Among the last into flower; pink buds opening pure ice-white
among green leaves.

6. Tibetan Cherry   *Prunus serrula*   293
Close-up of shining orange-brown bark, often mahogany-red.

7. Manchurian Cherry   *Prunus maackii*   300
Close-up of shining orange bark of young tree.

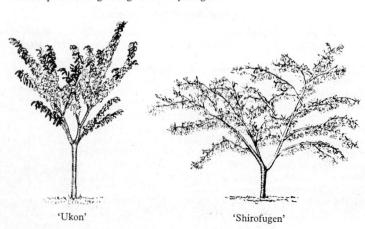

'Ukon'   'Shirofugen'

1

2

3

4

5

6 7

FRUIT TREES
Plate 28

Flowers of domestic fruit trees.

Old pear tree

Old orchard apple

Almond

Japanese Crab

pendulous, in June. Flowers of pea-flower type, white, fragrant, small, 2.5–3 cm. Pods to 8 cm, acuminate, variable in width.

Similar species. Resembles a species of ash more than any other – but leaf larger and petiole hides buds, and alternate.

SOPHORA

Twenty species in N. and S. America, Australasia and Asia. Evergreen or deciduous, several shrubby; leaf pinnate.

PAGODA or SCHOLARS' TREE   *Sophora japonica* L.

China; Korea 1753. Uncommon; collections, large gardens and a few suburban gardens and parks; S. England, E. Anglia, S. Ireland and Edinburgh R.B.G. 23 × 5m (Oxford B.G., felled 1973).

Bark. Dark brown or grey-brown, with willow-like broad ridges.

Crown. Irregular, open; heavy contorted branches; shoots nearly straight.

Foliage. Shoot blue-green, finely pubescent then green and glabrous. Bud small, scaly, hidden in bulbous base of petiole during summer. Leaves alternate, pinnate, 15–25cm long; 9–15 leaflets, entire, ovate to abrupt fine point, 3–5 cm; dark shiny green above, glaucous and pubescent beneath. Emerge pale yellow, almost white, in early June; fall late, and green.

Flowers. Only on trees some 30 years or more old and best during hot summers; start to open in early August, can be spectacular in September; spreading deep green, finely pubescent panicles 15–25cm long, longest branch 10cm, bearing white pea-flowers 1.5cm long. Fruit very rarely set, pod 5–8cm.

Growth. A very vigorous tree, to 20 × 2.3m in 63 years.

Pagoda Tree   'Pendula'

'PENDULA' Occasional in S. England. A mass of contorted branches grafted 2–3m high on stem of the type, with long-pendulous shoots to the ground. Flowering rare.

Similar species. *Robinia pseudoacacia* (p. 308) is best distinguished by the colour of the shoot and presence of spines as well as glabrous, round-tipped leaflet.

LABURNUM

Three species in S. Europe and W. Asia. Leaves trifoliate, alternate; flowers in long racemes.

COMMON LABURNUM *Laburnum anagyroides* Med.

Syn. *L..vulgare* Berchtold and Presl.

C. and S. Europe 1560. Very common in small and large gardens, parks, squares and streets; seeding itself freely. Largely replaced in modern plantings by the hybrid *L.* × *watereri* (below).

Bark. Smooth dark green then pale brown, patterned by small areas of fine orange flakes.

Crown. Ascending and arching branches, open, widest near top. Becomes thin with age and flower-racemes shorter.

Foliage. Shoot grey-green; long silky grey appressed hairs. Bud ovoid, pale grey-brown, hairy. Leaf trifoliate, petiole 2–6 cm, leaflets elliptic or obovate, 3–8 cm broad-cuneate, obtuse, grey-green above, silky and glaucous beneath.

Flowers and fruit. Flowers bright yellow, 2 cm long, crowded on pendulous racemes 15–25 cm long, mid-May–early June. Pods slender, twisted 5–8 × 0.7 cm, hang in bunches, dark brown in late summer, highly poisonous like all parts of the tree.

Growth. Rapid for a few years; very short-lived in most gardens although one is known to have been 176 years old when it was blown down.

'AUREUM' Infrequent, locally frequent, e.g. Edinburgh. Leaves on most branches bright pale yellow.

Similar species. First of the three laburnums in flower, with short and dense racemes. See *L. alpinum* (below), *L.* × *watereri* (below).

SCOTCH LABURNUM *Laburnum alpinum* Bercht. and Presl.

S. Europe 1596. Less common in England than the other two but frequent by roads in Scotland, where it reaches 12 × 2.2 m. Differs from *L. anagyroides* in much larger leaflets, 10–13 × 6 cm, ciliate but otherwise nearly glabrous, deep sub-shiny green both sides; long, slender racemes, 25–40 cm long, with flowers well-spaced down them, the flowers opening 2–3 weeks later than the Common Laburnum and pods with upper seam winged.

Scotch Laburnum

VOSS'S LABURNUM *Laburnum* × *watereri* Dipp. 'Vossii' **Pl. 29**

Syn. *L. vossii* Hort.; *L. parkesii.*

A hybrid between the two above species, this form raised in Holland and combining the best features of both in the flowers. These are conspicuously superior, especially noticeable in good laburnum years, with the long racemes of *L. alpinum* and the larger and densely borne flowers of *L. anagyroides*, opening with *L. anagyroides*. This hybrid is now the most commonly planted laburnum.

The dense curtains of flowers hang below branches much more densely leafed than in the more open, sparse *L. anagyroides*. Fruit scarcely developed, only 1–3 per catkin, curved, to 4 cm. This is a great advantage for planting near schools since they do not attract children like the bunches of filled fruit of Common Laburnum and so are very unlikely to poison them although equally toxic if eaten. Central leaflets 6–8 cm, underside pale, glabrous.

ADAM'S LABURNUM +*Laburnocytisus adamii* (Poit.) Schneid.
Syn. *Laburnum adami* Kirchn.
Vitry, Paris 1825. A curiosity popular in Victorian gardens, now less seen but in many parks and gardens and even by roads (e.g. Wallington, Surrey). A graft-hybrid, or "chimaera" of mixed tissues of *Laburnum anagyroides* and the dwarf shrub *Cytisus purpureus* Scop. Small tree like a small-leafed laburnum with occasional bunches of much smaller shoots bearing little *Cytisus* leaves and purple flowers in short bunches. Other parts bear copper-pink or pinkish-purple laburnum-like flowers, or smaller than normal, yellow laburnum flowers. Slow-growing tree of poor shape, but of unfailing interest when in flower.

LOCUST TREES Robinia

Twenty species in N. America and Mexico. Bud hidden in the base of the petiole; stipules usually spiny; leaf pinnate; flowers white or pink in pendulous racemes.

LOCUST TREE or FALSE ACACIA *Robinia pseudoacacia* L. Pl. 29
Eastern and mid-western USA *c.* 1636. Very common in gardens and parks and suburbs on sandy soils in S. England, spreading by root-suckers; less common on heavier soils in the same region; common in the Midlands, uncommon in the North, in Scotland and Ireland. 30 × 5 m.
Bark. Young trees rich brown and smooth, soon fissured and ridged; old trees dull grey with a network of thick, broad ridges.
Crown. Rough, open, broadest near the top; branches twisting; bole short, often double, or two or three stems fused; fluted and burred.
Foliage. Shoot dark red, ribbed; paired short spines at each bud. Winter bud small, naked, folded leaves hidden in petioles until leaf-fall. Leaf alternate, pinnate, 15–20 cm, usually 13–15 leaflets, opposite or sub-opposite. 3.5 × 2.5 cm on petiolule 2 mm; oval, entire, notched and minutely spined at rounded apex, dark or yellowish-green above; greyish-green, at first minutely pubescent, later glabrous, beneath. Leaves at first bright, pale yellow.
Flowers and fruit. Flowers mid to late June, white and fragrant, profuse in some years, pea-flower type, in dense racemes 10–20 cm long. Pod oblong 5–10 cm hanging into winter, dark brown, in bunches.

'AUREA' Rare, old form, to 20 m; leaves pale yellow turning greenish-yellow in midsummer (not to be thought a giant 'Frisia', (p. 309)).

'FASTIGIATA' ('Pyramidalis') 1839 France. Uncommon; very narrowly fastigiate; upright sinuous branches. 17 m.

'INERMIS' 1800 France. Thornless, dense, grafted on clean bole of the type, made into the non-flowering mop-headed trees of some suburban streets and parks.

'FRISIA' 1935 Holland. Now common in gardens in S. England. Good golden leaves remaining gold until autumn when they turn slightly orange. Greener in some shade, and mid-July before second growth.

Similar species. *Sophora japonica* (p. 306) is very similar in aspect and foliage, but green shoots distinguish it.

ROSE-ACACIA   *Robinia hispida* L.

South-eastern USA 1743. Properly a shrub but in some southern gardens as a small tree with a spreading head, grafted on a stem of *R. pseudoacacia*. Handsome in June or August when laden with short racemes of 5–6 of the largest flowers in the genus, 3 cm long and deep rose. The shoots and sepals are covered in crimson or purple bristles; leaf dark green, purplish on late growth, 10 cm; 9–13 elliptic mucronate-tipped leaflets 2.5 × 1.5 cm, slightly glaucous beneath on grooved finely bristly rachis.

Rose-acacia

RUE FAMILY   *Rutaceae*

About 1,000 species, mostly tropical.

EUODIA   (Evodia)

Fifty species in S. and E. Asia, Australia and Polynesia. Bud naked, leaf usually pinnate, opposite, flowers unisexual in flattened heads, open late in summer.

EUODIA   *Euodia hupehensis* Dode (*Evodia hupehensis* Dode)

C. China 1908. Rare; in collections but also in London parks and a few unexpected places; Ireland, S. and C. Scotland. (20 × 2 m, Glasnevin B.G. Dublin; 18 × 2.5 m Greenwich Park, London).

Bark. Very smooth, dark grey, speckled or streaked brown.

Crown. Low-domed, from short, stout bole and ascending lower branches.

Foliage. Shoot purple-brown with pale lenticels. Bud naked, a small *folded leaf* densely *hairy, red-brown*. Leaf opposite, pinnate, 20–25 cm, 5–9 leaflets, with oblique bases, short-acuminate, cupped and glossy dark green above; leathery; whitish-green below with long hairs in vein-axils; very shallow teeth, mere notches; rachis and midrib glabrous, may be pink.

Flowers and fruit. Flowers, with small white petals, sexes on separate

Euodia

inflorescences males with 5 yellow anthers, in *early September*, on broad-conic heads 10–15 cm across. Fruit small, erect pods red-brown, sometimes bright red.

Recognition. Smooth grey bark, opposite, pinnate, very glossy dark leaves and autumn-flowering. A choice tree. Several other species grown in a few collections are scarcely separable, except *E. velutina* Rehd. & Wils. with dense soft down.

PHELLODENDRON

Eight to nine species in E. Asia. Bud naked, leaf pinnate, opposite, flowers in big terminal panicles.

AMUR CORK-TREE *Phellodendron amurense* Rupr.

Amur Cork-tree

N. China, Manchuria 1856. Rare, collections in S. England only. 15 × 2 m. Gaunt tree with grey, corky bark in coarse, thick ridges; stout orange-brown wrinkled shoots; small, naked, hairy grey buds hidden in summer in petioles; leaves opposite, pinnate 25–40 cm long with 7–13 leaflets (sometimes 10), ovate, long-acuminate with curved point, 10 × 5 cm dark glossy green contrasting with yellow-green rachis and midrib; tuft of hair at the base of each midrib. Flowers on terminal panicles 15 × 8 cm irregularly branched; 8 mm, no petals, white stamens, brilliant yellow anthers. Fruit a bunch of 8–10 on each branch of panicle, smooth globose berries, 8 mm freckled pale and dark green.

JAPANESE PHELLODENDRON *Phellodendron japonicum* Maxim.

Japan *c*.1863. Rare; collections. 12 × 1.6 m. Differs from *P. amurense* in network of ridges on non-corky bark; uniformly dark yellow-green leaf and rachis, the latter densely pubescent, and leaflets *white-pubescent beneath*.

QUASSIA FAMILY *Simaroubaceae*

Some 150 species, mainly tropical. Only the very rare *Picrasma* and three species of *Ailanthus* are grown here.

TREES OF HEAVEN Ailanthus

Eight to nine species in S. and E. Asia and N. Australasia. Alternate, pinnate, long leaf, leaflets with few large teeth near the base.

TREE OF HEAVEN *Ailanthus altissima* (Mill.) Swingle   **Pl. 30**
Syn. *A. glandulosa* Desf.

N. China 1751. Common in London squares, streets and parks, frequent in gardens in S. England and E. Anglia, rare north to S. Scotland and in Ireland.

26 × 3.7 m (26 × 3.9 m at The Wakes, Selborne, Hants. Fine trees at Abbey, Bury St Edmunds; 30.5 × 2.9 m Endsleigh, Devon).

Bark. Young trees smooth grey-brown to blackish, patterned vertically with *white angular streaks*; old trees smooth but finely roughened, dark grey, streaked in pewter-grey or buff, often with a pattern of curving dark streaks scaling very finely.

Crown. Usually a good, straight, cylindrical bole, then stout, strongly ascending branches bearing a tall, irregular dome. Root-suckers may arise, some a great distance from the bole.

Foliage. Shoot stout, orange-brown, lenticelled; large grey leaf-scars. Bud small, ovoid, red-brown, becoming scarlet as it swells in late April. Leaf unfolds late, mid-June, bright deep red; alternate, pinnate, 30–60 cm (90 cm on young trees or sprouts after cutting back), 11–18(42) leaflets, very unequally cordate, one side overlapping rachis; oblong-lanceolate, entire except for 1–3 big teeth each side near the base, each with a raised wrinkled "gland"; crinkled and shiny, deep green above, pale and glabrous beneath, 7–15 cm long on red petiolule 0.5–1.5 cm long; emitting an unpleasant smell when crushed; rachis green or red; falling leaves late and green, the rachis remaining below the tree when leaflets rotted.

Flowers and fruit. Male and female usually on separate trees; males large greenish panicles, red in bud in early July, cream when open late July. four short broad petals. Fruit in big panicles to 30 × 30 cm, each seed in a membranous wing 4 × 1 cm, 1–5 wings on each stalk, bright crimson on outer side in late summer and autumn.

DOWNY TREE OF HEAVEN *Ailanthus vilmoriniana* Dode

W. China 1897. Rare; collections and a few gardens in S. England and at Edinburgh RBG. Small green spines occasional on new shoots; better distinguished by darker leaves, *drooping* to show consistently *deep red* rachis usually longer (1 m on pollards) with more leaflets, 20–23–35, *pubescent* beneath. The rachis is *finely pubescent* and the bole may have sprouts. 21 × 1.5 m.

Downy Tree of Heaven

QUASSIAS Picrasma

Eight species in tropical and subtropical regions. Bud naked, leaf pinnate alternate.

PICRASMA *Picrasma quassioides* (D. Don) Benn.
Syn. *P. ailanthoides* Planch.

China, Japan, India 1890. Rare, S. England. 12 × 1 m (9 × 1.6 m, Kew). Low rounded tree; shoot *dark chocolate-purple*, bud at first scarlet and minute, later pale brown, two leaves facing each other; leaf pinnate, 9–11 sub-sessile leaflets terminal one on long petiolule; heart-shaped, sharply serrated, glossy rich green on crimson rachis. Flowers four parted, yellow-green, or dark red, spaced on abundant, widely branched conic dark red panicles to 15 cm long, spreading from the axils. Fruit obovoid orange-red berry turning black. Handsome in leaf, colouring bright red and yellow in autumn.

Picrasma

MAHOGANY FAMILY *Meliaceae*

Six hundred species, nearly all tropical.

CEDRELA

About 18 species in tropical America, and S.E. Asia to Australia. Leaf usually evenly pinnate (no terminal leaflet).

CHINESE CEDAR *Cedrela sinensis* Juss.
N. and W. China 1862. Rare; collections and some large gardens in England, S. Scotland and C. and E. Ireland. 25 m in Cornwall, elsewhere 18 × 2 m.

Bark. Young trees rather like walnut, dark purplish or coppery-grey, coarsely fissured into smooth, lenticelled plates. Old trees dark pinkish-grey, coarsely shaggy.

Crown. Gaunt with few stout branches from straight bole and stout upcurved shoots; very open.

Foliage. Shoot stout, *pale orange*, warty, pubescent, at first. Bud squat globular, green; pointed scales project at tip. Leaf very large, 50–70 cm evenly pinnate (usually no terminal leaflet), borne in short whorls at the ends of the shoots, (10)20–30 leaflets 12 × 4 cm oblong-lanceolate, acuminate, slightly oblique broad-cuneate, on short red petiolule, very small distant teeth; crinkled; upper surface matt bright green, pale

Chinese Cedar

veins; pale and smooth beneath, dense pubescence each side of midrib, some hairs at first on veins.

Flowers. Big *pendulous* terminal panicles 50 × 20 cm, dense with small white flowers in July.

Similar species. *Rhus verniciflua* (p. 314).

BOX FAMILY *Buxaceae*

About 40 evergreen trees and shrubs, mostly tropical; unisexual flowers without petals, in hermaphrodite inflorescence.

BOXES Buxus

About 30 species in northern sub-tropical regions. Leaf evergreen, opposite; flowers without petals.

BOX *Buxus sempervirens* L.

Native on chalk and limestone in Kent, Surrey, Bucks. and Glos. Very common in gardens of all kinds, parks, churchyards and as hedge. S. Europe and N. Africa. 10 × 0.8 m.

Bark. Pale brown, deeply cut into small squares, weathering pale grey in old stands on hillsides.

Crown. Tree-form scarce north of native range; one or more sinuous boles; one-sided or leaning; dense above clean stems, rather narrow, often pointed.

Foliage. Shoot square in section, green, minutely orange-pubescent. Bud 1–2 mm cylindric, domed, pale orange-brown, densely pubescent, mostly hidden by leaves. Leaf evergreen, opposite, hard, leathery, elliptic, 2–3 cm long, entire, glossy dark green above, less glossy yellow-green or pale beneath, only midrib prominent with fine white speckling; emitting a peculiar sweet smell when damp and warm. Petiole 1 mm pale orange from pubescence.

Box

Flowers. Clustered at base of leaves, usually female flower in centre (three short styles) and 5–6 male flowers (four stamens) surrounding, open in April, a good yellow to look at, but "pale green" in books. Fruit a three-horned capsule, globose, blue-green, glaucous bloom.

Similar species. *B. balearica* (below).

BALEARIC BOX *Buxus balearica* Lam.

Spain, Balearic Is., Sardinia 1780. Rare; few collections and gardens north to East Lothian. 11 × 0.6 m. Differs from *B. sempervirens* in paler pinkish bark, *larger* leaf 3–5 cm, *dull*, in pairs farther apart (1 cm) and shoot flattened at nodes. Flowers larger, 1 cm, in terminal axils; males with broad white stamens (petalloid); females with 3–4 horns, becoming in the fruit as long as the capsule.

Balearic Box

CASHEW FAMILY *Anacardiaceae*

Four hundred species from warm regions.

SUMACS Rhus

About 150 species in all subtropical and temperate regions. Deciduous or ever-green, some climbers (Poison Ivy is *R. toxicodendron*). Leaf simple or large and pinnate.

VARNISH TREE *Rhus verniciflua* Stokes
The Himalaya, China, Japan 1874. Infrequent; large gardens and collections N. to Edinburgh and in Ireland. 15 × 1.7 m.

Bark. Dark grey with black diamonds joining to form vertical fissures; older trees flaking in curving patterns.
Crown. Upright, rather gaunt, on good straight stem; stout shoots bend down then curve up; open, domed; leaves whorled.
Foliage. Shoot very stout, *pale grey*, freckled orange-brown, rough. Bud like a nut of Sweet Chestnut, stout ovoid, shiny brown, terminal bud beaked. Leaf alternate, odd-pinnate, 50–80cm, basal 25cm of yellow and scarlet-striped rachis free of leaflets, 7–19 leaflets, terminal largest to 20 × 10cm others to 17 × 6cm sub-opposite, on petiolules 0.5cm; oblique at base, curly long-acuminate, entire, leathery, glossy bright green, darkening; lax, hanging at various angles; crushed give faint balsam scent. Autumn colours splendid reds and crimson. Sap is poisonous to some people and raises blisters.

Varnish Tree

Flowers and fruit. Flowers small, inconspicuous, yellowish-white on numer-ous prominent panicles, *radiating in whorls* from ends of shoots, each *50 cm long*, sparsely branched; fruit glossy, pale brownish-cream berry, 6 × 8mm. A fine vigorous tree, handsome in leaf.
Similar species. Another of these large, pinnate-leaved trees. Most like *Cedrela* (p. 312) but with a terminal leaflet, other leaflets larger, and bark and bud differ.

CHINESE VARNISH TREE *Rhus potaninii* Maxim.
C. and W. China 1902. Rare; collections as far north as Edinburgh. 18 × 2m. Usually on several curved stems with smooth grey-pink bark, and differing from *Rh. verniciflua* also in shorter leaf hanging with terminal *leaflet projecting* level, 40cm; 7–9 leaflets, narrowly cuneate, sessile and usually coarsely toothed. Flowers white with red anthers on panicles 12–15cm. Autumn colours pink to crimson.

HOLLY FAMILY *Aquifoliaceae*

Three hundred species from both hemispheres, in three genera.

HOLLIES Ilex

About 300 species in warmer parts of each hemisphere. Many evergreen, most dioecious; fruit a berry-like drupe.

HOLLY *Ilex aquifolium* L.　　　　　　　　　　　　　　　　　　**Pl. 30**

Native except in Caithness, Orkney, Shetland. Very common as understorey in beech and oakwoods, also in hedges and found on rocky hillsides to over 550 m. Planted in gardens for shelter, hedge or berries, and as cultivars for evergreen, coloured foliage. W., C. and S. Europe and Mediterranean. 22.5 × 1.8 m.

Bark. Smooth pinkish-grey freckled and striated buff; larger trees dull silvery-grey, often with large warts.

Crown. Young trees symmetrically narrow-conic, spired, small branches up-curved; older trees irregular, dense, rather pendulous.

Foliage. Shoot bright green or deep purple, grooved on outer half, thick; shoots 5–6 years old still green and by then, shiny. Bud a minute green, conic cap on the end of the shoot. Leaves show great variation within a single tree. In shade and lower parts of crown tend to have spines all over, but in open, toothing and buckled margin decline irregularly with height in crown and much of upper part bears plane, entire, ovate leaves. Normal lower leaves oblong-elliptic, 6–8 cm long, 6–8 spreading yellowish spines pointing alternately somewhat upwards and downwards due to buckling of margin, glossy dark green, pale midrib, other veins obscure; underside dead matt, bright green; petiole flattened above, stout, 1 cm.

Flowers and fruit. Flower-buds crowded in leaf-axils, pale purple until expanding, open in May, white, fragrant, almost wreathing stem, male and female on separate trees, 6–8 mm, similar except having either anthers only or styles only. Fruit globose, 7–10 mm on stalks 4–8 mm, scarlet, persisting through mild winters until next summer but may be raided suddenly, by Fieldfares especially, during hard weather in February.

'ALBOMARGINATA' and 'Argenteomarginata' Several forms with cream-margined leaves, including 'Silver Queen', 'Handsworth New Silver' (with deep purple shoots) and 'Argenteomarginata Pendula' or 'Perry's Weeping Holly' with a long-pendulous dome, rather striking. To 12 × 1 m. Common. See p. 325.

'AUREOMARGINATA' Yellow-margined leaves. To 17 × 1.5 m.

'BACCIFLAVA' ('Fructu-Luteo') Female form with bright, pale yellow berries, most attractive against the normal blackish leaves. Infrequent.

'CRISPA' Mainly entire leaves twisted and contorted. 14 × 1 m. Infrequent.

'Ferox'

'FEROX' Hedgehog Holly. Infrequent. Small leaves with rows of small spines along the upper surface. Variegated form about as frequent.

'GOLDEN QUEEN' Handsome male form with broad leaves widely margined yellow. Frequent.

'PENDULA' Domed and weeping to the ground. Female. Frequent.

'PYRAMIDALIS' Good conic, level-branched female form free with fruit. Leaves mainly entire, bright green. Frequent. 10m.

Similar species. Many other well-known cultivars, mainly of stronger growth, will now be found under *I. × altaclarensis* (below).

HIGHCLERE HOLLY   *Ilex × altaclarensis* Dallim.

A hybrid between the Common Holly and the Canary Holly, *Ilex perado,* Ait. apparently arising at Highclere, Berks. The various forms differ from Common Holly in greater vigour; shoots stout and flattened; broad plane leaves to 9 × 8 cm with *forward* spines 0–7 mainly towards the tip. Many common purple-shooted and flat-leaved, vigorous holly cultivars belong here. The type is now unknown; the common form is 'Hodginsii'.

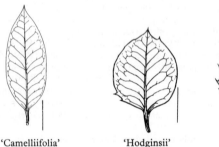 

'Camelliifolia'   'Hodginsii'   'Wilsonii'

'CAMELLIIFOLIA' Very handsome; big, glossy, ovate and ovate-lanceolate, largely entire leaves to 13 × 6 cm unfolding orange-brown. Crown conic. Female. Petals violet at base. Fruit 1.2 × 1 cm. 20 × 1.5 m. Infrequent.

'GOLDEN KING' Female form; leaves boldly margined rich yellow, with few spines. Frequent. Leaf oblong-elliptic, flat or margins down-curved, 10 × 5 cm, some with a few, small appressed teeth; margin deep yellow to varying widths, centre dark green; some new leaves entirely bright yellow. See p. 325.

'HENDERSONII' Less common than 'Hodginsii'; *female*, with big fruit; leaves dull, broad, oblong often decurved; Shoot usually green. 14 m.

'HODGINSII' Male; shoot purple (green in shade); leaf glossy, many entire, others with few teeth; oval or elliptic, slightly folded along midribs or quite plane, 8–9 × 4–8 cm, underside very matt pale yellow-green. Flowers big, 1.2 cm, outside of petals tinged purple. Common especially in industrial towns and near sea. Rather metallic sheen identifies at a distance. 14 m.

'LAWSONIANA' Leaf marbled with bright yellow, pale yellow and dark and light greens; to 10 × 6 cm, nearly entire. Female; a form of 'Hendersonii' liable to revert. Rare, bushy, low tree. 5 m. See p. 325.

'NOBILIS' Almost as 'Hodginsii' but more luxuriant, more spiny and purple; leaves mixed, lower (shaded) tend to be large and spiny, to 11 × 10 cm, some others small, entire, 5 × 3 cm.

'WILSONII' Female form with very handsome highly glossed, big broad leaves unfolding dark purple to 14×9cm, broad-elliptic, yellowish-green; minutely thickened margin, clear yellow; with 4–10 yellow spines each side, 5–6mm long; forward. Veins sunken, yellow. Rare. 10m.

PERNY'S HOLLY   *Ilex pernyi* Franch.
C. and W. China 1900. Rare; a few big gardens and collections. Curiously open, narrow, spiky crown with blackish glossy leaves crowded along stems; rhombic, 2–3 cm long, cordate 1–3 spined lobes each side and long terminal lobe. New leaves khaki-green. 17 × 0.3m.

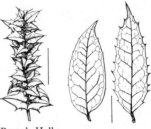

HIMALAYAN HOLLY   *Ilex dipy-rena* Wall.
E. Himalayas 1840. Rare; some large gardens in S. England. 12 × 1.5 m. Bark grey-brown, finely roughened. Usually

Perny's Holly

Himalayan Holly
(juvenile leaf toothed) juv.

forks low with curving boles and branches. Shoots angular; leaf dull, dark blue-green above: 8–12 ×3 cm, oblong-lanceolate, mostly entire, or with 1–8 spiny teeth each side, spreading or very closely appressed; bright green and sub-shiny beneath; often held regularly pectinate on shoot. Male flowers clustered in axils. Fruit dull red, numerous but well-spaced.

MAPLE FAMILY   *Aceraceae*

Variously reckoned as 115 to nearly 300 species of which all but two are maples in the genus *Acer*. The two are both *Dipteronia* from China; one is in cultivation.

DIPTERONIA

DIPTERONIA   *Dipteronia sinensis* Oliv.
China 1900. Shrubby tree in a few collections. Dark green pinnate leaves 40 cm long with 11–15 leaflets, the basal pair trifoliate, all coarsely crenate; dark red rachis; seed in circular membrane, 3.5 × 2.5 cm on wide-branched, open panicle 25 × 25 cm, deep red pedicels, following very small whitish flowers with reduced petals. Leaves emerge deep red. 10 m.

Dipteronia

MAPLES   Acer

The maples have opposite, mostly simple leaves, mostly lobed but a few entire or mixed, and fruit with two membranous wings. Flowers with or without petals, in racemes or panicles which may be unisexual or hermaphrodite or perfect.

Key to Acer species

1. Leaves unlobed, consistently, or mixed with lobed **2**
   Leaves consistently lobed or compound **11**

2. All leaves unlobed **3**
   Leaves mixed, lobed and unlobed on same tree **8**

3. About 25 pairs of parallel veins; oblong-lanceolate   *carpinifolium*, p. 341
   Mainly fan-veined, few parallel; ovate **4**

4. Lobulate or coarsely toothed **5**
   Crenate or serrulate; not lobulate **7**

5. Broad-ovate, to 5 × 7.5 cm; inflorescence erect   *tataricum*, p. 339
   Ovate-acuminate; inflorescence arched **6**

6. Petiole slender, bright red; leaves rounded at base   *tetramerum*, p. 346
   Petiole stout, yellow and pink; leaves cordate
   davidii 'Ernest Wilson', p. 342

7. Leaves nearly orbicular, thick; inflorescence erect   *distylum* p. 341
Leaves ovate-acuminate, not thick; inflorescence arched
                                                   davidii 'George Forrest', p. 342

8 Leaf margin entire   *sempervirens*, p. 327
Leaf margin toothed or partly and obscurely so   **9**

9. Leaves cuneate, three-nerved, glaucous beneath, partly and
    obscurely toothed   *buergeranum*, p. 338
Leaves cordate, fully toothed, not prominently three-nerved,
    green beneath   **10**

10. Shoot and petiole scarlet or dark red   *davidii* 'George Forrest' p. 342
Shoot and petiole yellow-green, rarely pink   *hersii*, p. 344

11. Leaves simple   **12**
Leaves compound   **48**

12. Leaves plainly three-lobed, rounded or cuneate; no basal
    lobules   **13**
Leaves 3–5 (11 +) lobed, lobuled or lobed near base   **27**

13. Margin entire or partly and obscurely toothed   **14**
Margin fully toothed   **17**

14. Leaves huge, 20 × 15; petiole stout 20-25 cm; lobes terminal
                                           platanoides 'Stollii', p. 323
Leaves small, less than 10 cm long   **15**

15. Leaves 5–9 cm, fresh green, glaucous beneath   *buergeranum*, p. 338
Leaves 3–5 cm, dark, blackish-green   **16**

16. Evergreen; leaves thick, hard; margin waved, ± lobulate
                                               sempervirens, p. 327
Deciduous; leaves not thick, margin plane and straight
                                            monspessulanum, p. 328

17. Leaves silvery beneath   *rubrum*, p. 347
Leaves green beneath   **18**

18. Leaves less than 8 cm long   **19**
Leaves more than 10 cm long   **20**

19. Lobes lobulate; very thin; veins pink   *crataegifolium*, p. 343
Lobes deeply and sharply toothed   *ginnala*, p. 338

20. Lobes terminal, very broad at base   **21**
Lobes in lower half or middle of leaf, not very broad   **22**

21. Leaves 10–12 cm long; lobes obtuse, coarsely toothed   *opalus*, p. 329
Leaves 15–20 cm long; lobes long-acuminate, evenly serrate
                                              pensylvanicum, p. 343

22. Vein-axils beneath with minute pegs   **23**
Vein-axils beneath with tufts of hair or orange stain   **25**

23. Leaves bright green; veins sunken; mid-lobe narrow-tri-
angular *capillipes,* p. 345
Leaves deep green, very smooth; mid-lobe ovate-acuminate **24**

24. Shoot, petiole and bud dark red *davidii* 'George Forrest', p. 342
Shoot, petiole and bud yellow-green or pink *hersii,* p. 344

25. Tufts in axils white; leaf plane, dark; veins pale *forrestii,* p. 345
Tufts or stains in axils rusty-orange; leaves crinkled **26**

26. Bud slender, red; leaves highly variable in size and shape,
shoot not bloomed *pensylvanicum,* p. 343
Bud ovoid, pale blue-grey; shoot bloomed, leaves only normal
in variations *rufinerve,* p. 343

27. Margin of lobes entire **28**
Margin of main lobes with one or more teeth **29**

28. All lobes ending in straight filament *cappadocicum,* p. 326
Basal lobes finely rounded; filaments of others twisted *lobelii,* p. 327

29. Teeth one, or few, scattered, $\pm$ asymmetrically **30**
Teeth a pair or several, symmetrical on main lobe, or fine serrations **32**

30. Main lobes filamented *lobelii,* p. 327
No lobes filamented **31**

31. Leaves blackish, veins and petiole dark red; tufts in axils
beneath at base only $\times$ *zoeschense,* p. 330
Leaves pale, thin; petiole bright red; tufts in all main axils
beneath $\times$ *dieckii,* p. 327

32. Teeth at shoulder of lobe very large **33**
Serrate, crenate or lobulate **37**

33. Lobes ending in filaments **34**
Lobes without filaments **35**

34. Teeth ending in filaments; lobes broad-based; bud green
platanoides, p. 321
Teeth finely rounded; mid-lobe narrows to base; bud dark
brown *saccharum,* p. 330

35. Lobes shallow, broad-based; leaves pale green *miyabei,* p. 323; *diabolicum,*
p. 346
Lobes deep, narrowed to base; leaves dark green **36**

36. Leaves very large, to 30 $\times$ 35 cm, thin texture *macrophyllum,* p. 330
Leaves small, 5–10 cm, hard *campestre,* p. 328

37. Leaves silvered beneath **38**
Leaves green or whitish-green beneath **39**

38. Leaves to 10 cm; lobes less than half blade, dark green,
crenate *rubrum,* p. 347
Leaves to 15 cm; lobes more than half blade, pale green,
deeply incised serrate *saccharinum,* p. 330

39 Lobes coarsely serrate   **40**
    Lobes finely and deeply serrate   **45**

40. Lobes broad, seldom as deep as half the leaf   **41**
    Lobes narrow and deep; well beyond half the leaf **44**

41. Petiole yellow or green, stout, to 22 cm; leaves yellow-green
                           velutinum var. *vanvolxemii*, p.335
    Petiole pink or red, not stout, to 15 cm, leaves dark green **42**

42. Petiole longer than blade, very slender, 9–11 cm   *hyrcanum*, p. 330
    Petiole equal to or shorter than blade, not slender **43**

43. Lobes scarcely toothed, shallow, rounded; bud conic   *opalus*, p. 329
    Lobes coarsely serrate, not shallow, acute; bud ovoid
                              pseudoplatanus, p. 331

44. Main lobes about equal, cut to 1.5 cm of base of leaf   *heldreichii*, p. 334
    Mid-lobe broadest, narrowed to base, cut to 3 cm of base
                            trautvetteri, p. 335

45. Three main lobes large, two to four basal ones small; main
    lobes drawn out into long, deeply serrated filaments; dark
    green, crinkled   *argutum*, p. 346
    Five-seven-nine lobes nearly equal $\pm$ two basal smaller;
    leaves round or oval   **46**

46. Lobes half or more of blade, long-acuminate, narrow-based   **47**
    Lobes less than half blade, short-acuminate, broad-based
                            japonicum, p. 340

47. Leaves shallowly serrate, truncate, five-seven lobes   *palmatum*, p. 339
    Leaves deeply incised, deeply cordate, nine-eleven lobes
                       pseudosieboldianum, p. 340

48. Leaflets three-five-seven on same shoot; shoot smooth, green
    often bloomed violet   *negundo*, p. 349
    Leaflets consistently three; shoot pubescent, red or brown **49**

49. Petiole glabrous; lateral leaflets stalked   *cissifolium*, p. 349
    Petiole woolly-pubescent; lateral leaflets sessile   **50**

50. Petiole stout; leaf dark and hard   **51**
    Petiole slender; leaf pale and soft   *triflorum*, p. 348

51. Prominent tooth at shoulder of leaflet   *griseum*, p. 349
    Teeth obscure, irregular or absent   *nikoense*, p. 348

NORWAY MAPLE *Acer platanoides* L.   **Pl. 31**
Europe north to S. Sweden and the southern tip of Norway; Caucasus. Before
1683. Common in S. England in gardens, shelterbelts, parks and sometimes in
streets; very numerous and seeding itself in some residential areas on sandy
soils; more confined to large gardens and parks in N. England and in Wales,
uncommon N. to Argyll and Perthshire. 27 × 4m.
Bark. Pale grey, smooth, finely *folded*, or shallowly ridged in a network.

Crown. Tall-domed, sometimes very broad on a short bole; open in winter with rather short perpendicular shoots and often thin bunches of persistent fruits; very densely leafed in summer.

Foliage. Shoot pinkish-brown or olive-brown. Bud tall-ovoid; terminals, dark red or red-brown, laterals green appressed. Leaf has five short-acuminate lobes, *filament-tipped* as are large teeth on the shoulders and from there to the tip; three main lobes nearly parallel-sided, basal two triangular; cordate, 12 × 15 cm, thin-textured, bright nearly shiny green, paler beneath with small white axil-tufts. Petiole 15 cm (8–10 on old trees, to 20 on young). Autumn colour generally a good butter-yellow towards end October, but odd trees scarlet in early October, and in some years most turn from yellow to orange.

Flowers and fruit. Flowers out before leaves late March, last well into April and until leaves out, bright acid-yellow-green; five oval petals and big, green disc; in erect pubescent panicles of about 30–40 flowers, each 8 mm across. Fruit yellow-green with widely spread flat wings, 6–10 cm across the pair.

Growth. Very rapid for some years; shoots to 2 m for 3–4 years but slows soon after. Growth in girth remains vigorous to 3 cm a year for 100 years. Not long-lived in general but one in Scotland, now thin, is 250 years old.

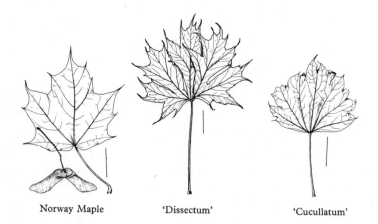

Norway Maple   'Dissectum'   'Cucullatum'

'DRUMMONDII' 1903 Stirling. Frequent and striking, variegated heavily with white blotches, spots and margins; leaves small, thin, densely held. Crown globular.

'SCHWEDLERI' 1870. All buds bright deep red; leaves unfold bright pinkish-red, turn dark purple-tinged green in summer and deep red-orange and purple in autumn. Flowers on dark red peduncles with large oblong bud-scales at base, 2 × 1 cm, dark red-purple, decurved; flowers with red-tinged sepals; petals elliptic, yellow-green smaller than in the type. Fruit a bright green seed, pale crimson wings. Common in parks, gardens and streets and on village greens. 24 × 2.5 m. 'Purple'-leaved forms are confused. Other books state that leaves of 'Schwedleri' are green in summer, but they are a very dark and purplish-green. Some trees too big to be any of the cultivars below, have red-purple leaves all summer and are labelled 'Schwedleri'.

'GOLDSWORTH PURPLE' 1936 marketed 1949. Seedling of 'Schwedleri' and far too common. Big leaves to 15 × 20 cm on petiole 20 cm; dark purplish-red above, green beneath with red veins; remaining a heavy dark offensive purple all summer.

'CRIMSON KING' 1946 Orleans. Now lost in 'Goldsworth Purple', which is sold under either name but, when found, has leaves a superior deep ruby-red, and red beneath.

'FAASSEN'S BLACK' 1936 Belgium. Slightly darker form of 'Goldsworth Purple' with large leaves tinged brownish. Frequent.

'LACINIATUM' **Eagle-claw Maple** pre-1792. Rare. Collections only. Slender, upright tree with arching high branchlets; leaves broad-cuneate on wire-thin 12 cm petioles; long-acuminate basal lobes, main lobes cut two thirds to base of leaf; lobe-ends curved down. 15 m.

'LORBERGII' ('Palmatum') 1845. Infrequent, broad little tree to 12 m with big, deep green leaves, 10 × 17 cm on red and yellow petiole 15 cm; main lobes narrow to mere wings at base and are themselves cut two thirds to base by secondary lobes; lobes and teeth ending in fine, upturned whiskers. Bole short and burred.

'DISSECTUM' ('Palmatifidum') 1845 Belgium. A low bushy tree, similar to 'Lorbergii' but more bushy and tips of leaves not raised. Bark rough, oak-like.

'CUCULLATUM' Pre-1880. A fine, tall, nearly fastigiate tree to 23 × 2 m in some collections (notably Westonbirt and Kensington Gardens). Leaf hooded, crinkled, nearly circular in outline with 7–10 veins fanwise; 12 × 13 cm; 10–12 spiked, shallow lobes with occasional teeth; cuneate or truncate to slender 10 cm petiole. In autumn splashed crimson on green.

'STOLLII' Seedling from 'Schwedleri'. 1888 Berlin. Very rare. Big leaf, 20 × 18 cm on 25 cm stout red petiole; three big terminal lobes, each 3.5 cm deep, acute; dark leathery green. 18 m at Kew.

Similar species. In winter bark and bud distinguish from *A. pseudoplatanus* (p. 331) and straight bole and branches from *A. cappadocicum* (p. 326). In leaf, the whiskered tip to every tooth differs from *A. saccharum* (p. 330) which is most similar. *A. lobelii* (p. 327), also similar, has fewer teeth, curled ends to lobes and bloomed shoots, as well as erect branching.

MIYABE'S MAPLE *Acer miyabei* Maxim.

Japan 1895. Rare; in most big collections of maples (and a big, bushy tree at Bedgebury National Pinetum). 16 × 1.5 m.

Bark. Orange-brown and grey, coarsely scaly; some deep, fine fissures.

Crown. Broadly domed; long main shoots with few, bunched, short shoots.

Foliage. Shoot brownish purple, clasped at nodes by joined swollen bases of petioles. Bud usually mostly hidden by base of petioles, ovoid acute, 3–5 mm, mottled yellow and brown-purple. Leaf five-lobed, terminal young leaf longer than broad, to 12 × 10 cm, very truncate; other leaves broader than long, to 20 × 28 cm, very deeply

Miyabe's Maple

324

Plate 29 JUDAS-TREE, LABURNUM, LOCUST TREE

Trees of the Pea Family.

1. Judas-tree *Cercis siliquastrum*

(a) Flowers, which are borne on shoots, branches and, often even on a stout bole, before and with the leaves.
(b) Shoot and leaf. (Katsura Tree Pl. 23 has opposite leaves).

2. Voss's Laburnum *Laburnum × watereri* 307

Leaves and flower catkin. Few seed-pods (often none) mature on each catkin, of this hybrid, unlike the prominent bunches on Common Laburnum.

3. Locust Tree *Robinia pseudoacacia* 308

The tree commonly called "Acacia"
(a) Outline of old tree 22 m tall, typically rough.
(b) Flower catkin in June.
(c) Leaf. The base of the petiole encloses the winter-bud.

Judas-tree　　　　　　　Voss's Laburnum

1a

2

3a

3b

3c

1

2a

2b

3a

3b

3c

TREE OF HEAVEN, HOLLY, MAPLE — Plate 30

1. Tree of Heaven *Ailanthus altissima* — 310

Leaf, showing 1–3 large teeth at the base of each leaflet.

A tall-growing tree whose leaves emerge bright red and late; a favourite in London squares, parks and gardens.

2. Common Holly *Ilex aquifolium* — 315

(a) Shoot of female tree with ripe fruit and fully spined leaves. Many old trees bear leaves with few teeth or none.
(b) Male flowers, known by the stamens and undeveloped pistil.

3. Paper-bark Maple *Acer griseum* — 341

(a) Shoot and leaves. This is one of the trifoliate maples.
(b) Underside of leaf, densely covered in blue-white hairs.
(c) Branch with peeling orange bark, like the bole.

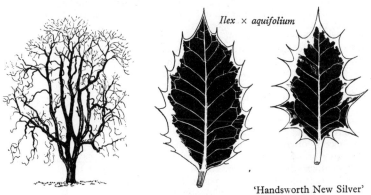

Ilex × aquifolium

Tree of Heaven 'Silver Queen' 'Handsworth New Silver'

'Lawsoniana' *Ilex × altaclarensis* 'Golden King'

cordate; lobes acuminate to blunt, rounded tip, centre lobe rectangular, one pair of large rounded lobules (or teeth); larger side-lobe with similar lobule usually on outer margin only; bright green and softly pubescent above; pale beneath, pubescent particularly on veins and in axils. Petiole stout, grooved, to 15 cm, yellow and pink, broadening at base into fleshy flattened part 1 cm across clasping shoot. Autumn colours: petiole becomes bright pink and red; blade bright clear yellow in mid-October; a few may remain bright green until they fall.
Flowers and fruit. Flowers yellow, on slender pedicels in narrow inflorescence 5–8 cm long. Fruit 5 cm across, each wing to 1 cm deep but very thin and fragile, quite level, pale pinkish brown; nutlets pubescent.
Similar species. *Acer diabolicum* (p. 346) has similar leaf (also resembling the London Plane), but always truncate, paler, ciliate, and base of petiole less enlarged, buds more visible, darker, scales free at tips.

CAPPADOCIAN MAPLE *Acer cappadocicum* Gleditsch **Pl. 33**
Caucasus Mts., through Hindu Kush and along the Himalayas to China (where separable as two varieties, very rare here) 1838. Frequent in large gardens especially in the west, less common in Scotland, N. to Ross-shire. Occasional as street tree in S. England. 24 × 2.5 m.
Bark. Grey, finely and smoothly folded.
Crown. A broad, dense dome of rather twisting branches on a short, *sinuous* bole which has large swellings around branch-scars. Base of bole surrounded by dense thicket of *suckers* for many metres, some occasionally reaching tree-size as tall as parent tree.
Foliage. Shoot green, often bloomed grey, then shiny, second or third year striped white; sucker-shoots often red. Bud small, blunt ovoid, grey-brown. Leaf 5–7 *entire*, ovate-acuminate, filament-ended lobes; cordate; old trees 8 × 12 cm on petiole 9 cm; young trees 12 × 16 cm; petiole yellow or pink, 12 cm; lobes one third of leaf in depth; pale bright green above, paler beneath with small tufts in vein-axils. Autumn colour, reliable uniform butter-yellow early to mid-October.
Flowers and fruit. Flowers pale yellow 6–8 mm with five slender obovate petals; 15–20 in small, wide erect, open panicles, 8 × 3 cm, rather hidden among unfolded leaves in mid to late May. Fruit widely spread wings, 7 cm.

Cappadocian Maple

'AUREUM' Rare as old tree, but now planted frequently. Leaves bright pale yellow when young, fading to green by August but in young trees growth restarts in July and gold leaves thus present through the season. 17 × 2 m.

'RUBRUM' 1846 Caucasus. Leaves unfold bright red. The margin of the leaf retains a pinkish colour. Suckers of the type tree also unfold red leaves.
Similar species. *A. lobelii* (below).

LOBEL'S MAPLE   *Acer lobelii*   Ten.

S. Italy 1838. Uncommon; collections, some large gardens in each country, and, rarely, in parks. 24 × 2.5 m (26 × 3.4 m at Eastnor Castle, Herefords.).
Bark. Young trees dark grey-green striped vertically buff or pink; older trees dark grey finely folded.

Crown. Young trees narrowly *fastigiate* with many long vertical, scarcely branched shoots; old trees semi-fastigiate broadening near the top. Several older trees have, mysteriously, many suckers of *A. cappadocicum* around the base and presumably must be grafts.
Foliage. Shoot purplish with a blue-white *bloom*, second year purple and green. Bud ovoid, brown base, green point. Leaf: five acute triangular lobes, basal pair with a few irregularly set acuminate teeth, other three forward-pointing, central with a tooth frequent on one shoulder only; leaves held level, points of lobes *curved upwards* or *twisted sideways*; crinkled, shiny light green above, sub-shiny beneath with small tufts of fine hairs in basal vein-axils. 10 × 12 cm on green petiole 10 cm long.

Lobel's
Maple

Flowers and fruit. Flowers 5 mm pale green in erect, open terminal panicle. Fruit bright green; wings widely spread, 3–7 cm across.
Similar species. Lobing most like *A. cappadocicum* (p. 326) but the presence of teeth and the twisted tips distinguish. A rare probable hybrid between these two species, *A.* × *dieckii* (Pax) Pax (1887) has big leaves to 15 × 18 cm on purple or red petioles; wide shallow ± entire lobes; tufts in all the vein-axils beneath, and fruit with long widely spread obovate wings each 4 × 1.2 cm, pale green, curved upwards towards the tip.

CRETAN MAPLE   *Acer sempervirens*   L.

Syns. *A. creticum* L.; *A. orientale* L.

E. Mediterranean 1752. Rare; collections northwards to S. Scotland. 9 × 1.5 m (12 × 1.5 m at Tregothnan, Cornwall). An *almost evergreen* maple with dark grey bark with a few orange fissures or patches of cracking blisters; a low crown of twisting branches, brown shoots and hard, shiny, dark, small, variable three-veined leaves 3–5 cm long, unlobed, irregularly lobulate, or with three entire lobes; wavy-edged, oblong-ovate, equally dark and shiny beneath; on yellow petioles 1 cm long. Fruit on

Cretan Maple

axillary racemes, bunched, on 3 cm yellow-green peduncle; wings acute, nearly vertical, pale green; brown then crimson. 2 cm across.

MONTPELIER MAPLE   *Acer monspessulanum* L.

S. Europe, W. Asia 1739. Uncommon: collections and large gardens N. to Perthshire; in a few London parks. 15 × 2 m (15 × 1.6 m in Kensington Gardens, London).

Bark. Dark grey and black, finely cracked, with bigger vertical fissures.

Crown. Very densely twigged, broad dome.

Montpelier Maple

Foliage. Shoot pale brown, smooth, lenticelled, slender. Bud ovoid, small, 3 mm, dark orange-brown. Leaf: three lobes widely spread, round-tipped, *ovate* entire; slightly cordate on 4 cm peach-coloured petiole; dark green, 4 × 7 cm, unfolding bright green in late May; hard; glaucous beneath with tufts in basal vein-axils.

Flowers and fruit. Flowers yellow, in small panicles in June. Fruit small, fat glossy wings each 1.2 cm held vertically and overlapping or parallel, on slender 4 cm pedicel. Nutlet brown by August, wings green, often tinged crimson.

Similar species. *A. sempervirens* (p. 327).

FIELD MAPLE   *Acer campestre* L.   **Pl. 31**

Native. Locally common on calcareous soils in S. England to N. Midlands, rare in Wales and N. England, not native in Scotland or Ireland. Mostly in hedges, trimmed or left to grow as tree, infrequent in gardens. Europe to N. Persia and N. Africa. 26 × 3 m (24 × 2.6 m at Mote Park, Maidstone, Kent).

Bark. Pale brown with wide orange fissures or cracked into squares; older trees grey-brown or dark grey with fine cracks and pale ridges.

Crown. Domed, usually low, sometimes high; short side-shoots; bole sinuous and sometimes burred; branch ends droop, then turn upwards.

Foliage. Shoot dark brown above, light brown beneath, finely pubescent; second year striated and roughened, often thickly *corky* and winged by fifth year. Bud red-brown with grey, pubescent tip; 3 mm. Leaf unfolds pinkish (new growth in hedges in summer bright red briefly), soon bright green then dark; five-lobed, basal lobes small with two irregular teeth on basal edge, three main lobes large, either cut half way to base and parallel inner half or, on big leaves, cut *almost to base* and *wedge-shaped* narrowing to base, each lobe with a rounded tooth at the shoulder, or sinuate margin, triangular end and finely rounded tip; to 8 × 12 cm, deeply cordate; sub-shiny beneath, tufted vein-axils, petiole slender, green or bright pink, 5 (9) cm. Autumn colour rich gold over long period, some red and some later purple.

Field Maple

Flowers and fruit. Flowers with leaves late April-mid-May; small, about ten widely spaced in erect head, yellow-green, in hermaphrodite heads; fruit four in a bunch, finely pubescent or glabrous, wings horizontal, 5–6 cm across, bright yellow-green *stained crimson*.

'POSTELENSE' *c.* 1896 Postel, Silesia. Very rare. Leaves emerge bright gold; mature leaves nearly normal green, but if growth continues during summer, the new shoots make the exterior of the crown partly golden.

ZOESCHEN MAPLE *Acer × zoeschense* Pax

Syn. *A. neglectum* Lange

Pre-1870. Hybrid between *A. campestre* and *A. lobelii*. Rare; collections and some large gardens especially in Ireland. 17 × 2 m. A broadly domed tree, usually surrounded by suckers; with large leaves 10 × 14 cm held very flat from shoot, on long 10 cm smooth, slender *dark ruby-red* petioles. The leaves are *shiny deep reddish-green* with sunken red veins, cordate, five-lobed; the three main lobes lobulate but entire, narrowing to acute tip; pale and smooth beneath with white pubescence on veins and basal axils tufted. Flowers: small erect terminal raceme,

Zoeschen Maple

5 × 2 cm, bearing 10–12 flowers with slender sepals, yellowish-green, without petals. Fruit: wings yellow-green flushed pink, nearly level; 5 cm across.

ITALIAN MAPLE *Acer opalus* Mill.

C. and S. Europe 1752. Infrequent; collections and some large gardens, mostly in S. England but one of biggest is in East Lothian. 20 × 3 m.

Bark. Dark pinkish-grey or orange-pink; young trees with small squares scaling away to leave orange patches, old trees with large plates adhering in middle, curving away at each end, coarsely shaggy.

Crown. Broad dome on low, spreading, twisting branches.

Foliage. Shoot glabrous, dark red-brown with pale lenticels. Bud narrowly conic-ovoid, pointed, 5 mm, pale and dark brown. Leaf: three broad obtuse lobes with coarse irregular teeth; mid-lobe shallow, sides nearly parallel, side lobes ill-defined by curved shallow sinuses; two basal lobules; hard, dark green, veins impressed above, variably woolly or pubescent beneath at least along the sides of the veins; 10–12 × 10–13 cm on 10 cm petiole red above, green beneath.

Flowers and fruit. Flowers a striking feature in April as the leaf-buds expand; large, pale yellow, hanging on long pale yellow-branched stalks in slender bunches 3–4 cm below opening leaves. Fruit about 8–15 in slender nodding bunch, on

Italian Maple

stout, curved, red peduncle; pedicels 3.5 cm long, wings nearly parallel, pale green, tinged pink, 2.5 × 1 cm; nutlets 1 × 1 cm bright green, ripening dark red-brown glabrous (with dense white long hairs in var. *tomentosum* (Tarsch) Rehder).

Recognition. In flower recognisable at great distance by large, pale yellow, hanging flowers. In leaf, like *A. pseudoplatanus* (p. 331) with smaller, much more shallowly three-lobed leaf and more coarsely scaling bark.

BALKAN MAPLE *Acer hyrcanum* Fisch. and Mey. S.E. Europe, Crimea, Caucasus 1865. Rare; in a few collections and a few elsewhere. 16 × 1.7 m. A domed tree rather intermediate between *A. opalus* and *A. campestre* with campanulate flowers in bunches of 20, yellow-green; dull dark green leaves notable for their long *very slender* pink or yellow petioles 9–11 cm long and very *parallel-sided* three main lobes like obtuse triangles on squares, the triangular part shallowly toothed; 7–10 × 10–13 cm; bud dark red-brown and grey, few-scaled. Fruit 6–8 in pendulous bunch on slender 4 cm pedicels, wings nearly parallel, bright green, 1.5 cm each.

Balkan Maple

SUGAR MAPLE *Acer saccharum* Marsh.   **Pl. 33**

E. Canada to Texas 1735. Infrequent but often overlooked and thought not to grow well or even at all. A fine, vigorous tree; a dozen at Westonbirt alone exceed 20 m and one at Bulstrode Park, Buckinghamshire is 27 × 3.3 m. In collections and some large gardens in all parts north to Perthshire, where frequent, and in C. and E. Ireland.

Bark. Smooth grey finely ridged until fairly big when long wide fissures develop and broad ridges lift away in big shaggy plates.

Crown. Irregularly domed; open with wide-spreading branches; slender straight shoots.

Foliage. Shoot bright pale green with pale lenticels and often *a band of purplish-red* by each pair of leaves or buds. Later olive-brown. Bud ovoid-conic, 5–6 mm, many dark brown scales with pale margins and fine pale brown pubescence.

Leaf deeply cleft into five lobes, the three main lobes reaching two thirds to the centre, often *wedge-shaped* to their base, long-acuminate to a small whisker but the few, large teeth at the shoulder and beyond are acuminate to a *finely rounded* tip; very thin texture, sometimes rather hard; soon tattered by insects; unfold pale green late in May, fresh green; pale or glaucous beneath, variably pubescent on veins; 12 × 18 cm; petiole 8–12 cm pale bright green, sometimes red. Gold and scarlet colours early in autumn.

Sugar Maple

Flowers and fruit. Bunches of slender 2 cm pedicels bearing pale yellow flowers. Discs without petals. Fruit rare; level slender wings 4 × 1 cm each.

Similar species. Often mistaken for *A. platanoides* (p. 321) but differences emphasised above.

OREGON MAPLE *Acer macrophyllum* Pursh   **Pl. 33**

Alaska to California 1827. Infrequent; in a few large gardens N. to S. Scotland and in Ireland, occasional in London parks. 22 × 3.8 m (28 m Monteviot).

Bark. At first brownish-purple with small pink lenticels, later, smooth dark grey ridges networked above orange-brown, or dark orange; then deeply fissured into square-plated ridges.

Crown. Tall narrow dome on ascending branches from sturdy bole, sometimes with strong basal suckers; branches *arching* out high up.

Foliage. Shoot stout for a maple, deep green with small white lenticels, sometimes green only beneath, deep purple above. Bud on strong shoots almost hidden until autumn in the clasp of *swollen bases of petioles*; stout, low-conic; scales with red-brown bases and green margins. Leaf huge but thin in texture, very deeply 5–7 lobed, 19–27 × 25–35 cm on yellow-green or red petiole 20–30 cm long; main lobes cut three quarters or more to base of leaf, long wedge-shaped inner portion, a spiky tooth at the shoulder and 2–3 obscure teeth beyond, 12 cm across at shoulders; dark yellowish-green and rather shiny above, pale beneath with tufts in axils along each main vein. In Oregon, autumn colour is a fine orange, but here mostly pale, dull brown.

Oregon Maple

Flowers and fruit. Flowers pale greenish-yellow on thick, hanging catkins 25 cm long in late April; fruit large, in dense, heavy bunches on short thick pale bright green stalk, pale green; nutlets covered in dense, whitish bristles; wings 5 × 2 cm at 90° or less. A handsome, vigorous tree unlikely to be confused with any other.

SYCAMORE, GREAT MAPLE or "PLANE" (Scotland)

Acer pseudoplatanus L.   **Pl. 32**

C. and S. Europe, north to Paris. Around 1550 (possibly in Roman times). Abundant and seeding freely almost everywhere; gardens of all sizes, town and city gardens and parks and railway embankments. Fine trees notably in N. Yorkshire, Lincolnshire and S. Scotland. 35 × 7 m (31 × 7.1 m at Birnam, Dunkeld, Perths.; 34 × 6.5 m at Drumlanrig Castle, Dumfries-shire).

Bark. At first dark grey and smooth, soon cracked into squares which later curl away at the edges; old trees pinkish-brown, scaling coarsely rather like that of the Horse Chestnut.

Crown. Hugely and densely domed; in the open often broader than tall with massive low branches; small shoots short and twisting; in leaf very dark and dense, foliage often somewhat separated into layers.

Foliage. Shoot greenish-grey-brown striated lengthwise with pale lenticels. Bud 8–10 mm *ovoid*, few *green* scales, margin reddish, open with basal scales red and decurved. Leaf varying much in size and depth of lobing with the age and vigour of the shoot. Young and vigorous trees: petiole scarlet to 15 cm; leaf to 18 × 26 cm, five lobes cut one to two thirds to base, long-acuminate, very coarsely and unevenly toothed, veins impressed above, deep blackish sub-shiny green, pale green beneath with pale buff pubescence each side of main veins. On old trees: petiole yellow-green or pink 5–10 cm, three main shallow lobes and two minor basal lobes, down to 8 × 10 cm but a

Sycamore

332

Plate 31   **MAPLES** (Contd.)

Opposite leaves and winged fruits.

1. Norway Maple   *Acer platanoides*   321

    (a) Outline of tree of 23 m.
    (b) Fruit in summer.
    (c) Flowers, which precede the leaves, in late March.
    (d) Leaf. The thin texture and finely pointed lobes and teeth
        easily distinguish this from Sycamore (Pl. 32). The Sugar
        Maple (Pl. 33) resembles it more closely, but has finely
        rounded teeth and deeper lobes.

2. Field Maple   *Acer campestre*   328

    (a) Leaves; some may have the lobes divided to the base.
    (b) Inflorescence. The female flowers, mixed with males can be
        seen showing the developing winged fruit.

3. Silver Maple   *Acer saccharinum*   347

    (a) Upper surface of leaf.
    (b) Lower surface of leaf.

A tree of very rapid growth quite frequently planted by roads
and in public parks.

4. Red Maple   *Acer rubrum*   347

    (a) Upper surface of leaf.
    (b) Lower surface of leaf. This is often nearly as silvered as in
        the Silver Maple, but the leaf is smaller, less deeply lobed
        and less deeply toothed.

This tree is rarely planted by roads, and is less common in
parks than the Silver Maple. Young trees turn fiery scarlet in
autumn, but the name comes from the bright red flowers.

Norway Maple   Field Maple   Silver Maple

1a

1b

1c

1d

2a

2b

3a

3b

4a

4b

1a

1b

1d

2a

2b

3

MAPLES (Contd.)

Plate 32

1. Sycamore *Acer pseudoplatanus* 331

Introduced long ago, this behaves like a native tree, seeding abundantly, even in the far north.

(a) Winter outline of mature tree 25 m tall.

(b) Leaf of young tree. On most of the older trees the leaf is smaller, less deeply lobed and has a shorter, yellow or pink petiole. The leaf is leathery and dark unlike that of the Norway Maple (Pl. 31) and has quite different toothing.

(c) Inflorescence. The flowers open when the leaves are nearly fully out, and have very short petals.

(d) Fruit. On some trees these ripen bright red.

2. Red Snake-bark Maple *Acer capillipes* 345

(a) Buds and leaf, showing distinctive parallel veins. Underside of leaf, a paler, yellowish-green, or slightly glaucous, has little pegs in the lower vein-axils.

(b) Bark. This is usually the best of the snake-barks and is very bright when young.

3. Ash-leafed Maple *Acer negundo* 349

Commonly planted in the white-variegated form, in towns. Leaf with the normal five leaflets, but three or seven may be found.

few old trees bear leaves twice this size. Leaves unfold orange, brownish or reddish, particularly bright in late-summer growth on sprouts; seldom achieve any autumn browns of note before falling. They are usually affected by "tar spot", a fungus (*Rhytisma acerinum*) which causes large thick black patches.
Flowers and fruit. Flowers yellowish on hanging racemes 6–12 cm long, in mid-April, thin-looking as the petals are very short. Fruit in short-stalked bunches, green variably tinged red, on some trees conspicuously bright red in summer; glabrous; wings at about 90°, each 3 × 1 cm.
Growth. Very rapid indeed when young with shoot in fourth year to 2 m but soon decreasing greatly. Buds may open overnight. Shoot-growth from late April to early August.

'VARIEGATUM' 1730. Frequent; in town parks and gardens. Slow-growing; very dull grey, dry-looking scaly bark. Pale green leaf blotched and spotted with white. 24 × 4 m.

'CORSTORPHINENSE' 1600 Corstorphine, Edinburgh. Original tree still healthy and 17 × 3.8 m. Infrequent in parks and gardens. Leaves unfold bright yellow and fade gradually to normal by mid-July, occasional shoots of new yellow leaves in August.

'WORLEEI' A more recent form than the foregoing, with leaves soon rich gold and pale yellow on red petioles, and largely retaining these colours. Bark smooth; lobes on leaf regular and triangular. Infrequent. 18 × 1.7 m.

'PURPUREUM' 1828 Jersey and 'Atropurpureum' 1883 Berlin. Too frequent, by roads and in parks and gardens and village greens. Leaves variably dark purple beneath tinged grey; rich dark purple in 'Atropurpureum'. 20 × 2 m.

'BRILLIANTISSIMUM' Unknown British origin; since 1900. Much planted in parks and small gardens; slow-growing, somewhat densely globose-crowned, grafted on a stem of the type sycamore. Leaves emerge bright pink, turn gradually with some orange to bright yellow then white until July then dark green with faint sickly yellow marbling around the veins; sharply lobed to about half way. A longer season of bright colour than most flowering trees and very attractive.

'PRINZ HANDJERY' 1883 Berlin. Similar to 'Brilliantissimum' but a more open crown and leaves persisting a dull bronzy-gold, *purple beneath*.
Similar species. Not really like *A platanoides* (p. 321) which has thin, bright green leaves and large, whisker-ended teeth and lobes. Much more like *A. heldreichii* (below), and the Caucasian *A. trautvetteri* (p. 335) and *A. velutinum* var. *vanvolxemii* (p. 335) in increasing order of resemblance, but differs from all of these in the green ovoid bud, scaly bark and hanging racemes.

HELDREICH'S MAPLE *Acer heldreichii* Orph.
Balkan States and Greece 1879. Rare, confined to collections, in all four countries. 22 × 2.3 m.
Bark. Smooth, greyish-pink, darkening with age and becoming finely fissured in patches or striated with black.
Crown. Tall-domed, rather narrow; branches upswept, sparsely twigged.
Foliage. Shoot pale mahogany-brown, olive or deep red-brown. Bud ovoid-conic, sharply *pointed*, small, *dark red-brown*. Leaf to 17 × 24 cm on pink 15 cm petiole, deeply five-lobed, the three main lobes cut *almost to base*; two basal

lobes cut half way; cordate, the big lobes each side
of the central lobe with 2–3 sharp triangular lobules
or coarse teeth; dark green above, glaucous beneath
with forward white hairs on veins or fine buff pubescence also in axils. Buds open in mid-May, the bright
red scales enfolding brilliant green leaves. Autumn
colour a good yellow and some reds.

Flowers and fruit. Flowers small, yellow in erect
ovoid panicle; fruit glabrous, wings erect, often incurved and overlapping, each 2.5–5 cm long.

Similar species. *A. trautvetteri* (below).

Heldreich's Maple

TRAUTVETTER'S MAPLE   *Acer traut-*
vetteri Medwed.

Caucasus 1866. Rare and confined to collections throughout the British Isles. 19 × 2.6 m.
Similar to *A. heldreichii* but leaves lobed only
three-quarters to base or less and coarsely for-
ward-toothed on pink petiole to 18 cm long;
glaucous beneath with orange pubescence on
veins and in axils beneath. Flowers in loose
erect panicles, 8 × 8 cm, males yellow, campanulate, 5 mm; about one third of total are
females; followed by big fruit, *rosy-pink* in
summer, like flowers from a distance, pubescent
at first, wings nearly parallel, very broad 5 × 2 cm,
peduncle to 6 cm.

Trautvetter's Maple

VAN VOLXEM'S MAPLE   *Acer velutinum* var. *vanvolxemii* (Mast.)
Rehd.

Caucasus 1873. Rare; in the larger maple collections of
each British country. 24 × 2.6 m (16 × 2.4 m at Edinburgh R.B.G.).

Bark. Smooth, light or purplish-grey; branch-scars
prominently ringed.

Crown. Broad, rather low dome in open; a long clean
bole when amongst other trees.

Foliage. Shoot shiny olive-brown; very small lenticels.
Bud sharply conic-ovoid, many scales, brown, edged
very dark brown, basal scales of terminal buds free.
Leaf like a thick pale yellowish-green large sycamore
leaf on a stout yellow-green or pinkish-yellow petiole to
27 cm long, blade 15 × 18 cm, cordate, three main lobes
broad, acute, cut nearly half way; unevenly and coarsely
toothed with curved teeth; two short, broad basal lobes;
glaucous beneath with soft, pale brown pubescence later
on veins only.

Van Volxem's Maple

Plate 33   **MAPLES** (Contd.)

1. Cappadocian Maple   *Acer cappadocicum*   326

  (a) Mature tree, 15 m tall, in late October.
  (b) Shoot, leaves and fruit. Young leaves frequently have red
       margins. Five-lobed leaves are common.

2. Coral-bark Maple   *Acer palmatum* 'Senkaki'   340

  Red shoots in early spring. The leaf is like **3.** but tinged
  yellow.

3. Smooth Japanese Maple   *Acer palmatum*   339

  Leaf of this highly variable tree, near the type. Most of the
  varied forms grown are bushes (but see 'Osakazuki' p. 339).

4. Oregon Maple   *Acer macrophyllum*   330

  (a) Leaf (reduced).
  (b) Buds opening with inflorescence erect before expanding to
       hang down 20–25 cm.

5. Sugar Maple   *Acer saccharum*   330

  Leaf, showing finely pointed lobes but bluntly pointed teeth.

  A tree of brilliant but early autumn colours, rare, but in many
  gardens especially perhaps in Scotland.

Norway Maple

Sugar Maple

2

3

4b

5

1b

HORSE CHESTNUTS, PRIDE OF INDIA   Plate 34

Showy panicles of flowers and compound leaves.

1. Horse Chestnut   *Aesculus hippocastanum*   351

    (a) Fruit opening to show ripe conker.
    (b) Leaf.
    (c) Flowers.

2. Red Horse Chestnut   (Briott's form) *Aesculus × carnea* 'Briottii'   354

    (a) Flowers.
    (b) Leaf; darker, more crinkled and more coarsely toothed
    than that of the Horse Chestnut. The leaflets may have short,
    reddish stems.

Superior to the type Red Horse Chestnut.

3. Pride of India   *Koelreuteria paniculata*   356

    (a) Flowers on part of terminal panicle.
    (b) Leaf. Some are doubly compound, some basal leaflets,
    being again fully divided rather than deeply lobed.

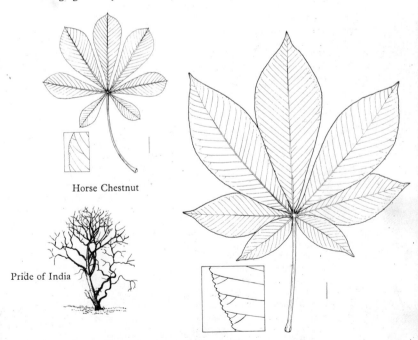

Horse Chestnut

Pride of India

Japanese Horse Chestnut, distinguished from Horse Chestnut
by size and gently tapered apex (see p. 354)

Flowers and fruit. Flowers in big open upright panicle 8 × 6 cm; each flower small, 4–6 mm pale green, without petals; stamens whitish, anthers bright yellow. Fruit with wings slightly raised.

Similar species. *A. velutinum* itself has similarly yellowish leaves, but much smaller, and on a *scarlet* 8 cm petiole. It is in only one or two collections. *A. pseudoplatanus* (p. 331) has ovoid green buds, rough bark and smaller, dark leaf and catkin-like racemes.

TRIDENT MAPLE *Acer buergeranum* Miq.

Syns. *A. trinerve* Dipp.; *A. trifidum* Hook.

E. China, Japan 1896. Rare; collections and a few large gardens in S. England and E. Anglia. 16 × 1.5 m (*c.* 11 × 1.5 m at Norham House, Oxford).

Bark. Buff-brown, pinkish and flaking when young, soon deeply fissured into *shaggy* rectangular plates becoming *orange* or dark brown and grey or blackish.

Crown. Densely leafy small dome; epicormic shoots often on bole and branches.

Foliage. Shoot slender, brownish-grey, lenticelled. Bud slender, conic, pointed, 5–6 mm, red-brown. Leaf unfolds yellow-orange with silky hairs; soon glabrous; three-lobed broad-cuneate, *three-nerved base*; central lobe ovate, long-acuminate; side-lobes at 45°, triangular, all entire or with occasional small rounded teeth. Occasional leaves on a few trees irregularly lobulate or without lobes; leathery, dark green above, bluish-*glaucous* beneath, to 9 × 7 cm on pink or yellow petiole 8 cm long; size highly variable on the same tree. Sprout-buds open scarlet. Autumn colour red then crimson, coccineal colour.

Trident Maple

Flowers and fruit. Hairy, terminal umbels of yellow flowers open in early April; fruit small, in arched panicle 7 cm across, nutlet prominent bright green, wings raised or parallel, 1–2.5 cm, tinged pale crimson; purple disc at the base of the fruit.

Recognition. A very distinct elegant and desirable small tree known readily by the bark and small leaves with forward triangular side-lobes and prominently three-nerved base.

AMUR MAPLE *Acer ginnala* Maxim.

China, Manchuria, Japan 1860. Infrequent in collections and large gardens; more frequent in small semi-suburban gardens. 10 × 0.8 m. Often a slender-branched, rather upright shrub, sometimes a small tree on a short sinuous bole. Bark: dark grey, smooth. Leaf opening pale yellow (late leaves bright red at first), 7.5 × 6 cm deeply three-lobed with *central lobe* much the longest, 5 cm, side-lobes near base 2 cm, forwards; mid-lobe parallel-sided or narrowing lower half, long-acuminate outer half; all lobes jaggedly, deeply and irregularly toothed; petiole 4 cm. Autumn colour early, deep crimson in September, soon shed. Flowers conspicuous in late May; erect panicles 4 cm across of

Amur Maple

about 50 yellow-green flowers. Fruit in small nodding bunches; wings translucent, nearly parallel, 2.5 cm.

TARTAR MAPLE   *Acer tataricum* L.

S.E. Europe, W. Asia 1759. Rare; a few collections and gardens. A small shrubby domed tree to 6 m resembling a bright-leaved thorn-tree from a distance. Bark smooth, brown, striped pale buff. Leaf fresh green, unlobed, ovate-acuminate or shallowly 3–5 lobed like a currant-leaf; irregularly toothed or lobulate, 5 × 7.5 cm, veins impressed above, pale and prominent below, petiole to 3.5 cm, grooved, whitish or red. Flowers 20–30 on

Tartar Maple

erect, domed panicles, 7–8 spreading stamens, in late May; fruit *deep red* by August, wing 2.5 cm with thick green outer edge, on a wire-like stalk.

SMOOTH JAPANESE MAPLE   *Acer palmatum* Thunb.   **Pl. 33**

Japan, Korea 1820. Common in gardens of all kinds, often as one of the small-growing cultivars. 16 × 1.3 m.
Bark. Rich brown, smooth, striped pale buff; old trees grey.
Crown. Tall-domed bushy tree, bole seldom 2 m long, sinuous; ascending branches curving out bearing slender, level shoots.

Foliage. Shoot slender, smooth, without lenticels, dark red above, bright green beneath. Bud ovoid, 2–3 mm, green and bright red. Leaf 5–7 lobes, cut more than half way, ovate, long-acuminate, sharply and finely forward serrate, about 7–9 cm on a slender glabrous petiole 3–5 cm long; truncate or broad-

Smooth Japanese Maple: various leaf shapes

cuneate, perpendicular basal lobes, the other lobes radiating.
Flowers and fruit. Flowers dark purple-pink, 6–8 mm across in small spreading or erect panicles of 12–15 flowers on very slender green or dark red pedicels 4 cm long. Fruit 2 cm across, wings at obtuse angle, pale red in erect bunches (pendulous in many cultivars).

'ATROPURPUREUM' To 9 × 1 m. Leaves five-lobed, dark purple. Best forms open sufficiently bright reddish-purple to be permissible.

'OSAKAZUKI' 1861 Japan.

'Osakazuki'

10 × 1 m. Leaves mostly seven-lobed, to 9 × 12 cm, the broad-ovate, long-acuminate lobes cut to within 1–4 cm of leaf-base; soft green often tinged pink at margin, until mid-October when, in sun or in shade the whole crown turns blazing scarlet. During the summer the fruit hangs scarlet beneath the green leaves.

'SENKAKI' Coral-bark Maple, Japan. *c.* 1920. Becoming frequent. Shoots glowing crimson in winter; small deeply lobed leaves slightly yellowish in summer, pale orange-yellow in autumn. Extremely attractive and much in demand but in short supply. 11 m. **Pl. 33.**
Similar species. *A. japonicum* (below).

DOWNY JAPANESE MAPLE *Acer japonicum* Thunb.
Japan 1864. Common in gardens but less so than *A. palmatum*; similarly with the cultivars. Scarcely a tree except in the cultivar given.

'VITIFOLIUM' 1864 Japan. Numerous at Westonbirt, infrequent elsewhere. 14 m. The type differs only in the smaller size of the plant and smaller leaf and lacks the brilliant, mixed autumn colours.
Bark. Smooth grey.
Crown. Broadly ovoid; a stout bole branching strongly or dividing at about 1 m, sinuous with level then upcurved branches.

Foliage. Shoot pinkish red-brown and bloomed above, sea-green beneath. Bud ovoid-conic sharply pointed, dark red, scales fringed grey. Leaf oval or circular in outline cut one quarter to one half to centre by narrow sinuses into 7–11 broad, acute, ovate-triangular lobes usually broadest at their bases, coarsely and irregularly forward-crenate, 9–13 × 11–17 cm (very rare variant to 22 × 24 cm); petiole pubescent at first, 4–6 cm. Unfold covered in silky hairs but pubescent only on some veins beneath, by mid-summer. In mid-October leaves in sun have outer parts intense scarlet, those immediately behind, bright gold; leaves in shade mixed green, yellow and pink; later all deep ruby-red.

Downy Japanese Maple

Flowers and fruit. Flowers conspicuous before leaves in mid or late April, purple, 1.5 cm across in nodding long-stalked bunches. Fruit 5–6 cm across, pubescent at first, wings horizontal or at wide angle, outer margin and seed bright green; pedicel 3 cm, red; peduncle, 4 cm, red.

'AUREUM' Probably 1861 Japan. A slow-growing form frequent in gardens, especially in small-scale plantings like heath and rock-gardens. Foliage as in the type, but held markedly in layers; butter-yellow throughout the season.
Similar species. The type (only) might be confused with *A. palmatum* (p. 339) but is much more like *A. pseudosieboldianum* (below).

KOREAN MAPLE *Acer pseudosieboldianum* Komar
Manchuria, Korea 1903. Rare, shrubby tree in some collections. Differs from *A. japonicum* in 9–11 acuminate, triangular lobes cut into lobules or large teeth each

with exceedingly *slender-pointed* fine teeth; sinuses between lobes often reduced to a slit for half their length; 8 × 10 cm; circular or elliptic, deeply cordate; pubescence remains on veins beneath; autumn colour a most distinct fiery *crimson* with *orange* and *purple* shades. Flowers purple. Known in autumn at a distance by leaf colours alone. (Confused with *A. sieboldianum* which has yellow flowers.)

Korean Maple

LIME-LEAFED MAPLE *Acer distylum* Sieb. and Zucc.

Japan 1879. Rare; collections only. 9 × 0.4 m. Grey-green bark striped orange; broad crown with slender arching branches. Best known by thick, stiffly *erect* 8–10 cm spikes with small dark yellow flowers on upper half with minute, broad petals, or pink-buff fruit with 2 cm incurved wings and unlobed, large *lime-like leaf*, 13 × 11 cm on 4 cm stout, scarlet or yellow-pink petiole; leathery, unfolding buff-pink with long hairs; oblong-ovate, crinkled, dark green, deeply cordate, short-acuminate, shallowly serrate, dull green beneath, scarlet at base of veins.

Similar species. Unlobed leaves of *A. davidii* (below) are less broad with less stout petiole and the tree has arched, then pendulous flower-heads.

Lime-leafed Maple

HORNBEAM MAPLE *Acer carpinifolium* Sieb. and Zucc.

Japan 1879. Rare; collections and a few large gardens in S. England and Ireland. A broad, bushy little tree to 10 × 0.6 m with foliage unique among maples. The smooth brown shoots bear long lanceolate-oblong leaves to 17 × 5 cm with 20 *or more pairs of parallel veins* each ending in a forward triangular tooth itself with 4–6 minute very sharp teeth; dark green above, shiny beneath with raised veins, hairy at first, bright pale green. Autumn colours bright pale yellow and some brown. About 15 flowers on very slender catkins, 10–12 cm long, open star-like 1 cm across, as green as the leaf, with five broad petals.

Hornbeam Maple

PÈRE DAVID'S MAPLE *Acer davidii* Franch.

C. China 1879, 1902. Frequent, a few parks and smaller gardens, many large gardens and collections everywhere. 16 × 1.2 m. The Snake-barked Maples are a difficult and confused group. *A. davidii* is the most variable and confused of them all and can be found labelled *A. forrestii* (a different tree; confusion with Forrest's form of *A. davidii*), *A. horizontalis* or *A. laxiflorum* (a species of which only three trees have been found in Britain). Conversely several trees of *A. crataegifolium* are labelled *A. davidii*. *A. davidii* is in cultivation in at least four recognisable forms, two of which have been named, 'George Forrest' and 'Ernest Wilson' (described below). A third form seen in several gardens has ovate or oblong-lanceolate leaves to 15 × 8 cm, truncate or rounded (very truncate in a narrow-leaved variant with leaves 13 × 5 cm), gradually acuminate, some faintly lobulate and all colouring a good orange in autumn. The fourth form has narrowly ovate, unlobed leaves, 6 × 3 cm on slender red petioles.

'GEORGE FORREST' The largest-growing and most frequent. 16 × 1.1 m at Holkham Hall, Norfolk.

Bark. Smooth, bright olive-green with broad white stripes made up of minute lines of brilliant blue-white densely massed in the middle and more spread towards the edges. Older trees cracking into dark grey fissures at base, an oak-like bark rising with age.

Crown. Typically rather radiating branches, lower ones level, upper ones arched, but some crowns parachute-shaped with ascending branches.

Foliage. Shoot dark red, striped with chalky white. Bud narrowly conic appressed, 1 cm, bright dark red; when expanding patterned with whitish-pink. Leaf broadly ovate, 15 × 10 cm, cordate, short-acuminate, irregularly finely crenate, very dark *blackish* shiny green above, leathery, lax, distant, unlobed, an obscure lobe on one side or on both just above half way or, on late growth, markedly 3–5 lobed (all can be on one tree); pale whitish-green beneath, soon glabrous; tiny *peg-like processes* in major vein-axils; major veins red; petiole 6 cm, bright red. Leaves unfold rich orange with rusty pubescence in vein-axils but are glabrous and dark green when full size. The leaves remain green late and fall with negligible colour.

Flowers and fruit. Flowers as leaves unfold in late May, profuse, *arching racemes* 7–10 cm long each with 20–30 campanulate green-yellow flowers; terminal on short shoots. Wings of fruit nearly horizontal, each 2.5–3 cm long.

'ERNEST WILSON' is very different: a low, spreading tree with densely bunched yellowish-green leaves with pink veins and short pink petioles; "V"-folded at base, lobulate and long-acuminate, not hanging; rather glaucous beneath. It is in a few collections and colours brilliant orange in autumn.

Similar species. *A. distylum* (p. 341) although not truly a Snake-bark; *A. capillipes* (p. 345), *A. hersii* (p. 344).

Père David's Maple

Small-leafed form   'Third form'   'George Forrest'   'Ernest Wilson'

HAWTHORN-LEAFED MAPLE *Acer crataegifolium*
Sieb. and Zucc.

Japan 1879. Infrequent; large gardens and collections. 14 × 0.5 m. A very slender little tree, the crown often leaning to one side near the top; few, level branches and foliage in layers close above them on short, *twisting dark red* shoots, striped white. Leaf to 6 × 3 cm long-acuminate, unevenly finely crenate, a short, rounded lobe near the base each side, *tinged pink* all summer, matt green finely white pubescent beneath on a scarlet 2 cm petiole. Fruit soon red, wings nearly level, flat and thin, 2.5 cm across the pair.

Hawthorn-leafed Maple

MOOSE-BARK *Acer pensylvanicum* L.

E. Canada and north-eastern USA 1755. Infrequent; some collections and large gardens in each country. 12 × 1 m. (The single "n" in "pensylvanicum" is the original spelling and should be preserved.)

Bark. Light grey, rarely more green; brilliantly striped white.

Crown. Ascending branches at narrow angles, curving out to horizontal.

Foliage. Shoot smooth, olive to brown above, sea-green beneath. Bud two-scaled, 1 cm, dark red and yellow-brown. Leaf peculiarly variable, from ovate-lanceolate, 13 × 9 cm with long acute triangular main lobe and two short triangular lobes below the middle, to almost square 22 × 20 cm, mid-lobe very broad, short-acuminate with a similar lobe terminally each side. Cordate, very unevenly and sharply serrate; flushes brilliant green and sheds bud-scales early; petiole 6–12 cm, stout, grooved, pink. Autumn colour early, clear gold. Winter shoots red. A short-lived tree.

Moose-bark

Flowers and fruit. Copious even on small trees: flowers on 10–12 cm pink pendulous raceme; broad-petalled, campanulate, yellow-green. Fruit hanging in bunches, wings curved, 5 cm across.

Similar species. Small-leafed forms similar in leaf to *A. rufinerve* (below) but fruit much bigger.

GREY-BUDDED SNAKE-BARK MAPLE
Acer rufinerve Sieb. and Zucc.

Japan 1879.
Frequent; in many large and some small gardens in each country. 13 × 1 m.

Bark. Either green with greyish-white stripes or distinctively *grey* with *pink* stripes; soon rough dull grey, losing the stripes and becoming pitted.

Crown. Opening out from a short bole to a high-spreading bush.

Foliage. Shoot bloomed blue-white, then lilac, finally

Grey-budded Snake-bark Maple

dull green striped white. Buds on older wood prominent, ovoid, *bright grey-blue*.
Leaf three-lobed, often broader than long to 14 × 15 cm, usually 9 × 10 cm,
central lobe broadly triangular or ovate, short-acuminate; side-lobes spreading
at 60–90°, narrower, about half way up leaf; sharply and unevenly serrate; dark
matt bluish-green, after unfolding yellowish; paler beneath with at first *rusty*
pubescence at base of veins and in axils, by late summer reduced to a rust-
coloured spot in the basal axils. Petiole pink, grooved, 5–7 cm. Autumn colours
orange and dark red or crimson.

Flowers and fruit. Fairly prolific from early age, flowers mid-April as leaves
unfold, on pubescent upright racemes, yellow-green; fruit small, 1–2 cm across
in dense bunches; wings at an obtuse angle.

Growth. Often short-lived. Upper branches liable to colour early and die.
Form with grey and pink bark seems more healthy and vigorous.

'ALBOLIMBATUM' Japan about 1860. Nearly as frequent as the type, and
differing only in fine silvery margin and splashes and dots of white, also patches
of light greens on the leaf, paler shoots and bud more white.

Recognition. Broad leaf and small fruit. A Snake-bark with grey and pink
bark is always this species.

HERS'S MAPLE   *Acer hersii* (Rehd.) Rehd.

China 1924. Fairly frequent and much planted in parks and gardens recently in
England; collections and some gardens in each country. 15 × 1.3 m.

Bark. Rich, smooth, *olive-green* with white stripes tinged green; oldest trees
still smooth but with some triangular pits.

Crown. Ascending branches
from a short bole, arching out
and hanging at an angle as
long shoots with few and
short laterals.

Foliage. Shoot *olive-green*;
sprouts and strong young
growth may be pale pink.
Bud small, flattened, ap-
pressed and *green*, opening
pink. Leaf unfolds *olive-green*,
becomes thick, rubbery, 12

Hers's Maple

Fruit

× 9 cm dark green with yellow-green veins, shallowly and unevenly crenate,
usually three-lobed with a short, acute lobe or lobule each side near the middle,
but often mixed with unlobed or slightly lobulate leaves; cordate; at first may
have long rusty pubescence at base of blade and adjacent part of the *green* 3–6 cm
petiole, soon glabrous with small whitish pegs in vein-axils, often marked purple
in basal axils. Autumn colours yellow to orange and sometimes crimson.

Flowers and fruit. Campanulate *green* flowers ten to fifteen on arching 12 cm
green raceme. Fruit with horizontal broad pale green wings, *large*, 5 cm across,
tinged pink late in season.

Recognition. The only Snake-bark that is green in every feature except a
few pink vigorous shoots. The big, broad wings on the fruit also help to distinguish.

RED SNAKE-BARK MAPLE *Acer capillipes* Maxim.   **Pl. 32**

Japan 1894. Infrequent; mainly in large gardens and collections, recently more in smaller gardens. 15 × 1.1 m.

Bark. Bright green striped bright white lasting well with age; oldest with buff stripes at base.

Crown. Branches ascend at narrow angle from short bole.

Foliage. Shoot green-striped white, slightly bloomed lilac at first. Bud narrow, compressed ovoid, 7 × 4 mm, purple to dark red occasionally bloomed grey. Leaf three-lobed: mid-lobe a *long, acute triangle* or ovate short-acuminate; side-lobes small, about 1 cm long acuminate, at 45° half way along the leaf; shallowly and unevenly crenate, truncate to rounded at base, 10–15 × 8–11 cm, *shiny rich green* above with 8–10 pairs *parallel sunken veins*; whitish-green beneath with small *yellow pegs* in axils on the main vein. Leaf often slightly folded in a "*V*"; petiole 4–8 cm *scarlet* and grooved above, orange beneath. Autumn colours, yellow, orange, red and crimson.

Red Snake-bark Maple

Flowers and fruit. Very copious on older trees, fewer on young; 25 yellow flowers on arched raceme 10–12 cm long; 6 mm across, five obovate petals, late May/early June. Fruit hanging in long bunches, small, 2.5 cm across, very pale yellow-green turning pink and, by October, crimson; wings at obtuse angle or nearly level.

Similar species. Quite distinct, but still confused with *A. rufinerve* (p. 343); some features in common with *A. davidii* 'George Forrest' (p. 342).

FORREST'S MAPLE *Acer forrestii* Diels

China 1906. A rare tree of great beauty which has branches arching out and long scarlet shoots hanging from them with few laterals. Slender *scarlet* 5–7 cm petioles bear three-lobed rather ivy-like leaves, dark green with pale around the veins; lobes triangular-ovate, long-acuminate, *mid-lobe longest*, side-lobes spreading widely, to 3 cm long on a leaf 11 × 10 cm; cordate, very finely forward-crenate. Another form has an even more cascade-like crown and leaves to 13 × 8 cm coarsely and unevenly crenate and with basal lobules. Neither shows much autumn colour. The flowers are on upright, arched, small, slender racemes; each flower 1 cm across; petals yellow, calyx and centre of flower reddish.

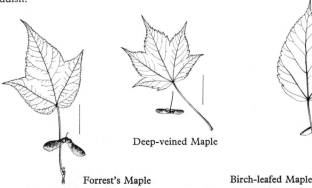

Deep-veined Maple

Forrest's Maple   Birch-leafed Maple

DEEP-VEINED MAPLE   *Acer argutum* Maxim.

Japan 1881. A many-stemmed small tree in a few large gardens, with dark green-grey bark blistered or lenticelled, and attractive, five-lobed *hard crinkled* dark yellowish-green leaves with ovate lobes drawn out into *long, very jaggedly toothed tails*; leaf similarly toothed; 10 × 10 cm, truncate, turning bright yellow in autumn. Petiole very slender, 10 cm yellow. Fruit: by late May fully developed, bright-green, terminal, sparse, pendent racemes from short shoots; 15 cm long, bearing 12 thin narrow-winged fruit 2.5 cm across; wings level.

BIRCH-LEAFED MAPLE   *Acer tetramerum* Pax

China, Tibet and Burma 1901. A tall slender many-stemmed open tree in collections and a few gardens, to 14 m. Resembles a Snake-bark in having ovate leaves on scarlet petioles but is in a different group and the bark although sometimes striped green and white is usually rough with brown lenticels. Leaf unlobed 10 × 6 cm, ovate-acuminate, usually slightly lobulate but variable, coarsely crenate, very *round at base*, petiole *slender, scarlet* 6 cm, leaf light green above, pale beneath with white tufts in basal axils, thin texture. Flowers green and white, 9–10 on 5 cm yellow pedicel. Fruit. By late May pendent racemes 12 cm long, terminal on short shoots, bearing 12 fruit on pink pedicels; bright green spreading wings, 4 cm across the pair; wrinkled seed red.

HORNED MAPLE   *Acer diabolicum* K. Koch

Japan 1860. Rare; collections and some large gardens. 12 × 1 m.

Bark. Pale pinkish-grey, smooth, older trees slightly fissured at base.

Crown. A tall, fairly broad dome with slender whippy shoots.

Foliage. Shoot bloomed purple becoming dark brown. Bud sharply conic, dark brown, basal scales spreading, free. Leaf five-lobed, usually broader than long to 15 × 19 cm on pale pink 8 cm petiole; three main lobes broadly rectangular with blunt obtuse tooth at each shoulder and 1–2 from there to the tip, basal lobes entire small ovate-triangular; main lobes cut half way into leaf blade; truncate, *hard, dull matt light green*, paler beneath with soft white pubescence on

Horned Maple

veins *and around margins* (ciliate). Autumn colours biscuit, often splashed crimson.

Flowers and fruit. Flowers hang in bunches below raised opening leaves resembling together an *open parachute;* yellow, male flowers lack petals; fruit bristly, wings upright or spreading.

     var. *purpurascens* (Franchet and Savatier) Rehder. 1878 Japan. About equally frequent; female flowers dark red and very attractive.

Recognition. Unmistakable when in flower. Leaf also distinct, broad lobes like some London Planes, ciliate edge; hard, pale green.

RED MAPLE *Acer rubrum* L.   **Pl. 31**

E. and C. North America, Newfoundland to Texas 1656.
Frequent in many parks and gardens and sometimes in
churchyards and road-side gardens. Fast-growing, very
desirable tree. 23 × 2m (20 × 3.2m at Bagshot Park,
Surrey).

Bark. Pale grey and smooth until old when darker and
cracking into slightly lifting long plates.

Crown. Irregular ovoid; ascending whip-like curved shoots.
shoots.

Foliage. Shoot slender, red to coppery-brown. Bud very
small, pointed, dark red-brown. Leaf opens reddish-green,
very shiny above and below, soon yellowish-green then dark
green above and *silvery beneath;* rounded or truncate, 3–5
lobed, main lobes forward, nearly terminal, parallel-sided
at base, acuminate-lobulate or very coarsely toothed,
8–10 × 7–11 cm, cut by lobes to less than half way; petiole

Red Maple

7–9 cm *red above,* yellow-green beneath. Autumn colour starts early, even
before September on the ends of a few branches, scarlet and gold, deep wine-
red all over by late September.

Flowers and fruit. Flowers wreathed closely at first along bare shoots in
March; last several weeks and stalks lengthen to 6–10cm. Male, 8 scarlet stamens
and deep red disc; females often on separate tree, larger disc, bright red. Fruit
bright red, wings narrowly parted; shed early; 1 cm

Similar species. *A. saccharinum* (below) is the only other hardy maple with
silver undersides to the leaves.

SILVER MAPLE *Acer saccharinum* L.   **Pl. 31**

Syn. *A. dasycarpum* Ehrh.

E. and C. N. America, Quebec to Florida 1725. Frequent in large gardens and
often by arterial roads and in town parks. 30 × 3.7m (31 × 2.8m at Westonbirt,
Glos.).

Bark. Grey, smooth except for a few shallow fissures and frequent burrs and
sprouts, later flaking and may be slightly shaggy.

Crown. Very tall-domed, open, spreading towards the top, many strongly
ascending, rather slender branches arching out with pendulous shoots from high
up.

Foliage. Shoot bright brownish-red with some grey bloom, then deep purple.
Bud long-ovoid slightly angled; terminal 1 cm, bright red. Leaf opens orange or
dark red with thick white pubescence beneath, becomes pale brown then
greenish-yellow above, *silvery beneath,* five-lobed, the central lobe narrowing
somewhat towards its base, cut half way or more to the base of the leaf, two
main side-lobes at 45° to main lobe, all three with *acuminate* lobules or large
teeth; basal pair of lobes perpendicular, acuminate, also
lobulate; truncate or cordate on slender pink petiole
8–13cm long; leaves from 8 × 9 to 15 × 16cm. Autumn
colours soft gold, occasional scarlet and crimson.

Flowers and fruit. Flowers greenish-red or dark red,
before leaves unfold in March; 4–5 bunched at nodes; on
1 cm dark red pedicel. Calyx 5mm bright red. Fruit on
3–5cm stalks; wings twisted each 5–6cm, broad tipped;
thick pink veins. (USA – rare here, falling very early.)

'Laciniatum'

'LACINIATUM' Becoming more frequent in towns and shopping centre precincts; pendulous pinkish-brown shoots glossy at base; petiole red or pink; leaf deeply and sharply lobed, mid-lobe to 10 cm deep in 14 cm leaf, dark green.
Growth. A very fast-growing tree with shoots to 1.5 m but brittle branches and relatively short-lived; big boles soon hollow stumps covered in sprouts.

NIKKO MAPLE   *Acer nikoense* Maxim.
Japan, C. China 1881. Infrequent; large gardens in S. England, E. Anglia, Wales and all parts of Ireland. Rare in Scotland. 13 × 1.2 m.
Bark. Smooth, greenish-grey then pink-grey finely speckled rufous.
Crown. Broadly conic with level lower branches; domed with age.

Foliage. Shoot dark purple-grey; short dense pubescence, longer at nodes. Bud ovoid-conic, blunt narrow tip; black-purple scales pale grey at tips where pubescent. Leaf *trifoliate*; leaflets to 10 × 3.5 cm elliptic-oblong, entire, obscurely toothed or sinuate; mid-leaflet on 1 cm stalk, side leaflets sub-sessile, oblique at base; midrib twice as far from outer edge as from inner; all short-acuminate leathery and thick, dark grey-green above, bluish-white usually with dense long pubescence beneath. Open in late April, turn crimson and deep red late in October. Petiole *stout pink* densely long-pubescent, 7 cm.

Nikko Maple

Flowers and fruit. Flowers out well after leaves in early May, terminal on short shoots, in threes, straight-sided cups, yellow on hairy stems; wings of fruit prominent in the centre of female flowers; fruit big thick densely pubescent nutlets with broad glabrous wings at more than 90°, 4–5 cm across.
Similar species. *A. triflorum* (below).

ROUGH-BARKED MAPLE   *Acer triflorum* Komar.
Manchuria, Korea 1923. A rare tree grown in a few collections and gardens for its brilliant crimson colour in autumn. Differs from *A. nikoense* in its rough grey-brown shredding bark, instantly recognisable, and in 1–2 large ovate teeth on each leaflet of the thin, paler leaf. 6(11) × 0.8 m.

Rough-barked Maple

Paper-bark Maple

PAPER-BARK MAPLE *Acer griseum* (Franch.) Pax   **Pl. 30**
W. China 1901. Now much planted in gardens of all sizes; big trees confined to
large gardens. 13 × 1 m (12 × 1.6 m at 1 m Hergest Croft, Herefords.).
Bark. *Dark red, rich chestnut or coppery-brown*, peeling and rolling away sideways to leave smooth areas on bole branches and twigs.
Crown. A slender high open dome on ascending sinuous branches.
Foliage. Shoot dark red-brown. Bud ovoid-conic, pointed, minute, 1 mm,
nearly black. Leaf *trifoliate*, mid-leaflet on 1 cm stalk and long-cuneate, to 10
× 4 cm, ovate-oblong, a large rounded tooth at each shoulder and 0–2 more
smaller beyond; side leaflets sub-sessile, oblique at base with one very large
rounded tooth on the outer margin and 0–1 beyond it, 0–2 small teeth on inner
margin; dark grey-green and hairy above, blue-white densely pubescent beneath. Petiole dark pink, densely hairy, 5 cm. Leaves unfold pale orange-buff
late in May, become pink-brown, then yellowish, finally dark green; late-season
growth unfolds scarlet; autumn colour begins at ends of some shoots in early
October, cochineal crimson, whole crown deep crimson or deep red by end of
October.
Flowers and fruit. Flowers open as leaves unfold in late May hanging on 3 cm
pubescent pedicels in bunches of 3–5, pale greenish-yellow, campanulate,
1.5 cm across. Fruit large, each wing 3.5 × 1.5 cm, nearly parallel; seed seldom
fertile.
Similar species. The bark identifies instantly in the field; leaves like *A.
nikoense* (p. 348) but smaller with large teeth, and differ from *A. triflorum*
(p. 348) in being darker, thicker, narrower with lobes more toothed.

VINE-LEAFED MAPLE *Acer cissifolium*
(Sieb. and Zucc.) K. Koch
Japan 1875. Rare, collections and a few gardens.
Bark smooth grey developing large white patches.
Flat *wide crown* of dense level shoots. Leaf
trifoliate 20 cm including *wire-thin* red petiole to
10 cm long; each leaflet 8–10 cm on a wiry stalk
1–2 cm long; ovate, cuneate with long-acuminate
point and very large uneven long-pointed
teeth; flowers prolific on paired racemes stiffly
spreading 12 cm early May. Wings of fruit
parallel, 2 cm pale red; seed bright glossy green.
Foliage in autumn pale yellow. To 9 × 1 m.

Vine-leafed Maple

ASH-LEAFED MAPLE or BOX-ELDER *Acer negundo* L.   **Pl. 32**
E. N. America, Ontario to Florida and, as varieties, to Alberta, California and
Texas 1688. Common in town gardens, parks, car-parks and streets, usually
planted as a variegated form but allowed to revert to the type by failure to cut
out the stronger-growing, green-leafed shoots. 15 × 1.5(2.4) m.
Bark. Smooth grey-brown becoming dark grey, greened with algae and shallowly
cracked.

Crown. Irregularly domed; interior thickened by sprouts from branches and bole; older trees leaning or lying down.

Foliage. Shoot straight, green, bloomed violet in second year. Bud small, two-scaled, *silky white*. Leaf 3–7 *foliate*, to 20 × 15 cm when pinnate (5–7 leaflets), basal pairs on slender 1–2 cm stalks, upper pair sessile sometimes not completely divided, larger leaflets with a broad lobule, all shallowly and very irregularly toothed, pale green, thin-textured; petiole pale yellow or pink 6–8 cm. Autumn colours negligible, some pale yellow and brown, falling early.

Ash-leafed Maple

Flowers and fruit. Male and female on separate trees: male flowers prominent in March, bunch of 12–16 minutely slender hanging pedicels, green; pink near red anthers at tips, 5–8 cm long; females 6–12 per bunch, 5 cm long on pink pedicels. Fruit ripen early, brown, and persist after leaves have fallen; 2 cm; wings incurved at acute angle.

'AURATUM' 1891 Berlin. Leaves unfold rich yellow, bright gold until fading a little in August. Said to be less hardy; a splendid tree, frequent in S. London.

'AUREOMARGINATUM' Commonly planted but less striking than the next; leaf variegated with pale yellow.

'VARIEGATUM' 1845 Toulouse. The commonest form, female, leaves heavily margined and variegated with pure white; green sucker-shoots often taking over. Flowers 5–6 in 3 cm raceme, pale pink. Fruit develop as leaves unfold in late May; slender pendent racemes 10 cm, bearing five fruit, bright green with cream and pink wings 2 cm vertical, incurved.

'CALIFORNICUM' As usually seen these are one of two forms, properly 'Violaceum' and 'Pseudo-californicum', stronger-growing trees with bloomed young shoots, those of 'Violaceum' violet and the leaves dark green and petioles red; 'Pseudo-californicum' has green shoots, bloomed whitish and pale green leaves. The true var. *californicum* has densely pubescent shoots. ('Violaceum' is var. *violaceum* from S. Rocky Mts.)

HORSE CHESTNUT FAMILY   *Hippocastanaceae*

Three genera, only one in cultivation.

AESCULUS

About 25 species, most in N. America where numerous natural hybrids occur and a few in S. Europe, the Himalaya, China and Japan. Medium to large trees (one shrubby) with big, digitate leaves and erect panicles of flowers.

HORSE CHESTNUT   *Aesculus hippocastanum* L.   **Pl. 34**
Albania, Greece 1616. Very common as parkland and garden tree, in town parks, squares, churchyards and particularly on village greens in England, less common in Scotland and in Ireland. 38 × 6 m (38 × 6.1 m at Petworth House, Sussex; 32 × 6.4 m at Hurstbourne Priors Church, Hants.).
Bark. Reddish-brown or dark grey-brown breaking into long plates whose ends rise away from the bole or into large scales.
Crown. Huge tall dome branching at narrow angles; very old trees with low spreading then sharply upturned limbs, sometimes layering in vast circles.
Foliage. Shoot stout, pale pink-brown or reddish-purple with pale lenticels. Bud dark shiny red-brown, 2.5 × 1.5 cm, 'sticky buds' in spring. Leaf digitate; 5–7 obovate, long-cuneate, *sessile,* abruptly acuminate leaflets from stout yellow-green petiole to 20 cm long; central leaflet to 25 × 10 cm, doubly and obtusely toothed, bright fresh green at first, soon darker; yellowish-green beneath. Autumn colour very variable: occasional trees scarlet early, soon bare; others gold and orange, mid-September to early November. The leaf-scar is large and like an inverted horse-shoe, complete with apparent "nail-holes".
Flowers and fruit. Flowers abundant every year, odd trees always much ahead, flowering at the beginning of April, general flowering from late April to mid-May. Flowers with five, fringed, ciliate petals, white with large blotch at base bright purple-red or yellow; 2 cm across, on panicles 15–30 cm, with radiating peduncles each with five closely held flowers opening 1–2 at a time. Fruit green, globular, 6 cm, with short, sharp flexible spines; splitting when ready to fall in September to show soft white lining and either one, big flattened-globular "conker" or 2–3 with flat sides, bright shiny, grained, mahogany-brown with a large white circular area soon pinkish-brown.
Growth. Buds open on a few early trees in early March, but mainly in early April. Young trees may grow 60–80 cm from mid-April to late July but slow markedly with age. A few trees are known to be over 300 years old and in good health but many only about 150 years old shed branches and break up.

'BAUMANNII' ('Flore plena') 1820 Geneva. Double, white flowers on shorter panicles lasting longer and producing no conkers and hence sometimes planted in public places.
Similar species. The "sticky buds" and stalkless leaflets distinguish from all other *Aesculus* species except *Ae. turbinata* (p. 354).

RED HORSE CHESTNUT   *Aesculus × carnea* Hayne   **Pl. 34**
A fertile true-breeding hybrid between *Ae. hippocastanum* and *Ae. pavia.* Europe before 1818. All too commonly planted in parks, gardens, avenues and

Plate 35 HORSE CHESTNUTS (Contd.), LIMES

1. Indian Horse Chestnut *Aesculus indica* 356

Grey-brown shoot in summer. The leaves have slender leaflets on relatively long, often red stalks.

2. Yellow Buck-eye *Aesculus flava* 354

(a) Inflorescence. The flowers can be quite bright yellow.
(b) Leaf, showing the five, slender, long-stalked leaflets which are glossy bright green and very finely toothed.

3. Caucasian Lime *Tilia euchlora* 360

(a) Shoot and leaves. The shoot remains yellow-green in winter. The leaf is very glossy above, paler beneath with prominent orange-buff tufts in the vein-axils.
(b) Fruit hanging from bract.

4. American Lime *Tilia americana* 360

Leaf. This is very large but thin, and is the same green each side, the only lime in which this is so.

1

2a

2b

3a

3b

4

LIMES (Contd.)

Plate 36

1. Common Lime *Tilia europaea* 359

    (a) Shoot and leaves, one showing pale underside with pale buff tufts in vein axils.

    (b) Fruit and bract.

2. Small-leafed Lime *Tilia cordata* 358

    (a) Leaf with glaucous underside with pale orange tufts in vein-axils.

    (b) Leaves, flowers and young fruit. The inflorescences may be all erect or at random angles.

3. Silver Pendent Lime *Tilia petiolaris* 362

    (a) Leaf. The petiole is as long or longer than the blade.

    (b) Leaf, underside, densely covered in white pubescence.

A taller, narrowly crowned and pendulous form of *Tilia tomentosa*.

4. Large-leafed Lime *Tilia platyphyllos* 358

    (a) Outline of tree 23 m tall.

    (b) Shoot and leaf. The shoot, petiole and both sides of the leaf are pubescent at first, but by autumn only the veins beneath the leaf are densely hairy, the other parts may be nearly glabrous.

Common Lime   Silver Pendent Lime

streets and as commemorative tree. An inherently dull, dark tree of poor crown, foliage and flowers, and fruit of no interest. It grows slowly and suffers from a canker disease so is, fortunately, not long-lived. 22 × 2 m.

Bark. Dark grey-green at first, striped pale pink, later reddish-brown, finely roughened and lenticelled, often cankered and burred. Often grafted at 1.5 m on *Ae. hippocastanum.*

Crown. A low dome of rather twisting, spreading branches.

Foliage. Shoot pale greenish-grey or pinkish-grey with raised orange-buff lenticels. Bud: weaker shoots end with a *pair of buds*, strong shoots with a single bud, 1.5–2.5 cm, ovoid, sometimes shiny, usually dull, grey-green scales with dark pink or purplish broad margins. Leaf darker, rougher, usually smaller than in *Ae. hippocastanum* but sometimes as big, with centre leaflet to 25 × 13 cm and petiole to 23 cm. Leaflets sub-sessile or with stout 1 cm petiolules radiating from thickened sunken centre; blackish-green and crinkled, *broad*, *jaggedly* toothed, hard, obovate or elliptic, yellowish-green beneath. Autumn colour nil.

Flowers and fruit. Flowers dull, muddy red on panicles 12–20 cm long in May. Fruit smaller with fewer spines than *Ae. hippocastanum*, sometimes all but smooth, containing 2–3 dull, small seeds.

'BRIOTII' 1858 France. A definite improvement on the type and of better health. Flowers brighter red; inflorescence 15 × 8 cm with ruby-red peduncle; petals crimson-red, style white, 3 cm drooping or spreading. Leaf more glossy.

JAPANESE HORSE CHESTNUT   *Aesculus turbinata* Bl.
Japan. About 1880. Infrequent; some large gardens north to S. Scotland, and in Ireland. 21 × 2.3 m.

Bark. Young trees corky grey-pink with sinuous *white streaks* in fissures; old trees smooth pink-grey, a few wide fissures.

Crown. Rather broadly domed; branches at wide angles.

Foliage. Shoot pink, bloomed grey-brown, very stout. Bud ovoid, pointed; glossy chocolate red-brown, 2.5 × 1.5 cm. Leaf seven enormous *sessile* leaflets, obovate *gradually* acuminate, to 40 × 18 cm on petiole to 42 cm, the whole leaf to 65 cm across, variably shiny dark grey-green above and pale green, sometimes silvery beneath, *orange tufts* often in axils along the midrib; fine rounded uneven teeth on margin. Autumn colour bright orange, the veins remaining white and pale green at first, then all-over orange-brown.

Flowers and fruit. Inflorescence domed, conic or narrowly cylindric panicle, some upcurved, 8–30 cm; flowers white with red blotches on strongly recurved petals; stamens downswept. Fruit small, seeds dark brown, small, 1.5 cm.

Similar species. *Ae. hippocastanum* differs in bark, size of leaf and abrupt acuminate tip.

SWEET or YELLOW BUCK-EYE   *Aesculus flava* Soland.   Pl. 35
  Syn. *Ae. octandra* Marsh.
South-eastern USA 1764. Infrequent; large gardens and a few parks mainly in England. 20 × 2 m.

Bark. Pink-grey or red-brown, large smooth areas with lenticels, parts shedding small, thick scales.

Crown. Domed with twisting branches.

Foliage. Shoot shiny grey-fawn; few scattered lenticels. Bud smooth nonresinous, pale pinkish-fawn scales edged pink, paired at ends of less strong shoots. Leaf five (rarely four or three) leaflets, *fully-stalked,* finely serrate, narrow-elliptic, acuminate, 10–15 cm long, *shiny,* bright or dark green above, often cupped, variably pubescent especially on the veins beneath. Autumn colour bright orange-red.

Flowers and fruit. Flowers yellow, occasionally pink, tubular, 4 cm long in dense bunches of 5–6 each, on small panicles 10–15 cm long; fruit lumpy, oblique globose, smooth. Many trees are grafted on to *Ae. hippocastanum* and the union is apparent.

Similar species. *Ae.* × *hybrida* (below), otherwise the five, glossy, cupped leaflets are quite distinct.

HYBRID RED BUCK-EYE   *Aesculus* × *hybrida* DC.

Syns. *Ae. versicolor* Wender, *Ae. lyoni* Hort., *Ae. discolor* Hort.

Hybrid *Ae. flava* × *pavia* pre-1815. Infrequent, grafted tree very like *Ae. flava* with broader coarser leaflets on much shorter petioles or subsessile with tufted axils beneath and flowers variously pink or red, which differ from *Ae. flava* in having glandular petals.

SUNRISE HORSE CHESTNUT   *Aesculus neglecta* 'Erythroblastos'

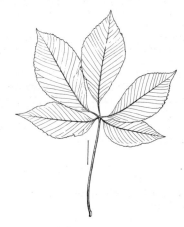

c. 1932 Berlin. Cultivar of an American species, grown for the spectacular colouring of the unfolding leaves. Prominent at Westonbirt, Glos. (biggest tree behind the office); young trees in many gardens; still rare. 8 m. Crown: a broad low dome. Shoot grey. Bud pale green, grey and orange, *tips of scales spreading free,* pale orange. In late April leaves unfold bright pink, redder in older trees and fade over the next two weeks. Five leaflets, 15 × 8 cm, obovate-lanceolate, tip finely acuminate; doubly serrate; bright yellow-green above when the bright pink is lost,

Sunrise Horse Chestnut

main vein prominent and densely pubescent; paler underside with sparse down on prominent veins. Leaflet on bright green petiolule 1 cm long; rachis bright green, 8–10 cm. Some leaves retain central areas of whitish-green.

RED BUCK-EYE   *Aesculus pavia* L.

South-eastern USA 1711. Very rare, small tree with pale grey-green shoots, five stalked leaflets to 18 × 7 cm on yellow-pink petiole to 18 cm; occasionally small leaves have winged petioles. The tree sometimes grown in gardens as

"*Ae. pavia*" has 10 cm ruby-red petioles, pale blue-grey shoots, five leaflets to 13 × 5 cm, dark shiny yellow-green and bright red flowers. This is another hybrid with *Ae. flava*.

INDIAN HORSE CHESTNUT   *Aesculus indica* Colebr.   **Pl. 35**

The Himalayas 1851. Infrequent; in some large gardens in each country, more planted recently in parks, by roads and in other public places to extend season of flower of horse chestnuts. 19 × 2.3 m.

Bark. Young trees grey-green striped white, older trees smooth pink-grey.

Crown. Tall-domed on ascending radiating branches; sometimes very short-boled or many-stemmed.

Foliage. Shoot pale yellowish-fawn, to yellowish grey-brown, rough with lenticels. Bud red-brown and pink-brown, shiny, resinous, pointed ovoid, 1.5 cm. Leaf unfolds bright orange, fades to deep green, 5–9 *slender, stalked leaflets*, often hanging like slender spread fingers on pink or reddish long, 10–18 cm petiole; centre leaflet to 32 cm long, all obovate-lanceolate, finely serrated; often waved, hard and crinkled; underside glabrous and glaucous.

Indian Horse Chestnut

Flowers and fruit. Flowers towards end of June, some trees rosy-pink, others with lower petals white, upper yellow or red; stamens long-exserted, bent down, then curved up at tip; panicles 13(30) × 8 cm; fruit smooth leathery, husk supple and thin; seeds glossy blackish-brown, flattened-globular, wrinkled, to 4 cm across, 2.5 cm high with a small circular pale brown area 1.5 cm across.

'SIDNEY PEARCE' 1928 Kew. 15 × 1.7 m (Original, Kew). Sturdy form with dark green petioles and leaves, and abundant cylindric panicles 30 × 8 cm; flowers dark pink in bud, opening to 2.5 × 3 cm pale pink, blotched yellow, orange, red or purple on same panicle.

SOAPBERRY FAMILY   *Sapindaceae*

A large and variable mainly tropical family of which only one genus grows into trees hardy here.

KOELREUTERIA

Four species in E. Asia. Leaf large pinnate or doubly pinnate, alternate; flowers yellow in large terminal panicles.

PRIDE OF INDIA or GOLDEN RAIN TREE   *Koelreuteria paniculata*
Laxm.   **Pl. 34**

China, Korea, Japan 1763. Infrequent; large gardens in S. England, E. Anglia and N.W. Herefordshire, rare in Ireland. 14 × 1.6 m. By main road at Tintern, Glos.

Bark. Brown to purple-brown, rough with short narrow orange fissures.

Crown. Slender high dome on ascending sinuous branches.

Foliage. Shoot pale copper-brown. Bud 2mm like squashed spinning-top with short, curved beak. Leaf to 45 cm, pinnate, usually bi-pinnate at base and imperfect at the tip, 11–13 leaflets; leaflets from 18 cm lobulate, lobed or pinnate, to 8 cm, oblong-ovate, doubly toothed near tip; matt dark green above, sub-shiny beneath with pink midrib. Whole leaf on red rachis grooved above, flanged at sides and green below; unfolding dark red in late May, soon turning pale whitish-yellow, then dark green.

Flowers and fruit. Flowers July–August, small, bright yellow, 1 cm across on open, widely branched panicles 30–45 cm long above and beyond the crown. Fruit a papery bladder containing three black seeds, the bladder conspicuous and pink in autumn.

'FASTIGIATA' 1888. A rare, narrowly fastigiate form with sinuous, erect branches. Original tree at Kew now 14 × 0.7 m.

Similar species. The leaf is unique, resembling *Gymnocladus* (p. 303) only in being bi-pinnate but toothing, dark colour, flanged red rachis and flowers all quite different.

LIME FAMILY *Tiliaceae*

Three hundred species in 35 genera; one genus of hardy trees with fragrant flowers in cymes on stalks with a bract attached.

LIMES Tilia

About 30 species in the temperate northern hemisphere except in N.W. America. Leaf oblique at base, flowers in cyme adhering half way along a large bract.

Key to Tilia species

1. Underside silvery or grey with dense very fine pubescence	**2**
Underside pubescent only on veins or tufts in axils	**5**
2. Dense white pubescence also on shoot and petiole	**3**
Shoot green, glabrous; petiole nearly glabrous	**4**
3. Petiole half length of blade; foliage spreading	*tomentosa*, p. 361
Petiole + half blade; foliage pendulous	*petiolaris*, p. 362
4. Leaf very flat, pale green; silver beneath	*oliveri*, p. 361
Leaf dark green above, greyish beneath	× *moltkei*, p. 361
5. Shoot, petiole coarsely pubescent at first; both sides of leaf pubescent along veins	*platyphyllos*, p. 358
Shoot, petiole glabrous; underside with pubescence in axil-tufts or absent	**6**
6. Underside nearly glabrous; small white tufts; leaf big, same green both sides; coarse toothing	*americana*, p. 360
Axils prominently tufted buff or orange; leaf paler beneath than above	**7**

7. Leaf glossy deep green above, big orange-brown tufts beneath;
  shoots bright yellow-green   *euchlora*, p. 360
  Leaf dull green above; shoots green or red   **8**

8. Leaf neatly cordate, small; bud red   *cordata*, p. 358
  Leaf coarsely oblique, often large; bud brown-red or green   × *europaea*, p. 359

LARGE-LEAFED LIME *Tilia platyphyllos* Scop.   **Pl. 36**

Native to limestone soils in the Wye Valley and S. Yorkshire or perhaps early introduction. Europe from N. Spain and Sweden east to Crimea, Caucasus and Asia Minor. Common as street tree in towns where it occasionally equals *T. europaea* in numbers; frequent as park, avenue and garden tree. 31 × 5.8 m.

Bark. Dark grey, finely fissured, sometimes ribbed, or with small, flat ridges; rarely with sprouts at base (although it is often stated that they never occur).

Crown. Tall, narrow dome on clean, grey branches ascending at narrow angles; more hemispherical when young; rarely very spreading.

Foliage. Shoot reddish-green, markedly pubescent but hairs may be confined to tip by autumn. Bud ovoid, dark red. Leaf rounded-ovate, abruptly acuminate, obliquely and deeply cordate, sharply crenate-serrate, hard, dark green and *pubescent above*, pale and densely pubescent on veins beneath; size very variable 6–15 × 6–15 cm, petiole 2–5 cm *pubescent*. An un-named form locally frequent in gardens has very small dark leaves held densely in level layers, each leaf curved down from the centre and up at the edges, very pubescent.

Flowers and fruit. The first lime in flower, flowers hanging in threes or fours (fives, sixes) in late June, 12 mm, five yellowish-white sepals, five yellower petals, from prominent whitish-green bract; fruit five-ribbed, densely pubescent, globose, 8–10 mm.

'Laciniata'

  'RUBRA' ('Corallina'). Frequent as small tree, rare as large tree, to 30 m. Shoots dark red in winter, normally green in summer. Flower-bracts large, 9 × 2 cm, pale cream to greenish-white. Crown nearly globular or broadly domed; denser and brighter green than in the type, when in leaf.

  'LACINIATA' ('Aspleniifolia') A fairly frequent form, grafted, to 16 × 1.5 m with a more dense crown and leaves 5–6 cm long, long-acuminate and lobed or coarsely toothed, cut almost to the midrib. Reverts freely. A variegated form of this seemingly almost confined to Irish gardens, is fastigiate.

Similar species. The name "Large-leafed Lime" is misleading as leaves on sprouts of *T.* × *europaea* are often larger and the small-leafed variant mentioned has leaves the size of those of *T. cordata*, the Small-leafed Lime. The hairy petiole and veins and big-bracted flower-stalks with only 3–4 flowers or fruit, readily distinguish. Usually a much cleaner and more shapely tree than *T.* × *europaea*. (p. 359)

SMALL-LEAFED LIME *Tilia cordata* Mill.   **Pl. 36**

Syn. *T. parvifolia* Ehrh.

Native in England and Wales especially on limestone cliffs, north to Lake District. Frequent in parks and gardens north to S. Scotland and in Ireland, occasional in suburban gardens, streets and churchyards, the last notably in Suffolk. Great avenues at Hampton Court. N. Spain to Caucasus and Siberia. 32 × 6 m (30 × 5.4 m at Oakley Park, Salop.).

Bark. Young trees very smooth, grey with few pale brown cracks; old trees dark grey or brown, much cracked into shallow plates.

Crown. Tall irregular dense domes; old trees with heavy downward-arched branches and burrs and sprouts on bole.

Foliage. Shoot mahogany-red above, olive-brown beneath with raised, buff lenticels; old trees green-brown. Bud smooth, dark, shiny red, ovoid. Leaf nearly round, cordate, abruptly acuminate, 4–7 × 3–5 cm on 3.5cm yellow-green or pinkish petiole; finely and sharply serrate, dark shiny green (yellowish in old trees) above, rather thick and hard in young trees, pale often *glaucous beneath* with large buff or *orange tufts* in vein-axils and, in a small-leafed and very floriferous form, long thick orange hairs around the petiole and base of leaf. An uncommon form has long-triangular leaves.

Flowers and fruit. Flowers in short, dense bunches of 5–10, erect or, more usually, *spreading at random angles*, open in early July. Bract 6cm, bright pale green; sepals 5–6, elliptic, 3mm, white; petals five, lanceolate, 7–8mm, translucent white; stamens widely spread, 2 cm across, about 40, white with short, bright yellow anthers. Fruit small, 6mm globose, scarcely or not at all ribbed, glabrous.

Similar species. A variant of *T. platyphyllos* (p. 358); *T. × europaea* (below) and *T. euchlora* (p. 360). The dense yellowish-green crowns of old trees can be identified at a distance.

COMMON LIME   *Tilia × europaea* L.   **Pl. 36**
  Syn. *T. vulgaris* Hayne

A hybrid, *T. platyphyllos × cordata*, of natural origin, probably introduced long ago but possibly native. Abundant especially in streets and avenues, for which it must be the least suitable tree of any; by roadsides, on village greens, in parks and churchyards in towns and cities, in deer-parks, large gardens and town gardens, where a victim of hideous lopping and mutilation. The tallest broad-leafed tree in most areas and in Britain as a whole. 40 × 7 m (46 × 3.7 m at Duncombe Park, Yorks.).

Bark. Dull grey, smooth at first, finely fissured or with network of flat, shallow ridges; burred and densely sprout-infested especially at the base.

Crown. Tall, billowing domes on ascending then arching branches, the centre often partly filled by huge masses of sprouts and the tops much bedecked with mistletoe. Oldest trees with huge low branches, and upper ones thickened and bent.

Foliage. Shoot green, often tinged dark red, rarely slightly pubescent. Bud ovoid, reddish-brown; green on sprouts. Leaf broad-ovate, short-acuminate, obliquely cordate to truncate, 6–10cm long (15 × 15 on sprouts), sharply crenate, dull green above, often infested with Nail-gall like red dunces' hats; sub-shiny beneath, glabrous except for *small white or buff tufts* in main axils; petiole 2–5 cm glabrous, green. Autumn colour usually nil; rarely some leaves bright yellow, then brown. During the summer, foliage is shiny with honey-dew from the aphids which swarm on the trees and this rains down on to anything beneath the tree, where it then goes black with Sooty-mould.

Flowers and fruit. Flowers pendulous in 4–10 flowered cymes, yellowish-white in early July; bract yellowish-green; fruit broadly ovoid, 8mm faintly ribbed, pubescent.

Similar species. *T. platyphyllos* (p. 358), *T. cordata* (p.358).

CAUCASIAN LIME   *Tilia euchlora* Koch   **Pl. 35**

Caucasus about 1860. Possibly a hybrid between
T. cordata and another Caucasian lime (*T. dasystyla:*
found here in a few collections only). Infrequent;
parks, sometimes streets (e.g. Cambridge) and large
gardens; in favour for replacing Common Lime in
streets but although the insect-free foliage is handsome, the crown at length becomes unattractive.
18 × 2 m.

Bark. Smooth, pewter-grey, striated dark grey; big
boles with a few deep brown fissures.

Crown. A fine clean bole for 2–3 m then a sprawl of
sinuous, generally ascending branches twisting over
and down in a toadstool-like dome with pendulous
shoots around the edge. The down-curved branches
become grossly thickened when the tree is about 40
years old.

Caucasian Lime

Foliage. Shoot typically bright *chlorine-green* ("lime-green") or dull yellowish-
green but some trees have the exposed outer shoots pink or
red. Bud smooth, terminal red and yellow, lateral yellow-
pink. Leaf rounded-ovate, abruptly short-acuminate,
obliquely cordate, 5–10 cm long (to 15 × 14 cm on sprouts),
finely and sharply mucronate-crenate; petiole 5 cm, yellow-
green; upper side of leaf rich deep *glossy green* with pale
teeth, underside pale green with *large tufts of brown hairs* in
axils and, at first, long straight brown hairs perpendicular
from the basal veins. Autumn colour bright gold usually only
in parts of the crown.

Flowers and fruit. Flowers mostly after other limes in
late July but some trees early in July; 3–7 in a pendulous
cyme, rather rich yellow; bract greenish-white, 8 cm   Caucasian Lime
oblanceolate; fruit pubescent, somewhat five-ribbed, ovoid, narrowed at end.

Similar species. *T. cordata* (p. 358) and some shoots of *T. × europaea*
(p. 358) may resemble this but the species is readily distinguished.

AMERICAN LIME   *Tilia americana* L.   **Pl. 35**

E. Canada and USA 1752. Rare; a few collections in each country. 23 × 2 m.

Bark. Rich, dark brown sometimes grey, rough and pitted, craggy with broken
scales.

Crown. Tall, open dome on few upcurved large branches.

Foliage. Shoot apple-green, bright and smooth. Bud apple-green, smooth and
bright, ovoid. Leaf big, to 20 × 18 cm, floppy but quite hard, broad-ovate,
abruptly acuminate, obliquely cordate, coarsely edged by triangular acuminate
teeth; distinctive yellowish-green *above and below; glabrous*, except for minute
tufts along each main vein beneath; petiole stout, dull yellow, 5 cm.

Flowers and fruit. Flowers 10–12 in pendulous cyme, 1.5 cm each; bract
10 × 2.5 cm, green with pink midrib; fruit smooth, glabrous. Rarely grows well
or lives very long here.

Similar species. *T. × moltkei* (below); big, coarsely toothed leaf, glabrous and
similar colour each side and rich green appearance distinguish *T. americana*.

VON MOLTKE'S HYBRID LIME *Tilia × moltkei* Spaeth

Hybrid *T. americana × petiolaris*, Germany before 1880. 25 × 3 m. A rare tree in a few large gardens especially in S.W. Ireland. Probably includes the smaller-leaved *Tilia × spectabilis* which makes such fine trees at Kew. Similar to *T. americana* with a very big leaf to 25 × 15 cm, dark matt and rough above but with soft *grey very close pubescence beneath* and on petiole. Rather pendulous and very handsome; more thriving and vigorous than *T. americana*.

OLIVER'S LIME *Tilia oliveri* Szysz.

C. China 1900. A rare tree in some large gardens and collections, with superbly handsome foliage. 23 × 1.8 m (Westonbirt).

Oliver's Lime

Bark. Smooth, soft grey with brown hair-streaks; branch-scars marked by *dark folds* curved over them ("Chinaman's moustache").

Crown. Clean ascending branches to a high dome; open as a young tree.

Foliage. Shoot stout, slightly zigzag, apple-green to pink-brown. Bud 7 mm, ovoid, smooth apple-green and red, grey pubescence at tip. Leaf elegant, *very plane*, pale *fresh green*, matt, smooth, with nearly white small peg-like mucronate teeth; oblique, slightly cordate, rounded-ovate, short-acuminate; curved, entire tip; 13 × 11 cm on 6 cm petiole (to 20 × 18 cm on 8 cm petiole high on big trees), *bright silvery* beneath. Leaves rather distant and well held out level from down-curved stalk. When leaves first unfolded, the bud-scales adhere, decurved, dark red, oblong-lanceolate, 3 × 1 cm.

Flowers and fruit. Flowers 2–4 on 4 cm peduncle from big bract of 10 × 2 cm which is bright green above, whitish beneath. Fruit large smooth globular, 1 cm grey-green with short, dense pubescence.

SILVER LIME *Tilia tomentosa* Moench

S.E. Europe, S.W. Asia 1767. Frequent; in London and other city and town parks and in many large gardens. 25 × 3 m (29 × 4.2 m at Tortworth Church, Glos.).

Silver Lime

Bark. Dark grey-green at first with buff *striae*; older trees dark to pale grey with shallow network of smooth flat ridges.

Crown. Younger trees remarkably regularly hemispheric on good boles; old trees broadly domed, branches steeply ascending, often some heavy and low.

Foliage. Shoot whitish with dense close pubescence, later dark grey-green above, bright green beneath. Rather zigzag. Laterals short and perpendicular. Bud ovoid, green and brown, 6–8 mm, pubescent. Leaf rounded, abruptly acuminate, cordate one side, truncate the other, fairly big sharp forward teeth; thick, dark green and rather crinkled above, pale *grey densely pubescent* beneath, and curved up at edges; 12 × 10 cm on 5 cm densely short-pubescent whitish petiole. Leaves held level, rather densely.

Flowers and fruit. Flowers late, very fragrant, towards end of July 7–10 on
3 cm peduncle, short-cylindric; five, ovate, pale yellow petals; rich golden
anthers; on yellow-green obovate bract of 9×2 cm; fruit 8–10 mm slightly
warted and five-angled.
Similar species. *T. petiolaris* (below) which has longer petioles and pendulous,
thinner leaves.

SILVER PENDENT LIME   *Tilia petiolaris* DC.   **Pl. 36**

Origin not known, probably Caucasian but possibly of early garden origin. Pre-
1840. Frequent, large gardens, parks in towns and cities, churchyards; more
frequent than *T. tomentosa* 27.5×3.6 m (by Magdalen Bridge, Oxford). $33 \times$
3.6 m (Bath B.G.) 33×4.2 m Orchardleigh, Somerset.
Bark. Dark and pale grey with smooth, shallow ridges.
Crown. *Grafted at* 2 m from which point usually 2–3 strongly ascending rather
sinuous branches rise to form a tall narrow dome with exterior branchlets
pendulous. In summer dense with dark leaves, patterned silver by the underside
of leaves on hanging shoots.
Foliage. Shoot pale greenish-grey with close, dense pubescence. Bud dull green,
ovoid, 5 mm. Leaf deeply cordate, rounded-ovate, sharply serrate, plane, increasing in size on later growth as season progresses, on hanging shoots; to
12×12 cm on *slender* densely white-pubescent petiole 6–12 cm long; upper
surface dark green, underside white with dense pubescence. Autumn colour
bright yellow in patches.
Flowers and fruit. As *T. tomentosa* (above).

EUCHRYPHIA FAMILY   *Eucryphiaceae*

A family of a single genus with four species in the southern hemisphere, in
Australia, Tasmania, Argentina and Chile.

NYMANS HYBRID EUCRYPHIA   *Eucryphia* $\times$ *nymansensis* Bausch
   'Nymansay'

1915 Nymans, Sussex. The selected seedling 'A' of a number raised which were
hybrids between *E. glutinosa* and *E. cordifolia* both from S. America. Frequent
in large gardens, particularly in western regions where it attains 15 m.
Bark. Smooth, pale-brown, striated buff.
Crown. Dense, irregular broad column; upper branches upswept, lower
drooping. Nearly black, evergreen.
Foliage. Shoot pale green, ribbed, densely pubescent. Bud ovoid-conic, pale
green, 6 mm. Leaves evergreen, vari-
able: large ones trifoliate, smaller may
have one minor leaflet, smallest are
simple. Larger leaf: central leaflet,
oblong-ovate, 8×3.5 cm, crenately
toothed, deep, somewhat glossy green
above, pale beneath, densely pubescent
on veins. Side-leaflets spreading widely,
may overlap central leaflet, sessile to
5×2 cm. Rachis 1–2 cm, pale green,
densely pubescent.

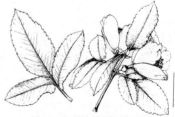

Nyman's Hybrid Eucryphia

Flowers. Late August to mid-September, mostly on upper half of tree, large, white, 4–5 petals, orbicular or ovate, 4 cm long; large boss of slender stamens with pink anthers.

TEA FAMILY   *Theaceae*

About 200 species mainly tropical but a few temperate shrubs e.g. *Camellia*, and *Stewartia*.

STEWARTIA

A genus of eight species from Eastern USA and E. Asia, named after John Stuart, Earl of Bute, so sometimes given as "*Stuartia*". Deciduous, rather small trees valuable for handsome white flowers in midsummer and often for coloured, smooth bark.

DECIDUOUS CAMELLIA   *Stewartia pseudo-camellia* Maxim.

Japan 1874. Infrequent; some large gardens in S. England. 17 × 1.2 m. Usually a slender, open-crowned little tree with orange-brown bark becoming *bright orange* where purple-grey scales have fallen. The dark, ovate-lanceolate, cuneate, acuminate leaves are remotely crenate and waved, 3–8 cm long, densely set, *dull above*, *shiny beneath* with small tufts in vein-axils. The white, cup-shaped flowers, 5–6 cm across open to show orange anthers in late July from erect buds between two oval, green bracts edged dark red. Good autumn colours, yellow to dark red.

Deciduous Camellia

CHINESE STEWARTIA   *Stewartia sinensis* Rehd. and Wils.

C. China 1901. Rare, in collections in S. England and Ireland. 10 × 1 m. A striking small tree, upright branched at first, then wide-spreading, in which the bole and branches shed all scales and outer bark and stand naked, flesh-pink to grey or creamy-orange, very smooth with a few rounded wrinkles. Shoot crimson-purple. Petiole 1 cm, red and pubescent, leaf 10 × 4 cm, oblong-lanceolate, rounded or cuneate base, curved acuminate tip, forward serrulate, bright green both sides; flower-buds erect in involucre of five lobes, each bright green, edged dark red, ovate, 1 cm; buds opening in late July, 4–5 petals, thick, fleshy, broad, 3.5 × 2 cm, white; bunches of white stamens with yellow anthers. Good reds and crimson autumn colour.

Chinese Stewartia

FLACOURTIA FAMILY *Flacourtiaceae*

Some 500 species mainly tropical with three species each in a different genus in cultivation here, but two are too rarely seen to include.

IDESIA

Single species in Japan and China, dioecious.

IDESIA *Idesia polycarpa* Maxim.
Japan, China 1864. Rare; a few large gardens in England and Ireland. 16 × 1.3 m (Abbotsbury, Dorset). At first glance resembling a Catalpa but with very level, wide branches; *scarlet petioles* 12–30 cm long, and coarse, distant *hook-tipped teeth* on the big, broadly ovate, acuminate, cordate leaves which are dark, glossy, yellowish-green, glabrous, thickly veined, to 20 × 20 cm and glaucous beneath with tufts in the basal axils. Small, yellow fragrant flowers on open, conic, terminal spreading or pendulous panicles 10–25 cm long, followed by orange-brown fruit 8 mm across. Bark smooth, grey-green and pink, lenticelled, and wrinkled horizontally.

Idesia

PITTOSPORUM FAMILY *Pittosporaceae*

A genus of 150 small evergreen trees mainly from Australasia but also from Japan and South Africa. Flower parts in fives.

PITTOSPORUM *Pittosporum tenuifolium* Gaertn.
New Zealand *c.* 1850. Frequent in Ireland and Cornwall; infrequent to uncommon near the west coast; becoming rare eastwards to Surrey and Sussex. 16 × 1.5 m.
Bark. Dull grey, smooth.
Crown. Ovoid, somewhat erect, finely branched, bushy, but not dense.
Foliage. Shoot slender, *dark purplish* brown, finely pubescent. Bud 2 mm, conic, pale yellow-green, tipped crimson-purple. Leaves alternate, well-spaced, mostly on outer half of shoot; oblong-elliptic to 5 × 2.5 cm; margin entire but deeply *waved and crinkled*; bright *pale green* with prominent

Pittosporum

whitish midrib, slightly glossy above; whitish beneath and very matt. Petiole 1–5 mm, whitish-green.

Flowers and fruit. In leaf axils, May, dark purple, cup-shaped with outcurved tips to the five petals; 6–7 mm across, highly fragrant in the evening. Fruit a green capsule ripening black, 1.5 cm.

'VARIEGATUM' A pale cream-variegated form, growing to the same size as the type, in Ireland and Cornwall but very rare elsewhere. (One at Muncaster Castle, Cumberland.) 'SILVER QUEEN' has silvery-green leaves.

Recognition. The bright pale green, crinkled leaves make this an attractive and distinctive plant. The foliage is commonly seen in florists' shops.

TUPELO FAMILY *Nyssaceae*

A small family closely related to Cornaceae (Dogwoods).

TUPELOS Nyssa

Six species: four in N. America, and two in E. Asia.

TUPELO or BLACK GUM *Nyssa sylvatica* L.

E. N. America pre-1750. Infrequent; mainly in large gardens in S. England (north to Chatsworth, Derbyshire); notable planting 1909, Sheffield Park, Sussex. 15(24) × 1(2.3)m.

Bark. Fawn-grey or dark grey, almost at once coarsely fissured into vertical, rough, broad ridges.

Crown. Broadly conic, branches level, curved up towards the tip; lateral shoots spiky, perpendicular, short, slightly curved.

Foliage. Shoot smooth greenish-brown, some tinged purple; few small lenticels. Bud small, pointed conic, red-brown. Leaf variable in shape and size from obovate and acute to elliptic and obtuse, 5–12 cm long, rarely to 18 × 7 cm; petiole 1 cm, dark red; leaf glossy dark or yellowish-green, *entire,* rarely a few coarse teeth; whitish-green beneath, usually glabrous. Very late into leaf-buds open in late May; autumn colours vivid scarlet and gold, still glossy, finally deep red.

Flowers. On 4–5 upcurved, green 3 cm peduncles at base of new growth in mid-June. Males in globular heads 3 mm across; yellow-green sepals and anthers. Females 2–3 on each peduncle, cylindric or conic 4 mm green; style exserted 3 mm pale yellow, tipped purple. Less commonly only two pendulous peduncles per node (var. *biflora* Sargent). Usually dioecious. Fruit 8 × 5 mm ovoid plum-purple, bloomed.

var. *biflora*
Female flowers
(x 2)

Tupelo. *Left,* female flowers

Recognition. Spiky, curved shoots and glossy, entire leaf.

DAVIDIA

Single species (often regarded as two) in China.

DOVE-TREE or GHOST-TREE *Davidia involucrata* Baill. **Pl. 37**
W. China 1904. Infrequent; large gardens mostly in the south and west.
18 × 1.3 m. Most trees so labelled are var. *vilmoriniana*. Also regrettably known
as "Handkerchief-tree".
Bark. Purple finely flaking pale brown, or grey-brown; finely fissured vertically.
Crown. Conic, becoming a high dome on radiating branches, the lower branches
level; shoots rather few and stout.
Foliage. Shoot dark brown, glabrous; pale lenticels. Bud ovoid, bright, *shiny
deep red*, 1.5 cm. Leaf broad-ovate, deeply cordate, acuminate, to 17 × 15 cm,
5–9 pairs of sub-opposite impressed veins; teeth big, 5 mm, *triangular acuminate;*
petiole 15 cm pink, yellow-green or rarely dark red; leaf deep, sub-shiny green
above, pale with soft, *white, dense pubescence* beneath.
Flowers and fruit. Flower, as leaves emerge, globose, purple head 6 mm
across under pale green bract, opens to yellow in a dense head 2 cm across on a
7 cm stalk with bract now large, very thin, veined like the leaf, white, oval,
17 × 10 cm, hanging on one side and one about half that size on the other side.
Flowers copious on trees more than about 20 years old, a few from ten years,
spectacular in late May. Fruit 3 × 2.8 cm, obovoid, much ribbed, deep green,
slightly glossy, speckled buff, ripening dark purple. Pedicel 10–14 cm, dark red,
much swollen at fruit-end.

var. *vilmoriniana* (Dode) Wanger.
C. and W. China 1897 (to France) 1901. Frequent in parks and gardens, particularly in the west and in Ireland. The common form. As the type, except
leaf *glabrous* and *shiny pale green* beneath, may be oval to 20 × 17 cm and fruit
narrower, 3 × 2.3 cm on shorter 7 cm pink and yellow pedicel. 19 × 2 m.
Recognition. Leaf like a large, dark lime leaf with deep prominent veins, big
sharp teeth, and pinkish petiole.

MYRTLE FAMILY *Myrtaceae*

A vast group of aromatic trees and shrubs from warm regions.

MYRTLES Myrtus

A large genus of evergreen plants, mostly shrubby; none reliably hardy in E. England.

ORANGE-BARK MYRTLE *Myrtus apiculata* Niedenz.

Syns. *M. luma* Molina, *Eugenia apiculata* DC.

Argentina., Chile 1843. Frequent in Ireland generally, colonising shrubberies in the south-west; in Britain confined to extreme south and west; hardly survives east of Dorset, rare Devon and Cornwall; north to Ayrshire and, probably, Argyll. 13 × 1.3 m.

Orange-bark Myrtle

Bark. Orange, flaking finely to leave areas of white; old trees with broad, tapering streaks of white 2–3 m long.
Crown. Evergreen, loosely conic, nearly black.
Foliage. Shoot dark pink above, green and pale brown beneath, densely pubescent. Bud minute, deep shining red. Leaf opposite, sub-sessile, oval, with pronounced mucro; 2.5 × 1.5 cm, entire, deep green; midrib deeply impressed, few side-veins impressed; beneath, pale green, minutely pubescent; midrib prominent. Crushed foliage aromatic, sweet and spicy.
Flowers and fruit. Flowers solitary, from axils, on very slender, dark pink 15 mm pedicel; globose in bud, red and green; opening 2 cm across, white, four petals in a cup shape, in masses in late summer. Fruit a small berry, briefly red then black.

GUMS Eucalyptus

Evergreen trees confined to Australasia. A large assembly of species and hybrids, perhaps 800. Juvenile foliage of most species large and clasping stem, very different from adult, usually lanceolate leaves; retained by a few species throughout life. No winter bud; growth continuous except in cold spells. Flowers, bunches of stamens from hard capsule which forms fruit with shapes useful in identification. Tallest broad-leaved tree, known now to 100 m. Fastest-growing tree, to 30 m in five years, 10 m in one year, in tropics.

CIDER GUM *Eucalyptus gunnii* Hook. f.

S. Australia, Tasmania 1846. The most widespread *Eucalyptus*. Infrequent; large gardens and some small, north-east at least to Morayshire. 35 × 4 m.
Bark. Large pinkish-orange strips peeling to leave smooth grey.
Crown. Conic at first on upswept sinuous branches, old trees tall-domed irregular, heavily branched.
Foliage. Shoot yellowish-white, bloomed pinkish-grey. No bud. Tiny growing leaves stop as they are for the winter. Leaf: juvenile foliage for 2–3 years, op-

Plate 37   **DOVE-TREE, STRAWBERRY TREES, EUCALYPT**

1. Dove-tree   *Davidia involucrata*   366

(a) Ripening fruit.
(b) Leaves, large and coarsely toothed; dense pale pubescence beneath.
(c) Bracts each side of and hiding flower.

The more frequent var. *vilmoriniana* differs in the leaf being shiny and glabrous beneath, and fruit on stalk half as long.

2. Strawberry Tree   *Arbutus unedo*   375

(a) Shoot, leaves and one flower. The nodding inflorescence has about twelve flowers which open few at a time through the late autumn as the fruit of the previous year ripen.
(b) Ripe fruit.

3. Madrona   *Arbutus menziesii*   376

(a) Large leaf and panicle of ripe fruit. The fruit ripen in late summer from flowers of the immediately preceding spring.
(b) Small leaf, showing entire margin.

4. Snow Gum   *Eucalyptus niphophila*   370

Foliage. Young leaves may be a luminous orange-brown for a few weeks. The shoot soon becomes blue-white.

Dove Tree

Strawberry Tree

Madrona

Snow Gum, a young tree

Cider Gum

1a

1b

1d

1e

2a

2b

2c

ASH TREES

Plate 38

Opposite compound leaves, fruit with single wing.

1. Common Ash   *Fraxinus excelsior*   380

    (a) Winter outline of tree of medium age, about 20m tall.
    (b) Leaf. The midrib of the underside of each leaflet has dense
        rows of white hairs each side, near the base.
    (c) Male flower-buds opening.
    (d) Female flowers open; well before the leaves.
    (e) Ripe fruit.

2. Manna Ash   *Fraxinus ornus*   379

    (a) Ripe fruit.
    (b) Leaf.
    (c) Part of inflorescence; the flowers open in June when the tree
        is in full leaf.

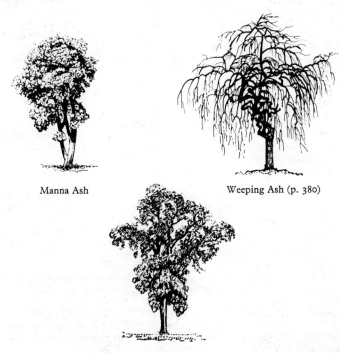

Manna Ash   Weeping Ash (p. 380)

Narrow leafed Ash (p. 381)

posite, rounded, sessile pale blue
grey, 3–6 cm across; often seen in
florists' shops; adult foliage alternate, oblong-lanceolate, acute,
broad-cuneate or rounded base,
entire, 8–10 × 3–4 cm, dark blue-

Cider Gum: *left,* adult; *right,* juvenile

grey above, yellow-green, much veined beneath; petiole 2.5 cm, pale yellow.
Flowers and fruit. Flower-buds short-stalked in clusters of three along
shoots of trees from 4–5 years old; ovoid-cylindric with broad projecting
rounded rim near apex, blue-white, opening to white fluffy flowers in July; seed
capsule top-shaped, flat-ended, 5 mm long, white.
Growth. May to mid-August except in mild areas where growth may stop only
during coldest spells; shoots to 2 m, tree can be 15 × 1 m in ten years.
Recognition. The only species of any size likely to be seen in the eastern half
of England and Scotland (where mostly var. *whittingehamensis* with narrower
leaves). Known by small, flat, oblong, broad-cuneate leaves on yellow petioles.

SNOW GUM *Eucalyptus niphophila* Maiden and Blakey   **Pl. 37**
Australia, to tree-line at 2,000 m. 1929. Recently planted in many gardens as
apparently very hardy and soon has brilliant bluish-white stem and branches
(but may be reddish-brown). Shoot yellow then dark red then bloomed violet;
leaves *adult from first year,* may unfold rich orange then brown, finally grey-
green, *elliptic,* 7 × 5 cm, or oblong-lanceolate, *falcate,* 14 × 5 cm, thick, hard,
three veins parallel each side of midrib, *margin red,* petiole thick, wrinkled, red
above, yellow beneath, 1.5–2 cm. Flowers in bunches 9–11 on common stalk
1 cm, yellow-green in bud, open white and can be 5 cm and spectacular, pure
white. Growth very moderate for a Eucalypt, seldom more than 1 m a year.

BLUE GUM *Eucalyptus globulus* Labillardère
S. Australia 1829. A few in Falmouth; many in Ireland where even on the east
coast it is a towering magnificent tree in small and large gardens. 42 × 6 m.
Bark. Large, slightly spiralled areas of grey-brown strips falling to leave white,
fawn, coffee-brown, pink, greenish-grey and dark brown very smooth, bald
areas.
Crown. Narrowly conic high on a bole as cylindric as a machined pole; biggest
trees broader with narrow dome arising from each heavy branch. Dense with
hanging dark leaves.
Foliage. Leaf sickle-shaped, deep blue-green, 20–25 × 5–8 cm when adult.
Seedlings, used as annual spot-plants in bedding, have *square, winged* pale blue-
green stems and opposite, clasping juvenile leaves, floppy and blue-white,
oblong-elliptic, 10–15 cm.
Fruit. Capsules carpet the ground under Irish trees, far larger than those of
any other species, top-shaped, blackish with lid bloomed grey-blue, 2–3 × 1.5
cm.
Growth. Remarkably rapid, particularly in Co. Kerry and Co. Cork. The biggest, 42 × 6 m, at Glengarriff, Co. Cork, is believed to be about 50 years old.
Seedlings from this spring up at 2–3 m a year all round. A tree of six years'
growth was 15 × 0.6 m in Co. Kerry.
Recognition. Crown; long dark leaf and huge capsule.

URN-FRUITED GUM   *Eucalyptus urnigera* Hook. f.

Tasmania pre-1860. Rare in Cornwall and Argyll, frequent in Ireland, very rare elsewhere. 32 × 3 m. Bark streaked orange, grey, green, and cream. Juvenile leaves opposite, cordate, orbicular, 2–5 cm, bright blue-white; adult leaves alternate *ovate*, 8–15 cm long, *dark glossy green*. Petiole red; new leaves purplish. Flowers in threes. Capsule 5–6 mm, *constricted* to make urn shape.

Recognition. Safely, only by the very small, urn-shaped capsules, which are abundantly produced; but dark green crown a useful guide.

FUNNEL-FRUITED GUM   *Eucalyptus coccifera* Hook. f.

Tasmania 1840. Rare; widespread but in few gardens, from Devon to Wester Ross and from Sussex to Norfolk; infrequent in Ireland. Bark very *spiralled* greenish-white, grey, cream and brown; crown low and spreading; shoot *white, spotted red*; leaf small 3.5 × 1.2 cm ovate, abruptly *short-acuminate*; petiole pale yellow. Fruit small, long-obconic, 1 cm. Original tree in Devon died in 1964 when 26 × 6.1 m.

Recognition. Spiralled bark, twisting bole, and small leaf and fruit.

Funnel-fruited Gum: *left,* juvenile; *right,* adult

IVY FAMILY   *Araliaceae*

A widespread family of more than 500 species represented here by evergreen climbers and shrubs and deciduous spined trees and shrubs, all with flowers in umbels. *Hedera* (Ivy), *Fatsia*, *Aralia*, *Acanthopanax*. One species makes a large tree here.

KALOPANAX

Single species in Eastern Asia. Bole with short stout spines, leaf palmately lobed, large.

PRICKLY CASTOR-OIL TREE   *Kalopanax pictus* (Thunb.) Nakai

Syn. *Acanthopanax ricinifolius* Seem.

China, Manchuria, Korea, Japan 1865. Infrequent; large gardens in S. England and north near the west coast to Argyll, east to Peebles and north-east to Aberdeen and in Ireland; nearly always as the variety given.

var. *maximowiczii* (van H.) Hara. Japan 1874. 15 × 1.8 m.

Bark. Dull grey with thick, interwoven purple-grey ridges and numerous, large, spined warts; fewer and smaller on old trees.

Prickly Castor-Oil Tree

Crown. Gaunt, broad-columnar; branches few, level; leading shoot often leaning; laterals spur-like, perpendicular, tipped by long, sharply pointed buds.
Foliage. Shoot stout, green, smooth with bright, blue-green, soft-pointed
spines; ripening blue–grey, pink and brown; older shoots dark grey transversely
wrinkled. Bud conic, 3–4 cm; lateral buds perpendicular. Leaf opens red in mid-
May, expands late May, dark green, *hanging* on red-brown, rough and hairy
petiole 10–20 cm long and bulbous at base; palmate, deeply 5–7 lobed, nearly
round, 20 × 20 cm but variable; lobes cut *two thirds* to base of leaf, mid-lobe
obovate, acute, side-lobes oblong-ovate; hard,
thick, very sharp fine forward serration; underside with dense curly white pubescence and
stout prominent veins.

The type, seen in a few gardens from Hampshire to Ayrshire, has smaller leaf 13 × 14 cm on
slender petiole 12–15 cm and five *broad*, triangular,
acuminate lobes, the larger three about 6 cm
across at base, sinuses wide, obtuse, about *one
third* to base of leaf, underside at first pubescent
at base of veins only and in axils. To 14 × 2 m.
Flowers and fruit. Terminal inflorescence 20 cm
across, about 30 smooth, slender, white peduncles
each 8 cm long, radiating from 3 cm of shoot and
bearing an umbel 3 cm in diameter of 25 small white
flowers in late summer. Fruit obovoid, 5 mm, black;
prominent on tree after leaves fall, until December.
Recognition. Both forms are strange, gaunt trees
with spined boles and foliage of a kind more

var. *maximowiczii*

familiar in a hot-house. The type resembles a coarse sort of maple with alternate
leaves. Many trees are intermediate between the type and the variety. They
have lobes of various depths.

DOGWOOD FAMILY *Cornaceae*

About 90 species, mostly shrubs, including *Aucuba japonica* (Spotted Laurel).
Cornus mas (Cornelian Cherry) familiar with its small yellow flowers in February and March is very rarely a tree to 15 m.

DOGWOODS   Cornus

About 40 species in northern temperate region. Flowers small, four-parted, in
some species surrounded by 4–6 large white or pink bracts. Fruit a berry.

TABLE DOGWOOD   *Cornus controversa* Hemsl.
Japan, China and the Himalaya pre-1880. Infrequent; a few gardens in
each county N. to Edinburgh, especially in Sussex, also in Ireland. 15 × 1.5 m.
Notable for the way the foliage is held in *level layers* well separated from each
other. Bark smooth, grey with folds and short pink-buff fissures, becoming

networked with broad ridges. Shoots dark
red. Leaves *alternate*, rather pendulous shiny,
fresh then deep bright green, 6–9 pairs
prominent basal veins; ovate, abruptly acute;
waved margin, 9–13×7cm, pale and soft
pubescent beneath; on curved, 4cm petiole
red above, white beneath. Flowers, white,
1cm on inflorescence 5 × 10cm, thick, green
pubescent peduncles; can be spectacular in
mid-June in wide layers above hanging foliage.

Table Dogwood

    Some specimens are grown as *Cornus macrophylla* which differs only in having
opposite leaves.

    'VARIEGATA' Rare, slow-growing, much prized form with small lanceolate,
twisted leaves 4cm, broadly margined pale cream. Seldom 3m, but one in Co.
Kerry 10 × 1m and most spectacular.

BENTHAM'S CORNEL *Cornus capitata* Wall.

    Syn. *Benthamia fragifera* Lindl.
The Himalaya and China 1825. S. coast of England rarely, more frequent
in Ireland. Semi-evergreen spreading tree
to 14 × 1.7m with grey-brown, shallowly
scaly bark, whitish-green shoot, *opposite,*
softly leathery, oblong-lanceolate leaves, abruptly narrowed to curved tip, waved margin
remotely and obscurely toothed, pale, soft
green above, *glaucous beneath, densely fine
pubescent both sides.* Flower bracts (6) pale
yellow on erect stalks in late June; fruit bright
green ripening crimson, strawberry-like,
13×18mm, flattened globose, erect on 3cm
stalk.

Bentham's Cornel

NUTTALL'S DOGWOOD *Cornus nuttallii* Audub.

British Columbia to S. California 1835. Infrequent; large
and a few small gardens mainly in the west. 10 × 1m. Conic,
rather ascending, whorled open-branched crown on a fluted
straight bole with dark purple bark; fine, upcurved shoots on
the upper sides of the branches. Flower-heads are present at
shoot-ends all winter, greenish-white, 1cm across. Leaf oval or
obovate, cuneate, 7–12 × 4–7cm, short-pubescent on both
sides, glaucous beneath. Flowers in dense green and purple
head 2.5cm across, surrounded by six large oval or obovate
pointed bracts, 4×4cm, white or cream, later tinged pink,
opening in May, a few in October. Tends to be a short-lived
tree.

Nuttall's Dogwood

HEATHER FAMILY *Ericaceae*

A family/of more than 1,500 species in 70 genera, including *Rhododendron*, *Pieris* and *Vaccinium*, but only two genera with trees grown here.

SORREL-TREE Oxydendrum

Single species in N. America. White flowers in terminal panicles late in the year.

SORREL-TREE *Oxydendrum arboreum* (L.) DC.

South-eastern USA 1752. Infrequent; large gardens and a few small, mainly in S. England and in Ireland. 16 × 1.3 m.

Bark. Grey, at first with short buff-orange interwoven fissures, later all grey with thick interwoven ridges.

Crown. Flat, high dome, broadest near the top, on rather ascending sinuous branches from a straight bole.

Foliage. Shoot smooth, reddish-brown or purplish above, sea-green beneath. Bud small, few-scaled, 2 mm, narrowly conic, yellow-green. Leaf alternate, elliptic-oblong, cuneate, 10–15 × 5 cm, the few veins curved away from margin; slightly cupped, finely serrated, deep glossy green above; very smooth, grey-green below with *only the white mid-rib showing*, petiole pink and white, 1.5 cm. Autumn colour scarlet to deep red late in October.

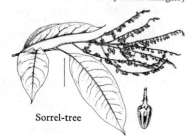

Sorrel-tree

Flowers. From fourth or fifth year, end of July, small, ivory-white, pendulous, urn-shaped with a narrow mouth, on slender panicles to 25 cm with six or more white branches, each 10–15 cm long, the whole gently curving down and outwards from near the tips of branches.

Fruit. Ivory coloured conic-ovoid capsule with persistent style, looks like a flower.

Similar species. In flower unique; leaf resembles *Nyssa* (p. 365) *but is serrated.*

STRAWBERRY TREES Arbutus

About 12 species in N. and C. America and Mediterranean region. Fruit a sub-globose, berry-like drupe with mealy flesh.

Key to Arbutus species

1. Adult leaf serrate   **2**
   Adult leaf entire   **3**

2. Leaf 6 cm, pale green beneath (bark soon brown and grey)   *unedo*, p. 375
   Leaf 9 cm, yellowish glaucous beneath (bark bright deep red)
      petiole broad, fleshy   × *andrachnoides*, p. 375

3. Bud 1 cm, conic; leaf to 12 × 5 cm   *menziesii*, p. 376
   Bud 3 mm, ovoid; leaf to 8 × 4 cm   *andrachne*, p. 375

STRAWBERRY TREE   *Arbutus unedo* L.   **Pl. 37**
Native, locally abundant in Co. Kerry, W. Cork and Co. Sligo. Medit. Frequent
in villages and country gardens, more rarely in town parks and gardens; mainly
in S. England and Ireland. 10 × 1.2 m.
Bark. Dark red at first, shredding and soon obscured by grey-brown scaling
ridges.
Crown. Very short bole; ascending sinuous branches and dense low rounded
head; sometimes only a bush, often leaning.
Foliage. Shoot pink-red above, pale green beneath, with long hairs. Bud very
small, 1–2 mm, flattened conic, purple-red. Leaf evergreen; elliptic or obovate,
acute, cuneate, sharply forward serrate to within 5–6 mm of tip, nearly black,
± shiny above, pale green beneath with prominent white midrib, 5–10 × 2–3 cm,
petiole dark pink above, pale green beneath, long-pubescent, 5–7 mm.
Flowers and fruit. Inflorescence terminal, sharply nodding or pendulous,
5 cm, whitish-green with long, scattered pubescence, 15–20 flowers opening
few at a time in October and November, greenish-white to ivory with greenish
lips to the bell-mouth in which are brown anthers; 8 × 8 mm. Fruit of previous
year colour when flowers out, yellow then deep scarlet dotted with grey-tipped
papillae; flattened-globose, 1.8 × 1.5 cm, edible but unpalatable (*unedo*: "I eat
one", only).
Similar species. Crown may be mistaken for blacker, smaller-leafed, grey-
barked *Phillyrea* (p. 383). Serrate leaf only found in one other adult *Arbutus*,
A. × *andrachnoides* (below) which may be distinguished by orange or red bark.

CYPRUS STRAWBERRY TREE   *Arbutus*
andrachne L.
E. Mediterranean region 1724. Very rare; S. England.
12 × 1.8 m. Bark red and dark brown, largely shed
to leave bald pinkish-yellow areas, *yellow-green* on
upper branches. Shoot yellow-green, turning brown;
glabrous. Leaf *entire*, obovate, 5–10 × 4–5 cm,
obtuse, slightly oblique cuneate at base, glossy dark
green with prominent white midrib above, pale,
slightly glaucous beneath. Flowers April, similar to
A. unedo; fruit smoother, smaller, 1 cm. Seedlings
have serrated leaves.
Similar species. *A. menziesii* (p. 376).

Cyprus Strawberry Tree

HYBRID STRAWBERRY TREE   *Arbutus* × *andrachnoides* Link
   Syn. *A. hybrida* Ker-Gawler
A natural hybrid between *A. andrachne* and *A. unedo*
occurring wild in Greece, also raised in Fulham in
about 1800. Infrequent; in large gardens in England
and Wales, rare in Scotland. 13 × 1 m. Intermediate
between parents in most respects but more vigorous
than either. Bark *deep ruby-red* or dark orange-red,
ridged vertically and scaling blackish; sometimes bald
orange-brown areas. Leaf sharply forward, *serrate*,
paler, especially the veins, than *A. unedo*, ovate, 9 ×
4.5 cm, about 16 pairs parallel veins; uniform matt

Hybrid Strawberry Tree

yellow-green beneath; petiole dark red above, pale green beneath, may be winged and 3 mm across, 7 mm long. Flowers in late autumn or in spring on leafy panicle 7 cm long, with nine green branches, fruit smaller and smoother than *A. unedo*.

MADRONA *Arbutus menziesii* Pursh   **Pl. 37**
British Columbia to California 1827. Infrequent; large gardens, except in Scotland where very rare. 19 × 3 m.
Bark. At base dark purple finely cracked into squares, above this usually stripping or bare, very *smooth yellow-pink; branches red,* peeling. Young trees smooth, orange.
Crown. *Tall ovoid* on upswept sinuous branches; rather open.
Foliage. Shoot smooth, glabrous, pale green; second year and later bright orange. Bud relatively large, 6–10 mm green or pale brown, conic. Leaf evergreen, rather distant except near tip of shoot, *leathery,* oval or oblong-ovate, *entire,* rarely finely serrated, (always for the first two or three years from seed); 5–14 × 5–7.5 cm, lax, often rather twisted; shiny rich green above, *glaucous* to blue-white beneath; petiole fleshy, 2–2.5 cm, bright red above with basal part of midrib; pale green beneath.
Flowers and fruit. Flowers late April to mid-May, white, 3 × 3 mm, like little buckets on *erect,* terminal whitish-green much-branched panicles to 20 × 15 cm; fruit small, 1 cm, orange-red.
Similar species. *A. andrachne* (p. 375).

EBONY FAMILY   *Ebenaceae*

A largely tropical family of 300 species only three of which are grown here and two of these are confined to one or two collections.

PERSIMMONS   Diospyros

About 200 species, mostly tropical and evergreen, a few deciduous. Dioecious; females usually solitary; males in cymes. Fruit a large, juicy berry.

DATE-PLUM *Diospyros lotus* L.
China and Japan to W. Asia 1597. Infrequent; collections and some large gardens in each country, rarely as a shrub in small gardens. 13 × 1 m.
Bark. Blackish or dark pink-grey, regularly cracked into thick, small, square plates.
Crown. Dark, shiny dome, looks evergreen but sheds leaves late, often forked low down
Foliage. Shoot green or light brown, glabrous. Bud appressed, small, pointed conic-ovoid, yellow and green. Leaf, younger trees: ovate-oblong, broad-cuneate, acuminate, usually 10 × 4.5 cm but to 18 × 5 cm; margin entire and waved, upper side *very glossy,* dark green with impressed veins, underside slightly glaucous, hairy on veins; petiole 1 cm, green or pale red-brown, pubescent. Very old

Date-plum

trees: smaller, broader leaf, more crinkled; yellowish-green with pink margin. Black and prominent bud-scales adhere to new foliage.

Flowers and fruit. Dioecious. Male trees have flowers 1–3 together in leaf-axils, females solitary hanging in dense rows, both *urn-shaped*, pale cream down to the constriction, pink below it, 5–8mm long, open in July. Fruit globose, 1–2cm, yellow or purple.

PERSIMMON *Diospyros virginiana* L.

Eastern and central USA pre-1629. Rare; in a few collections in S. England. Differs from *D. lotus* only in longer petiole 1.5–2cm, and longer flower 1–1.5cm. Leaves on a single shoot vary from 1cm and oval to 20cm ovate-oblong, the small ones at the base, and nearly as small mixed with the large towards the tip. Leaves emerge pale yellow.

Recognition. *Diospyros* species are known by the bark: very glossy dark entire waved leaf, and, in season, the hanging urn-shaped flowers. Rotting leaves can give off a heavy, fruity scent.

Persimmon

STORAX FAMILY *Styracaceae*

A hundred species from N. and S. America, Mediterranean and E. Asia. A few hardy species reach small tree size.

STORAX Styrax

About 100 species in northern warm temperate and tropical regions, flowers white, fruit a fleshy drupe.

SNOWBELL TREE *Styrax japonica* Sieb. and Zucc.

China, Japan 1862. Frequent as an attractive small tree in gardens. 11 × 1m.

Bark. Young trees fawn-grey, striated buff-pink. Older trees dull grey, thick ridges between orange fissures.

Crown. Neatly rounded, rather dense; lower branches level, upper branches arching out rather flat.

Foliage. Shoot slender, zigzagged, purplish-brown or orange-brown, slightly pubescent and black-speckled. Bud small, 2–4mm, narrowly conic, appressed, pale brown-green, pubescent; black scurfy warts. Leaf alternate, ovate-acuminate, broad-cuneate, 6–8cm long, margin waved; few irregular, shallow remote teeth; dark or mid-green shiny above, paler less shiny beneath, tufted axils; usually cupped. Petiole 2–6mm, pale yellow-green with some black scurf.

Snowbell Tree

Flowers and fruit. A mass of white flowers hanging close beneath the branches in mid-June, in bunches of three or four on slender 2–4cm pedicels, campanulate, five (four) oval petals 12mm; stamens held together, pale orange. Fruit on pedicels with conic swelling to *round-lobed, star-like* calyx which is bright green tipped purple; the globular fruit is 1.4 cm long, smooth, greenish-grey.

BIG LEAF STORAX *Styrax obassia* Sieb. and Zucc.

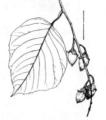

Japan 1879. Infrequent, in S. England in many large gardens; rare elsewhere. An open-crowned, upright, grey-barked tree to 14 m. Young plants have curiously shaped leaves to 15 × 15 cm with three pairs of *large triangular teeth near the apex*, or truncate across the top like the Tulip-tree; older plants with *nearly round*, pale green leaves densely *pubescent* and glaucous beneath, 10 × 10 (20 × 15) cm; petiole stout, 2 cm; dense long hairs; base of petiole encloses a leaf-bud. Flowers white,

Big Leaf Storax

2–3 cm across, 20–25 on one side of erect, pale green raceme 10–20 cm long. Fruit ovoid 1–1.5 cm, covered in dense, short, pale brown wool.

HEMSLEY'S STORAX *Styrax hemsleyana* Diels

China 1900. Similar to *S. obassia*; differs in bright orange buds; leaf ovate or obovate, abruptly acuminate, 15 × 10 cm with small distant peg-like teeth, and flowers on 3–5 cm pubescent racemes, one terminal, one from axil beneath, 4–8 small flowers on one side of each. Infrequent; mainly southern gardens. 12 m. Often very profuse in flowers.

Hemsley's Storax

SNOWDROP-TREES Halesia

Three to four species in N.E. America and E. China. Flowers white; fruit winged.

SNOWDROP-TREE or SILVERBELL-TREE *Halesia monticola* (Rehd.) Sarg.

South-eastern USA 1897. Infrequent, in larger gardens north to C. Scotland. 14 × 1 m.

Bark. Pale grey with widely spaced short pink or orange fissures; later dark grey, deeply fissured.

Crown. Broadly conic; wide, spreading lower branches; curved bole.

Foliage. Shoot grey-brown. Bud minute, dark purple. Leaf alternate, ovate-oblong, acute or short-acuminate, finely serrulate, 15 × 6 (25 × 10) cm, veins deeply impressed above; pubescent below; petiole grooved, pubescent, green, 1 cm.

Flowers and fruit. Flowers white from pale pink bud, hanging in clusters, mostly of three

Snowdrop Tree

in late May, shaped more like a crocus than a snowdrop, 3 cm long on 2 cm pedicel, profuse in good years. Fruit on 2 cm stalk, pale green until November, 4 cm long, four-winged, each 1 cm wide. Finally brown.

Similar species. *H. carolina* L. is shrubby with smaller parts and is about equally frequent. 'Rosea' is a form of the western population var. *vestita* Sarg. with leaves downy beneath, which has pink flowers.

OLIVE FAMILY *Oleaceae*

A large and widespread family of 400 species, mostly with opposite leaves. Species of many genera are familiar shrubs – Lilac, Privet, Forsythia, Osmanthus and Jasmine.

ASHES Fraxinus

About 65 species in N. hemisphere south to Mexico and Java. Trees of moderate or large size, many with flowers lacking petals and pollinated by the wind, all with winged fruit and opposite, pinnate leaves.

MANNA or FLOWERING ASH *Fraxinus ornus* L. Pl. 38
S. Europe, W. Asia pre-1700. Frequent in all parts in gardens, town parks and, in some areas, alongside roads. 24 × 3 m (23 × 2 m in Kensington Gardens, London).

Bark. *Dark grey* (black in city parks) and *very smooth*. Grafted trees have the ridged bark of the root-stock, Common Ash, below the union which is thus very obvious.

Crown. Hemispherical or flattened, rarely rather upright; branches *sinuous*. Suckers of Common Ash often around the base of grafted trees.

Foliage. Shoot olive-green, speckled white. Bud squat, domed, blunt, like a bishop's mitre, two very dark outer scales, two *pale brown* inner scales with *dense grey pubescence*. Leaf 25–30 cm, pinnate, opposite, 5–7–9 leaflets on slender bending rachis which is widely grooved above and pubescent at the joints; leaflets on 1.5 *cm stalks*, unequal at base, to 10 × 3.5 cm, oblong-ovate, terminal one obovate; obscurely toothed on outer half, abruptly acuminate, pale beneath with woolly *brown or white pubescence each side of the white veins*.

Flowers and fruit. Inflorescence bright green, glabrous, with about seven main branches and two leaves; brilliant green in bud. Flowers *creamy-white*, fragrant, in late May, in dense, conic, terminal panicles to 15 × 20 cm; petals very narrow, 6 mm long. Fruit on wiry peduncle 3–10 mm long, wing lanceolate, *slender*, 1.5–2.5 cm long, the bunches prominent, green until just before leaf-fall, then brown.

Similar species. *F. excelsior* (p. 380) when not in flower; *F. mariesii* (below).

CHINESE FLOWERING ASH *Fraxinus mariesii* Hook. f.
C. China 1878. A rare tree, in some collections, similar to *F. ornus*, but with 3–5 sub-sessile leaflets, what petiolules there are being *purple*, and the fruit dark purple-red during summer, on a smaller, more open panicle. Petals linear; anthers pink. 6 × 1 m.

COMMON ASH   *Fraxinus excelsior* L.   **Pl. 38**

Native, abundant wherever the soil is base-rich and damp as in northern limestone areas, less so on sandy soils, common in towns and city parks and churchyards. Europe and Asia Minor. 45 × 6 m (35 × 4.6 m at Longleat; 6 m in girth
at Holywell Hall, Lincs.). 7.5 m at Tynan Abbey, Co. Armagh.

Bark. Pale grey, very smooth when young, later interwoven ridges, thick in old
trees.

Crown. Tall-domed, open; branches strongly ascending at a narrow angle
from a long bole; biggest trees often pollards or many limbs from 2–3 m up.
Burrs and sprouts on some trees; large cankers commonly on smaller trees.

Foliage. Shoot stout, green-grey with white lenticels, much flattened at nodes.
Bud squat, conic, angled and *black*. Leaf opposite, pinnate, 20–35 cm with 9–13
leaflets, the terminal pair largest, terminal leaflet on 2 cm petiole, side ones 2 mm
petiolules; to 12 cm long, ovate-oblong or lanceolate, acuminate; sharp shallow
forward toothing; dull dark green above, pale beneath with *white pubescence*
densely each side of white midrib. Buds on sucker and coppice-growth open in
mid-April, uncurling like two opposite bracken-fronds; trees leaf out 2–3
weeks later. In hedges late shoots growing in July have new leaves dark purple.
Autumn colour brief, yellow or none.

Flowers and fruit. Total sexual confusion: some trees all male, some all
female, some male with one or more female branches, some *vice versa*, some
branches male one year, female the next, some with perfect flowers. Male

flowers in dense globular bunches along shoots of
previous year, purplish then dark red in bud, open
yellow with slender anthers in early April well before
leaf-buds; female flowers similar but open more
widely into a filigree of purple then pale green. Fruit
abundant every few years, scarce in others, pale
bright shiny green, wing 4 × 1 cm, oblanceolate, tip
deeply or unevenly notched with terminal spine,
pedicel slender 2.5 cm; hang shiny deep green in
summer, brown after leaf-fall until eaten by bullfinches.

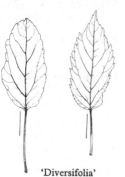

'JASPIDEA' Rare, to 20 × 3 m; *shoots* yellow or
golden-brown in winter and spring. Leaves yellow,
spring and autumn. Fruit yellow on 15 cm yellow
peduncle.

'Diversifolia'

'DIVERSIFOLIA' ('Heterophylla', 'Monophylla')
Single-leafed Ash. Arises in wild populations now
and again; infrequent in large gardens and parks. 27 × 4 m. Bark smoother, crown
more open, leaf *simple*, ovate-oblong, deeply and sharply toothed, or scarcely
toothed, 15–20 × 5–12 cm on petiole 8–10 cm. A good trick question for students,
puzzling at first sight.

'PENDULA' **Weeping Ash**. Frequent in gardens, parks and churchyards,
often in towns. *Grafted* as high as possible on Common Ash, usually 2 m up but
occasionally 10 m and once at 27 m. Long vigorous shoots grow *straight down to
the ground* from a *globose head* of *twisting* branches. Foliage as in the type.

Similar species. *F. americana* (p. 381). Distinguished from other species of
ash by the black buds.

NARROW-LEAFED ASH   *Fraxinus angustifolia* Vahl
S. Europe, N. Africa, W. Asia 1800. Infrequent; town parks mostly in S.
England. 23 × 2 m (26 × 3 m at Chiswick House).
Bark. Dark grey, closely and finely networked ridges becoming deep and
knobbly with age.
Crown. Tall, irregular dome of dense foliage on few upcurved branches, some
spreading widely before curving up; shoots slender, short, pendulous.
Foliage. Shoot olive-brown to olive-green. Bud dark brown-purple, pubescent
outer scales, yellow-brown inner, also grey-pubescent. Leaf a slender version of
Common Ash, 15–25 cm long, 7–13 slender, lanceolate leaflets 3–8 cm long
1–2 cm wide, with *jagged* teeth on outer half, shiny green above, completely
glabrous beneath. Leaves tend to hang; leaflets far apart in one form.

'VELTHEIMII' (*F.a. monophylla* Henry). A rare form analogous to *F.
excelsior* 'Diversifolia', found in some big gardens and in at least one London
park to 20 × 2.3 m, with a simple leaf, lanceolate 5–12 × 2–5 cm, coarsely toothed.
Distinguished from *F.e.* 'Diversifolia' by *rough dark bark*, dense upswept brushes
of stout shoots and much smaller, more slender leaves quite *glabrous* beneath.

Narrow-leafed Ash   'Veltheimii'   Caucasian Ash

CAUCASIAN ASH   *Fraxinus oxycarpa* Willd.
S. Europe, Caucasus to Persia 1815. 18 × 1.5 m. A rare but increasingly planted,
extremely attractive tree similar to *F. angustifolia* but with nearly *smooth, pale
grey* bark and bright *shiny* green *cupped* leaflets, hairy at the base of the midrib
beneath.
'RAYWOOD' is a recent form from Australia, very rapid in growth, so far to
15 m, the leaves turning purple in autumn.

WHITE ASH   *Fraxinus americana* L.
E. N. America 1724. Rare; collections, a few gardens and London parks.
26 × 2.3 m.
Bark. Mostly finely and deeply fissured into very small,
short, grey ridges but a few have broad, smooth ridges
like Common Walnut.

Crown. Tall domed, open and poplar-like (not Lombardy Poplar); straight slender shoots.

Foliage. Shoot smooth, shiny brownish-green, green or brown. Bud small, *pale brown*, conic. Leaf heavy, hanging, 35 cm, seven leaflets *on stalks 1–1.5 cm long*; rachis terete, whitish, often bending sideways at first two leaflet pairs and upwards at the third; leaflets to 15 × 7 cm; terminal one on 4 cm petiole, cuneate, obovate, acuminate; other leaflets abruptly short-acuminate, all entire, obscurely toothed or sharply toothed, sub-shiny

White Ash

rich green above, *silvery-green* beneath, glabrous or with hairs each side of white veins beneath. Autumn colours striking bronze-purples in America.

Flowers and fruit. Very similar to *F. excelsior*.

Similar species. *F. pennsylvanica* (below) and *F. excelsior* (p. 381). A very variable species.

RED ASH   *Fraxinus pennsylvanica* Marsh.

E. N. America 1783. Rare; collections and a few gardens. Differs from *F. americana* in *pubescent* shoot, petiolules and beneath the leaflets, where it is also *green*; purplish-grey bark. The dense dark hairs on the petiolules make dark patches along the rachis.

    var. *lanceolata* (Borkh.) Sarg. Green Ash. 1824. Occurrence here the same as the type. Differs in *stout, bright green, glabrous* shoot, dense heavy foliage of rich green leaves 22 cm long wih slender, long-acuminate leaflets on 1 mm stalks (sub-sessile). Male flowers 3 each bud, 6 cm rich yellow.

Red Ash

PRIVETS   Ligustrum

Fifty species mainly in E. Asia, one in Europe and N. Africa. Mainly evergreen shrubs or small trees with fragrant white flowers in dense, conic inflorescence.

GLOSSY or CHINESE PRIVET   *Ligustrum lucidum* Ait.

China, Korea, Japan 1794. Infrequent and mostly in cities, town parks and by roadsides. 12 × 1 m (15 × 2 m stood near Winchester Cathedral until 1970). A most attractive tree with ovoid or hemispherical crown of large, dark *glossy evergreen* leaves on radiating branches and fine straight shoots. Bark smooth, dull grey, streaked buff. Leaf thick, ovate-acuminate, opposite, entire 10 × 5 cm, pale and matt beneath, only midrib showing. Crown usually partly obscured

Chinese Privet

by *profuse panicles* of buds or flowers, 8–15 × 3 cm, broadly conic, the very small flowers opening creamy-white and intensely fragrant from August until about January and the new buds and panicles visible soon after these fall, pale green until July.

PHILLYREA

Four species in the Mediterranean region. Evergreen, leaves opposite, flowers small, white.

PHILLYREA   *Phillyrea latifolia* L.   **Pl. 40**
S. Europe, Asia Minor 1597. Infrequent in village front-gardens along the S. coast of England also in the Midlands and S.W. Less often in large gardens. A grey-barked densely rounded tree to 9 m with very small nearly black evergreen leaves; sometimes mistaken for *Arbutus unedo*. Shoot slender, grey-brown, densely pubescent; bud minute, pointed, grey-green, densely pubescent; leaf 3–4 × 1.5 cm lanceolate, broad-cuneate,

Phillyrea

with shallow forward teeth, very dark glossy green above with midrib raised, matt beneath with well-marked veins. Flowers small, 5 mm across, whitish-green, cup-shaped; anthers brown; in groups in axils, March-April.

FIGWORT FAMILY   *Scrophulariaceae*

A large family mainly of herbs like Figwort and Foxglove with one genus of about ten trees in China.

PAULOWNIA

About ten species in China. Leaf large, opposite, on long petiole; flowers tubular in terminal panicle.

PAULOWNIA or FOXGLOVE-TREE   *Paulownia tomentosa* (Thunb.)
Steud.   **Pl. 39**
Syn. *P. imperialis* Sieb. and Zucc.
China 1838. Infrequent; in large gardens mostly in S. England and S. Ireland. 12 m (26 × 2.2 m at Westonbirt).
Bark. *Smooth,* grey in old trees; young trees often purplish-grey finely striated grey and marked by broken orange blisters.
Crown. Gaunt and few-branched from a good but slightly sinuous bole making a domed crown, sometimes low, usually fragile and much broken by storms and by woodpecker borings.
Foliage. Shoot pale pinkish-brown, lenticelled, fairly stout. Bud: terminals lacking; laterals above big leaf-scars, minute, purplish. Leaf opposite, *deeply cordate,* ovate, *long-acuminate,* to 35 × 25 cm, entire except on very young trees when 2–3 large acuminate teeth each side near the base; softly pubescent pale

Plate 39   LARGE-LEAFED FLOWERING TREES

1. Foxglove Tree   *Paulownia tomentosa*   383

    (a) Flowers on erect terminal panicle.
    (b) Leaf, much reduced. Leaves on young trees have more
       basal lobes.
    (c) Part of leaf. The central lobe may be much longer.
    (d) Immature fruit, which is glutinously sticky.
    (e) Tree 7 m tall.

2. Hybrid Catalpa   *Catalpa × erubescens*   387

Leaf, much reduced. Much thinner in texture than in Foxglove
Tree and hairs beneath largely confined to the veins.

3. (Red) Indian Bean Tree   *Catalpa bignonioides*   386

    (a) Leaf, much reduced.
    (b) Flowers, flower-buds and part of leaf. The inflorescence is
       squat globose. That of the Hybrid Catalpa is conic-cylindric
       and open.
    (c) Tree 7 m tall.

4. Cucumber-tree   *Magnolia acuminata*   262

    (a) Leaf.
    (b) Ripening fruit.

A tree of large stature, with a rich brown bark.

Paulownia   Paulownia leaf, typical of mature tree.   Hybrid Catalpa

Indian Bean Tree

1a

2

1b

3a

1d

3b

1c

1e

3c

4a

4b

1a

1b

2

3

4

PRIVET, PHILLYREA, CABBAGE PALM, Plate 40
PALM

1. Glossy or Chinese Privet *Ligustrum lucidum*   382

(a) Foliage. Leaves glossy.
(b) Inflorescence. The flowers open in autumn over a long period and are very fragrant. They are prominent and pale cream in bud for much of the summer.

2. Phillyrea *Phillyrea latifolia*   383

Foliage. A low, rounded evergreen tree with a dark bark most frequent in southern villages especially near the sea.

3. Cabbage Palm *Cordyline australis*   389

A much-branched tree, 7m tall showing that it flowers frequently and is growing in the far west of Britain. In less warm areas they flower infrequently and for years, until they flower, they remain as a single stem.

4. Chusan Palm *Trachycarpus fortunei*   390

A tree 7–8m tall. The lowest leaves may turn a bright yellow before they fall.

A very hardy tree of slow growth.

Glossy Privet

Phillyrea

green above, densely pubescent with prominent veins beneath; petiole pink-yellow, *densely pubescent*, 10–15 cm. Leaves fall early without autumn colour. On a young plant growing 2.5 m in the year, leaves to 45 × 45 cm on petioles of 45 cm had five to nine small acuminate lobes.

Flowers and fruit. Flowers on terminal erect panicles 20–30 cm long, visible from midsummer, densely brown-pubescent buds, open in late May before the leaves, to pale violet or rich purple-blue narrowly campanulate flowers 6 cm long, profuse after mild winter if no frost when opening. Fruit 2–10 per panicle, glossy whitish-green ovoid constricted to broad curved beak, sticky, 3 × 1.8 cm on very stout pubescent stalk of 1.5 cm.

Similar species. *Catalpa speciosa* (p. 387) and *Catalpa bignonioides* (below) but smooth bark distinguishes the tree, even if flower-buds not present.

BIGNONIA FAMILY *Bignoniaceae*

A large family, mainly tropical and subtropical, the few hardy species including the Trumpet-vines and *Catalpas*, the latter divided between E. Asia and N. America.

CATALPA

Ten species in Eastern N. America, West Indies, and E. Asia. Leaf large, opposite, or in whorls of three; fruit a long slender pod.

(RED) INDIAN BEAN-TREE *Catalpa bignonioides* Walt. **Pl. 39**
South-eastern USA 1726. Frequent in S. England in parks, gardens, city squares and sometimes in streets, uncommon northwards to S. Scotland and in S. Ireland. Large trees only where hot summers can occur, notably in London, Bath and Cambridge areas. 18 × 3.4 m.

Bark. Usually dull pink and brown scaling into fine flakes but some more grey and fissured into flat ridges.

Crown. Low, wide-spreading dome from a short, bent, stout bole. A few tall-domed on longer bole; oldest may lean badly.

Foliage. Shoot fairly stout, smooth grey-brown with large leaf-scars. Bud: terminal lacking; laterals minute orange-brown, above leaf-scars. Leaf in whorls of three on strong growth, opposite on weaker shoots, shallowly cordate or rounded, ovate, *short*-acuminate, to 25 × 22 cm but some half this size; margin waved, entire, veins impressed; bright light green; deep purple on young trees when emerging minute at the tip of the shoot, then a satiny sheen; pale, with close, dense pubescence beneath; petiole flattened, smooth, *glabrous*, pale green, 10–18 cm. Leaves falling fairly early without autumn colour.

Indian Bean Tree

Flowers and fruit. Flowers in a broadly conical, or bun-shaped panicle 15–20 cm high, each flower opening to 5 cm across to make panicle nearly opaque in mid-July; campanulate with frilled margin, white, spotted yellow and purple. Fruit a slender pod 15–40 cm long 6–8 mm wide, persisting on the tree dangling from the panicles, dark brown, through the winter.

Growth. Rapid but short-lived; young trees make rods over 1 m long which are cut back at the tips by frost each year then, after a few years, branch; after this growth in height is slow, but in girth it becomes quite rapid. Decay and breakage set in when the girth exceeds about 3 m which may take less than 100 years. Usually the *last tree to leaf*, scarcely showing green until late in June, the minute leaves continue to emerge at the tip of the shoot until September when, with some still developing, growth stops and the immature shoot-tips are killed by the first frost; in hard winters they are killed back 3–4 whorls.

'AUREA' Usually a more spreading tree seen in a few gardens and parks and especially in nurseries, with leaves bright yellow in the open, more greenish in shade and later in the season. New leaves brownish-purple or coppery. A fine sight during its short season in leaf and, fortunately, seldom flowering, for white flowers are no ornament among rich golden foliage.

Similar species. Resembles *Paulownia* (p. 383) but more difficult to distinguish from *Catalpa speciosa* (below); also quite like *C.* × *erubescens*.

WESTERN CATALPA *Catalpa speciosa* Engelm.

Central USA 1880. Rare; in a few collections and also in a few London parks and gardens. 10 × 1 m (18 × 3 m at Radnor Gardens, Twickenham).

Bark. Dark *grey*, deeply *fissured into scaly ridges*. The largest, mentioned above, is grafted on to *C. bignonioides* and the change in bark at the union is striking.

Crown. *Conic*, fairly narrow, sometimes rounded, on a straight bole; branches and shoots twisting; dense.

Foliage. Shoot green-brown, leaf-scars raised, concave, grey, knobbly. Terminal bud lacking; laterals above leaf-scars, dark red, flattened. Leaf cordate, usually very deeply so the blade starts after the veins have spread from the petiole, but can be rounded; ovate-lanceolate, *long-acuminate, leathery*, smooth shiny deep green, to 27 × 23 cm; dense pale brown pubescence beneath; petiole stout, yellow and dark pink, *finely pubescent* at first, 13–18 cm.

Western Catalpa

Flowers and fruit. Flowers open in late June and early July, 6 cm across but sparsely borne on the 15 cm panicle; white, with yellow and a few purple spots; fruit pods 20–45 cm long, 1.5 cm wide.

Similar species. *C. bignonioides* (p. 386).

HYBRID CATALPA *Catalpa* × *erubescens* Carr.   **Pl. 39**

Syn. *C.* × *hybrida* Spaeth

Hybrid *C. ovata* × *bignonioides* 1874. Indiana. Introduced 1891. Infrequent in S. and W. England, locally frequent in W. Surrey and E. Anglia. 19 × 2.7 m.

Bark. Grey or *grey-brown* coarsely and *deeply fissured* into a network of thick ridges.

Crown. Huge, spreading dome or tall and conic.

Foliage. Leaf emerges deep purple; cordate, broad-ovate, often *broader than long*, 22 × 27 (38 × 33) cm, vaguely *five-cornered* or with short-acuminate ends to broad lobes, short-acuminate tip; thin, translucent light green, slightly pubescent above and strongly so at the sides of the veins beneath; petiole 10–15 cm. (This form is sometimes distinguished from others of the same cross as 'J. C. Teas', the name of the man who first raised it.)

Flowers and fruit. Flowers late, early August to early September, small, white tinged yellow and spotted purple, intensely fragrant with the scent of *Lilium speciosum*, close on the branches of a tall *open panicle*, to 32 × 20 cm with wide branching at base, whorls of three small branches above. Fruit profuse dark brown pods, to 40 cm long, filled only with cotton-wool.

YELLOW CATALPA   *Catalpa ovata* Don

China 1849. Infrequent; collections N. to Edinburgh and a few gardens in S. England. Known at a distance by the very *dark green* leaves and *yellow flowers*. Leaves to 20 × 25 cm, roughly pentagonal with acuminate corners, main veins reddish at base, petiole *dark red, hard-pubescent* 10–15 cm, new leaves dull purple; flowers whitish-yellow, small, on panicles 25–30 cm high, in late July.

FARGES'S CATALPA   *Catalpa fargesii* Bur.

W. China 1900. Rare; a few large gardens in S. England and Ireland. 18 × 1.5 m. A *slender, upright* tree with twisting shoots and dark pinkish-grey fissured slightly shaggy bark and small leaves (for a *Catalpa*), very variable in shape. Leaf hard, leathery, sub-shiny, 12 × 10 cm on 8 cm petiole, ovate-acuminate and finely pointed or truncate and deltoid, long-acuminate, or with 2–3 acuminate teeth or lobes each side; soft white pubescence beneath; shoot and petiole *densely pubescent*. Flowers 7–15 on a panicle 15 × 15 cm, rosy-pink from distance in late June, densely borne, each 5 × 5 cm, finely speckled pale purple and splashed deep yellow at the mouth. Very showy in a good season.

Yellow Catalpa

Farges's Catalpa

Monocotyledoneae

Stems without central pith or annual layers; first leaf a single slender cotyledon; leaves always alternate usually parallel-veined; parts of flowers in threes or sixes. Includes the grasses, lilies, amaryllids and other familiar bulbous plants and the palms. Those with tree-form have scarcely tapered stems often unbranched because of the method of growth (see p. 21) and can branch only where a flowering stem arises. Secondary thickening in palms by diffused bundles of cells, not from a cambial layer.

LILY FAMILY *Liliaceae*

Large, widespread and varied family of 2,000 species, mostly herbaceous, including lilies, onions, agaves, asparagus and *Yucca*.

CABBAGE PALM or CABBAGE TREE *Cordyline australis* Hook. f.
Pl. 40

New Zealand 1823. Restricted closely to the W. and S. coasts of England and to the coasts of Wales and W. Scotland and, less closely, to all coasts of Ireland. Common around Dublin, Wicklow and Cork in front gardens in towns and villages; frequent in parts of West Scotland notably in Ullapool, also found on the extreme N. coast at Tongue. 10 m.

Bark. Fawn-grey, finely fissured into small, deep corky ridges.

Crown. A straight stout stem partly hidden by the drooping lower leaves of a huge single, central radiating plume; with age, after flowering, upcurved branches begin to proliferate and in areas with very mild winters build up a large-domed crown. Root-suckers frequently arise to form a clump.

Foliage. Leaf linear-lanceolate, tapering from near the base to a fine, sharp point; 60–90 cm long, 3–8 cm wide, dark green, often yellowish-tinged, hard and extremely strong under tension (related to Sisal and used as temporary belt or braces by western gardeners), new leaves erect, older lax leaves fray at the tips, grey-brown.

Flowers and fruit. Flowers small, with six petalloid stamens making a starry white flower 8–10 mm across, creamy-white, fragrant, on huge, much-branched panicle, 60–120 × 30–60 cm, arching out from centre of leaf-plume; the main stem very stout, ribbed, flattened, deep green. Fruit small bluish-white berry, 6 mm. These germinate like grass in Ireland but seldom seem to survive.

Similar species. Only confusion possible is with the tender *Dracaena indivisa* used in summer bedding as a spot-plant but this has leaves twice as long and wide and with a purple or yellow midrib.

PALM FAMILY *Palmaceae*

Large family widespread throughout the tropics. Only two are hardy here, one being the usually dwarf *Chamaerops humilis* L. from S. Europe, but a few others survive in occasional gardens in the south.

CHUSAN PALM *Trachycarpus fortunei* Wendl. **Pl. 40**
S. China 1836. Infrequent; in gardens along the S. coast of England and in Ireland, more frequent near the W. coast north to Wester Ross, rare inland. 11 × 1 m.
Bark. A mass of hard brown fibres and upward-projecting woody bases of leaves which have been shed.
Crown. An unbranched, stout cylindrical stem with a crown of radiating leaves.
Foliage. Leaf fan-shaped, 45–80 × 80–120 cm, divided to within 20–25 cm of the base into 50–60 narrow, long-pointed lobes each folded down the middle, rich dark green, turning bright yellow, then dull brown before falling; petiole 60–100 cm long 2.5 cm wide, flat-convex upper side with a row of small sharp teeth along each edge, deeply convex underside. The lobe-ends soon become frayed into two brown points.
Flowers and fruit. Flowers prolific, very small, yellow on four or more large, drooping, much-branched conic panicles, pale orange at first, 60 cm long with very stout sharply tapering sinuous yellow then white central stem; male and female usually on separate panicles; fruit seldom seen except in the far west and in Ireland; blue-black, globular, 1–1.5 cm.

GLOSSARY

Acicular Needle or awl-shaped.
Acuminate Tapering to a fine point.
    abruptly a. Round or blunt towards end then suddenly drawn out to a fine point.
    long a. Uniformly acuminate from well down the leaf.
    short a. Acuminate only for a short distance below the tip.
Acute Sharply pointed; ending at a narrow angle.
Anther The pollen-bearing part at the tip of the stamen.
Appressed Lying flat and close against.

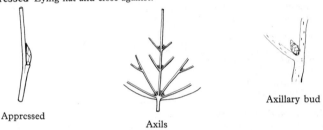

Appressed

Axils

Axillary bud

Aril A fleshy appendage partly covering a seed.
Aristate With the tip drawn out into a fine whisker-like point.
Auricle Ear-shaped extension at the base of the leaf, curving back to the petiole.
Awl-shaped Tapering, and often curved, to a stiff, slender point.
Axil Upper angle between midrib and vein or shoot and leaf.
Axillary Situated in an axil.
Axis The line of the main stem carried to the apex.

Back-cross The offspring of a hybrid crossed with one of the parents of that hybrid.
Blade Flat part of the leaf; leaf excluding petiole.
Bloomed Overlain with a layer, usually waxy and violet or purple, which is removed
    by rubbing or with age.

Chimaera A plant formed of the tissues of two different forms or species. Usually
    originates from a bud forming at the union of stock and scion after grafting and
    composed of part of each. E.g. + *Laburnocytisus adamii*. (Graft-hybrid, denoted
    by the prefix " + ".)
Ciliate With a projecting fringe of hairs.
Clone A single plant propagated vegetatively (by cuttings, grafting, budding or
    layering), and therefore growing in many places although genetically a single
    individual. Cultivars are usually clones.
Columnar Tall and narrow, with straight sides.
    broad-c. Tall and rather broad, with straight sides.
Conic Tapering evenly from base to apex. This and "columnar" are the correct de-
    scriptions for plants described elsewhere as "pyramidal".
Cordate Heart-shaped; particularly used for bases of leaves which curve back each
    side from the petiole.
Corolla The petals collectively.

Crenate Toothed with broad-based, rounded teeth.
Cultivar See p. 17.
Cuneate Wedge-shaped at base; tapering evenly to the petiole.
  broad-c. Wide-angled wedge-shape at base.
  long-c. Wedge-shaped for a good proportion of the blade.
  narrow-c. Long, narrow wedge of blade drawn out to petiole.
Cyme Flat or convex flower-head with central flowers opening first.

Decumbent Leaning to and resting on the ground.
Decurved Curving downwards (see "recurved").
Deltoid Triangular, D-shaped with curved basal angles.
Digitate (Lobes) radiating from a point, like spread fingers.
Dioecious Male and female flowers on separate plants. (See p. 27.)
Distal The end farther from the base, or petiole.
Distant Widely separated (cf. "Remote").
Doubly toothed With teeth which themselves have teeth. Merges into "irregularly toothed" where big and little teeth alternate.
Drupe A fleshy fruit enclosing one or more seeds.

Elliptic Outline of an ellipse, about twice as long as broad.
Entire Margin without teeth or lobules.
Epicormic Growing from buds on large stem or shoot, which buds did not expand when first laid down on the growing shoot. (See p. 24.)
Exserted Projecting beyond surrounding organs (usually from cone or flower).

Falcate Curved sideways (of a leaf); scythe-shaped.
False rings Rings in timber which are among, and look like annual rings (see p. 21) but are not complete. They may be caused by severe frost, defoliation or other damage.
Fasciated Growing as a congested bunch on a broad, antler-like shoot.
Fastigiate With branches nearly erect.
Flush Leaf-out; extend buds.

Globose

Fusiform

Fluted

Fluted (Of a bole) with rounded grooves running vertically.
Forward Pointing forwards, along the shoot towards the tip, rather than perpendicular or backwards.
Free Not adherent to; projecting.
Fusiform Spindle-shaped; tapering to each end from a swollen middle.

Glabrous Without hairs; not pubescent.
Gland A secreting organ; often used for any swollen organ or an appendage.
Glaucous Grey-blue or whitish.
Globose More or less globular; irregularly globular.
Globular Spherical.

Hermaphrodite With male and female flowers distinct but borne in the same inflorescence.

Hybrid The offspring of parents of different species or forms of a species. (See p. 18).

Incise-serrate Sharply and deeply, usually irregularly, toothed.
Inflorescence Part bearing the flowers; flower-head.
Internode See "Node".

Juvenile cone A cone-shaped region in which some juvenile features are retained. Notably in some *Fagus, Quercus* and *Carpinus* where dead leaves are retained in winter within a cone whose apex is about 2.5 m up the stem.

Lanceolate Shaped like the blade of a spear; about 4 times as long as broad, tapered at each end.
Layer A branch bending to the ground, rooting there and growing up as a new plant.
Lenticel A pore on a shoot, usually elliptical and white or corky and raised.
Linear Long and narrow, with parallel sides.
Lobe Segment of a leaf or petal, divided from adjacent segments by sinuses.
Lobulate Bearing lobules.
Lobule A small lobe; a division of the margin larger than a tooth, and usually itself toothed. Lobules may decrease in size towards the tip of a leaf and merge into teeth.

Matt Without gloss; dull.
Median Along the central line dividing an organ into two equal halves.
Monoecious Bearing male and female flowers as separate organs but on the same plant.
Mucro A short, abrupt point or spine.
Mucronate Tipped by a mucro.

Node The point on a shoot at which a leaf or shoot or whorl arises; nodes are separated by "internodes".

Oblanceolate Lanceolate with the broadest part towards the tip.
Oblique Unequal-sided at the base (of a leaf or cone).
Obovate Ovate with the broadest part beyond the middle.
Obovoid Ovoid and broadest beyond the middle.
Orbicular Circular in outline.
Ovate Egg-shaped in outline.
 -acuminate Egg-shaped to beyond the middle and then drawn out to a long, narrow point.
 -deltoid D-shaped at base, then ovate.
 -orbicular Nearly round but broadest below the middle.
Ovoid Egg-shaped; ovate in section (three-dimensional).
 -conic Egg-shaped to beyond the middle, then pointed.
Ovule The body which after fertilisation becomes the seed.

Palmate With lobes or leaflets radiating from a point. (= Digitate.)
Panicle An inflorescence with stalked flowers branching from a central stem.
Papillate (Papillose) Bearing minute hemispherical projections.
Pectinate Arranged like the teeth of a comb. In conifers, with leaves in flat ranks each side of the shoot.
Pedicel The stalk of a flower or fruit.
Peduncle The stalk of a flower or cluster of flowers.
Perfect (Flower). With the organs of both sexes in the one flower; bisexual.
Petiole The stalk of a leaf.
Petiolule The stalk of a leaflet.

These examples show the named features fully developed. Some of these
shapes are intermediate and are named accordingly, e.g. obovate-lanceolate.
Many leaves have the features much less marked than those shown.

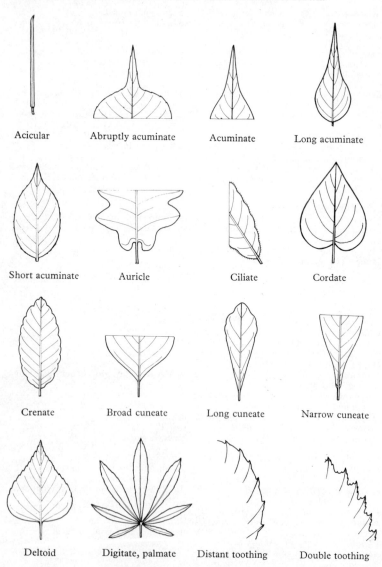

Acicular   Abruptly acuminate   Acuminate   Long acuminate

Short acuminate   Auricle   Ciliate   Cordate

Crenate   Broad cuneate   Long cuneate   Narrow cuneate

Deltoid   Digitate, palmate   Distant toothing   Double toothing

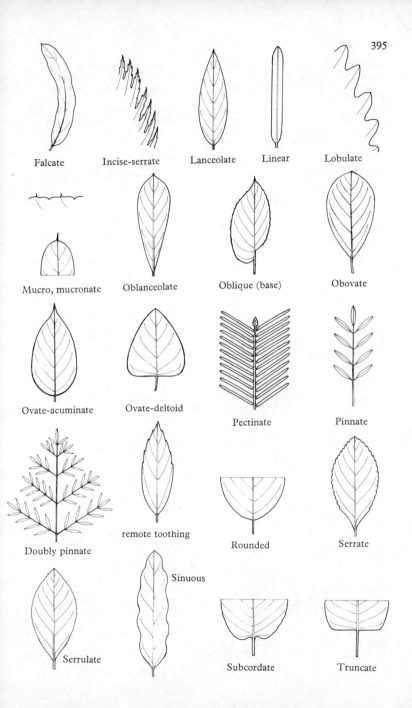

Falcate

Incise-serrate

Lanceolate

Linear

Lobulate

Mucro, mucronate

Oblanceolate

Oblique (base)

Obovate

Ovate-acuminate

Ovate-deltoid

Pectinate

Pinnate

Doubly pinnate

remote toothing

Rounded

Serrate

Serrulate

Sinuous

Subcordate

Truncate

Pinnate (Leaf). With leaflets each side of the common stalk or rachis.

　-doubly Pinnate with each leaflet itself pinnate.

Pistil The female organs of a flower; ovary, style and stigma.

Plane Flat; not cupped nor waved.

Pollard A tree which has been pollarded, i.e. cut, often repeatedly at intervals, at 2–3 m above the ground. Still practised on willows; formerly on hornbeam, beech oak and elm, it shows for the rest of the tree's life by a swelling at 2–3 m from which many stems arise.

Pubescent Covered with hairs, usually short and soft.

　-long Covered in long hairs, pilose.

Pulvinus (Conifers). The swelling on the shoot from which each leaf arises; basal part of the petiole.

Ovoid conic

Pulvinus

Raceme An inflorescence of stalked flowers borne on a common stalk (or rachis).

Rachis The central stalk of a compound leaf or of an inflorescence.

Radial-compound A compound leaf with leaflets radiating from a point; digitate; palmate.

Radiating Spreading from a common centre.

Receptacle The swollen end of a stalk bearing a flower.

Recurved (In this book). Curving upwards (cf. "decurved").

Remote (Toothing or lobing). At the far end of the leaf.

Reticulate Prominently networked.

Revolute Curved sharply down at the margin.

Rounded (Base of leaf). Curving regularly away from the petiole.

Rugose Wrinkled or puckered.

Scion The shoot used in grafting which is put on the rootstock to make the new tree.

Sepal A division of the calyx, outside the petals. In Magnolia, sometimes indistinguishable from petals in colour and texture and so called "tepals".

Semi-double With more than the normal complement of petals, but with the centre still of stamens, style, etc.

Serrate Toothed like a saw.

Serrulate Minutely saw-toothed.

Sessile Without a stalk.

Sinuate With a strongly waved margin.

Sinuous Curving in various directions; snaky.

Sinus The recess between lobes.

Solitary (Flower). One to a stalk.

Spike Simple inflorescence of nearly sessile flowers on a common stalk.

Spur A short branchlet with much shortened internodes (see "node") usually bearing a whorl of leaves.

Stamen A male organ in a flower, bearing the anthers with pollen.

Stellate (Hairs). Branched and star-like.

Stigma A female organ in a flower, which receives the pollen, on the end of the style.

Stipule An appendage, often leafy, at the base of the petiole, usually soon shed.

Stomata Plural of stoma. In conifers these pores in the leaf are white with resin.

Striated Marked with fine vertical lines.

Style A female organ in a flower, the lengthened part of the pistil between the ovary and the stigma.

Stool-shoot The annual shoots made when a tree is cut back to base each year, seen mostly in "stool-beds" where willows and poplars are propagated.

Subcordate Only just cordate; rounded with a small indentation to the petiole.

Sub-evergreen With some of the leaves remaining green through the winter, or all remaining green through part of the winter.

Sub-sessile With a minute stalk.

Sub-shiny A term coined to describe the undersides of leaves which are matt but so smooth that there is a slight shine.

Tepal The term for corolla lobes in some Magnolias where sepals and petals not distinguishable.

Terete Smoothly rounded in cross-section; without projecting ends (of scale-leaves.)

Terminal At or near the end (of the leaf or stalk).

Tomentose With a dense, woolly pubescence.

Translucent Allowing the passage of light, but not transparent.

Truncate Ending abruptly as if cut; base of leaf perpendicular to petiole, straight across.

Umbel An inflorescence of pedicels or branches radiating from a common point.

Umbo The rough, raised centre of the scale in a pine cone.

Unisexual With inflorescences entirely of male or female flowers, at random on a single tree.

Whorl An arrangement of three or more organs in a circle around an axis.

COLLECTIONS OF TREES OPEN TO THE PUBLIC

The Botanic Gardens are usually open every day.

Westonbirt and Bedgebury and the London parks are always open.

The National Trust gardens (NT) maybe open all the year or closed in winter. Scottish (ST) gardens likewise.

Gardens open under the National Gardens Scheme (NGS) are included only where they are open for several days each year, and these should be found in the current "Gardens of England and Wales". Scottish gardens marked (SGS).

The new Countryside Parks (CP) may open only in the summer.

ENGLAND

Bedfordshire

Woburn Abbey. Pleasure Grounds. Big Cornish Elms; Sessile Oaks; Golden Swamp Cypress; big Deodars; mixed collection.

Berkshire

Windsor Great Park. Big collection of rare conifers.

Savill Gardens. Mixed collection; notable Metasequoia.

Valley Gardens. Mixed collection of young trees.

Titness Park, Sunninghill (NGS). A few big conifers; young broadleafed trees.

Buckinghamshire

Waddesdon House, Aylesbury (NT). Good variety.

Cliveden House, Taplow (NT). Remarkable Butter-nut; fine Cypress oaks, etc.

Cambridgeshire

Cambridge Botanic Garden. Wide collection; notable Catalpas, Metasequoias; Tetracentron, maples.

Clare College Garden. Fine Metasequoia, Swamp Cypress.

Cheshire

University of Liverpool Botanic Garden. Ness, Wirral. Good young trees.

Cornwall

Glendurgan, Mawnan Smith, Falmouth (NT). Many big and rare trees.

Boconnoc (Lostwithiel), Penjerrick (Falmouth) and Carclew (Mylor) open for a few days in spring, and are included because of the many outstanding specimens in each garden.

Tresco Abbey, Isles of Scilly, is an extraordinary collection of S. hemisphere trees.

Cumbria

Patterdale Hall, Ullswater. Fine conifers; remarkable Western White Pine.

Derbyshire

Chatsworth House. A pinetum with notable specimens.

Devon

Bicton, East Budleigh. Wide selection of outstanding specimen conifers, oaks and many others, many unequalled elsewhere – Cunninghamia, Leyland Cypress, Deodar, Cypress Oak.

Knightshayes Court, Tiverton (NGS). Many fine and rare trees; largest Turkey Oak; fine Cornish Elms.

Killerton, Silverton, Exeter (NT). Large, rare and tender trees.

Powderham Castle, Kenford, Exeter. Notable Cork Oaks, Turkey Oaks.

Dartington Hall, Totnes (NGS). Notable Davidia, Lucombe Oak.

Arlington Court, Barnstaple (NT). Garden trees.

Streatham Drive, Streatham Hall, Exeter University. Conifer collection; notable Santa Lucia Firs.

Saltram House, Plympton (NT). Some fine trees, notable Monterey Pine, Dutch Elms.

Dorset

Abbotsbury. Many large and rare; Idesia, Pterocarya.

Minterne, Cerne Abbas (NGS). Some fine conifers; Davidias; maples.

Forde Abbey, Chard. Some large and rare.

Essex

Hatfield Forest. Some large and uncommon trees.

Gloucestershire

Westonbirt, nr. Tetbury (Arboretum). 100-acre landscaped planting of immense variety, plus (Silk Wood) 2 km walk lined both sides all the way with rare trees and bays of collections.

Batsford Park, Moreton-in-Marsh (NGS). Large and varied collection; some very big trees; new collection of rare oaks.

Stanway, nr. Winchcombe (NGS). Good pinetum.

Hidcote Manor, Chipping Campden (NT). Rare broadleafed trees.

Speech House, nr. Coleford. Good collection of groups of less usual and rare trees, mainly conifers; others being added.

Cirencester Park and Abbey. Fine broadleafed trees.

Hampshire

Rhinefield Terrace. Public (gated) road from A35 to Brockenhurst. 1859 planting of conifers, now huge; younger trees added.

Bolderwood Arboretum. Below gated road from A35 east to A31. 1861 and later; notable Noble Fir (42 m).

Exbury, nr. Beaulieu. Many rare and big trees.

Jermyn's House, Ampfield (NGS). Immense collection of young trees, verging on the completely comprehensive. Utmost rarities galore.

Avington House, nr. Itchen Abbas. A few fine unusual trees; big Ginkgo, Wheatley Elm, Honey-locust.

Osborne House, Isle of Wight. Avenue of Lucombe and Holm Oaks; big Cork Oaks; varied young trees.

Herefordshire

Hergest Croft, Kington (NGS). Huge collection, especially of conifers, maples and oaks, many very rare.

Queenswood, Hope under Dinmore, on hill by A49. New planting; many unusual trees.

Whitfield, Wormbridge (NGS). Some very big trees; notable Ginkgo, redwood
grove, cedars, tallest oak, Pendulous Oak.

Eastnor Castle, Ledbury (NGS). Vast collection of mostly huge conifers; some
maples, oaks, etc. Notable Santa Lucia Firs, Deodars, original Blue Atlas
Cedar; *Acer lobelii.*

Hertfordshire

Cassiobury Park, Watford. Finest Red Oak; many other trees.

Kent

The National Pinetum, Bedgebury, nr. Goudhurst. Nearly comprehensive
collection of hardy conifer species and many cvs, landscaped; and over 100
forest plots of different species, mostly conifers. Some rare oaks, maples and
other hardwoods.

Scotney Castle, Lamberhurst (NT). Some fine, big conifers, etc.

Sandling Park, nr. Hythe. Some old and large conifers; outstanding Alder,
26 × 3.7m.

Godinton Park, nr. Ashford (NGS). Fine hardwoods in park.

Crittenden House, Matfield (NGS). Rare young trees.

Mote Park, Maidstone (Public Park). Some big hardwoods; notable Black
Walnut, Liquidambar and Field Maple.

The Grange, Benenden (NGS). Famous collection of flowering cherries, with
many other rare trees; notable *Eucalyptus gunnii, Fagus englerana* and
Nothofagus spp.

Dunorlan Park, Tunbridge Wells (Public Park). Some big conifers.

Lancashire

Wythenshawe Park, Manchester. Fine Metasequoias; Western White Pine;
Lucombe Oak.

Lincolnshire

Brocklesby Park. Limber pines, many conifers; Turkish hazel, etc.

London

Hyde Park and Kensington Gardens. Remarkable trees of rare oaks, maples,
ash and many other species.

Regents Park. Many fine Cornish and Dutch Elms and other trees.

Syon House, Brentford. Garden Centre. Famous big and rare oaks, maples,
Catalpas, Zelkova and many other trees; Swamp Cypresses.

Osterley Park, Hounslow. Some very fine and rare oaks.

Waterlow Park. Good hardwoods of many kinds.

Kenwood, Highgate. Notable Zelkova; Swamp Cypresses, oaks.

Chiswick House. Many large trees; notable *Fraxinus angustifolia.*

Marble Hill, Twickenham (Public Park). Notable huge Black Walnut; tallest
Lombardy Poplar and Italian Alder.

Greenwich Park. Many good trees; notable *Euodia hupehensis* and *Betula
papyrifera.*

Middlesex
Capel Manor. Tall Zelkova; huge Purple Beech.
Forty Hall, Enfield. Cedars, pines, etc.

Northumberland
Cragside, Rothbury (NT). Big planting around 1860 of conifers now immense.
White fir 46m; Low's firs.

Norfolk
Lynford Arboretum, nr. Mundford. Wide variety of groups of less usual
conifers; maples, etc., being added to since 1949, growing fast; big old Crimean
and Corsican Pines.

Oxfordshire
Oxford Botanic Gardens. Some old trees of rare species.
University Parks, Oxford. Many fine trees; Zelkova, poplar spp.
Blenheim Palace, Woodstock (NGS). Notable Cedar of Lebanon, Sugar Maple,
London Planes.

Somerset
Bath Botanic Garden. Many rare species; notable Ginkgo, Golden Catalpa.
Victoria Park, Bath. Many good trees.
Nettlecombe, nr. Willaton. Outstanding Himalayan Cypresses and many other
trees.
Orchardsleigh. Frome. Tall specimens of many conifers and broadleaves.

Staffordshire
Sandon Park Hall, nr. Stafford (NGS). Many good trees.

Suffolk
Abbey Gardens, Bury St Edmunds. Some big and unusual trees; notable Trees
of Heaven and Buckeye.

Surrey
Royal Botanic Gardens, Kew. The largest specimens of numerous of the rarest
species; unequalled collections of most genera, notably oaks, Celtises, limes,
Zelkovas, Catalpas.
Royal Horticultural Society's Gardens, Wisley, Ripley. Very good pinetum;
wide range of other trees.
Claremont, Esher (NT). Notably splendid Cedar of Lebanon; oldest Cunning-
hamia; fine Sequoia and Bishop Pine.
Grayswood Hill, Haslemere (NGS). Many fine trees of wide range; notable
Montezuma Pine; *Nothofagus betuloides, N. obliqua*, etc.
Winkworth Arboretum, S. of Godalming (NT). Notable collections of Sorbus
and Acer; groups of Nyssa, Oxydendrum; rare oaks.
Moss's Wood and Leith Hill Place below Leith Hill. Public road. Some fine
conifers at each place.
Riverside Park, Richmond. Many fine trees.
Ravensbury Park, Morden (Public Park). Fine London Planes, English Elms
and smaller trees.

Sussex

Hollycombe, nr. Liphook (but Sussex). Remarkably big specimens of rare trees; Black Birch, Chinese Wingnut, Chinese Cork oak, etc.

Wakehurst Place, Ardingly (out-station of Kew RBG). Immense collection of conifers and broadleafed trees; many fine specimens of extremely rare trees.

Borde Hill, N. of Haywards Heath (NGS). Huge park and six woods full of rare trees, some unknown elsewhere. Most notable maple collection, also collections of oaks, pines, spruces, etc.

Nymans, Handcross (NT). Two pinetums, three gardens and a large Wilderness filled with rare and some tender trees. Outstanding specimens of rare Nothofagus species; Austrocedrus.

Leonardslee, Lower Beeding (Open in May and October). Many very fine conifers, Magnolias, oaks; notable Sassafras, etc.

Sheffield Park, Uckfield (NT). Wide variety of fine conifers, and unique planting of Nyssa; notable Maritime and Montezuma Pines; Pseudolarix, Serbian Spruce, Pond Cypress.

Highdown, Goring. The famous chalk-garden has many rare trees; notable *Acer griseum*, a hornbeam and a juniper too rare to include in this book (*Carpinus turczaninowii; Juniperus cedrus*).

Cowdray Park, Midhurst (NGS). Many very big conifers; notable Wellingtonia (in avenue); *Acer buergeranum;* Sawara Cypresses.

West Dean Arboretum (Roche's Arboretum). Wide collection, mainly of conifers, some of great size, to over 46m (Douglas Firs).

Tilgate Park (Crawley). Rare trees in dell and 1905 pinetum; splendid specimens of wide variety.

Wiltshire

Stourhead, nr. Mere (NT). Large collection of very big conifers and hardwoods. Largest Macedonian Pine; Noble Fir, Tiger-tail Spruce, Thuja, Tulip-trees.

Wilton House, Wilton. Many fine old trees; Concord Oak by bridge.

Longleat, nr. Warminster. Many big conifers by roads and in the Paradise.

Worcestershire

Spetchley Park, E. of Worcester (NGS). Notable Metasequoia.

Yorkshire

Studley Royal and Fountains Abbey, nr. Ripon. Many big trees; notable Sweet Chestnut, oaks.

Thorpe Perrow, Bedale. Extensive plantings of collections of genera with notable rare maples, oaks, limes, cherries, poplars and conifers.

WALES

Breconshire

Gliffaes Country House Hotel (NGS. Daily in summer).

Denbighshire

Bodnant, Tal y Cefn, Conway (NT). Huge collection of conifers, magnolias, maples. Notable *Nothofagus obliqua*, Low's Fir, Lodgepole Pines, Grecian Fir, etc.

Vivod Forest Garden, above Vivod House, nr. Llangollen. Young arboretum of many rare species; forest plots of wide range.

Glamorgan
Roath Park and other public areas, Cardiff. Wide selection.

Montgomeryshire
Powis Castle, Welshpool. Gardens (NT). Park has big trees, including tallest Douglas Fir and *Pinus ponderosa,* but not all visible to public at present. Gardens have Ginkgo, big Silver Firs and Sequoias, Davidia, *Populus lasiocarpa.*

SCOTLAND

Argyll
Strone, Cairndow (SGS). Tallest tree in Scotland in group of very big conifers. (Grand Fir, 54 m.)
Inveraray Castle Gardens. Many fine conifers; notable Leyland Cypress, Grand Fir and Sitka Spruce by bridge and across river visible from terrace.
Benmore, Younger Botanic Garden (Royal Botanic Garden, Edinburgh). Large areas of huge conifers and new garden with comprehensive collection. Notable Western Hemlock (48 m), Wellingtonia avenue, *Abies amabilis, Picea jezoensis.* Very tall trees (to 50 m) in Glen Masson nearby.
Crarae Gardens and Forest Garden, Furnace. Wide collection of rare trees; plots of rare conifers.
Kilmun Forest Garden, nr. Benmore. Plots of rare conifers and Eucalypts growing fast. (Forestry Commission.)

Ayrshire
Culzean Castle, Girvan (ST and CP). Many fine conifers and other trees, especially in Happy Valley.
Glenapp, Ballantrae (CP). Small group of big conifers in valley off main valley.
Kilkerran, Maybole (CP). Small pinetum above House; notable Scots Pine, Noble Fir. Big Araucarias, Wellingtonias. Big Larch and Silver Firs in Lady's Glen.

Bute
Brodick Castle, Arran (ST). Many trees; rare maples.

Edinburgh
Royal Botanic Gardens. Notable collections of birches, maples, limes, conifers Notable trees of *Corylus colurna,* Tetracentron, *Quercus dentata, Fagus orientalis,* etc.

East Lothian
Smeaton House, E. Lothian. Wide range of notable conifers; big Italian Maple.
Whittingehame, nr. Haddington. Many large conifers.

Inverness-shire
Moniac Glen, nr. Beauly (Forestry Commision picnic site). Small area of very tall Douglas Firs, to 51 m and a few other conifers.

Peebles-shire

Dawyck, Stobo (SGS). Extensive collection of conifers, maples, and many rare
trees. Original Dawyck Beech, very early larch, Douglas Fir, Western Hemlock; fine Asiatic silver firs.

Perthshire

The Hermitage, Inver, Dunkeld (ST). A few very big trees; one Douglas Fir of
53 m.

Blair Castle, Blair Atholl. Diana's Grove full of conifers 45 m tall; outstanding
Japanese Larch; outside are an early European Larch (more at far end), and
original hybrid larch. St Brides, just above, has immense *Abies procera* and
A. magnifica side by side.

Keir House, Dunblane (SGS). Large number of big conifers and rare maples.
Notable *Abies spectabilis, Cupressus torulosa*.

Doune House, Dunblane. Valley near Motor Museum. Well-spaced huge
conifers; small maple and oak collection. Notable Western Hemlock, Wellingtonia (44 m); largest Lawson and Nootka Cypresses in Scotland.

Scone Palace, nr. Perth. Garden has original Douglas Fir; huge pinetum in
widely spaced lines planted 1860 among 1852 trees. Notable Jeffrey's pine,
Western Hemlock, Wellingtonia, 4 massive Sitka Spruces, Noble Firs;
younger rarities.

Roxburgh

Monteviot. Pinetum of big conifers and Oregon maple.

Wigtownshire

Castle Kennedy and Lochinch. Large scale early planting of wide range of
conifers, also tender hardwoods. Avenues of unusual species (e.g. Emboth-
rium, Eucalyptus, Araucaria). Notable Bishop pine, line of Cordyline, Nothofagus spp.

NORTHERN IRELAND

Castlewellan, Newcastle, Co. Down. (Forestry Service) An immense collection
rich in rare and tender conifers and other trees, many of great size.

Rowallane, Saintfield, Co. Down. Many fine rare and tender trees; notable
Nothofagus collection.

Tullymore Park, Co. Down. Mixed big conifers; plots of Eucalypts.

Bangor Castle, Co. Down. Fine Monterey Pines, Blue-gums and other trees.

Gosford Castle, Markethill, Co. Armagh. Big conifers; record Himalayan Fir,
huge Noble Fir.

Drum Manor, Co. Tyrone. Record Western Hemlock and Cripps's Cypress,
big Monterey Pines, etc.

Mount Stewart, Co. Down. (NT). Big Eucalypts, Monterey Pines and less
usual trees.

Powerscourt, Co. Wicklow. Huge collection, mainly conifers many very well-grown, rare and big.

The John F. Kennedy Memorial Arboretum, New Ross, Co. Wexford. New, but rapidly expanding collection on a vast scale. Forest plots.

Glasnevin Botanic Garden, N. Dublin. Large collection with many fine, very rare trees; outstanding *Euodia* spp., good rare maples, etc.

Birr Castle, Co. Offaly. Enormous and widespread general collection; numerous extreme rarities; notable wing-nuts, limes, maples, etc.

This is a tiny fraction of the gardens with notable trees. Some of the best collections are around what are now schools (especially girls' schools, for no obvious reason), or hotels. Some of these will be opened at various times but cannot be included here. Many others are privately owned and may be opened occasionally or with change of ownership, or in the future. Hundreds more, open under the national gardens schemes, will have trees of interest but have not yet been visited by the author.

INDEX TO ENGLISH NAMES

INDEX TO SCIENTIFIC NAMES